PIRACY

In Comparative Perspective
Problems, Strategies, Law

Charles H. Norchi
Gwenaële Proutière-Maulion
Editors

Editions A.Pedone & Hart
2012

For Alexander Kieran Norchi

---CHN

For each member of the CDMO,

for the happiness of working together.

To those we love.

---GPM

© Editions A.Pedone
13 rue Soufflot
75005 Paris
France
Tel.: +33 (0) 1 43 54 05 97
Fax: +33 (0)46 34 07 60
librairie@apedone.net
http://www.pedone.info
Ean 978-2-233-00650-9

Hart Publishing Ltd
16C Worcester Place,
Oxford, OX1 2JW
United Kingdom
Tel.: +44 (0)1865 517530
Fax: +44 (0)1865 510710
mail@hartpub.co.uk
http://www.hartpub.co.uk
Ean 978-1-849-

-

Hart Publishing
c/o International Specialized Book Services
920 NE 58th Avenue, Suite 300
Portland, OR 97213-3786
USA
Tel: +1 503 287 3093 or toll-free: (1) 800 944 6190
Fax: +1 503 280 8832
orders@isbs.com
http://www.isbs.com

TABLE OF CONTENTS

Acknowledgements

The editors gratefully acknowledge the support of their colleagues and staffs of the Center for Maritime and Oceans Law in the University of Nantes, and the Center for Oceans and Coastal Law in The University of Maine School of Law. They especially thank Cédric Leboeuf of the University of Nantes who served as European coordinator for this project, and from the University of Maine school of Law Christopher J. Rauscher who served as US coordinator and editorial assistant, graphic designer Tara Wheeler, librarian Julie Welch and financial manager Tina Claypoole. The editors gratefully acknowledge the support of the Partner University Fund (PUF), a program of the FACE Foundation of New York City that is managed by the Cultural Services of the French Embassy to the United States. PUF provided the seed funding in support of the Nantes-Maine oceans and maritime law partnership, including this book and related programs.

puf Partner University Fund

About the Authors

Charles H. Norchi, co-editor of this volume, is Professor of Law and Director of the Center for Oceans and Coastal Law in the University of Maine School. Professor Norchi serves as Chair of the Admiralty and Maritime Law Section of the American Association of Law Schools (AALS), Co-Chair of the Institute for Law and Development Policy in Geneva, Switzerland, is a Fellow of the Explorers Club and a member of the Advisory Committee of the Hong Kong Centre for Maritime and Transportation Law. Professor Norchi holds an A.B. from Harvard University, a J.D. from Case Western Reserve University School of Law, an LL.M. and J.S.D. from Yale Law School.

Gwenaële Proutière-Maulion, co-editor of this volume, is Vice President for International and European Relations in the University of Nantes, France. Previously Dr. Proutière-Maulion was Senior Lecturer at the University of Western Brittany and subsequently at the University of Nantes. From 2004 she was director of the Center for Maritime and Oceanic Law (CDMO) until assuming her current university position in 2012. Her research and teaching specialties include French and European Union fisheries law, maritime labour law including the International Labour Organization Convention, seafarers' rights and ,marine resources. Dr. Proutière-Maulion manages the FEMMAR Project of the CDMO which researches gender and women's working condititions in the maritime sector.

Valerie Boré-Eveno is a lecturer at the Faculty of Law and Political Sciences at the University of Nantes (France) and member of the Center for Maritime and Ocean Law (CDMO). She is author of numerous articles on the Law of the Sea and International Protection of Human Rights. Dr. Boré Eveno holds a Doctor of Laws from the University Paris 1 Panthéon Sorbonne, where she completed a dissertation on "treaty interpretation by international tribunals."

Arthur Bowring is Managing Director of the Hong Kong Shipowners Association. He has eight years of seagoing experience, worked for Lloyds Register of Shipping, Cargill International SA, Geneva, Orient Ship Management, Hong Kong and as a Marine Consultant. Mr. Bowring serves as Arbitrator for Shipping and Commercial disputes, and is a member of the Panel of Arbitrators maintained by the Hong Kong International Arbitration Centre. He is a Fellow of the Institute of Chartered Shipbrokers, the Nautical

Institute, the Royal Institute of Navigation, the Royal Institution of Naval Architects, the Chartered Institute of Arbitrators and the Hong Kong Institute of Arbitrators, and a Member of the Hong Kong Mediation Council.

Emmanuel Chassot has worked at the French Research Institute for Development (IRD) since 2008 in the Mixed Research Unit 212 on "Exploited Marine Ecosystems." He member of a research team of the "Tuna Fisheries Observatory", responsible for monitoring French tropical tuna fisheries of the Indian and Atlantic Oceans. He participates in the working groups of the tuna Regional Fisheries Management Organisation. His research focuses on tuna biology and ecology, as well as fisheries dynamics to promote an Ecosystem Approach to Fisheries Management.

Patrick Chaumette is Professor of Labor Law at the University of Nantes, France and Director of the Center for Maritime and Ocean Law (CDMO) in the University of Nantes. Professor Chaumette specializes in labor and social security as well as in social rights of the Seafarers. He contributed to *Droits Maritimes,* Beurier JP (Eds.), Action Dalloz, Paris, 2th ed., 2008. Among his many publications are *The Repatriation of Seamen*, in A Right to Free Men, Studies in Honor of Professor Alain Fenet, Litec, Paris, LexisNexis; *Reflagging a Vessel in the European Market and Dealing with Transnational Collective Disputes*: ECJ, 11 December, 2007, *ITF & Finnish Seamen's Union v. Viking Line*, Case C-438/05, "trans. Janet Heard-Carnot, Ocean & Coastal Law Journal, University of Maine School of Law; *The ILO Maritime Labour Convention 2006 (MLC, 2006): An Example of Innovative Normative Consolidation in a Globalized Sector*, with A. Charbonneau, in European Labour Law Journal, Intersentia, Mortsel, 2010.

Simon Delfau, is Security Adviser, CMA CGM, France. For seven years was safety advisor for all maritime and land matters within the Safety Management – Safety – Environment Direction of the Company GMA CGM. Simon Delfau holds a degree in maritime law with specialization in maritime security and safety from the University of Nantes, France, and has earned two advanced degrees in International Maritime Management from the School of Business and the School of Merchant Marine in Marseille, France.

Dominique Gaurier is Senior Lecturer, University of Nantes. Dr. Gaurier recently published a textbook on Legal History of International Law, and has translated from Latin into French, classical works, such as Gentili's *De Jure Belli* and *De Légationibus*. He has also translated works on Maritime Law from Latin into French, *inter alia*, *De Dominio Maris* by Cornelis van Bijnkershoek, and the 17th century *Dominio Maris* by the Scot Willam

Welwod. Professor Gaurier holds a Doctor of Law from the University of Nantes.

Edward Girardet is a writer and journalist based in Geneva. A former reporter for *The Christian Science Monitor*, he has reported widely on humanitarian and conflict situations in Africa, Asia and elsewhere. He is author of several books including the 2011 *Killing the Cranes – A Reporter's Journey Through Three Decades of War in Afghanistan* (Chelsea Green, Vermont). He is co-founding director of the Institute for Media and Global Governance/Media21 in Geneva. Mr. Girardet hold degrees from Nottingham University and Yale Law School.

Patrice Guillotreau is an economist at the University of Nantes, France. He has published numerous scientific articles and books on the economics of the sea, of which his *Mare Economicum* was awarded the *Place de Fontenoy* Prize. He has worked at the IRD as a researcher in Sète, France, and in Seychelles. He was vice-President of a national working group at the Grenelle de la Mer (French Ministry of Ecology and is the current Deputy-Director of the Research Cluster on marine and coastal sciences in Nantes (FR CNRS 3473) encompassing 430 scientists.

Claude Kirongozi Ichalanga is Associate Professor in the University of Kinshasa School of Law, University of Kisangani and Visiting Professor in University Kongo, Bas-Congo in the Democratic Republic of the Congo. He is also Visiting Scholar in the University of Maine School of Law. His fields are international law, maritime law, public law, history of law and international development. Dr. Ichalanga has previously published on international law and maritime issues including Nation-Building in Democratic Republic of the Congo and the law of maritime ports. He holds university degrees in law from the University of Kinshasa (Congo) and a Doctorate in Law from Dalian Maritime University, China.

James Kraska is the Howard S. Levie Chair in Operational Law, member of the faculty of the International Law Department, and senior associate in the Center for Irregular Warfare and Armed Groups at the U.S. Naval War College in Newport, Rhode Island. A commander in the U.S. Navy Judge Advocate General's Corps, Commander Kraska also serves as a senior fellow at the Foreign Policy Research Institute (USA) and as guest investigator at the Marine Policy Center, Woods Hole Oceanographic Institution. Commander Kraska served in four Pentagon staff assignments, including deputy legal adviser to the Deputy Chief of Naval Operations, law of the sea attorney for the Judge Advocate General of the Navy, and oceans policy adviser and chief of international negotiations on the Joint Staff, where he was the principal military adviser for piracy policy. Dr. Kraska holds a J.D.

from Indiana University Maurer School of Law, and an LL.M. and S.J.D. from the University of Virginia School of Law.

David Kaplan is a researcher at the French Research Institute for Development (IRD). His research field is modeling effects of marine reserves on fish populations. He is also a lecturer at the University of Montpellier, France, and spent many years in the United States and Chile as an assistant professor.

Cédric Leboeuf is a Research Fellow in the Center for Maritime and Ocean Law (CDMO) in the University of Nantes, France. He holds degrees from the Universities of Lille, France and Leuven (KUL), Belgium where he concentrated in European and international law and politics as applied to security and safety. He is Laureate of the Institute of High Studies of National Defense (IHEDN), Military School of Paris, France, in 2009-2010, and an *ad hoc* legal advisor to the French School of Merchant Marine, DCNS. Mr. Leboeuf served as European Coordinator for this book project. His doctoral thesis was written under the supervision of Prof. Patrick Chaumette, University of Nantes and is entitled "Treatment and authentication of the threats and risks at sea".

Fozia Lone is Assistant Professor of Law in the City University of Hong Kong School of Law where she teaches International Law, Common Law Torts, Humanitarian Law and Advanced Issues in Public International Law. Dr. Lone has tutored international law at the University of Aberdeen (Scotland) and practiced law in Kashmir where she was a Member of the Bar Council of Jammu and Kashmir. She has authored articles on various aspects of public international law, contributed an entry to the Oxford Bibliography on international law, and is currently writing a book on the common law of torts. Dr. Lone holds a Bachelor of Laws (B.A.) from the Faculty of Law, University of Kashmir; a Masters of Laws (LL.M.) and a Doctor of Philosophy (Ph.D.) from the School of Law in the University of Aberdeen, Scotland.

Alexander McKinnon, is a non-resident Visiting Scholar of the Center for Oceans and Coastal Law in the University of Maine School of Law and candidate for a Masters of Law (LL.M.) in the University of Cambridge, United Kingdom. He previously served as a Visiting Fellow in the Hong Kong Centre for Maritime and Transportation Law in the City University of Hong Kong; as an Associate in the Supreme Court of Queensland, Australia; and Lecturer and Tutor in Law at CQ University Australia. Mr. McKinnon has published monographs on maritime ports and piracy.

Martin Murphy is an internationally-recognized expert on piracy and unconventional conflict at sea. His published works include three books:

Somalia, the New Barbary? Piracy and Islam in the Horn of Africa (2011), *Small Boats, Weak States, Dirty Money: Piracy and Maritime Terrorism in the Modern World* (2009), both with Columbia University Press, and *Contemporary Piracy and Maritime Terrorism*, Adelphi paper 388 (2007), for the London-based International Institute for Strategic Studies. Dr. Murphy is currently writing two further books: *Piracy, Terrorism and Unconventional Warfare at Sea: Navies Confront the 21st-Century* and *The Maritime Trinity: A History of Piracy, Trade and War.*

Oya Özcayir, Maritime Law Consultant & Member of Äzmir Law Bar, Turkey and associate professor of maritime law. She studied law in Turkey and continued her studies in England for her LLM and PhD in Maritime Law. She is an experienced lawyer, trainer and lecturer. Dr. Özcayir has taught Maritime Law in Turkey and at Cardiff University Law School in England. She has published numerous articles on aspects of maritime law in various journals. Dr. Özcayir is the author of two books: *Liability for Oil Pollution and Collisions* and *Port State Control*, published by Lloyd's of London Press. She is a member of the Editorial Board of Maritime Risk International and the editor of the International Maritime Organization section of *the Journal of International Maritime Law*. Dr. Özcayir is a Member of Äzmir Law Bar in Turkey and a frequent speaker at international conferences.

Poomintr Sooksripaisarnkit, LL.B. (Thammasat), LL.M. (International Commercial Law) (Leicester), PhD (Leicester), is Assistant Professor in the School of Law, City University of Hong Kong and Maritime Specialist in The Hong Kong Centre for Maritime and Transportation Law in City University of Hong Kong.

Michael J. Stepek is a partner in the London and Geneva offices of the international law firm of Akin, Gump, Strauss, Hauer & Feld LLC and Co-Chair of the Institute for Law & Development Policy in Geneva, Switzerland. Mr. Stepek has more than 25 years of experience in the practice of international public and private law counseling clients on international commercial, investment and trade, multilateral investment treaties and commercial agreements and other matters. He holds a Juris Doctor with Honors from the University of Notre Dame.

Timothy Steigelman is an attorney at the law firm Kelly, Remmel & Zimmerman in Portland, Maine. He holds a Juris Doctor (J.D.), *summa cum laude*, from the University of Maine School of Law; a Master of Arts in Government and Politics from the University of Maryland; a Diploma from the United States Naval War College; and a Bachelor of Science, with Distinction, from the United States Naval Academy. He previously served on active duty in the United States Navy, and continues serving as a Lieutenant in the U.S. Navy Reserve.

Captain Tom Tulloch, MSM CD Royal Canadian Navy, serves on the staff of NATO's Maritime Command Headquarters in Northwood, United Kingdom. A career Naval Officer, he has commanded HMC Ships at sea. He served as the Chief of Staff to the Commander of Standing NATO Maritime Group One on two occasions for counter-piracy operations off the Horn of Africa in 2010 and 2011. Captain Tulloch was awarded the Meritorious Service Medal for his leadership in action against pirates.

Thomas Vallée is Professor of Economics at the University of Nantes. He is a researcher at the Laboratory of Economics and Management Nantes Atlantique (LEMNA). His research interests concern the dynamic game theory, industrial economics, economics of fisheries and governance. He is a member of the International Society of the International Dynamical Games (ISDG). He has been published in numerous international journals, including, *Journal of Evolutionary Economics, Journal of Economics Dynamics and Control, Macroeconomics Dynamics,* and *Annals of Operations Research.*

FOREWORD

THE PIRACY PROBLEM: THE PUNTLAND PERSPECTIVE

The President of Puntland State of Somalia
His Excellency Abdirahman Mohamed MOHAMUD (FAROLE)

Pirate attacks originating from the coast of Somalia have surged to new heights since 2007, and have become a worldwide challenge. The problem of piracy is a relatively new phenomenon in Somalia. Piracy is a product of the prolonged Somali conflict following the state's collapse in 1991, and the subsequent failure of public institutions, including the disappearance of Somali coastal defense.

Today, the organized crimes of piracy and terrorism complement each other. Piracy has contributed to overall insecurity in Somalia and has aggravated economic hardships for the Somali people by disrupting the livelihoods of coastal communities.

Initially, the Illegal Unregulated Unreported Fishing (IUUF) in Somali territorial waters triggered the pirate insurgency. It was foreign trawlers that destroyed the fishing boats and gear of Somali coastal communities. This catalyzed an armed resistance by Somali fishermen against foreign trawlers, which led eventually to ransom payments and to the escalation of pirate attacks against commercial vessels and innocent seafarers.

Piracy has tarnished our image internationally, as the Somali people are unfairly labeled as living in a piracy-prone society, even though piracy is not unique to Somalis, both historically and in modern times. The recent surge of pirate attacks in West Africa, particularly around the Gulf of Guinea, demonstrates this point. Piracy gangs have taken advantage of Puntland's geographic vulnerability and it has become a favorite hunting area. Puntland is located at the crossroads of international waterways where an estimated 22,000 commercial vessels pass through annually. Puntland's tip at the narrow waterway, where the Gulf of Aden and the Indian Ocean intersect, is an ideal hunting area, as it allows pirates to hijack vessels and easily escape to the open sea.

The security and socio-economic impact of piracy in Somalia has been tremendous, particularly in the Puntland State. First, piracy has impacted our security as the ransom payments have led to the proliferation of weapons and increased the recruitment of criminal gangs. Second, piracy has disrupted our once vibrant fishing economy and created inflation in the area where pirates operate. Third, piracy has spoiled our cultural values by introducing new social problems, such as drugs, alcohol, and Sexually Transmitted Diseases.

International naval warships from different countries will not unilaterally end the piracy phenomenon in Somalia. The pirates are becoming more violent and cunning, and they are increasingly using sophisticated technology, such as GPS satellite phones, and international connections, including foreign-based brokers, facilitators and ransom money transporters.

I believe that we can no longer afford to deny that there are international connections to Somali piracy. There are networks in many world capitals that are connected through piracy proceeds. For example, in May 2011, the world awoke to the surprising news of foreigners arrested in Mogadishu while attempting to smuggle over three million U.S. dollars in ransom cash to pirates.

Since my election as President of Puntland State of Somalia on 8 January 2009, my Administration has adopted a unique combined approach to tackle the piracy problem. This includes strengthening our security and law enforcement capacity. Puntland security forces, including the Puntland Maritime Police Force, have raided pirate locations, arrested piracy suspects, and seized vehicles and equipment, including speedboats, ladders, satellite phones and weapons. In 2010, the Puntland Parliament passed Somalia's first Anti-Piracy Law to deal specifically with piracy related crimes. The high concentration of jailed pirates has created a backlog of criminal cases congesting the judiciary's workload and prison space in Puntland State.

The Administration's second tack features community engagement programs to rehabilitate pirates and prevent piracy recruitment. This combined approach has worked effectively to eradicate piracy from Puntland's Eyl coastal town, which was once internationally notorious as a piracy hub. More recently, in early March 2012, Puntland government officials and community elites engaged in successful efforts to expel pirate gangs from Puntland's southern coastal town of Gara'ad. NATO naval commanders deployed on counter-piracy missions along Somalia's coast arrived along the Gara'ad coast to meet the Puntland government officials and community elites.

As we look at solutions, we need to develop alternative livelihoods for coastal communities affected by piracy and illegal fishing. Peace-building development programs, such as vocational schools, job opportunities, and reviving the fishing activities which were disrupted by piracy and by illegal fishing, have proven to be effective long-term solutions to the piracy problem.

The geography of Puntland's territory also poses a big challenge, due to difficulties accessing pirate hideouts among valleys, mountains and a long coastline that is difficult to monitor. Access to coastal areas can be improved through construction of feeder and paved roads, and jetties along the coast for the dual purpose of economic development and enhancing coastal monitoring capabilities.

Thirdly, there is the legal challenge of jurisdiction and piracy prosecutions in foreign countries. By early 2012, there were over 1,000 Somali piracy suspects jailed in over 20 countries around the world. Many countries have been troubled by pirate detentions and trials, and in fact, some Western countries opted to fund piracy prosecutions in African nations, such as Kenya and the Seychelles. Moreover, specialized international courts based in foreign countries have been proposed as a legal remedy. But these propositions are temporary in nature and fail to take into account the long-term legal, jurisdictional and moral challenges surrounding piracy prosecutions.

As a remedy, in May 2010, the Puntland Government proposed to the international community to transfer Somali pirates jailed in foreign countries to prisons in Somalia; subsequently, in April 2011, the Puntland Government signed a piracy-transfer agreement with the Seychelles Government. This proposal was conditional to tangible support for upgraded and new correctional facilities, as well as human resource development in the judiciary sector, such as training programs and incentives for judges, prosecutors and lawyers in Puntland State. Indeed, we were encouraged that many nations, including the United Kingdom, welcomed piracy-transfer agreements as the "most sustainable solution," according to UK Minister for Africa, Henry Bellingham.

Fourthly, I firmly believe that education and security are interlinked. Education is the new battleground of the Digital Age. We need to re-establish a viable public school system, in Puntland and Somalia as a whole, which follows a curriculum that teaches a program of civic competence and responsibility among our young people. This is the only way that we can guarantee a future generation that believes in the values of peace, justice, democracy and freedom.

This presents long-lasting solutions to piracy problems, as governance and development create opportunities for youth who are vulnerable to joining the pirates or other criminal groups, such as al-Shabaab. We have already recorded the worrisome trend of growing ties between pirates and al-

Shabaab, a relationship that exasperates the threat to regional and global security and stability.

After more than two decades of lawlessness, Somalia has begun to export its problems – particularly piracy and terrorism. It remains vitally important that the international community develop genuine partnerships with Somali institutions to advance the process of stabilization, state building and reconstruction. Dealing with piracy alone – for example, through international military action – will not suffice, as piracy constitutes simply a part of the whole problem in Somalia.

I believe that expensive naval patrols off the coast of Somalia will remain ineffective to eradicate piracy, as long as the world continues to neglect the domestic conditions that produce this scourge. Without addressing such conditions, military action alone is not a panacea and is indeed merely a short-term remedy to effectively addressing the piracy problem. The costs and legal ramifications associated with piracy prosecutions in foreign countries pose more obstacles. These are problems that can be overcome by pursuing a new comprehensive approach to tackling piracy in full partnership with the Somali people and their institutions.

The future of Somalia depends on the continued development of the regional administrations like Puntland, and our ability to combat the two greatest threats to stability: piracy and terrorism, the latter generally perpetrated by al-Shabaab. While we have made real progress in these areas, we need greater assistance, both financial and technical, to more effectively counter this dual threat to peace in Somalia.

INTRODUCTION

PIRACY IN COMPARATIVE PERSPECTIVE

When political entities – empires, nations and states – first engaged in trade and war they sought to preserve a public order of the world community on land and on sea. The laws of war and the law of the sea were early attempts to secure minimum order including the public order of the oceans.[1] Piracy, a critical disruption of the order of the oceans, has been recorded as far back as ancient Greece and Persia, the first Empire of India and the Han Dynasty of China. The early European seafaring powers spawned norms proscribing piratical acts that became codified in contemporary international law. However, contemporary maritime piracy is a more complex phenomenon then its historical antecedents of claims and efforts to suppress unauthorized non-state coercion on the high seas. In addition to power, the contemporary piracy problem implicates other values such as well-being, respect, skill and the human dignity of seafarers taken hostage and of the coastal communities coping with poverty and armed conflict. An overwhelming number of piracy incidents today are entwined with conditions in Somalia. This inspired the Government of the United Kingdom to convene the London Conference on Somalia in February 2012. Addressing piracy the final communiqué urged that "the problem requires a comprehensive approach on land as well as sea."[2] This book is a quest for such a comprehensive approach.

The piracy problem can be viewed from a multiplicity of standpoints. Each bears upon perception, appraisal and ultimately the choice of strategies and legal instruments selected to address the problem. Thus *Piracy in Comparative Perspective: Problems, Strategies, Law* approaches maritime piracy from the perspectives of contributors from four continents, diverse legal cultures, and from multiple disciplines. This work appraises the piracy problem from the comparative perspectives of those disciplines, and also from key participants in the social processes that are plagued by piracy—mariners, navies, ship owners and operators, policy makers and lawyers. The contributors bring clarity to the piracy problem through the lenses of history,

---

[1] See, *Myres S. McDougal & William T. Burke*, The Public Order of the Oceans: A Contemporary International Law of the Sea, 1962 (1987, with new introductory essay).

[2] Final Communiqué of the London Conference on Somalia, paragraph 14, 23 February 2012. Available at http://www.fco.gov.uk/en/news/latest-news/?id=727627582&view=PressS.

law, maritime security, fisheries, economics and ocean commerce. They appraise strategies – the range of available modalities to address and correct the problem – through the lenses of naval power, port state control, penal systems and development. And they appraise law – both national and international authoritative decision-making – viewing state practice, international regulations, tribunal judgments, custom and international conventions from the comparative perspectives of Africa, India, England, France and the United States.

The Problem and the Trends

While piracy has a long ancestry, its contemporary manifestation is epiphenomenal of an intensely globalized social process that has security and commerce at its core. At the center of trade and commerce is shipping, because nearly all consumer goods and hydrocarbon resources move on water. The vessels that transport resources demanded by the end user globally are susceptible to pirate attacks. Shipping is one component of a global social process that includes states, naval forces, and coastal communities that struggle to meet basic human needs. Many of these communities are abandoned by, and precluded from, the fruits of 21st Century globalization. They have become spawning grounds for piracy. Their weal and woe of life unfolds adjacent to an ocean transit corridor of Western and Asian wealth, that, for impoverished coastal communities, represents a potential source of income and power. At the same time, contemporary piracy unfolds in a post-September 11th security environment in which state elites increasingly allocate substantial assets to avert existing and emerging threats to world order. In sum, piracy is a complex problem in an environment of intense and conflicting demands of states, consumers, seafarers, impoverished coastal communities and increasingly sophisticated private armies that employ force against vessels and mariners on the seas.

To understand the piracy problem, it is important to comprehend the historical and contemporary trends that are the subject of Part I of this book. The authors frame the problem by appraising trends in piracy beginning in the ancient world. Drawing upon Roman, English, French and international law through history, Dominique Gaurier describes the pirates path from rogue adventurer and robber to the enemy of all mankind. Fozia Lone explains that piracy is discussed in the Indian Sanskrit text of Vedas and in the *Arthashastra* written by Kautilya around 300 B.C.E. Contemporary trends are appraised by the contributors including Tom Tulloch who discusses the conditions that enable the piracy problem to proliferate and explains pirate tactics and international maritime security responses. Today maritime piracy has cost the global economy between $7 and $12 billion annually, as explained by Emannuel Chassot, Patrice Guillotreau, David Kaplan and Thomas Vallée. In particular, they explain the effect of piracy on fisheries using an economic analysis. Piracy expert Martin Murphy describes trends in economic costs, human security, privatization of maritime security, naval force protection, and projects geo-strategic and political outcomes. He concludes by identifying means to reverse the current trend, invoking short term and mid to longer term strategies.

The Participants and Their Perspectives

A participant observing or affected by the piracy problem will view it variously depending upon his or her standpoint and perspectives. Thus, in this book multiple standpoints and perspectives are presented. The first perspective, in the Foreword, is, appropriately, Somali. The President of Puntland State of Somalia, His Excellency Abdirahman Mohamed Mohamud (Farole), explains the piracy problem from the Puntland perspective. President Mohamud Farole underscores that piracy is both a land-based and a sea-based problem. Hence, the solution will require strategies and legal instruments calibrated for each context. Patrick Chaumette in his chapter "Seafarers: Piracy Protection," addresses the problem from the seafarer's perspective explaining the applicable legal and regulatory regimes and strategies for protection. The seafarer is a key actor and decision-maker in pirate incidents. Mariners face intense physical, psychological and workplace challenges as they operate on the frontlines of piracy. Challenges to the industry, from the perspectives of ship owners and the industry, are presented in chapters by Simon Delfau and by Arthur Bowring and Alexander McKinnon. Because perspectives on the piracy problem are also shaped by culture, geography and crisis, two chapters explain the views from India and West Africa. Fozia Lone presents an Indian perspective on counter-piracy indicating distinct views of piracy incidents, counter-strategies and applicable law. West African piracy receives less attention than East African Somali piracy. Thus, Claude Ichilanga writes of perspectives from Central and West Africa with a particular focus on incidents in the Gulf of Guinea.

Counter-Piracy Strategies

Strategies, the range and use of instruments and modalities to wage counter-piracy, are the subject of Part III. Maritime security law specialist James Kraska presents the larger security strategic framework in a chapter comparing European, American, African and Asian counter-piracy strategies. Cédric Leboeuf focuses on an important maritime security feature of the framework in his chapter appraising Operation Atalanta. Although piracy is largely conceived as a high seas activity, there is a role for ports and instruments of port-state control for strategic deterrence. Thus Oya Özçayır describes how port-state control is an effective counter-piracy strategy. Insurance, a strategic instrument intended to restore economic loss, performs a special role in our globalized commercial system. Thus "The Global Insurance Industry and Piracy," Poomintr Sooksripaisarnkit discusses the global insurance industry and piracy including specialized kidnap and ransom (K&R) insurance that has been available in varying guises since the early part of the 20th Century. Pirate organizations, states, NGOs and international organizations use media strategically. How media is strategically used and its actual and potential media impact on piracy is assessed by journalist Edward Girardet.

Law

Part IV appraises law understood as all pertinent authoritative decisions and their potential application to piracy. The international legal framework, its attributes and pathologies, is appraised. This framework includes the 1982 United Nations Convention on the Law of the Sea (UNCLOS), which defines the crime of piracy and provides a legal basis for jurisdiction and state cooperation, the Suppression of Unlawful Acts Against the Safety of Maritime Navigation (the Rome Convention) which proscribes acts of violence including robbery at sea that threaten navigation, and the relevant United Nations Security Council Resolutions that authorize multilateral mobilization of armed forces and which are designed to also insure respect for human rights. Thus Gwenaële Proutière-Maulion urges a reconsideration of the law of the flag and a holistic approach to piracy incorporating greater corporate social responsibility and implementation of the new maritime labour convention. Michael J. Stepek appraises international and national legal arrangements and mechanisms in his chapter, "Challenges of Prosecution and Jurisdiction." Mr. Stepek examines the fractured nature of the international legal architecture, its relationship to domestic law, prosecution pitfalls and possible solutions. The two subsequent chapters focus specifically on national legal systems. Noting that "some gestation periods can be long," Valérie Boré Eveno presents the new French law on piracy which was negotiated and drafted over a period of sixteen months. Dr. Boré Eveno discusses French law in reference to UNCLOS and in the context of the broader legal framework. Attorney Timothy Steigelman appraises historical and contemporary United States law on piracy with reference to the international legal system. Cumulatively, these national and international legal systems, instruments and mechanisms comprise the contemporary counter-piracy law repertoire.

Outcomes

Because of gaps in strategies, and an appreciation of diverse perspectives and inadequacies of the legal framework, there is a discrepancy between counter-piracy goals and desired outcomes. Outcomes accruing from the cumulative application of law and strategy to contemporary piracy problems are appraised in a concluding chapter that explores our public order of the oceans in this contemporary age of piracy. Coordinated strategic responses are producing some measurable results as the number of successful attacks has decreased. But as noted in the final Communiqué of the 2012 London Conference on Somalia, these have not fully addressed the fundamental issues of piracy.[3] There is a need for new strategies in new combinations accounting for diverse identifications, expectations and demands to achieve a comprehensive and thus more effective approach. Such an approach will account for all those who live with the piracy problem daily. These perspectives and problems are treated in the pages that follow. The editors have sought to insure that the cumulative result would be multi-method, multi-cultural and multi-national with a view to addressing the problem of maritime piracy in the global common interest. It is hoped that the following pages will inform the reader, and encourage a consideration of maritime piracy problems through a fresh lens.

---

[3] Final Communiqué of the London Conference on Somalia, 23 February 2012. Available at http://www.fco.gov.uk/en/news/latest-news/?id=727627582&view=PressS.

I. The Problem and the Trends

1. The Enemy of All Mankind

Dominique GAURIER[1]

Over the last thirty years, Western industrialized countries have witnessed a renascent piracy that has endangered maritime traffic. Today, piracy is no longer limited to the south-eastern regions of the globe, as it was for a long time. Now, piracy is present in maritime zones neighboring on commercial routes used by Western nations, particularly along the coast of Somalia. Consequently, the problem of piracy is becoming more and more serious, causing a great anxiety in many nations.

This chapter is a brief sketch of the historical grounds of piracy, in three sections. The first will show how piracy was, in ancient times, considered an honorable activity, but then became a calling of ill repute, especially under the influence of the Romans. The second section will then discuss the definition of the pirate as the enemy of all mankind. Finally, the third section will discuss the pirate conceived as an outlaw, a kind of buccaneer, among so-called "lawful pirates," or privateers.

I. Piracy in the Ancient World

Piracy is discussed in numerous ancient texts. The Homeric corpus contains many allusions to piracy, which was described as "robbery on the seas." Such robbers of the seas were among Odysseus's Achaean comrades as well as among the troops of the Achaean's enemies. In one mention a woman from Sidon tells how she was captured in Phœnicia by "sailors from Taphos, by pirates."[2] In fact, during ancient times, many heroes could have been accused of practicing piracy. For instance, Telemachus, Odysseus's son, is asked by Nestor after having gone up to unfamiliar coasts:

> If it is a convenient time for asking the guests for their names, it is surely when they have enjoyed the pleasures of the table. My visitors, [what is] your name? Where do you come from to us on the wat'ry ways? Are you in business? Aren't you only pirates who, with some

---

[1] D. LL, University of Nantes C.D.M.O.-EA 1165 "Droit Maritime et Océanique."

[2] *Odyssey*, XV, verse 427 (our own translation from the Greek and the French).

> folly, are running and cruising on the seas, and, while you were risking your lives, you are going and plundering foreign coasts?[3]

Poets were not the only ones concerned with piracy, historians dealt with it as well. In his introduction to the *Peloponnesian War*, Thucydides shows that piracy was probably the most ancient trade of the world, when he says that,

> ancient Greeks, those Barbarians who were living along the coasts of the seas and those who were residing in the isles, when they started to associate with each other through the seas, indulged in piracy; the most powerful ones looked there for a way of becoming richer and feeding the weak people; they attacked the towns which had no walls and people who resided within villages, they plundered them and extracted from these expeditions the greatest part of their resources, because piracy did not include any mark of dishonor; much more on the contrary, piracy could even bring some glory. It is easy to see it today, when some contemporary maritime people honored themselves to indulge in it and ancient poets let the seafarers be asked by the figures of their poems whether they were pirates. Those who were questioned in such a way do not deny such an activity and those who were asking it do not consider the question as insulting. . . . From this ancient robbery the custom of circulating with arms exists among the inhabitants of the inland.[4]

As suggested here by Thucydides piracy was not *prima facie* considered a roguish pursuit; when Homer wrote, piracy was seen as a meritorious, perhaps even glorious, means of enrichment. In fact, the Homeric poems describe piracy as belonging to the common law; piracy was not to be condemned except if done between citizens. It was lawful, if not honorable, when perpetrated on foreign people. Piracy was then just a way of living, along with fishing or hunting.

Hugo Grotius, who was himself an excellent student of ancient literature, wrote in his famous treatise, *The Law of War and of Peace*:

> It was thought [in the ancient world] that robbing and sacking the foreigners was permitted without declaring war on them. From this it follows, as Thucydides remarks, that foreigners were asked whether they could be either crooks or pirates, without offending them; of these things there are many examples in Homer. And in an old law of Solon it is spoken of some communities of men who were associated

---

[3] *Odyssey*, III, verses 69-74 (our own translation from the Greek and the French).

[4] Thucydides, *History of the Peloponnesian War*, I, 5 (our own translation from the French).

for the purpose of thievery. Justinian observed that in the time of Tarquinius, the profession of piracy was still attended with a degree of glory. It is also said in the Roman Law that, if there exists no friendship, no hospitality, no treaty of alliance, the members of this Nation are not really enemies, but that what was come into their hands from the Romans became under their ownership; that the Roman freeman, if made prisoner by them, be enslaved; that it is the same if something comes into the power of the Romans and that, in this case, the *postliminium* was conceded.[5]

Further, the "communities of men who were associated for the purpose of thievery," which Grotius spoke of, are indirectly suggested as lawful by an Imperial Constitution of Justinian edicted in the year 533 A.D. This Constitution was certainly evoked in an extract from the *Digest of Justinian*, where it was provided that:

> Co-members are those who belong to the same association, what the Greeks call an hetaireia. A statute gives them the power to enter into any agreement they like, so long as they do not contravene the public statute. This statute appears to have been adopted from the law of Solon which says: "If the inhabitants of a city district or precinct are in association for the purpose of holding religious feasts or of dining together or to provide for their burials or as mariners or for the purpose of selling wheat or of inhabiting together or if they are co-members of the same club or they combine to engage into some enterprise or for profit, anything that they agree betwixt themselves will be valid unless if it is forbidden by public statutes.[6]

---

[5] Grotius, *De jure belli ac pacis Libri tres*, b. II, chapt. XV, § 5, nb 2 (our own translation from a French version translated by Pradier-Fodéré, *Le Droit de la Paix et de la Guerre*, PUF, coll. Léviathan, Paris 1999, p 381). As regards the French translations of the main work of Grotius, three are actually existing. The first one was made by Antoine de Courtin, published in 1686, 1687 and the last edition in 1703. That translation is certainly the more reliable and the best ever made during the 17th and 18th century. In the 18th century Barbeyrac published a new French translation, but much more unreliable, because he not only translated, but freely interpreted the very difficult Latin text of Grotius which he did not understand very well, adding therefore many from his own. The last translation, probably the most reliable, is the one that is quoted above, made by Pradier-Fodéré made in the 19th century.

[6] The Latin text says:

Sodales sunt, qui eiusdem collegii sunt ; quam Græci hetaireian vocant. His autem potestatem facit lex, quam velint, sibi ferre; dum ne quid ex publica lege corrumpant. Sed hæc lex videtur ex lege Solonis tran, slata esse: nam illuc ita est: (text in Greek translated into Latin) "Si autem plebs, vel fratres, vel sacrorum sacramentales, vel nautæ, vel confrumentales, vel qui in eodem sepulchro sepeliuntur, vel sodales, qui et multum habitantes sunt: enimvero ad negocium, aut quid aliud; quidquid disponent ad invicem firmum sit, nisi hoc publicæ leges prohibuerint.

We have completed the English translation of the Latin text published by Alan Watson, *The Digest of Justinian*, D. 47, 22, 4, University of Pennsylvania Press, Philadelphia 1998, vol. 2.

In other words, that rule clearly means that associations contracted for the purpose of piracy, because they were not prohibited by any public statute, were consequently permitted!

Moving forward in time, during the classical Hellenic period, piracy was condemned as a common crime at the same level of armed and highway robberies. The emergence of the Greek cities, and of their constitutions, led piracy to slowly diminish on the main maritime routes, and to be relegated to the marginal countries of the Greco-Roman world. During the 5th century B.C. Athenians began the fight for more secure maritime routes, followed two centuries later by Alexander the Great, the kings of Egypt and the Rhodians.

Regarding this period, Diodorus of Sicily quotes the case of a Tyrrhenian pirate who entered the port of Syracuse with twelve pirate-vessels in the year 399 B. C., as well as the example of Philip of Macedonia who had enlisted an Aetolian in the purpose of practicing piracy in the Greek isles and in Crete.[7] Additionally, Polybius, in his *History*, accuses the Aetolians and denounces their exactions; reproaching that they answered derisively when charged to be accountable for their acts before arbiters.[8] Illyrians also had a strong reputation as pirates. In fact, their queen, Teuta, was reproached as having murdered two Roman plenipotentiary envoys just before embarking, "disregarding all the recognized principles of the law of nations."[9]

From the middle of the 4th century B.C., Romans had attempted to secure the occidental part of the Mediterranean Sea, but with limited success. The reason was perhaps that the Romans were not a genuine maritime people; they only began to build ships during the maritime war against the Punics, in the middle of the second century B. C. Further, they were instructed by the people of the southern maritime cities of the Italian Peninsula, who were of Greek origin and had a good knowledge of the art of navigation. Rome fought against the Tyrrhenians who sacked a large zone extending from the coasts of Tuscany to the Aegean Sea and the strait of Gibraltar, with the help of sundry Italic people.

With the conquest of Etruria, Rome was more effectively able to contend with pirates; nevertheless, Rome ought to have waited for the conquest of Liguria, when Carthage was completely defeated. Along the Adriatic Sea, the Illyrian coasts came then in the foreground. Rome could only obtain the peace with the defeat of the Illyrian king Genthos (168 B.C.), especially

---

[7] Diodorus of Sicily, *Historical Library*, XXIV, xxv ; XVI, lxxxi ; XX, xxviii.

[8] Polybus, *History*, II, i, 16.

[9] Polybus, *History*, II, i, 8.

around the region of Otrante, which was the favorite area for Illyrian pirates. Rome was obliged to intervene here, because other peoples, the Lapydes and the Dalmats, took advantage of the Roman Civil Wars and renewed their piratical activities.

But Rome had another growing anxiety. The wild geography and the aggressive character of the inhabitants of the Cilician countries allowed them to be largely independent of the Seleucid and Sassanid empires. Cilicia became a true haven for pirates. In a first stage, the Romans did not fight against an activity that was rather beneficial to the slave markets of the region of Delos. Rome only began to react when it was itself directly threatened by the pirates, knowing that it could not hope for any significant help from the Hellenistic kings. In fact, one of these kings, Mithridates 4th Eupator, the king of Pontus, was associated with Cilician pirates and actively sacked the Roman oriental trading posts.

Moving ever forward, in the year 67 B.C. the tribune of the Roman plebs, Aulus Gabinius, let an act be adopted, the *Lex Gabinia*, with which the Roman general Pompeius was given, for three years, full power to fight against pirates.[10] Pompeius lead this war with so great an efficiency that the pirates were totally destroyed and expelled from the area. He consequently won a high reputation, of which Cicero gave testament when he related Pompeius's campaign and the great merits of the man.[11]

---

[10] We know only the main chapters of this act from J. Calvinus, *Lexicon Iuridicum Iuris Cæsarei*, Genevæ 1640, p 999, *s. vbis* Gabinia, *De Piratis Persequendis*. These chapters may be translated as follows:

"Here are the chapters of that act: 1. in order that the command of the war against pirates be given to Cnæus Pompeius during three years; 2. in order that there be a power to command shelters, to garrisons and cities on the sea near the Herculean columns within a radius of forty stades from the sea; 3. in order that they assist their allies in all things regarding the administration of that war."

The Latin text says:

Huius hæc sunt capita: ut bellum adversus piratas Cnæio Pompeio in triennium ita madaretur; ut toto mari, quod est juxta columnas Herculis, et in maritimis provonciis usque ad quadrigente finium a mari stadium potestatem haberet imperandi tegibus, præsidis civitatibusque; ut se rebus omnibus ad eius belli administrationem necessariis iuuarent.

[11] See Cicero, *Pro Lege Manilia*. This oration, which clearly had political goals, was intended to support the purpose of the tribune Manilius; the tribune wanted Pompeius to be the supreme commander of the fleet and of the oriental maritime provinces. But that act was firstly strongly disapproved, because it was thought of as being too strong a support of ambitions which could be dangerous for the Republic. The opponents said that the power of the Senate, which was the general administrator of the Roman conquered provinces, was therefore lowered. Cæsar curiously supported this act, Cicero as well, probably influenced by some personal interest; he set his heart on becoming consul and was then an objective ally of Pompeius. This oration was extremely skilful and well-argued, so that Pompeius could obtain the asked supreme power. See peculiarly in this oration, XI, 31 ; XII, 33-34 ; XIII, 36-37.

Nevertheless, this fight exceeded its first goal, the elimination of a real danger: the Romans had also undertaken it in order to impose a new political pattern on the world they were conquering. Comparatively, pirates themselves largely adopted the preexisting frames from the barbarian communities, because they were driven back on the geographical borders of the Roman lawfulness. The Roman state, which was on the point of having hegemony over the Mediterranean area, could not do otherwise than to eliminate those pirate-states, in order to secure the coming *Pax Romana*. This period of relative stability left a firm remembrance after the collapse of the Roman empire, up to the 5th century A.D.

The moral concern for peace lingering in the people of the Empire was still very clear in Saint Augustine's work. In the *City of God*, Augustine shows how the values supported by the robberies could give birth to new states with a simple reversal of perspectives, if one is not careful of it. He says:

> Without any justice actually, are kingdoms other than great troops of robbers? And what is a troop of robbers, if not a little kingdom? For it is a gathering of men in which one chief commands, in which a social compact is recognized, and in which some conventions rule the partition of the booty. If this disastrous troop, with recruitment of malfeasants, gets accrued to such an extent that it occupies a country, it establishes important places, it takes cities, it subdues people, then it openly assumes the name of kingdom, a name which does not warrant him the renouncement of cupidity, but the conquest of impunity. . . . Waging war against neighbors for making a rush at new fights, crushing, reducing people who did not offend us only with a desire for domination, is that something different from a huge robbery?[12]

[12] Here is the Latin text, directly translated by us:

Remota itaque iustitia quid sunt regna nisi magna latrocinia? quia et latrocinia quid nisi parua regna? Manus et ipsa hominum est, imperio principis regitur, pacto sociétatis astringitur, placiti lege præda dividitur. Hoc malum si in tantum perditorum hominum accessibus crescit, ut et loca teneat sedes constituat, ciuitates occupet populos subiuget, euidentius regni nomen adsumit, quod ei iam in manifesto confert non dempta cupidita, sed adita impunitas . . . . Inferre autem bella finitimis et in cetera inde procedere ac populos sibi non molestos sola regni cupiditate conterere et subdere, quid aliud quam grande latrocinium nominandum est?

City of God, IV, iv et vi.

II. THE PIRATE AS *HOSTI HUMANI GENERIS* – THE ENEMY OF ALL MANKIND

Cicero, that great orator, appealed strongly to morals. Thus, he severely condemned the pirate as being the "enemy of all mankind," *hostis humani generis*. In the second judicial action against Verres, while Verres was *proprœtor* in Sicily, *i.e.* a governor commissioned by the Roman senate for three years, Verres was reproached by Cicero for having exploited the province and having satisfied his lowest instincts in shamelessly plundering and sacking the public and private wealth between 73 and 70 B.C. Even though this judicial action never came before the judges, Cicero wrote five orations; in the last one, called *De suppliciis*, Verres was reproached for having given shelter to a chief pirate. This became, for the advocate Cicero, the major focus of his towering rage. Cicero developed a lyric flight of oratory and questioned the law, the customs and the precedents that could have allowed Verres to give shelter to an "enemy who was fighting desperately and very relentlessly against the Roman people, or rather the common enemy of all races and all people."[13] Ever since then variations of that expression were adopted by authors, and continually repeated.

The first subsequent mention of this expression can be found in Alberico Gentili's great work on international law, *De Jure Belli Libri Tres*, or *The Three Books on the Law of War*, which was first published in 1598 and republished in Germany by his younger brother in 1612. In the first book, Gentili speaks of pirates in these terms: "Pirates are the common enemies of all mortals."[14] A contemporary of Gentili, the great English Judge Edward Coke, justified his definition of piracy as a "petit treason, for which he was to be drawne and hanged: because *pirata est hostis humani generis*."[15] In English, "because a pirate is the enemy of all mankind."

[13] *Actio in Verrem Secunda*, V, xxx, 76. The Latin text is as follows: *"Quod est huiusce rei ius, quæ consuetudo, quod exemplum? Hostem acerrimum atque infestissimum populi Romani seu potius communem hostem gentium nationumque."*

[14] *De Jure Belli Libri Tres*, Hanau 1612, lib. I, cap. IV, Latin text p 33: *"Piratæ omnium mortalium hostes sunt communes."* It must be remembered that Alberico Gentili was appointed as *Regius professor* at Oxford, where he gave lectures on Roman law, after having fled Italy because of religion, for he was a Protestant. An English translation of that work was published by the Carnegie Endowment for International Peace by the Clarendon Press Oxford, London 1933. But the English or American reader has to be very attentive, because the translator did not know at all the Roman law, *i.e.* the major ground, if not the only one, of Gentili's developments, and made a lot of misinterpretations. We have made a translation into French of that work, to which we joined the complete translation of the Roman sources used by Gentili. It will be published by the end of the year 2011 or in the beginning of 2012.

[15] *3 Third Part of the Institutes of the Laws of England Concerning High Treason and Other Pleas of the Crown and Criminal Causes*, cap. 49 *Of Piracy*, 113. Note that Matthew Hale, in his *History of the Pleas of the Crown*, defines piracy as a "crime not made felony, whereof the common law can take notice," ed. by G. Wilson Serjeant at law, London1778, vol. 2, p 18.

In the 17th century, Charles Molloy, who was the author of *De Jure Maritimo et Navali,* or a *Treatise of Affairs Maritime and of Commerce*, defines the pirate as follows:

> A Pirate is a Sea-Thief, or *hostis humani generis*, who for to enrich himself, either by surprise or open force, sets upon Merchants and others trading by Sea, ever spoiling their Lading, if by any possibility they can get the mastery, sometimes bereaving them of their lives, and sinking of their Ships; the Actors wherein, Tully [Cicero] calls Enemies of all, with whom neither Faith nor Oath is to be kept.[16]

A century later, the same was repeated by Blackstone in his *Commentaries*:

> Lastly, the crime of piracy, or robbery and depredation upon the high seas, is an offence against the universal law of society; a pirate being, according to Sir Edward Coke, *hostis humani generis*. As therefore he has renounced all the benefits of society and government, and has reduced himself afresh to the savage state of nature, by declaring war against all mankind, all mankind must declare war against him.[17]

In French legal literature, which contains a paucity on Maritime law, the bad reputation of pirates is also echoed. Pirates are not precisely qualified as "enemies of all mankind," but rather as "the avowed enemies of the society, violators of the public faith, armed public robbers with open force."[18] This characterization was adopted by René-Josué Valin, the great commentator of the French *Royal Ordinance 1681*, concerning maritime commerce. This opinion was given afresh, *verbatim*, in the 19th century by another French author, Beaussant, in his *Code Maritime* in a chapter concerning piracy.[19]

The pirate being then commonly defined as an enemy, an important question remained to be asked whether a pirate could be sued and punished as a common robber. The mediaeval customary provisions provided, in the *Rolle of Olayron*, that

[16] Molloy, *De Jure Maritimo et Navali, or a Treatise . . .*, printed for John Bellinger and George Dawes, 3d ed., London 1682, p 52.

[17] *4 Black. Comm.*, 5, 71. Blackstone explains that piracy was at his time ruled by statute 11 and 12 W. III, c. 7, completed by statute 4 Geo. I c. 11 and 8 Geo. I c. 24.

[18] Valin, *Nouveau Commentaire sur l'Ordonnace de la Marine du Mois d'Aoust 1681*, La Rochelle 1766, t. 2, Liv. III, tit. IX, art. 3, p 236.

[19] A. Beaussant, *Code Maritime ou Lois de la Marine Marchande, Administratives, de Commerce, Civiles et Pénales, Réunies, Ordonnées et Expliquées*, Edouard Legrand Libraire-commissionnaire, Paris 1840, t. 1, p 244.

> Likewise, the thynges preceding[20] ought to be understood yf the said ship was not engaged in the practice of pillage, that the crew of her were not pirates or sea-rovers, or enemies of our Holy Catholic Faith. For in that case yf they be pirates, pillagers, or sea-rovers, or Turks, or other opposed to and enemies of our Holy Catholic Faith, *every one may take from suche manner of men as from dogs, and may strip them and despoil them of their goods without any punishment*. This is the judgement.[21]

The French commentator of this provision, Cleirac, who wrote the first French book on Maritime law, said:

1. The right of wrecks against pirates is fully of justice, the agony or penalty of which is to be break on the road, *ordinance of Admiralty 1584 art. 64*.
2. Piratæ communes generis hiumani hostes sunt, quos idcirco omnibus rationibus persequi incumbit [Pirates are the common enemies of the human mankind whom one applies oneself to prosecute with all reasons for that] the Chancellor of England says, *Bacon De Bello sacro p. 346,* after all the ancient authors . . . . Therefore, sunt ipso iure diffidati, cumquibus publice bellum habemus [By the law itself, those with whom we have a public war are to be mistrusted], our Doctors say.
3. Consequently it is lawful, even commendable to spoil them . . . . Indeed it is a crime to have any commiseration or to make the pirates good . . . .
4. For them there is legally no action and no exception in justice against those who are sueing them quia in omnium furum persona constitutem est, ne eius rei nomine furti agere possint, cuius ipsi fures sunt [because it is enacted against the person of all robbers that they could not sue for the stealing of that good of which the robbers themselves are the owners], *D. 47, 2, 14 § 4 ; D. 47, 2, 48 § 4 and the constitution of the Emperor Friedrich under C. 6, 2, 18* by which Navigantium bona qui naufragium passi sunt, illis reservantur is added by exception that judgement nisi piraticam exerceant pravitatem [The goods of navigant crew who have endured a shipwreck are reserved for them, unless they have carried on the fault of piracy].

[20] *I.e.* as regards the wrecking of a ship.

[21] Sir Travers Twiss, *The Black Book of Admiralty*, Reprint 1985 Professional Books Ltd, Oxford, vol. 2, p 479-481 (emphasis added).

5. So that they have no action between themselves; on the contrary the prize between rovers is good and without any right of complaint . . . [22]

If no precise penalty was provided for in the maritime customs, except the mention of the torment on the road for pirates made by Cleirac, then robbery against a robber was for a long time esteemed lawful. But Valin thought it absolutely unlawful in the 18th century,23 because the king had imposed a new order since then: he was liable for the conservation of the goods from a ship which had run-aground, and the goods coming from shipwrecks, in order to allow their restitution to their owners.

A statute of the 7th of December 1373 enacted by the French king Charles the Fifth, gave the Admiral of France a full competence on crimes committed by pirates. It was then the first statute on maritime prizes and its first article provided that:

> to amend the bad will of those who could be attracted by a blameworthy covetousness suggested by enemies to commit against our friends, subjects and other allies, murders and larcenies . . . our Admiral and his lieutenants in every region of our kingdom will diligently inquire about occurred cases and the persons whom they will find guilty of such misdeeds, they will sentence them and make quickly or without delay justice against them so that it will be an example for all others.[24]

No punishment was however provided for. Nevertheless the mention of a quick inquiry means clearly that no feeling of impunity was suggested. This urgency was also recalled in another contemporary English text emanating from the *Royal Commission of Inquiry* given by the English king Edward the Third in April 1375 in Queensborough:

> It be inquired about all thieves who rob on the sea some lieges of our Lord the King or some of his alliance or of his friendship or some under truce or under his protection, about the names of the robbers and of the owners and masters of the pirate-ships, about the stolen goods, their value and into which hands they were kept, about all their keepers, recipients and comforters.[25]

In France, under the Ancient regime, a distinction was made between piracy on public rivers and bays and piracy on the high seas. As regards the pirates who entered the public rivers or bays and were consequently

[22] E. Cleirac, *Us et Coustumes de la Mer*, Guillaume Millanges, Bordeaux 1647, p 158-159.

[23] R.-J. Valin, *Commentaire . . .*, *op. cit.*, t. 2, b. III, tit. IX, art. 3, p 236.

[24] Sir Travers Twiss, *The Black Book . . .*, *op. cit.*, vol. 1, p 431-432. The original text is quoted in old French and translated into English by us.

[25] Sir Travers Twiss, *The Black Book . . .*, *op. cit.*, vol. 1, p 148.

captured, an Edict of July 1691 ruled that they were considered as pirates, sentenced to penal servitude by the judges of the admiralties. The pirate on the high seas was considered as a ship-owner who practiced an unlawful activity. A Royal Ordinance of the 5th of September 1718 sentenced such pirates to capital punishment. A little time before, the great Ordinance on Maritime Commerce of 1681 forbade all subjects to serve on warships commissioned by foreign princes under the same penalty as the pirates. Another article of the same ordinance declared that ships seized either from enemies or from pirates were good prizes, and a last one said that all ships which were fighting under a flag other than that from her commissioning state, were also good prizes.

However the exact definition of a pirate was not so precise as could be desired, and some vagueness remained between pirates, privateers, or in French "corsaires," sea-rovers and other men of such quality.

III. WHO WAS A TRUE ENEMY OF ALL MANKIND? UNLAWFUL, VERSUS LAWFUL, PIRATES

Throughout history, pirates were commonly defined as sea-rovers, or in old English statutes "robbeurs sur mer." They were generally recognized as wrongdoers practicing on the seas but were distinguished from other men who could practice the same activity, but lawfully. In the French language, a pirate may be known by three names: pirate, corsaire, and forban, *i.e.* a pirate, a privateer and a buccaneer. In ancient French dictionaries of law and in French dictionaries on Maritime law of the 18th and 19th centuries, those three appellations are quite equivalent, because they were undecided as regards the exact meaning of each term. But in English, more precision seems to have been exercised.

Let us begin with a well-known English dictionary from the 18th century, *Jacob's New Law Dictionary*. The pirates are therein clearly defined as

> Sea Rovers, without any fixed Place of Residence, who acknowledge no Sovereign and no Law, and support themselves by Pillage and Depredations at Sea. . . . They are denied Succor by the Law of Nations, and by the Civil Law, a Ransom promised to a Pirate, if not complied with, creates no Wrong; for the Law of Arms is not communicated to such, neither are they capable of enjoying that Privilege, which lawful Enemies are entitled to in the Caption of another.[26]

---

[26] *Jacob's New Law Dictionary*, by Woodfall and Strahan, London 1762, no pagination, *s. vbo* "Pirates."

The definitions of piracy in French dictionaries are generally not far from the above, albeit much less precise. In the *Dictionnaire de Trévoux*, a dictionary made by the Jesuits in 1703, some interesting but equivocal characterizations are given:

> PIRATE: privateer, buccaneer, who practices privateering on the sea, without any license or authority of the Prince or the Sovereign. . . . The first Pirates known in France were the Normans.[27] All were not coming from Normandy: French people who disagreed with their lords united with them and called themselves with the same name.[28]

A century before, in the second part of the 17th century, an author from the Netherlands, Johan Voet, defined the pirate in Ordinance of the States of Holland of 29th of January 1658. In that work he said, "must also be considered as pirates those who are using with duplicity commissions of princes fighting reciprocally between them, having a ship fitted out for taking preys, commonly, die op dubbele commissie varen [those who are sailing with a double commission]."29

A conclusion commands here some attention: maritime nations, as both the English and the Dutch ones were, adopted precise and clear definitions of piracy. It was absolutely not the case with the French nation. In spite of a wide maritime border, France was never a true maritime nation because of its greater interests in territorial conquests of neighboring European countries

[27] The fame of piracy against the Normans seems to go back to the mediaeval times and was also evoked in a case of piracy from the time of King Edward 3rd in 1367. In this case, a difference was laid down between piracy as practiced by an English subject against one of his fellow citizens, an act termed a treason because of the natural faith owed to the king by an English subject, and where piracy was practiced by a foreign subject. If he was a Norman, the crime was termed a felony, sentenced to seizure of property or capital punishment. The case is reported in the Maynard edition of the Year Books, in the *Livre des Assises et Pleas del Corone, en Temps du Roy Edward le Tiers*, London 1679, reprint Professional Books Ltd 1981, *anno quadragesimo*, 25, p 245. The words are from the counsel of a party in Lawfrench:

Il dit que ils furent les servants de la mort de la mort . . . . Car il dit que devant Shard et Anglois un Norman qui fuit Ductor d'une nef Anglois qui avoit gens Anglois, robbe les gens sur le mer; et sur ceo ils fuerent pris et trové culpables: et pur le Norman, en tant que il fist ceo felonie à son langue de Normandie, envers luy ne fuit accompt forsque felonie, il fuit pendu; et les Anglois, en ce que ils le firent en la langue [anglaise], il fuit devers eux adjuge Treason: et issint fuerent ils treies et pendus.

If the issue of the case was the same for both men, nevertheless the English pirate was sentenced through a regular trial, of which the Norman could not have the advantage. It must be remarked that the same king Edward 3rd had however abolished that distinction by the Statute of Treason 1352 (25 Edw. III c.2), not taken in account in that case and making piracy a felony, whoever commits it.

[28] *Dictionnaire de Trévoux*, Paris 1752, t. 5, col. 637-638.

[29] J. Voet, *Commentarius ad Pandectas*, Apud Abrahamum de Hondt, The Hague 1746, t. 2, lib. XLVII, tit. IX, nb 4, p 984.

than in maritime spaces or ultramarine conquests. The few French authors who wrote on maritime law were generally vague in the matter of definitions.

As regards the French corsaire, or the English privateer, both words have exactly the same meaning. But once more, there is more exactitude in the English works than in French ones. In Jacob's New Law Dictionary, we read that,

> Privateers are a Kind of private Men of War, the persons concerned wherein administer at their own Costs a Part of a War, by fitting out these Ships of Force and providing them with all Military Stores; and they have, instead of Pay, Leave granted them to keep what they can take from the Enemy, allowing the Admiral his Share.[30]

Compared with this clear and straight definition, the one given in a French dictionary of the same time seems rather undecided:

> The corsairs are men who run the seas without any commission for robbing and pillaging all what they can take (this word comes from Italian corsaro, which was said from corsis or corsibus - i.e. Corsicans). That kind of men, who are also sometimes called pirates, are not too distinguished from highwaymen; so they are approximately sentenced in the same manner.[31]

Such a definition is not as exact as could be expected from a law-dictionary. First of all, there is nothing emphasizing that a corsair was seen as a private entrepreneur who fit out a ship at his own costs, but with a public commission, because he was granted to keep what he could take from the enemy. In the French dictionary, the corsair is only defined as a pirate or as a highwayman. It must also be pointed out that the word *corsair* was itself supposed to have been extracted from the name of Corsican, in 1768, a time when Corsica was just integrated into France. The same dictionary concludes the definition and says that, "corsairs who are running with the commissions of several powers may be treated as buccaneers and hanged without any ceremony."[32] It may be said that regarding the French authors, a pirate, a corsair and a buccaneer are the same, because they sack and pillage on the seas without any commission from anybody and practice on their own behalf, even if there were no murders of passengers or sailors.

Nevertheless a new element emerged when several nations gave pirates commissions for fitting out ships, and to make and keep prizes made on

---

[30] *Jacob's . . ., op. cit., s.vbo* "Privateers," no pagination.

[31] Denisart, *Collection de décisions nouvelles relatives à la jurisprudence actuelle*, Chez la Veuve Desaint, Paris 1771, t. 1, *s. vbo* "Corsaires," p 734 (our translation from the French).

[32] Denisart, *loc. cit.*

enemy-ships. If the corsair or privateer practices with the commission of a single state, he is deemed to perform to the detriment of enemy cargoes or enemy ships, say the French authors, and supposedly the English ones. That is to say that the corsair is not considered as a pirate when he fits out a ship with an official commission given by a single state, but he can be recognized as such if he has commissions from more than one power or state, and be sentenced to the same penalties as the pirate or buccaneer.

As regards these commissions, they were known under many appellations: letters of mark, free booter, commissions for reprisals and warrants. In French it is called something which cannot be found in English, *lettres de course*, which may literally be translated as "letters for cruising." Such an expression being surely never used in English, where the expression "letters of mark" was commonly used. These letters of mark were a document which a private person was given, who wanted to recover his investment from the people of an enemy prince. The word *mark* comes from the Provençal *marca*, which means a seizure. Nevertheless the English meaning of "letters of mark" applies itself both to the warrant given to the sailor who carries on reprisals, and to the privateer himself, with some confusion.

It was not until the 19th century that a French author could give a clearer definition with a better distinguishing betwixt a pirate and a privateer. This author, who may well be considered as the last commentator of the French Royal Ordinance 1681 on Maritime Commerce, said that:

> Piracy is the act of a sea-rover, who runs without any commission of his government after the ships which he encounters for sacking them. . . . The Government gives this commission to one of its subjects; then the subject who runs on the seas with this power is not anymore a pirate, but a shipowner whose cruising is allowed by the law of nations and confirmed by the State. But, since the law of nations wants that a Government does not give such commissions without the shipowner having performed the formal procedures required from him, all Government which does not regard for these formal procedures infringes the social compact and falls itself into the case of piracy which it lets to be practiced by its subjects; consequently that Government is thus in this case a pirate.[33]

[33] Boucher, *Institution au droit maritime, Ouvrage complet sur la législation maritime, ayant pour base l'Ordonnance de 1681, à laquelle sont adaptées les Lois de l'ancien et du nouveau régime; des Réflexions, des jugemens, étayés des autorités les plus respectable; notamment d'Emerigon, Valin et Pothier; des Formules de divers Actes, Traités, Comptes; des Intsructions nouvelles sur la course maritime*, A Paris an XII (1803), nb 1363-1364, p 360.

If this definition is well understood, it clearly means that there are two categories of pirates: lawful pirates, who practice with the official warrant which they were given by a government, and unlawful pirates, who practice without any warrant and exclusively for their own interests. Such men were, for a long time, the subjects of famous and glorious legends. Some adventurers have even looked for their abandoned or concealed treasures. But it is only a dream that was never as romantic as it seemed. A life on board was harsh for the sailor, the ship being lawful or pirate, with no comfort at all, suffering from hunger and many diseases. When captured, unlawful pirates or buccaneers were generally sentenced to be hanged without great ceremony, and their ships seized or destroyed.

However, in the 19th century, such a sentence was more rarely applied and, as an author remarks: "Today it is no need to say that the law does not allow the crime and that it was not more permitted to pillage than to kill the captured pirates or the shipwrecked men. Justice must rule on their fate and the fruit of their depredations."[34]

Contrary to today, the competent jurisdictions for such judgments were only national. In France, piracy was referred to the regional Admiralties, today to the common criminal court. In 1537, in Great Britain, it was given to a new jurisdiction, which was created by a statute of Henry the Eighth. In this statute, the procedure of the common law was applied and the cases were to be heard by the Lord Admiral's court, to which the Lord Chancellor added three or four other judges appointed for the case. The crime of piracy was then sentenced as a felony and as highway robbery.

In France, two reforms were undertaken in the 19th century: firstly, a new statute in 1825 mandated a death sentence when the crime of piracy was committed, but only a sentence of hard labor when there was neither a homicide nor wounds and when the attack was only on the crew of the pirate ship, who were neither the chiefs nor the captain of the ship. The second reform was one of international character. The Treaty of Paris of 1856 forbade privateering between all signatory states, with the exception of the United States of America. The USA rejected such a provision because it wanted to retain the ability to sanction privateers during a time of war. The USA also argued that it should not be deprived of resources which the patriotism of their subjects could provide, in the absence of true naval forces.

[34] Cf. A. Beaussant, *Code maritime ...*, *op. cit.* t. 1, p 245 (our translation from the French).

IV. CONCLUSION

This historical sketch of piracy, and of its lawful and unlawful forms, could lead one to believe that piracy lives in the past. Nevertheless, it never totally disappeared in some parts of the world, especially in South-Eastern Asia, around the Philippines, in Malaysia, and in some straights in the southern part of China. Today, a new and very offensive piracy emerges on the Eastern coasts of Africa along Somalia. This new piracy was fed by the poverty of local populations, civil and religious wars, and many other horribles. And all under the eyes of a world that remained indifferent where its interests were not concerned. However, western nations are increasingly concerned because piracy is now practiced on the world's great maritime routes, in particular around the Suez Canal. To the great concern of western nations, piracy is now jeopardizing the world's supply of fuel.

Yet, this increasingly complex problem presents increasingly complex questions. Is piracy merely a crime? Could it be, for some destitute peoples, just a means of subsistence? Or is it becoming, through funding, arms, and commissioning, a means to further a vague ideo-religious cause in the region?

2. Plague of Pirates – A Primer

Tom TULLOCH[1]

In February 2011 Somali pirates held 30 merchant vessels in anchorages off the east coast of Somalia and 664 innocent merchant seamen hostage. Many of these vessels and men have since been ransomed, netting the pirates over $137 million USD for 2011, and the scourge continues. Three of the vessels and crews currently held have been in pirate hands for over a year, with one (M/V ICEBERG) dating back to March 2010, almost two years in captivity. Somali pirates have taken hundreds of millions of dollars in ransom payments since hijackings began off the Horn of Africa in 2004, the majority since the pace accelerated in early 2008. In response, the nations of most of the developed world have sent naval forces to the region to disrupt piracy. Between 15 and 20 warships currently operate there under various coalitions and alliances such as NATO and the European Union, with an additional dozen or so deployed under national authority, such as from Russia, China, India and Japan, for counter-piracy. Yet the problem has not been solved; in fact the number of ships successfully captured by Somali pirates continues to average nearly one per month and attacks continue apace. How can this be?

In order to understand why Somali piracy continues to enjoy success it is necessary to examine the conditions under which it flourishes, the tactics and procedures employed by the pirates, and the limitations on and of the naval forces sent to deal with the problem.

Somalia – A Failed State

Somalia is a failed state, having been without an effective central government since President Siad Barre was deposed in 1991. The current internationally recognized authority in Somalia is the Transitional Federal Government (TFG), which was established in 2004. The TFG however has been battling Al Shabaab insurgents for control of the capital Mogadishu and a limited footprint in Southern Somalia for some years. Even with the

---

[1]Captain Tulloch, MSM CD Royal Canadian Navy.

assistance of African Union troops only minimal headway has been made; the TFG has therefore little to no ability to exert control over the country at large. The offensive against Al Shabaab in Southern Somalia by Kenyan forces that began in October 2011 has assisted the TFG to broaden its sphere of control, however, the struggle for control continues. Years ago north-west Somalia declared itself the Independent Republic of Somaliland and, although not officially recognized internationally, has enjoyed a relative degree of stability. A second region, Puntland, occupying north-east Somalia proclaimed itself autonomous in 1998; however scant control over its territory or coastal waters has been able to be exercised by the Puntland Authority to date. Furthermore, Somalia, in addition to being fragmented and fought over by various official and unofficial government bodies and insurgent forces, is also divided into a number of clan groupings which exercise varying degrees of control over the activities in their regions. What little local authority exists is virtually ineffective. Economically Somalia is one of the poorest countries in the world, with a Gross Domestic Product (GDP) per capita in the mere hundreds of dollars and the vast majority of the population living in poverty. The current situation in Somalia therefore is one of limited fragmented control by a broad spectrum of disparate groups, with much of the country essentially lawless and destitute – the perfect situation to permit piracy to flourish.

Geographically Somalia lies adjacent to one of the busiest shipping routes in the world. The shortest route by sea between south/southwest Asia and Europe/eastern North America is through the Suez Canal, the eastern approach to which is through the Gulf of Aden off Somalia's north coast. Over 20,000 merchant ships transit this route annually – some 400 per week. The Gulf of Aden separating Somalia and Yemen is only 500 miles long and 150 miles across at its widest point – essentially a chokepoint through which maritime traffic must pass. The initial forays into piracy in the region occurred here, where the lack of maritime and government authority combined with the close proximity to the Somali coast of lucrative targets, the means to hunt and capture them, and a willingness to undertake piracy merged to great effect. Initially taking the form of sporadic, often violent maritime robbery beginning in 1989, it evolved into hijacking for ransom around 2004, as the potential for high payoffs escalated and pirate leaders gained experience and refined their practices. Somali pirates in the early days styled themselves as a makeshift "coast guard," asserting that they had taken to the seas to defend Somalia against over-fishing and toxic waste dumping by foreign vessels; whatever tenuous truth these claims may have held then are clearly non-existent now, as the pirate business model has fully embraced capture for profit as its sole aim.

ALLIED FORCES

Naval and maritime air forces assigned to the counter-piracy mission operate either as part of one of three alliance groupings, or under independent national control in the case of nations such as Russia, China, India, Japan and Malaysia. NATO maintains a Combined Task Force (CTF 508) in theatre comprised of one of its two Standing NATO Maritime Groups (SNMG) of three to eight frigates or destroyers. The European Union has deployed a force of similar size (CTF 465), and a third multinational group operates under the auspices of the US-led Combined Maritime Forces (CMF - CTF 151). In addition to surface forces, NATO has periodically employed submarines to conduct covert coastal surveillance, and various nations have contributed maritime patrol aircraft to operate either as part of one of alliances, or independently like Japan. These surveillance assets are vital to the task of maintaining situational awareness over the vast operating area. While nations and alliances exercise command over their own forces, the overall military counter-piracy effort is coordinated via regular Shared Awareness and Deconfliction (SHADE) meetings in which all parties participate. At-sea coordination between these different groups, independent deployers and transiting merchant vessels is achieved via a secure Internet based system called Mercury.

NATO's plan of operation consists of three main objectives. Firstly it aims to disrupt piracy in the region by interdicting pirate activity at sea. The second objective is to ensure the protection of merchant shipping, both by promoting self protective measures within the shipping community as well as by undertaking the active defence of vessels against pirate attacks. The third is to optimize counter-piracy operations through regional and international cooperation and the encouragement of capability amongst the nations of the region. By progressing these objectives simultaneously it is intended to reduce piracy to a more acceptable level, acknowledging that the outright solution lies beyond the scope of the current mission.

CANADA

Canada has contributed two frigates to the NATO force in recent years; HMCS WINNIPEG in early 2009 and HMCS FREDERICTON in late 2009/early 2010. Additionally there are 12 Canadian officers and petty officers permanently on the staff at NATO's Maritime Headquarters in Northwood, which exercises operational command over Operation OCEAN SHIELD, the NATO counter-piracy mission, and one officer permanently filling a seagoing position on the staff of the Commander of SNMG 1. In addition and specifically for OCEAN SHIELD Canada contributes three Naval Reserve officers to augment the manning of the NATO Shipping Centre in HQ Northwood. Canada has however not sent vessels or aircraft to participate in counter-piracy for the past two years. There are a number of reasons for this. The Royal Canadian Navy is in the midst of a multi-year programme to modernize its 12 frigates, the workhorse of the fleet, with resulting low numbers of available vessels for deployment; the RCAF's ageing CP-140 Aurora maritime patrol aircraft have seen their scarce flying hours all but used up in recent operations off Haiti and Libya; and Canadian submarines are not yet in a state to be deployed. Furthermore, the Canadian government is reluctant to engage in counter-piracy operations without a comprehensive legal framework in place to prosecute pirates. It views the de facto catch-and-release policy as inadequate; but is unwilling to attempt prosecution of pirates in Canada because of the cost and likelihood of associated claims for refugee status, or to hand them over for regional prosecution where their human rights cannot necessarily be guaranteed or monitored.

PIRATE TACTICS AND COUNTER-PIRACY – GULF OF ADEN

Pirate tactics vary across the region. Pirates in the Gulf of Aden generally operate in single, fast "attack" skiffs of between 6 and 14 metres long, with a crew of 5 to 9 armed with easily-obtained Kalashnikov (AK-47) assault rifles and rocket-propelled grenade (RPG) launchers. Their tactics are to loiter in the main shipping lane between Somalia and Aden for up to 3 or 4 days until a suitable vessel is located. They then rapidly bring their craft alongside and swarm aboard by means of aluminum ladders, quickly overpowering the crew with their weapons. If the ship is undefended, this can be accomplished normally in about 15 minutes. The ship is then diverted to an anchorage while the pirates make their demands for ransom – a process that can take many months but can net the pirates as much as $10 million.

The priority of naval forces since their arrival in the region has been the safety of shipping in the Gulf of Aden, as merchant vessels have no choice but to transit this body of water unless they opt to go around the southern tip of Africa, which is not a cost-effective option in most cases. An Internationally Recommended Transit Corridor (IRTC) has been established in the Gulf of Aden for merchant traffic, enabling naval vessels to focus their defensive patrols there. Nations such as China, Russia, Japan and India have chosen to escort shipping through the Gulf convoy-style. The NATO Shipping Centre (NSC), part of the Northwood Headquarters, is

NATO's link to the merchant shipping community and serves also to advise them of risk areas. Merchant ships have been encouraged to adopt self-defence measures such as employing extra lookouts, rigging fire hoses and barbed wire to deter access, manoeuvring at speed when under attack, and as a last resort, having a "panic room" or safe compartment to which the crew can retreat if pirates are able to board. Additionally, many shipping companies have begun to hire commercial armed protection teams to defend their vessels. The combination of merchant practices and naval patrols has made it significantly harder for pirates to achieve success in the Gulf of Aden; in the last 8 months of 2011 there were only 6 merchant vessels taken by pirates. By comparison 17 vessels were captured in the first 4 months of 2011. None of the vessels captured to date has employed armed protection teams.

PIRATE TACTICS – SOMALI BASIN AND ARABIAN SEA

As piracy in the Gulf of Aden has become more difficult, pirates have adapted and broadened their range of activity; indeed they have ventured considerably further afield. The entire east coast of Somalia overlooks the Indian Ocean, and pirates have been unafraid to venture hundreds of miles out to sea to hunt. Weather here has played a factor, since the seasonal monsoons periodically create seas in the Western Indian Ocean that are too rough for small pirate skiffs to operate. These monsoons occur twice yearly, from June to September, and again from December to March. When the seas are calmer during the transition periods between monsoons, pirates put to sea in small attack groups, generally consisting of a large "whaler" or mother-skiff loaded with supplies, weapons and fuel accompanied by two smaller attack skiffs – sustainable for 3 to 4 weeks. With merchant shipping able to avoid the east coast of Somalia by a considerable distance, these attack groups have enabled pirates to reach the areas where shipping must transit: the Mozambique Channel, off Madagascar, near the Seychelles, towards the Maldives, and into the Arabian Sea. Pirate attacks have occurred within 200 miles of India, some 1500 miles from Somalia. Pirates have also taken to capturing dhows, the indigenous cargo vessels that ply the region, and fishing vessels, and using them as motherships with their crews held hostage on board to transport their attack skiffs well out into the broader Indian Ocean. In a number of cases there has been evidence of collusion between pirates and dhow crews for a share in the profits. Thus the area of pirate activity now stretches across thousands of miles, from the Southern Red Sea to India, and from the Arabian Sea to Madagascar – an area comparable in size to the whole of continental Europe from Lisbon to Moscow.

Pirates have realized a degree of success by using captured merchant vessels, in addition to dhows and fishing vessels, as motherships, to increase their range and transit speed and to negate the effect of the monsoon, thereby permitting them to operate year-round. January and February 2011 saw unprecedented numbers of attacks taking place in the Arabian Sea, previously too difficult for pirate operations due to distance and sea state - these attacks were facilitated by using motherships. Naval forces have since been quicker to mark and shadow identified motherships with a warship, which has minimized their effectiveness in recent months.

INTERVENTION OPTIONS

Pirates use a series of camps scattered along the coast of Somalia, predominantly on the east side of the Puntland region, to amass their supplies for launching attack groups and as base anchorages to hold their captured merchant vessels awaiting ransom. Rules of Engagement (ROE) granted by most western governments to their navies prohibit mounting hostage rescue operations against pirated merchantmen for fear of hostage injury or death; as such, once pirates have taken the crew of a ship hostage they generally find themselves safe from attack by naval forces. Pirates have grown to understand this restriction and they regularly threaten to harm their hostages should naval vessels come too close for their liking. This restriction prevents action to recover any pirated merchant vessels, whether they are being held at anchor or are being used as motherships, and has had the effect of providing the pirates with a great deal of freedom of action once they have taken hostages. The pirates have shown willingness to torture and even kill hostages, although this has to date not been widespread. The increasing use of "panic rooms" has been an effective development, as it has meant that naval forces can launch assaults, and have done so, to retake ships boarded by pirates. In these cases it has been assessed that the pirates have not yet been able to take the crew hostage, and so there is little likelihood of the crew being harmed in the process.

Naval forces in the region have been permitted, by United Nations Security Council Resolutions, to operate within the territorial waters of Somalia (normally extending 12 miles offshore) for counter-piracy operations. This enables them to go right up to the shore line, however ROE directed by western governments prohibit any operations ashore (a "no boots on the ground" policy). Thus, counter-piracy forces can only conduct surveillance and observe the build-up of pirate supplies ashore, but are powerless to do anything about it until they take to the water. Warships may intercept the vessels at sea and, if it can be determined that their intent is piracy, seize their weapons, boarding equipment, extra fuel and the skiffs themselves. Often, however, when naval forces approach the pirates simply jettison their incriminating evidence and claim to be fishermen – despite the lack of actual presence of fishing gear. Many are caught, however, with a coastline 1500 miles long and a vast number of dispersed pirate camps there will always be some that slip past, and once out into the vastness of the Indian Ocean they are very hard to find.

MEASURED SUCCESS

In the latter half of 2011 there has been a marked reduction in successful pirate attacks throughout the region. This may be attributed in part to a number of contributing factors. As naval forces have become better organized and increasingly cooperative, they have moved to focus their assets in areas where they will have the greatest effect. While maintaining the security of the IRTC in the Gulf of Aden as a priority, a number of vessels have been positioned in the vicinity of the pirate camps along the East coast of Somalia when those camps are active. When airborne surveillance gives an indication of a pirate attack group putting to sea, naval forces can swiftly intercept and disrupt it. Even captured dhows and fishing vessels have been pressured into surrendering by warships that have demonstrated resolve and tenacity. This has reduced the number of pirate groups that can operate freely in the region.

Undoubtedly the increasing prevalence of self-defence measures (referred to as Best Management Practices) by merchant vessels has had a major impact on pirate success rates. In particular the use of armed security teams has proven to be very effective, as pirates, looking for an easy capture, will usually leave a vessel alone if demonstrates this capability. Previously discouraged by governments and shipping companies, the use of armed security has gained increased acceptance - the International Chamber of Shipping (ICS) acknowledged the use of armed guards to combat piracy in February 2011; and the UK Government announced in October 2011 plans to license armed guards for merchant ships in pirate-infested waters. To date, no vessel employing an armed security team has been taken by Somali pirates.

It is generally acknowledged however that the key to success against the pirates lies ashore. Without the ability to interdict the pirates' supply chain or to disrupt their staging bases on land, all efforts at sea will be at best a band-aid measure to address the symptoms only.

LEGALITIES

Difficulty for naval forces lies in the legal framework (or lack thereof) for dealing with captured pirates. For centuries piracy was treated very harshly indeed, with pirates being executed when caught, their vessels sunk, and their hideouts destroyed. Nowadays however, in our more enlightened times, such ruthlessness is frowned upon. Pirates today are treated as civilian criminals, with all the expansive interpretations of individual human rights inherent in that status. If pirates are captured they must be tried in court, however there is no international court in place with the authority to do so. Thus, captured pirates (or rather "suspected" pirates) must be prosecuted in the court of whichever country is able and willing to take on the task, under the civilian criminal procedures of that nation and with all of the associated entitlements and requirements for evidentiary standards. However, the sheer logistical nightmare of ensuring the proper gathering and continuity of evidence, of administering rights, of transporting suspects, witnesses, translators and sufficient evidence to a location thousands of miles from the scene of the "crime" and of ensuring the availability of the naval expert witnesses at a trial that could stretch over years (and therefore tying up the associated naval vessel that made the "arrest" for an eternity) makes this a highly impractical option. The result of these huge hurdles is that many captured pirates who have been turned over to legal authorities have been able to avoid standing trial or being convicted. Furthermore, many western nations are reluctant to take on the prosecution task because of the fear of having to grant refugee status to the pirates once they are on home soil. Some agreements that were established with regional nations such as Kenya to try pirates have fallen through because of the excessive burden it places on its courts and prisons. Pirates cannot be handed over to Somalia authorities for prosecuting and imprisoning as there is very little authority in the first place and it is impossible to ensure their human rights would be respected. Some nations such as the Seychelles, while willing to try and imprison pirates, lack the capacity to do so. Other regional nations are simply unwilling to consider accepting pirates for prosecution.

The end result is that when caught, pirates are often simply disarmed and released freely ashore back into Somalia, as the legal considerations are deemed to be excessively onerous to be effective. This "catch and release" approach, while contentious to some procedurally-minded westerners, at least disrupts the potential for pirate activity from that particular pirate group for a period of time until they can reconstitute their resources. Moreover, the "threat" of incarceration in a western or even regional prison is of virtually no deterrent to pirates who are willing to venture into the far reaches of the ocean and risk death for a big payoff. While they are somewhat risk averse, what constitutes an acceptable level of risk to a Somali pirate bears no resemblance to a western understanding of risk.

There have been a few occasions when western nations have undertaken to try and imprison pirates themselves. This generally only occurs when the direct interest of a particular nation is involved. For example, Germany, the United States, Italy and the Netherlands are among western nations that have prosecuted pirates at home, as a result of attacks on merchant vessels from those nations. Nevertheless these instances are rare, as the majority of occurrences do not involve the happy coincidence of national interests and assets in place.

THE COST OF PIRACY

The ransom payments are but a small part of the overall economic impact of piracy. Increased insurance rates for merchant vessels; the added costs to shipping companies to avoid high risk areas, to hire security teams and to "harden" vessels against attack; the costs to deploy and sustain naval forces, and the prosecution costs, as well as the secondary economic impact to local tourism and fishing industries and from discouraged regional investment are substantial. While difficult to calculate accurately, conservative estimates place the total cost of Somali piracy in the range of \$2 to \$3 billion (US) annually – some assess this figure to be as high as \$12 billion. This in addition to the hundreds of seafarers who have been and continue to be held in captivity for up to a year, suffering deprivation, malnutrition, torture and on occasion, death.

STATUS QUO

The naval forces deployed to the Horn of Africa region have achieved a measure of success, despite the restrictions imposed upon them. Throughout the region in 2010, coalition forces disrupted 145 pirate groups and individual vessels. There were a further 176 pirate attacks on merchant vessels, of which 45 succeeded. In 2011 disruptions numbered 95, with the number of attacks reduced to 126, of which 23 were successful; these out of a total number of vessels plying the region of over 20,000 annually. The difficulties continuing to face the naval forces there are indeed significant – so much so that piracy continues despite the continuous presence of the world's navies off the Horn of Africa now for three years. The limitations imposed by western governments against rounding up pirates as they gather ashore and against attempting hostage relief operations has largely ceded the playing field to the pirates, who have displayed inventiveness and audacity; and the essentially non-existent legal framework to deal with pirates whose human rights have somehow trumped those of the innocent mariners on whom they prey continue to hamper the ability of counter-piracy forces to deal with them once caught. The pirate business model remains intact and until western democracies give their forces in theatre the means and ways with which to combat piracy effectively there will be no end to this plague.

3. The Tuna Fishery and Piracy

E. Chassot, P. Guillotreau, D. Kaplan, T. Vallée

Abstract

Maritime piracy is costing the international economy between $7 and $12 billion annually. Of all successful piracy acts that resulted in a ransom in 2010, a large proportion, i.e. 44 out of 48, stemmed from Somali pirates. Since April 2008, when the first piracy attacks against tuna purse seiners operating in the Indian Ocean occurred, vessels have been deterred to harvest in some fishing zones. According to European shipowners, the productivity of vessels has decreased by 50% since the extension of piracy acts up to 500 nautical miles off the Somalia coast, an area encompassing the most productive fishing grounds of the Indian Ocean.

The EU purse-seine fleet has responded to piracy attacks with different adaptive strategies: exit of the fishery for part of the fleet, security protection onboard, fishing by pair of vessels, new fishing grounds, shift of technique towards a more intensive use of fish aggregating devices (FADs), etc. Such changes have affected both costs and revenues for fishing companies.

Also, it is hypothesized in this chapter that the exclusion zone induced by piracy may have created some unexpected positive consequences for fishers. To a certain extent, the piracy area could act as a well-enforced marine reserve. Among the tuna stocks that are fully exploited or over-exploited in the Indian Ocean, the sheltered natural capital is under lower pressure, resulting in higher opportunities of profit for the remaining fishers.

A brief review of the economic literature on piracy is proposed in this chapter, followed by a detailed analysis of all of the changes experienced by the French fishing fleet since the large-scale development of piracy. The hypothetical impact of piracy acting as a large marine protected area (MPA) is further discussed, although a too short observation period and a too complex fishery do not allow for some empirical assessment of this assumption.

I. INTRODUCTION

In recent years, a steady growth of piracy acts and armed robbery has been observed in the world oceans. In the Western Indian Ocean (WIO), Somali pirate attacks have increased within the Gulf of Aden from the early 1990s onwards, but since 2008 have seriously threatened the oceanic tuna fisheries after the expansion of piracy acts towards the east of the Indian Ocean up to 500 nautical miles off the Somali coast, and even further.[1] Compared to other maritime operations, the fishing industry is particularly exposed to piracy risks because vessels like purse seiners or longliners are vulnerable to attacks during fishing operations. More importantly, the expansion of piracy now covers a vast area where the tuna fleet used to harvest a great proportion of their annual catches.

The economics of piracy is complex because of the hidden economic value which is deviated from legal activities and re-distributed, particularly in failed-state countries, the variety of social expenditures to fight against it (police, law), and the legal industries deterred by piracy. A few studies estimate the value issued by criminal activities at several points of national GDPs, and the worldwide value was recently estimated around 10 billion USD. Several theoretical frameworks and empirical analyses found in the literature attempt to explain the causes and consequences of criminal activities. The expected returns derived from criminal activities depend both on the level of the offender's income and the expected level of punishment (probability of conviction times the amount of the fine). A low opportunity cost (lack of alternative jobs) and a state failure can also create favourable conditions for piracy. For instance, some authors do establish a link between illegal and unreported fishing and the driving of spoliated domestic fishers to piracy.

Concerning distant fishing nations exploiting resources in the high seas where pirates now operate, several harmful effects of piracy on fisheries can be observed: ransoms, injuries, deaths, material damages, reduction of the nominal fishing effort (exit of vessels), avoidance of traditional fishing grounds, security costs incurred, etc. A more original input of this chapter considers the potential positive and indirect consequences of piracy for fishers through a marine reserve effect.

All of these different dimensions of the linkages between piracy and tuna fisheries (economics of piracy, analysis of piracy acts and consequences on tuna fishing strategies in the Western Indian Ocean, the economic loss for the

[1] UNOSAT 2009.

fishery and the marine reserve hypothesis) are further developed in the following sections of this chapter, before the conclusion.

II. THE ECONOMICS OF PIRACY

Maritime piracy represents a tremendous economic value for pirates as well as a major threat for legal activities such as shipping or fishing, costing the international economy between 7 and 12 billion USD.[2] Ransoms can be very profitable for pirates, reaching several million USD for a single boat,[3] with relatively high but volatile success rates (63% in 2009 and 20% in 2010 according to IMB 2011). The economic consequences of piracy are tremendous.[4] Pirates deter a lot of maritime activities, impose additional costs of military protection onboard or security equipment, represent important prosecution costs, increase insurance premiums, impose re-routing for ships, etc.

From a theoretical perspective, the economics of piracy can be analysed in terms of criminal activities. Gary S. Becker (1968) was one of the first economists interested in the economics of organized crime, followed by other authors a few decades later, like Fiorentini and Peltzman in 1995. Pioneers' contributions have been "targeted on individual agent's allocative choice between legal and illegal activities in the face of different detterrence systems and different opportunity costs."[5] Such contributions have been grounded in the belief of some economists (particularly among the U.S. economists) that the involvement in illegal activities can be derived from rational choice theory. Beyond the original decision of joining or not joining in piracy, pirates' behaviour itself could be considered as rational, leading Peter Leeson to create the neologism "*pirational* choice."[6] By adopting visible signs of piracy like a black flag with skull and cross bones (reputation building and signaling), pirates would prevent any resistance from the attacked ships which prefer to surrender, saving lives and gunpowder on both sides and thus saving useless costs for pirates. On a more general field, from one who is a fan of good witticism, Leeson (2009) writes about the "invisible hook of pirates" substituted for Adam Smith's invisible hand, comparing the role of piracy with that of free economy to achieve a socially desirable outcome from selfish interests. In the case of piracy of the 17th and 18th

[2] Bowden et al. 2010.

[3] In November 2010, the highest ransom on record, $9.5 million, was paid to Somali pirates to release the *Samho Dream*, a South Korean oil tanker (Bowden et al. 2010, p. 9). In the case of the Somali piracy, the average cost of ransom would be 5.3 million USD in 2010 (*Ibid.*, p 10).

[4] Anderson 1995, Bowden et al. 2010.

[5] Fiorentini and Peltzman 1995, p 1.

[6] Leeson 2010a.

centuries, pirates could be considered as more tolerant than merchants who used to employ slaves aboard when the equalitarian society of pirates would pay them like any crew member. In the same way, relationships between pirates and colonial governors during that period were mutually profitable, the former providing scarce goods against protection by the latter.[7]

An interesting question is addressed by Peter Leeson responding to some criticisms of his approach about the status of piracy: do pirates form a society or a firm? His answer tends to argue that piracy is certainly a mixture of both because the profit-seeking goal of piracy is combined with a set of social rules that classical firms externalize to society as a whole. Sharing the risk of a company (which risk is necessarily high in this case), pirate crews receive an equal share of the plunder and operate more like cooperatives than neoclassical firms. Nevertheless, because of the peculiar nature of this activity implying violence and theft, a pirate organization has to develop its own judicial and self-enforcement institutions, producing additional costs that legal private firms do not have to incur.[8]

Whatever the status of piracy, it represents an important economic value for society in terms of illegal revenues and judicial activities to fight against it, keeping in mind that prosecution and prison costs contribute to the Gross Domestic Product (GDP) of a country. Gary Becker evaluated the revenues of illegal activities and induced effects for the U.S. society in 1965 to 4% of the Gross National Product (GNP), considering crime as an economically important activity or "industry" (e.g. justice and police expenditure, revenues of illegal traffics, loss of earnings due to homicide, etc.). In 1999, this figure was re-evaluated by Anderson to 11.9% of the U.S. GDP.[9] In Italy, Detotto and Otranto (2010) evaluated the burden of a subset of crimes representing 65% of all crime offenses to 2.6% of the GDP in 2006. In their view, criminal activity acts as a tax on the economy, discouraging investment and consumption.

Like a damage function used in environmental economics, Gary Becker (1968) suggests to model the amount of harm (H) for society as a function of criminal activity level (O): $H=H(O)$, the latter being measured by the number of offenses. In his view, harm is positively influenced by this level ($H'=dH/dO>0$). The social value of the gain to offenders is assumed to increase with the number of offenses too: $G=G(O)$ with $G'>0$. Note that the social gain could also be expressed as a decreasing function of offenses, just like the de-pollution cost in environmental theory. The utility function for society, represented by the net cost or damage, is therefore the difference

[7] Leeson 2010b.
[8] Leeson 2010b.
[9] Anderson 1999.

between the harm and gain: $D(O)=H(O)-G(O)$. Like polluters, offenders receive diminishing marginal gains and cause increasing marginal harm ($G''<0$ and $H''>0$), therefore increasing net marginal damages for society ($D''>0$). The question becomes: how many offenses (crimes) should be permitted to minimize social loss? Even more interestingly, the individual supply function of an offender j includes, besides other influences (u), the level of punishment (f) and the probability (p) to be punished: $O_j=O_j(p_j,f_j,u_j)$. From that function can be derived the expected utility (EU) of a crime:

$$EU_j = p_jU_j(Y_j\text{-}f_j) + (1\text{-}p_j)U_j(Y_j) \quad (1)$$

Where Y_j is the offender's income, both derivatives of EU to p_j and f_j being negative. According to Becker (1968), an increase of the probability to be punished can be compensated by a proportional reduction in the level of punishment (f_j being converted in monetary terms) to leave the expected income unchanged:

$$EY_j = p_j(Y_j\text{-}f_j) + (1\text{-}p_j)Y_j = Y_j - p_jf_j \qquad (2)$$

However, it "could change the expected utility, because the amount of risk would change."[10] For most of criminal analysts, the probability of conviction is more detterrent than the amount of the fine itself, whatever the criminal's attitude toward risk.[11] This is particularly true in societies where the opportunity cost of piracy is low, i.e. when the alternative choice of becoming a pirate is limited by the low level of the economy and law enforcement.

When looking at the causes of piracy, the empirical literature stresses the major role played by a poor economic development or socio-political instability.[12] The economic situation measured by the GDP per capita would even prevail over the political situation estimated by an index of political rights or civil liberties (like the failed state index or *FSI*).[13] Somalia cumulated such conditions of poor economic standards (GDP per capita around \$600) and political instability since the fall of Siad Barre in 1991.

Some authors go further by extending the link between poor economic alternative jobs and piracy by looking for the cause of piracy in the decline of the domestic fishing industry.[14] Referring to Leeson (2009), these authors claim "that the absence of ownership over the high seas means that no one had much interest in preventing activities such as piracy which destroys the

---

[10] Becker 1968, p 11.

[11] Davis 1988.

[12] Anderson 1995, Mejia et al. 2009, Cariou et al. 2011.

[13] Cariou and Wolff 2011.

[14] Bawumia and Sumaila 2010.

value of the oceans," piracy being understood here as plundering marine natural resources.[15] They do not assert the hypothesis of a direct trade-off by Somali people deciding to become either pirate or fisher, but do consider that the increasing level of Illegal, Unreported and Unregulated (IUU) fishing in the Somalian Exclusive Economic Zone (EEZ) has indirectly spurred the local fishers, in the absence of state control, to organize themselves to board the foreign IUU vessels and demand monetary compensation for fish caught. "Somali fishers formed themselves into bands of local coastguards to ostensibly protect their livelihoods and Somalia's marine resources."[16] This hypothesis is somewhat confirmed by the rare surveys of Somali modern pirates.[17] However, the importance of fishing resources spoliation must not be exaggerated because the domestic fishing industry has always been almost negligible in Somalia with less than 30,000 mt of landings accounting for less than 1% of GDP, its traditional economy relying more on agriculture and pastoralism.[18] On the other hand, Somalia has an old tradition of piracy attacks against merchant ships and trawlers at least dating back from the 1950s.[19] Among others, tuna longliners and purse-seiners commissioned by distant fishing nations represent interesting targets for Somali pirates.

III. TUNA FISHERIES IN THE WESTERN INDIAN OCEAN AND SOMALI PIRACY

During the late 2000s, global tuna fisheries have represented more than 4.1 million metric tons (mt) of catches and have been dominated by three fishing gears, i.e. purse seine, longline, and pole and line, that accounted for about 60%, 15%, and 11% of the world tuna catches, respectively.[20] The tuna fisheries in the Indian Ocean currently concentrate about 25% of global tuna catch and are dominated by two major industrial fleets, i.e. Asian longliners from Japan, Taiwan and South Korea, and European purse seiners (see Figure 1). The small-scale fishery component in the Indian Ocean is substantial, representing approximately 50% of total catch, primarily in coastal waters.[21] The deep-freezing longline fishery started in the early 1950s and expanded rapidly over the whole Indian Ocean to target yellowfin (*Thunnus albacares*), bigeye (*Thunnus obesus*), albacore (*Thunnus alalunga*), and southern bluefin tuna (*Thunnus maccoyii*). It represented an

---

[15] Bawunia and Sumaila 2010, p 5.
[16] Bawunia and Sumaila 2010, p 21.
[17] Murphy 2011.
[18] The expression "fish eater" is even considered as an insult for a Somali (Murphy 2011).
[19] Murphy 2011.
[20] Source FAO: http://www.fao.org/fishery/statistics/tuna-catches/en).
[21] Herrera et al. 2011.

annual average of more than 100,000 mt in the recent years. The tuna purse seine fishery, dominated by the European Union (EU) fleet, has been operating in the WIO since the early 1980s and targets yellowfin, skipjack (*Katsuwonus pelamis*), and bigeye tunas. Over the last decade, the total catches of the EU purse seine fishery reached a maximum of about 400,000 t in 2003 and have fluctuated around 290,000 t in recent years.

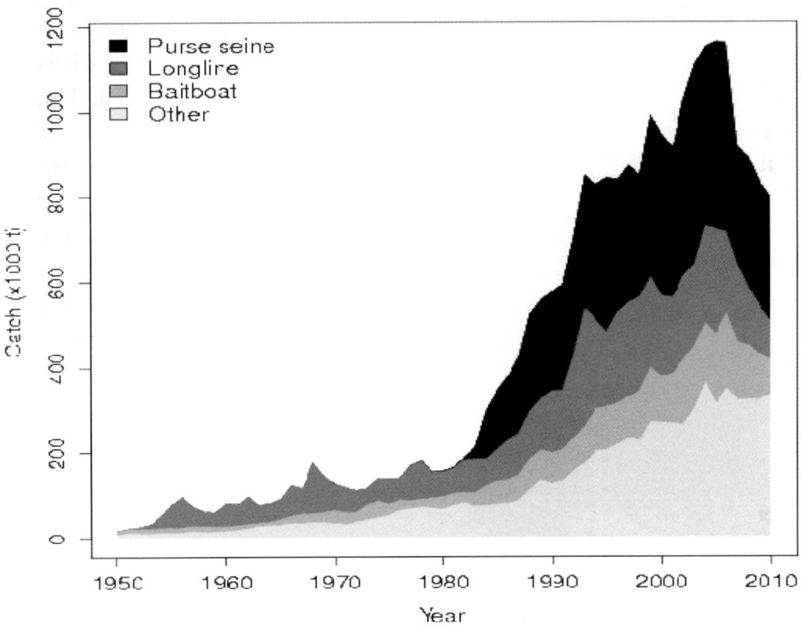

Figure 1: Tuna catch (in thousand mt) in the Indian Ocean by fishing gear (Souce: IOTC)

Between 2001 and 2007, Asian longliners mainly operated off of the Somali coast during the December-May season with annual catches of yellowfin and bigeye varying between 20,000 and 60,000 mt, i.e. an average 25% of their production in the Indian Ocean. The EU purse-seine fleet mainly operates between August and late October in the fishing grounds off the Somali coast where localized upwelling occurs in relation with the alongshore alignment of summer monsoon winds during the boreal summer. The 500 nautical mile area off Somalia represented 30-50% of the total catch of the EU purse seine fleet during 2000-2007 with an annual average of 140,000 mt. Most purse seine catches in the area are made on schools associated with fish aggregating devices (FADs) which are man-made bamboo rafts equipped with satellite buoys that are deployed at sea to aggregate tuna and facilititate their capture.[22]

[22] Scott et al. 1992, Dempster and Taquet, 2004.

FAD-fishing targets mostly skipjack (63%), though catch of juveniles of yellowfin (28%) and bigeye (9%) tunas are not negligible.[23] As a consequence, the 500 nm area off Somalia concentrated 50% of purse seine skipjack catches during 2000-2007 and more than 25% of all skipjack catches of the Indian Ocean (see Figure 2).

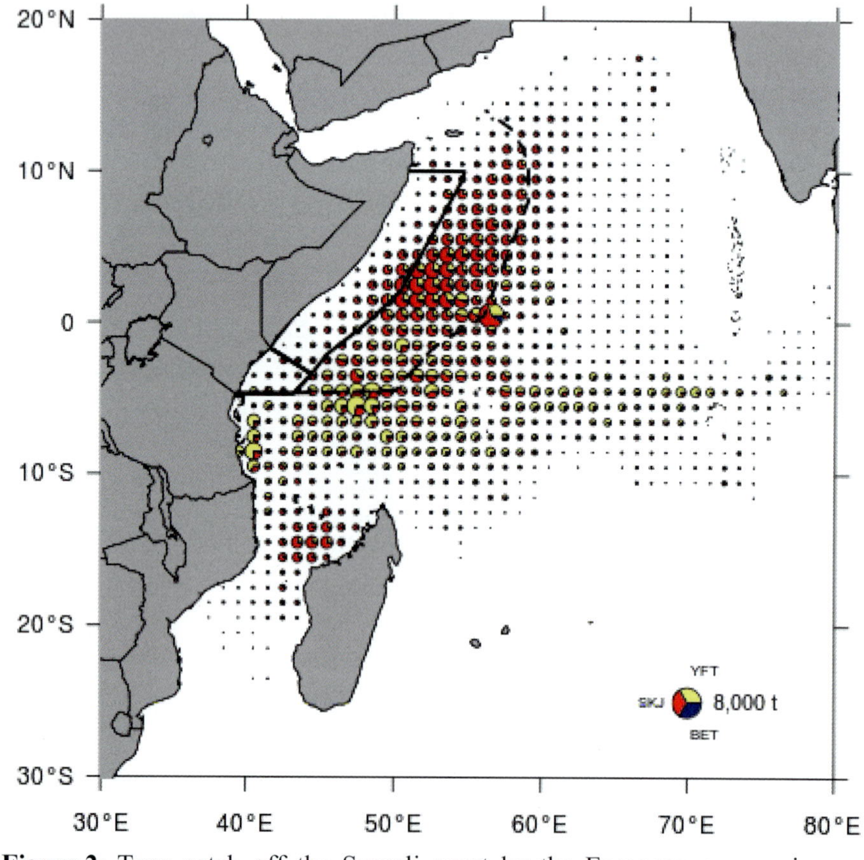

Figure 2: Tuna catch off the Somali coast by the European purse-seiners during 2000-2007, i.e. before the onset of piracy acts. Solid lines delineate the Somalia and Kenya Economic Exclusive Zones (EEZ). Dashed line indicates an extended area at 500 miles off the Somali coast within which purse-seiners were excluded during the peak of piracy attacks (mid-2008 to mid-2009). Source: IRD-IEO-SFA

[23] Pianet *et al.* 2011.

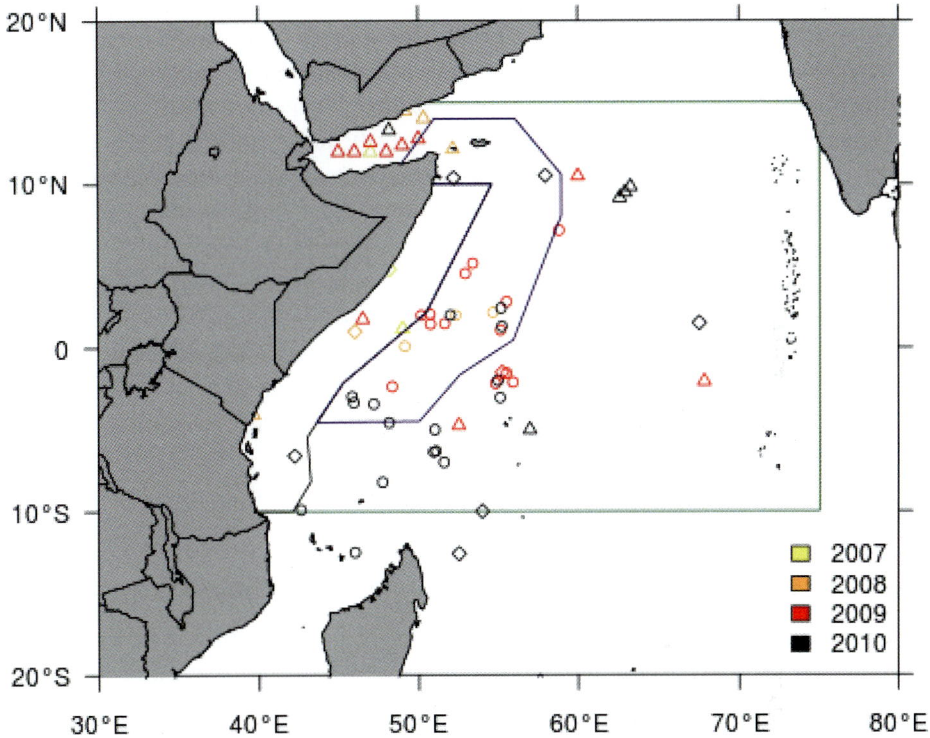

Figure 3: Pirate attacks of fishing vessels by category in the Western Indian Ocean between 2007 and 2010. Legend: circles = purse-seiners; diamonds = longliners; triangles = other fishing vessels. The lines delineate 3 areas: the East-African EEZs (Area 1), the 500-mile purse-seine exclusion zone (Area 2) and the northeast equatorial part of the Western Indian Ocean (Area 3). Source: IMB and UNOSAT

Recently, the fisheries of the WIO have been subject to Somali piracy with at least 5 attacks of longliners and 30 attacks of purse seiners and their supply vessels between 2007 and 2010 (see Figure 3). Thereafter, the longline effort in the Somalia basin has strongly decreased since 2008, with several vessels leaving the Indian Ocean for other oceans, and some effort being redistributed in the southern Indian Ocean.[24] Piracy attacks have been particularly dramatic for purse seiners. In April 2008, the 26 crew of the Spanish vessel "Playa de Bakio" were captured and held as hostages by Somali pirates for a few days before being released in exchange for a ransom. In September 2008, the French purse seiner "Drennec" was attacked

[24] IOTC 2011, Okamoto 2011.

by pirates at a distance of 420 nm off the Somali coast. The pirates failed to board the purse seiner but fired two rockets without causing any injury or major damage. After this attack, all European fishing vessels came back to their port of call in Mahé, Seychelles, to claim assistance to their respective governments. As a result, the European fishing companies restricted their fishing grounds by extending eastward a security line from 300 nm to 500 nm off the Somali coasts (see Figure 3). The attack of the "Felipe Ruano" in March 2009 as far as 59°E, however, showed the limits of establishing such a safety zone.

Regarding the lack of detailed spatial information for longliners (available catch and effort data are aggregated at a spatial resolution of 5° by 5°) and the overall small contribution of Somali fishing grounds for this fishery, our analysis mainly focuses on European purse seiners for which fine-scale data (by vessel per fishing operation) have been collected in a consistent way since the early 1980s by the Institut de Recherche pour le Développement (IRD), the Instituto Español de Oceanografía (IEO) and the Seychelles Fishing Authority (SFA).

IV. THE ECONOMIC LOSS FOR EUROPEAN TUNA FISHERS DUE TO PIRACY

The rise of piracy in the Somali basin and the associated threat to crews and materials has resulted in adaptive strategies from European purse seine companies that are accompanied by increasing costs and changes in fishing strategies. From July 2009, military personnel boarded French purse seiners to ensure protection of the crew during fishing operations. By mid-October, similar measures were implemented by Spanish and Seychelles-flagged ships with private security guards. Military and private security intervention imposed additional costs to the fleet of around €60,000 per fishing trip.[25] Considering an average number of 8 fishing trips per vessel per year, we estimated that these extra-costs represent more than 20% of total annual costs (our own estimation from survey data). This expenditure has been fully borne by the French fishing firms, the Spanish vessels receiving a 50% contribution from the state or the Region.[26] The boarding of military personnel also imposed some logistic constraints for the French purse-seiners: (i) a reduction in crew aboard small vessels so as to board the military staff, (ii) a reduction in fishing trip duration from 7 to 5 weeks from July 2009 and July 2010, and 6 weeks thereafter according to military rotations, (iii) the

[25] Orthongel for the French military protection and http://bruxelles2.over-blog.com/210-categorie-10532258.html for the Spanish/Seychelles security guards.

[26] Yves Riva, CEO of Saupiquet-Armement, one of the French shipowners, and President of Orthongel, the French tuna Producer Organization (Reportages Ouest-France n°2, February 2011, p 19).

necessity for the vessels to operate in pairs with some maximum distance allowed between them (25 nm at day and 7 nm at night) and alternative fishing in some areas from July 2009 to June 2011, and (iv) the boarding of military guards in some cases in La Réunion island, adding some extra voyage costs. Such constraints have affected both the strategies and tactics of the fleet and resulted in changes in effort level, spatial distribution of effort, and resulting catches.

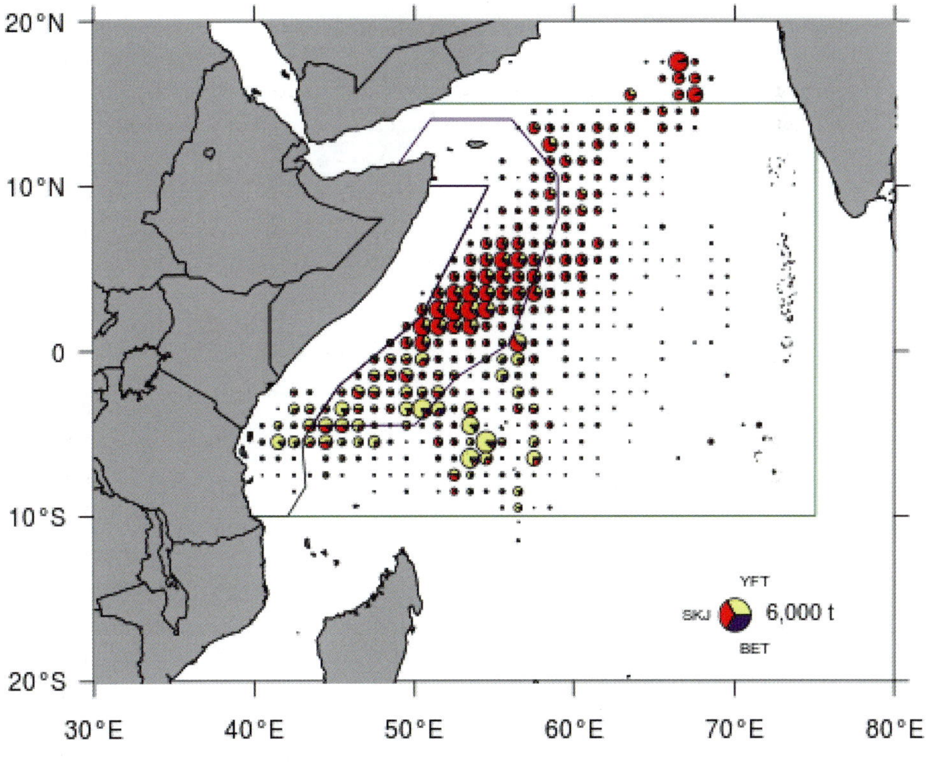

Figure 4a: Spatial distribution of tropical tuna catch during the FAD-dominated "Somali season" (June-November 2007). Source: IRD-IEO-SFA.

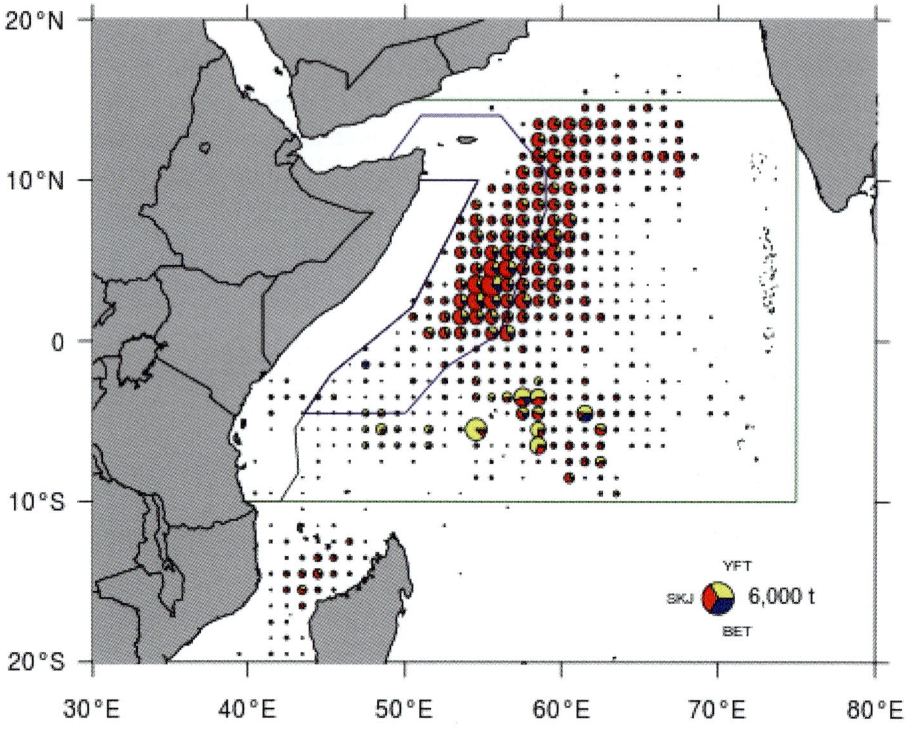

Figure 4b: Spatial distribution of tropical tuna catch during the FAD-dominated "Somali season" (June-November 2008). Source: IRD-IEO-SFA.

The number of EU purse seiners in the Indian Ocean decreased from a mean annual number of 48 between 2001 and 2008 to 35 in 2010.[27] Between 2008 and 2010, European fishing companies reallocated 14 EU purse seiners and 3 supply vessels from the Indian to the Atlantic and Pacific Oceans as a direct response to the threat of piracy. A few other EU purse seiners were sold to non-EU companies and also departed towards the Atlantic Ocean. Since 2008, the overall decrease in the number of EU vessels corresponded to a 22% decrease in fleet capacity, i.e. from about 60,000 GRT in 2008 to 46,000 GRT in 2010.[28] This resulted in a 30% and 19% decrease in fishing effort expressed in searching days and fishing sets, respectively.

[27] Pianet *et al.* 2011.

[28] *Id.*

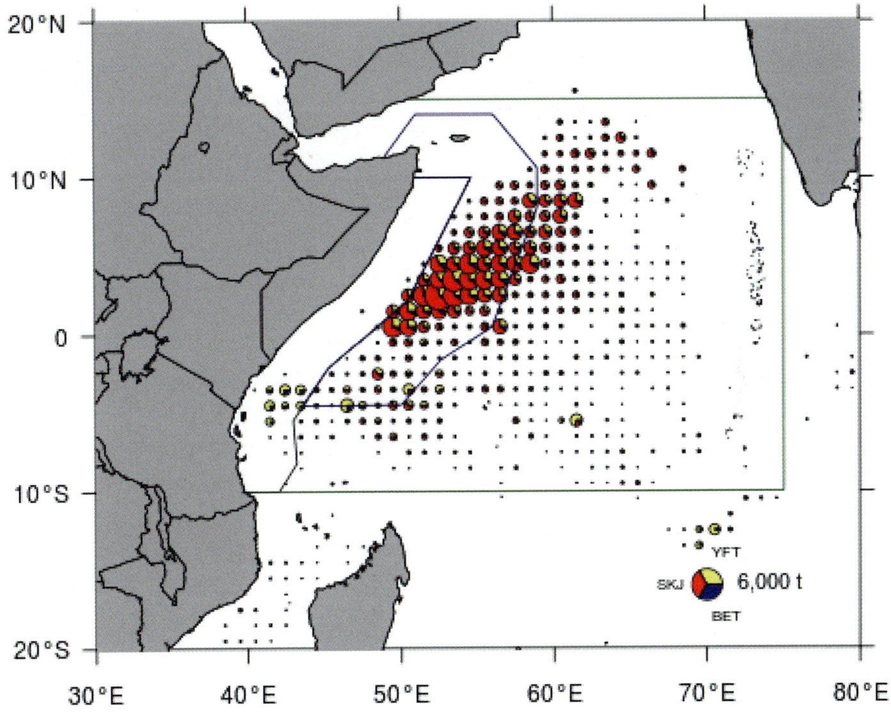

Figure 4c: Spatial distribution of tropical tuna catch during the FAD-dominated "Somali season" (June-November 2009). Source: IRD-IEO-SFA.

The number of distinct 1-degree squares where vessels operate is a good indicator of spatial effort reallocation and shows the exclusion effect caused by piracy. In the EEZs of Somalia, Kenya, and Tanzania (Area 1), there were only 17 squares with catch from the EU purse seine fleet in 2009, compared with 60 in 2002 (see Figures 4a and 4c). This is mainly due to changes in fishing agreements between the EU and Eastern coastal African countries, i.e. end of the agreement between EU and the former state of Somalia. In Area 2, the decrease in the number of squares with catch from about 70 during 2005-2007 to 60 in 2009-2010 is essentially explained by the avoidance of the piracy zone (see Figure 4b). By contrast, and despite the decrease in the number of vessels, the number of squares visited in Area 3 did increase from an average of about 280 squares during 2001-2007 to more than 340 squares in 2008-2009. New fishing grounds, sometimes less productive, were therefore visited by the European fleet because of the risk of piracy attacks in the vicinity of the Somali coast. A large area off Mogadiscio has been clearly avoided by fishers in 2008, before a partial come-back in 2009 and close-to-full come back in 2010 under military protection (see Figures 4c and 4d). Overall, the fleet moved significantly further east in 2009 compared to past years, resulting in substantial and unusual catches of yellowfin as far as 70°E (see Figure 4c).

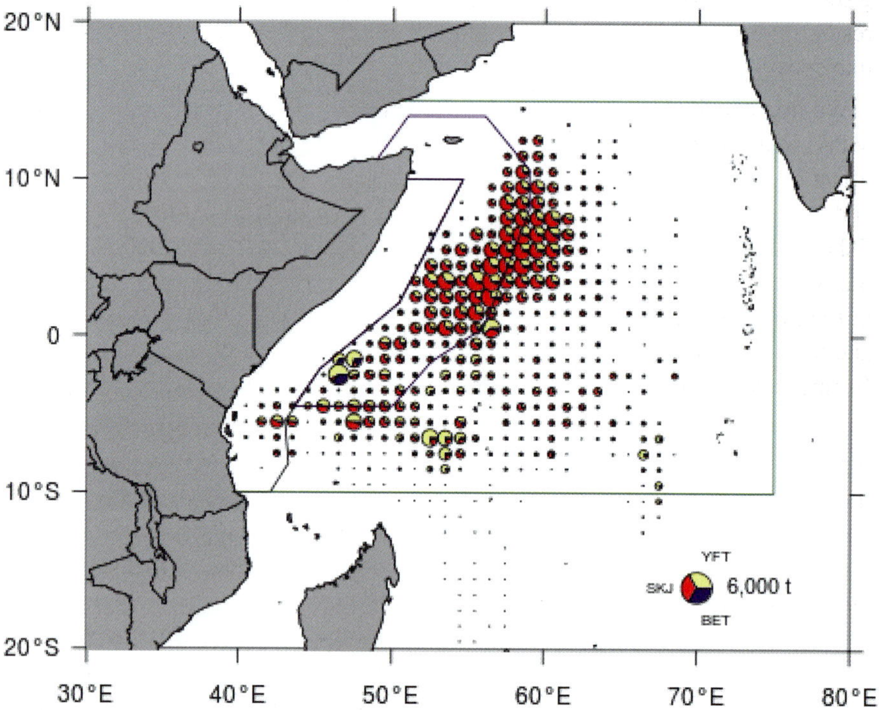

Figure 4d: Spatial distribution of tropical tuna catch during the FAD-dominated "Somali season" (June-November 2010). Source: IRD-IEO-SFA.

The catch of the European purse-seine fleet in Area 2 decreased from an average 90,000 mt in 2001-2007 to less than 50,000 mt in 2008 (-45%) and 60,000 mt in 2009. The transfer of effort to Area 3 resulted in an increase of catch there, from an average of 134,000 mt y^{-1} during 2001-2007 to 157,000 mt (+15%) in 2008. Area 3 represented about 57% of total catch in 2008 compared to 38% in the past. Because of the new constraints on fishing operations, particularly the reduction of fishing trip length, the proportion of sets on free swimming schools significantly decreased while the number of FAD-associated sets increased, thus modifying the species composition of catch towards more skipjack and less large yellowfin.[29]

[29] Chassot et al. 2010.

V. IS THERE ANY MPA EFFECT OF PIRACY?

As a paradox, piracy may have indirect positive consequences for fishers. By creating a vast exclusion zone, pirates virtually enforce a large-scale marine protected area (MPA) in which the fish population may spawn and grow out of any fishing mortality pressure, increasing the recruitment for the residual fishing zone through the dispersal of eggs, juveniles or adults, just like conventional MPAs.[30]

We hypothesize in this section that the piracy zone could act as a *de facto* MPA. With a controlled level of piracy, the risk of hijacking for fishers is offset by the growth and the transfer of biomass between the exclusion zone and the fishing zone, thus increasing both fishing effort and profits for fishers. A too high level of piracy deters the fishing effort and may eradicate the whole fishery, leaving no opportunity of ransoming fishing vessels. The mitigation measures against piracy (security equipment, military protection) and the risk attitude of fishers prove to play a key role in keeping a profitable fishing industry despite the risk of piracy.

Assuming that pirates preferably target fishing boats rather than any other type of vessel,[31] a three-actor game links narrowly fish, fishers and pirates, thus creating a complex set of externalities (see Figure 5). The fish stock is enhanced by the presence of pirates deterring fishing in the unsafe zone, thus increasing biomass and fishers' profits outside the zone. By reducing the number of fishers, piracy increases the amount of fish per vessel, thus creating a strong incentive for fishers to remain in the fishery. Fishers reduce the fish stock by their catches and are ransomed by pirates. Fishers are therefore trapped in the dilemma of being hijacked by pirates and the perspective of higher catches and higher revenues. The price of fish itself could also be higher because of the piracy threat.

The EU purse seine effort decreased by about 20-30% after the onset of Somali piracy while overall catches only decreased by 8% during the same period. This suggests that catch per vessel increased despite the constraints imposed on fishing operations (e.g. fishing in pairs, reduction of fishing trip length, etc.). Any increase in catch per unit effort outside Area 2 could possibly reveal different intricate dynamics: (i) an increase in tuna biomass due to good recruitment or migration, (ii) a change in fishing strategy,

[30] Sanchirico and Wilen 2005, Sumaila *et al.* 2007, Smith *et al.* 2009.

[31] This assumption is unrealistic because most of the acts of piracy having occurred in the Indian Ocean for the last three years targeted preferably tankers and merchant vessels. It is estimated that 40% of piracy attacks have been directed on bulk carriers and general cargo vessels. Mejia *et al.* 2009. However, more than 30 attacks concerned the European purse-seine fleet between 2007 and 2010 (Chassot *et al.* 2010) and the deterrence of fishing is considered as a major threat. Bowden *et al.* 2010.

assuming that fishing more on FAD-associated schools would increase catch rates as measured by catch per day-at-sea, or (iii) a reduction in overcapacity: fewer vessels catch a larger quantity per vessel with the same biomass level.

We selected a subset of 24 vessels active during 2001-2010 to untangle the effects of effort variation and analyse the changes in purse seine fishing strategy linked to Somali piracy. The overall effort in searching days exerted by the vessels in Areas 2-3 did not change between 2007 and 2008 but about 300 searching days were allocated from Area 2 to Area 3 in 2008, corresponding to an increase by 20% of the effort in the latter area. This resulted in a 35% decrease of catches in Area 2, from 24,000 mt during 2001-2007 to 15,500 mt in 2008. Despite increased effort in Area 3, total catches in 2008 were within the average range due to catch rates smaller than those of 2001-2007, which would rather bring opposite evidence to the MPA hypothesis.

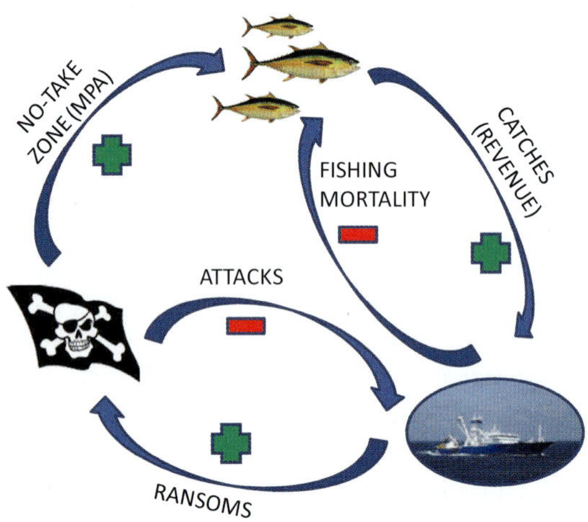

Figure 5: Interactions between fish, fishers and pirates

Under military and private security protection, purse seiners came back in Area 2 in 2009-2010 during which the effort re-increased by 20% compared to 2008 (i.e. "back to normal"). Catches increased in 2009 to the average level observed during the period 2001-2007, due to a combined increase of a high number of sets per searching day (more than 1 d^{-1}) and good catch rates on log-associated schools, i.e. 30.3 mt d^{-1} and 12.9 mt d^{-1} for skipjack and yellowfin, respectively. Catches decreased to 16,300 mt in 2010 due to low catch rates for skipjack (18.5 mt d^{-1}) caught on log-associated schools. The percentage of sets on log-associated schools in Area 2 increased from an average of 75% during 2001-2007 to more than 90% and 80% in 2009 and

2010, respectively. This did not significantly modify the species composition of the catch in Area 2 that has been predominated by skipjack (62% ± 6%) throughout the whole period 2001-2010.

The effort, number of sets, total catches, and catch rates in Area 3 during 2009-2010 were all within the range of values observed during 2001-2007. A shift in fishing strategy was however observed in this area after 2008. The reduction of fishing trips (45 to 30 days) increases the opportunity cost of searching time: the higher efficiency of FAD sets thus represents a better strategy than free school fishing (personal communication of an industry representative). Indeed, while this area was predominated by fishing on unassociated schools during the period 2001-2007 (i.e. 2/3 of the sets), the percentage of sets on log-associated schools sharply increased from about 38% during 2001-2008 to 64% and 74% in 2009 and 2010, respectively. This shift caused a major change in the catch species composition of Area 3, with skipjack increasing from an average of 35% during 2001-2007 to 50% during 2009-2010.

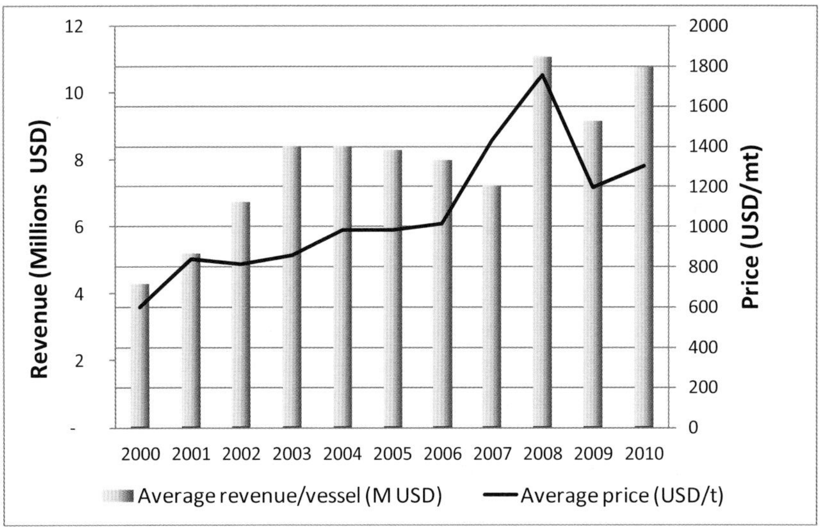

Figure 6: Average revenue per vessel in the European purse-seine fleet Source: IRD, IEO, SFA and IOTC for landings by species and the number of vessels; Thailandese Customs for reference prices of tuna species for canneries.

Finally, in spite of the new constraints imposed by piracy, the changes have not affected the average revenue of the European vessels, thanks to the very good tuna prices obtained since 2007 (above 1200 USD per metric tonne) (see Figure 6). Average revenue per vessel has never been as high as it has been for the last three years. Even the average tonnage per vessel in

2010 (> 8000 mt) is comparable to the catch levels of the very productive years of 2002-2006, as though piracy had not caused any detrimental impact on fishing yields. More surprisingly, the monthly series of catches show another effect since 2007: the seasonal variability of catches (peak of October for the FAD season and peak of January for the free school season) has been significantly smoothed down, presumably because of the exit of several vessels (making the fleet more homogenous) and because of the increasing use of FADs for the last years of the period (> 80% of sets for all areas in 2009 and 2010), after the first piracy attacks against the fleet.

VI. CONCLUSION

Piracy represents a serious threat for legal maritime activities, deterring shipping, offshore investment, fishing, etc. All expenditures aiming at fighting against it, but also the economic effects in very poor countries that piracy may have, result in a significant economic value (between 7 and 12 billion USD worldwide). For both legal and criminal activities, a new risk component affects costs and revenues, i.e. the probability of being captured and even killed.

Because of this risk, the progressive spatial expansion of piracy acts from coastal to high-sea areas, and increasing attacks on fishing vessels in recent years, have strongly modified the tuna fisheries of the Western Indian Ocean. The adaptive response of fishing companies has fallen into two categories. On one hand, all Asian longliners and about 20 purse seiners have left the Somali basin to other fishing grounds of the Indian Ocean, or other oceans, to avoid the human and financial risks associated with piracy, like material damages, ransom, injury, hostaging, and death. On the other hand, investments in security allowed European and Seychelles purse seiners to mitigate the threat of piracy and keep their major historical fishing grounds off the Somali coast. For fishers, the risk can therefore be managed through additional costs of security protection as long as they can afford it,[32] but also through the avoidance of the exclusion zone caused by piracy, incurring additional costs to explore new grounds and use more Fish Aggregating Devices.

At least four effects of piracy on tuna fishing have been observed in the present study:

(i) A strong reduction in the fishing effort exerted on tropical tunas since 2007,

[32] For instance, what is affordable for large purse-seiners is not for smaller boats like long-liners or even supply vessels which had to exit the fishery.

(ii) A temporary redistribution of effort outside the 500 nm area off Somalia before security intervention in July-October 2009,

(iii) A trend toward more fishing on log-associated schools resulting in an increase in catches of skipjack and juveniles of yellowfin and bigeye,

(iv) A significant increase in the unit cost of fishing effort.

On the basis of the first two effects, a possible MPA-like impact of piracy on the biomass level was hypothesized. However, the consequences of changes in effort and fishing strategy on the status of tuna stocks in the IO are too complex to be evaluated given the limited time-area closure following the inception of piracy acts, the high seasonal and interannual variability in tuna dynamics, and our still limited knowledge about their natural mortality and movements/migrations.[33] The effectiveness of MPAs for pelagic ecosystems that are highly dynamic in time and space needs careful attention[34] and, presumably, a longer period of observation than that of the present case study.

Whatever the impact in terms of population dynamics, the whole WIO tuna fishery has undoubtedly been transformed lastingly by the introduction of piracy. Beyond the maritime security problem, further research is needed for a specific assessment of the bioeconomic consequences of piracy.

Acknowledgements.

This work was supported by the AMPED project (www.amped.ird.fr) through a grant from the French National Research Agency (ANR), Systerra Programme, grant number 595 ANR-08-STRA-03. Purse seine fisheries data analysed in this publication were collected by UMR 212 'Exploited Marine Ecosystems' of the *Institut de Recherche pour le Développement* (IRD), the *Instituto Español de Oceanografía* (IEO) and the Seychelles Fishing Authority (SFA) through the EU-funded Data Collection Framework [DCF, Reg (EC) 1543/2000 and 199/2008]. We wish to acknowledge the contributions of the staff of the 'Observatoire Thonier', ORTHONGEL, and all technicians and fishers who have been involved in data collection, processing, and management. We are particularly grateful to Patrice Dewals (IRD) for fruitful discussion on the IO purse seine fishery. Data for other tuna fisheries were obtained from the Indian Ocean Tuna Commission (http://www.iotc.org).

---

[33] IOTC-WPTT13 2011. A large amount of information recently collected in the Indian Ocean through a large-scale tagging program might help address some of these issues and provide insights into some major demographic parameters that drive tuna populations.

[34] Kaplan et al. 2010, Grüss et al. 2011.

References

Anderson, J.L. (1995), *Piracy and World History: An Economic Perspective on Maritime Predation*, Journal of World History 6: 175-199

Anderson, D.A. (1999), *The Aggregate Burden of Crime*, Journal of Law and Economics 42: 611-642.

Bawumia M. and Sumaila U.R. (2010), *Fisheries, Ecosystems and Piracy: A Case Study of Somalia*, The University of British Columbia Fisheries Centre, Working Paper 2010-04, 29 pp

Becker G.S. (1968), *Crime and Punishment: An Economic Approach*, Journal of Political Economy 76: 169-170.

Bowden A., Hurlburt K., Aloyo E., Marts C., Lee A.(2010), The economic cost of maritime piracy, One Earth Future Working Paper, December 2010, 26 pp.

Cariou P., Mejia Jr, M.Q., Wolff F.-C. (2011), *Piracy in Shipping*, *in* W.K. Talley (Ed.) Maritime Economics, Blackwell Publishers, Oxford.

Cariou P., Wolff F.-C. (2011), *A Longitudinal Analysis of Piracy in Shipping*, *Economics Bulletin*, Vol. 31 no.2: 1055-1062.

Chassot, E., Dewals, P., Floch, L., Lucas, V., Morales-Vargas, M., Kaplan, DM. (2010), *Analysis of the Effects of Somali Piracy on the European Tuna Purse Seine Fisheries of the Indian Ocean*, IOTC SC-09, 26 pp.

Davis M.L. (1988), *Time and Punishment: An Intertemporal Model of Crime*, Journal of Political Economy, 96(2): 383-390.

Dempster, T., Taquet, M. (2004), *Fish Aggregation Device (FAD) Research: Gaps in Current Knowledge and Future Directions for Ecological Studies*, Reviews in Fish Biology and Fisheries, 14(1), 21-42.

Detotto C., Otranto C. (2010), *Does Crime Affect Economic Growth?*, Kyklos 63(3): 330-345.

Fiorentini G., Peltzman S. (1995), *The Economics of Organised Crime*, Cambridge University Press, 303 p.

Grüss, A., Kaplan, D., Guenette, S., Roberts, C. M., Botsford, L. W. (2011), *Consequences of Adult and Juvenile Movement for Marine Protected Areas*, Biological Conservation 144: 692-702.

Herrera, M., Pierre, L., Million, J. (2011), *Review of the Statistical Data Available for the Tropical Tuna Species*, IOTC-2011-WPTT13-06, 26p.

IMB 2011. http://www.icc-ccs.org/home/imb

IOTC-WPTT13 2011. Report of the Thirteenth Session of the IOTC Working Party on Tropical Tunas. Lankanfinolhu, North Malé Atoll, Republic of Maldives, 16–23 October 2011. IOTC–2011–WPTT13–R[E]: 85 pp.

Kaplan, D., Chassot, E., Grüss, A., Fonteneau, A. (2010), *Pelagic MPAs: The Devil is in the Details*, Trends in Ecology and Evolution 25: 62-63.

Leeson P.T. (2009), *The Invisible Hook: The Hidden Economics of Pirates*, Princeton University Press.

Leeson P.T. (2010a), *Pirational Choice: The Economics of Infamous Pirate Practices*, Mimeo, http://www.peterleeson.com/Pirational_Choice.pdf

Leeson P.T. (2010b), Pirates, *Review of Austrian Economics* 23: 315-319.

Mejia, M.Q., Cariou P., Wolff F.-C. (2009), *Is Maritime Piracy Random?*, Applied Economics Letters 16: 891-895.

Murphy M.N. (2011), *Somalia: The New Barbary?: Piracy and Islam in the Horn of Africa*, Columbia University Press.

Okamoto, H. (2011), *Preliminary Analysis of the Effect of the Piracy Activity in the Northwestern Indian Ocean on the CPUE Trend of Bigeye and Yellowfin*, IOTC Proceedings, (IOTC-2011-WPTT13-44), 9 pp.

Pianet, R., Delgado de Molina, A., Dewals, P., Lucas, V., Floch, L., Chassot, E., & Ariz, J. (2011), *Statistics of the Main Purse Seine Fleets Fishing in the Indian Ocean* (1981-2010). IOTC Proceedings, (IOTC-2011-WPTT13-24), 30 pp.

Sanchirico J.N., Wilen J.E. (2005), *Optimal Spatial Management of Renewable Resources: Matching Policy Scope to Ecosystem Scale*, Journal of Environmental Economics and Management 50: 23–46.

Scott, M.D., Bayliff, W.H., Lennert-Cody, C.E., & Schaefer, K. (1992). *Proceedings of the International Workshop on the Ecology and Fisheries for Tunas Associated with Floating Objects*. IATTC Special Report (IATTC., Vol. 11). La Jolla, California (USA): IATTC.

Smith M.D., Sanchirico J.N., Wilen J.E. (2009), *The Economics of Spatial-Dynamic Processes: Applications to Renewable Resources*, Journal of Environmental Economics and Management 57(1): 104–121.

Sumaila U.R., Zeller D.,Watson R., Alder J., Pauly D. (2007), *Potential Costs and Benefits of Marine Reserves in the High Seas*, Marine Ecology Progress Series 345: 305–310.

Taquet M., Sancho G., Dagorn L., Gaertner J.-C., Itano D, Aumeeruddy R., Wendling B., Peignon C. (2007), *Characterizing Fish Communities Associated with Drifting Fish Aggregating Devices (FADs) in the Western Indian Ocean Using Underwater Visual Surveys*, Aquatic Living Resources 20(4): 331-342.

UNOSAT (2009) *Analysis of Somali Pirate Activity in 2009*. Available: http://unosat.web.cern.ch/unosat/freeproducts/somalia/Piracy/2009/UNOSAT_Somalia_Pirates_Analysis_Q1_2009_23April09_v1.pdf. Accessed 13 July 2009

4. Concerns, Consequences, and Resolutions to Somali Piracy

Martin MURPHY

People in developed countries are fascinated by the damage a bunch of, what they perceive as, savages, has inflicted on international shipping. They cannot believe the world's navies are unable to defeat them. Many people cannot understand why pirates are not being shot on sight, but when no coherent answer is forthcoming, they dismiss the problem until the next incident when the cycle of incredulity followed by outrage followed by indifference starts all over again.

But why should hugely expensive navy ships plough the seas in defense of merchant vessels that often have at best only the remotest connection with national interests? What possible concern can this arid and inhospitable patch of earth that the pirates call home have for powers outside the region above and beyond a charitable willingness to succor the victims of periodic famines? Why should they even do that given that the aid that is provided is often expropriated and subject to political bargaining by internal groups who have little or no concern for the welfare of their own kind?

This chapter argues that there are powerful reasons why concerns about the immediate impacts of Somali piracy are justified. Moreover, that the pirates' actions have raised more serious concerns about international security regimes, the changing balance of power in the Indian Ocean and a reordering of the balance between state and private security in the maritime domain that has not been seen for nearly two centuries. This argument will be pursued along six axes:

- Economic cost
- Human security
- Privatization of naval force
- Naval performance
- Geo-strategic issues
- Political implications.

ECONOMIC COST

The free movement of raw materials and finished goods is vital to the world economy. Somali piracy is the most substantial threat to that peaceful movement by sea since World War II. It has been more prolonged than the "Mines of August" episode when a Libyan ship seeded the Red Sea with mines in July 1984, although unlike that outrage, shipping has not as yet refused to sail through the affected area.[1] Compared to the Iran-Iraq "Tanker War," that started in 1985 and reached its height between 1987 and 1988, Somali piracy has evoked an uncertain state response militarily and politically, which has raised important questions about the limits of trade protection.[2]

Shipping sailing anywhere in the Arabian Sea is potentially at risk. This sea area is as large as Western Europe or Australia. Pirates have attacked and, in many cases, hijacked successfully all types of merchant vessel from oil tankers to dhows, although it is neither the vessel nor its cargo that is of interest to the pirates of Somalia. Their focus is the crew and the value they can yield in ransom.

Piracy had taken place off the Somali coast since the Somali state failed in 1991. By 2006, evidence of a new and well-organized piracy group had emerged. The rise in the number of incidents (actual and attempted) since then has been truly remarkable. In 2006 the International Maritime Bureau (IMB) recorded 18 incidents in the region; in 2009 that number had risen to 148 (62 per cent of the global total); in 2010 there were 100 (51 per cent); up until the end of July 2011 there were 163 (61 per cent).[3] These numbers need to be contextualized. First, by acknowledging that the number of ships attacked amounts to around half of one per cent of the total number of transits through the region, which are generally believed to be about 30,000 annually. Secondly, that the number actually hijacked and taken to Somalia to be exchanged for ransom is an even smaller number: in 2010, 49 ships were hijacked; up to July 2011 the number was 21.[4] The pirates, however, have compensated for this lower capture rate by increasing the ransom

---

[1] Martin N. Murphy, *Small Boats, Weak States, Dirty Money: Piracy and Maritime Terrorism in the Modern World*, New York and London: Columbia University Press/Hurst, 2009, p 237.

[2] *See* Martin S. Navias and E.R. Hooton, *Tanker Wars: The Assault on Merchant Shipping During the Iran-Iraq Crisis, 1980-1988*, London: I.B. Tauris, 1996 and on the U.S. Navy response in particular Lee Allen Zatarain, *Tanker War: America's First Conflict with Iran, 1987-1988*, Philadelphia & Newbury: Casemate Publishers, 2008.

[3] *Piracy and Armed Robbery Against Ships*, January-June 2011, London: ICC International Maritime Bureau, 2011, pp 5-6.

[4] *Piracy and Armed Robbery Against Ships*, January-June 2011, p 9; *Piracy and Armed Robbery Against Ships*, 2010. London: ICC International Maritime Bureau, 2011, p 8.

"take": in 2006 the average ransom was around $150,000, but by 2011 it had increased to between $4.5 and $5 million.

Estimates of the loss to the global economy have varied widely over the years. In 2010 the One Earth Foundation (OEF) published a report entitled "The Economic Costs of Maritime Piracy" which attempted to fill this knowledge gap.[5] It acknowledged difficulties in arriving at a definitive figure, including data limitations, which forced the use of "proxies, averages, and estimations in some areas in order to fill some . . . gaps," incomplete incident reporting and the incredible difficulty of disaggregating the effects of piracy on "macroeconomic variables such as reductions in foreign direct investment (FDI), tourism, or commodity price inflation."[6] Despite these obstacles, the report concluded that maritime piracy costs the world economy between $7 and $12 billion annually. Included in the mix were ransom payments, naval costs, re-routing expenses, insurance premiums, security equipment purchases, prosecutions, the cost of international bodies such as the Contact Group on Piracy off the Coast of Somalia (CGPCS) and the UN Office on Drugs and Crime (UNODC), and costs to regional economies.[7] OEF rightly regarded the report as provisional and called for further research.

Even if the OEF range is accurate, the economic impact of modern piracy globally amounts to no more than a rounding error when compared to an estimated worldwide maritime commerce total of $12.2 trillion in 2010.8 This remains true even when the maximum estimated cost is compared to trade across the Somali Basin/Gulf of Aden alone, which on the basis of about eight percent of world trade, amounts to just short of $1 trillion, yielding a distressing but not disastrous loss rate of 1.2 percent. A useful comparison might be with the retail industry's global loss rate of 1.36 percent due to fraud and shoplifting.[9]

The economic cost of piracy will, however, become very real for everyone if ransom payments are made illegal. The proponents of this position argue

---

[5] Anna Bowden, *The Economic Costs of Maritime Piracy*, One Earth Future Foundation Working Paper, December 2010 at http://oneearthfuture.org/images/imagefiles/Cost%20of%20Piracy%20Final%20Report.pdf.

[6] Bowden, *The Economic Costs of Maritime Piracy*, pp 7-8.

[7] Bowden, *The Economic Costs of Maritime Piracy*, p 25.

[8] The WTO worldwide merchandise export total of $15.2 trillion for 2010 has been adjusted on the assumption that 85 percent moves by sea. World Trade Organization *World Trade 2010, Prospects for 2011*, Press/628, 7th April 2011, Table 3 at http://www.wto.org/english/news_e/pres11_e/pr628_e.htm.

[9] As a rough-and-ready comparison, the global average rate in 2010 for retail "shrinkage," that is to say losses due to theft by shoppers, employees and vendors, fraud, or administrative and logistical error, was 1.36 percent. *The First Worldwide Shrinkage Survey*, Nottingham: Centre for Retail Research, 2010 at http://www.retailresearch.org/grtb_globaltrends.php.

that without the prospect of reward, pirates will not put to sea. They acknowledge that seafarers will be trapped in Somalia, but suggest that the long-term gain of piracy eradication outweighs the short-term misery and potential loss of life felt by only a few hundred sailors at most. In reality any decision to withhold ransom would affect millions of people worldwide.

The outcome is unlikely to be "no ransom no pirates," but rather "no ransom no seafarers." If seafarers refused to go to sea, then no trade would cross the region; Arabian Gulf oil and gas shipments would cease as well. Depending upon how such a legal bar were enacted, three outcomes, or a muddled mixture of all of them, are possible. If the ban comes about through a United Nations Security Council resolution, then maritime traffic across the Arabian Sea could cease almost immediately because shippers would not accept the liability without the safety-net provided by the general average mechanism. If the United States took action unilaterally then at least parts of the marine insurance market would leave London and New York for Asia, beyond the reach of U.S. law, probably never to return. Thirdly, labor unions would boycott the region, something that the powerful Indian union and the Anglo-Danish union have already warned may happen.[10] If ship movements across the Indian Ocean fell significantly, even if they did not cease altogether, the economic damage inflicted on an already fragile world economy would be severe and could quite possibly lead to widespread social unrest. The United States has already put in place the legal authority and the administrative apparatus for such a ban, although it has so far refrained from implementing this measure in full.[11]

HUMAN SECURITY

The human cost of Somali piracy is a blot on the world's conscience. Crews have a right to be protected by their own governments and the maritime powers whose goods they carry. Despite this, many states, and some shipping companies, fail to address the problem with the honesty it demands. Consequently, seafarers even on large ships are apprehensive and even afraid when they pass through pirate-prone areas.

---

[10] *See Indian Seafarers May Boycott Pirate-Infested Gulf of Aden*, The Brunei Times, 16th May 2011 at http://www.bt.com.bn/news-asia/2011/05/16/indian-seafarers-may-boycott-pirate-infested-gulf-aden. and Paul Redfern, *Shippers Have Paid $110m in Ransom This Year*, The East African, 6th November 2011 at http://www.theeastafrican.co.ke/news/Shippers+have+paid++110m+in+ransom+this+year+/-/2558/1268008/-/10atban/-/index.html.

[11] Executive Order 13536 can be accessed at http://edocket.access.gpo.gov/2010/pdf/2010-8878.pdf. Detail on OFAC can be found at http://www.treasury.gov/about/organizational-structure/offices/Pages/Office-of-Foreign-Assets-Control.aspx.

In 2010 alone, 4,185 seafarers were subjected to armed attack off Somalia, 1,432 were on ships boarded by pirates of which 1,090 were held hostage and 516 were used additionally as human shields.[12] While 342 escaped capture by hiding in the secure on-board rooms known as "citadels," the experience of being locked in a steel box on a ship occupied by pirates, wondering what they are planning, whether or not an RPG round will be fired at the door or air inlets blocked by fire, and if naval support will arrive in time, can be terrifying.[13] Pirates have also reportedly abused crews physically and psychologically through beatings and mock executions, as in the cases of the MV *Marida Marguerite* and MV *Samho Jewelry*. Official and industry sources admit to other incidents, which they prefer not to discuss publically, that suggest the willingness to apply pressure has increased.[14] EU NAVFOR and others have gone further, suggesting that abuse had become systematic.[15] The UN Monitoring Group on Somalia and Eritrea (UNMG), on the other hand, found "no evidence that the use of violence or mistreating of hostages" during 2010 had become either more frequent or more widespread than previous years.[16] However Kaija Hurlburt, the author of a second OEF report, makes a telling point when she compares the rates of broadly equivalent crimes committed at sea and on land: on a per capita basis, the rate of major assault off Somalia was the world's highest at 697.7 per 100,000 in 2010 compared to 576 per 100,000 in South Africa. The 2010 hostage rate was equally appalling at 181.7 per 100,000, making it twelve times higher than that of Turkey, the most kidnap-prone country, in which approximately 15 out of every 100,000 people were abducted.[17]

In addition to the seafarers, at least two other groups are affected. First is the seafarers' families, who in the main suffer day after day the agony of not knowing what is happening, but in some cases suffer immediate financial hardship when wages are stopped.[18] Onshore Somalia, moral hazards have become widespread with an increasing use of drugs (principally the local narcotic called *khat,* a green leaf that people chew) and alcohol. That influx of pirate money has stoked price inflation, which has sent the cost of food and

---

[12] Kaija Hurlburt. *The Human Cost of Somali Piracy*, One Earth Future Foundation Working Paper, 6th June 2011, p 8 at http://www.oceansbeyondpiracy.org/sites/default/files/human_cost_of_somali_piracy.pdf.

[13] Hurlburt, *The Human Cost of Somali Piracy*, p 15.

[14] On the filtering of information see Hurlburt *The Human Cost of Somali Piracy*, p 10.

[15] Katharine Houreld, *Somali pirates torturing hostages*, Associated Press, February 1, 2011 at http://www.businessweek.com/ap/financialnews/D9L44TR80.htm.

[16] United Nations *Report on the Monitoring Group on Somalia and Eritrea Pursuant to Security Council Resolutions 751 (1992) and 1907 (2009)*, S/2011/433, 18th July 2011, p 35 and pp 27-32 at http://www.un.org/ga/search/view_doc.asp?symbol=S/2011/433. It noted a 1.15 per cent injured rate in 2009 vice 1.2 percent in 2010 and 0.57 percent killed or missing in 2009 vice 0.78 percent in 2010.

[17] Hurlburt, *The Human Cost of Somali Piracy*, p 22.

[18] Hurlburt, *The Human Cost of Somali Piracy*, pp 19-20.

other commodities soaring.[19] Moreover, the dream of young Somali women to marry a pirate is being replaced by prostitution, with pirates often using girls brought in from abroad, that has led ineluctably to the spread of STDs including AIDS.[20] The cost of piracy, in other words, is not purely economic.

PRIVATIZATION OF NAVAL FORCE

Clearly, if governments are unable or unwilling to provide protection, seafarers have an inherent right of self-defense. Because merchant shipping cannot rely on navies to protect them, the owners and crews of vulnerable vessels have had to adopt protective measures of their own. For the most part these have been passive, including enhanced watch-keeping, maintaining best possible speed, installation of upper-deck lighting, better bridge protection against gunfire, fire hoses rigged to spray a continuous stream of water and foam over likely pirate access points, anti-climb paint, conventional or electrified razor wire, and the construction of citadels to which the crew can retreat if these impediments prove inadequate.[21] Each passive defense method currently employed has been overcome in one incident or another. Citadels are not designed to survive sustained assault. In practice, naval help has to arrive within three days, largely because of the psychological pressure induced by not knowing what the pirates might be planning. Pirates have fired RPGs at citadel doors in attempts to break in and have lit fires over air intakes to smoke crews out. To lessen the chance that such eventualities will occur, ship-owners have begun to embark armed guards.

The full import of a change this rapid cannot be understated. Owners are being presented with no option other than to protect their ships militarily.[22] This is not about the deployment of what are called Vessel Protection Detachments (VPDs) consisting of small teams of regular armed forces personnel placed on board merchant vessels under government command. This is about the privatization of naval force. States have, one by one, begun to back away from their claim to monopolize the use of force at sea, because they are no longer willing to provide their navies with the resources

---

[19] Martin N. Murphy, *Somalia the New Barbary? Piracy and Islam in the Horn of Africa*, New York and London: Columbia University Press/Hurst, 2011, pp 112-3.

[20] Yahya Mohamed. *The Real Cost of Piracy on Locals*, SomaliaReport, 27th March 2011 at http://www.somaliareport.com/index.php/post/390/The_Real_Costs_Of_Piracy_On_Locals?PHPSESSID=4f976f989ab5ea41904deb12334fb8fd.

[21] *BMP3: Best Management Practices to Deter Piracy off the Coast of Somalia and in the Arabian Sea Area*, Edinburgh: Witherby Seamanship International, 2010.

[22] *See, e.g., Piracy: Prepare to repel boarders*, The Economist, Schumpeter Blog, 13th October 2011 at http://www.economist.com/blogs/schumpeter/2011/10/piracy.

necessary to do so.[23] Western navies, in particular, have been forced to make a choice: either prepare to fight high intensity war, or secure the seas. The relentless decline in escort ship numbers makes clear the choice they have made. It is a false one.

It represents a reversal of a trend *towards* naval protection and *away* from ship self-protection that began in the early Eighteenth Century.[24] The overwhelming argument in favor of using Private Security Contractors (PSCs) at sea, which is the one the shipping industry has reluctantly acceded to, is that so far at least no ship with an armed detachment on board has been hijacked. Most observers, including the more thoughtful private security providers, believe that it is only a matter of time before one is taken down. Once the private armed detachments come under sustained attack difficulties the following questions will demand resolution: who has actual command, the armed guards or the ship's master, who has the clear legal authority and responsibility, how the guards interact with naval forces in the area, and where the liability lies as and when pirates or crew members are killed, injured or captured. The latest estimate is that around 35 percent of ships now carry armed details. Given that naval capacity is being cut, there is a real concern that armed guards will become a permanent feature for all ships transiting "at risk" areas worldwide.

NAVAL PERFORMANCE

Historical experience suggests that navies have rarely been able to exert sufficient dissuasive pressure at sea alone; to be effective they have had to deny pirates access to their bases on land. Governments with navies operating off Somalia have not minded this age-old lesson. They have refused to sanction operations to neutralize pirate bases, forcing navies to confront the problem solely at sea. Governments desire the end of piracy, but refuse to commit the political and material resources needed to bring it about. The results have been predictable, even though they know full-well what is required. The US, Britain and France engineered passage of UN Security Council resolution 1851 in 2008 which gave any force permission to suppress piracy within Somalia, provided the agreement of the UN-mandated Transitional Federal Government (TFG) in Mogadishu had been secured

---

[23] Meredith Buel, *US Admiral: Commercial Ships Need Armed Guards to Fight Pirates*, VOANews.com, 21st April 2010 at http://www.voanews.com/english/news/US-Admiral-Commercial-Ships-Need-Armed-Guards-to-Fight-Pirates-91719979.html.

[24] Douglass C. North, *Sources of Productivity Change in Ocean Shipping, 1600-1850*, Journal of Political Economy, 76, No. 5, September-October 1968, pp 959-60.

beforehand.[25] This power has never been invoked. Although the UK mounted a raid in July it is not clear that this was piracy-related.[26]

Apart from *ad hoc* interventions by the US Navy following the *Seabourn Spirit* attack in November 2005, navies focused initially on protecting food aid shipments from Mombasa, in Kenya, to Mogadishu. The first escorts were provided in November 2007 but the program only became systematic when NATO, and then the EU, took over the mission in November 2008. The arrival of warships off the Indian Ocean coast prompted the pirates to shift their attacks into the Gulf of Aden, which, because of the density of commercial traffic, proved a most rewarding hunting ground. In response, the naval forces, which were now divided into three groups led separately by the US, NATO and the EU, supplemented by vessels from other nations under national control, initiated two Internationally Recognized Transit Corridors (IRTCs) in July 2008, one for eastbound traffic, the other for westbound. These took time to work, partly because not all ships' masters and owners either understood the procedures or accepted the need to alert the navies to their presence. Without notification, and the opportunity this gave to assess a vessel's vulnerability, navies could not respond effectively. Once more ships began to alert MTO the navies' success rate increased and the pirates' declined. In response, the pirates returned many of their operations to the Indian Ocean, eventually using larger vessels as mother ships to cover the vast distances involved.

The problem has been that no more than 30 warships – supported by even fewer aircraft - have been at sea at any one time, too few to adequately patrol the vast spaces involved. The number has usually been nearer 20, when 50 was estimated to be the minimum needed to patrol the Gulf of Aden alone.[27] Comments made more recently suggest that if all the modern warships in the world were assembled in theatre, it would still be insufficient to contain the problem. In the view of Spyros Polemis, the chairman of the International Chamber of Shipping (ICS), the "current military response - with only a

---

[25] UN Security Council Resolution 1851 (2008) at http://daccess-dds-ny.un.org/doc/UNDOC/GEN/N08/655/01/PDF/N0865501.pdf?OpenElement. France reportedly pushed for the mandate to intervene on-shore be extended to other pirate-prone regions such as the Gulf of Guinea under similar terms but this was opposed by Vietnam, Libya and China. *Navies to Tackle Somali Pirates*, BBC News, 2nd June 2008 at http://news.bbc.co.uk/2/hi/africa/7432612.stm.

[26] *Marines in Daring Amphibious Raid in Somalia*, Daily Telegraph, 29th October 2011 at http://www.telegraph.co.uk/news/uknews/defence/8857071/Marines-in-daring-amphibious-raid-in-Somalia.html.

[27] John Knott, *Somalia, the Gulf of Aden, and Piracy*, Mondaq.com, 20th January 2009, p 9 at http://www.mondaq.com/article.asp?article_id=72910&lk=1.

handful of navy ships available to provide protection on any given day - has just been sticking plaster on a gaping wound."[28]

If, as appears likely, improved self-protection measures, including armed guards in the case of the most vulnerable vessels, are the key variable, not deterrence or faster naval reaction times, then the justification for a continuing naval presence, and certainly the assertion that it will bring piracy to an end, must be open to doubt.[29] Navies have, in short, allowed themselves to be used as an alternative to an effective political policy. "Governments have so far failed to protect shipping, and the smooth flow of world trade, from being literally held to ransom by Somali criminals," as Polemis said in September 2011.[30] Shippers, crews and, potentially, legislators and voters want to know how and why navies can justify the money expended upon them if they can longer fulfill what is widely regarded as a basic naval task. The answer to this question will remain inadequate so long as governments refuse to craft a policy to confront piracy on land, or *from* the sea, which permits naval force to be deployed effectively.

GEO-STRATEGIC ISSUES

The Gulf of Aden has been an important waterway since the age of the Pharaohs. Thirty-five percent of all traded oil and gas passing through the Bab el-Mandeb (BAM) is destined for the European market, about eight percent of the world total. Approximately half of the world's container traffic also passes through the BAM, of which around 80 percent is accounted for by Europe-Asia trade. This vital waterway bisects a region which, while linked by economic exchange, migration and Islam, is now fraught with actual and potential conflict from the Red Sea to Kenya.

Piracy is a symptom of this instability and not a cause. The longer it is allowed to persist, however, the more pernicious and the harder to eradicate it will become. It is also, alongside large-scale migration and its inevitable concomitant, illegal human trafficking, the most obvious way in which the region exports harm to individuals and political and economic interests that otherwise would have no direct engagement in the region's problems. However, it is the destabilizing potential of militant Islamist groups al-Shabaab, in Somalia, and al-Qaeda in the Arabian Peninsula (AQAP), in Yemen, and the possibility that they might find some common cause, that worries many outside the region most.

---

[28] Saul, *Somali Piracy Set to Surge as Monsoon Ends: EU navy.*

[29] Murphy, *Somalia the New Barbary?* pp 135-6.

[30] Saul, *Somali Piracy Set to Surge as Monsoon Ends: EU navy.*

This challenge should not be over-estimated. Al-Shabaab, like so many groups in Somalia, is a coalition whose constituent parts have varying degrees of loyalty to the core that has pledged its alliance to Al-Qaeda. It is, moreover, weak domestically; if anything, the famine, al-Shabaab's own policies have done so much to engineer, has undermined its domestic position still further.

On the other hand it appears to have amassed substantial financial reserves. Its 2009-10 income was believed to be between $70 and $100 million, which was drawn from various sources including taxation, extortion, port dues from Kismayo, commercial activities and smuggling, external assistance, and, to a limited and uncertain extent, the "taxation" of piracy. If accurate, then al-Shabaab's income stream was greater than Somaliland's. Outside Somalia the group is connected to Kenyan criminal groups and has a growing presence amongst Somali diaspora communities. Its recruitment efforts in East Africa have been intensive. It has already carried out one deadly attack in Uganda. It has also developed links with AQAP, the nature and strength of which are yet unclear.[31]

Yemen is not a failed state. Its plight is not yet as dire as Somalia's, but it is politically fragile and economically weak.[32] In the judgment of the Bipartisan Policy Center, "History, demography and geography have conspired to bequeath Yemen a legacy of factionalism and civil conflict, distrust and resource competition" while the country's rulers have found it "easier to maintain a semblance of stability by playing various factions off against each other."[33]

It is fair to say that it is unclear how substantial a threat AQAP actually presents, certainly within Yemen. The bare facts are that it was formed, in its present guise, in January 2009 by the coming-together of two previous al-Qaeda groupings: al-Qaeda in Yemen (AQY) and the Saudi Arabian-based al-Qaeda in the Arabian Peninsula to launch attacks across the whole region. Attacks on Western targets included the plan to blow-up a flight from Amsterdam to Detroit on Christmas Day 2009 using the so-called "underwear bomber," Umar Farouk Abdulmutallab, and also a series of

[31] United Nations, *Report on the Monitoring Group 2011*, pp 24, 27-32, 38-9, 140-179, 181-203.

[32] United States Senate, Committee on Foreign Relations. *Al Qaeda in Yemen and Somalia: A Ticking Time Bomb*, 21st January 2010, pp 8-9 at http://foreign.senate.gov/imo/media/doc/Yemen.pdf.

[33] *Fragility and Extremism in Yemen*, Bipartisan Policy Center, Stabilizing Fragile States Project, Staff Paper, February 2010, p 1 at http://bipartisanpolicy.org/library/staff-paper/fragility-and-extremism-yemen.

bombs packed into printer cartridges, discovered before they were loaded aboard a cargo flight in 2010.[34]

To what extent al-Shabaab and AQAP might be cooperating is a matter of intense speculation, most of it uninformed. Al-Shabaab has reportedly sworn to support AQAP and to exploit the opportunity for the conflicts on either side of the Gulf of Aden to become "increasingly intertwined."[35] The links between the two organizations revealed by Ahmed Abdulkadir Warsame, during his interrogation, heightened these concerns because he reportedly brokered weapons deals between al-Shabaab and AQAP.[36] Subsequent reports based on material retrieved from Bin Laden's Abbotsbad compound, and interrogations conducted with al-Shabaab members captured in Mogadishu, suggested that AQAP had acted as the go-between for Bin Laden and al-Shabaab and that before his death Bin Laden had agreed to grant al-Shabaab the same al-Qaeda franchise status as AQAP. Despite this inducement, al-Shabaab's leaders apparently refused to shift the focus away from Somalia and onto US and Western targets, or to change the group's name to al-Qaeda in East Africa, fearing heightened US interest.[37]

Whatever the extent and future direction of the relationship between al-Shabaab and AQAP, Yemen-based Islamist terrorism will remain an international threat that cannot be ignored, in part because the shipping has to pass through the BAM to access the Red Sea. Islamist groups are far from blind to the opportunity that disrupting shipping may present. Comments by the al-Qaeda strategist al-Suri, and on Islamist websites, suggests more than a passing interest in what the pirates have achieved.[38] Material taken from Bin Laden's compound after his death indicated a continuing interest in attacking oil and gas supplies, perhaps using the small boats tactics used against the *Limburg* off Yemen in 2002, and against the *M Star* in the Strait of Hormuz in 2011.[39]

---

[34] *Al-Qa'ida in the Arabian Peninsula*, The National Counterterrorism Center, Counterterrorism Calendar 2011 at http://www.nctc.gov/site/groups/aqap.html.

[35] Scott Baldauf, *Is al Qaeda in Yemen Connected to al Qaeda in Somalia?*, Christian Science Monitor, 7th January 2010 at http://www.csmonitor.com/World/2010/0107/Is-Al-Qaeda-in-Yemen-connected-to-Al-Qaeda-in-Somalia.

[36] Pam Benson, *Official: Somali Terrorist Suspect was in Contact With Anwar al-Awlaki*, *CNN Justice,* 8th July 2011 at http://www.cnn.com/2011/CRIME/07/07/somali.terror.suspect/.

[37] Brian Bennett, *Al Qaeda's Yemen Branch Has Aided Somali Militants, US Says*, Los Angeles Times, 18th July 2011 at http://articles.latimes.com/2011/jul/18/world/la-fg-bin-laden-somalia-20110718.

[38] *See, e.g.*, Brynjar Lia, *Architect of Global Jihad: The Life of Al-Qaida Strategist Abu Mus'ab al-Suri*, London: Hurst & Co, 2007, p 401; *Jihadist Website Commentary Argues "Maritime Terrorism" Strategic Necessity*, Biyokulule Online, 29th April 2008.

[39] Eileen Sullivan and Matt Apuzzo, *Al-Qaida Eyed Oil Tankers As Bombing Targets*, Associated Press, 20th May 2011 at http://www.msnbc.msn.com/id/43115189/ns/us_news-security/t/al-qaida-eyed-oil-tankers-bombing-targets/#.TmU_u2rtcZs.

If contact between al-Shabaab and AQAP were to turn into cooperation, that would be made both easier and potentially much more threatening to shipping if they gained effective control of the northern and southern shores of the Gulf of Aden.[40] The pirates have demonstrated how maritime security there, and across much of the western Indian Ocean, could be compromised. Attacks at sea, if not countered effectively, could unsettle the littoral states of East Africa to the south and as far north as Egypt and Israel. Djibouti could become an isolated outpost for United States and Coalition based operations. While any realistic threat of complete closure of these vital trade routes would provoke a major political and military response, much the same effect could be achieved using low-level attacks to persuade the international shipping and insurance companies that the transit risks were too great. If maritime traffic did have to divert around Africa, then re-routing costs would go up. If one shore of the Gulf were to fall into hostile hands that would be worrying, but if coordinated attacks could be mounted from both coasts the threat could become substantial. Like almost everything else relating to terrorism, the threat must not be over-stated; attacking large merchant vessels requires specialized training, tailored weapons and a logistic base that is potentially detectable.[41] One of the principle reasons why al-Qaeda was unable to build on its initial successes against shipping along the Yemen coast was that it was unable to establish such a base.[42] However, the increasing availability and rapidly decreasing cost of lightweight guided weapons small enough to be mounted on and fired from small craft, and sophisticated naval mines, could alter this calculation.[43]

Popular perceptions to the contrary, the situation on the southern shore of the Gulf of Aden is for the most part more stable than its northern neighbor. Somaliland has changed governments three times democratically and peacefully in the two decades since it broke away from the rest of Somalia. Puntland lacks governmental capacity, but is not wracked by violence. If al-Shabaab was to gain a foothold in the north, then stability could be undermined, bringing with it many of the privations that now affect only the south.

---

[40] *Al-Qaeda Vows to Block Strategic Al-Mandeb Strait*, BRIEFS, The Jamestown Foundation, Terrorism Monitor, Vol. 8, Issue No. 7, 19th February 2010 at http://www.jamestown.org/single/?no_cache=1&tx_ttnews[tt_news]=36058&tx_ttnews[backPid]=228&cHash=bd9014a6ad.

[41] For a discussion of the difficulties and a review of some of the weapon options see Murphy, *Small Boats, Weak States, Dirty Money*, pp 231-241 & 254-259; Jonathan Saul, *ANALYSIS – Vital Shipping Lanes Can Weather Turmoil in Yemen*, Reuters, 3rd June 2011 at http://af.reuters.com/article/energyOilNews/idAFLDE7520RS20110603?sp=true.

[42] Martin N. Murphy, *Piracy and the Exploitation of Sanctuary*, in Jeffrey H. Norwitz (ed.), *Armed Groups: Studies in National Security, Counterterrorism, and Counterinsurgency*, Newport, RI: U.S. Naval War College, 2008, p 167.

[43] Murphy, *Somalia the New Barbary?* pp 177-8.

The Sool-Sanaag region lies between Somaliland and Puntland and is disputed by both. It had been described as the Horn's Tora Bora, partly because of its rugged, mountainous terrain riddled with caves, and partly because of the groups that use it as a base and hiding place.[44] It is here that disruptive forces may find a beachhead.

The Sool-Sanaag Cayn Army (SSCA), which is the smaller of two groups, was founded in 2007. In its 2011 report, the UNMG described the SSCA as being "conceived, funded and led by members of the Dhulbahante clan diaspora." Over the years the clan divided its loyalties between Somaliland and Puntland, but, having been let down by both, now claims its objective is to establish a separate existence as part of a unitary Somalia. Despite this, the SSCA appears to be another typical Somali group that uses political rhetoric to disguise its use of violence for economic ends. The UNMG characterized it as an "opportunistic and arguably mercenary militia force," which, like several other largely notional Somali "states" and "authorities," is "largely conceived, funded and led by members of the Somali diaspora, who have appropriated legitimate local grievances to advance personal political ambitions and – in some cases – to enrich themselves."[45]

The larger and more capable group is led by Mohammed Sa'iid Atom of the Warsengeli clan, who has a long history as an arms trader linking Eritrea and other arms suppliers with Islamists groups, including al-Shabaab and the now defunct Hizbul Islam.[46] His essentially criminal militia, which emerged as the principal military presence in this remote area, was quickly linked to a number of violent incidents and to al-Shabaab. It was rumored to have protected a pirate group, who had captured and held hostage a German couple in June 2008, against Somaliland and Puntland forces.[47] During 2009, Atom reportedly strengthened his ties with al-Shabaab, naming his militia the "Eastern Sanaag Mujahidicen," while remaining, in UNMG's words, "essentially a Warsengeli clan warlord."[48] He established a training base at Galgala where he met with delegations from al-Shabaab and where both non-Warsengeli recruits and foreign trainers were observed, established two further training camps over the border in Puntland, continued to ship arms to southern Somalia from Eritrea and Yemen, and was apparently ready to

---

[44] Mustafa Haji Abdinur, *Fears of a New Tora Bora in Northern Somalia*, AFP, 22nd July 2010 at http://www.google.com/hostednews/afp/article/ALeqM5gPIGk5KHvnkayhRfOBd4W_7HzkfQ.

[45] United Nations, *Report on the Monitoring Group 2011*, pp 32 & 130.

[46] United Nations, *Report on the Monitoring Group on Somalia 2008*, p 33; United Nations, *Report on the Monitoring Group on Somalia 2010*, p 24.

[47] United Nations, *Report on the Monitoring Group 2008*, pp 21 & 33; *Germans Freed After Five Week Somali Kidnap Ordeal*, AFP, 9th August 2008 at http://afp.google.com/article/ALeqM5hgJLzwByWDnZYKGjAWPR4k8UAbwA.

[48] United Nations, *Report on the Monitoring Group on Somalia 2010*, p 45.

confront both Somaliland and Puntland directly.[49] Between April and September 2010, however, his militia confronted Puntland forces and lost. A search of his camp reportedly revealed evidence of extensive links to al-Shabaab. This setback seemingly forced Atom to rely on al-Shabaab support even more; support which they delivered despite the fact they were under pressure themselves. Early in May 2011 Atom returned to Sanaag and engaged Puntland forces again. It is clear that his militia would not survive without support not only from al-Shabaab, but from Warsengeli clan interests and, possibly, members of the Bosasso business community in Puntland itself. The UNMG now consider that Atom's militia has become part of al-Shabaab and not merely an affiliate. In its judgment "it is possible that the remote and mountainous region of eastern Sanaag, with its access to the Gulf of Aden and proximity to Yemen, may increasingly appear to be an attractive alternative to areas of southern Somalia where al-Shabaab has recently been placed on the defensive."[50]

The geo-strategic threat is not therefore related to piracy directly. Piracy has, however, exposed a weakness in maritime security, which naval forces have so far been unable to address effectively, that can be exploited by non-state groups and even state proxies for political ends. The problems that straddle either side of the Afghan-Pakistan border shows what happens when corruption and disorder are left unaddressed politically and, if necessary, militarily. The groups fighting in the Sool and eastern Sanaag are trying to establish havens from which they can undermine whatever stability Somaliland and Puntland have achieved. Neither is fighting to establish a haven from which they can attack shipping. This will, however, be the eventual result if they are not defeated.

POLITICAL CONSEQUENCES

Piracy's political significance has generally exceeded its economic impact. State reluctance to act, observable at times throughout history, is evident just as clearly off Somalia today. The modern view of piracy is that it is a crime that needs to be punished. This has closed minds to the political and economic aspects of piracy, both of which need to be addressed on their own terms. Modern states have pursued narrow rule-based approaches that lack the flexibility to attack all aspects of the problem and leave modern pirates with the initiative.

---

[49] United Nations, *Report on the Monitoring Group on Somalia 2010*, p 45.

[50] United Nations, *Report on the Monitoring Group 2011*, pp 19-23; Abdi Sheik. *Islamist Rebels Vow Jihad on Somalia's Puntland*, Reuters, 28th July 2010 at http://af.reuters.com/article/topNews/idAFJOE 66R0F220100728?sp=true.

Piracy has shared characteristics wherever it occurs, but in each case these are ordered according to local circumstances and arise out of local conditions. Provided outbreaks remain local they can be confronted locally or, in many cases, ignored. But piracy has another characteristic, its mobility, which can make it a threat to international shipping. When pirates operate outside a state's territorial waters they can present a challenge to international good order at sea. Somali piracy is merely the current outstanding example.

The U.S. reluctance to engage with political actors on land in Somalia clearly originated in the battle that became known as "Black Hawk Down." Thereafter, Somalia's problems were relegated by the fight against al-Qaeda, Iraq and Afghanistan. When compared to these events, Somalia's problems, of which piracy was often the most visible but not necessarily the most significant component, were regarded as largely insignificant. Indeed, if there was any detectable American political strategy towards Somalia post-1995, it was to *avoid* landward engagement.

Ken Booth described navies as having three functions: military, diplomatic and policing.[51] Ever since the Civil War, the U.S. Navy has focused on the military and diplomatic aspects, and downplayed policing. Consequently, when the U.S. took over Britain's position as the world's supreme naval power in 1945, it did so only partially. It adopted Britain's military and diplomatic roles, but failed to take over its policing responsibilities. Lacking an empire it had no need to develop such a capability. Since 1945, and certainly since Britain and other imperial powers withdrew from their possessions, piracy has been able to survive and prosper by exploiting differences in political will between states in the international system. The United States, the current naval hegemon, has not generally seen it as its role to help resolve these differences. The collective security arrangements that have enabled it to lead and manage the core inter-state dimension of international security successfully for over half a century have no equivalent in the maritime domain.

In spite of the fact that all, or almost all, states have an interest in the safe and secure operation of the world's maritime system and the elimination of non-state and state-based threats, one state alone has a truly global interest in securing free navigation everywhere and in maintaining the system-of-systems that sustains all the rest: The United States is the ultimate guarantor of maritime security, just as Rome and Britain were in the past. It is a role loosely

[51] Ken Booth, *Navies and Foreign Policy*, London & New York: Croom Helm and Crane, Cusack, 1977, p 16.

analogous to the dollar's position as the world's reserve currency; it gives the United States a huge advantage, one that the U.S. should fight to retain.

The most damaging effect the Somali pirates have achieved is to show up shortcomings in United States maritime leadership. Somali pirates have been *allowed* to achieve what they have because of U.S. distraction or indifference. The U.S. Navy's failure, in tandem with its coalition partners, to curb their activities raises doubts about America's willingness to devote the political resources that are necessary to make maritime security a reality; doubts that in turn raise questions about its position as the natural leader of global or regional maritime security regimes.[52] Yet the rationale for U.S. military action against Somali piracy, framed in the context of a coherent *political* strategy for those parts of Somalia that are willing and able to engage in a productive dialogue, is compelling because, as Jakob Grygriel has pointed out, failed states "are not only a source of domestic calamities; they are also potentially a source of great power competition" and that "America's global rivals are doing what aspirant powers have done at moments of transition for millennia . . . probing the top state on the outer limits of its power commitments . . . reading America's responses to gauge how much latitude they have to make low-cost revisions to the system in their favor."[53] Somalia, and the presence of rival navies off its coast justified rhetorically by a common need to suppress piracy, fits these descriptions well.

So, What Needs to be Done?

Solving Somali piracy demands a layered approach that mixes long-term and short-to-medium term actions. Overall, the context needs to be focused on changing the balance of economic incentives away from piracy and towards alternatives; it means increasing the risk of piracy and decreasing its reward.

Over the long-term this can only be achieved by building on the not inconsiderable antipathy to piracy within Somalia, which is concentrated in local communities, women's groups and amongst imams. These groups and local business interests need to be enrolled in multiple, generally small-scale, programs that work from the bottom-up to expand employment in existing industries, such as livestock rearing, fishing, and construction, and the

[52] Murphy, *Somalia the New Barbary?* p 167.

[53] Jakob Grygiel, *Vacuum Wars: The Coming Competition Over Failed States*, The American Interest, July-August 2009 at http://www.the-american-interest.com/article.cfm?piece=622; A. Wess Mitchell and Jakob Grygiel, *The Vulnerability of Peripheries*, The American Interest, March-April 2011 at http://www.the-american-interest.com/article.cfm?piece=923.

creation of new opportunities in occupations that local people will identify.[54] It will also involve the development of small-scale infrastructure projects such as clinics, schools, roads, air-strips and electrical capacity.

Inevitably, it will also mean interacting with regional political entities. With Somaliland that should be straightforward: they have proved over two decades that they deserve international recognition as a separate state, recognition that has been consistently denied because of the desire by the international community, in particular the African Union, to achieve a one-state solution to Somalia. This flies in the face of reality and threatens to reverse all that Somaliland has accomplished as it gives heart to those who wish to see it undermined.

The requirement elsewhere in Somalia – including Puntland - is to avoid picking winners or choosing sides; doing so almost always provokes disputes. The "take-me-to-your-leader" attitude that has typified so much foreign involvement in Somalia has severely limited opportunities for wider engagement. Bronwyn Bruton has labeled what should be done as "constructive disengagement": Somali processes of clan and national reconciliation and the political compromise leading up to it will, she argues, "be largely imperceptible to Western eyes."[55] Consequently, external powers need to refrain from attempting to impose their preferred solutions because, as experience has shown, they do not yield the outcomes desired, but ignite Somali resentment and competition instead. The alternative approach is not to pick winners, but to offer potentially all Somali actors, regardless of whether these are government entities, regional authorities, civil associations, clan or business groups, equal access to assistance based on their demonstrable ability to deliver services and assistance to local populations. This would reinforce the Somali tradition of "bottom-up" governance and avoid the problems of "top-down" imposition that bedeviled so many previous initiatives.[56] Implicit in such a recommendation is the recognition that some recipients will lack the political and managerial expertise necessary to overcome the problems that will inevitably arise. These entities must be allowed to fail. Somalis will respond to failure by transferring their

---

[54] *See, e.g.*, Martin N. Murphy and Joe Saba, *Countering Piracy: The Potential of Onshore Development*, in *Global Challenge, Regional Responses: Forging a Common Approach to Maritime Piracy*, Selected Briefing Papers. Dubai: Dubai School of Government, 2011, pp 46-51 at http://counterpiracy.ae/briefing_papers/Murphy%20and%20Saba%20The%20Potential%20of%20Onshore%20Development.pdf.

[55] Bronwyn E. Bruton, *Somalia: A New Approach*, Council Special Report No. 52, New York: Council on Foreign Relations, March 2010, p 35.

[56] Bronwyn Bruton and J. Peter Pham, *How to End the Stalemate in Somalia*, Foreign Affairs SNAPSHOT, 30th September 2011 at http://www.foreignaffairs.com/articles/68315/bronwyn-bruton-and-j-peter-pham/how-to-end-the-stalemate-in-somalia?page=show.

allegiance to more successful and better-managed options. For this process to work efficiently, each entity must be made accountable in ways that the TFG is not. In short, any approach needs to work with the grain of Somali society, not against it.

Short-to-medium term measures need to focus first on taking down the pirate leaders. Who they are is largely known. What is needed is a detailed understanding of the networks that enable them to finance their operations and pay-off their backers within Somalia and overseas. This effort has barely started. Secondly, it will mean disrupting pirate support networks, primarily those that supply weapons, fuel, outboard motors, skiffs and other equipment, all of which is imported into Somalia primarily though Yemen, but also from the Gulf States. Thirdly it will mean that the information gathered on and from suspects held on board ships and then released as part of "catch-and-release" programs will need to be analyzed and distributed more systematically, unencumbered by military classification. If states desire a law enforcement solution based off of naval platforms, then they need to provide the equipment, systems and procedures that will enable this relatively new hybrid to work properly; the Key West-based Joint Interagency Task Force South which operates against Caribbean drug smugglers provides an effective, albeit expensive, model.

However attractive offshore non-engagement might appear to be, longer-term landward engagement can only be delayed, not ignored, if piracy - and Somalia's more deep-seated problems - are to be addressed. Somalia has made plain the risks that are run if maritime security is ignored. It has also demonstrated that the solution is not purely naval. It never was and never has been at any point in history. Suppressing piracy and securing the seas from the predations of criminal and quasi-criminal enterprises means securing the land. Securing the land demands engagement, which in turn requires a realistic political strategy out of which the subordinate development, judicial, law enforcement and naval strategies can derive their own strength and purpose, and achieve the unity of effort which has been sorely lacking so far.[57] A challenge this substantial demands a response that matches its seriousness.

[57] Murphy, *Somalia the New Barbary?* pp 179-80.

II. Participants and Perspectives

5. SEAFARERS: PIRACY PROTECTION

Patrick CHAUMETTE[1]

Piracy is an international scourge, grabbing headlines and costing millions. Yet, suffering from the attacks falls disproportionately on seafarers. Seafarers have many reasons for complaining about being at the center of these attacks; they are not simple spectators in the violence. In October 2011, there was an increase of attacks against offshore gas and oil rigs and supply ships in the Gulf of Guinea. These attacks even took place against oil tankers within miles from Lagos port. Since the start of 2011, there were attacks counted. In the Indian Ocean, pirate attacks started around 2001, and since then their numbers have gradually risen. In 2010, a report from the International Maritime Bureau listed, worldwide, 445 attacks, a number that corresponded to an increase of 10% from 2009. These attacks included the capture of 53 ships and 1181 seafarers. While the different counter-piracy naval forces have reduced the efficiency of attacks, they did not decrease the occurrences.[2] On the contrary, there has been a rise of violence and an expansion of bad treatment toward captive crews, with some resulting deaths. Since the start of 2011, the P&I Clubs are said to have paid 90 million dollars for ransoms. Every year, the amount of ransoms increases, attacks are more violent, and more prisoners are taken and held in Somalia. Indian shipowners have estimated the cost of piracy for international shipping to be 9 billion dollars (6.55 billion euros), without even taking into account the public cost due to Operation Atalanta or other military interventions.

Piracy in the Indian Ocean has become durable and structural. It has demanded defensive strategies, armaments, technical adaptations of ships, crew training, management of stress and anxiety, and psychological follow-up for post-traumatic disorders. This situation not only disturbs shipping but also tuna fishing in the Indian Ocean, particularly when attacks happen near

---

[1] Patrick Chaumette is Professor of Labor Law at the University of Nantes, France.

[2] A. Bellayer-Roille, *Montée en Puissance de la Lutte Contre la Piraterie Maritime. Sus à l'Hostis Humanis Generis!*, Annuaire de Droit Maritime et Océanique, *ADMO*, université de Nantes, T. XXVII, 2009, pp 309-311. M.D. Fink & R.J. Galvin, *Combating Pirates off the Coast of Somalia: Current Legal Challenges*, NILR, 2009, pp 367-395. M. Manouvel, *Piraterie Maritime, Droit International, Droits Internes et Volonté Politique*, *Annuaire du Droit de la Mer*, Pédone, Paris, 2009, t. XIV, pp 171-200; Ashley J. Roach, *Countering Piracy of Somalia: International Law and International Institutions*, AJIL, 2010, vol. 104, afl. 3, pp 397-416.

the Seychelles. The tuna seiners have to navigate two together, when one fishes; the other looks out for pirates and does not fish. The consequence is a productivity loss and a cost increase. Further, the presence of guards on board some French fishing ships, requires more stopover and cohabitation on board. The period French soldiers are available to stay on board does not correspond to the tuna fishing period; the fishing industry had to adapt itself to the working conditions of these new "passengers."

The "Best Management Practices for Protection against Somalia Based Piracy (BMP-4)" booklet, revised in 2011 and jointly published by Atalanta Chain of Command of EU-NAVFOR and the shipping industry, considers the entire Indian Ocean as a high risk area. The High Risk Area is bounded by the Suez Canal and the Strait of Hormuz to the North (10°S and 78°E) and extends to the Mozambique Channel in the South. The "Best Management Practices" recommend to shipping companies and vessels to register on the website of the Maritime Security Centre Horn of Africa,[3] before transiting the Gulf of Aden. Registered vessels receive all available information concerning the situation in the navigation area and are escorted by the EU-NAVFOR-Atalanta operational forces. This diminishes the risk of attacks. However, more than a third of the vessels transiting do not register at the Maritime Security Centre Horn of Africa and therefore cannot benefit from the measures implemented to secure their transit in the area.

The European Union asks its Member States to adopt the Convention of Rome of March 10, 1988, on the repression of illicit acts against navigation.[4] The measures adopted by the EU are part of the European space of freedom, security and justice project that ensures free movement of persons and goods. It aims to fight organised crime and terrorism - the development of maritime piracy is a new form of organised crime. The communitisation of the IMO ISPS Code, inserted in the annexes of the SOLAS Convention, is regulated by the Commission regulation EC n°725/2004 of the European Parliament and of the Council of March 31, 2004 on enhancing ship and port facility security.[5] Resulting from the 9/11 attacks, the IMO ISPS Code tries to prevent eventual terrorist attacks, but partially ignores piracy acts. Following the Resolution 1814 of the United Nations of May 15, 2008 that protects the World Food Program, the Resolution 1916 of June 2, 2008 aims to protect maritime navigation. On September 19, 2008, the Council of the EU has

---

[3] http://www.mschoa.org.

[4] Ramos B. Sanchez, *Action undertaken by the International Maritime Organization in the Struggle Against Maritime Piracy and Armed Robbery*, *Sûreté Maritime et Violence en Mer; Maritime Security and Violence at Sea*, Heredia J.M. Sobrino, dir., Bruylant, Editions de l'université de Bruxelles, 2011, pp 211-233.

[5] Joue, n° L 129, 29 April 2004, p 6.

adopted a joint action in order to coordinate the military actions lead by Member States (EU-NAVCO)[6]. On the 10th of November 2008, the new joint military action is named Atalanta.

Interventions of naval forces, capture of pirates and cross-fires have worsened the violence of the attacks. For several years, gunfire is no longer simply shot in the air to impress, but is now shot towards the bridge. Crews have therefore asked for protection, willing to navigate only if armed guards are on board, whether they are soldiers or working for private security companies (Private Military Company – PSC). Sometimes covered in the media, the treatment of captive crews has worsened. The first execution of a captive seafarer happened in 2011 following the intervention of Swedish coast guards. There are no longer only hundreds of pirates, but now thousands; thousands who are younger and ready to take greater risks.

Until recently, regional agreements between States have been concluded without real efficiency. In January 2009 the Djibouti Code of Conduct was adopted, sponsored by the IMO. Nine States out of 21 signed it at the end of the conference.[7] To date, the "Code of Conduct Concerning the Suppression of Piracy and Armed Robbery against Ships in the western Indian Ocean and the Gulf of Aden" has been signed by 12 countries in the area. It says:

> Consistent with their available resources and related priorities, their respective national laws and regulations, and applicable rules of international law, the Participants intend to cooperate to the fullest possible extent in the repression of piracy and armed robbery against ships with a view towards:
>
> (a) sharing and reporting relevant information;
>
> (b) interdicting ships and/or aircraft suspected of engaging in piracy or armed robbery against ships;
>
> (c) ensuring that persons committing or attempting to commit piracy or armed robbery against ships are apprehended and prosecuted; and
>
> (d) facilitating proper care, treatment, and repatriation for seafarers, fishermen, other shipboard personnel and passengers subject to piracy or armed robbery against ships, particularly those who have been subjected to violence.

---

[6] A. Cudennec, *Terrorisme et Piraterie Maritimes: L'affirmation du Statut de l'UE sur la Scène Internationale, Sûreté Maritime et Violence en Mer – Maritime Security and Violence at Sea*, précité, pp 191-209.

[7] Ramos B. Sanchez, *Action undertaken by the International Maritime Organization in the Struggle Against Maritime Piracy and Armed Robbery, Sûreté Maritime et Violence en Mer – Maritime Security and Violence at Sea*, préc.

the IMO is currently evaluating the results of this Code.

The policy of prevention by armaments is integrated in International Law, as well as in regional cooperation policies, especially in Europe. The multiplication of approaches at different scales aims to prevent an escalation of piracy.

INTERNATIONAL DIMENSIONS IN MARITIME RISK PREVENTION

The three pillars of maritime security were issued during the IMO's Conventions: SOLAS, MARPOL and STCW. The fourth one is the ILO's Maritime Labour Convention held in 2006[8].

The first Convention for the Safety for Life at Sea (SOLAS) was adopted in 1914, the second in 1929; a third revision was made in 1952 and a fourth in 1960. The actual text was adopted on the 1st of November 1974 and entered into force on the 25th of May 1980[9]. This Convention has only thirteen articles. Most of the technical measures are presented in an annex organised in 12 chapters. Regulation 14 in Chapter V underlines that "all ships shall be sufficiently and efficiently manned." The numerous and always more detailed technical requirements could not be sufficient; the insert on management imposed an integrated management of safety. A ship must belong to a well-managed armament. These recommendations on management were added to the annex of the SOLAS Convention in the aftermath of maritime accidents.[10]

The International Safety Management Code for the management of maritime safety and pollution prevention was adopted in 1993 by IMO resolution A.741/18 and was then integrated in Chapter IX of the SOLAS Convention. It recommends to the Company (the shipowner or any person, such as the manager or bareboat charterer, who has assumed responsibility for operating the ship) to establish safeguards to prevent exhaustion on board. It entered into force on the 1st of July 1996 for the Member States of

---

[8] C. Doumbia-Henry, *The Consolidated Maritime Labour Convention: A Marriage of the Traditional and the New*, Les normes internationales du travail: un patrimoine pour l'avenir, Mélanges en l'honneur de Nicolas Valticos, Genève, OIT, p 319 et s.; D. Fitzpatrick & M. Anderson, dir., *Seafarer's Rights*, Oxford University Press (2005); O. Fotinopoulou-Basurko, *Aspectos Generales del Convenio Refundido Sobre el Trabajo Marítimo*, Gobierno vasco, Departamento de Transportes y Obras publicas, Vitoria-Gasteiz (2006); A. Charbonneau, *Marché International du Travail Maritime - Un Cadre Juridique en Formation*, Presses universitaires d'Aix-Marseille, PUAM, Aix-en-Provence, coll. Berthold Goldman (2009), pp 177-191.

[9] Ph. Boisson, *Politiques et Droit de la Sécurité Maritime*, Edition Bureau Veritas, Paris, 1998, pp 238- 352.

[10] A. Lefrancois, *L'Usage de la Certification – Nouvelle Approche de la Sécurité dans les transports Maritimes*, Presses universitaires d'Aix-Marseille, PUAM, Aix-en-Provence, coll. Centre de Droit Maritime et des Transport, 2011, préface Ph. Boisson, Avant-propos P. Chaumette sp. pp 83-89 et 182-189.

the European Community following the Regulation 3051/95 of December 8, 1995 on the safety management of roll-on/roll-off passenger ferries.[11] The captain must be "given the necessary support so that the master's duties can be safely performed" (ISM Code, § 6.1.3). ISM Code enforces the obligations and responsibilities of the shipowner or the shipmanagers, liable for the state of the ship. However, the integration of the ISM Code is not complete as the Regulation 1 of Chapter IX only references the IMO ISM Code.

Part A of the Code presents its implementation, part B its certification and verification. The verification of the implementation of the ISM Code is mandatory for the Flag State, *i.e.* the State where the ship is registered and that has granted the flag it flies. The Document of Compliance (DOC), the Safety Management Certificate (SMC) can also be delivered by an organisation recognised by the Flag State. Port States have to ensure good implementation of the ISM Code by controlling the SMC certificate and a copy of the DOC that should be on board. Despite their similarities, the norms ISO 9002 are relative to quality management systems of organisations while the ISM Code concerns the safety and protection of the environment.[12] The ISM Code imposes the certification of armament management processes. It implements a referential of prescriptions that leave room to formal respect and documentary certification, that are out of step with reality and the objectives.

The preamble of the ISM Code finishes with the following acknowledgment: "The cornerstone of good safety management is commitment from the top. In matters of safety and pollution prevention it is the commitment, competence, attitudes and motivation of individuals at all levels that determines the end result".

In the aftermath of the 9/11 attacks in New York, the IMO adopted the International Ship and Port Facility Security Code (ISPS Code) on December 12, 2002. It amends the SOLAS Convention by adding a new chapter (XI-2) and it entered into force on July 1, 2004. A predefined security plan varying according to the alert levels must be applied to the interfaces ship/port.[13]

ISM and ISPS Codes take into account the famous "human factor" in maritime transport. Considering the extensiveness of their approach, their

---

[11] L. Joce 320, 30 December 1995, p 14.

[12] A.M. Chauvel, *Sécurité en Mer – Le Code ISM*, Ed. Préventique, 1996; M. Lassagne, *Management des Risques, Stratégies d'Entreprise et Réglementation: le Cas de l'Industrie Maritime*, thèse en sciences de gestion, Ecole Nationale Supérieure des Arts et Métiers, Paris, 2004.

[13] P. Marionnet, *Sûreté Maritime et Portuaire – Vade-mecum ISPS*, InfoMer, Rennes, 2006; R. Cuisigniez, *La Réglementation de Sécurité à Bord des Navires Marchands*, InfoMer, Rennes, 2004.

implementation on board has transformed the working conditions in both the engine room and the bridge. So says one captain: "the total trust of the shipowner in its officers, starting with the captain, has changed in systematic wariness. The numerous procedures, activity reports and audits, as well as the instructions and orders from the direction, constantly pressure the working teams. This is worsened with the instant telecommunication tools and the multiplication of external controls."[14] If the ISM Code contributes to improving safety (person in charge, clarification of roles, maintenance planning, training for emergencies), it also creates a large number of questions on its implementation.

The Best Management Practices for protection against Somalia based Piracy (BMP-4), revised in 2011, provide accurate guidance concerning navigation in the Indian Ocean:

> This guide presents an aide-memoir that summarises in one page the instructions simplified in six major advices: do not be alone, do not be detected, do not be surprised, do not be vulnerable, do not be boarded, and do not be controlled. A vessel must report to UKMTO by email or phone and register with the European system MSCHOA. It must use the International Recommended Transit Corridor (IRTC, in the Gulf of Aden). According to the guide, it is recommended to keep AIS turned on (at the contrary of certain marine practices), to keep track of NAVWARNS, the system of naval alert that indicates the positions of the pirates, to use only navigation lights, to implement the protection measures on board and to provide additional protection to bridge teams. To avoid boarding, two methods have been proved to be efficient: increase speed to maximum and manoeuvre the vessel.
>
> It also lists recommended practices to avoid boarding: use visible and physical ship protection such as razor wire or foam around bridge windows; control the access to the deck, the accommodation and machinery spaces (all the doors should be properly secured; use water spray and foam monitors, input a closed circuit television

[14] R. Baumler, *L'Instrumentation des Codes ISM et ISPS*, *Annuaire de Droit Maritime et Océanique*, Université de Nantes, T. XXIII, 2005, pp 95-108. Cl. Durand & A. Pichon, dir., *La Puissance des Normes*, coll. Logiques Sociales, L'Harmattan, Paris, 2003; R. Baumler, *La Sécurité de Marché et Son Modèle Maritime – Entre Dynamique du Risque et Complexité des Parades: les Difficultés pour Construire la Sécurité*, Thèse de doctorat en Sciences de gestion, université d'Evry Val d'Essonne, 2009.

(CCTV)…). When pirates have boarded, nothing is over. To use citadels and destroy the equipments can be useful.[15]

In June 2009, the IMO adopted the "Guidance to Shipowners and Ship Operators, Shipmasters and Crews on Preventing and Suppressing Acts of Piracy and Armed Robbery against Ships."[16] This preventive approach is part of the implementation of the ISPS Code and proposes communication procedures and technical measures to ship operators. The aim is to go beyond State interventions and recommendations to governments in order to secure the best safety for crews. The circular MSC.1/Circ. 1332 of June 16, 2009 take up the "Best Management Practices to Avoid, Deter or Delay Acts of Piracy in the Gulf of Aden and off the Coast of Somalia" that shipping partners had developed on a voluntary basis and that the contracting parties have supported and encouraged considering the urgency to counter the menace off the Somalia coast. The shipping partners have updated these measures in a second version, published in the IMO circular MSC.1/Circ. 1335 of September 29, 2009. Although the measures in these circulars are not obligatory, the evident interest in the improvement of maritime security endeavours to make sure ships flying a Member State flag are protected and informed in the best way when exposed in high risk piracy and armed robbery navigation areas.[17]

The Maritime Safety Committee revised in June 2009 the "Guidance to shipowners and ship operators, shipmasters and crews on preventing and suppressing acts of piracy and armed robbery against ships" (MSC/Circ.623/Rev.3); a temporary guide was adopted on May 23, 2011.[18] It insists on the importance of long-term use of armed guards and the increase of security personnel companies providing services to ships transiting through High Risk Areas. Hiring Privately Contracted Armed Security Personnel (PCASP) raises difficulty for shipowners, because of the uncertainties present in most of the Flag States' legislations and in the regulations concerning the transport and use of weapons in coastal States.[19] It requires an evaluation of the risks because self-protection measures cannot be neglected. As the quality of services depends mostly on the quality and

---

[15] N. Gros-Verheyde, *Piraterie: Tout l'Océan Indien en Zone à Haut Risque*, *Bruxelles2,* [online] : www.bruxelles2.eu/piraterie-golfe-daden-ocean-indien/piraterie-tout-locean-indien-en-zone-de-haut-risque.html consulted on the 24-10-2011.

[16] MSC.1/Circ. 1333, 26 juin 2009.

[17] European Commission Recommendation of the 11 March 2010 on measures for self-protection and the prevention of piracy and armed robbery against ships (2010/159/UE).

[18] IMO, MSC.1/Circ.1334, 23 June 2009 – MSC.1/Circ.1405, 23 May 2011.

[19] F. Gouttefarde, *Aspects Particuliers de la Lutte Contre la Piraterie – Réflexions sur l'Usage de la Force par les Sociétés Privées de Sécurité Maritime sur des Navires Battant Pavillon Français*, Annuaire du Droit de la Mer, Pédone, Paris, T. XIV, 2009, pp 201-217.

experience of the persons working as PCASP on board, the selection of the team is essential. The selected company must also provide professional insurance. Ship owners have to consult their P&I. Before boarding armed guards, the shipowner must check that the captain and the crew are informed and ready, that exercises are planned and practised by everyone on board. If force is used, it should be done respecting enforceable laws. The use of force should never be more than what is minimally necessary, and in any case, it should be proportionate to the threat and adapted to the situation. Armed guards have to give to the shipowner a detailed report concerning their time on board.

In the USA, President George W. Bush, resurrecting the practice of raiding, delivered letters of marque to *Pristris Incorporated* in order to arm two 65 meter vessels, with an armed helicopter and very fast boats going up to 50 knots and carrying 50 people. These vessels are also connected to military observation satellites. The United States' Constitution gives to Congress the ability to declare war and to issue letters of marque as the U.S.A. has not signed the Paris Declaration of April 16, 1856, which included the abolition of privateering.

THE PREVENTION OF RISKS AT WORK

European Law on health protection, safety at work and the prevention of professional risks is presented in the Council Directive 89/391/EEC of June 12, 1989.[20] This directive has improved the technical rules, controlled by the administration of work and developed since the end of the 19th century, by re-establishing a general obligation of prevention, imposed on the employer, in all the sectors employing workers. It concerns industrial and commercial activities but also administrative and maritime ones.

Safety and improvement of the working conditions on board ship depend, above all, on the habitability of the boat and the protection of human life at sea; i.e. of the dispositions taken in the SOLAS Convention of the IMO which are transposed in French Law in the code des Transports.[21] This rule defines the terms concerning the delivering, renewing and validating of safety deeds, pollution prevention certificates, and the control and penalties measures. These maritime particularities, due to navigation at sea and ships,

---

[20] R. Baldwin & T. Daintith, ed., *Harmonization and Hazard – Regulating Workplace Health and Safety in the European Community*, Graham & Trotman, London, 1992; L. Vogel, *L'Impact des Directives Communautaires sur l'Harmonisation du Droit de la Santé au Travail des Etats de l'Union Européenne*, Thèse Droit, Nantes, 1998; P. Chaumette, *La Sécurité pour Autant que ce Soit Raisonnablement Praticable?,* CJCE 14 June 2007, aff. C-127/05, Commission c/ Royaume-Uni, *Droit Social* 2007, n° 9/10, pp 1037-1043.

[21] Art. L 5241-1 à L. 5242-15 Code des Transports.

are integrated within the general framework concerning companies that are regulated by the general obligation to prevent risks.[22]

The employer must assess professional risks, plan prevention, provide employees with information and training and take into account people's prevention abilities.[23] These measures apply to vessels registered on the French International Register.[24] Shipowners name a qualified member of the crew to be in charge of the prevention of professional risks, under the command of the captain and a copy of the document of prevention is carried on board.[25] Depending upon their training and abilities, each employee must provide for his own safety and health as well as that of all the people affected by his acts or omissions at work.[26] All employers must provide practical and accurate training in safety procedures; employees with a non-permanent contract benefit from enhanced training in safety when there are specific risks.[27] In the maritime sector, these safety trainings have been integrated into the regulation of the maritime diploma.

An employee has the right to opt-out from his post when high danger is imminent.[28] This is applicable to maritime shipping companies, according to interpretations of the law.[29] This extension has been developed par Law n° 97-1051 of November 18, 1997. Neither a sanction nor a salary deduction can be applied to an employee or a group of employees that have validly exercised their right of opt-out. This exercise must be immediately followed by an inspection of the working place by a representative of the management and a representative of the employees, member of the *Comité d'hygiène, de sécurité et des conditions de travail* (CHSCT).[30] This Committee should also meet within the following twenty-four hours. Further, the work-place inspector and the prevention service of the *Caisse régionale d'assurance retraite et de la santé au travail*[31][32] should be informed. For the sailors, there

---

[22] P. Chaumette, *De la Prévention à la Pêche Maritime - Protéger les Marins Autant que la Ressource Halieutique?*, Rev. Française des Affaires Sociales, Paris, n° 2-3, *Santé et Travail: Connaissances et Reconnaissances*, 2008, pp 323-339.

[23] Art. L 4121-1 à L. 4121-5 Code du Travail – art. L. 5545-1 à L. 5545-14 Code des Transports.

[24] L. n° 2005-412, 3 May 2005, relative à la création du registre international français, art. 4, *JORF* 4 May 2005 – art. L. 5612-1 Code des Transports.

[25] Décret n° 2007-1227, 21 August 2007, relatif à la prévention des risques professionnels maritimes et au bien être des gens de mer en mer et dans les ports, *JORF* 22 August 2007.

[26] Art. L. 4122-1 Code du Travail.

[27] Art. L. 4141-2 Code du Travail.

[28] Art. L. 4131-1 et L. 4132-1 Code du Travail.

[29] L. n° 82-1097, 23 December 1982, art. 9, relative aux comités d'hygiène, de sécurité et des conditions de travail, *JORF* 26 December, p 3858.

[30] Hygiene, Safety and Working Conditions Committee.

[31] Regional Pension and Health Insurance Company.

[32] Art. L. 4131-3 et L. 4131-4 Code du Travail.

were no adaptations taken involving the intervention of the *Etablissement National des Invalides de la Marine*,[33] that does not have a prevention service, or the intervention of a ship safety and professional risks prevention inspector who depends of the Maritime Administration.

If there is a prevention failure, civil responsibility, and eventually penal responsibility, may ensue. The gross misconduct of an employer, as defined in article L.452-1 of the French *Code de la sécurité sociale*, is presumably established for the employee who is a victim of a professional accident or a professional illness, when he or a member of the CHSCT had informed the employer of the risk that manifested.[34] The same rule applies to non-permanent employees[35] if they are victims of a professional accident or a professional illness when they did not benefit from an enhanced training in safety[36] if their jobs involved particular risks. Very recently, these dispositions allowing a complementary compensation for injured employees or members of their families were extended to sailors in French Law.[37]

ARMAMENT'S POLICIES

Armament's policies are made according to the applicable international, European and national juridical context. The French Association of Captains carefully follows the preventive measures implemented by ships and the modification of working conditions on board.[38] On September 29, 2011, during the *Journées de l'Observatoire des Droits des Marins*,[39] Mr. Simon Delfau, Security Manager of the armament CMA-CGM, presented the guidelines of their prevention policy.[40] Since 2005, the company has been subjected to 26 attacks in the Indian Ocean, including the hostage-taking of the crew of *Le Ponant*,[41] as well as 11 attacks in 2011. In 2011, the use of mother ships, especially cargos working with captive crews in charge of

---

[33] Health Insurance of the sailors.

[34] Art. L. 4131-4 Code du Travail.

[35] Under a fixed term contract or a temporary contract.

[36] Art. L. 4154-3 Code du Travail.

[37] Conseil Constitutionnel, 6 May 2011, Décision n° 2011-127 QPC, *Droit Maritime Français*, 2011, n° 727, observations P. Chaumette, *Du Recours en Faute Inexcusable de l'Armateur en Cas d'Accident du Travail Maritime*, pp 623-628; Droit Social 2011, n° 7-8, pp 862-864 – Cour de cassation, 2è chambre civile, 22 September 2011, n° 09-15756, exposition d'un marin décédé aux poussières d'amiante.

[38] www.afcan.org consulté le 25 October 2011 – "La Piraterie Maritime – Les Entretiens de Royan – 7 May 2011" - "Naviguer en 2011 dans l'Océan Indien," Juin 2011.

[39] Observatoire des Droits des Marins, Maison des Sciences de l'Homme Ange Guépin, Nantes, France, www.obs-droits-marins.fr/.

[40] S. Delfau, *Mode d'Action des Pirates Somaliens*, AFCAN Informations, February 2010 - www.afcan.org/dossier_piraterie1.html.

[41] Cdt P. Marchesseau, *Prise d'Otages sur le PONANT*, Ed. Michel LAFON, Paris, p 272.

navigation, has resulted, at the end of the monsoon, in an expansion of attack locations nearly to Mayotte and the Mozambique Channel.

A safe ship is a container ship, sailing at knots, with a freeboard between 5 and 8 meters. They are nearly inaccessible due to their speed and height. All the ships report to the coordination centre, to the head office and to the Navy present in the zone. Further, the Routing Meteo, that also became a Routing Safety that takes into account the monsoon, has been implemented as safety measures.

Passive protection is developed referring to Best Management Practices that include barbed tape necessary when the ship cannot reach 19 knots, a portcullis, water sprays (less efficient since the improvements of weapons), bullet-proof vests, safety helmets on the bridge, safety procedures, training of the crews by security companies, debriefing, emergency contacts, and exercises near the Djibouti coast conducted by the French Navy. Bridges tend to transform into fortresses, with secured doors: they become a place where the crew can find refuge after stopping the engines and can stay in contact with the rescue operations while hoping to delay the control of the ship by the pirates for as long as possible. The creation of a citadel necessitates the reinforcement of the walls.

Active protection is created through the use of Military Vessel Protection Detachment when, as in France, the recourse to Private Military Company is not allowed by the Flag State. It is the same case in Cyprus. Carrying a weapon is heavily regulated in French Law regarding the rule n° 83-629 of July 12 1983 on the activity of private security companies.

This "terrestrial" law is not a mandatory rule that applies on board a ship sailing under the French flag.[42] It is only for regulating the access and exercise of a profession. However, the weapons security guards or building safekeepers can use under the decree n° 95-589 of May 6, 1995 are not adapted for fighting maritime piracy. French Law restricts the use of legitimate violence by private people for self-defence to what is proportionate to the aggression. The use of Military Vessel Protection Detachment or Private Military Company requires the information of coastal States, the authorisation of insurance companies and P&I clubs, the consulting of the company personnel institutions (such as the work council, the Hygiene, safety and working Conditions Committee) connected to the sailors' union organisations. When an armament asks for embarking a Military Vessel Protection Detachment of a State which is not the Flag State,

[42] F. Gouttefarde, *Aspects Particuliers de la Lutte Contre la Piraterie – Réflexions sur l'Usage de la Force par les Sociétés Privées de Sécurité Maritime sur des Navires Battant Pavillon Français*, Annuaire du Droit de la Mer, Pédone, Paris, T. XIV, 2009, pp 201-217.

it requires the agreement of the Flag State. By unilateral declaration, in Atalanta operation, the Flag State gives a protective status of immunity to the embarked military personnel. These safety measures must be evaluated, and require regular reports and feedback on the experience that will be part of the training of the crews. The armament has used the military engagement rules concerning the use of weapons and opening fire. As the armed personnel on board are under the commandment of the captain, it is logical that ship captains and armaments reflect upon their eventual responsibilities.

By doing bridge watch in the Indian Ocean, some officers develop psychosis as they navigate with the AIS switched off to prevent the ship from being detected by satellite means. Sometimes the main-beam headlights are even switched off. False echo from the radar oftens frightens. Should the navigation rules of the COLREG Convention (International Regulations for Preventing Collisions at Sea) still be in force when they might facilitate the location and subsequent attack of a ship? Bridge watch officers should be doubled; this would require extra people working on board or it would result in the exhaustion of the crew. Changing the water ballast is more complex when the ship comes close to the Indian coast and increases its speed. VHF radio-watch is more and more complicated in this risk area: there are not even 5 minutes of silence in a 4 hour watch.[43]

Hostage-taking and negotiation with intermediaries are the most difficult, especially because the negotiators are not always different from the attacking forces. When the *Ponant* was taken hostage, another armed group attacked the first assailants to gain their spoils. Only the proximity of the military vessel *Jean Bart* helped to solve these tensions. The commandant Patrick Marchessau succeeded in calming the attackers when the pirates discovered the women, who were members of the crew and were hidden before. However, the music continuously broadcast on canal 16 hardly allows for a call for help concerning an attack.

The tuna seiners based in the Indian Ocean face similar obstacles. For historical reasons, these French fishermen are registered in Concarneau, Brittany, but also because there is a know-how that justifies the recruitment of French crews, supported by sailors from Africa, Seychelles, Madagascar, and Mauritius. In fact, an Italian tuna seiner has registered in France in order to benefit from military protection. Two Spanish tuna seiners were captured while Spain refused the system of Military Vessel Protection Detachment and the armaments could not use PSC services. In April 2009, Constantino Mendez, the Spanish Defense Secretary, declared that he authorised private

[43] Cdt H. Ardillon, *Naviguer en 2011 dans l'Océan Indien*, AFCAN Informations, June 2011.

armed guards to defend the safety of Spanish tuna seiners and carry short-range rifles. On September 16, 2009, long-range rifles were authorised. In March 2011, the *Draco*, a Spanish tuna seiner was defended by Israeli PSC. The Royal decree 1628/2009 of October 30, 2009 establishes a framework for these interventions. These ships navigate in tandem, when one fishes, the other stays manoeuvrable. Traditionally, work at sea would last 5 weeks, but militaries must disembark after 3 weeks. The company Orthongel covers the cost for the onboard protection teams working on its ships. It results in about a 20% activity loss that strongly impacts the profitability of the armaments. Whether a ship is attacked or not, stress is high and a psychological follow-up has been implemented by the Maritime Social Service.

In shipping, the *International Bargaining Forum* was agreed on November 13, 2003, between the International Transport Workers' Federation (ITF) and the Joint Negotiating Group. It brought together 75 shipowners based in 24 member-countries of the International Maritime Employers' Committee and Japanese shipowners, represented by the International Mariners Management Committee of Japan. In 2007, during the IBF in London, 70,000 sailors were covered and 3,500 ships concerned. The *Report on activities 2006-2009/Organising Globally* (§ 41) made by ITF for its 42nd congress on union norms that was held in Mexico between the 5th and the 12th of August 2010, states that there are 10,500 agreements made that cover 175,636 sailors. This corresponds to around 33.5 % of the fleet sailing under flags of convenience.[44] In 2008, the development of piracy off the coast of Somalia resulted in a specific negotiation in order to double the salaries in this war risks area. The company CMA-CGM decided in December 2008 to implement this agreement, using bonuses, as sailors unions are opposed to risk primes and claim for an increase of the shore leaves length.

This exchange goes on. On March 25, 2011, the International Bargaining Forum (IBF) decided to add a new risk zone to the existing one in order to

---

[44] N. Lillie, *Global Collective Bargaining on Flag of Convenience Shipping*, British Journal of Industrial Relations, vol. 42/1, March 2004, pp 47–67; N. Lillie, *Union Networks and Global Unionism in Maritime Shipping*, Relations Industrielles/Industrial Relations RI/IR, Université Laval, Québec, 2005, vol. 60, n° 1, pp 88-111 (www.erudit.org/revue/ri); N. Lillie, *A Global Union for Global Workers. Collective Bargaining and Regulatory Politics in Maritime Shipping*, New York, Routledge, 2006; A. Charbonneau, *Marché International du Travail Maritime - Un Cadre Juridique en Formation*, Presses Universitaires d'Aix-Marseille (PUAM), coll. "Berthold Goldman" 2009; P. Chaumette, *Du Statut du Navire. En Mer, Comme Nulle Part Ailleurs*?, Justice et mondialisation en droit du travail - Du rôle du juge aux conflits alternatifs, M.A. Moreau, H. Muir-Watt & P. Rodiere (dir.), Dalloz, 2010, coll. "Thèmes & Commentaires," pp 293-310; A. Charbonneau, *L'Action d'ITF dans le Secteur du Transport Maritime. Bilan et de Venir d'une Négociation Collective Internationale*, Annuaire de Droit Maritime et Océanique, Université de Nantes, t. XXIX, 2011, pp 361-383.

improve the protection of seafarers on board ships that transit the always wider area under the pirates' threat.

> The new agreement renews the existing conditions in the high risk area first agreed by the IBF in 2008 and since amended (Gulf of Aden covered in 2008, increased to 400 nm off Eastern Somali seaboard in 2009) – a 100 per cent wage increase, doubled compensation in case of injury or death and the right to sign off and be repatriated if a vessel does not follow the internationally recognised transit corridors through the Gulf of Aden – and recognises the existence of pirate danger in a huge additional swathe of ocean, now known as the extended risk zone. Within this area increased protective measures that surpass those of the existing Best Management Practice (BMP: cross industry guidance on piracy prevention) must be adopted based on vessel size, type, speed and freeboard. These can include the provision of personnel or systems to prevent or combat an attack. The enhanced pay and compensation also applies in this new extended risk zone area on any day in which a ship is attacked.[45]

Dave Heidel, president of the seafarers section in ITF, has declared:

> The first IBF agreement on piracy risk came in 2008 and was a major breakthrough, but the problem of piracy has worsened and expanded since then, and so we keep having to revisit it. This latest phase commits operators to significantly beefing up their security measures in this new extended risk zone. This was the big concern that seafarers tasked us with taking to the IBF, and we're gratified that their worries have been addressed. What this means on board may be armed guards – there's no doubt that a lot of seafarers now would go for that option, although there are cases and routes where they may not be appropriate – or it may mean new preventative/defensive technologies.[46]

In 2006, one out of 3 piracy attacks was successful and resulted in the storming of the ship. In 2010, only one out of 6 attacks was successful. However, in 2010, ship attacks have increased by 10 % compared to the previous year. Can piracy urge a "substantial" change of flag towards a flag state that can provide military protection, or will it contribute to an extension of private "militia" in more and more private seas?

---

[45] http://www.itfglobal.org/news-online/index.cfm/newsdetail/5823 www.marisec.org/piracy-gulf-of-aden-indian-ocean-industry-best-management-practice.

[46] www.itfglobal.org/press-area/index.cfm/pressdetail/5818.

6. SHIPOWNERS: THE PIRACY CHALLENGE

Simon DELFAU[1]

By way of introduction, it must first be acknowledged that there exists not one monolithic piracy, but several piracies sprinkled throughout the seas and with different *modi operandi*. Thus, shipowners must face piracy (or armed robbery[2]) worldwide, in sea areas as disparate as South America, South East Asia, West Africa, and, famously, East Africa, where piracy is particularly worrying. In fact, off the coast of East Africa pirates are now attacking ships throughout the whole of the Indian Ocean, from the southern Red Sea to the subcontinent's coasts, and throughout the Gulf of Aden, the Mozambique Channel, off the Tanzanian and Kenyan coasts, in the Seychelles Islands, and the Arabian Sea. East Africa is the global navel of piracy;, the number of pirates and attacks have increased significantly in the last few years and the amount of ransoms are skyrocketing. East Africa is the epicentre – there, as of November 2011, pirates are holding some 46 vessels and 480 hostages.

Consequentially, shipowners trading in East Africa face difficult questions: how can one perform efficient business operations without jeopardizing the safety and security of vessels and crewmembers while transiting the Indian Ocean? How can a merchant vessel face the threat of piracy when military vessels and Operation Atalanta[3] cannot even control pirate activities in the Gulf of Aden?

In order to meet these challenges, all responsible shipowners must strictly apply international standards and requirements of the International Ship and Port Facility Code (ISPS), and must perform security assessments and update ship security plans. As will be discussed below in section I, these assessments presuppose that shipowners understand the *modus operandi* of

---

[1] Security Adviser, CMA CGM, France.

[2] From a legal perspective, as per Montego Bay Convention 1982, piracy is taking place in high seas, while armed robbery takes is usually defined as taking place within territorial seas or port areas. Despite this semantic difference, consequences are generally the same for shipowners, as their vessels are attacked.

[3] Operation Atalanta was launched by European Countries in 2008. Headquarters of the Operation are in Northwood, United Kingdom, and purpose of this operation is firstly to protect vessels of the World Food Program delivering food aid to Somalia, then to protect vulnerable vessels (mainly in Gulf of Aden) and fight against piracy in the area, and to finish with, to monitor fishing activities off the coast of Somalia.

East African pirates and the potential consequences of attacks, and, as section II will cover, shipowners must implement relevant security procedures and measures on board their vessels and ashore.

I. UNDERSTANDING PIRACY – MODUS OPERANDI AND CONSEQUENCES

Modus Operandi

Understanding the pirates' *modus operandi* is the first step in understanding the consequences of piracy on shipowners' operations. Pirate attacks have spiked in the High Risk Area off of East Africa over the past four years; 220 attacks and 49 hijackings[4] occurred in 2010, while "only" 111 attacks and 42 hijackings occurred in 2008. As of November 2011, more attacks were recorded than for the whole year of 2010.[5]

High-Risk Area

In order to fully understand the contours of this spike in attacks, one must observe that seasonal weather accounts for a wide variance in the frequency and location of attacks, as well as a difference in pirate tactics and organization. In the Indian Ocean, monsoon periods have a strong effect on the location of attacks. During the two monsoon periods, approximately from January to March, and from June to mid-September - when sea conditions can be very rough- most pirate attacks usually take place within the Gulf of Aden and in the southern Red Sea (up to 17° North)[6].

By contrast, during the non-monsoon periods from April to May and mid-September to December, when sea conditions are more favourable, pirates attack throughout the whole Indian Ocean. Thus, during these periods, the Gulf of Aden, the southern Read Sea, areas off of Yemen, Oman, Somalia, Kenya, Tanzania, the Seychelles, Madagascar, and off of Mozambique are of great concern, as well as the whole Indian Ocean through West and South India and the West Maldives. For example, in 2010, during non-monsoon periods, the first attacks to ever take place in Mozambique Channel occurred (three attacks and one hijacking in December 2010). Additionally, close to the Seychelles Islands attacks occurred in March and October of 2010; in June of 2011 pirates conducted attacks up to 76° East in 2011. Thus, there is

[4] International Maritime Bureau, *Piracy and Armed Robbery against ships*, Annual Report, 1 January – 30 December 2010.

[5] Keeping in mind that all attacks are not systematically reported to the Authorities by shipowners.

[6] It has to be noticed however that such an assessment may need to be reviewed following 2011 attacks. Indeed, if attacks during second monsoon period from June to mid-September 2011 occurred only within Gulf of Aden and Southern Red Sea, many attacks occurred off Oman Coasts during January - February monsoon period (as sea conditions were favourable), which was clearly not the case during the same period in 2009 and 2010, when nearly all attacks occurred within Gulf of Aden.

a massive amount of the Indian Ocean that is now part of the High Risk Area. This High Risk Area, as defined by Military Forces and the Shipping Industry, bounded by the Suez Canal and the Strait of Hormuz to the north (10°S and 78°E) covers nearly the whole of the Indian Ocean.

Source: Best Management Practices Version 4

Pirate Tactics

Although there are now more and more pirates operating in the Indian Ocean, using hijacked vessels as mother ships, characteristics of these attacks remain relatively unchanged. In 2008 the number of Somali pirates was estimated to be between two and four hundred. Currently, some sources suggest that there are around one thousand to fifteen hundred pirates operating in the Indian Ocean and Gulf of Aden. This obviously translates into a dramatic increase in the number of vessels attacked and hijacked. Further, organization and coordination between pirate bands are gotten more efficient.

Pirates are now using merchant or fishing vessels they previously hijacked as mother ships. The use the captured crewmembers both to operate the vessel, and to serve as "human shields," to deter any military intervention to recover the hijacked vessel. These vessels are usually small or medium sized ships such as fishing boats and dhows, but are sometimes bigger vessels like general cargo ships and bulk carriers. By using such mother ships, pirates can increase their range of action, as long as they have enough fuel. This is why in 2010 some Somali pirates attacked vessels very close to India.

However, over the past four years, the characteristics of attacks have not changed much. Attacks take place during daylight, mainly at dawn or dusk (they only happen at night when moonlight is sufficient), and once pirates have targeted a vessel to be hijacked, they usually launch one or two skiffs from their mother vessel to chase their prey. When closing on their target, they often open fire, either with AK 47s or Rocket Propelled Grenades (RPG), or both, in order to intimidate the vessel's master and force him to stop. The use of these weapons is generally focused on the bridge and accommodation area. If the vessel stops, the pirates get on board and proceed to hijack her. If the vessel does not stop, the pirates do not hesitate to chase her for some time (some pursuits have lasted up to three or four hours), and attempt to climb on board with aluminium ladders put against the vessel's freeboard. Consequently, the lower the freeboard and the slower the speed of the targeted vessel, the easier a time of hijacking the pirates will have. As the International Best Management Practices have stated: "there have been no reported attacks where pirates have boarded a ship that has been proceeding at over 18 knots" [7] and "vessels with a minimum freeboard that is greater than 8 metres have a much greater chance of successfully escaping a piracy attempt than those with less"[8]. That is why most of the hijacked merchant vessels are tanker vessels, chemical carriers, bulk carriers, general cargo and

[7] *Best Management Practices for Protection against Somalia Based Piracy, Version 4*, August 2011, p 6.

[8] *Best Management Practices for Protection against Somalia Based Piracy, Version 4*, August 2011, p 7.

fishing vessels, as these ships which tend to have relatively lower top speeds and less freeboard. Finally, when pirates manage to hijack a vessel, they then bring it along the Somali coast, close to one of several pirate camps that exist. The vessel will then stay at anchorage during negotiations, unless the pirates decide to use it as a mother vessel.

Example of pirate skiff:

Pirate organization

An activity at such a level of organization (sometimes up to more than twenty large merchant vessels remain at anchorage along Somali coasts) would be totally impossible in other pirate infested. This is because West African countries and countries around the Malacca Strait have real authority and military assets, and are able to perform maritime interventions. However, Somalia is currently weaker than ever, and their pirates do not encounter any difficulties in "business development," at least from the Somali side. Somalia based piracy is indeed a real business now, with criminal structures in place ashore. For instance, when a group of pirates arrive with a hijacked vessel off of Somalia, another group of pirates come on board to relieve the first group, and keep watch over the vessel's captive crew. Moreover, maintaining several vessels at anchorage complete with their crew over several months while negotiating ransoms for these vessels evidences that a dedicated organization is in place, leaving no room for the dilettante. Furthermore, pirates understand that as long as they are "trustworthy," and release the vessel and her crewmembers once a ransom is paid, shipowners will continue to pay, and the pirates' business will continue to burgeon.

Consequences of piracy

Although great for Somali pirates, this piracy business has become a real burden for the shipping industry and its operations in Indian Ocean. The consequences of the pirates' activities for the shipping industry are numerous, with both human and economic impacts.

Human consequences

The primary consequences of piracy are human ones, as stated by the IMO Secretary-General Efthimios E. Mitropoulos: "*piracy and kidnapping have blighted the maritime community for too long and it is seafarers who bear the brunt.*"[9] Indeed, for most seafarers, transiting the Indian Ocean causes constant constant anxiety. To compensate for this, shipowners and unions have signed agreements to ensure that bonus pay is provided to seafarers when in a piracy area, and that an extra bonus is paid in case of an actual pirate attack[10].

When a ship is hijacked, the human consequences can be dramatic; detentions are now longer than ever, with seafarers being kept in captivity sometimes more than one hundred and fifty days.[11] Even worse, a bulk carrier, pirated on the 1st of January 2011, was not released until the beginning of November 2011; the crew was in pirate hands for more than ten months. Further, negotiations are lengthening with the increasing of ransoms, which, in turn, increases the duration of captivity. Shipowners have to deal, on the one hand, with the negotiation of the ransom, and, on the other hand, with the well-being of the captive crewmembers and with the obvious and understandable anxiety of their families. Furthermore, the conditions of captivity are becoming ever more harsh, as the level of violence employed by pirates has increased over the past few years. Consequently, hijacked seafarers, once released, must be tended to with efficient follow-up care. However, symptoms of such a traumatic event may not manifest until long after the release. For these reasons, it is paramount that shipowners prevents hijackings in the first place.

Economic consequences

The consequences of pirate attacks are also of an economic nature; piracy is reported to cost the international economy between US$7 and $12 billion

[9] IMO Secretary-General Efthimios E.Mitropoulos, *Situation Unacceptable IMO Launches Anti-Piracy Agenda for 2011*, IMO News, Issue 1, 2011, p 11.

[10] http://www.itfglobal.org/press-area/index.cfm/pressdetail/5818.

[11] One Earth Future, Oceans Beyond Piracy, "*The Economic Cost of Maritime Piracy*", One Earth Future Working Paper, December 2010, available at: http://oceansbeyondpiracy.org/sites/default/files/documents_old/The_Economic_Cost_of_Piracy_Full_Report.pdf.

per year,[12] mainly due to piracy in Indian Ocean. This impacts not only the shipping industry, but all economies, both in East Africa and throughout the world. As reported by United Nations Secretary General Ban Ki-moon, piracy in the Indian Ocean "*has had an immense impact on the economies of East Africa and also the wider world. International trade routes are threatened and goods in the region as well as in Somalia are becoming more expensive. This is made worse by the bleak state of the global economy.*"[13] For example, it is reported that losses due to piracy, per year, represent US$642 million for Egypt (loss of revenues from Suez Canal fees), US$414 million for Kenya (general trade impact) and US$6 million for the Seychelles (losses to fishing and tourism industries).[14]

For shipowners, the main economic consequences of piracy, apart from measures put in place to protect vessels against attack, are, of course, related to insurance, routing and ransoms, but also detention of vessels. Thus, when a vessel is hijacked, she is said to be "off hire," which means that shipowners, charterers, operators, etc., cannot use it. A shipowner then has to face an obvious loss of business activity and capacity as the vessel is out of service. Moreover, having a ship out of service for an extended period of time may not be economically feasible for some shipping companies, with regards to their small size and charter hire rates. Further, a vessel which has been hijacked and held for a long period of time will not be fit to operate as soon as she is released, and will need repair, which will again add more cost and more delay.

Insurance

Insurance costs related to piracy, such as War Risks, Kidnap and Ransom (K&R), cargo and hull insurances, have increased sharply in recent years. In 2008, the Gulf of Aden has was designated as a War Risk Area by the Joint War Committee[15] and the Indian Ocean became a War Risk Area in January 2011. These War Risk Areas come with additional insurance premiums for vessels plying these waters. Thus, the premiums have increased from

---

[12] One Earth Future, Oceans Beyond Piracy, "*The Economic Cost of Maritime Piracy*", One Earth Future Working Paper, December 2010, available at: http://oceansbeyondpiracy.org/sites/default/files/documents_old/The_Economic_Cost_of_Piracy_Full_Report.pdf.

[13] United Nations, Security Council, *Report of the Secretary-General pursuant to Security Council resolution 1897 (2009),* 27 October 2010, available at: http://unpos.unmissions.org/Portals/UNPOS/Repository%20UNPOS/S-2010-556%20%2827OCT10%29.pdf.

[14] One Earth Future, Oceans Beyond Piracy, *The Economic Cost of Maritime Piracy*, One Earth Future Working Paper, December 2010, available at: http://oceansbeyondpiracy.org/sites/default/files/documents_old/The_Economic_Cost_of_Piracy_Full_Report.pdf.

[15] http://www.lmalloyds.com/Web/market_places/marine/JWC/Joint_War.aspx.

US$500 per ship, per voyage, in 2007, to US$20,000 in 2008,[16] and to US$150,000 in 2010 (excluding injury, liability, and ransom coverage).[17] Shipowners desiring to transit the Gulf of Aden and Indian Ocean have to pay these premiums to be covered against piracy risks. Furthermore, while Best Management Practices Version 4 define the High Risk Area as being bounded by the Suez Canal and the Strait of Hormuz to the north, 10°S and 78°E, the Joint War Committee defines the same area as being a War Risk Area, but up to latitude 12°S,[18] adding again some insurance costs. Further, K&R[19] insurance premiums are estimated to have increased tenfold between 2008 and 2009.[20] Cargo and hull insurance premiums have also increased. Cargo premiums are estimated to have increased by between US$25 and US$100 per container and hull premiums have doubled.[21]

Routing

To avoid piracy, some shipowners have decide to re-route their vessels. Instead of passing through the Suez Canal, their vessels now transit around the Cape of Good Hope, off of South Africa. Such a re-routing is usually done for vulnerable vessels with low speed, such as oil tankers. But such a re-routing represents substantially increased costs. For example, routing a tanker from Saudi Arabia to the United States via the Cape of Good Hope adds about 2,700 miles to the voyage.[22] With regards to the current price of fuel oil, such a measure is clearly expensive for the shipowner, who will lose ship-use time through the increased length of transit.

Moreover, many vessels transiting the High Risk Area are currently doing so either at full speed for low speed vessels, or at a minimum speed of eighteen knots for bigger vessels, as recommended by Best Management Practices. Maintaining such speeds for long periods of time leads to

---

[16] MARAD, *Economic Impact of Piracy in the Gulf of Aden on Global Trade*, 2008, available at: http://www.marad.dot.gov/documents/HOA_Economic%20Impact%20of%20Piracy.pdf.

[17] UNODC (United Nations Office on Drugs and Crime), *The Globalization of Crime, a Transnational Organized Crime Threat Assessment*, 2010, available at: http://www.unodc.org/documents/data-and-analysis/tocta/TOCTA_Report_2010_low_res.pdf.

[18] Joint War Committee, *Hull War, Strikes, Terrorism and Related Perils Listed Areas*, JWLA/018, 1 August 2011, available at: http://www.lmalloyds.com/Web/market_places/marine/JWC/JW_Bulletins/JWLA018.aspx

[19] K&R policies usually aim at covering the crew in case of hijacking in addressing ransom demands.

[20] One Earth Future, Oceans Beyond Piracy, *The Economic Cost of Maritime Piracy*, One Earth Future Working Paper, December 2010, available at: http://oceansbeyondpiracy.org/sites/default/files/documents_old/The_Economic_Cost_of_Piracy_Full_Report.pdf.

[21] One Earth Future, Oceans Beyond Piracy, *The Economic Cost of Maritime Piracy*, One Earth Future Working Paper, December 2010, available at: http://oceansbeyondpiracy.org/sites/default/files/documents_old/The_Economic_Cost_of_Piracy_Full_Report.pdf.

[22] One Earth Future, Oceans Beyond Piracy, *The Economic Cost of Maritime Piracy*, One Earth Future Working Paper, December 2010, available at: http://oceansbeyondpiracy.org/sites/default/files/documents_old/The_Economic_Cost_of_Piracy_Full_Report.pdf.

drastically increased fuel consumption, which is another additional costs for shipowners. For instance, a container vessel of 8500 TEUs proceeding at a speed of eighteen knots will consume nearly twice as much fuel as the same container vessel proceeding at a speed of fourteen knots.

Ransoms

Since 2005, ransoms have increased considerably, from an average of US$150,000 in 2005 to US$5.4 million in 2010 (in 2009 the average ransom was around US$3.4 million). Total ransom payments for 2009 and 2010 are estimated around US$415 million.[23] Reportedly, as of the beginning of November 2011, ransom payments paid by shipping companies to Somali pirates in 2011 had already reached nearly US$110 million[24]. The largest ransom ever, US$12 million, is reported to have been paid in June 2011 for the release of an oil tanker hijacked in March 2011. All of these ransoms are first paid directly by shipowners (usually dropped by plane), before reimbursement can be sought from a K&R insurer. Obviously, each time a shipowner has to pay a ransom, premiums of his K&R insurance will increase.

II. FACING PIRACY

Once the shipowner has assessed the security of his trade within pirate infested waters, he must assess the vulnerability of each one of his ships by taking into account their speed and freeboard, among other criteria. Once done, he will then be able to put in place relevant security measures, both on board and ashore. In order to face piracy, shipowners have adopted two different sets of measures, which can be complementary. These measures are termed passive and active measures.

Passive Measures

Passive measures implemented on board and ashore are generally related to tracking and reporting of vessels when in the High Risk Area. They also include measures related to the training of crewmembers and the defensive protections installed on vessels. These measures are deemed "passive" because there is no "action" performed against pirates.

Tracking of Vessels

Some shipping companies have installed systems on board their vessels to track them twenty-four hours a day, worldwide, from ashore. These systems, originally used for weather routing, appear to be very efficient for piracy

[23] One Earth Future, Oceans Beyond Piracy, *The Economic Cost of Maritime Piracy*, One Earth Future Working Paper, December 2010, available at: http://oceansbeyondpiracy.org/sites/default/files/documents_old/The_Economic_Cost_of_Piracy_Full_Report.pdf.

[24] http://www.tmcnet.com/usubmit/2011/11/07/5911124.htm.

routing as well. As soon as the shipowner is aware of an attack, through the IMB[25] for instance, he can immediately advise all his vessels in the vicinity to change their routes. Moreover, all vessels are equipped with Automatic Identification Systems (AIS), as required by the International Maritime Organization (IMO). When switched on, AIS allows all vessels in the vicinity equipped with the system to receive information on each other. When in the High Risk Area, depending on a shipowners' instructions, vessels either switch off the AIS[26] and switch it on only in case of an attack, or they leave the AIS transmitting across the entire area, but with a transmission restricted to the ship's identity, position, course, speed, navigational status and safety-related information.

Besides this daily tracking, all vessels, per ISPS Code requirements, are equipped with Ship Security Alert Systems (SSAS), to be activated in case of attack. Once activated, an alert is sent to any destination previously selected, which is usually the shipowner and the flag administration. This alert can be delivered to email, fax, GSM phone, telex, or other Inmarsat terminals.

Mandatory reporting

All vessels transiting the High Risk Area have to report to different authorities, under the obligation of the shipowners. Prior to entering the High Risk Area, and before departure from a port in the area, vessels have to submit a Vessel Movement Registration Form to the Maritime Security Centre - Horn of Africa (MSCHOA). The MSCHOA was put in place together with Operation Atalanta in 2008, and is the planning and coordination centre for the EU Naval forces (EUNAVFOR). This centre monitors all vessels transiting through the International Recommended Transit Corridor (IRTC) in the Gulf of Aden. The corridor is 492 miles long and has an East and a West bound lane. Each lane is five miles wide with a two mile separation between the lanes. Depending on a vessel's speed, "Group Transits" are designed to put ships in different flotillas of passage within the IRTC. This allows the military forces in the area to best position their assets so as to protect ships against piracy and to give assistance in case of attack.[27]

---

[25] International Maritime Bureau (IMB). Based in Kuala Lumpur, the IMB monitors all piracy attacks worldwide and advise immediately vessels and shipowners of the nature and position of the attack.

[26] As per IMO Resolution A.917(22) which allows master to switch off the AIS when the Master believes that its use increases the ship's vulnerability.

[27] http://www.shipping.nato.int/SiteCollectionDocuments/Group%20Transit%20explanation.pdf.

The International Recommended Transit Corridor (IRTC)

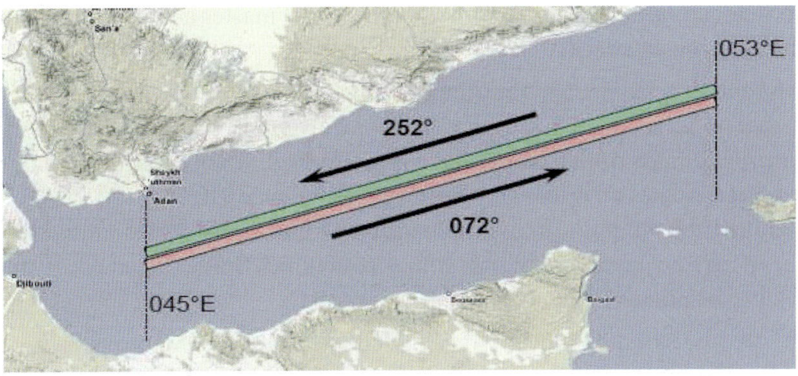

Meanwhile, vessels are also encouraged to report their position when entering the High Risk Area to the United Kingdom Maritime Trade Organization (UKMTO), in Dubaï, through a *Position Reporting Form – Initial Report*. They are then encouraged to report their position daily to the UKMTO via a *Vessel Position Reporting Form – Daily Position Report*, and to issue a *Final Report* when leaving the High Risk Area. All vessels must contact the UKMTO immediately in case of attack, as the UKMTO is in charge of coordinating actions of military forces in the High Risk Area. Some flag states also have their own requirements. This is the case for instance for the French flag, which requires that all French flag vessels in the High Risk Area report their position to the French Navy.

Crew training

It is essential that crew expected to transit the High Risk Area are properly trained in piracy risk, and the behavior to adopt in case of a hijacking. Consequently, regular briefings and drills must be performed on board vessels, to ensure that all crewmembers are perfectly aware of their duties in case of an attack.

Dedicated piracy instructions on how to prevent piracy and how to act in case of an attack and hijacking are also provided to crewmembers. These instructions, which are confidential, regard lighting on board, radio communications, watch on bridge, instructions for officers on watch, speed during transit and in case of attack, among other things.

Defensive protections

In order to deter attacks, many shipowners have installed defensive protections on board their vessels. Such measures may consist of enhanced bridge protection or fire hoses permanently installed along the freeboard of the vessel. They may also include Kevlar helmets and vests and a dedicated in-bridge navigation room, in order to protect the master and crew from stray bullets during an attack.

More and more vessels transiting the High Risk Area, whatever their size, are also protected with razor wire (and some even with electric fences), used to prevent pirates from boarding the vessel. Indeed, when carefully deployed, razor wire creates an effective barrier against attacks. The wire is fitted either all around the vessel or in areas identified as vulnerable to boarding, and is usually affixed outboard of the ship's structure in order to make it more difficult for pirates to hook on a boarding ladder.

Lastly, the shipping industry recently adopted the use of citadels on board. Per Best Management Practices Version 4, a "*Citadel is a designated pre-planned area purpose built into the ship where, in the event of imminent boarding by pirates, all crew will seek protection. A Citadel is designed and constructed to resist a determined pirate trying to gain entry for a fixed period of time.*"[28] In case pirates succeed in boarding a vessel, all crew will then gather in the citadel, where they will be insulated from the pirates, and will be able to get in close contact with the shipowner and military forces. Thus, specific communication equipment, among other equipment, must be installed in the citadel. Citadels have proven their efficacy; in 2011 more than ten vessels managed to avoid hijacking due to the use of citadels. The pirates abandoned the vessels either because the citadel bought the crew enough time for a military to intervene or because they could not reach the crewmembers at all.

Active Measures

In addition to passive measures, shipowners have adopted active measures in order to protect their vessels and crewmembers. Active measures consist in taking actions against pirates in case of attack, e.g. by embarking privately contracted armed security personnel.[29] Statistically, out of three vessels

[28] *Best Management Practices for Protection against Somalia Based Piracy, Version 4*, August 2011, p 38.

[29] IMO Circular MSC.1/Circ.1405/Rev.1: *Revised Interim Guidance to Shipowners, Ship Operators and Shipmasters*. The International Maritime Organization has adopted in September 2011 several circulars dealing with piracy topic, in order to assist Shipping Industry and Administrations: MSC.1/Circ.1406/rev.1 : *Revised Interim Guidance Recommendations for Flag States Regarding the Use of Privately Contracted Armed Security Personnel on Board Ships in the High Risk Area*; MSC.1/Circ.1408 : *Interim Recommendations for Port and Coastal States Regarding the Use of Privately Contracted Armed Security Personnel on Board Ships in the High Risk Area;* MSC-FAL.1/Circ.2: *Questionnaire on Information on Port and Coastal States Requirements Related to Privately Contracted Armed Security Personnel on Board Ships in the High Risk Area.*

attacked in the High Risk Area in 2011, two of them managed to prevent pirates from boarding due to the use of armed guards.

In the last few years, many private maritime security companies (PMSC)[30] have been created, but some doubt remains about the capability and maturity of some of these companies. To avoid any doubt, responsible shipowners must use only reliable PMSCs, which are chosen after a stringent selection process, which includes relevant risk assessments in a legally binding context. It must be emphasized that shipowners operate merchant vessels, not military ones, and as such, the purpose of shipowners in having armed guards on board is not to make war on pirates, but only to protect vessels and crewmembers. Consequently, privately contracted armed security personnel are not mercenaries; they are used only as a deterrent force, acting only in self-defense, with strict rules of engagement, and always under the authority of the vessel's master.

Moreover, shipowners use PMSCs because they do not have any other choice, as military forces are unable to ensure security in the whole High Risk Area. Further, it is inconceivable to ask seafarers on board merchant vessels to carry and use weapons, as seafarers are not soldiers and should never be seen as such. Armed guards, then, are necessary to allow the crew to perform their daily duties peacefully, knowing that active measures are in place to protect them. Additionally, responsible shipowners use PMSCs with total transparency in regards to Insurance, and Flag and Port States, as well as crewmembers and unions. Without authorization of their insurers, shipowners cannot embark armed guards on board their vessels. Some P&I Clubs have even developed vetting processes in order to help shipowners to choose the right PMSC.

There are still some flag states, however, albeit very few, that refuse to allow armed guards on board. As a consequence, to protect these vessels in piracy areas, shipowners have no other choice but to change their flag. Fortunately, the main flag states are now well-aware of piracy's risks and allow shipowners to protect their vessels with armed guards, requesting ship operators to provide them with details of the privately contracted armed security personnel to be placed on board.

Further, shipowners must always advise port states of call that they have private guards and weapons on board, for port state control authorities must come on board and check that the vessel is in compliance with local regulations regarding security companies and the carriage of weapons and

[30] Defined by IMO Circular MSC.1/Circ.1405/Rev.1 as "Private contractors employed to provide security personnel, both armed and unarmed, on board for protection against piracy."

ammunitions. Finally, responsible shipowners usually embark armed guards with the agreement of the crewmembers, as it would be counterproductive if the crew were not in accord: the daily operations would not be efficient and during an attack the situation could become uncontrollable.

III. CONCLUSION

As discussed, despite military efforts piracy in East Africa has been growing dramatically over the last three years. Yet, it is obvious and proven today that long term solutions against piracy in East Africa will not be found at sea, but ashore. Somalia must be stronger than she is now. For this, Somalia needs to be assisted in capacity-building, and legal and economic development, among other things, before she will turn from piracy.

Nevertheless, the situation at sea can still be improved. From a shipowner's perspective, captured pirates must be prosecuted and not simply released. A better system to track ransom money must be put in place, as we do not know precisely where all these millions of dollars go. Further, as the International Transit Corridor in the Gulf of Aden proves its utility, it may be useful to have the same kind of militarily protected corridor between East Africa and the Seychelles. This vulnerable sea-lane is vital for the shipping industry, East Africa economies, and the world economy as a whole.

To conclude with a word of warning: in these troubled times, the development of the political and security situation in Yemen is very worrying. If Yemen becomes a *Somalia bis*, security in the Gulf of Aden will become particularly difficult to ensure, threatening even further one of the world's most important sea passages.

7. THE SHIPPING INDUSTRY AND PIRACY

Arthur BOWRING[1] and Alexander MCKINNON[2]

I. INTRODUCTION

The threat of piracy and armed robbery at sea is a major concern of maritime industry groups, shipowners, ship operators and the wider sector supporting the shipping industry. The statistics are disturbing: in Somalia toward the end of 2011, at least nine vessels were being held against the will of the owners and an estimated 246 hostages (mostly seafarers) were at the whim of Somali pirates.[3] Even more troubling is that the first quarter of 2011 was labelled as the worst on official record. Almost three times the number of attacks occurred as compared to the same quarter in 2010.[4] But piracy is not geographically isolated, nor is it a new phenomenon. It is an ever-present danger in the waters of South East Asia – although regional efforts have yielded positive results – and piracy off Nigeria on Africa's west coast is becoming as serious a concern as that originating from Somalia.

The dissemination of information concerning piracy to the shipping industry, governments, and other stakeholders has surged in recent years. There now exists copious recommendations, industry guidance and best management practices; almost all freely accessible. While shipowners, operators and the wider industry applaud international efforts to assist efforts to combat piracy, it is possible that much-needed clarity will be lost in a sea of detail. It is crucial that the recommendations and guidance provided to the industry is relevant and realistic; and perhaps just as importantly, concise.

---

[1] Managing Director, Hong Kong Shipowners Association.

[2] Visiting Scholar, Center for Oceans and Coastal Law, University of Maine School of Law, LL.M. Candidate, University of Cambridge, UK. An earlier version of this chapter appeared in volume 41(3) of the Hong Kong Law Journal (2011).

[3] Statistics taken from the EU NAVFOR Somalia "Pirated vessels" update dated 13 October 2011 available at <http://www.eunavfor.eu/downloads/> as at 28 October 2011. It is to be noted that the International Maritime Bureau most recently reported that as at 31 March 2011, 596 seafarers were being held for ransom on board 28 ships. In the first quarter alone, pirates killed seven crew and wounded 34: International Maritime Organisation (IMO), "International Shipping Facts and Figures – Information Resources on Trade, Safety, Security, and the Environment" (Maritime Knowledge Centre Report, 2011) p 19.

[4] Reported in the International Chamber of Commerce – International Maritime Bureau's (ICC-IMB) Piracy Report: "Piracy and Armed Robbery Against Ships" (ICC-IMB Report for the period 1 January – 31 March 2011, United Kingdom, April 2011).

The International Maritime Organisation (IMO) produces valuable recommendations and the international industry's Best Management Practices (BMP) guidance is germane. However, confounding issues such as the use of private armed guards on board vessels is not simplified by voluminous guidance.

A number of the world's most significant shipping registries have entered the foray by publishing information specifically targeted at shipowners, masters, and ship and company security officers. The information is often, but not always, consistent with other international publications: registries must work with domestic legislation and the advice naturally varies. As the fourth largest registry in the world – and certainly in terms of publishing information, one of the most active shipping registers – the Marine Department of the Hong Kong Special Administrative Region's (HKSAR) guidance is an appropriate example of State-industry interaction with the problem of piracy. Notwithstanding the guidance, Hong Kong vessels continue to be at risk and the uncertainty surrounding the adoption of measures to combat piracy trouble the local industry.

This chapter investigates the approaches taken by the international shipping industry in attempting to protect ships from piracy and armed robbery. As international guidance calls upon states to react to piracy by implementing measures and recommendations, it is important to consider whether the approaches of states are assisting the development of successful anti-piracy measures by the industry. In this respect, Hong Kong serves as a relevant case study. This chapter therefore begins by summarising some recent piratic incidents involving Hong Kong-registered ships before proceeding to canvass the guidance provided to shipowners, masters and security officers and governments in the context of international and Hong Kong law. The paper concludes by highlighting some controversial and emerging issues with reference to international industry guidelines and recommendations.

II. PIRATIC ACTIVITY

In the 1990s the South China Sea was identified as one of the most active piracy zones in the world.[5] Certain areas in South East Asian waters are still considered "piracy prone areas." With over 17,000 islands in its archipelago, Indonesian waters continue to pose risks for ships. Significant patrol efforts in the Singapore and Malacca Straits have reduced the number of incidents

---

[5] Zou Keyuan, *Law of the Sea in East Asia* (Routledge, 2005) p 140.

although mariners are urged to exercise caution.[6] The reduction is critical to the region as there are over 60,000 ships movements in the Straits each year accounting for a significant percentage of world trade and world energy needs.

Without doubt, Somalia today attracts the most attention, and deservedly so. Not only does Somalia and the Gulf of Aden account for the most reported piracy incidents in the world at present,[7] the ferocity and number of attacks – pirates commonly fire automatic weapons and Rocket Propelled Grenades (RPGs) at merchant vessels[8] – continue to rise despite significant international efforts to curb the threat.[9] Pirates are suspected of using "mother ships" which enable them to operate much farther from the coast. The mother ships launch smaller, heavily-armed skiffs to attack and hijack passing vessels. Even dangerous seas do not appear to hinder pirates: the International Maritime Bureau's (IMB) Piracy Reporting Centre reported a recent incident where pirates attempted to attack vessels in Force 7 conditions.[10] Additionally, Somali pirates have shown increased brazenness with the attack a chemical tanker in Omani territorial waters in August 2011. The vessel was anchoring at the port of Salalah when it was hijacked.[11] Although it had armed guards on board during its transit of the Gulf of Aden, the guards were left at Oman prior to proceeding to Salalah. Some progress has been made with the IMB's 2010 report noting that attacks within the Gulf of Aden had reduced by 50 per cent. On the other hand, other areas

---

[6] International Maritime Bureau Piracy Reporting Centre, "Piracy Prone Areas and Warnings" <http://www.iccccs.org/piracy-reporting-centre/prone-areas-and-warnings> as at 15 August 2011. See also Catherine Zara Raymond, "Piracy and Armed Robbery in the Malacca Strait: A Problem Solved?" (2009) 62(3) *Naval War College Review* 31. The Tripartite Technical Experts Group (TTEG) was established in 1977 between Indonesia, Malaysia and Singapore following a littoral arrangement of 1975. It has taken proactive steps to improve navigational safety in the Straits of Malacca and Singapore including taking anti-piracy measures.

[7] Attacks are widespread reaching the seas off Kenya, Tanzania, Seychelles, Madagascar, Mozambique, the Indian Ocean and Arabian Sea near Oman. A number of attacks have occurred more than 1000 nm from the Somali coast.

[8] It seems that the pirates take this action to encourage vessels to stop rather than intending to harm seafarers.

[9] In 2010 a total of 219 out of a total of 445 actual and attempted attacks were attributed to Somali pirates: International Chamber of Commerce – International Maritime Bureau (ICC-IMB), "Piracy and Armed Robbery Against Ships Annual Report" (ICC-IMB Report for the period 1 January – 31 December 2010, United Kingdom, January 2011).

[10] International Maritime Bureau Piracy Reporting Centre, "Piracy Prone Areas and Warnings" < http://www.icc-ccs.org/piracy-reporting-centre/prone-areas-and-warnings> as at 15 August 2011.

[11] Marine Department of the Hong Kong Special Administrative Region, "Recent Pirate Attempt to board Hong Kong Registered Ship" (Security and Quality Advisory No. 19, 31 August 2011). The advisory states that "The seizure represents a bold new departure for Somali pirates who have tended to hijack ships in international waters, now extended to within territorial waters of neighboring states."

farther out to sea without close naval protection have seen a substantial increase in piratic incidents.[12]

Contemporary piracy has been categorised into three broad areas: opportunistic hit and run attacks ("maritime mugging"); kidnap for ransom; and ship hijacking for ransom or to steal the cargo.[13] Of most concern to shipowners are the latter two: in 2010, pirates captured 1181 seafarers and 53 ships were hijacked.

As one of the world's largest shipping registries, Hong Kong faces the threat of piracy on an ongoing basis. In 2010 its vessels were among the eight flag states whose ships were attacked 12 times or more.[14] As recently as May 2011 in the Arabian Sea, the Marine Department of Hong Kong reported the unsuccessful attack of a Hong Kong-registered bulk carrier.[15] The Master was able to avoid the attack by taking evasive action after alerting the relevant authorities. The vessel suffered some damage to the wheelhouse and a lifeboat. Another unsuccessful attack on a chemical tanker was reported in June 2010.[16] The incident came amid the increasing use of "multi-skiff" attacks from vessels disguised as fishing boats and the capture by pirates of a large chemical tanker. Other incidents include a suspicious vessel approaching a Hong Kong-flagged container ship in March 2011 in the Arabian Sea[17] and on 13 April 2010 another container vessel was chased by "suspected pirate skiffs." The skiff aborted after the Master took an evasive manoeuvre and notified nearby coalition warships.[18] A similar attempt by skiffs was reported on 21 March.[19]

---

[12] International Chamber of Commerce – International Maritime Bureau (ICC-IMB), "Piracy and Armed Robbery Against Ships Annual Report" (ICC-IMB Report for the period 1 January – 31 December 2010, United Kingdom, January 2011) p 19.

[13] James Kraska, "Developing Piracy Policy for the National Strategy for Maritime Security" in Myron H. Nordquist, Rüdiger Wolfrum, John Norton Moore and Ronán Long, *Legal Challenges in Maritime Security* (Martinus Nijhoff, 2008) 341, pp 341-2.

[14] International Chamber of Commerce – International Maritime Bureau (ICC-IMB), "Piracy and Armed Robbery Against Ships Annual Report" (ICC-IMB Report for the period 1 January – 31 December 2010, United Kingdom, January 2011).

[15] Marine Department of the Hong Kong Special Administrative Region, "Recent Pirate Attempt to board Hong Kong Registered Ship" (Security and Quality Advisory No. 18, 23 May 2011).

[16] Marine Department of the Hong Kong Special Administrative Region, "Somali pirates try new techniques as monsoon season starts" (Security and Quality Advisory No. 10, 29 June 2010).

[17] After manoeuvring the ship and increasing speed the Master was able to lose the suspicious boat. This incident was reported to the Information Sharing Centre, a body created by the Regional Cooperation Agreement on Combating Piracy and Armed Robbery against Ships in Asia (ReCAAP).

[18] Marine Department of the Hong Kong Special Administrative Region, "Recent Pirate Attempt to board Hong Kong Registered Ship" (Security and Quality Advisory No. 9, 13 April 2010).

[19] Marine Department of the Hong Kong Special Administrative Region, "Recent Pirate Attempt to board Hong Kong Registered Ship" (Security and Quality Advisory No. 8, 21 March 2010).

In the Asian region, on 30 August 2010 a Hong Kong bulk carrier was boarded by pirates in the vicinity of Pulau Mankai in the South China Sea. The attack was the sixth such incident in the region in August of that year.[20] Another Hong Kong bulk carrier was approached by a speed boat and mother ship in the Bay of Bengal in February 2011. The master managed to avoid the suspected pirates through evasive manoeuvres. That month was identified as having a greater number of attacks as compared to February 2009 and 2010; however, it was largely due to an increase in "less significant" and "moderately significant" attacks.[21] This is consistent with ReCAAP's half-yearly report for 2011 which describes "an increase in the number of incidents reported during this period compared to the same period in the past four years."[22] Again, the increase was largely attributable to Category 3 (small scale) incidents, most apparent in Indonesia and the Straits of Singapore and Malacca. ReCAAP immediately orchestrated a step-up in the number of patrols and warned of the threats. An August 2011 report by the Regional Cooperation Agreement on Combating Piracy and Armed Robbery Against Ships in Asia (ReCAAP) concluded there had been a decrease in the number of incidents in comparison to the same period in 2010.[23] It has been reported that "pro-active and evasive successful measures undertaken by ship masters and crew" has led to a decrease in the number of actual incidents in the South China Sea.[24]

III. KEY SECURITY INITIATIVES

The United Nations General Assembly has recognised the "crucial role of international cooperation at the global, regional, subregional and bilateral levels in combating, in accordance with international law, threats to maritime security" including piracy and armed robbery at sea.[25]

---

[20] Marine Department of the Hong Kong Special Administrative Region, "Boarding by armed pirates at 2° 59.7'N 105° 12.2'E" (Security and Quality Advisory No. 13, 2 September 2010). For more information on security in the region see Kevin X Li and Jin Cheng, "Maritime Law and Policy for Energy Security in Asia: A Chinese Perspective" (2006) 37 *Journal of Maritime Law and Commerce* 567.

[21] ReCAAP Information Sharing Centre, "Report for February 2011" <www.recaap.org>.

[22] "Half Yearly Report: 1 January 2011 – 30 June 2011" (Report by the ReCAAP Information Sharing Centre, Singapore, 2011) p 3.

[23] The reference period is 1 – 31 August. ReCAAP Information Sharing Centre, "Report for August 2011" <www.recaap.org>.

[24] *Ibid* p 23.

[25] See resolution 64/71 of 4 December 2009: *Oceans and law of the sea*, GA Res 64/71, UNGAOR, 64th sess, UN Doc A/RES/64/71 (12 March 2010) para 69.

A. *The Maritime Safety Committee of the International Maritime Organisation (IMO)*

The International Maritime Organisation (IMO) was established by Convention in 1958[26] and its functions include encouraging and facilitating the general adoption of the highest practicable standards in "matters concerning . . . maritime safety" and the consideration of "any matters concerning shipping" (art 1). It may (directly or through its organs) make recommendations on such matters and draft conventions, agreements or other suitable instruments and recommend them to Governments. The IMO Assembly first adopted a resolution concerning piracy in 1983.[27] The IMO has played an integral role in the development of regional cooperation agreements including the ReCAAP, MOWCA and the Djibouti Code of Conduct[28] and its Maritime Safety Committee (MSC) continues to dominate efforts to reduce piracy and armed robbery at sea.

The Maritime Safety Committee (MSC) is established under part VII of the IMO Convention and is empowered to consider, amongst other things, "maritime safety procedures and requirements" and "any other matters directly affecting maritime safety" (art 28). Although the article does not specifically mention "security" (as distinct from "safety"), the MSC has dealt with maritime security issues since the 1980s.[29] The MSC may consist of all members of the IMO and is responsible for a wide range of maritime safety matters. It submits to the Council of the IMO proposals for safety regulations

---

[26] *Convention on the International Maritime Organisation*, opened for signature 6 March 1948, 289 UNTS 3 (entered into force 17 March 1958) ("IMO Convention").

[27] *Measures to Prevent Acts of Piracy and Armed Robbery Against Ships*, IMO Ass, 13th sess, Res A.545(13) (17 November 1983). Other similar resolutions were passed in 1991 (Resolution A.683(17)) and 1993 (Resolution A.738(18)).

[28] The *Code of Conduct concerning the repression of piracy and armed robbery against ships in the Western Indian Ocean and the Gulf of Aden* ("the Djibouti Code of Conduct"), IMO Council, 102nd sess, C.102/14 (3 April 2009) was adopted on 29 January 2009. The State signatories to the Code agreed to cooperate in the investigation, arrest and prosecution of pirates, the interdiction and seizure of suspected pirate vessels, the rescue of ships, persons and property subject to piracy and armed robbery and providing care to the crews affected, and the conducted of shared operations with signatories and navies outside the agreement. It also extends to sharing information through centres and focal points (see art 8 which deals with Coordination and Information Sharing).

[29] Klein recognises that the distinction between safety and security has not always been clear within the IMO: "Maritime safety refers to preventing or minimizing the occurrence of accidents at sea that may be caused by substandard ships, unqualified crew or operational error, whereas maritime security is related to protection against unlawful, and deliberate, acts": Natalie Klein, *Maritime Security and the Law of the Sea* (Oxford University Press, 2011) p 8. Reference is made to Proshanto K Mukherjee and Maximo Q Mejia Jr, "The ISPS Code: Legal and Ergonomic Considerations" in Maximo Q Mejia Jr (ed), *Contemporary Issues in Maritime Security* (World Maritime University, 2004) 33, p 34.

or amendments to existing regulations, recommendations and guidelines developed by the committee, and reports of the committee.[30]

Significant developments have been made by the MSC in an attempt to enhance maritime security. At its 88th session in December 2010, the MSC established the Working Group on Maritime Security, including Piracy and Armed Robbery Against Ships.[31] Amongst other things, the group has considered the development of guidance on the use of privately contracted armed security personnel on board merchant ships. Recent guidance in the form of Circulars has been approved by the MSC covering issues such as ensuring private security personnel comply with national regulations and standards, what guidance is to be given to port and coastal States, and what guidance is to be given to Governments dealing with the import, export, embarkation and disembarkation of firearms.[32] A manual intended to provide consolidated guidance on maritime security measures was considered at the 89th session.[33] Although the original maritime security measures, especially those under the International Ship and Port Facility Security (ISPS) Code,[34] were developed to deal with perceived terrorist threats, the proliferation of piracy in the past decade has necessitated the application of the measures to anti-piracy activities. The manual has been adopted by the Committee as the "User Guide to SOLAS chapter XI-2 and the ISPS Code."

B. *International Maritime Bureau Piracy Reporting Centre*

The IMB's Piracy Reporting Centre[35] is a voluntary-funded 24 hour operation based in Kuala Lumpur, Malaysia. Its main objective is "to be the first point of contact for the shipmaster to report an actual or attempted attack or even suspicious movements."[36] It works with governmental organisations, including law enforcement agencies, as part of its information sharing

---

[30] Article 29. The Council is established by Part VI of the *Convention*.

[31] Refer to "Report of the Maritime Safety Committee on its Eighty-Eighth Session", MSC, 88th sess, Agenda item 26, MSC 88/26 (15 December 2010) para 4.34.

[32] "Report of the Maritime Safety Committee on its Eighty-Ninth Session", MSC, 89th sess, Agenda item 25, MSC 89/25 (27 May 2011) para 18.60.

[33] See MSC Circulars MSC.1/Circ.1339 (14 September 2011), MSC.1/Circ.1405/Rev.1 (16 September 2011), MSC.1/Circ.1406/Rev.1 (16 September 2011) and MSC.1/Circ.1408 (16 September 2011). See also "Maritime Security Manual – Guidance for port facilities, ports and ship", Maritime Safety Committee, 89th sess, Agenda item 4, MSC 89/INF.13 (5 March 2011).

[34] International Convention for the Safety of Life at Sea (SOLAS), opened for signature 1 November 1974, International Maritime Organisation (IMO), chapter XI-2 (entered into force 25 May 1980; as amended by the Conference of Contracting Governments to the International Convention for the Safety of Life at Sea, 1974: 9 - 13 December 2002) ("ISPS Code"). Part A of the Code is mandatory and part B provides guidelines on compliance with part A.

[35] The IMB, established in 1981, is a special division of the International Chamber of Commerce (ICC).

[36] IMB Piracy Reporting Centre <http://www.icc-ccs.org/piracy-reporting-centre> as at 15 August 2011.

function. The Centre receives reports from crews, provides advice to masters, publishes warnings and information on piracy prone areas, and publishes reports on piracy. Part of the Centre's reporting function includes maintaining a "Live Piracy Report" which outlines all incidents reported to the Centre and a "Live Piracy Map" displaying all incidents of piracy and armed robbery.[37] IMO's MSC recommends contacting the Piracy Reporting Centre in the event of an incident and has endorsed the information it disseminates as "vital . . . upon which precautionary measures should be based."[38]

C. *Regional Cooperation Agreement on Combating Piracy and Armed Robbery Against Ships in Asia (ReCAAP)*

The ReCAAP is the preeminent regional agreement directed at combating piracy in Asia. Seventeen states are parties to the Agreement which entered into force on 4 September 2006.[39] It has been reported that the Agreement "has led to a dramatic decline in the incidence of maritime piracy in the Straits of Malacca and Singapore."[40] As the first treaty dedicated to combating piracy from a regional perspective, ReCAAP has become a model for other similar agreements such as the Maritime Organization of West and Central Africa (MOWCA), although none is as successful.[41]

The Agreement creates a number of general obligations for Contracting Parties including taking measures to prevent and suppress piracy and armed robbery against ships, make arrests, seize ships or aircraft, and rescue victim ships and persons.[42] One of the key components of the ReCAAP is the establishment of an Information Sharing Centre (ISC), based in Singapore, which is effectively a 24-hour tactical command centre.[43] Like the IMB's Piracy Reporting Centre, the Information Sharing Centre has been endorsed

---

[37] The incidents are colour-coded to differentiate actual attacks, attempted attacks and suspicious vessels.

[38] IMO Circular, Maritime Safety Committee, 86th sess, MSC/Circ. 1334 (23 June 2009) annex, paras 2, 10.

[39] The 17 States are Bangladesh, Brunei Darussalam, Cambodia, China, Denmark, India, Japan, South Korea, Laos, Myanmar, the Netherlands, Norway, Philippines, Singapore, Sri Lanka, Thailand and Vietnam. Hong Kong is a party through China's accession.

[40] James Kraska and Brian Wilson, "The Pirates of the Gulf of Aden: The Coalition is the Strategy" (2009) 45 *Stanford Journal of International Law* 243, p 271.

[41] *See* James Kraska and Brian Wilson, "The Pirates of the Gulf of Aden: The Coalition is the Strategy" (2009) 45 *Stanford Journal of International Law* 243.

[42] Art 3.

[43] *See* pt II of the Agreement.

by the MSC.[44] In 2007 the ISC was formally recognised as an international organisation. Its functions include:

- managing and maintaining the expeditious flow of information relating to incidents among the Contracting Parties;
- collecting, collating and analysing the information;
- preparing statistics and reports and disseminating them among the Contracting Parties, the international shipping community and the IMO;
- providing appropriate alerts and warnings of threats whenever possible; and
- facilitating cooperation between Contracting Parties in detecting pirates and offenders.

Notwithstanding that the Agreement has other provisions concerning extradition, mutual legal assistance, capacity building, and cooperative arrangements (for example, joint counter-piracy exercises), at its core is information sharing which supports the critical function of facilitating cooperation between the states. The provisions deal with more than merely sharing details about incidents; they extend to requiring a "Focal Point" in a Contracting Party responsible for communicating with the ISC.[45] This enables information concerning threats to be quickly disseminated among the parties via the Information Network System. The Focal Points are linked together through the system: a local agency will first receive an incident report and manage it according to its national policies and response procedures. The agency will then forward the information to its Focal Point which in turn feeds the information to the ReCAAP ISC and neighbouring Focal Points. This procedure provides a significant degree of autonomy to states in dealing firsthand with incidents; and it gives the advantage of obtaining possible assistance from other Focal Points and the ISC which may include the deployment of assets to assist in controlling an incident.

The reporting of incidents is emphasised by the User Guide to SOLAS chapter XI-2 and the ISPS Code which incorporates guidelines on the drafting of a Ship Security Plan (SSP).[46] A SSP "shall address . . . procedures

---

[44] IMO Circular, Maritime Safety Committee, 86th sess, MSC/Circ. 1334 (23 June 2009) annex, paras 2, 10, 11, 39. Appendix 2 contains a flow chart for reporting incidents in Asia. The flowchart is also available through ReCAAP's website: <http://www.recaap.org/>.

[45] *See* art 9.

[46] A SSP is a plan developed to ensure the application of measures on board the ship designed to protect persons on board, cargo, cargo transport units, ship's stores or the ship from the risks of a security incident: ISPS Code, pt A, s 2.1.4.

for reporting security incidents."[47] Security incidents, according to the Guide, generally fall into two categories:[48]

1. Those considered sufficiently serious that they should be reported to relevant authorities by the Company Security Officer. Incidents in this category may include unauthorised carriage or discovery of stowaways, weapons or explosives; incidents of which the media are aware; attempted or successful boardings; and damage to the ship caused by explosive devices or arson.

2. Those of a less serious nature but require reporting to, and investigation, by the Ship Security Officer; for example, damage to equipment through sabotage or vandalism; suspicious behaviour or packages near a ship when at a port facility; and unsecured access points to the ship.

Governments are required to indicate the types of security incidents that must be reported to them and should provide guidance on the procedures to be followed.[49] As alluded to above, it is acknowledged in the Guide that, "Maritime Security Measures were developed in response to perceived terrorist threats. However, to varying degrees, the measures are applicable to countering other forms of security threats, notably piracy and armed robbery in international and territorial waters . . . ."[50] It concludes that "the fundamental purpose of the ISPS Code can be considered to reduce the vulnerability of the maritime industry to security threats, regardless of their nature." As the responsibility for the development and revision of a SSP rests with the shipping company's Company Security Officer (CSO),[51] shipowners must remain up to date with reporting requirements and procedures.

D. *Maritime Organisation of West and Central Africa (MOWCA)*

Established in 1975, the Maritime Organisation of West and Central Africa (MOWCA) arose out of a need for cooperation at an inter-governmental level on maritime security and safety issues, marine environmental protection and the implementation of relevant international conventions.[52] Present projects under the auspices of the organisation include an integrated sub-

---

[47] ISPS Code, pt A, s 9.4.12.

[48] "Maritime Security Manual – Guidance for port facilities, ports and ship", Maritime Safety Committee, 89th sess, Agenda item 4, MSC 89/INF.13 (5 March 2011) para 4.8.35.

[49] "Maritime Security Manual – Guidance for port facilities, ports and ship", Maritime Safety Committee, 89th sess, Agenda item 4, MSC 89/INF.13 (5 March 2011) para 2.9.37.

[50] "Maritime Security Manual – Guidance for port facilities, ports and ship", Maritime Safety Committee, 89th sess, Agenda item 4, MSC 89/INF.13 (5 March 2011) para 1.5.6.

[51] See Guide para 2.9.15. CSO is defined as "the person designated by the Company for ensuring that a ship security assessment is carried out; that a ship security plan is developed, submitted for approval, and thereafter implemented and maintained and for liaison with port facility security officers and the ship security officer": para 1.8.1(i).

[52] MOWCA's website is accessible at <http://www.mowca.org/>.

regional coastguard network, an information and communications centre, a transit transport management system (aimed specifically at road transport), a regional maritime fund, and a regional maritime bank. At a regional meeting held in Ghana in 2002, it was agreed between regional Governments that the MOWCA should be used as the coordinating body "for developing a regional strategy on cooperation and coordination against piracy and armed robbery against ships."[53]

The Integrated Sub-Regional Coast Guard Network was established by a Memorandum of Understanding in 2008 to respond to maritime security threats in the African region.[54] Articles of the agreement provide for the synchronising of national legislation and policies directed at ensuring the security of maritime trade and long-term protection of the marine environment. The region's size has necessitated the establishment of four distinct coastguard zones which each has its own Coastguard Coordinating Centre; these Centres operate under two Principal Coordinating Centres. Similar to ReCAAP, the MOWCA agreement places an emphasis on information sharing between states. This example of cooperation between "sovereign entities that have rarely, if ever, cooperated on a common footing" demonstrates a collective interest in rectifying the situation as efficiently as possible.[55]

E. *Maritime Security Centre – Horn of Africa (MSCHOA)*

The Maritime Security Centre – Horn of Africa (MSCHOA) was established on 8 December 2008 by the European Union Naval Force (EU NAVFOR) Somalia with support from the shipping industry. Its genesis is due to UN Security Council Resolutions 1814 (15 May 2008), 1816 (2 June 2008) and 1838 (7 October 2008).[56] Acting under Chapter VII of the Charter of the United Nations, the Security Council decided in Resolution 1816 that, for a period of six months, states cooperating with the Transitional Federal Government of Somalia could enter and use the territorial waters of Somalia for the purpose of repressing acts of piracy and armed robbery at sea, in a

---

[53] Note by the Secretariat, "Piracy and Armed Robbery Against Ships", Maritime Safety Committee, 76th sess, MSC 76/16/1 (Agenda item 16, 25 March 2003) para 27.

[54] Memorandum of Understanding on the Establishment of a Sub-Regional Integrated Coast Guard Network in West and Central Africa, 13th sess, MOWCA/XIII GA 08/8 (29-31 July 2008). The history of discussions prior to the MOU is summarised in the Report of the Maritime Safety Committee, 83rd sess, MSC 83/28 (26 October 2007) para 19.25 and following.

[55] Peter Chalk, "Piracy Off the Horn of Africa: Scope, Dimensions, Causes and Responses" (2009) 16(2) *Brown Journal of World Affairs* 89, p 99.

[56] It has been reported that in 2008, the Security Council "adopted more resolutions on piracy than on any other subject": Ved P Nanda, "Maritime Piracy: How can international law and policy address this growing global menace?" (2010) 39 *Denver Journal of International Law & Policy* 177, pp 183-4.

manner consistent with such authorized action on the high seas.[57] Resolution 1846, which renewed the initial authorization, extended its application from states cooperating with the Transitional Government to include regional organisations.[58] The authorization has been repeatedly renewed, most recently in November 2010.[59]

The mandate of the operation – Operation Atalanta – is to protect shipping involved with the transportation and delivery of humanitarian aid to Somalia, the World Food Programme (WFP) and the African Military Mission in Somalia,[60] cooperate to deter acts of piracy and armed robbery at sea in the Red Sea, Gulf of Aden and part of the Indian Ocean,[61] and protect vulnerable shipping. The taskforce also monitors fishing activities off the Somali coast.[62] It has been stated that the "main strength of Operation Atalanta is the clarity of its mandate."[63]

The MSCHOA Centre provides round-the-clock monitoring of vessels transiting the Gulf of Aden and issues guidance to the industry on best practices to combat piracy. A critical element of MSCHOA's monitoring function is registration: crews are strongly encouraged to register their vessels' movements through the region. The Centre passes this information on to the United Kingdom Maritime Trade Operations (UKMTO) base in Dubai which tracks vessels and records positional information. This enables the naval forces in the region and headquarters (including the CTF, discussed below) to assess overall risk and pass relevant information directly to ships. The Centre also arranges "Group Transits" whereby merchant ships transit together (sometimes but not always accompanied by a naval escort) through the Internationally Recommended Transit Corridor (IRTC) in the Gulf of

---

[57] SC Res 1816, UNSC, 5902nd mtg, UN Doc S/RES/1816 (2 June 2008) para 7.

[58] SC Res 1846, UNSC, 6026th mtg, UN Doc S/RES/1846 (2 December 2008) para 10.

[59] SC Res 1950, UNSC, 6429th mtg, UN Doc S/RES/1950 (23 November 2010).

[60] SC Res 1814, UNSC, 5893rd mtg, UN Doc S/RES/1814 (15 May 2008) paras 11,

[61] SC Res 1816, UNSC, 5902nd mtg, UN Doc S/RES/1816 (2 June 2008) para 2. Paragraph 3 concerns rendering assistance to vessels threatened or under attack; para 4 extends to States cooperating to provide appropriate guidance and training on avoidance, evasion, and defensive techniques; and para 5 calls on States and interested organizations to provide technical assistance to Somalia and nearby coastal States to enhance the capacity of those States to combat piracy and armed robbery at sea.

[62] The Security Council expressed grave concerns about the "recent proliferation of acts of piracy and armed robbery at sea against vessels off the coast of Somalia, and by the serious threat it poses to … commercial fishing activities" in Resolution 1838.

[63] Omer Elagab, "Somali Piracy and International Law: Some Aspects" (2010) 24 *Australian and New Zealand Maritime Law Journal* 59, p 71. The operation is being conducted under the European Security and Defence Policy.

Aden.[64] Escorts are also provided to WFP vessels. According to MSCHOA, "[s]ince escorts began in late 2007, not a single ship carrying WFP food to ports in Somalia has been attacked by pirates."[65]

F. *NATO*

The North Atlantic Treaty Organization (NATO) responded to a request of UN Secretary-General, Ban Ki-moon, in 2008 to provide escorts to WFP vessels.[66] Currently it is operating under Operation Ocean Shield which has a wider mandate than earlier operations: it provides maritime security in the region (including escorts and deterrence activities) in addition to offering anti-piracy training to regional countries.[67]

G. *Combined Maritime Forces*

The Combined Maritime Forces is a 25 nation coalition operating in accordance with the UN Security Council Resolutions.[68] Combined Task Force (CTF) 150 (maritime security and counter-terrorism) operates in the Red Sea, Gulf of Aden, Indian Ocean, Arabian Sea and Gulf of Oman; CTF 151 (counter piracy) operates in the Gulf of Aden and off the eastern coast of Somalia; and CTF 152 conducts security operations in the Arabian Gulf. CTF-151 is commanded on a rotational basis meaning it is not always under the control of a particular state. Its primary role is to "deter, disrupt and suppress piracy in order to protect global maritime security and secure freedom of navigation for the benefit of all nations."[69] The Maritime Liaison Office Bahrain (MARLO) operates as a conduit for information exchange between the CMF and industry and organisations in the region.

---

[64] The IRTC was endorsed by the Sub-Committee on Safety of Navigation at is fifty-sixth session in July 2009. The IRTC is "subject to change by military authorities according to prevailing circumstances": International Maritime Organisation, Sub-Committee on Safety of Navigation circular, SN.1/Circ.281 (3 August 2009). The MSC endorsed the action of the Sub-Committee in approving SN.1/Circ.281: see "Report of the Maritime Safety Committee on its Eighty-Seventh Session", MSC, 87th sess, Agenda item 26, MSC 87/26 (27 May 2011) para 9.7.

[65] Maritime Security Centre – Horn of Africa, "World Food Programme" <http://www.mschoa.org/ Pages/ About.aspx> as at 17 August 2011.

[66] In a 2008 resolution, the Security Council unanimously welcomed "the decision by the North Atlantic Treaty Organization (NATO) to counter piracy off the Somalia coast, including by escorting vessels of the WFP": SC Res 1846, UNSC, 6026th mtg, UN Doc S/RES/1846 (2 December 2008) para 6.

[67] The operation was approved by the North Atlantic Council on 17 August 2009. At present it will continue until end-2012.

[68] Member nations: Australia, Bahrain, Belgium, Canada, Denmark, France, Germany, Greece, Italy, Japan, Jordan, Republic of Korea, Kuwait, the Netherlands, New Zealand, Pakistan, Portugal, Saudi Arabia, Singapore, Spain, Thailand, Turkey, United Arab Emirates, United Kingdom and United States.

[69] Combined Task Force (CTF) 151 <http://www.cusnc.navy.mil/cmf/151/index.html> as at 17 August 2011.

H. *Shared Awareness and Deconfliction (SHADE) and the Contact Group*

Shared Awareness and Deconfliction (SHADE) meetings, held on a monthly basis, provide an opportunity for the various international militaries, nations and organisations to coordinate anti-piracy operations. Established in December 2008, it initially involved the CMF, EU NAVFOR and NATO but now includes a number of regional nations and other navies. It is responsible for the introduction of the IRTC including the IRTC Coordination Guide, advanced military communications systems, improved coordination with the industry, and the sharing of military assets.[70]

The Contact Group on Piracy off the Coast of Somalia (Contact Group) was set up on 14 January 2009 and meets three times each year at the UN. Security Council Resolution 1851 (2008) encouraged all States and regional organisations to "establish an international cooperation mechanism to act as a common point of contact between and among states, regional and international organizations on all aspects of combating piracy and armed robbery at sea off Somalia's coast."71 The Contact Group has established five working groups: (1) Military and Operational Coordination, Information Sharing and Capacity Building; (2) Judicial Issues; (3) Strengthening Shipping Self-Awareness and Other Capabilities; (4) Public Information; and (5) Financial Flows. Nearly 60 countries and a number of international organisations participate in the group. It has recently considered transfer agreements for convicted pirates to serve out their sentences in Somalia and called upon Somali authorities to pass and implement anti-piracy legislation.[72]

IV. STATE SPECIFIC LEGISLATION

The United Nations Convention on the Law of the Sea (UNCLOS) requires states to cooperate in the repression of piracy and provide for the seizure of a pirate ship and the arrest of the persons on board.[73] The International Chamber of Shipping, in collaboration with the European Community Shipowners Association, has produced a table of certain flag State rules for

[70] "8th SHADE meeting sees largest international participation so far", EU NAVFOR Somalia, 1 October 2009 < http://www.eunavfor.eu/2009/10/8th-shade-meeting-sees-largest-international-participation-so-far/> as at 28 October 2011.

[71] SC Res 1851, UNSC, 6046th mtg, UN Doc S/RES/1851 (16 December 2008) para 4.

[72] United Nations, Press Conference by Contact Group on Piracy off Somalia Coast (21 March 2011) available at <http://www.un.org/News/briefings/docs/2011/110321_Piracy.doc.htm> as at 28 October 2011.

[73] *United Nations Convention on the Law of the Sea*, opened for signature 10 December 1982, 1833 UNTS 3 (entered into force 16 November 1994) arts 100, 105. The Convention has 157 signatories and over 160 parties.

armed guards.[74] As one of the world's largest shipping registers, Hong Kong is a useful jurisdiction for analysis.

Part III of Hong Kong's Crimes Ordinance deals with "Piracy and Other Offences at Sea" and punishes piratical acts with life imprisonment.[75] Pursuant to s 20, a person may commit a piratical act under the Ordinance if either:

(1) he is a resident of the HKSAR [Hong Kong Special Administrative Region] and commits any piracy or robbery or any act of hostility or robbery against other residents of the HKSAR on the sea; or
(2) being on board any Hong Kong ship, he: turns pirate, enemy or rebel; voluntarily yields up the ship or its contents to any pirate; brings any seducing message from a pirate, enemy or rebel; assaults the master; confines the master; or makes or endeavours to make a revolt on the ship.

Trading with pirates is criminalised under s 21; s 22 concerns persons found within Hong Kong on board any vessel equipped for the purposes of piracy; and s 19 refers to "piracy with violence."

Section 23B(1) deems an act of a person on board a Hong Kong ship on the high seas an offence under the law of Hong Kong just as if the act constituting the offence were to take place in Hong Kong. For the purposes of this section, the person's nationality is irrelevant. A similar provision applies in respect of an act committed in Hong Kong waters on board a non-Hong Kong ship (s 23B(2)); and an act committed by a resident of the HKSAR on board a Hong Kong ship in any port or harbour outside Hong Kong, or on board a ship which is neither a Hong Kong ship nor a ship to which the person belongs (s 23B(3)).[76] The aforementioned provisions are subject to two provisos.[77]

The Theft Ordinance applies where a person "dishonestly appropriates property belonging to another with the intention of permanently depriving

---

[74] Refer to the International Chamber of Shipping, "Flag State Rules and Requirements on Arms and Private Armed Guards On Board Vessels: Combined ICS/ECSA Table" (December 2011) available at <http://www.marisec.org/ICS-ECSA%20Private%20Armed%20Guards%20Flag%20State%20Laws%20 December%202011%20final.pdf> as at 19 January 2012.

[75] Crimes Ordinance (Hong Kong) cap 200, s 20.

[76] Subsection (4) states that "Where an offence against the person or against property is committed, either ashore or afloat, in any place outside Hong Kong by any master, seaman or apprentice who at the time when the offence is committed is, or at any time within the previous 3 months was, employed in any Hong Kong ship, the matter may be inquired into, and the person by whom the offence was committed may be punished and otherwise dealt with in the same manner as if the offence had been committed in Hong Kong."

[77] *See* ss 23B(5) and (7). Subsection (5) provides that this section does not apply to acts expressly or impliedly authorised under Hong Kong law or not otherwise prohibited by it. Subsection (7) deals with hovercraft.

the other of it."[78] Sections 9, 10 and 11 concern theft, robbery and burglary respectively. Under s 11, a person commits burglary if he enters a building as a trespasser either with intent to commit an offence of stealing, inflicting on any person therein grievous bodily harm or rape of a woman, or doing unlawful damage to the building; or, having entered a building, steals or attempts to steal anything in it or inflicts or attempts to inflict grievous bodily harm on a person in it. References to "building" also apply to an inhabited vehicle or vessel.[79]

V. GUIDANCE AND RECOMMENDATIONS FOR SHIPS IN THE GULF OF ADEN AND OTHER DANGEROUS AREAS

This part identifies the key guidance and recommendations disseminated to the shipping industry and flag states. It first outlines the key materials before focusing specifically on Hong Kong's application and extension of the guidance.

A. *Best Management Practices*

The international shipping industry publishes a set of Best Management Practice (BMP) guidelines for ships transiting the waters around Somalia and the Gulf of Aden. The purpose of the BMP guidelines, now in its fourth edition, is to "assist ships to avoid, deter or delay piracy attacks in the High Risk Area."[80] The High Risk Area is defined by "where pirate activity and/or attacks have taken place."[81] It is noted that the level of pirate activity varies with weather conditions, military operations and the monsoonal season. The BMP "complements piracy guidance provided in the latest IMO MSC Circulars"[82] but it warns that the advice given is always subject to the overriding authority of the master to protect his crew, ship and cargo. The

[78] Theft Ordinance (Hong Kong) cap 210, s 2(1). Note: s 23B of the Crimes Ordinance does not appear to be limited in its reach to that ordinance, which is itself a consolidation of criminal laws. It would therefore apply to cap 210.

[79] Theft Ordinance (Hong Kong) cap 210, s 11(3): "References in subsections (1) and (2) to a building shall apply also to an inhabited vehicle or vessel, and shall apply to any such vehicle or vessel at times when the person having a habitation in it is not there as well as at times when he is."

[80] *Best Management Practices to Deter Piracy off the Coast of Somalia and in the Arabian Sea Area* (version 4, August 2011) ("BMP") para 1.1. Signatories to the BMP (fourth edition) are BIMCO, Cruise Lines International Association, the International Chamber of Shipping, International Group of P&I Clubs, IMB, International Maritime Employers' Committee Ltd (IMEC), Intercargo, InterManager, Intertanko, International Shipping Federation, International Transport Workers' Federation (ITF), International Parcel Tankers Association, Joint Hull Committee, Joint War Committee, Oil Companies International Marine Forum, the Society of International Gas Tanker and Terminal Operators, the Mission to Seafarers, and the World Shipping Council (WSC). There are also a number of naval/military forces and law enforcement organisations supporting the BMP.

[81] BMP para 2.4.

[82] BMP para 1.7.

guidelines are updated as necessary "based upon operational experience and lessons learned."[83]

The MSC also supports "full compliance" with the BMP.[84] Moreover, the UN Security Council, in Resolution 1976 (April 2011),

> *Commends* the efforts of the shipping industry, in cooperation with the CGPCS [Contact Group on Piracy off the Coast of Somalia] and IMO, in developing and disseminating the updated version of the Best Management Practices to Deter Piracy off the Coast of Somalia and in the Arabian Sea Area (BMP) and *emphasizes* the critical importance for the shipping industry of applying the best practices recommended in the BMP.[85]

Despite the evident support, the BMP remain voluntary;[86] however, there is nothing to prevent individual states making it compulsory and the guidelines are fast becoming the industry norm.[87] The Philippines, for example, has mandated piracy training for seafarers since early 2010.[88] Moreover, recommendation 10 in MSC Circular 1334 acknowledges that the shipping industry would benefit from consulting other recommendations including those produced by the ReCAAP ISC, the IMB Piracy Reporting Centre, BIMCO, ICS and other industry bodies.[89]

---

[83] BMP para 13.1.

[84] The BMP are circulated via MSC Circular 1339 (MSC.1/Circ.1339, 14 September 2011). See also "Report of the Maritime Safety Committee on its Eighty-Ninth Session", MSC, 89th sess, Agenda item 25, MSC 89/25 (27 May 2011) paras 18.1, 18.47.

[85] SC Res 1976, UNSC, 6512th mtg, UN Doc S/RES/1976 (11 April 2011) para 12.

[86] The "Terms of Use" set out on p ii of the BMP states that the advice and information given is "intended purely as guidance to be used at the user's own risk." Furthermore, a thorough risk assessment should be carried out by the company and master prior to the ship entering the High Risk Area.

[87] "Piracy and Legal Issues: Reconciling Public and Private Interests" (Report of the Africa Programme and International Law Conference, London, 1 October 2009) p 15. The report notes that "Insurers are not making compliance compulsory but there is little doubt that if they are not followed and a hijacking arises, questions may be asked. This also applies to charterers and cargo interests who may look to non-compliance as a justification for alleging that a vessel is unseaworthy, thereby giving a potential defence to any claim for a contribution to the costs of the ransom. Importantly, following the BMP also ensures that the owner is fulfilling its obligations towards the crew in terms of the duty of care that is owed to them under the employment contracts."

[88] Department of Labor and Employment, Republic of the Philippines available at <http://www.dole.gov.ph/secondpage.php?id=1269> as at 19 August 2011. See also "Anti-piracy training for Filipinos after 470 deaths", Maritime Union of Australia News (5 January 2010) <http://www.mua.org.au/news/anti-piracy-training-for-filipinos-after-470-death/> as at 19 August 2011; "Philippines orders sailors to take anti-piracy classes", BBC News (4 January 2010) <http://news.bbc.co.uk/2/hi/8439198.stm> as at 19 August 2011.

[89] IMO Circular, Maritime Safety Committee, 86th sess, MSC/Circ. 1334 (23 June 2009). For example, the IMB's Piracy Reporting Centre recommends following company and ship specific procedures, advice in Circular 1334 and the BMP. It also adds a number of other recommendations: "Advice to Masters", IMB Piracy Reporting Centre <http://www.icc-ccs.org/piracy-reporting-centre/advice-to-masters> as at 23 August 2011.

B. IMO Maritime Safety Committee (MSC) Circulars

The Committee first published detailed recommendations to Governments concerning maritime piracy in June 1999.[90] Circulars 1333 and 1334 have replaced the original documents and are apropos guidance; for instance, the European Commission has noted:

> Although the measures set out in these IMO circulars are not compulsory or binding, the clear need to improve maritime security means that ships flying the flag of a Member State should protect themselves as best they can using current know-how when they are exposed in navigation regions with a high risk of piracy and armed robbery.[91]

Circular 1334, released in conjunction with 1333, provides guidance to shipowners and ship operators, shipmasters and crews on preventing and suppressing acts of piracy and armed robbery against ships.[92] Circular 1333 constructs the guidance in the form of "recommendations" to governments for preventing and suppressing piracy and armed robbery against ships. Aside from dealing with armed guards (see below), Circular 1333 covers the use and implementation of action plans and criminal jurisdiction of states concerning a person apprehended at sea outside the territorial sea of any State for committing acts of piracy or armed robbery against ships. Circular 1333 commends the recommendations to member states affected by piracy and armed robbery at sea. The Circulars' recommendations do not stand alone; they are to be read with and implemented alongside the BMP.[93] Revised Circulars 1405 and 1406 (hereinafter "Circular 1405/06") were published by the IMO on 16 September 2011 and provide "revised interim guidance" to states and industry on the use of privately contracted armed security personnel on board ships in the high risk area (they replace the initial versions of the circulars which were in the form of interim guidance).

C. Other industry guidance

Other organisations also publish additional guidance and recommendations which may assist shipowners, operators and masters in coping with the threat

---

[90] IMO Circular, Maritime Safety Committee, 71st sess, MSC/Circ. 622/Rev.1 (16 June 1999). Revised Circular 622 urged Governments to "involve representatives of shipowners and seafarers in developing measures to prevent and suppress piracy and armed robbery against ships"; it was issued with Circular 623 which directed guidance to shipowners and ship operators, shipmasters and crews.

[91] *Commission Recommendation of 11 March 2010 on measures for self-protection and the prevention of piracy and armed robbery against ships* [2010] OJ L 67/13, para 4. This statement is in the context of "these IMO Circulars" which refers to Circulars 1332, 1334 and 1335. Evidently the term "IMO Circular" is used interchangeably with "MSC Circular".

[92] Circular 1334: IMO Circular, Maritime Safety Committee, 86th sess, MSC/Circ. 1334 (23 June 2009).

[93] IMO Circular, Maritime Safety Committee, 86th sess, MSC/Circ. 1335 (29 September 2009) paras 5-6.

of piracy. For example, the IMB Piracy Reporting Centre suggests that masters first follow company and ship specific procedures; follow advice in Circular 1334; and while transiting pirate-prone waters near Somalia, follow BMP. It then adds 23 additional recommendations and provides information on some commercially-available anti-piracy options available to shipowners such as electric fencing for vessels and vessel tracking technology.[94]

MSCHOA has published "Guidance relating to the Construction and Use of Citadels in Waters Affected by Somalia Piracy."[95] A Citadel is a "designated pre-planned area purpose built into the ship where, in the event of imminent boarding by pirates, all crew will seek protection."[96] A number of attempts by pirates to take control of a vessel have been thwarted by the presence of a citadel (generally the crew radio from within the citadel for the assistance of nearby naval vessels).[97] The guidance outlines risk assessment processes to determined whether to use the citadel; citadel criteria including location, survivability time frame, construction, ventilation, equipment such as medical supplies, navigational aids, food and communication devices; and the use of a citadel. It concludes with a stark warning: "Somali Pirates knowledge and *modus operandi* continues to evolve over time. As their knowledge on Citadels increases, then their ability and methodology in attempting to defeat a citadel will also change, and therefore more robust protection will be required."[98]

D. Marine Department of Hong Kong Guidance

The Marine Department of Hong Kong regularly updates masters, shipowners and ship security officers of piratic incidents and arrangements for safe passage of Hong Kong ships in and around the Gulf of Aden and throughout other areas of known piratic activity, such as the South East Asian seas. Some of the measures are outlined below:

---

[94] See IMB Piracy Reporting Centre, "Advice to Masters" available at <http://www.icc-ccs.org/piracy-reporting-centre/advice-to-masters> as at 26 August 2011.

[95] July 2011. The information is available to registered users via the MSCHOA website <http://www.mschoa.org/ >.

[96] BMP para 8.13. The Citadel "is designed and constructed to resist a determined pirate trying to gain entry for a fixed period of time." The BMP notes that detailed guidance and advice on the use and construction of Citadels is included on the MSCHOA and NATO Shipping Centre websites.

[97] The MSCHOA "Guidance relating to the Construction and Use of Citadels in Waters Affected by Somalia Piracy" puts the estimate, since January 2010, at 26 cases where pirates have actually boarded vessels, but have been unable to take control because of the use of the citadel (p 1).

[98] Guidance p 8.

D.1 Ship Security Plan

The Singapore Navy Information Fusion Centre (IFC)[99] Shipping Advisory 1/2010 recommends ship masters adopt a Ship Security Plan (SSP) in accordance with the ISPS Code for transit through the Malacca Strait. It is suggested that such SSP be in conformity with those in use when transiting the Gulf of Aden.[100] In general, a Ship Security Plan details security vulnerabilities and identifies possible solutions in order to mitigate risks.[101] The Marine Department makes reference to this requirement in the Hong Kong Merchant Shipping Information Note 15/2009 ("Prevention and Suppression of Piracy and Armed Robbery Against Ships").

According to the User Guide to SOLAS chapter XI-2 and the ISPS Code ("the Guide"), the plan must make provision for three security levels: ships will usually apply the same security level set by the government responsible for the relevant port; however, a ship may operate on a higher (but not lower) security level.[102] Relevantly, SSPs should provide details of:

- Measures designed to prevent weapons, dangerous substances and devices intended for use against persons, ships or ports from being taken on board;
- Measures and procedures required for each of the three security levels;
- Procedures for evacuation in case of security threats or breaches of security;
- Security-related duties of shipboard personnel assigned security responsibilities and other shipboard personnel; and
- Procedures for testing security equipment, training, reviewing the SSP and reporting security incidents.

It is clear from the Guide that an SSP is an extensive document covering numerous scenarios and adequate training of its documented procedures must be undertaken.

---

[99] The IFC, opened in April 2009, works closely with ReCAAP's ISC and coordinates information obtained by the Western Pacific Naval Symposium Regional Maritime Information Exchange and the Malacca Straits Patrol's Information System.

[100] Marine Department of Hong Kong, "Advisory to shipping on improving security measures while transiting the Malacca Strait" (Security and Quality Advisory No. 7, 5 March 2010).

[101] As noted above, in any event, the SSP is required by the ISPS: *see* pt 9 of the ISPS Code: *International Convention for the Safety of Life at Sea (SOLAS)*, opened for signature 1 November 1974, International Maritime Organisation (IMO), chapter XI-2 (entered into force 25 May 1980; as amended by the Conference of Contracting Governments to the International Convention for the Safety of Life at Sea, 1974: 13 December 2002) (*"ISPS Code"*). China is a signatory to the *SOLAS Convention*.

[102] Refer to pts 4.3 and 4.8 of the Guide: "Maritime Security Manual – Guidance for port facilities, ports and ship", Maritime Safety Committee, 89th sess, Agenda item 4, MSC 89/INF.13 (5 March 2011).

D.2 Preventing Piratic Activity

The Marine Department has provided to all masters, ship security officers and company security officers of Hong Kong registered ships "sample reference measures" to be taken to prevent pirate activity. "Ships are encouraged to make reference to them when considered applicable" and they generally appear to be in line with those contained in the Best Management Practices guidelines (discussed below).[103] At the outset of the sample measures it is noted that "pirates are generally untrained" and the "only motivation is money"; consequently, the pirates search for "easy prey," that is, vessels with low freeboard, low speed and a low level of alertness. The sample measures include:[104]

(i) *Situational awareness*: Pirates have been known to track vessels via the Automatic Identification System (AIS) and may have the capacity to jam radio frequencies prior to an attack. Additionally, the mother ships they launch from are generally well-equipped with radar, communication equipment and AIS. It is essential that the crew is aware of the pirates' level of sophistication so as to avoid complacency. The measures also point out that the pirates do fire at vessels from time to time. Mostly, the pirates use war relics such as the Kalashnikov (AK-47) rifle and rocket propelled grenades.

(ii) *Precautions*: Precautions include the use of razor-bladed barbed wire around the vessel; securing the accommodation areas completely in every aspect and removing external access ladders from the main deck; securing all doors from inside; keeping an efficient lookout while ensuring all lookouts are well rested and briefed in detail;[105] and staggering the switch-over to new officers and lookouts.[106]

(iii) *Standard Operating Procedures*: The Standard Operating Procedures (SOPs) should comprise five parts:

- Physical duration and preparation of the vessel prior to entering the danger zone;

[103] Marine Department of Hong Kong, "Recent pirate attempt to board HK registered ship" (Security and Quality Advisory No. 9, 27 April 2010). The sample measures are contained in the appendix.

[104] The measures are listed under the subheading "What a vessel must do?".

[105] The measures note: "Navy found that a lookout's efficiency normally starts to fall after 2 hours and the lowest after 3 hours when under pressure. It is recommended that Master and 3/O keep 6 hrs relieved by C/O and 2/O for next 6 hrs. For lookouts it is recommended that period on watch be restricted to 2 or maximum 3 hours. Lookouts must be briefed in detail what to look for and procedure for scanning the horizon and seas."

[106] It is reported that most attacks and accidents occur in the last 30 minutes and first 30 minutes of a watch. By staggering the changeover, at least one crew member on duty will have current situation awareness while the new member absorbs the situation.

- Actions required 96 hours before the vessel's arrival into the zone. For example, details of information to be transmitted, briefings, drills, and testing of emergency and communications equipment;
- Procedures to follow in the event of a suspicious sighting. For example, raise the alarm and upgrade the security measure on the vessel,[107] inform authorities patrolling the area, maintain a high speed (never below 10 knots unless there is a naval vessel nearby), steer the vessel in such a way as to create a wake sufficient to deter an approaching small craft etc.;
- What the crew must do if the vessel is boarded by pirates. It is noted that the nearby naval authorities may be asked to board the vessel to repel the pirates if the crew is secure. It is vital that the master or an officer who can remain calm under pressure mans the radio or communications device in order to send out prepared messages with updates of the vessel's position and details of the attack; and
- The post-attack period.

(iv) *Checklist*: A checklist for each crew member should detail the assigned tasks during an incident.

(v) *Rest*: All crew must be well-rested during the passage.

(vi) *Automatic Identification System (AIS)*: Even though pirate mother ships often rely on AIS to track vessels, the sample measures recommend it be kept on as naval forces in the region may be unable to monitor the vessel's progress and provide updates. If a situation requires that it be switched off, the naval monitoring centre must be updated every hour with the vessel's position, heading and speed.[108]

(vii) *Briefing the crew*: Regular crew briefings are important in raising awareness of the situation and encouraging the early detection and reporting of threats.

(viii) *Notification of progress*: Regular reports to the company security officer are required. The regularity of reports depends on the vessel's location (and any other requirement the CSO may impose).

D.3 Chinese Naval Escort

The Marine Department has advised ships seeking protection in the Gulf of Aden to join the Chinese Naval Vessels Escort Arrangement.[109] China has sent a naval unit consisting of two destroyers and a supply ship to the Gulf of Aden on an anti-piracy mission. Its primary role is "to protect Chinese ships

[107] This may be a reference to the security level required by the ISPS Code.

[108] It is noted that "AIS is normally seen put off when vessel leaves a convoy and duration is normally 6 hrs. This is normally when vessels are most vulnerable."

[109] Marine Department of Hong Kong, "Chinese and Navy Escort in Gulf of Aden" (Security and Quality Advisory No. 13, 19 August 2010).

and crew on board, as well as ships carrying humanitarian relief material for international organizations, including the World Food Programme."[110] The Chinese Navy has escorted around three thousand merchant vessels since deploying the first unit to the region in 2009.[111]

The Hong Kong Maritime Rescue Coordination Centre (HKMRCC) receives ship movement reports and works with the escort arrangement to coordinate the convoy. Approximately 10 convoys are organized each month.[112] During the escort, vessels must comply with instructions given by Chinese escorting warships and must not make an early departure from the convoy without consent. The Marine Department adds that on "very vulnerable" ships armed Chinese naval officers may be offered to board; it recommends the master accept any such offer.[113]

Hong Kong registered ships seeking assistance from Chinese naval warships and ships scheduled to transit the Gulf of Aden are reminded of the need to submit a "ship movement report" via email to the HKMRCC.[114] An updated report came into use on 4 April 2011.[115] Information required by the report includes general ship and crew details such as Inmarsat numbers, draft and cargo; communications equipment; whether a security consultant is on board; whether any firearms or munitions are on board; whether there is a citadel on board; and the ship's present position, course and speed. Hong Kong shipowners of non-Hong Kong registered ships may also apply for Chinese naval escorts by applying directly to the Beijing Maritime Rescue Coordination Centre. Satellite phone numbers of the Chinese Navy ships in the Gulf of Aden are provided to all relevant parties.[116] It is also to be noted that the Best Management Practices (outlined below) require all vessel

---

110 Marine Department of Hong Kong, "New Movements Report for Ship on Entering and Leaving the Gulf of Aden and the Somali Waters" (Security and Quality Advisory No. 15, 16 March 2011). It is noted in the information circular that: "In this context, Chinese ships include ships registered in Hong Kong."

111 Li Yancheng, "Chinese Navy escorted over 3,000 merchant vessels in Gulf of Aden", *People's Daily Online*, 10 March 2011 <http://english.peopledaily.com.cn/98666/101812/101886/7314838.html>.

112 For instance, in June 2011 five Eastbound and five Westbound convoys were arranged: Marine Department of Hong Kong, "Chinese Naval Vessel Arrangement – Update" (Security Circular No. 6/2011, 20 May 2011).

113 Marine Department of Hong Kong, "Placing Security Personnel on Board Hong Kong Registered Ships" (Security and Quality Advisory No. 14, 16 February 2011).

114 Marine Department of Hong Kong, "New Movements Report for Ship on Entering and Leaving the Gulf of Aden and the Somali Waters" (Security and Quality Advisory No. 15, 16 March 2011).

115 Marine Department of Hong Kong, "New Movements Report for Ship on Entering and Leaving the Gulf of Aden and the Somali Waters" (Security and Quality Advisory No. 16, 4 April 2011).

116 *See*, eg, Marine Department of Hong Kong, "Recent Pirate Attempt to board Hong Kong Registered Ship" (Security and Quality Advisory No. 18, 23 May 2011) and Marine Department of Hong Kong, "Chinese Naval Vessel Arrangement – Update" (Security Circular No. 6/2011, 20 May 2011).

movements to be registered with MSCHOA when in the High Risk Area even if the vessel is part of a National Convoy such as the Chinese Naval Vessels Escort Arrangement.

D.4 Best Management Practices (BMP)

The Marine Department recommends shipowners apply the BMP guidance at all times when within known "piracy areas."[117] Further, it encourages registering with MSCHOA irrespective of the freeboard or speed of the ship. Prior to proceeding, a risk assessment should be undertaken; this should at the least analyse crew safety, freeboard, speed, sea state, and pirate activity but may vary depending on the particular vessel.[118] The three fundamental requirements of the BMP are (1) registering the vessel with MSCHOA, (2) reporting to the United Kingdom Maritime Trade Operations (UKMTO), and (3) implementing Ship Protection Measures. Company counter piracy planning is vital: according to the BMP, it is to be developed in line with the Ship Security Assessment and Ship Security Plan as required by the ISPS Code.[119] The plan should include procedures for a passage through the high risk area and a Company Security Officer (CSO) should ensure that it is exercised, briefed and discussed with the master and Ship Security Officer (SSO). Evidently the BMP, while containing detailed provisions on master's planning,[120] emphasises the company's role in counter piracy preparation.

It is essential under the BMP that ships liaise with the naval forces in the region such as MSCHOA, UKMTO and MARLO. "This is to ensure that Naval/Military forces are aware of the sea passage that a ship is about to embark upon and how vulnerable that ship is to pirate attack."[121]

D.5 Private Security Personnel on board Hong Kong registered ships

The Marine Department "encourages the carriage of experienced security consultants to assist in following BMP requirements."[122] The MSC, in its circular directed to governments, leaves the decision of whether or not to carry unarmed security personnel in the hands of individual shipowners, companies and operators.[123] Similarly, the BMP leaves it to the discretion of individual ship operators following a voyage risk assessment; and, of course, the national laws of the flag state must be considered. The guidance surmises

---

[117] Marine Department of Hong Kong, "New Movements Report for Ship on Entering and Leaving the Gulf of Aden and the Somali Waters" (Security and Quality Advisory No. 16, 4 April 2011).

[118] BMP pt 3.

[119] BMP pt 6.

[120] See BMP pt 7.

[121] BMP para 5.1. It is important that ships continue to advise of progress during the passage.

[122] Marine Department of Hong Kong, "Placing Security Personnel on Board Hong Kong Registered Ships" (Security and Quality Advisory No. 14, 16 February 2011).

[123] IMO Circular, Maritime Safety Committee, 86th sess, MSC/Circ. 1333 (26 June 2009) annex, para 6.

that "[t]he use of experienced and competent unarmed Private Maritime Security Contractors can be a valuable addition to BMP."[124] The principal justification appears to be that they give confidence to the crew in the event of a pirate attack. In at least some cases it appears these consultants provide anti-piracy training enroute to the Gulf and shift focus to attack prevention as the ship passes through it.

D.6 Possession of weapons on board Hong Kong registered ships

Circular 1406, approved by the MSC in September 2011, provides that "Flag States should have in place a policy on whether or not the use of PCASP [privately contracted armed security personnel] will be authorized and, if so, under which conditions."[125] The Marine Department does not encourage the carriage of weapons on board any Hong Kong registered ship.[126] There is a significant degree of sentiment throughout the industry which tends to the view that carriage of weapons will lead to an escalation of the severity of attacks. Nonetheless, "where ships are passing through known piracy areas with no naval protection and it is felt to be in the best interest of crew and ship safety and security to carry weapons," the Marine Department recommends that:

(i) a thorough due diligence is done on the security consultants, as there is no established organization to vet such companies;
(ii) the lawyers are consulted on the legal consequences and liabilities, especially in the event that innocent parties are injured;
(iii) all other parties involved in the voyage, such as charterers and insurers, are in agreement;
(iv) the line of command and rules of engagement are clearly understood and conform with the legal advice;
(v) the crew are fully briefed and consulted; and

---

[124] BMP para 8.14. The use of Private Maritime Security Contractors is only mentioned twice: once in the context of unarmed guards and once in respect of armed guards (para 8.15).

[125] IMO Circular, Maritime Safety Committee, MSC.1/Circ.1406/Rev.1 (16 September 2011) annex, para 5. If the use of PCASP is determined "appropriate and lawful", a policy should be established which may include: (1) the minimum criteria or minimum requirements with which PCASP should comply; (2) a process for authorizing the use of PCASP; (3) a process by which shipowners, ship operators or shipping companies may be authorized to use PCASP; (4) the terms and conditions under which the authorization is granted and the accountability for compliance with that authorization; (5) references to any directly applicable domestic laws pertaining to the carriage and use of firearms by PCASP, and the relationship of PCASP with the Master while on board; and (6) reporting and record-keeping requirements.

[126] Marine Department of Hong Kong, "Placing Security Personnel on Board Hong Kong Registered Ships" (Security and Quality Advisory No. 14, 16 February 2011). It does, however, recommend vulnerable vessels accept any offer by the Chinese Navy of armed Chinese naval officers as discussed above.

(vi) the weapons are possessed by the master, or by a person who is authorised by the owner or person in charge of the vessel to have such possession.[127]

Once the Department receives a request from the shipowners addressing the above points it will issue a letter for the carriage of weapons on board the vessel.[128]

VI. PRIVATE MARITIME SECURITY AND THE CARRIAGE OF WEAPONS ON BOARD SHIP

Of the 136 reported incidents of pirate attacks by EU NAVFOR since 10 January 2011, approximately 28 per cent have been repelled by the use of armed force from the merchant vessel.[129] It is not known whether there has been a corresponding increase in ferocity of attacks but over the same period more than a third of the attacks involved the firing of weapons by pirates.[130] The prevailing view throughout the industry is that on-board guards should not be armed: there is a risk that armed engagement will result in a greater number of injuries and/or fatalities and will escalate the use of dangerous, warlike weaponry.[131] The MSC has similarly recognised that the use of armed guards may result in the "possible escalation of violence" and that armed guards may become the targets rather than the ship and/or crew.[132] On the other hand, highlighting the industry's desire for better protection on board vessels, seamen's unions from Hong Kong, China, the Philippines, Singapore, Indonesia, Vietnam and Russia agreed at the Asian Seafarers' Summit in Hong Kong in August 2011 that their seafarers had the right to refuse to board ships sailing through "high-risk pirate areas."

---

[127] Marine Department of Hong Kong, "Placing Security Personnel on Board Hong Kong Registered Ships" (Security and Quality Advisory No. 14, 16 February 2011).

[128] *Ibid*: the Marine Department notes that "confidentiality regarding this matter is beneficial to the safety of the ship and crew involved". The BMP recommendations on the use of PMSC is discussed below.

[129] Based on known details published by EU NAVFOR to 6 November 2011: "Weekly Piracy Incident Summary: 10 January – 6 November 2011" available at <http://www.eunavfor.eu>. EU NAVFOR does not specify if the use of armed force from the merchant vessel is attributable to military or private armed guards. Furthermore, it should be noted that many of the details provided in the Weekly Incident Summary are basic and little if any details are known of vessels that are successfully pirated.

[130] The MSC expressed concern in the report of its latest meeting that "in many of the reports received [for the period 1 January to 31 December 2010], the crews had been violently attacked": "Report of the Maritime Safety Committee on its Eighty-Ninth Session", MSC, 89th sess, Agenda item 25, MSC 89/25 (27 May 2011) p 74.

[131] See, eg, "Security guards in the Indian Ocean – to arm or not to arm?" (Hellas HiLights, UK P&I Club publication, July 2011, issue 21) p 7.

[132] IMO Circular, Maritime Safety Committee, MSC.1/Circ.1406/Rev.1 (16 September 2011) annex, para 3.

The possession of weapons and/or armed guards on board ships creates new problems. The latest edition of the BMP avoids recommending or endorsing the use of armed guards:

> 8.15 Armed Private Maritime Security Contactors *(sic)*
>
> The use, or not, of armed Private Maritime Security Contractors onboard merchant vessels is a matter for individual ship operators to decide following their own voyage risk assessment and approval of respective Flag States. This advice does not constitute a recommendation or an endorsement of the general use of armed Private Maritime Security Contractors.
>
> Subject to risk analysis, careful planning and agreements the provision of Military Vessel Protection Detachments (VPDs) deployed to protect vulnerable shipping is the recommended option when considering armed guards.
>
> If armed Private Maritime Security Contractors are to be used they must be as an additional layer of protection and not as an alternative to BMP.
>
> If armed Private Maritime Security Contractors are present on board a merchant vessel, this fact should be included in reports to UKMTO and MSCHOA.
>
> The International Maritime Organisation (IMO) have produced guidance in the form of IMO Circulars for ship operators and Masters and for Flag States on the use of Private Maritime Security Contractors on board ships in the High Risk Area.
>
> The current IMO Guidance on the use of armed Private Maritime Security Contractors is included on the MSCHOA website. (www.mschoa.org)[133]

This is a shift from the wording adopted in the third edition of the BMP which provided: "The use of additional private security guards is at the discretion of the company, but the use of armed guards is not recommended."[134] It is clearly an issue the BMP would rather leave to ship operators. In its twelfth report in the 2009-10 parliamentary session, the House of Lords' European Union Committee considered the issue of armed guards on board merchant vessels. The Committee endorsed "the view of the shipping industry, the IMO and the [UK] Government" that

---

[133] BMP para 8.15. This paragraph did not appear in the third edition of the BMP.

[134] BMP (3rd ed) para 6.11.

private security guards should not be placed on commercial shipping as this would increase the risks to which the ships and crew were subject. However, military personnel from national armed forces are occasionally placed on commercial shipping on a case-by-case basis, and we believe this should continue. The Government and the EU should ensure that any such personnel receive prior specialised training to a high standard for this role.[135]

It appears the position adopted in the United Kingdom will change as legislation is now proposed to licence armed guards on board commercial ships.[136] Notwithstanding the reluctance of organisations and governments to endorse the use of armed guards, because of the increased interest in and use of them, especially in armed conflict situations,[137] the international community has introduced a non-binding compilation of international laws, recommendations and good practices. These are relevant to the use of private security consultants in the maritime context.[138]

The UNCLOS extends state sovereignty to its territorial sea.[139] Furthermore, ships have the nationality of the state whose flag they are entitled to fly;[140] ships must sail under the flag of one state only and are, generally, subject to the exclusive jurisdiction of that state on the high seas.[141] Consequently the flag state's laws are critical to consider – private security guards will be subject to them.

---

[135] European Union Committee, *Combating Somali Piracy: the EU's Naval Operation Atalanta*, House of Lords Twelfth Report, Session 2009-10 (6 April 2010) para 50. See also Transport Committee, *Piracy*, House of Commons Eighth Report, Session 2005-06 (28 June 2006).

[136] Specific information is, as at the time of writing, unavailable. Details of British Prime Minister David Cameron's announcement are accessible at "Somali piracy: Armed guards to protect UK ships", BBC News (30 October 2011) <http://www.bbc.co.uk/news/uk-15510467> as at 12 November 2011. This is despite the government apparently endorsing the report of the European Union Committee, stating "The Government supports the view that armed security companies should not be used by the shipping industry to counter pirates": Foreign and Commonwealth Office, Letter to the Chairman of the House of Lords' EU Committee signed by Nicholas Harvey MP, Minister for the Armed Forces and David Lidington MP, Minister for Europe (undated).

[137] See, eg, Carolin Liss, "Private Security Companies in the Fight Against Piracy in Asia" (Working Paper No. 120, Asia Research Centre, Murdoch University, June 2005); IMO Circular, Maritime Safety Committee, MSC.1/Circ.1405/Rev.1 (16 September 2011) annex, para 2; Dana M Parsons, "Protecting the Booty: Creating a Regulatory Framework To Govern Increased Use of Private Security Companies in the Fight Against Pirates" (2010) 35 *Tulane Maritime Law Journal* 153, p 170.

[138] As noted above, para 8.15 of the BMP states "The International Maritime Organisation (IMO) have produced guidance in the form of IMO Circulars for ship operators and Masters and for Flag States on the use of Private Maritime Security Contractors on board ships in the High Risk Area. The current IMO Guidance on the use of armed Private Maritime Security Contractors is included on the MSCHOA website. (www.mschoa.org)".

[139] *United Nations Convention on the Law of the Sea*, opened for signature 10 December 1982, 1833 UNTS 3 (entered into force 16 November 1994) ("UNCLOS") art 2.

[140] Article 91.

[141] Article 92.

An appropriate starting point, however, is a consideration of the relevant MSC Circulars. At its 89th session, the Maritime Safety Committee of the IMO approved original Circulars 1405 and 1406 which provided interim guidance to shipowners, ship operators and ship masters, and flag states, respectively, concerning the use of PCASP on board vessels in the high risk area. They have recently been revised and replaced.[142] Circular 1406 reiterates that the IMO does not endorse the use of PCASP[143] on board ships, but due to the difficulty shipping companies may have in finding reliable and professional armed security providers, the guidance may be useful. The United Kingdom P&I Club notes that the circulars are based on guidelines produced by the industry.[144] The circulars were developed taking into account guidance contained in MSC Circulars 1334 and 1333[145] but did not explicitly replace or revoke them because the latter contain broader recommendations for preventing and suppressing piracy and armed robbery against ships. As far as we can ascertain, Circulars 1405 and 1406 represent the first time in which the MSC has issued "interim" guidance: when compared with the statements contained in the earlier circulars, a shift in industry needs is clearly identifiable. It is therefore useful to first refer to the more general circulars.

In May 2011 the MSC "reaffirmed its position that it did not endorse the use of armed personnel on board merchant ships."[146] Ultimately, and especially in light of the BMP guidelines, it seems the issue is left with some ambiguity to accommodate the needs of certain shipowners. The salient points of Circular 1333, entitled "Recommendations to Governments for preventing and suppressing piracy and armed robbery against ships", are outlined by the Report of the MSC's 89th Session:[147]

---

[142] MSC.1/Circ.1405/Rev.1 and MSC.1/Circ.1406/Rev.1 both dated 16 September 2011.

[143] Defined as "armed employees of PMSC." PMSC means private maritime security companies, defined as "private contractors employed to provide security personnel, both armed and unarmed, on board for protection against piracy": IMO Circular, Maritime Safety Committee, MSC.1/Circ.1405/Rev.1 (16 September 2011) annex, para 1.1.

[144] See "Industry Guidelines for the Use of Private Maritime Security Contractors (PMSC) as Additional Protection in Waters Affected by Somali Piracy" (Guidelines produced by BIMO, ICS, Intercargo, Intertanko, OCIMF and IG P&I Clubs for their members, May 2011) <http://www.ukpandi.com/fileadmin/uploads/uk-pi/Latest_Publications/Circulars/Industry%20PMSC%20Final%20May%202011.pdf> as at 22 August 2011.

[145] See, eg, IMO Circular, Maritime Safety Committee, MSC.1/Circ.1405 (23 May 2011) para 2.

[146] "Report of the Maritime Safety Committee on its Eighty-Ninth Session", MSC, 89th sess, Agenda item 25, MSC 89/25 (27 May 2011) p 81.

[147] "Report of the Maritime Safety Committee on its Eighty-Ninth Session", MSC, 89th sess, Agenda item 25, MSC 89/25 (27 May 2011) p 78. *See* also IMO Circular, Maritime Safety Committee, 86th sess, MSC/Circ. 1333 (26 June 2009).

- For legal and safety reasons, flag States should strongly discourage the carrying and use of firearms by seafarers for personal protection or for the protection of a ship (Circular 1333, para 5);
- The use of unarmed security personnel is a matter for individual shipowners, companies, and ship operators to decide (Circular 1333, para 6);
- The use of privately contracted armed security personnel on board ships may lead to an escalation of violence. The carriage of such personnel and their weapons is subject to flag State legislation and policies and is a matter for flag States to determine in consultation with shipowners, companies and ship operators, if and under which conditions this will be allowed. Flag States should take into account the possible escalation of violence which could result from carriage of armed personnel on board merchant ships, when deciding on its policy (Circular 1333, para 7); and
- The use of military, or law enforcement officers duly authorized by the Government of the flag State to carry firearms for the security of the ship is a matter for the flag State to authorize in consultation with shipowners, companies, and ship operators. Flag States should provide clarity of their policy on the use of such teams on board vessels entitled to fly their flag (Circular 1333, para 8).

If PCASP are to be deployed on a vessel transiting the high risk area, the guidance provided in Circular 1405 should be followed. Member Governments are "recommended to bring this circular to the attention" of agencies associated with anti-piracy activities and shipowners, operators, masters, crews and shipping companies.[148] Circular 1405 neatly summarises the problem facing flag States, shipowners, operators and masters in its introduction:[149]

> The decision on the employment of PCASP on board ships is a complex one for a ship owner. The absence of applicable regulation and industry self-regulation coupled with complex legal requirements governing the legitimate transport, carriage and use of firearms gives cause for concern. This situation is further complicated by the rapid growth in the number of private maritime security companies (PMSC) and doubts about the capabilities and maturity of some of these

[148] IMO Circular, Maritime Safety Committee, MSC.1/Circ.1405/Rev.1 (16 September 2011) para 5. Member Governments are "also urged to take any necessary action to implement, as appropriate, the interim guidance given in the annex". It is worthwhile to note that the revised circular has used the word "urged" whereas the original used "recommended".

[149] IMO Circular, Maritime Safety Committee, MSC.1/Circ.1405/Rev.1 (16 September 2011) annex 1, para 1 (footnote omitted).

companies. Significant competence and quality variations are present across the spectrum of contractors offering services.

Circular 1406 applies to flag states. As the circulars are revised interim guidance only, the MSC asks Governments, international organisations and non-governmental organisations to report on results of the experience gained in using the recommendations.

The circulars provide non-binding guidance for the employment of PCASPs and are not an alternative to the BMP. Initially a risk assessment process should be undertaken including consideration of any flag state requirements. Circular 1405 details criteria for selecting PMSCs and the guidance appears to be generally consistent with the *Montreux Document* recommendations (discussed below):[150]

(i) The usual due diligence must be undertaken covering company structure and place of registration, company ownership, financial position, extent of insurance cover, senior management experience and quality management indicators.

(ii) The company's background must be investigated. For example, the PMSC should be able to produce documentary evidence showing maritime experience, written procedures on topics such as chain of authority, responsibilities, etc., understanding of the flag State and coastal State requirements with respect to carriage and use of firearms, availability of written testimonials and references from previous clients in the maritime industry, availability of documentary evidence showing the legality of firearms carried on board, understanding of the Somalia-based piracy threat, understanding of BMP and in particular ship protection measures, and access to legal advice on a 24 hour basis.

(iii) The PMSC should demonstrate that they have policies and procedures for determining the suitability of employees.

(iv) PCASPs should be appropriately trained. It is critical that the company has adequate training procedures in place.

The Security Association for the Maritime Industry (SAMI) is presently working to develop standards and accreditation processes for PMSCs in line with the IMO guidance.[151]

It is important to consider how the deployment of a PCASP may impact on the shipowner's property and liability insurance cover.[152] It is suggested that

[150] The PMSC Selection Criteria is outlined in annex 1, para 2 of the Circular.

[151] For more information refer to <http://seasecurity.org/standards-accreditation>.

[152] Para 3.1.

shipowners consult with insurers prior to contracting with and embarking PCASP. The security company to be engaged should provide evidence of public and employer's liability insurance cover to an appropriate level in addition to personal accident, medical expenses, hospitalization and repatriation insurance. The UK P&I Club suggests that whether or not P&I cover is prejudiced by having armed guards on board is "likely to be dependent on the cause of loss on a case-by-case basis."[153] It is suggested the use of armed guards is unlikely to prejudice the cover unless the use is contrary to flag or port state regulations. Another factor to be considered is the size and composition of the PCASP team and the equipment the team will carry. Finally, the Circular considers the relationship between the PMSC and the master, the management of firearms and ammunition, rules for the use of force, and reporting and record keeping. Command and control structure, including any interaction with the master, is a critical element of the PMSC engagement and must be documented. The shipowner should ensure the master and crew are briefed and exercises planned and conducted so that roles and responsibilities are understood.

In terms of managing firearms and ammunition, the Circular records certain issues that must be addressed.[154] Any flag state requirements must be complied with, control procedures for the safe storage of firearms and ammunition should be in place, and detailed and exercised orders for when firearms can be loaded and "made ready" for use should be "confirmed, trained and documented." The rules for the use of force must be understood and followed.[155] All reasonable steps must be taken to avoid the use of force but if it is used, it should be "in a manner consistent with applicable law." In no case should it exceed what is strictly necessary – it should be "proportionate to the threat and appropriate to the situation."[156]

Under Hong Kong criminal law, self-defence and defence of persons or property operates as a defence to a charge of assault. An assault is any act which intentionally or recklessly causes another to apprehend immediate and unlawful personal violence.[157] There must be more than mere words[158] but

---

[153] "Security guards in the Indian Ocean – to arm or not to arm?" (Hellas HiLights, UK P&I Club publication, July 2011, issue 21) p 7. The Club recommends members consult fully with the War Risk insurers before entering into any arrangement.

[154] Para 3.4.

[155] Para 3.5.

[156] Para 3.5 of the Circular seems to provide further guidance by stating "PMSC should require that their personnel not use firearms against persons except in self-defence or defence of others against the imminent threat of death or serious injury, or to prevent the perpetration of a particularly serious crime involving grave threat to life."

[157] *Fagan v Metropolitan Police Commissioner* [1969] 1 QB 439.

[158] *Lam Leung-ping v R* (unreported; Crim App 579/1977).

almost certainly the pointing of a gun at a person will constitute an assault.[159] The critical element required to establish the defence is that no more is done than is necessary; and this has traditionally involved the concept of "reasonable force."[160] While this area of the criminal law is vexed, a few points may be distilled. "A person can use force to ward off an anticipated attack provided that it is anticipated as 'imminent.'"[161] In this sense, a pre-emptive strike may be permissible in certain circumstances. Furthermore, a person may act to protect his property from an "unlawful or criminal act."[162] In respect of the defence of one's house it has been noted that "[f]orceful resistance would no doubt be in order (which might unintentionally cause death) but deliberate killing would normally be hard to justify."[163] Underlying these principles is the overriding proviso concerning the degree of force permitted: disproportionate force will not be tolerated.[164]

In Hong Kong, s 13 of the Firearms and Munitions Ordinance makes it an offence for a person to have in his possession any arms or ammunition unless he holds a licence for it.[165] However, that section does not apply to the possession of arms or ammunition by the owner or person in charge of a vessel, or by a person who is authorized by the owner or person in charge of a vessel to have such possession, if the arms or ammunition (a) are carried on a vessel other than a specified vessel;[166] (b) are part of the equipment reasonably required to be carried on such vessel for the protection of life or property; and (c) remain at all times on the vessel while it is in Hong Kong.[167] Further, s 13 does not apply to the carriage of firearms on board a foreign ship so long as the person who holds them is authorised by the

---

[159] *R v Tsang Cheong* (1950) 34 HKLR 276.

[160] *See*, eg, *Williams* [1987] 3 All ER 411, 414. In *Beckford v R* [1988] AC 130, Lord Griffiths stated the test in these terms: "a person may use such force as is reasonable in the circumstances as he honestly believes them to be in the defence of himself or another".

[161] The Right Honourable Lord Justice Hooper and David Ormerod (general eds), *Blackstone's Criminal Practice 2010* (Oxford University Press, 20th ed, 2009) 56 referring to *Chisam* (1963) 47 Cr App R 130.

[162] *Ibid* 56 referring to *DPP v Bayer* [2004] 1 WLR 2856.

[163] *Ibid.*

[164] It is not the purpose of this article to fully canvass this area of the law. For further information refer to the Right Honourable Lord Justice Hooper and David Ormerod (general eds), *Blackstone's Criminal Practice 2010* (Oxford University Press, 20th ed, 2009) 54-60.

[165] Cap 238. A person who contravenes the section is liable to a fine of $100,000 and imprisonment for 14 years.

[166] Means a regular river trade vessel, fishing vessel, vessel used for pleasure purposes, vessel used in navigation solely in the waters of Hong Kong, etc.

[167] Firearms and Munitions Ordinance (Hong Kong) cap 238, s 5.

appropriate authority having jurisdiction over the ship and that they remain on the ship while it is in Hong Kong.[168]

The relevant wording has not been judicially considered. It is unclear, therefore, whether the words "reasonably required . . . for the protection of life or property" align with the Marine Department's recommendation as discussed above: "where ships are passing through known piracy areas with no naval protection and it is felt to be in the best interest of crew and ship safety and security to carry weapons." It would be prudent for those involved in any security and safety assessment to consider both. Detailed procedures governing the use, control and possession of the weapon/s on board the vessel would similarly be advantageous, especially in light of the IMO MSC Circulars.

An additional relevant, non-binding piece of guidance is the *Montreux Document.*[169] An initiative of the Swiss Government and International Committee of the Red Cross (ICRC), the *Montreux Document* draws on the experience of 17 governments across the world to address legal concerns arising from the use of private military and security companies.[170] It is not law but it seeks to clarify legal obligations and furnish guidance for states: indeed "[t]he heart of the *Montreux Document* lies in its recommended good practices."[171] Notwithstanding that it focuses on armed conflict, the Preface to the Document outlines certain "understandings" that guided its development. Paragraph 5 provides: "[t]hat existing obligations and good practices may also be instructive for post-conflict situations and for other, comparable situations; however, that international humanitarian law is applicable only during armed conflict."

In the first part of the *Montreux Document*, "existing international legal obligations of States regarding private military and security companies" are

---

[168] Firearms and Munitions Ordinance (Hong Kong) cap 238, s 7. It should be noted that the UNCLOS, art 27 provides that the criminal jurisdiction of a coastal State is only to be exercised on board a foreign ship in certain circumstances: (a) if the consequences of the crime extend to the coastal State; (b) if the crime is of a kind to disturb the peace of the country or the good order of the territorial sea; (c) if the assistance of the local authorities has been requested by the master of the ship or by a diplomatic agent or consular officer of the flag State; or (d) if such measures are necessary for the suppression of illicit traffic in narcotic drugs or psychotropic substances.

[169] *Montreux Document: On pertinent international legal obligations and good practices for States related to operations of private military and security companies during armed conflict* , International Committee of the Red Cross (17 September 2008).

[170] The document was finalized by consensus on 17 September 2008 by 17 States.

[171] Dana M Parsons, "Protecting the Booty: Creating a Regulatory Framework To Govern Increased Use of Private Security Companies in the Fight Against Pirates" (2010) 35 *Tulane Maritime Law Journal* 153, p 173 (emphasis added for consistency). The learned author also discusses the Document's limitations pointing out that it is directed to the employment of Private Security Contractors by government bodies.

distilled.[172] The part is organised into obligations relevant to Contracting States (states directly contracting for services), Territorial States (states on whose territory the private military and security companies operate) and Home States (nationality state of a private military and security companies). In addition to the obligations of those states, "all other States" have an obligation to ensure respect for international humanitarian law by implementing legislative and other measures to give effect to them.[173] In the second part of the Document, good practices are covered. Provisions cover contracting and selection (including criteria which is arguably useful for shipowners and operators),

Maritime piracy is an area where the *Montreux Document* may be relevant: the Document acknowledges that one example of its applicability "is the contracting of private military and security companies to protect merchant shipping against acts of piracy."[174] One author suggests its applicability to the use of armed guards on ships stems from the Document's practicality, its "not overly limiting or exclusive" language, and the benefit that shipowners may derive from referring to its good practices guidelines.[175] Reference to the good practices would potentially be very useful in establishing an overall SSP incorporating the armed guards, selection of security providers, drafting contractual terms, and developing rules of engagement and authority. Naturally the Document will be useful regardless of whether or not the security consultants are to be armed. Some private security companies have gone a step further in signing an *International Code of Conduct for Private Security Service Providers*.[176]

Finally, the MSC has published interim recommendations for port and coastal states regarding the use of PCASP on board ships in the high risk area.[177] Circular 1408 is a response to the need to develop recommendations

---

[172] *Montreux Document: On pertinent international legal obligations and good practices for States related to operations of private military and security companies during armed conflict* , International Committee of the Red Cross (17 September 2008) p 11.

[173] *Montreux Document: On pertinent international legal obligations and good practices for States related to operations of private military and security companies during armed conflict* , International Committee of the Red Cross (17 September 2008) part 1(D), paras 18-19.

[174] *Montreux Document: On pertinent international legal obligations and good practices for States related to operations of private military and security companies during armed conflict* , International Committee of the Red Cross (17 September 2008) p 39.

[175] Christopher Spearin, "A private security solution to Somali Piracy?" (2010) 63(4) *Naval War College Review* 56, pp 65-6. The Document was considered at the IMO MSC's latest meeting in May 2011: IMO MSC, 89th sess, Agenda item 18, MSC 89/INF.20 (8 March 2011).

[176] The Code was signed by 58 security companies in Geneva on 9 November 2010. Its aims include establishing objective and measurable standards for providing security services, and establishing external independent mechanisms for effective governance and oversight. See further: < http://www.icoc-psp.org/>.

[177] IMO Circular, Maritime Safety Committee, MSC.1/Circ.1408 (16 September 2011).

related to the embarkation, disembarkation and carriage of PCASP and the associated firearms and security-related equipment. While the circular explicitly does not address all the legal issues, it urges governments (specifically the governments of port and coastal States bordering the Indian Ocean, Arabian Sea, Gulf of Aden and Red Sea) to "have in place relevant policies and related procedures" to "facilitate the movement of PCASP and of their firearms and security-related equipment."[178] The policies and procedures should be disseminated to the IMO, shipping industry and PCASP service providers. In recognising that this area of the law is under development in many jurisdictions, Circular 1408 encourages governments to establish policies and procedures, consistent with international law and which do not hinder the continuation of maritime trade nor interfere with the navigation of ships, that take into account a number of considerations outlined in the circular.[179]

VII. OTHER ISSUES

A. Master's control of the vessel

Determining at the outset any conflict between the master's control of the vessel and the security consultant's, security guard's or naval force's responsibilities is necessary. Complications may arise owing to the operation of the SOLAS Regulations. Regulation 8(1) provides that "[t]he master shall not be constrained by the Company, the charterer or any other person from taking or executing any decision which, in the professional judgement of the master, is necessary to maintain the safety and security of the ship."[180] The International Ship and Port Facilities Security (ISPS) Code also clarifies that "[a]t all times the Master of a ship has the ultimate responsibility for the safety and security of the ship."[181] The fourth edition of the BMP do emphasise the overall discretion of the master.[182] From a practical point of

---

[178] IMO Circular, Maritime Safety Committee, MSC.1/Circ.1408 (16 September 2011) annex 1, para 5.

[179] IMO Circular, Maritime Safety Committee, MSC.1/Circ.1408 (16 September 2011) annex 1, paras 6-7. The considerations are bracketed under "Embarkation", "Disembarkation" and "Vessel calling".

[180] *International Convention for the Safety of Life at Sea*, opened for signature 1 November 1974 (entered into force 25 May 1980) (as amended) ch XI-2 (*'SOLAS Convention'*).

[181] *See* Guidance Regarding the Provisions of Chapter XI-2 of the Annex to the *SOLAS Convention* as amended, pt 4.10.

[182] In the introduction to BMP (p 2) a red box contains the following text: "Nothing in this booklet detracts from the Master's overriding authority to protect his crew, ship and cargo." MSC Circular 1332, which brought the original BMP guidelines to the attention of States, provided: "Nothing in the attached BMP should be read as limiting the Master's authority to take action deemed necessary by the Master to protect the lives of passengers and crew": IMO Circular, Maritime Safety Committee, 86th sess, MSC/Circ. 1332 (16 June 2009). Circular 1337, which brought the third edition of the BMP to the attention of States did not contain a similar statement (but it did not revoke Circular 1332): IMO Circular, Maritime Safety Committee, 87th sess, MSC/Circ. 1337 (4 August 2010).

view, if a ship is carrying experienced security personnel or navy personnel, it may be difficult for a master to enforce control during a pirate attack.[183]

The IMO MSC's Circular 1405 is a response to a conclusion by the Working Group on Maritime Security including Piracy and Armed Robbery against Ships (MSPWG) that "it was important to include, in contract documentation, a clear statement that at all times the master remains in command and retains the overriding authority on board."[184] As noted above, Circular 1405 contains a section on "Command and Control of Onboard Security Team – including relationship with the Master."[185] There must exist a "documented command and control structure" which provides "[a] clear statement that at all times the Master remains in command and retains the overriding authority on board"; "list of duties, expected conduct, behaviour and documentation of PCASP actions on board"; and "transparent two-way information flow and recognizable coordination and cooperation between the shipowner, charterer, PCASP, PMSC and the vessel's Master, officers and crew." Additionally, shipowners should ensure that the Master and crew are familiar with the guidance provided in Circular 1405.[186]

B. *Non-compliance with Best Management Practice guidelines and MSC Circulars*

Non-compliance with BMP and anti-piracy recommendations is concerning. The issue was raised at the IMO MSC's latest session in May 2011.[187] It has been reported that a "startling" number of "vessels and flag states are failing to comply with anti-piracy measures." [188] The report suggested, between September and November 2010, over three quarters of Hong Kong-flag ships were observed not to be following best management practices. A circular letter sent to all IMO members, UN and specialized

---

183 It is arguable though that the "Master's authority to take action deemed necessary by the Master to protect the lives of passengers and crew" could extend to transferring this authority to a more appropriate person on board the vessel. However, this issue is unclear. Captain Richard Phillips, the captain of the *Maersk Alabama*, which was attacked by pirates in April 2009, told the US Senate Committee on Foreign Relations "...I am not comfortable giving up command authority to others… including the commander of a protection force. In the heat of an attack, there can be only one final decision maker.": Statement of Captain Richard Phillips to the Senate Committee on Foreign Relations Hearing, *Confronting Piracy off the Coast of Somalia*, 30 April 2009.

184 "Report of the Maritime Safety Committee on its Eighty-Ninth Session", MSC, 89th sess, Agenda item 25, MSC 89/25 (27 May 2011) para 18.55.

185 IMO Circular, Maritime Safety Committee, MSC.1/Circ.1405/Rev.1 (16 September 2011) para 3.3.

186 Para 3.9: "Shipowners and ship operators should ensure that the Master and the crew receive familiarization in relation to this guidance".

187 *See* "Report of the Maritime Safety Committee on its Eighty-Ninth Session", MSC, 89th sess, Agenda item 25, MSC 89/25 (27 May 2011) p 73.

188 "Owners face being named and shamed", *InterManager News* (online), 11 March 2011 < http://www.intermanager.org/Resources/News/tabid/82/mid/500/newsid500/673/Default.aspx>.

agencies, intergovernmental organisations, and NGOs on 14 February 2011 adds:[189]

> Naval forces operating in the region off the coast of Somalia have reported that an unacceptably high proportion of the ships transiting the Gulf of Aden are not registered with the [MSCHOA]; are not reporting to UKMTO Dubai; show no visible deterrent measures and are not acting upon the navigational warnings to shipping promulgating details of pirate attacks and suspect vessels.

The Hong Kong Shipowners Association (HKSOA) has taken proactive steps to increase compliance with BMP. HKSOA receives a daily report which identifies Hong Kong vessels in the High Risk Zone that are not registered with MSCHOA. The Association attempts contact with the unregistered vessels and reiterates the requirement under BMP to register with MSCHOA even if the vessel is part of a convoy.

The issue should be a concern to local shipowners, operators and masters. The cause of the problem is not immediately evident. It could stem from the ever-increasing supply of recommendations, BMP guidelines and requirements of the various anti-piracy organisations. A shift toward consolidation and simplification may ultimately materialise.

VIII. CONCLUSION

The voluminous supply of statistics from numerous international organisations confirms the serious threat piracy poses to the world's merchant shipping fleet from economic, trade and crew-safety perspectives. Although the economic cost of piracy is notoriously difficult to accurately ascertain, it is unquestionably significant.[190] Recent piratic activity involving the use of armed force by pirates and attacks on vessels in port demonstrates the problem is far from coming under control despite the best efforts of international task-forces, navies and industry organisations. The mechanisms by which the international community is confronting piracy includes anti-piracy task-forces generally established in piracy prone areas, such as the IMB Piracy Reporting Centre, ReCAAP, MSCHOA and EU NAVFOR, NATO and the Combined Maritime Forces. Additionally, industry organisations and the IMO have published guidance concerning anti-piracy measures and best practices, including use of the Internationally

---

[189] International Maritime Organization, Circular letter No. 3164 (14 February 2011, Ref. T2-MSS 2.11.7) p 3 (references omitted).

[190] *See* Anna Bowden et al, "The Economic Cost of Maritime Piracy" (One Earth Future Working Paper, Oceans Beyond Piracy, December 2010). The paper estimates that maritime piracy is costing the international economy between USD$7 to $12 billion annually.

Recommended Transit Corridor in the Gulf of Aden, carriage of firearms and armed guards on board merchant vessels, recommended anti-piracy measures to be adopted on ships, and various other recommendations for States.

The evidence of vessels continuing to be at risk demonstrates the desperation and tenacity of the pirates. It is unsurprising therefore that industry is searching for better methods of protecting vessels, most notably the carriage of firearms and/or privately contracted armed security personnel. The issue is largely a grey area according to IMO MSC guidance and industry recommendations such as the BMP. There is the potential for an escalation of violence; and even if recommendations are followed, there is no guidance as to the legal consequences for the guards, crew, shipowners and the relevant states involved. No international conventions or regulations deal with the level of force that may be used to defend against a pirate attack. Thus it seems the best a shipowner can do is a thorough due diligence and risk assessment process involving, at least, consideration of national flag state laws[191] and all relevant policies, guidelines and recommendations – not an entirely easy task.[192]

Hong Kong is a leading international shipping centre – its shipping registry is ranked in the top 10 of the world's largest and its container port is the world's third busiest. It is an active participant in ReCAAP, its Marine Department regularly publishes piracy updates for the attention of masters, crew, shipowners and company security officers, and it promotes the use of China's naval escort through the Gulf of Aden. The advice and updates provided generally appear to be consistent with IMO MSC guidance and other international recommendations such as the *Montreux Document*. Despite the actions Hong Kong has taken, there remains a degree of uncertainty surrounding the use of private security personnel and armed guards, and the carriage of weapons on board vessels. The desire to carry armed guards and weapons may indicate that shipowners, charterers and crew are pessimistic about the effectiveness of the international community's current efforts and that owners are doing everything they can to protect their seafarers. However this may be, the fact that the IMO and BMP discourage the use of armed guards is significant. The Marine Department of Hong Kong has arguably tried to find a balance in empowering shipowners with

[191] UNCLOS art 94(1) requires every State to exercise its jurisdiction and control in administrative, technical and social matters over ships flying its flag. Shipowners would be prudent to also consider the laws of the State in which it is incorporated as well as the laws of the States at which the vessel will call (MSC Circular 1408 alludes to the latter issue).

[192] The UK may clarify the position of the carriage of firearms and use of armed guards on board merchant vessels in legislation foreshadowed by Prime Minister David Cameron in October 2011. Apart from that, in most jurisdictions the area is uncertain,

the option of carrying weapons (provided certain conditions are satisfied). The lack of regulation surrounding the use of Private Security Contractors exacerbates the risks for shipowners and companies engaging them.[193] Moreover, the preeminence of the Master's role in a legal sense complicates the use of Private Security Contractors and the presence of naval forces on board a vessel.

Piracy and armed robbery against ships remain major threats to international shipping centres such as Hong Kong. There appears to be a general consensus on how best to deal with piracy: the BMP and IMO Circulars are useful, but the identifiable ambiguity in the recommendations does not assist shipowners and security officers in clarifying their legal responsibilities. Whether many companies will adopt the measures promoted by individual registries, in addition to the BMP and the IMO MSC guidance, remains to be seen. The economic consequences and human cost of piracy must not be forgotten. The imperative to clarify ambiguities and promote further proactive measures by major shipping registries now exists.

[193] *See* further Dana M Parsons, "Protecting the Booty: Creating a Regulatory Framework To Govern Increased Use of Private Security Companies in the Fight Against Pirates" (2010) 35 *Tulane Maritime Law Journal* 153, p 177.

8. THE INDIAN SUBCONTINENT AND COUNTER-PIRACY: THE INDIAN PERSPECTIVE

Fozia NAZIR LONE[1]

I. INTRODUCTION: INDIA'S RISE IN THE WORLD COMMUNITY

India is a nation that was born of turbulent times after the Second World War. It is a land of a peculiar combination of enigmas, oddities and versatile resilience. From a geographical standpoint, India is situated at a strategic position between the Arabian Sea (Strait of Hormuz and Gulf of Aden) and the South China Sea (Strait of Malacca). With shifting global geopolitics, and the economic rise of the East, India has a remarkable opportunity to carve out for herself a place alongside the other powerful nations of the world – and their navies. India, being a democracy, remains the best bet for the United States in the region to counter China's growing economic and maritime power and presence, which are alarming to the global community. This might be the defining moment for India to demonstrate her viability and strength. The Prime Minster of India, Dr. Manmohan Singh underscores this:

> India's growing international stature gives it strategic relevance in the area ranging from the Persian Gulf to the Strait of Malacca. . . . India has exploited the fluidities of the emerging world order to forge new links through a combination of diplomatic repositioning, economic resurgence and military firmness.[2]

In her early years of existence, India adopted a policy of non-alignment in international affairs and survived, despite poverty and a lack of social development. During the Cold War era, India took a pro-Soviet position and distanced herself from the Association of Southeast Asian Nations (ASEAN) member states. However, in the 1990s, with the rise of Chinese influence, India recognized ASEAN's importance and launched her "Look East" policy, focusing to become actively engaged in Southeast Asian affairs in the post-

---

[1] Assistant Professor City University of Hong Kong School of Law.

[2] Cited in Admiral Sureesh Mehta (Chief of the Naval Staff), *Freedom to Use the Seas: India's Maritime Military Strategy* (India: Integrated Headquarters of Defence (Navy) 2007. Available at http://indiannavy.nic.in/maritime_strat.pdf. Accessed on 26th Feb 2012

Cold War era.[3] Today, India is transforming herself and is capable of acting multilaterally, unilaterally or bilaterally, which shows her versatility. India's interest in increasing her maritime capabilities is partly due to her worries of China's maritime expansion, which now reaches into the Indian Ocean. India may also be concerned about a potential hegemonic China, which has a long history of close cooperation with Russia, a nation that has championed freedom of navigation.[4] During the term of President Bush, India signed a series of international cooperation agreements with the U.S., which promised to bring India into a new strategic relationship with China.

India is now perceived as a power balance against China. India is aware of the rise of China and its power projection on the ocean; in reaction India is seeking developmental partners to project its own maritime power. For this reason India has intensified its bilateral anti-piracy cooperation with the Seychelles. Recently New Delhi became nervous with China's increased incursion into the Seychelles.[5] Last year the Seychelles offered China its harbour for refueling and stocking of Chinese warships stationed in the Gulf of Aden for anti-piracy operations. Manmohan Singh held talks on 2 February 2012 with President James Alix Michel of the Seychelles, who was in India for the *12th Delhi Sustainable Development Summit*, which focused on security issues, piracy and ways to expand developmental cooperation between the two countries. Defence cooperation between India and the Seychelles has been growing. Last year the Indian Navy deployed a *Dornier* maritime surveillance aircraft in the Seychelles for conducting anti-piracy operations in the Indian Ocean Region. The aircraft, stationed at the Seychelles' capital, Victoria, was to be operated by an Indian Navy crew on anti-piracy patrol duties in the Indian Ocean Region.

II. A HISTORY OF EASTERN PIRACY

In an historical sense, piracy is defined as unendorsed looting of vessels on the high seas, which was usually associated with the crimes of kidnapping, extortion, and ransoming of captives. Piracy, or larceny at sea, is a continuing crime, and its occurrence in Atlantic waters is ancient. However, it was in the early modern era (c. 1450–1750) that seaborne predation grew

---

[3] Zhao Hong, ***India and China: Rivals or Partners in Southeast Asia?***, Contemporary Southeast Asia (April 2007) Vol. 29, Issue 1; 121. Accessed on 8th November 2009 (Available through ProQuest).

[4] James Kraska, *Maritime Power and the Law of the Sea – Expeditionary Operations in World Politics* (Oxford University Press, 2011) 311.

[5] *With China Watching, India & Seychelles to up Anti-Pirate Operations*, Feb 2, 2012, The Times of India. Available at http://m.timesofindia.com/india/With-China-watching-India-Seychelles-to-up-anti-pirate-operations/articleshow/11728694.cms. Accessed on 2 Feb 2012.

most intense, giving rise to many legendary figures.[6] From the second half of the 17th century most popular images of pirates were drawn from the Golden Age of buccaneers, who were privateers, and attacked Spanish ships in the localized area of the Caribbean Sea.[7] It was followed by the Second Golden Age of "Pirate Round" by Anglo-American freebooters whose sailing route was from the western Atlantic, around the southern tip of Africa, stopping at Madagascar, then on to targets such as the coast of Yemen and India. In the early 17th Century, as wars started in Europe, the tobacco planters of colonial Virginia struggled against shrinking markets and pirates lurking off the coast. This prompted American seafarers to look for other sources of wealth, and they took the route of piracy, aiming toward the Indian Ocean and ships carrying tremendous treasure to the great Mogul of India.[8] The "Pirate Round" was largely co-extensive with the routes of the East India Company ships, of Britain and other nations. The final outburst of piracy was in the post-Spanish Succession period, which dated to the Treaty of Utrecht in 1713, which ended the War of the Spanish Succession, and an epidemic of pirate trials culminating around 1730.[9] These pirates were left unemployed after the War of Spanish Succession and comprised of the Anglo-American sailors and privateers. This Golden Age of piracy saw the emergence of some famous pirate figures such as Black Bart,[10] Black Bellamy,[11] Edward Teach or Thatch,[12] Anne Bonney,[13] Captain William Kidd,[14] and Mary Read.[15] Since piracy was a crime that took place on the high seas, which were generally regarded in early modern times as open spaces beyond the limits of traditional, land-based sovereignty, emergent nations such as England and the Netherlands established admiralty courts for the prosecution of crimes committed at sea, most importantly piracy.

---

[6] Kris Lane, Piracy, Entry in Oxford Bibliographies, http://www.oxfordbibliographiesonline.com/view/document/obo-9780199730414/obo-9780199730414-077xml?rskey=VhyWhD&result=1&q=piracy#firstMatch. Accessed on 29 Jan 2012.

[7] Alexandre Exquemelin, '*The Buccaneers of America' New York*, Frederick A. Stokes company, 1914 (English translation available on Internet Archive http://www.archive.org/details/buccaneersofamer01exqu Accessed on 29 Jan 2012).

[8] There were many stories written on this era of piracy, and among them is James L. Nelson's excellent book, *The Pirate Round: The Brethren of the Coast*, (Thomas Marlowe Book 3), Harper Collins, 2003.

[9] Kris E Lane, *Pillaging The Empire – Piracy in the Americas 1500-1750*, New York M. E. Sharpe Inc, 1998, 181.

[10] Bartholomew Roberts, Welsh Pirate.

[11] Samuel Bellamy, Famous English pirate.

[12] Also known as Blackbeard - English pirate.

[13] Famous Irish Female pirate.

[14] Scottish pirate.

[15] Famous English Female pirate. *See* John Biddulph, *The Pirates of Malabar, and An Englishwoman in India Two Hundred Years Ago*, London: Smith Elder & Co, 1907, xii. *Also see* Famous Pirates http://www.elizabethan-era.org.uk/famous-pirates.htm. Accessed on 29th Jan 2012.

During the wars of the 16th and 17th centuries, piracy gave rise to privateering which involved authorizing raiding by private individuals and commercial associations. Privateers were private sea raiders whose aim was to profit by capturing commercial vessels flying the flag of declared enemies. During the Elizabethan era, which was seen as the Age of Exploration, there emerged the famous Elizabethan pirates who attacked the Spanish treasure fleet and the Spanish colonies. These Elizabethan pirates brought wealth and power to England.[16] Famous Elizabethan Pirates included Sir Francis Drake, Sir Walter Raleigh, Sir John Hawkins, Sir Humphrey Gilbert and Sir Richard Grenville. However to be legal, privateering required a letter of Marque usually signed by a monarch or issued by local governors. In exchange for the letter of Marque, crown officials received a portion of booty. As such, there was a very thin line of demarcation between privateering and piracy, and many acts of piracy were committed under fabricated facades against friendly nations during peacetime. Hence the famous Elizabethan pirates, who were skillful at capturing and plundering ships, but who acted both as pirates and privateers in the course of their careers, such as Francis Drake, Henry Morgan, and William Kidd.

The instances of ancient Piracy in India are recorded in the Indian Hindu text of Vedas, which is written in Sanskrit. Even the *Arthashastra* (meaning "Science of Politics") mentions piracy. This book was written by Kautilya, around 300 B.C., who was the chief advisor to *Chandragupta Maurya*, the king who united the Indian subcontinent in an empire.[17] In the chapter on the Kautilyan state and society, he mentioned that the Chief Controller of Shipping was responsible for the welfare of sea-traders and seamen, elimination of piracy, ensuring the seaworthiness of vessels and rescuing vessels in distress.[18] By the 4th century, piracy in India had assumed such proportions that it became a menace to the State. It was therefore decreed that pirate ships *(himsrika)* or vessels bound for the country of an enemy, as well as those which had violated customs regulations and the rules relevant to port towns *(pattana),* were to be destroyed. Due to the high risks of sea voyages from pirates, the legal interest leviable among sea traders was high.[19] Instances of piracy are also recorded in the 7th century when the trade with Arabs started with Sindh. It is recorded that the immediate cause of war

---

[16] Famous Pirates http://www.elizabethan-era.org.uk/famous-elizabethan-pirates.htm Accessed on 29th Jan 2012.

[17] *See* Roger Boesche, *The First Great Political Realist – Kautilya and his Arthashastra*, Lexington Books, 2002 2.

[18] L N. Rangarajan (translated) *Kautilya's The Arthashastra*, India: Penguin Books, 1992.

[19] R. N. Saletore, *Indian Pirates* (Delhi: Concept Publishing Company) 1978, 15. *Also see generally*, W. J; Hatch, *The Land of Pirates of India* (Concept Publication) 1928.

between the Arabs and Sindh was the act of piracy on the entourage heading towards the capital of the Caliph.[20] Since the 14th century Deccan (South of current Indian peninsula) was ruled by the competing dynasties of the Muslim Bahmani Sultanate (1347–1527) and the Hindu Vijayanagar Empire (1336–1565) for at least two centuries.[21] The war between these two dynasties demanded frequent resupplies of horses, which were to be imported through sea routes from Persia and Africa. The Vijayanagar Empire employed a Hindu privateer and pirate *Timoji* (also referred to as *Timoja* or *Timayya*) against the Bahmani Sultanate during the first decade of the 16th century.[22]

As Vasco da Gama arrived on the west coast of India, it opened a new direct sea route from Europe to Asia that was significant economically, politically and religiously. Indeed current international law is the product of interaction with a number of Asian sovereigns (excluding China and Japan which remained isolated prior to 19th century), which accompanied the spectacular growth of East Indian trade during the sixteenth, seventeenth and eighteenth centuries. According to Alexandrowicz, *Mare Liberum* of Grotius was not strictly an academic exercise, but a lawyer's pleading at the request of the Dutch East India Company. Particularly chapter XII of the *De Jure Praedae* was a pleading from the Dutch East India Company in relation to a case in which the Dutch Admiral seized a Portuguese vessel in the Straits of Malacca. This chapter deals with the general aspects of the Portuguese-Dutch conflicts in the Indian Ocean, while the freedom of the high seas (was seen) as its central problem. Even the work of Franciscus Seraphin de Freitas refers to problems arising out of actual state practice in south Asia and the Indian Ocean in the 16th and 17th centuries. The same is true of the *Mare Liberum*, which, in spite of the generality of its propositions, concentrates on the Portuguese-Dutch conflict in Asia and the role played in it by the local rulers.

In relation to India, and more generally Asia, the capacity to inflict violence followed essentially from the immensely armed superiority of European ships over their indigenous counterparts.[23] The weak naval power of the Indian kings ultimately allowed the colonization of India. The

[20] Gobind Khushalani, *Chachnamah Retold – An Account of the Arab Conquest of* Sindh (Delhi: Promilla & Co Publishers) 2006, 186.

[21] *World and its Peoples: Eastern and Sothern Asia - India and its Neighbors* Part I (New York: Marshall Cavendish Co-operation) 335 and 337.

[22] *See* Geneviéve Bouchon, *Inde Découverte, Inde Retrouvée (1498-1630) Études d'Histoire Indo-Portugaise*, ISBN 972-8462-07-7, http://openlibrary.org/books/OL21771423M/Inde_d%C3%A9couverte_inde_retrouv%C3%A9e_1498-1630; N. Singh, *India and International Law* 1969 (referring to the agreement of the kings Bahmani and Vijaynagar in 1367.

[23] G. Parker, *The Military Revolution, Military Innovation and the Rise of the West 1500-1800* (Cambridge 1988) 107-108.

instances of uncontrolled European piracy in the Indian Ocean also increased in the 16th and 17th centuries against the Mughal Indian ships and merchants. Mughals attributed this to the East India Company. Tensions soared over the capture of the *Ganj-i- Sawai*, the largest vessel in the *Surat* mercantile fleet. Every year, protected by its eighty guns, this great vessel transported high status pilgrims to Mecca and then traveled to *Jedda* port to trade in Indian goods. In 1695, when this vessel was returning to *Surat* from *Mecca* (*Jedda* port), with a full load of passenger and treasure, it was attacked by the pirates; goods were plundered and women were raped. This was a cause of outrage. The Surat governor stormed the East India Company and jailed all the occupants.[24] In 1702 Aurangzeb reacted to the depredations of European pirates by interdicting all trade with the English, Dutch and French companies in the empire.[25] In 1612, six English ships congregated off the Arabic coast and hijacked, in succession, 15 passing Mughal ships from India, culminating in the capture of the great 1000-ton vessel *Rahimi* which belonged to Maryam-uz-Zamani (Jodha Bai), mother of the Mughal emperor Jehangir.[26] In 1613 AD the Portuguese came into direct conflict with the Mughals for capturing one of the ships despite the fact that the Portuguese issued a pass guaranteeing her against molestation. The Mughals were greatly angered by this highhanded behaviour and it led to the orders of stopping all traffic, and to laying siege to the Portuguese town of Daman.[27]

By the late 17th century and early 18th century, the design and hulls of Indian-built ships likely did not differ from those of European ones in any fundamental way, particularly those within the same range of commercial uses. In the 18th Century an independent mariner named Kanhoji Angria allied with the Maratha confederacy that had formed in resistance to the Mughal Empire and which became the great Maratha privateer.[28] He was also provided with the title of admiral by the Marathas.[29] He had large guns mounted on his ships, and in a calm sea he could lie outside the range of ordnance in European shipping, and tear them into pieces with his own heavy guns, which were in size of 15 cwt (Hundred Weight). This range far exceeded the 5 cwt that was stipulated in 1719 by the Court of Directors, who gave permission to the servants in Madras and Calcutta to sell guns on

---

[24] John. F. Richards, *The Mughal Empire*, (Cambridge University Press, 1995) 241.

[25] John. F. Richards, *The Mughal Empire*, (Cambridge University Press, 1995) 241.

[26] O. Prakash, *The New Cambridge History of India – European Conmmercial Enterprise in Pre-Colonial India* (Cambridge University Press, 1998) 140.

[27] S. Mukherjee, *Royal Mughal Ladies and Their Contribution* (Delhi: Gyan Publishing House, 2001) 238.

[28] Candice Goucher and Linda Walton, *World History: Journeys from Past to Present* (London: Routlege 2007) 278.

[29] R. J. Barendse, *Arabian Seas 1700-1763 Volume 1: The Western Indian Oceans in the Eighteen Century* (Leiden: Koninklijke Brill 2009) 408.

the Malabar Coast as part of their private trade.[30] He ruled the seas between Mumbai and Goa and commanded the *Konkan* Coast (rugged section of the western coastline of India from state of Maharashtra to Karnataka). Under the admiralship of Kanhoji Angria the Marathas attacked British shipping and asserted that the East India Company ships should pay taxes when they were in the waters off the western Indian coasts, which were claimed by the Marathas. These waters were ones also claimed by the Portuguese coastal fleets.[31]

During the middle of the 18th century there was additional tension in the Indian waters due to competition between the English and the French. The privations and dangers of the voyage to India were great, due to the presence of pirates.[32] There were pirates of every nationality, including English, French, Dutch, Danish, Portuguese, Arab, Malay or other local pirates, beset from the Cape of Good Hope to the head of the Persian Gulf, and from Cape Comorin to Sumatra. Even the Bay of Bengal was dangerous because of piracy.[33] This, to a large extent, was the result of the War in Europe and its financial exhaustion, they could not put a check on the pirates either in the East or in the West. During this time the greatest sufferers among European traders in India were the English, as there were a greater number of pirates of English nationality and many pirate captains of other nationalities sailed under the English colours.[34] Since native officials were unable to distinguish between them, they held the East India Company responsible.[35]

The large island of Madagascar became an ideal base for pirates. For a quarter century, from the 1680s onward, Madagascar was a thriving pirate haven.[36] Capitan Mission, a famous pirate, explored the Madagascar coast and found a bay ten leagues north of Diego Suarez. He erected a town, built docks and called the colony *Libertatia.*[37] Captain Mission was one of the forebears of the French Revolution and his career was based upon an initial desire to better adjust the affairs of mankind. The Constitution of *Libertatia* stated that the decisions with regard to the colony were to be submitted to a

---

[30] K. N. Chaudhuri, *The Trading World of Asia and the English East India Company 1660-1760* (Cambridge University Press, 1978) 202-203.

[31] J. Barendse, *Arabian Seas 1700-1763 Volume 1: The Western Indian Oceans in the Eighteen Century* (Leiden: Koninklijke Brill 2009) 411.

[32] *See* John Biddulph, *The Pirates of Malabar, and An Englishwoman in India Two Hundred Years Ago*, London: Smith Elder & Co, 1907, page vi.

[33] *Id.* at vii.

[34] *Id.* at xi.

[35] *Id.* at x.

[36] Angus Konstam, *The History of Pirates* (The Lyons Press 2002) 136 & 137.

[37] W. Burroughs, *Word Virus: The William S Burroughs Reader* (ew York: Grove Press, 1998) 415 (Edited by James Grauerholz and Ira Silverberg).

vote; slavery and the death penalty was abolished, and people had freedom of religion.[38] Hence, the liberal principles embodied in the French and American revolutions had already been put into practice by this pirate community a hundred years earlier.[39] Captain Mission's colony, which numbered about three hundred, was ultimately destroyed by attacks from the natives, and Mission was killed in a sea battle.[40] So, the Indian subcontinent has been a hot bed of piracy since the times when the first European started to arrive in India to colonize it.

III. MODERN PIRACY IN AND AROUND INDIAN SUB-CONTINENT WATERS

1. Arabian Sea (Strait of Hormuz) and Indian Ocean (Gulf of Aden)

In the second week of February 2011, there were the hijackings of the supertankers *Irene SL* and *Savina Caylin* in a spate of two days, which posed significant questions on various navies that patrolled the vital sea-routes in the Indian Ocean and Arabian Sea.[41] According to Rajan, since 2009 there have been instances in which piracy attacks took place just 350 nautical miles from India's west coast, which also falls within the sphere of influence of India's blue-water navy. Hence the Indian navy, being the world's fifth largest navy, needed to come up with some satisfactory counter-piracy measures.[42] This is partly due to naval patrolling getting tighter in the Gulf of Aden which is indeed pushing the pirates to areas closer to India's Lakshadweep Islands in the Indian Ocean. According to the Indian news channel, NDTV News, the Indian Coast Guard's Inspector General S P S Basra said that "close to Lakshadweep, there are three major sea lanes of communications, where the traffic diverges into three places. It is a good, ideal place for them to hunt." However, India also suspects that Pakistan could be playing a role in piracy in the Indian Ocean.[43]

The dangerous nature of piracy in the India sub-continent can be envisaged from the Foreign and Commonwealth Office's advice to citizens to not travel by yacht and leisure craft on the high seas (more than 12 nautical miles from

---

[38] *Id.* at 415.

[39] D. C. Seitz, *Under the Black Flag – Exploits of the Most Notorious Pirates* (Unabridged Dover 2002) 18-26 (Originally published in New York by The Dial Press in 1925).

[40] W. Burroughs, *Word Virus: The William S Burroughs Reader* (New York: Grove Press, 1998) 415 (Edited by James Grauerholz and Ira Silverberg).

[41] Pradeep Rajan, *India Should Lead Fight Against Piracy in Indian Ocean, Arabian Sea*, 18th Feb 2011 The Platts. Available at http://www.platts.com/weblog/oilblog/2011/02/18/india_should_le.html. Accessed on 12 Feb 2012.

[42] *Id.*

[43] Defence Forum of India: *Pakistan Playing Role in Piracy in Indian ocean* http://defenceforumindia.com/international-politics/16911-piracy-arabian-sea-pakistan-playing-role.html.

shore) in the Gulf of Aden, Arabian Sea and part of the Indian Ocean.[44] They generally advise all merchant shipping, including cruises, to comply with the shipping industry best practice on self-defence measures. It is also stipulated that the mariners must register with the Maritime Security Centre (Horn of Africa).[45] Piracy is becoming a real threat to regional trade and maritime security in the Arabian sea generally, which is costing a loss to the global economy of up to $12 billion per year.[46] Further, 80 percent of international maritime trade is moving through the Gulf of Aden to Europe.[47] With the rise of Somali pirates, crude oil tankers sailing through the Arabian Sea are constantly being targeted by pirates.[48] It also undermines the regional actors' ability to deal with maritime security in their waters. It has been argued that the piracy challenge provides a unique opportunity for the Gulf Cooperation Council (GCC) nations to exercise regional leadership by taking decisive action against this growing threat.[49] It is arguable that India also needs to show the regional leadership and cooperate with the other neighboring nations in and around the Arabian sea and the GCC to control piracy. Over the years, the confidence and tactics of pirates has increased to the extent that they can now attack a ship more than 1,000 miles off the coast.[50] Such attacks at times are closer to India than to Somalia.[51]

India has conducted independent maritime security operations in this region.[52] Apart from Indian initiatives there have been other international responses to this menace. At the moment there are three major international responses to piracy in the Gulf of Aden include Operation Atalanta, an EU deployment (EU-NAVFOR) originally tasked with protecting the UN World Food Program shipments to Somalia. Another response is Operation Ocean

---

[44] Indian Ocean bounded by the following latitude and longitude: 15°N in the Red Sea, 23°N in the Arabian Sea, 78°E and 15°S in the Indian Ocean.

[45] Foreign and Commonwealth Office http://www.fco.gov.uk/en/travel-and-living-abroad/staying-safe/river-safety/indian-ocean-piracy Accessed on 29th Jan 2012.

[46] Anna Bowden et al., *The Economic Cost of Maritime Piracy* (working paper, One Earth Future, Louisville, CO, December 2010), 25, http://oneearthfuture.org/images/imagefiles/The%20Economic%20Cost%20of%20Piracy%20Full%20Report.pdf.

[47] U.S. Maritime Administration and U.S. Department of Transportation, *Economic Impact of Piracy in the Gulf of Aden on Global Trade*, September 2010, http://www.marad.dot.gov/documents/Economic_Impact_of_Piracy_2010.pdf. Accessed on 12 Feb 2012.

[48] Rick Ozzie Nelson and Scott Goossens, *Counter-Piracy in the Arabian Sea: Challenges and Opportunities for GCC Action*, Center for Strategic and International Studies, Middle East Program, May 2011, 1 http://csis.org/publication/counter-piracy-arabian-sea. Accessed on 11th Feb 2012.

[49] *Id.*

[50] Jeffrey Gettleman, *Suddenly, a Rise in Piracy's Price*, New York Times, 26 February, 2011, http://www.nytimes.com/2011/02/27/weekinreview/27pirates.html. Accessed on 12 Feb 2012.

[51] The Economist, *Piracy: No Stopping Them,* 3 February, 2011, http://www.economist.com/node/18061574. Accessed on 12 Feb 2012.

[52] The Economist, *Piracy: No Stopping Them*, 3 February, 2011, http://www.economist.com/node/18061574. Accessed on 12 Feb 2012.

Shield, a NATO deployment with similar responsibilities, and the third is Combined Task Force 151 (CTF-151), a US-led initiative comprising 25 nations which is headquartered in Bahrain. Further there have been numerous Security Council Resolutions passed to manage this region, such as SCR 1816 that authorized naval vessels to enter Somali territorial waters in pursuit of pirates.[53] Other Security Council resolutions such as 1851 (2008)[54] and 1918[55] were also passed concerning Somali piracy. These resolutions allow states that had the consent of Somalia's transitional federal government to "enter the territorial waters of Somalia for the purpose of repressing acts of piracy and armed robbery at sea."

Further, some shipping companies are avoiding the Gulf of Aden by rerouting around the Cape of Good Hope. However, this approach is both time consuming and economically expensive. It has been estimated that this detour costs additional fuel expenses amounting to $3.5 million annually for a single tanker operating between Saudi Arabia and the US.[56] Since pirates are expanding their range, this rerouting does not guarantee that there will be no attacks by pirates.[57] The shipping companies are accepting the piracy risk, but they are trying to reduce it by either applying the shipping industry's Best Management Practices (BMP) or installing Self-Protection Measures (SPM). The shipping industry is also taking assistance from private security companies which offer armed escorts to merchant ships across the Gulf of Aden. However, private escorts are not only expensive but also lead to various legal complications.

2. Piracy in the South China Sea – The Malacca Strait

India is not a littoral state to the Malacca Strait, however it is contiguous and is linked through the Bay of Bengal and Andaman and Nicobar Islands to the South China Sea and Malacca Strait. In fact, the tip of the Andaman and Nicobar Islands is only 90 nautical miles from *Aceh* which is located at the western entrance to the Malacca strait. Piracy in the Malacca Strait decides to the large extent, the enforcement of security against pirates and possibly terrorists, and is a contentious issue not only for the littoral states of

---

[53] Chip Cummins, *Piracy Grips Gulf of Aden*, Wall Street Journal, 8th September, 2008, http://online.wsj.com/article/SB122083029536208391.html. Accessed on 12 Feb 2012.

[54] A Contact Group on Piracy off the Coast of Somalia (CGPCS) was created by this resolution.

[55] S.C. Res. 1918, UN Doc S/RES/1918 (Apr. 27, 2010).

[56] U.S. Maritime Administration and U.S. Department of Transportation, *Economic Impact of Piracy in the Gulf of Aden on Global Trade*, September 2010, http://www.marad.dot.gov/documents/Economic_Impact_of_Piracy_2010.pdf. Accessed on 12 Feb 2012.

[57] Rick Ozzie Nelson and Scott Goossens, *Counter-Piracy in the Arabian Sea: Challenges and Opportunities for GCC Action*, Center for Strategic and International Studies, Middle East Program, May 2011, page 4. http://csis.org/publication/counter-piracy-arabian-sea. Accessed on 11th Feb 2012.

Indonesia, Malaysia and Singapore, but also for China, India, Japan and the United States, which all maintain an active interest in the area.[58] India, being the 6th largest consumer of energy in the world, is concerned about the security of oil transportation in the Malacca strait. Vavro argues that the United States's interest in playing the largest role in the Malacca strait is not limited to piracy, but also involves overall geopolitical concerns in the region. The U.S. is prevented from playing any significant role because they cannot push the littoral states to accept their desires. The balance of power in the Malacca Strait is not traditional, therefore the littoral states are not likely to align with one power but to try to maximize their maneuverability and percent of regional domination.[59] In this regard, as mentioned earlier, the economic growth of China, India and Japan plays a significant role which reduces the chances of the littoral states aligning towards the U.S. This coexistence of three powers in Asia displays the dynamics of power politics. These local powers will try to dominate the seas to project their power. China, using the strategy of "String of Pearls," is increasing its involvement with littoral states around the Malacca region and is establishing ports and diplomatic ties with them. For example, China is constructing a port in *Gwadar*, Pakistan, and has been financially involved in the development of ports in Myanmar. China has also developed facilities on Coco Island, only 18 miles away from India's newly constructed naval base on the Andaman and Nicobar Islands.[60] However, India, as an external power, has the longest involvement in the Malacca region. India is also building ties with the littoral states of the region. For example, the Indian Navy has carried out joint anti-piracy exercises with the Singapore Navy for over a decade, with Indonesia since 2004, and Thailand since 2005. In 2002, the Indian and U.S. navies were also permitted to jointly escort vessels transiting the strait carrying high-value American cargo.[61] As a rising power, India is beginning to increase its presence in the region through its navies from the Strait of Hormuz to the Strait of Malacca.[62] Since 2006, India also began setting up a high-tech monitoring station off the coast of Madagascar, which is thought to be used for monitoring the sea-lanes of communications in the India Ocean.

The United States has fuelled the Indian fears of a possible Chinese encroachment on India's vital interests. In the post-9/11 era, Washington

[58] Caroline Vavro, *Piracy, Terrorism and te Balance of Power in the Malacca Strait*, Canadian Naval Review, Volume 4, Number 1 (Spring 2008) 13- 17 at 13.

[59] *Id.* at 15.

[60] *Id.* at 16.

[61] *Id.* at 17.

[62] Sudha Ramachandran, *Delhi All Ears in the Indian Ocean*, Asia Times Online, 3 March 2006, available at www.atimes.com.

encouraged and partly funded India's establishment of a *Far Eastern Naval Command (FENC)* Centre on the Andaman and Nicobar Islands. This command post is designed to streamline the surveillance capabilities of the Indian Army, Air Force and Navy under one command structure to improve India's monitoring capabilities in the area and increase its maritime reach. The United States's efforts to increase ties with India stems from its desire to provide stability and balance in the region in the face of growing Chinese power.[63]

IV. How Does India deal with Piracy?

There are various conventions, resolutions, regional codes and practices such as, the UN Convention on the Law of the Sea (UNCLOS), the Convention on the Suppression of Unlawful Acts against the Safety of Maritime Navigation, 1988 (SUA)[64] and some SC Resolutions have been adopted to deal with piracy. However, these international practices have not been uniform and governments, ship owners and other affected actors deal with piracy in their own ways ranging from anti-piracy missions to paying ransom to get back hostages. India is using a broad range of tactics to deal with piracy in the India Ocean and the piratic episode of *MV Stolt Valour* off the Gulf of Aden and the capture of the pirate ship *Alondra Rainbow* in November 1999 by the Indian Navy already points to the capability of the Indian Navy and its positive counter-piracy contribution.[65] However, at a much deeper level, India's approach to international law and diplomacy is guided by a formalist dualism which is a strategy of opposing imperialistic policies on one hand and at the same time using contemporary international law to bring changes in international system to the benefit of third world countries, and particularly for their own benefit.[66] A critical reflection on Indian understandings of international law shows essential elements of dualism and Eastphalia, which is the adoption of the defensive, security oriented sovereignty that arose in Europe in the 17th century, and which has always been the basis of military, as well as economic, competition among

---

[63] Caroline Vavro, *Piracy, Terrorism and te Balance of Power in the Malacca Strait*, Canadian Naval Review, Volume 4, Number 1 (Spring 2008) 13- 17 at 17.

[64] http://www.admiraltylawguide.com/conven/suppression1988.html Accessed on 16 Feb 2012.

[65] Cdr Ritu Raj Sahu, *At Crossroads in Changing Crosshairs*, Naval Dispatch, (The Indian Navy Journal) Sept 2009, 9. Available at http://indiannavy.nic.in/dnt_navaldespatch2009_100726.pdf. Accessed on 26 Feb 2012.

[66] *See*, particularly, B.S. Chimni, *International Law Scholarship in Post-colonial India: Coping with Dualism* (2010) 23 Leiden Journal of International Law 23-51.

the Western powers,[67] which spearheads India's contemporary international relations.

Today, India is member to both UNCLOS and SUA. However, India, upon ratification of UNCLOS, made a declaration on 29 June 1995 in relation to the part XV settlement of disputes. The declaration was as follows:

(a) The Government of the Republic of India reserves the right to make at the appropriate time the declarations provided for in articles 287 and 298, concerning the settlement of disputes;

(b) The Government of the Republic of India understands that the provisions of the Convention do not authorize other States to carry out in the exclusive economic zone and on the continental shelf military exercises or manoeuvres, in particular those involving the use of weapons or explosives without the consent of the coastal State.[68]

Indian Governmental Strategy to manage piracy involves surveillance, seizure of property, detention, trial and punishment of pirates. India, on a long term basis, has also cooperated with nations such as Japan, Djibouti, Seychelles, Mauritius and Australia to tackle piracy in the region, and to develop bilateral economic engagement, taking into account the regional (and global) economic context, infrastructure development and financing. However, it is significant to analyze the Indian approach towards the law of the sea generally.

1. The Law of the Sea: From its Inception to Implementation

After India gained its independence, scholars have consistently argued that India remained at the periphery of the mainstream international legal system because it had no role in formulating some of the basic principles of international law.[69] However, the law of the sea negotiations became a source of optimism for India to be involved in the process of making international law, and hence noted post-colonial scholars during the 1970s, such as Anand, and Khan,[70] and some senior civil servants, such as Rao,[71]

---

[67] *See* T. Carty & F. N Lone, *Some New Haven International Law Reflections on China, India and Their Various Territorial Disputes*, Asia Pacific Law Review, Vol. 19, No 1, 2011, 95-113 at 100; Sung Won Kim, David P Fidler, and Sumit Ganguly, *Eastphalia Rising? Asian Influence and the Fate of Human Security* (2009) World Policy Journal 53.

[68] UN Division for Ocean Affairs and the Law of the Sea http://www.un.org/depts/los/convention_agreements/convention_declarations.htm#India. Accessed on 16 Feb 2012.

[69] *See* V. G. Hegde, *Indian Courts and International Law*, Leiden Journal of International Law, 23 (2010) 55-77 at 55.

[70] R. P. Anand, *Tyranny of the Freedom of the Seas Doctrine*, (1973) 12 International Studies 417; R. Khan, The 200 Miles Exclusive Economic Zone: Indian Ocean Fisheries (1977).

[71] P. S Rao, *Legal Regulation of Maritime Military Uses* (1973) *13* AJIL 425.

wrote extensively on this subject. As Chimni argues in the law of the sea negotiations, it was believed that "Third World international lawyers could contribute to its evolution and final shape. It was a test case for what was seen as the transformation of international law from being a law of coexistence to a law of cooperation."[72] Anand argues that during the First United Nations Conference on the Law of the Sea in 1958, the Western maritime Powers being in majority "dominated the Conference and, through their political influence and divisive power, controlled a majority of the votes taken and proposed most of the amendments accepted."[73] However during the Third United Nations Conference on the Law of the Sea, the Third World Countries were determined to safeguard their economic interests as well as their national security and sovereignty.[74] India was one such nation as it has a long coastline and was determined to protect its national interests. Third World states were of the view that only a new international law in place of the present "lawless" *laissez faire* system could be fair because they knew that "between the strong and the weak, it is freedom which oppresses and law which protects."[75] The law of the sea convention renewed the faith of the Indian international law community in international law and institutions; however the refusal of the Reagan administration to ratify this convention came as a setback for all those who invested hopes and energies in the Convention.[76]

2. *No Municipal Anti-Piracy Law in India: Initiatives in Progress*

The inefficiency of India to deal with piracy and maritime hostages became clear when Somali pirates attempted to bargain with the Indian government to swap seven Indian hostages for their men imprisoned in Indian jails.[77] India has no specific municipal law to deal with piracy, and they still use the criminal law (Indian Penal Code 1860) and the British colonial admiralty law to tackle piracy. However, none of these provisions define piracy and they fall short of the international standards that are set in UNCLOS Sections 101 to 107. It is interesting to note that as early as 1868, Hong Kong had enacted its independent law (Hong Kong Ordinance No 1 of

---

[72] BS Chimni, *International Law Scholarship in Post-colonial India: Coping with Dualism*, (2010) 23 Leiden Journal of International Law 23-51 at 38.

[73] Ram. Prakash. Anand, Origin and Development of the Law of the Sea, History of International Law Revisited (The Hague: Martinus Nijhoff, 1983) 184.

[74] *Id.* at 209.

[75] Raharijaona (Madagascar) cited in Warioba (United Republic of Tainzania) Third UN Conference on Law of the Sea, *Official Records*, Vol I, UN Publications Sales no E 75, v. 3 (New York, 1975) 106.

[76] B. S. Chimni, *International Law Scholarship in Post-colonial India: Coping with Dualism* (2010) 23 Leiden Journal of International Law, 23-51 at 39.

[77] *India's Anti-piracy Laws are Medieval: Experts*, 18th April 2011. Available at http://www.rediff.com/news/report/indias-anti-piracy-laws-are-medieval-say-experts/20110418.htm.

1868 - Suppression of Piracy Amendment Ordinance, 1927) with respect to piracy.[78] Most of the common law countries, including India, follow the Victorian era admiralty law such as the Admiralty Court Act 1861.[79] While Pakistan has now developed its specific admiralty law, the Admiralty, i.e. Jurisdiction of High Courts Ordinance, 1980 (Ordinance XLII of 1980),[80] it is still partly based on old English admiralty law, namely the Administration of Justice Act 1956. For this reason English case law is still useful. On the other hand, states like Panama do not follow the English statute and have their own maritime courts. The courts have an exclusive jurisdiction over cases arising from or connected to maritime trade and navigation occurring within the territory of the Republic of Panama, its territorial sea, the navigable waters of its rivers and lakes and the Panama Canal waters.[81]

In India it is difficult to prosecute captured pirates. Even if the Navy or the Coast Guard captures them they cannot be prosecuted, and they have to be handed over to the police. The police then start the legal procedure. In prosecuting, the Indian Penal Code, section 380, is applied to pirates. This section deals with "Theft in Dwelling House, etc." and is used for piracy. This section says: "Whoever commits theft in any building, text or Vessel, shall be punished with imprisonment of either description for a term which may extend to seven years, and shall also be liable to fine." The commentary on this section provided by Misra suggests that the object of this section is to provide a greater security to any property deposited in a house, tent or vessel.[82] However, the term "vessel" has not been defined and it is not clear what approach Indian courts will take if the vessel in question does not have any property which could warrant such a security, or if the pirates only kidnap people for ransom purposes.

The current rudimentary admiralty law in India comprises the following laws: Admiralty Offences (Colonial) Act, 1849; Admiralty Jurisdiction (India) Act, 1860; Admiralty Court Act, 1861; Colonial Courts of Admiralty Act, 1890; Colonial Courts of Admiralty (India) Act, 1891 and the provisions of the Letters Patent, 1865 applicable to the admiralty jurisdiction of the Bombay, Calcutta and Madras High Courts. All the matters of marine

---

[78] *See* S. Morrison (ed), *A Collection of Piracy Laws of Various Countries*, 26 Am. J. Int'l L. Sup 887 1932, 929.

[79] The current statute dealing with the Admiralty jurisdiction of the England and Wales High Court is the Supreme Court Act 1981, ss. 20-24, 37. The provisions in those sections are, in turn, based on the International Arrest Convention 1952.

[80] http://www.vakilno1.com/saarclaw/pakistan/admiralty_jurisdiction_ordinance/admiralty_jurisdiction_of_high_c.htm. Accessed on 23 Feb 2012.

[81] Admiralty Law in Panama. http://www.pardinilaw.com/publications/admiralty/booklet/ admiralty.pdf. Accessed on 24 Feb 2012.

[82] S. N. Misra, *Indian Penal Code* (11th ed., India: Central Law Publications 2003) 531.

commerce, marine navigation, shipping, sailors, and the transportation of passengers and goods by sea are governed by these laws in India even today. Nonetheless, India is also seeking to consolidate the Admiralty law in India by the Admiralty Bill, 2005.[83]

However, after the decision of the Supreme Court in *M.V. Elisabeth-v-Harwan Investment & Trading Pvt Ltd*[84] the Supreme Court of India, interpreting Article 225 of the Constitution of India (and Articles 215 and 226),[85] held that the High Courts in India are superior courts of records and have original and appellate jurisdiction. They have inherent and plenary powers, and unless they are expressly or impliedly barred, and subject to the appellate or discretionary jurisdiction of the Supreme Court, the High Courts have unlimited jurisdiction, including the jurisdiction to determine their own powers.

The Indian High Court can arrest a "sister ship" for securing any maritime claim.[86] However, the exercise of jurisdiction of the High Courts of India is based on Admiralty law as it was applied by the English Court of Admiralty as defined in the Admiralty Court Act 1861.[87] Admiralty courts in India assume jurisdiction by virtue of the presence of the vessel in its territory. The High Court by an action *in rem,* can also exercise jurisdiction on the foreign vessel owned by a foreign company, which does not have residence or business in India. Such a cause of action could arise by reason of a breach of obligation arising from the carriage of goods from a port in India to a foreign port.[88]

India has not yet adopted formal municipal legislation to tackle piracy and to integrate the provisions of UNCLOS 1982 and the IMO Convention on the Suppression of Unlawful Acts against the Safety of Maritime Navigation 1988. Hence, to fill this present lacuna there are many discussions[89] on this issue and the Indian Government has, since last year, decided on formulating

---

[83] The Admiralty Bill, 2005. Available at http://www.prsindia.org/print.php?bill_id=160 &category=44. Accessed on 24 Feb 2012.

[84] 1993 AIR 1014, 1992 SCR (1)1003. Available at http://indiankanoon.org/doc/1515069/. Accessed 25 Feb 2012.

[85] The Constitution of India, http://lawmin.nic.in/coi/coiason29july08.pdf. Accessed on 24th Feb 2012.

[86] *M.v. Mariner IV -v- Videsh Sanchar Nigam Limited*, decided on 15th December 1997 Bombay High Court.

[87] *Kamlakar v The Scindia Steam Navigation Co Ltd* AIR 1961 Bom 186, (1960) 62 BOMLR 995. Available at http://indiankanoon.org/doc/1816963/. Accessed on 25 Feb 2012.

[88] *See*, Shrikant Hathi and Binita Hathi, *Maritime Practice in India*, (6th ed., Mumbai BRUS CHAMBERS Advocates & Solicitors, 2010) 12 – 13. Available at http://www.maritime practice.com/. Accessed on 24th Feb 2012.

[89] *See*, Global Maritime Security and Anti-Piracy Conference 2011 (GMSAC 2011) Gandhinagar (Gujarat), INDIA 26 November 2011. Available at http://www.gmsac2011.com/docs/provisional_ program.pdf. Accessed on 25 Feb 2012.

a new express municipal law to tackle piracy, called the Anti-piracy Bill 2011. The exact provisions of this bill are not known; however the general idea is to tackle acts of piracy and other complicated issues on the high seas. The draft legislation also prescribes punishment for different acts that constitute piracy under the law. The draft law would define piracy, and list out the legal framework for apprehending the pirates, be they in Indian or international waters, and for prosecuting them in Indian courts.[90] It is also anticipated that new domestic legislation will have elements of both the Indian Penal Code as well as the Admiralty Law that will make it focused, effective, and easier to tackle these issues.[91] At this moment, the ship owners enter into negotiations with the pirates for the interest of their sailors and the merchandise they carry. The pirates also generally do not harm the hostages for their own interest of securing their ransom.[92]

The advancement is that India does realize the absence of law and hence there has been advancement of the Admiralty Bill 2005 and the Anti-Piracy Bill 2011. This advancement is a result of the fact that India is traditionally a maritime nation with a long coast from the state of West Bengal on the East to state of Gujarat on the West. Today, India, with the rise in its economy, moves 95% of its traded goods, by volume, to the rest of the world, and ports and shipping form an integral part of the maritime sector which also immensely contributes to the economic growth of India.[93] India realizes the value in expanding its maritime knowledge and created the Indian Maritime University (IMU)[94] in 2008. This university was founded pursuant to the Indian Maritime University Act, 11th November 2008 (No 22 or 2008), establishing and incorporating:

> A teaching and affiliating University at the national level to facilitate and promote maritime studies and research and to achieve excellence in areas of marine science and technology, marine environment and other related fields and to promote for matters connected therewith or incidental thereto.

Dr. P. Vijayan, the first Vice-Chancellor of IMU, said that this university was the first of its kind in the country and it would cater to the educational requirement of the maritime fraternity. It is a teaching and affiliating

---

[90] India: A Case Study, http://piracy-law.com/2011/09/24/india-a-case-study/. Accessed on 25 Feb 2012.

[91] *Government to Frame Law to Tackle Piracy on the Seas*, The Hindu, 13 March 2011. Available at http://www.thehindu.com/news/national/article1532398.ece. Accessed on 25 Feb 2012.

[92] *Id.*

[93] Indian Maritime University http://www.imu.tn.nic.in/aboutus.html.

[94] The headquarters of the University shall be at Chenni with its campuses at Mumbai, Kolkata, Chennai, Vashakhapatnam ans such other places within its jurisdiction as it may deem fit. *See* Sec 3 (2) of The Indian Maritime University Act, 2008.

University, which will offer degree, postgraduate degree and research programmes in all disciplines of the maritime sector.

3. Piracy, General Maritime Security and the Right to Navigation

In the area of maritime security there exists clear security convergence between ASEAN countries, Australia and India. India is increasingly seen as an emerging geopolitical partner of Australia to counterweight the rising power of China. The concept of maritime security in Asia is hypothesized as an issue related to traditional maritime defence and naval concerns, such as a right to navigation. For this reason it is difficult to achieve in practice comprehensive maritime security at a regional level in Asia. India has a traditional approach to international law, and as such she has a strong stance on the sovereignty over the Exclusive Economic Zone (EEZ) and to regulate the foreign flagged activities well beyond her legitimate coastal competence.

India has consistently claimed the EEZ jurisdiction for the construction, maintenance or operation of artificial islands, offshore terminals, installation and other structures and devices necessary for the exploration of the resources of the zone.[95] Further, before passage of any hazardous and dangerous goods is allowed through its EEZ, India requires at least 24-hour advance notice. This is seen internationally as India's move to restrict foreign military activities.[96] The U.S. has protested in the past over the Indian EEZ legislation which is seen to restrict the right of navigation of the U.S.[97] Chris Rahman argues that India, as well as many ASEAN countries, remains highly suspicious of the military activities by foreign defence forces in and around their exclusive economic zones and straits used for international navigation.[98] Hence, in the ASEAN-Australia – India "triangle," states assert jurisdiction on the security zones to restrict the activities of the foreign warships or other military activities in their claimed zones of jurisdiction.[99]

In fact the assertion of such jurisdiction falls well outside the UNCLOS freedom of navigation rights. Kraska argues that since India is now assuming a position alongside the other powerful navies in the Indian Ocean, it will be

---

[95] The Territorial Waters, Continental Shelf, Exclusive Economic Zone and other Maritime Zones Act 1976, Act No 80 of 28 May 1976.

[96] James Kraska, *Maritime Power and the Law of the Sea – Expeditionary Operations in World Politics* (Oxford University Press, 2011) 310.

[97] *American Embassy New Delhi Diplomatic Note* delivered May 13 and 16, 1983, State Department Telegram 128220 9 May 1983 quoted in James Kraska, *Maritime Power and the Law of the Sea – Expeditionary Operations in World Politics* (Oxford University Press, 2011) 310.

[98] *See*, Chris Rahman, *Australia and Maritime Security in the Northeast Indian Ocean*, in William T. Tow and Chin Kin Wah, *ASEAN India Australia Towards Closer Engagement in a New Asia*, (Singapore: Institute of Southeast Asian Studies 2009) 185 at 192.

[99] *Id.*

in the interests of India to have a more liberal approach to the oceans.[100] However, maritime competition in the region and in the world is centered on China's growing maritime power. The Indian Navy's 2004 Maritime Doctrine identified the Chinese Navy's rise as a significant "military threat" due to its naval missions. This vision confidently stated that "the Indian maritime vision for the first quarter of the 21st century must look at the arc from the Persian Gulf to the Straits of Malacca as a legitimate are of interest."[101] So, India is realigning its political and security interests beyond South Asia to fit its widening economic and diplomatic activities.[102] It is argued that such a tight stance may also affect the curbing of piracy in the region, as foreign warships will need to ask for permission every time they need to conduct anti-piracy operations.

4. India's Efforts to Fight Piracy: Indian Ministry of External Affairs

In India, on combating piracy the Cabinet Committee on Security (CCS)[103] considers proposals with regard to conduct of anti-piracy operations in the Gulf of Aden and off the Coast of Somalia.[104] In 2011, the CCS approved a series of mid-term and long-term measures to be taken by the Ministries of Shipping, External Affairs and Defence to address legal, executive and operational aspects of combating piracy. The CCS approved the following immediate steps: to intensify diplomatic efforts through consultations with the governments of regions where the owners of hijacked vessels reside and those governments whose nationals are held hostage; establishing an Inter-Ministerial Group under the chairmanship of the Cabinet Secretary to monitor the early release of Indian ships or cargo or crew, and to formulate suitable operating procedures for the Indian Navy and its coordination with the navies of friendly foreign countries in the Gulf of Aden to fight piracy.[105]

---

[100] James Kraska, *Maritime Power and the Law of the Sea – Expeditionary Operations in World Politics* (Oxford University Press, 2011) 196.

[101] Indian Navy, Indian Maritime Doctrine (INBR 8), April 2004, 56.

[102] Rahul Roy- Chaudhury (International Institute for Strategic Studies, London), *Maritime Ambitions and Maritime Security: India*, (Discussion Paper), 5th Berlin Conference on Asian Security (BCAS), Berlin 30th Sept to 1st Oct 2010 (published by - German Institute for International and Security Affairs Stiftung Wissenschaft und Politik).

[103] The Prime Minister, Manmohan Singh, constituted two crucial sub-committees of the Cabinet — the committee on security and another committee on political Affairs — to initiate and oversee crucial decision-making. Harish Khare, *Manmohan Constitutes Key Cabinet Committees*, The Hindu, Friday, Jun 11, 2004 http://www.hindu.com/2004/06/11/stories/2004061103871100.htm. Accessed on 26 Feb 2012.

[104] Indian Ministry External Affairs, Statement by EAM in Lok Sabha on combating piracy, March 11, 2011, http://www.mea.gov.in/mystart.php?id=100517373. Accessed on 23 Jan 2012.

[105] *Id.*

On 17 August 2011, the Minister of State[106] in the Ministry of External Affairs, Smt Preneet Kaur, said that according to the IMO, since 2008, the Gulf of Aden, the western part of the Indian Ocean and the Arabian Sea have seen a major spike in attacks by pirates operating from Somalia, which has emerged as a serious problem for merchant shipping.[107] She said that the Indian Navy has been involved in anti-piracy patrols off Somalia since 2008.[108] She said India has the full support of Somalia and the Transitional Federal Government to fight piracy. India also held discussions in the Second India Africa Forum Summit 2011.[109] A Declaration was adopted at the Summit stressing the importance of addressing the threat posed by piracy off the coast of Somalia and the suffering caused by the taking of hostages, and it called on all states to cooperate in combating and eradicating the menace of piracy. In addition, India also contributed to non-UN multilateral organizations and groups such as the Non-Aligned Movement (NAM),[110] the Commonwealth and the Contact Group on Piracy off the Coast of Somalia (CGPCS).[111]

India is also participating actively in international counter-piracy efforts at the UN level. For example, India is a founding member of the Contact Group on Piracy Off the Coast of Somalia (CGPCS).[112] The Working Group II on legal issues of the CGPCS accomplished assigned tasks such as continuous exchange of information on legal challenges arising from piracy off the coast of Somalia, examination of the possibility of establishing additional mechanisms for prosecution of suspected pirates, and establishment of an international legal network consisting of legal experts. The Working Group was also involved in the compilation of the international legal basis for prosecution and in the development of generic templates on evidentiary standards, "ship rider" agreements, and in the drafting of a Memorandum of Understanding on the conditions of transfer of suspected pirates and armed

[106] In India Minister of State is a junior Minister in the Council of Ministers in the Central Government who assist a cabinet minister.

[107] India Ministry of External Affairs, Lok Sabha, Unstarred question no.2587, Shri Balkrishna K. Shukla, Shri Ramashanker Rajbhar: August 17, 2011, http://www.mea.gov.in/mystart.php ?id=100518048. Accessed on 23 Jan 2012.

[108] India-Somalia Relations, July 2011, http://www.mea.gov.in/mystart.php?id=50049955. Accessed on 23 Jan 2012.

[109] Conference was held in Addis Ababa in May 2011.

[110] External Affairs Minister Shri S. M. Krishna participated in the Ministerial meeting of the NAM Coordinating Bureau and Meeting of Commonwealth Foreign Ministers held in the margins of the 65th UN General Assembly in September 2010.

[111] Ministry of External Affairs, Annual Report 2010-11, http://www.mea.gov.in/mystart .php?id=500417371. Accessed on 23 Jan 2012.

[112] Established in January 2009, India participated in the Plenary meetings of the Contact Group in New York in November 2010 and its four Working Groups. CGPCS is an international forum consisting of 45 countries and seven international organizations.

robbers. The Working Group is also examining proposals for establishing international tribunals for dealing with the crimes of piracy.

India also attended the 12th Crime Congress[113] held under the auspices of the United Nations Office of Drugs and Crime (UNODC). The main theme of the 12th Crime Congress was "comprehensive strategies for global challenges: crime prevention and criminal justice systems and their development in a changing world." India took the lead in raising a number of issues, including the issue of new and emerging forms of crime like cyber-crime, maritime piracy etc.

India is also a member of the Indian Ocean Rim Association for Regional Cooperation (IOR-ARC).[114] India participated in its tenth meeting held in Sana'a, Yemen, on 5 August 2010. The Indian delegation was led by the Minister of State for Human Resources Development Smt. D. Purandeswari. The Sana'a Communiqué stressed greater cooperation among IOR-ARC member countries in areas such as promotion of trade and investment, tourism, culture, and education, combating communicable diseases and natural disasters, and tackling the challenges posed by climate change. The Council of Ministers also expressed their support for the initiatives for combating piracy in the Gulf of Aden and other parts of the Indian Ocean. India also has liaison with the Civil Societies to combat piracy and terrorism.[115]

5. *Bilateral Activities with Neighboring Nations and Civil Societies*

India, on a long term basis, has cooperated with nations such as Japan, Djibouti, the Seychelles, Mauritius and Australia to tackle piracy in the region and to develop bilateral economic engagement. In doing so, India is taking into account the regional and global context, and coordinating economic issues of cross-cutting nature, including infrastructure development, maneuvering and financing. India also has signed maritime boundary agreements with Sri Lanka, Indonesia, Maldives, Thailand, Malaysia and Burma to solve various disagreements with these nations.[116]

During the Annual Summit in October 2010, Japan's Defense Minister, Mr. Toshimi Kitazawa, and the Indian Defence Minister, Mr. A. K. Antony, agreed

---

[113] The 12th Crime Congress held in Salvador, Brazil from 12-19 April, 2010.

[114] India will assume the Chair of the Indian Ocean Rim Association for Regional Cooperation (IOR-ARC), in 2011.

[115] The second India-EU Forum on Effective Multilateralism, jointly organized by ICWA and the European Union Institute for Security Studies (EUISS), was held in Brussels from 11-12 October, 2010. Participants from both sides discussed issues related to India-EU relations covering counter terrorism, climate change, cooperation in antipiracy operations etc.

[116] J. Kraska, Indian Ocean Security and the Law of the Sea, 43 *Georgetown Journal of International Law* (2012) 433 – 493 at 493

to establish a Ministerial Level Economic Dialogue to give strategic and long-term policy orientation to their bilateral economic engagement and to coordinate economic issues of a cross-cutting nature, including infrastructure development and financing. Within the framework of the October 2008 India-Japan Joint Declaration on Security Cooperation a concrete Action Plan is provided which covers a wide range of issues, including maritime safety and security, fights against piracy and trans-national crimes, safety of transport, protection of marine environment and non-traditional security threats like disaster management through consultation and cooperation in multilateral frameworks in Asia.

From 12-14 December 2010, on the ports of Djibouti, Indian Naval Ships have made port calls in their operational turn around, and anti-piracy patrols. Likewise India has defence and security co-operations with Mauritius and Indian Naval ships have visited on a goodwill basis. For example, Indian Naval ship *INS Trishul* was deployed in Mauritian waters to conduct EEZ surveillance and joint anti-piracy patrols from 23 May-12 June 2010. Further, *INS Mysore* and *INS Tabar,* two Indian Naval Ships, were in Mauritius to carry out EEZ surveillance and anti-piracy patrols of Mauritian waters. India has also from time to time cooperated with Seychelles on bilateral cooperation,[117] security interest in Indian Ocean, fights against piracy and economic development. The Indian Navy has been a leading force to suppress piracy in the western Indian Ocean under the Security Council resolutions for counter-piracy operations in the Somali Basin. [118] Indian coast guards in 2011 intercepted pirates from Somalia, Burma, and Thailand, operating in the Indian Ocean.[119]

V. INDIA'S INTEREST IN FIGHTING PIRACY IN THE INDIAN OCEAN

According to a 2011 IMB report on piracy, there was an improvement in response to armed robbery at sea in South East Asia and the Indian subcontinent.[120] On 14 March 2011, the Indian navy, on its west coast some 600 nautical miles off Mumbai, neutralized a mother ship, the *MV Vega-5*, and captured 61 pirates. This vessel was hijacked by Somali pirates on 28 December 2010, and its position and the number of pirates found onboard suggested that the vessel was used to stage multiple attacks on shipping in the

---

[117] For example, External Affairs Minister Shri S. M. Krishna paid a visit to the Seychelles from 5-6 July, 2010 and held discussions with President James Alix Michel.

[118] J. Kraska, Indian Ocean Security and the Law of the Sea, 43 *Georgetown Journal of International Law* (2012) 433 – 493 at 437

[119] *id*

[120] Piracy Attacks in East and West Africa Dominate IMB Report, 20 Jan 2012 http://www.triton-risk.com/2012/01/20/1245/. Accessed on 6 Feb 2012.

Indian Ocean and that they were planning attacks against ships on an industrial scale. IMB Director, Pottengal Mukundan, was of the view that the Indian Navy's action prevented many potential attacks against merchant vessels. He was also of the view that "similar actions against known pirate action groups are vital in an area which is simply too vast for close monitoring by naval assets. For too long pirate gangs have been operating with relative impunity."

India can play a dual role to stop piracy in the Indian Ocean: firstly, to strengthen her position as an emerging economic powerhouse; and secondly, to secure her interests against pirates. This interest is based on economic, political and military reasons. With the rise of her economy, India is expanding her footprint in the Indian Ocean to counter piracy, which is targeting commercial shipping on the high seas. The Deputy Chief of Naval Staff, Vice-Admiral R.K. Dhowan, states that the Indian Navy is moving beyond the piracy-hit Gulf of Aden and Indian warships are working under the multilateral Shared Awareness and Deconfliction (SHADE)[121] mechanism. The regularly rotated Indian warships can access ports in 30 Indian Ocean countries, including the Seychelles and Mauritius, so that their movement is not interrupted. A promulgation message was first issued designating the specific point along the 500 nautical miles east-west piracy-prone transit corridor, where commercial ships seeking escort can assemble. Naval ships then escort the convoy before it enters a safety zone.[122]

Maitra argues that India's security provisions in the strait are not expanded to the same degree as those adopted by Japan and the United States, but the country will be "ready to provide assets when asked for."[123] India is however growing its presence in the Indian Ocean for security purposes, which is shown by India's maritime doctrine that reflects the forwarding naval presence from the Strait of Hormuz to the Strait of Malacca.[124] India has also expanded its ties with countries in the region such as Japan, the Seychelles, and Djibouti etc. Since 2006, India also began setting up a high-tech monitoring station off the coast of Madagascar, to monitor the sea-lanes of communications in the Indian Ocean. Monitoring the sea lanes in the region is important as India is wary of energy competition with China, having already lost in purchasing oil from Angola, Ecuador, Kazakhstan and

---

[121] SHADE comprise of more than 23 countries, including Russia, China, Egypt and the European Union.

[122] *See*, Atul Aneja, *India Expands Anti-Piracy Footprint in Indian Ocean*, The Hindi. Available at http://www.thehindu.com/todays-paper/tp-national/article934576.ece. Accessed on 13 Feb 2012.

[123] Ramtanu Maitra, *India Bids to Rule the Waves*, Asia Times Online, 19 October 2005, available at www.atimes.com.

[124] Cited in Admiral Sureesh Mehta (Chief of the Naval Staff), *Freedom to Use the Seas: India's Maritime Military Strategy*, (India: Integrated Headquarters of Defence (Navy)) 2007. Available at http://indiannavy.nic.in/maritime_strat.pdf. Accessed on 26th Feb 2012.

Myanmar.[125] India has also upgraded its Andaman base. This decision was indeed in retaliation of China's increasing presence in the Indian Ocean Region.[126] India has decided to upgrade two fighter bases in the Andaman and Nicobar Islands that will increase its reach in South Asia by more than 1,200 km.[127] The two airstrips, one at Shibpur in the Andaman and the other at Campbell Bay in Nicobar Islands, will be turned into all-weather bases that can support fighter operations. [128]

India's endeavors in the region are partly supported by the US such as the establishment of a Far Eastern Naval Command (FENC) Centre on the Andaman and Nicobar Islands. This command post is designed to streamline the surveillance capabilities of the Indian Army, Air Force and Navy under one command structure to improve India's monitoring capabilities in the area and to increase its maritime reach. The US's desire to increase ties with India stems from its desire for the country to provide stability and balance in the region in the face of growing Chinese power. This in a way is the United States's stance to attempt to balance power in the region in relation to China. India is concerned about China's strategic interests and growing influence in the region.[129]

India aspires to become a permanent member of the UN Security Council.[130] The Indian reform of the UN SC as argued by Patel is based on the theory of realism and India views that "the Council tends to behave in a manner wherein the P5 try to maximize their national interests."[131] India believes that by becoming a permanent member of the Council, the new status offers India an opportunity to maximize its own national interests.

VI. CONCLUSION

The Indian navy, amidst changing geopolitics, is determined to upgrade its technological and fighting capabilities and skills.[132] India is also taking a

---

[125] Caroline Vavro, *Piracy, Terrorism and the Balance of Power in the Malacca Strait*, Vol 4, Number 1 (Spring 2008). Available at http://naval.review.cfps.dal.ca/archive/7345817-2223651/vol4num1art4.pdf. Accessed on 1 Jan 2012.

[126] *India to Upgrade 2 Fighter Bases in Andamans*, The Indian Express, Mon Feb 08 2010 http://www.indianexpress.com/news/india-to-upgrade-2-fighter-bases-in-andamans/576971/.

[127] *Id.*

[128] *Id.*

[129] *Balancing on Shifting Sand: Perspectives on Singapore's Strategic Engagements With the Major Powers in the Asia-Pacific*, Journal of the Singapore Armed Forces, Vol. 34 No. 2, 2008. http://www.mindef.gov.sg/imindef/publications/pointer/journals/2008/v34n2/feature3.html.

[130] Charles Grant, *India's Role in the New World Order*, Briefing Note, Centre for European Reform, September 2008, http://www.cer.org.uk/pdf/bn_india_cg_26sept08.pdf.

[131] *Id.* at 59.

[132] *The Indian Navy's Vision Document*, Integrated Headquarters of the Ministry of Defence (Navy) May 2006. Available at http://indiannavy.nic.in/vision.pdf. Accessed on 26 Feb 2012.

flexible approach and is cooperating with its neighbors. In 2011, the President of India conducted the International Fleet Review[133] in the Mumbai headquarters of the Western Naval Command, which attracted large international participation of the navies of Singapore, Malaysia, Indonesia, Thailand, and Vietnam. It is also believed that India may take a more positive anti-piracy role by participating in internationally organized initiatives such as CTF-151 and by taking on strategic and leadership roles that are more suited to an emerging economy and not limited it to patrols. In the absence of taking a leadership role, and overcoming its structural weaknesses and corruption, a new study by the London School of Economics and Political Science (*India: the Next Superpower?)* declares that India cannot become a super power.[134]

It is to be noted that India is already trying to expand its fleet of coastal vessels and helicopters. India is also a party to the initiatives by ASEAN, and their collective efforts have already reduced piracy in the Strait of Malacca. Today the Indian navy is equipped to support its policy objects. The major goal is to become strong enough to counter the Chinese naval influence, to combat piracy and to become a major power in the region. The Indian navy is willing to take the constabulary role and to revisit its comfort levels to enforce antipiracy law.[135] Justice Chinnappa Reddy, in the Supreme Court case of *Gramophone Company of India Ltd v Birendra Bahadur Pandey,*[136] held that "nations must march with the international community and the municipal law must respect rules of international law as nations respect international opinion." He further observed that "the doctrine of incorporation itself recognizes the position that the rules of international law are incorporated into national law and considered to be part of the national law, unless they are in conflict with an Act of Parliament."[137] It is argued that in light of these developments India needs to back up its forward thinking by enacting a robust domestic anti-piracy law. The presence of anti-piracy law will demonstrate India's greater commitment to promote regional maritime security. It indeed is also an opportunity for India to demonstrate its leadership, which will benefit her as an emerging regional power.

---

[133] Indian Navy PFR 2011, http://indiannavy.nic.in/PFR2011/wnc.html. Accessed on 26 Feb 2012.

[134] Hasan Saroor, *India May Never Be a Super Power: LSE Study*, The Hindu, 7 March 2012. *See*, http://www.thehindu.com/news/international/article2969252.ece. Accessed on 7 March 2012.

[135] Cdr Ritu Raj Sahu, *At Crossroads in Changing Crosshairs*, Naval Dispatch, (The Indian Navy Journal) Sept 2009, 9. Available at http://indiannavy.nic.in/dnt_navaldespatch2009_100726.pdf. Accessed on 26 Feb 2012.

[136] (1984) 2 SCC 534.

[137] (1984) 2 SCC 534 at 540.

While interrogating apprehended pirates last year, the Indian police said that "rampant poverty and unemployment back home in Somalia pushed them into piracy," and "the police sources said that the pirates were promised a hefty reward if they managed to bring back a hijacked vessel."[138] Hence, poverty plays a significant role in piracy and thus a pure procedural approach to this problem can never exterminate it. Rather, taking some degree of a sociological approach to counter piracy laws would assist in building a relationship of reality with the current international and domestic laws. Opening the Third United Nations Conference on the Law of the Seas, Carlos Andres Perez, the President of Venezuela, said that the seas could not be permitted to "be used in such a way that a few countries benefited from it while the rest lived in poverty, as had been done with the rich of the land."[139] It is believed that taking a criminological approach to tackle piracy would not gratify poor nations such as Somalia, and their concerns would not be purely seen as criminal wrongdoing but a sociological problem. The recent one-day "*London Conference on Future of Somalia*" (23 February 2012) to a large extent reflected this view. About 55 countries and organizations participated in this conference, and world leaders pledged to boost support for measures to fight piracy, terrorism and political instability in Somalia.[140] UK Prime Minister David Cameron said that "setting up an inclusive government" in Somalia was vital. He further stated that:

> It must work alongside African Union military action . . . those young people who take up guns for al-Shabab need to be able to see that there is a future in a prosperous stable Somalia that offers them what everyone wants, which is a job and a voice . . . so the connection between military action to put huge pressure on Shabab, which has been happening, and the political process, they are two sides of the same coin.'[141]

This pledge resonates Koskenniemi's argument that a single act of piracy triggers a number of legal fields simultaneously such as maritime, shipping, contract, insurance, human rights, trade and criminal law etc.[142] For that reason, a holistic approach to fight piracy is required.

---

[138] Surabhi Vaya, *Poverty, Lack of Jobs Pushed Them to Piracy*, Hindustan Times, March 28, 2011 http://www.hindustantimes.com/StoryPage/Print/678393.aspx. Accessed on 23 Feb 2012.

[139] *See*, Warioba (United Republic of Tainzania) Third UN Conference on Law of the Sea, Official Records, Vol I, UN Publications Sales no E 75, v. 3 (New York, 1975) 36.

[140] *See*, BBC News, http://www.bbc.co.uk/news/mobile/uk-politics-17131208. Accessed on 24th Feb 2012.

[141] *Id.*

[142] Martti Koskenniemi, *Fragmentation of International Law: Difficulties Arising from the Diversification and Expansion of International Law*, REPORT OF THE STUDY GROUP OF THE INTERNATIONAL LAW COMMISSION ¶ 8, A/CN.4/L.682.

Anand described oceans and the law of the seas as follows:

> The sea is no longer a mere navigational route, a recreation centre or a dumping ground. It is the last phase of the man's expansion on earth and must become an area of cooperation for orderly progressive world development in which all will share equally and equitably.[143]

These words catch the spirit of counter-piracy operations equally because the menace of piracy is an international problem affecting every country and consumer in the world, and it can be tackled only by cooperation and balancing power and interests of all the nations.[144]

---

[143] Ram. Prakash. Anand, *Origin and Development of the Law of the Sea, History of International Law Revisited* (The Hague: Martinus Nijhoff, 1983) 219.

[144] In 2010, in the case of *Medvedyev v France (*3394/03) (2010) 51 E.H.R.R. 39 (Judgment 29th March 2010) the Grand Chamber of the European Court of Human Rights addressed in a limited manner the legal implications of the interception of a suspect pirate vessel. This case raised and settled the questions of state jurisdiction and of the detention of pirates in the Europe. However, this case also shows that piracy is dealt from a limited perspective.

9. Perspectives From Central and West Africa

Claude Kirongozi Ichalanga[1]

The world has recently witnessed many acts by extremists - whether they are terrorists or genocidal killers. The end of the last century was characterized by such acts of extremism; for example, the war in the former Yugoslavia, the war in Rwanda and consequently in the whole African Great Lake Region. There have also been acts of terrorism, such as the September 11, 2001 attacks and the attacks in London and Madrid. The acts of pirates can be categorized with these other acts - pirates are, in truth, extremists, just as terrorists and genocidal killers are.

But if we look carefully, it seems the ocean has been a place where security has never completely existed because it has always been a *res nullius*, such that no one has responsibility to control or to secure it.[2] If this is true for all mankind, it is very true for the African people who have suffered from slavery and Niger's trade. Both unforgotten issues richen Africa through the wild frontier that is the ocean. This continues today, with certain constituencies in Nigeria becoming increasingly wealthy by shipping its resources away, while the average Nigerian remains destitute.

Piratical acts by extremists have increasingly jeopardized maritime navigation and commerce off the coasts of Africa. African piracy is the result and consequence of the phenomenon of the failed and collapsed state in Somali, but also the bad governance and mismanagement of other African countries, such as Nigeria. Thus, this chapter will focus on the occurrence, law, and policy of West African piracy.

I. West African Piracy

The Gulf of Guinea in West Africa has long been a high-risk area, according to IMB-ICC annual Reports from 2003-2009.[3] Recently, however, the number of attacks has been surging. The International Maritime

---

[1] Dr. Claude Kirongozi Ichalanga is Associate Professor at the University of Kinshasa School of Law in Kinshasa, Democratic Republic of the Congo, and Visiting Scholar at the University of Maine School of Law.

[2] See the theory developed by Hugo Grotius on *Mare Liberum*, 1609.

[3] IMB-ICC annual Reports 2003-2009 on Maritime Piracy, in www.unodc.org, visited on October 24, 2011.

Organization is reporting that there was a twenty-eight percent increase in pirate attacks in 2011 over 2010 – 64 attacks were reported, up from a total of 46 in 2010.[4] However, as will be discussed below, armed robbery at sea and piracy are two overlapping, yet distinct acts. Armed robbery at sea is increasingly common in the Gulf of Guinea – Nigeria alone recorded 102 armed robberies at sea in 2010, with an attendant 80 people killed.[5] For efficiency, armed robbery at sea and piracy will be referred to collectively as piracy.

Piracy activities are increasing in the Gulf of Guinea due, in part, to an increase in maritime commercial traffic, discovery of oil, installation of additional offshore extracting infrastructure, and on-going instability in various coastal areas.[6] Even though the piracy phenomenon in the Gulf of Aden and the one in the Gulf of Guinea are both occurring in Africa, it has been commented that:

> the nature of the attacks [in West Africa] appears to differ with those off the Somali coast, encompassing an equal amount of armed robberies or hijackings and hostage takings. In addition to the immediate financial effect on oil and natural resource exploration and exploitation, the increased piracy activity appears to have a substantial impact on a set of traditional economic activities, such as commercial trade, regional travel and fishing.[7]

Further, the government of Nigeria and the oil companies "split profits roughly 60/40, and the money is supposed to benefit the Delta inhabitants, but this rarely occurs."[8] Piracy off of West Africa appears to be centered on resource imbalance – with the pirates attempting to viciously even the scales. In fact, the region is becoming increasingly important with more and more resources – the Gulf of Guinea is expected to supply fully one quarter of United States oil imports by 2015, with Nigeria accounting for most of it.[9] The International Maritime Bureau has pointed out Nigeria as an area of particularly high concern, for many oil companies are operating there.[10]

---

[4] Neena Rai, *Shippers Cautious on Piracy's Emerging Market – West Africa*, Associated Press, February 3, 2012.

[5] *Piracy in The Gulf Of Guinea: Getting Worse Before it Gets Better*, Business Monitor Online, February 6, 2012.

[6] Theo Neethling, *Piracy Around Africa's West and East Coasts: A Comparative Political Perspective*, Scientia Militaria, South African Journal of Military Studies, Vol. 38, Nr 2, 2010, p 103.

[7] *Id.*

[8] *Id.* at 99.

[9] *Piracy in The Gulf Of Guinea: Getting Worse Before it Gets Better*, Business Monitor Online, February 6, 2012.

[10] Neethling at 99.

The pirates in the Gulf of Guinea are much less "diplomatic" than their Somali counterparts. For example, in February of 2012, pirates summarily killed a captain and his chief engineer on a Tawainese owned and Danish managed heavy cargo ship in order to commandeer it, some 120 miles from the coast of Lagos.[11] As far as piracy is concerned, "Nigerian politics on land directly result in offshore actions, causing the hub of insecurity."[12]

This strain of piracy has been ascendant for a number of years. In November of 2009, the Ghanaian navy intercepted a Nigerian oil tanker, which had been hijacked and was laden with a cargo of stolen oil.[13] No ransom was demanded; it was clear that the pirates desired the oil.[14] Given Ghana's recent embarkation into the oil business, this brand of criminality is alarming; and compared with Somali piracy, it is unique.

West Africa has a very important sea-lane that connects not only with newfound energy sources, but also diamonds, rainforest products, and cocoa. This confluence of industry, channeled through a small segment of society, creates an atmosphere ripe for crime, instability, and conflict. This conflict should be understood

> "in the context of poverty, political disenfranchisement and the easy availability of firearms and armed conflict over oil. It should further be understood against the background of previous governments largely ignoring the Niger Delta, partly because its geography made it relatively inaccessible, and also following bad governance and corruption in Nigeria after years of military rule."[15]

Thus, West African piracy is different in kind, origin, and impetus than its Somali counterpart. Far from fighting over resources, Somali pirates are taking hostages because there are no resources. Piracy activities off of the Horn of Africa are explained by the failure of the Somali government; the collapsed state is why the civil population carries guns and turns to piracy. However, "piracy and insecurity in the Gulf of Guinea manifests[] in the form of attacks on ships, hostage-takings and destruction of energy infrastructure by rebels who – in some instances – extended their political agendas offshore."[16] Though this may be true, or perhaps because it is so, piracy in the Gulf of Guinea will likely not reach the levels seen off of

---

[11] *Violence Against Shippers New Norm off West Africa*, Associated Press, February 2, 2012.

[12] Neethling at 99.

[13] Frances Kokutse, *Concern Grows in Ghana Over Rise in Piracy*, BBC International Reports (Africa), November 30, 2009.

[14] *Id.*

[15] D. Bekoe, *Strategies for Peace in the Niger Delta*, United States Institute for Peace Briefing, December 2005, available at www.usip.org/pubs/usipeace_briefings/2005/1219_nigerdelta.html.

[16] Neethling at 102.

Somalia. Though the local governments of Benin, Nigeria, Ghana, Cameroon, etc., are somewhat weak, there is simply no West African pirate safe-haven like Somalia.

The ocean is considered by Africans as a place where there occurs many activities such as navigation, trade, fishing, oil exploitation, etc. Not only positive activities take place on the sea, but also nefarious ones such as armed robbery, illegal fishing, and piracy. To this list we can add the trading of slaves that Africans will not forget soon, so brutal were those illegal and amoral acts. Yet, the ocean is also a place where people go to look for essential sustenance. The solution to the problem of piracy is finding a middle path between maintaining the freedom of navigation while eliminating threats to that very navigation, thus ensuring a "minimum world public order of the oceans."[17] The solutions to the problems of West and East African piracy, however, cannot be the same, for the problems are very different.

II. THE LAW OF WEST AFRICAN PIRACY AND ITS EFFICACY

Piracy is as old as maritime navigation, and domestic laws banning piracy almost as old. International law on piracy evolved much later. As important as domestic law is, this chapter will not discuss it because West and Central African countries' laws are largely modeled on customary international law. Most of these countries are parties to the United Nations Convention on the Law of the Sea (UNCLOS), with UNCLOS forming part of their domestic law.

Piracy activities in West and Central Africa take place in both territorial and internal waters. This is true because pirates in the Gulf of Guinea are not as well equipped and not as well trained as Somali pirates who commit their acts on the high sea.[18] Technically, most West African piracy should not be defined as piracy but as armed robbery because the coastal state, which exercises jurisdiction over its territorial and internal water, is competent to sanction it.[19] Thus universal jurisdiction can be difficult to apply, domestic law will often govern, and the domestic definition of piracy may differ from UNCLOS.

Much of the West and Central African counter-piracy capacity is at the regional level. In 2002 the African Union (AU) succeeded the Organization

---

[17] Myres S. McDougal & William T. Burke, *The Public Order of the Oceans: A Contemporary International Law of the Sea*, VII (1962).

[18] Roger L. Phillips, *From the Gulf of Aden Back to the Gulf of Guinea Piracy Reports in West Africa on Rise*, www.piracy-law.com, visited on October 24, 2011.

[19] *See* Article 101 of the United Nation Convention on the Law of the Sea, UNCLOS III.

of African Unity (OAU), which was created in 1963, just three years after independence of most African Countries. How was the OAU to continue to struggle against colonial power, when in the new century all African countries are formally enjoying sovereignty and independence? [20] The purpose of the OAU was out of date. And so, African leaders thought of a new continental organization. After a long vacillation between the European and United States model, African leaders expressed their preference for the European Union model and created the African Union in the Republic of Togo in 2000.

Regarding maritime activities, the former OAU had created some sub-regional organizations to deal with specific issues - for example, the Maritime Organization for West and Central Africa (MOWCA). MOWCA, which is an intergovernmental cooperative institution, is comprised of 25 countries stretching from Mauritania to Angola and was established in 1975. MOWCA

> "aimed at reinforcing cooperation between member States in the face of mounting problems of piracy, armed robbery and other illicit acts against ships (SUA Convention), combating illegal immigration, terrorism and marine pollution (MARPOL), illegal exploitation of the resources of the exclusive economic zones of member States, the implementation of United Nations Conventions on Maritime Security and Safety (SOLAS and ISPS Code), Search and Rescue (SAR Convention), protection of marine environment as well as the implementation of the Convention on the Law of the Sea."[21]

MOWCA has undertaken a number of projects, including protecting vessels from piracy and terrorism and thus, in 2008, its member states established a Sub-Regional Integrated Coast Guard Network whose members "have assumed obligations to coordinate their national legislation, practices and procedures, and policies related to safeguarding maritime trade, providing security for safe operation of port facilities and ships, and effective protection of the marine environment."[22] Members of this Network must prosecute all manner of pirates and illegal actions against those involved in the maritime industry.[23]

---

[20] Claude Kirongozi Ichalanga, *L'Organisation de l'Unité Africaine: Fin de l'Histoire et Nouvelles Perspectives à Travers l'Union Africaine*,Revue Congo-Afrique, N°296, July 2002.

[21] *Developing Stake-Holders-Driven Approach to Addressing Maritime Piracy*, www.oceansbeyondpiracy.org, visited on February 5, 2012

[22] Ved P. Nanda, *Maritime Piracy: How Can International Law and Policy Address This Growing Global Menace*, 39 Dev. J. Int'l L. & Pol'y 177, 191.

[23] *Id.*

Further, piracy increases maritime risk, and drives maritime insurance and freight costs up. In order to address these issues, the AU has certain measures such as the African Charter on Maritime Transport and The Durban Resolution. The African Charter on Maritime Transport was adopted by the Conference of African Ministers of Maritime Transport, which

> "meeting in its Third Session in Addis Ababa from 13-15 December 1993, reiterated the importance of co-operation among African countries in the Sector in finding appropriate solutions to the problems impeding the development of the Maritime Transport Sector as well as in facing the challenges brought about by the abovementioned changes. The Conference, therefore, adopted an African Charter on Maritime Transport to provide the framework for cooperation, on one hand, among African countries and on the other hand, between African and non-African countries."[24]

The African Charter on Maritime Transport serves as the legal framework of African countries in the maritime transport sector and provides basic principles of cooperation among African countries such as

> "solidarity and independence of States; harmonization and cooperation of Member States in all areas connected with international maritime transport and ports; the need to make maritime and ports activities and services more efficient in order to promote economic and social development; the right of free access to the sea for every land-locked member State with the proviso that they comply with the laws and regulations of transit States."[25]

African states' policy on maritime transport improved after the September 11 terrorist attacks, which showed that no state can escape from the risk of an attack. These deplorable events confirmed that the freedom of navigation is threatened and the entire world public order is challenged.[26] Thus, African states decided to adopt the Durban Resolution on Maritime Safety, Maritime Security and Protection of Marine Environment – it was adopted by African ministers in Durban, October 2009. Further, African countries should comply with ISPS Code in order to meet international standards on maritime security matters. But the main problem is that African countries are not well equipped

---

[24] CM/Res. 1520 (LX) of December 15, 1993, Resolution of Conference of Ministers of Maritime Transport of OAU, Preface of the African Charter on Maritime Transport, p 1.

[25] Article 3 of the African Charter on Maritime Transport.

[26] James C. Kraska, *The Law of the Sea Convention: A National Security Success – Global Strategic Mobility Through the Rule of Law*, 39 The Geo. Wash. Int'l Rev. 543, 552.

or trained, and sometimes do not express the clear political will to deal with maritime security issues.[27]

In the maritime sector, the same maritime joint patrols are held by European Union and African countries. This is true of the Joint Action 2008/851/CFSP known as Atalanta. In addition, the US Navy, with its Africa Partnership Program (now part of the US Africa Command), is in a strong working relationship with the Nigerian Navy, as well as other relevant African navies.[28] US Africa Command is a partnership between the United States of America and Africa to deal with security issues such as terrorism, piracy, and armed robbery. Without this partnership African countries will not be able to pursue pirates and bring them to trial.

Africa's West and Central coasts used to be quite safe in contrast to the Horn of Africa and the Gulf of Aden. Theo Neethling is correct when he considers that:

> "Of special importance is that maritime insecurity in general, and in African waters in particular, has been growing at a disturbing rate and threatens the global flow of goods and services across the world's shipping lines. In this regard, globalisation and maritime trade show a close interface since the bulk of international goods and services – more than 80 per cent – travel by sea. In view of this, Potgieter rightly argues that pervasive maritime insecurity is a significant threat to security in Africa, to its development, to the shipping around Africa's coast and to maritime resources".[29]

Thus, despite the regional, sub-regional, and domestic capacity, West and Central African piracy is surely a growing concern.

Prosecution of pirates seized in the Gulf of Guinea remains very problematic. It seems that universal jurisdiction is partly to blame because it gives jurisdiction to every state and no specific state feels obligated to prosecute pirates. Additionally, African Union member states have the problem of instability, when trying to implement legal norms in domestic and external affairs. That is why African countries often defer to their partners for prosecution and in order to improve capacity. African countries have

---

[27] Neethling, at 103. The author underlines that: "in the African context in general, where the absence of effective navies, coupled with a lack of co-operation among littoral states in the relevant regions is the order of the day, piracy has proliferated and poses serious challenges to the international community."

[28] US Africa Command, *Plans Underway for Fourth Year of Africa Partnership Station*, available at www.africom.mil/getArticles.asp?art=4709&, last visited February 19, 2012.

[29] Neethling at 91.

adopted different counter-piracy legal documents, but the implementation of such documents remains problematic.

> "The transnational nature of piracy makes regional cooperation (and international actors) crucial. For example, Benin's Chief of Defence Staff claims that joint patrols with Nigeria significantly reduced the number of attacks in late 2011. The US, France and China have also become more involved in anti-piracy efforts, training and investing in local navies. While this bodes well for the future, substantial improvements will take time."[30]

West and Central African countries have no problem with signing or ratifying treaties. They always do it. But effective implementation is another thing. The difficulty in implementation is due to a number of factors, including limited governmental capacity and institutional framework, and also instability. To attempt to address this, most African countries have cooperative relationships with Western countries. The only effective solution remains capacity building with partners such as the European Union, NATO and the United States government.

Piracy has jeopardized the Gulf of Guinea these last 5 years, especially the Niger Delta where off-shore oil exploitation by western companies does not improve the life of people in even the nearest villages. Some reports have indicated that:

> "the period 2008 to 2009 will be remembered for a surge in piracy not seen in generations. In May 2008, the BBC reported that, according to statistics provided by the IMB, Nigeria accounted for 10 of the 49 attacks registered worldwide in the first quarter of 2008, which translates into a figure of more than 20 per cent. Despite the prevalence of maritime piracy off the Nigerian coast and in the wider Gulf of Guinea, piracy in this region tends to receive less public attention than in the case of the Horn of Africa and in the Gulf of Aden."[31]

This lack of attention is alarming – and may not continue. In November of 2011 a supply ship named *Endeavor* was attacked and its crew was kidnapped.[32] Further, there are rumors that Boko Haram in Nigeria and al-Qaeda in the Islamic Maghreb may be allying with al-Shabab. In light of this, western countries must intervene in Africa's West and Central Coast. This

---

[30] *Piracy in The Gulf Of Guinea: Getting Worse Before it Gets Better*, Business Monitor Online, February 6, 2012.

[31] Neethling at 98.

[32] *Piracy in The Gulf Of Guinea: Getting Worse Before it Gets Better*, Business Monitor Online, February 6, 2012.

intervention could be by the European Union, or it could be US intervention. Further, African countries must cooperate with each other in implementing security measures. Everything must be done in order to ensure the freedom of navigation and to maintain the world public order of the oceans.

III. CONCLUSION

The piracy occurrences in the Gulf of Guinea are largely catalyzed by the mismanagement of national wealth in the Niger Delta, and the inability of the Nigerian government to share the wealth from oil exploitation with local institutions and people. The armed robbers and pirates in the Niger Delta are not professional criminals looking for ransoms, like their Somali counterparts. They are individuals giving vent to their desire for attention from the government of Nigeria and an equitable sharing in national resources, as well as an increased capacity for the delivery of social goods like education, health, running water and electricity, public transportation, and employment opportunities. Absent meeting these demands, it will be difficult for the international community to end what we so deplore in the Gulf of Guinea.

Of note, meeting violence with violence will not solve this issue – embarking armed guards is not the solution. It is in severe contrast with long practice and may even be against customary international law which forbids carrying weapons on board. Capacity building as a policy implemented by Western countries is one of the key solutions to the West African piracy problem. Additionally, although it has its detriments, universal jurisdiction remains the most efficient response mechanism to piratical acts.

III. Strategies

10. Comparative Counter-Piracy Strategy: European, American, African, and Asian Approaches

James KRASKA[1]

I. Introduction

Since 2006, warships from Europe, North America, and Asia, and, more recently, offshore patrol vessels and even larger corvettes from Africa, have converged on the western Indian Ocean to patrol against Somali pirates. The Western navies began concerted counter-piracy operations after the M/V *Seabourn Spirit*, a luxury passenger liner, was attacked on November 5, 2005. The pirates circled the beleaguered ship in two high-speed skiffs, training machine gun and rocket propelled grenade fire on the vessel for 30 minutes. Miraculously, none of the 151 passengers was injured, although the ship's master-at-arms was hurt in the melee. The attack on the *Seabourn Spirit* elevated piracy from a relatively obscure regional threat to a major issue of international security. Throughout 2006 and 2007, merchant ships faced increasing numbers of attacks. Somali pirates began operating farther from shore, attacking ships beyond 200 nautical miles. Ransom amounts soared and larger ships were made vulnerable as the pirates utilized mother ships–often captured tramps or dhows–to extend their range.

In the fall of 2008 several high-profile attacks, including the September 25 capture of the Ukrainian M/V *Faina*, a roll-on/roll-off cargo ship carrying 33 T-72 Russian main battle tanks and registered in Belize. The pirates repeatedly sought to offload associated small arms and ammunition from the *Faina*, but were deterred by nearby warships. The hijacking prompted the UN Security Council to adopt resolution 1838 on October 7, 2008, which called on nations concerned with maritime security to deploy naval surface and air forces to the western Indian Ocean to suppress Somali piracy. On November 15, 2008, pirates seized the M/V *Sirius Star*, a Saudi Aramco very large crude carrier-class tanker carrying 2.2 million barrels of oil and registered in Liberia. Two weeks later, on December 2 the UN Security

---

[1] James Kraska holds the Howard S. Levie Chair in Operational Law in the United States Naval War College. The views presented are those of the author and do not reflect the official policy or position of the Naval War College or the Department of Defense.

Council adopted resolution 1846–followed by resolution 1851 on December 16. These resolutions provided additional legal authority and political support for nations to deploy naval forces to the region.

By late-2008 and early-2009, the multinational naval presence in the area significantly expanded. Warships from some Asian nations joined the effort, complementing Western maritime patrols. Russia sent the Baltic fleet missile frigate *Neustrashimy* (Fearless) to the Horn of Africa to fight piracy the day after the *Faina* was captured.[2] China entered the fight against Somali piracy by deploying ships to the area in December 2008; Japan made the decision to provide assistance in 2008 and sent aircraft and warships to the area beginning in 2009. Singapore, Malaysia, South Korea, and the Philippines also responded to the call by the UN Security Council to support counter-piracy operations off the Horn of Africa.

Today ships and manned and unmanned aircraft are operating from South Africa to India, patrolling against roving gangs of Somali pirates. Thirty nations have deployed naval and maritime law enforcement forces to the region, and warships and aircraft from all the great powers–the United Kingdom, France, Germany, the United States, China, India, Japan, and Russia, among others, are participating in the effort. The nations that have sent forces to the region are interested in suppressing maritime piracy, but they do so within a distinct political and strategic context. Because piracy is a heinous crime of universal jurisdiction, all nations regard pirates as *hostis humani generis*–enemies lying outside of the social compact of mankind. Taking action to patrol the seas against pirates, therefore, is a politically low-cost venture that can pay rewards beyond merely helping to keep safe the international sea lanes. Ironically, some of the greatest beneficiaries are farthest from the high-risk areas in the western Indian Ocean.

Which countries and institutions have gained from the international fight against piracy, and how has counter-piracy operational art and strategy differed among the nations patrolling? For the Philippines, for example, protection of the large numbers of Philippine seafarers is a major concern. South Korea, dependent upon the flow of oil from the Persian Gulf and international exports to Europe that travel by sea, sought to protect critical sea lines of communication. China shares these concerns, but the emerging giant plays at a high level of global politics in which piracy is but a sideshow.

---

[2] *Russia Sends Warship to Fight Piracy Near Somalia*, RIA Novosti, September 26, 2008, http://en.rian.ru/russia/20080926/117144421.html.

For Beijing, counter-piracy patrols draw attention to the burgeoning People's Liberation Army (Navy) or PLAN, which in only a decade has been transformed from a defensive, littoral force into an instrument of power projection. Thus, China has been a big winner, converting its two-warship deployments into a "coming out" party for the PLAN. Beijing has been able to augment its orchestrated "peaceful rise" campaign by showcasing how the PLAN can play a constructive role in enforcing the rule of law in the oceans. Operationally, the deployments to the western Indian Ocean are a golden opportunity for blue water training for Chinese sailors. Operationally, the two ships provide additional depth to a coalition force straining under the challenge of ridding half the Indian Ocean of pirates. Strategically, China's counter-piracy deployments have outflanked India, reassured Pakistan, and displayed to the United States and Japan that Beijing has the ability to project power along the sea lines of communications connecting the Persian Gulf to China.

It is no accident that once China succeeded in deploying to the region, Japan was close behind. For Japan, which has long operated a highly advanced and well-maintained naval force, the counter-piracy operations have less to do with influencing the operational effectiveness of the force than with signaling a political maturation inside the Government of Japan. Inhibited by its constitution from assuming a political role commensurate with its economic and military, Japan's counter-piracy deployment constitutes another toe in the water, testing the boundaries of the concept of "self-defense." Japan is, furthermore, deeply concerned about promoting rule of law in the oceans and preserving the concept of freedom of the seas. As the leader in counter-piracy cooperation in Asia during the early- and mid-2000s, no nation has done more to suppress piracy than Japan. An island nation wholly dependent on Persian Gulf oil and international shipping trade, Japan is a reliable leader for developing new approaches to maritime security.

But Asian nations are not alone in using Somali piracy to think about new naval roles and missions. If the maritime piracy threat off the Horn of Africa proved to be a golden opportunity to develop new missions and celebrate new capabilities for China and Japan, the North Atlantic Treaty Organization (NATO) has also proved adept at taking advantage of the crisis in maritime security. Building on the success of the maritime interception operations conducted pursuant to Operation Active Endeavor in the Mediterranean Sea, NATO broadened its ability to conduct asymmetric maritime security operations utilizing naval forces configured for more conventional roles. The deployment of Standing NATO Response Force Maritime Group 1 (SNMG1) to circumnavigate Africa in the summer of 2007, in advance of a counter-piracy patrol, heralded NATO's first maritime out-of-area mission.

Similarly, the European Union has deployed its first out-of-area naval force to fight piracy in the western Indian Ocean. The European Union decided to send naval forces to the region on November 10, 2008, and the Naval Force has been conducting Operation Atalanta in direct support of UN Security Council resolution to suppress maritime piracy. As an added bonus, the effort serves as a demonstration project for the European Union's goal of fashioning a common security and defense policy.

This chapter highlights some of the counter-piracy strategies developed by nations in Europe, Africa, and Asia. Each approach bears a distinct political-military imprint. The first turns toward the European multilateral initiatives to combat piracy, focusing on the European Union's Naval Force Somalia–Operation Atalanta, and NATO's effort, now called Operation Ocean Shield.

Next, the focus shifts to Africa itself, where the states of East Africa are marshaling their resources to address Somali piracy and the greater problem of instability in Somalia. Finally, the chapter closes with analysis of China and Japan's mobilization to combat piracy off the coast of Somalia. In the conclusion some assessment is made of the naval efforts. Although the naval force presence has had some effect on decreasing rates of hijacking, it is likely that merchant ship passive and active defensive measures, and especially the deployment of privately contracted armed security personnel (PCASP) has been an even more effective deterrent. In the end, the cost of the naval operations can scarcely be justified if the metric is the number of pirates that have been suppressed. Instead, the enormous resources that nations from Europe and Asia especially have poured into the fight against Somali piracy suggest that the patrols are more about exercising naval power projection than ending the ages-old crime of armed robbery and ship hijacking.

II. EUROPE–THE EU AND NATO

A. European Union

European nations contribute a large number of international coalition warships to patrol the western Indian Ocean to deter and disrupt piracy. European Union states have contributed to the U.S.-fashioned counter-piracy coalition task force 151 (CTF 151), which reports to U.S. Central Command's three-star Navy component commander forward deployed to

Bahrain. The Joint Strategy Paper for Somalia for 2008-2013 allocates €215.8 million under the 10th European Development Fund (EDF).

With characteristic multilateralism, European states are most likely to conduct counter-piracy operations under the aegis of a broad international effort. European interest in the threat of Somali piracy emerged in 2005-06 out of concern over the vulnerability to Somali pirates of World Food Program (WFP) shipments. For 3.2 million people in Somalia–43 percent of the population–humanitarian assistance is necessary to meet basic human needs. In many areas of south and central Somalia, 15 to 20 percent of the population suffers from acute child malnutrition. But 90 percent of the UN World Food Program (WFP) aid into Somalia is carried by sea. Because of the general state of disrepair of the Somali road infrastructure and the relative efficiency of moving bulk goods by ship, food from donor nations outside East Africa arrives by port into Somalia.

In order to husband scarce funds, the WFP typically leases older, smaller vessels to carry humanitarian aid to the Somali population. These vessels are particularly vulnerable to Somali piracy since they lack speed and sit low in the water. In a country where food security is a risk for millions of people, the WFP shipments are attractive targets for Somali pirate gangs operating from the beach in Puntland. Somali pirates began attacking WFP shipments in 2006. If the shipments are seized, the pirates will use the food as a weapon, withholding it from needy populations and dispensing it based on political patronage. Furthermore, the ransom to free the ship and crew constitutes a nice bonus.

Thus, the initial impetus for EU involvement in counter-piracy operations was to protect the vulnerable WFP ships from Somali pirates. France, the Netherlands, Canada and Denmark offered naval escorts to ensure that humanitarian food aid reached Somalia. By November 2007, naval escorts began to accompany WFP ships carrying food aid to Somalia, and these missions were formalized in December 2008 with the inception of Operation Atalanta.[3]

Operation Atalanta is an initiative of the EU Naval Force (EU NAVFOR) conducted within the framework of the European Common Security and Defense Policy (CSDP). The 27 countries of the EU are working to establish a single voice on security issues. The CSDP is managed through a handful of permanent EU politico-military bodies based in Brussels, including the

[3] Acts Adopted Under Title V of the EU Treaty, Council Decision of 2008/918/CFSP, December 8, 2008, Official Journal of the European Union, September 12, 2008, at L 330/19.

ambassadorial-level Political and Security Committee, which monitors threats and develops integrated responses. The EU Military Committee is the high military body with the Council of the European Union and consists of chiefs of defense of the various states. Finally, two additional bodies–Civilian Aspects of Crisis Management and the EU Military Staff–play a role in integrating national responses into a cohesive effort under the EU banner.

In 1999 the EU dispatched its first peacekeepers–helping to stabilize the situation in Bosnia and Herzegovina. The deployment was followed by Operation Concordia, a peacekeeping effort in Macedonia. In 2005, a rule of law mission was established in Iraq, and an EU police mission was set up in Afghanistan in 2007. Further peacekeeping involvement in Chad and the Central African Republic was followed in August 2008 by a brokered ceasefire and deployment of observers to stop hostilities between Russia and Georgia.

The EU counter-piracy effort began in December 2008. Since its origin, the scope of Operation Atalanta has expanded from protecting WFP ships delivering humanitarian aid to Somalia to broader support for the African Union Mission in Somalia (AMISOM). The resolution under which EU NAVFOR operates sets forth a commitment to conduct operations in accordance with relevant UN Security Council Resolutions (UNSCR) and international law:

> The European Union shall conduct a military operation in support of [UNSCRs] . . . consistent with action permitted with respect to piracy under Article 100 *et seq*. of the United Nations Convention on the Law of the Sea . . . ., hereinafter called "Atalanta" in order to contribute to:
>
> - the protection of vessels of the WFP delivering food aid to displaced persons in Somalia, in accordance with the mandate laid down in [UNSCR] 1814 (2008);
> - the protection of vulnerable vessels cruising off the Somali coast, and the deterrence, prevention and repression of acts of piracy and armed robbery off the Somali coast, in accordance with the mandate laid down in [UNSCR] 1816 (2008)[4]

Adhering to the Security Council mandates, Operation ATALANTA conducts patrols to protect both WFP and AMISOM shipping. While this

[4] European Union Council Joint Acton 2008/851/CFSP of November 10, 2008 on a European Union military operation to contribute to the deterrence, prevention and repression of acts of piracy and armed robbery off the Somali coast, November 11, 2008, Official Journal of the European Union, at L 31/304.

sort of mission creep is perhaps inevitable in order to defeat pirates, it begins to place EU forces on one side of a multi-dimensional internal struggle for power inside Somalia. Other nations–e.g. Uganda, which has provided the bulk of troops in support of AMISOM–have paid a price for disrupting the operations of the Somali Islamic terrorist organization, *Harakaat al-Shabaab al-Mujaahidiin*, which is also known as "Al Shabaab." Al Shabaab claims responsibility for a 2010 bombing in Kampala that killed 76 people–an attack that was in retaliation for Uganda's leadership in AMISOM. There is still uncertainty over whether the kidnappings and murders of European tourists that occurred in coastal resort areas in Kenya in September and October 2011 are related to Somali piracy, or even more ominously, the Al Shabaab Islamic terrorist organization.[5] In response to the violence inside Kenya, two battalions of Kenyan Army troops supported by helicopter gunships crossed into Somalia on October 16 to conduct a pincer maneuver against the Shabaab stronghold at Kismayo.[6]

The EU NAVFOR also monitors fishing activities off the coast of Somalia to ensure that foreign-flagged ships from distant water states are not poaching Somalia's fish stocks. Some Somali pirates, especially in the "early" years of 2004-2006, claimed that they were operating as an informal coast guard to suppress illegal, unreported, and unregulated (IUU) fishing.

The force elements of EU NAVFOR consist of surface navy vessels and auxiliary ships, such as oilers, manned Maritime Patrol and Reconnaissance Aircrafts (MPRA), and individual Vessel Protection Detachment (VPD) teams embarked on commercial ships transiting the area.[7] The air and sea forces are orchestrated out of the EU NAVFOR Operational Headquarters in Northwood, United Kingdom, and through members of the armed forces serving on board ships in theater.

---

[5] Four European women were kidnapped in the span of less than a month. One United Kingdom national was kidnapped in Kenya in September, and her husband was murdered during the abduction. A French national was seized from her coastal home only two weeks later, and she was confirmed dead on October 19, 2011. Two Spanish aid workers from the humanitarian group *Médecins Sans Frontiéres* were kidnapped from the Dadaab refugee camp on October 13, 2011. Lauren Gelfand, *Kenya Opens Ground War in Somalia against Shabab*, Jane's Defence Weekly, October 26, 2011, p 5.

[6] Id.

[7] Council Joint Acton 2008/851/CFSP of November 10, 2008 on a European Union military operation to contribute to the deterrence, prevention and repression of acts of piracy and armed robbery off the Somali coast, Official Journal of the European Union, L 31/304, November 11, 2008, Council Decision 2009/907/CFSP of December 8, 2009 amending Joint Action 2008/851/CFSP on a European Union military operation to contribute to the deterrence, prevention and repression of acts of piracy and armed robbery off the Somali coast, Official Journal of the European Union, L 322/27, September 12, 2009.

Funding for EU NAVFOR totaled € 8.4 million in 2010 and € 8.05 million in 2011. The financing is derived from a formula based on the Athena Mechanism, which distributes assessments among the EU member states based upon their gross domestic product. Common costs are shared among the participating states, and include the operation of the Northwood command center and embarked at sea NAVFOR headquarters located aboard a flagship. Medical services and transportation are also shared expenses. Each individual state, however, shoulders the cost of deployment of ships, aircraft and military personnel.

The size of EU naval forces on station in the western Indian Ocean varies according to the threat level. The cyclical ebb of the monsoon seasons affects the prevalence of piracy. Generally, Operation Atalanta consists of five to ten surface combat vessels, one or two auxiliary ships, and as many as four MPRAs. Including those based on land, approximately 2,000 military personnel are assigned to EU NAVFOR. Since its inception, more than 20 vessels and aircraft have participated in the effort.

EU NAVFOR patrols an area that stretches from the south of the Red Sea and the Gulf of Aden to the Western part of the Indian Ocean extending to the Seychelles. This region is comparable in size to the Mediterranean Sea and is 2,000,000 square nautical miles (almost 4,000,000 square kilometers), or the equivalent of 30 times the size of England, ten times the size of Germany, or seven times the area of France or Spain. Since the launch of the initiative, EU NAVFOR has had a 100 percent success rate providing escorts to WFP vessels delivering over 520,000 tons of food that has fed 1.13 million Somalis per day. The force has also participated in protecting the Internationally Recommended Transit Corridor through the Gulf of Aden, ensuring safe passage to and from the Suez Canal. The EU also operates Maritime Safety Center–Horn of Africa (MSC–HOA) to help to coordinate international merchant shipping through the region.

Any long-term solution will have to involve the African states, and the EU is heavily involved in developing regional capacity to counter Somali piracy. The mission has broadened to include land-based programs designed to build state institutions and broaden the rule of law in Somalia and the surrounding states. After adoption of UNSCR 1872 in 2009, for example, the EU began a program for training of Somali security forces in Uganda.[8] The Political and Security Committee decided on April 21, 2009 to accept contributions of

[8] S/RES 1872 (2009), May 26, 2009.

third states to EU NAVFOR,[9] and established a Committee of Contributors.[10] Norway was the first non-EU country to contribute to the operation. Croatia and Ukraine provided staff officers to the headquarters, and Montenegro entered into a Participation Agreement with the EU on March 22, 2010.[11]

On January 25 2010 the EU Council approved a programmed military mission to help train Somali security forces. On April 7, 2010, this decision resulted in the establishment of the EU training mission (EUTM) as part of the overall effort to strengthen the Transitional Federal Government (TFG) and governmental authority and institutions of Somalia. The actual training, which takes place in Uganda, began in May 2010, and includes coordination with AMISOM, the TFG, Uganda, the African Union, the United Nations and the United States. Training has been provided to 2,000 Somali recruits up to and including the platoon level, including appropriate modular and specialized training for officers and non-commissioned officers. On December 7 2010, the EU Council agreed to extend its military mission in Somalia until December 12, 2012.[12]

The EU also signed an agreement to assist the Seychelles.[13] The comprehensive Status of Forces Agreement specifies that EU personnel, ships, and aircraft may be used in the Seychelles, and throughout the territorial sea of the country, against pirate ships.[14] The Seychelles grants "EUNAVFOR personnel freedom of movement and freedom to travel within its territory, including its waters and its air space."[15] "Freedom of

---

[9] Political and security Commitee decision ATALANTA/1/2010 of March 5, 2010 amending Political and Security Committee Decision ATALANTA/2/2009 on the acceptance of third States' contributions to the European Union military operation to contribute to the deterrence, prevention and repression of acts of piracy and armed robbery off the Somali coast (Atalanta).

[10] EU Political and Security Committee Decision ATALANTA/3/2009 on the setting up of the Committee of Contributors for the European Union military operation to contribute to the deterrence, prevention and repression of acts of piracy and armed robbery off the Somali coast (Atalanta).

[11] EU Council Decision 2010/199/CFSP, March 22, 2010, on the signing and conclusion of the Agreement between the European Union and Montenegro on the participation of Montenegro in the European Union military operation to contribute to the deterrence, prevention and repression of acts of piracy and armed robbery off the Somali coast (Operation Atalanta), Official Journal of the European Union, August 4, 2010, at L 88/1-/2.

[12] EU Council Decision 2010/766/CFSP of December 7, 2010, amending Joint Action 2008/851/CFSP on a European Union military operation to contribute to the deterrence, prevention and repression of acts of piracy and armed robbery off the Somali coast, Official Journal of the European Union, November 12, 2010, L 327/49-50.

[13] Council Decision 2009/916/CFSP of October 23, 2009 concerning the signing and conclusion of the Agreement between the European Union and the Republic of Seychelles on the status of the European Union-led force in the Republic of Seychelles in the framework of the EU military operation Atalanta, Official Journal of the European Union, L 323/12-13.

[14] *Id.*

[15] *Id.*

movement" for EU forces includes "stopping and anchoring under any circumstances."[16] EU forces also have permission to use any "military device" on land or at sea, but subject to host nation rules on flight safety.[17] The agreement also contains standards privileges and immunities from the Seychelles's civil law process.

B. NATO

The North Atlantic treaty Organization (NATO) consists of 28 nations, but not all are involved in the counter-piracy effort. For a decade NATO has been conducting a maritime anti-terrorism operation in the Mediterranean named Active Endeavour.[18] The objective of Active Endeavour is to target terrorists involved in the conflicts in Afghanistan, the Balkans, and Iraq. NATO warships have boarded thousands of ships in the Mediterranean Sea, providing technical and legal experience for the more recent counter-piracy operations. Even before the EU became involved in counter-piracy, NATO responded to the threat with its first out-of-area maritime mission. In a September 25, 2008 letter, UN Secretary-General Ban Ki-moon asked NATO to provide warship escorts to WFP vessels transiting through the waters of the Horn of Africa, bound for Kenyan ports. The request was intended to fill a gap in security escorts until the European Union (EU) could pick up the mission. In response, NATO's Operation Allied Provider conducted its first escorts from October to December 2008, utilizing a deployed Standing NATO Maritime Group (SNMG).

From March to August, 2009, NATO continued the more modest Operation Allied Protector, but then transitioned to Operation Ocean Shield.[19] On August 17 2009, Operation Ocean Shield was initiated to extend the work of Operation Allied Protector, which ended the day before. Ocean Shield entails the following military missions:

- Deter and disrupt pirate attacks and come to the aid of ships *in extremis*.
- Search for suspected pirates, detaining them and seizing their vessels–delivering both to law enforcement authorities.
- Build local and regional maritime security capacity.
- Collaborate with EU NAVFOR and other international organizations conducting counter-piracy operations.

---

[16] *Id.*

[17] *Id.*

[18] NATO also used maritime forces in support of policing the arms embargo against the toppled regime of Muammar Quadafi in Libya under authority of UNSCR 1970 and 1973.

[19] Counter Piracy Operation Ocean Shield, http://www.shipping.nato.int/CounterPir

Operation Ocean Shield has been extended into the end of 2012.

NATO has two principle maritime groups, which are multinational, scalable and flexible, integrated maritime forces comprised of warships from member nations that train and operate as a single unit. Under the command of a commodore or rear admiral, the SNMGs can perform the gamut of missions, from peacekeeping exercises, maritime security operations and major combat operations. From March to June 2009, NATO deployed five warships of the SNMG1 as part of Operation Allied Provider. Since then, the counter-piracy mission has rotated between SNMG1 and SNMG2. Command of the SNMGs periodically rotates among NATO nations, but the command element for Operation Ocean Shield is located in Northwood Middlesex, United Kingdom. The NATO Shipping Centre also is at the Allied Maritime Command Headquarters Northwood. The North Atlantic Council approved Operation Ocean Shield on August 17 2009, and the effort expands Operation Allied Protector.

Operation Ocean Shield also operates an Internet website that includes emergency contact telephone numbers for the NATO Shipping Centre, MSC–HOA and the International Maritime Bureau Piracy Reporting Center, the last of which is operated by the International Chamber of Commerce. The NATO website also maintains a daily piracy overview, weekly assessments, updated advice on vessel safety precautions, use of onboard citadels, and locations of suspected pirate action groups (PAGs) that are stalking merchant ships. Ocean Shield is also contributing to public diplomacy by broadcasting on Somali radio to correct disinformation that the pirates pass on to the Somali population. The NATO force operates beyond the Gulf of Aden and the International Recommended Transit Corridor (IRTC), sending forces to patrol the Somali Basin.

Portugal, for example, operates a P-3 Orion Maritime Patrol and Reconnaissance Aircraft from the Seychelles. While at-sea counter-piracy operations and aerial surveillance will continue to be the focus, a new element of regional-state counter-piracy capacity building has been developed for Operation Ocean Shield. NATO's capacity building effort will aim to assist East African states in developing local and regional capabilities to combat piracy activities.

III. UNITED STATES

The United States has a well-developed strategy for ensuring maritime security. In December 2004, the White House issued a joint National Security Council and Homeland Security Council directive to organize the

Nation's maritime security efforts.[20] The presidential directive established the Maritime Security Policy Coordination Committee (MSPCC), which the Obama administration has renamed the Maritime Security Interagency Policy Committee (MSIPC). The purpose of the MSIPC is to coordinate maritime security policy for the National and Homeland Security Councils, and the committee is co-chaired by representatives from the Department of Defense and the Department of Homeland Security. The MSIPC also developed a National Strategy for Maritime Security (NSMS), which complemented the National Security Strategy of the United States. The NSMS was released in 2005, and it is supported by eight plans that relate to specific tasks in the maritime domain, such as port and transportation infrastructure protection.[21] Perhaps the most enduring of the eight supporting plans is the Maritime Operational Threat Response (MOTR) protocols, which provide a road map for ensuring interagency coordination within the U.S. government during or after a piracy attack or other maritime incident or crisis. The MOTR protocols are implemented by all departments and agencies with a maritime security mission, and the entire collaborative effort is orchestrated from an interagency command center located in Washington, D.C.

The Oceans Law & Policy Advisers in the Department of Defense led an effort at the National Security Council to augment the NSMS with a specific policy addressing U.S. interests in counter-piracy. The effort was undertaken in response to the increase in piracy attacks off the coast of Somalia in 2006, and it culminated in the U.S. Maritime Security (Piracy) Policy, which was signed by the president in June 2007. The Piracy Policy identified the range of American interests in countering maritime piracy, including freedom of navigation and regional stability.

In response to the high-visibility attacks on the *Sirius Star* and *Faina* during the fall of 2008, the National Security Council hastily wrote and published a "partnership and action plan" that supplemented the Piracy

---

[20] National Security Presidential Directive (NSPD) 41/ Homeland Security Presidential Directive (HSPD) 13 Maritime Security Policy (December 2004).

[21] The eight supporting plans of the NSMS are:

1. National Plan to Achieve Maritime Domain Awareness, October 2005.
2. Global Maritime Intelligence Integration Plan, July 2005.
3. Maritime Operational Threat Response Plan, October 2006.
4. International Outreach and Coordination Strategy, November 2005.
5. Maritime Infrastructure Recovery Plan, April 2006.
6. Maritime Transportation System Security Plan, October 2005.
7. Maritime Commerce Security Plan, October 2005.
8. Domestic Outreach Plan, October 2005.

These plans constitute "Annex A" of the NSMS.

Policy, with a specific focus on the Somali threat. The document broke new ground, but appeared to fill a public diplomacy need by the administration to explain to legislators, the American people, and friends and allies abroad, that the United States was focused specifically on the problems gathering off the Horn of Africa.[22]

The Action Plan was approved in December 2008, setting forth three distinct approaches to suppressing Somali piracy. First, there was an immediate need to prevent pirate attacks by reducing the vulnerability of the maritime domain, and this included working with flag states and the major international shipping organizations to "harden" merchant shipping. Second, the U.S. recommitted to disrupting piracy attacks "consistent with international law and the rights and responsibilities of coastal and flag States." Third, there was a new focus on criminal prosecution of suspected pirates, although this was always understood not to be a panacea given the inexhaustible supply of potential pirate recruits in Somalia.

In order to bring the heralded but never achieved measures of effectiveness to the effort, the Action Plan assigned 14 tasks. At the time of its inception, ten of the tasks were in execution phase, two were in the planning phase, one was in the assessment phase, and one task was considered no longer necessary.

Since the release of the U.S. Action Plan a number of developments have converged to yield significant progress in international coordination. After creation of an international coordinating forum was recommended in UNSCR 1851 of December 16, 2008, two dozen nations formed the Contact Group on Piracy off the Coast of Somalia (CGPCS). The Contact Group was created on January 14, 2009 and has become the primary focal point for international counter-piracy policy coordination. The CGPCS has grown to include nearly 50 nations. The International Maritime Organization (IMO), a specialized maritime agency of the United Nations, has been placed in a rather awkward position by the success and strength of the CGPCS, and some have suggested that the Contact Group is encroaching on the mandate of the IMO. But as a leaner effort lacking in the formal trappings of an international organization, the Contact Group has been more nimble and responsive to nations' concerns, producing numerous breakthroughs in international coordination.

[22] The National Security Council, Countering Piracy off the Horn of Africa: Partnership & Action Plan (2008).

Today most merchant vessels use the Internationally Recognized Transit Corridor (IRTC) to transit the Gulf of Aden, which grew out of the Contact Group. The CGPCS has also been effective at sufficient interdiction-capable vessels based on national priorities and missions and they are successfully seizing and destroying, or retaining for evidence, suspected pirate vessels and equipment. Part of the early effort was to reach bilateral agreements with area nations to prosecute captured pirates. After Kenya suspended such an agreement with the United States, however, Washington has had to think more seriously about bringing suspects before a U.S. federal court.

The counter-piracy effort also unfolds within the context of the tri-service seapower strategy. The Cooperative Strategy for 21st Century Seapower was signed by the chiefs of the Navy, Marine Corps and Coast Guard in October 2007, and it has set the tone for the contemporary U.S. approach to global maritime security. Counter-piracy patrols off the Horn of Africa were the first attempt to realize naval operations in accordance with the collaborative principles of the Cooperative Strategy.[23] Finally, tactical guidance for the U.S. Navy, Marine Corps, and Coast Guard is provided in the Naval Operations Concept.[24]

With these policy authorities in mind, the commander of naval forces for U.S. Central Command established Combined Task Force 151 (CTF 151) in January 2009 as a dedicated multinational task force focused exclusively on countering maritime piracy in the Horn of Africa. Located in Bahrain, Commander, Naval Forces, U.S. Central Command is also "double hatted" as Commander, U.S. Fifth Fleet and Commander, U.S. Maritime Forces (CMF). Although CTF 151 is nominally under the overall authority of the CMF, the task force has great operational independence and has been led by naval officers from a variety of nations. Previous commanders of Task Force 151 include officers from the Republic of Korea Navy, the Turkish Navy, and Rear Admiral Harris Chan Weng Yip of the Singaporean Navy.

The Department of Defense has two geographic combatant commanders led by four-star general officers that are responsible for planning and conducting U.S. military operations to suppress Somali piracy. U.S. Africa Command, located in Stuttgart, Germany, was established in 2007. There is a

---

[23] James Kraska and Brian Wilson, *The Cooperative Strategy and the Pirates of the Gulf of Aden*, 154 RUSI Journal (Royal United Services Institute) 74, 77 (April 2009).

[24] *Naval Operations Concept: Implementing the Maritime Strategy* (General James T. Conway, USMC, Admiral Gary Roughead, USN, and Admiral Thad W. Allen, USCG, 2010), at http://www.navy.mil/maritime/noc/NOC2010.pdf. "*Naval Operations Concept 2010* (NOC 10) describes when, where and how U.S. naval forces will contribute to enhancing security, preventing conflict and prevailing in war." *Id.* at Preface.

seam between the two combatant commands along a line that runs due south of Yemen, complicating the counter-piracy response by American forces. Still suffering from a maladroit roll-out, not all nations on the continent are entirely trustful of U.S. Africa Command, with South Africa being perhaps the most reticent. Meanwhile, just as some Africans complain that establishment of African Command presages a militarization or even neo-colonization of U.S. Africa policy, others express dismay that a combatant command designed to broaden engagement on the continent is located in Germany.

The most often cited reasons for locating the command in Europe are force protection and logistics. The transportation infrastructure in Africa is sometimes fairly limited, so it often is easier and fast, for example, to fly from one African capitol to another by flying through Europe. Furthermore, political, safety and security considerations may preclude a large footprint of U.S. service members, not to mention a large number of associated family members. Nonetheless, if the U.S. military experience in Asia has taught anything, it is that virtual presence is actual absence and there is no substitute for U.S. forces being forward-deployed and integrated into the region.

IV. AFRICA–THE EAST AFRICAN COMMUNITY

Ironically, no nation outside Somalia suffers more from the effects of piracy than land-locked Uganda. Piracy has created a shortage of consumer goods in the country that has caused rapid inflation, with some household goods costing four times as much as similar items in Tanzania. In essence, piracy is tantamount to an economic embargo on Uganda, and there appears no end in sight.

AMISOM has about 7,000 Ugandan military forces and 2,000 from Burundi. There are sixty staff members from African countries–for example, Kenya has sent four advisers. The United States is training troops from Djibouti to participate in the mission. But the East African states envision a force of 20,000. Nigeria and Sierra Leone have declined to participate due to a lack of resources, and provisioning and training their forces for peacekeeping operation (PKO) duty in Somalia is among the most cost effective measures we could take in the region.

The United Nations Monitoring Group has reported that Al Shabaab generates $70 to $100 million per year in duties and fees levied at airports, seaports, through local sales taxes, and *ad hoc* "jihad contributions," and checkpoint extortions justified in terms of religious obligation or *zakat*.[25] The Uganda forces that participate in Peacekeeping in Somalia have observed that Al Shabaab is being financed from the ransom proceeds obtained by piracy. When large ransoms are paid there is an increase in Al Shabaab activity, including noticeable increases in the expenditure of ammunition. Al Shabaab is reliant on the use of improvised explosive devices, grenades, and small arms sniper fire to create havoc, so a small amount of money from piracy provides cash infusion into the force.

The PKO in Somalia wants and needs equipment and training to facilitate the mission and assist the TFG in stabilizing the country, which everyone agrees is the only long-term solution to the problem of Somali piracy. Some African states, such as Djibouti and Sierra Leone, have indicated a desire to participate in Somali peacekeeping operations, but lack the resources to do so. During a multilateral exercise in September 2011, which was sponsored by U.S. Africa Command, counter-piracy was a feature of regional readiness and response. The exercise included military forces from Burundi, Kenya, Rwanda, Tanzania, and Uganda. Military leaders of several of these states complained to the author that the naval missions are ineffective, merely "swatting the bee." Two of Uganda's generals, General Okello and Lieutenant General Katumba expressed a lack of patience with the current approach. The armed forces in East Africa are motivated to acquire the resources to "go after the beehive" in Somalia and stop the scourge of piracy in the region.

Leveraging the PKO in the fight against piracy treats the maritime threat at sea as much more like a war than a law enforcement operation, although East African military forces understand that piracy is regarded as a crime of universal jurisdiction, and not generally considered an act of war. But while the threat of piracy poses a relatively minor inconvenience to most states, the effect on East Africa has been devastating–tantamount to a blockade. From the perspective of the United States and Europe, piracy looks like a crime spree, but here on the ground in East Africa, it is war. Under this theory, pirates are acting in sustainment of Al Shabaab, and therefore become lawful targets in international humanitarian law.

The naval coalition operating in the Indian Ocean is described to the author by African military leaders as mere "window dressing." The East African forces could use assistance now, and the problem of piracy can be resolved in a few months. Not only is this approach the humane and efficient method of

---

[25] S/2011/433, ¶ 60, p.27.

addressing the threat of Somali piracy, it is also the most prudent. General officers in East Africa want to get the job done now before the disrupting effect of piracy ransoms, powerful criminal organizations, and a wealthier Al Shabaab throw the country into even worse condition than it already is. Al Shabaab is evolving into a powerful pseudo-political criminal cartel with a religious message that reverberates throughout the Muslim communities of East Africa–if it successfully makes the transition, the threat to the regional stability will dwarf the rag-tag pirates.

Al Shabaab, not piracy, is the most acute threat to security and stability in East Africa. The group already has conducted attacks in Addis Ababa, Ethiopia and coordinated double suicide bombings at two nightclubs in Kampala on July 11, 2010. The nightclub attacks were committed by non-Somalis from Uganda and Kenya; 79 people died in the attacks and scores were injured.[26]

The naval coalition, being relatively cost-ineffective, is the wrong tool for the job of suppressing piracy, even at sea. The naval forces patrolling the International Recommended Transit Corridor in the Gulf of Aden have helped to reduce piracy attacks by 50 percent in that area. But implementation of Best Management Practices by merchant ships and use of private security companies have also had an impact on reducing piracy in the Gulf of Aden–perhaps even a larger impact than naval patrols. In any event, attacks have increased significantly in areas where there are fewer naval patrols, such as the Red Sea and the Western Indian Ocean.[27] The answer is not to concentrate high-end warships, but rather to create a diffuse network consisting of private security and small boat coastal security and naval forces. The fleet commander of Kenya, for example, indicated to the author that his naval force consists of two fast attack ships and two offshore patrol vessels (OPVs). The OPVs are 70-meters in length and weigh about 700 tons, a much more precise and cost-effective solution to piracy than billion-dollar capital warships. The versatile boats have 14-day operational endurance. The Kenyan naval base at Manda Bay sits on the northern edge of Kenya, next to the Somali coast. If the Kenyan Navy had four additional OPVs and just some additional training, it could divide its existing crews among the new platforms and completely control piracy along the Somali coast as far north as Kismayo.

Finally, the West has waffled on whether to commit to the long-term viability of the TFG. While multiple UN Security Council resolutions,

[26] S/201/443, ¶ 46, p. 24.
[27] S/2011/433, at ¶ 88 at p.33.

binding on all nations under Chapter VII, have called on the international community to back the TFG, actual support has been tepid. The reason that states are relatively reticent about the future of the TFG is that, at times, the organization has been remarkably incompetent, suffers from rampant corruption, and is woefully lacking in vision and capability. But the TFG has hung on–long after many Africa observers thought it would. In early August 2011, TFG forces with the great assistance of AMISOM, ejected Al Shabaab from Mogadishu in a show of strength that provides a glimpse of promise for its future. Perhaps most importantly, there is no option other than the TFG. For all its faults, the TFG is viable, and the UN Security Council and our East African partners have put their eggs in the same basket with the TFG. We should too.

The first of three information-sharing centers (ISCs) developed pursuant to the Djibouti Code of Conduct opened in Mombasa, Kenya, in early 2011. The Mombasa ISC is co-located with the Regional Maritime Rescue Coordination Center, which operates around-the-clock. [28] The Maldives, Seychelles, Mauritius, Kenya, and eventually, Somalia, will be linked with the Mombasa ISC. The Mombasa MRCC was established in 2006 and covers a vast area of the Western Indian Ocean extending to the Seychelles. The Mombasa MRCC is linked with the Dar es Salaam MRCC sub-center, which was commissioned in 2009. The ISC also shares information with the Sana'a ISC and Dar es Salaam ISCs to form a three-ISC network, as envisioned under the Djibouti Code.[29] The centers receive and respond to piracy alerts and requests for information or assistance. Each center is also designed to share information with maritime authorities and the international coalition of warships operating against piracy in the Western Indian Ocean, including EU NAVFOR, the United Kingdom Maritime Trade Operations (UKMTO), and the Maritime Liaison Office (MARLO), Bahrain.

It is often overlooked that the fight against piracy has to begin and end in Somalia. Although much of the country has been in political chaos since the early-1990s, other parts are relatively stable and secure, and governed by responsible authorities. Somaliland, for example, has maintained a piracy-free coastline and authorities are consolidating nascent democracy after the free and fair presidential election of June 2010. The trend in Southern Somalia is less promising. The TFG, allied militias and AMISOM are engaged in a war against Al-Shabaab. The TFG security forces are largely devoid of a sense of patriotic nationalism, and instead retain clan-based

---

[28] *Piracy Information-Sharing Centre in Mombasa Commissioned*, IMO News, Issue 2, 2011, at p. 9.
[29] Id.

loyalties to individual commanders who look to AMISOM rather than the Government for leadership and support.[30] Unlike Al-Shabaab, the TFG relies on external forces for security.

Today, Al-Shabaab is the principal impediment to peace and security in Somalia.[31] But Al-Shabaab is not unstoppable. Even after conducting several spectacular suicide attacks in 2010–one on August 24 at the Muna Hotel that killed four members of Parliament and another on September 9 at Mogadishu International Airport coinciding with the arrival of a high-level international delegation–Al Shabaab has experienced hard setbacks. In 2010, the influx of 2,000 Ugandan peacekeepers and an aggressive counter-offensive by TFG forces reversed Al Shabaab's gains. In 2011, Al Shabaab was kicked out of Mogadishu, beginning with an offensive by AMISOM's Burundi detachment complemented by TFG forces. Finally, the aforementioned Kenyan incursion into Somalia to drive at Al Shabaab's southern operations is rolling back previous gains by the Islamist group. Operation Lindi Nchi (Defend the Country) was originally aimed at defeating Shabaab forces crossing into Kenya from Somalia, but a side benefit is that the mission has placed the pirate's business model at risk. Fearing that hostage seafarers might be released or pirate camps overrun by the Kenyan army, pirates are lowering their ransom demands in order to reach a quick deal with shipping companies. Al Shabaab provides protection to the pirates for cash, weapons, and logistical support that is all worth $4.9 to $8.3 billion.[32] But with Al Shabaab on the run and facing a strong Kenyan force, the pirates are more vulnerable and thus interested in closing a deal. The Algerian-flagged M/V *Bilda*, for example, was hijacked on January 1, 2011 while on its way to Dar es Salaam, Tanzania. The ship and its multinational crew of 27 seafarers were being held under a $6 million demand for the release of the ship. But after Al Shabaab suffered setbacks from the Kenyan incursion, the ship was released upon payment of $3.5 million.[33] These defeats of Al Shabaab, possibly exacerbated by a reliance on inexperienced conscripted child soldiers, have forced the group to focus on nurturing clan alliances rather relying on ideology to attract supporters.[34]

[30] S/2011/433, ¶ 15, p. 16.

[31] S/2011/433, ¶¶ 17-18, p. 17.

[32] Benard Sanga, *Kenya's Somali Incursion Cuts Piracy Costs in Indian Ocean, Business Daily*, November 9, 2011.

[33] *Id.*

[34] S/2011/433, ¶ 19-24, p. 18.

V. ASIAN CONTRIBUTIONS TO THE FIGHT AGAINST SOMALI PIRACY– JAPAN AND CHINA

A. Japan

Each year about 2,000 ships flagged in Japan or owned by Japanese corporations transit the Gulf of Aden and coast of Somalia. The Gulf of Aden is a particularly important sea lane, connecting Japan to Europe. Responding to an urgent need to protect the lives and property of Japanese nationals, the Japanese Prime Minister, acting upon Cabinet decision, approved a maritime security order on March 13, 2009, to deploy Self-Defense Forces to the region.[35] The destroyers *Sazanami* and the *Samidare* departed Japan on March 14 and began escort operations in the Gulf of Aden on March 30.[36] A detachment of Japan Coast Guard officers was embarked on each warship. During their first 90 days on station, the destroyers escorted 100 ships, including Japanese-flagged ships, foreign-flagged ships with Japanese crew or operated by Japanese carriers, or transporting important Japanese cargo.

On May 15, 2009, an order was issued to supplement the destroyers with the deployment of P-3C maritime patrol aircraft (MPA). On May 28, two P-3C maritime patrol aircraft left Japan and began conducting surveillance and reconnaissance throughout the Gulf of Aden. The Ground Self-Defense Force is charged with protecting the P-3C aircraft at the apron, the Air Self-Defense Force maintains an airlift group consisting of C-130H and U-4 support sorties into the airport, and the entire package associated with the Djibouti deployment constitutes the first joint task force to be dispatched overseas since World War II. The next month, the adoption of a June 19 law provided authority for Japan to escort foreign-flagged ships at risk of piracy attack. The law also provides authority for JMSDF ships to fire on private ships as a last resort to prevent piracy.[37]

The legal authority for the Japanese response is grounded in the United Nations Convention on the Law of the Sea and the UN Security Council resolutions addressing the threat of piracy off the coast of Somalia. The Diet passed an Anti-Piracy Measures Law on June 19, 2009, and it was enacted on July 24, 2009. The law provided authority for the Minister of Defense to determine, with the approval of the Prime Minister, the scope of Japan's anti-piracy operations for a period of one year. The first deployment under the

---

[35] The measure was issued under Article 82 of the Self-Defense Forces Law, providing stopgap authority until a law was enacted. Defense of Japan 2009 128-29 (Ministry of Defense, Government of Japan, 2009).

[36] Defense of Japan 2009 129 (Ministry of Defense, Government of Japan, 2009).

[37] Asahi Shimbun, June 3, 2011, Kyodo News Service, June 1, 2011 and Jiji, July 2009.

new law was made by the destroyers *Harusame* and *Amagiri*, which left Japan on July 6, 2009, and arrived on station in the western Indian Ocean on July 29, 2009.

On July 1, 2011, the JSDF unveiled its first overseas military base since World War II–the Japanese Facility for Counter-Piracy Mission–located in Djibouti in the Horn of Africa.[38] The facility operates two maritime patrol aircraft and includes approximately 200 personnel. American and French military forces already operate small bases in Djibouti, and the Japanese facility is adjacent to the U.S. and French installations, both of which are co-located with the international airport. Japan has assiduously avoided calling the facility a "base" because the word implies a permanent deployment. Still, the Japanese government plans to operate the facility for as long as a decade. The JSDF initially staged from the neighboring US. Camp Lemonnier, but then moved to its own facility to broaden its capacity to conduct operations and improve logistical support to the counter-piracy effort. When the facility was opened on July 7, the president of the Japanese Shipowner's Association, Akimitsu Ashida, was present, underscoring the close relationship that the Japan Maritime Self-Defense Force has with commercial industry. The day after the opening, Japan announced that it would continue to deploy two P-3C aircraft and two destroyers to patrol the Horn of Africa. The Japan military forces may use force in accomplishing the counter-piracy mission in accordance with Article 7 of the Police Officer Duties Execution Law, which is applied *mutatis mutandis* to the provisions of Article 93 of the Self-Defense Forces Law.[39]

The Japanese public has supported the deployment by a ratio of about two-to-one, and the deployment has resulted in more than 800 messages of gratitude by ship masters and ship owners who have been escorted.[40] On November 23, 2010, the IMO conferred a bravery award for Japanese successes–a testament to the high degree of professionalization of the Japan Maritime Self-Defense Force. The counter-piracy mission has drawn the attention of the international community, and already there is an expectation that Japan Self-Defense Forces may play a greater role in maintaining regional political stability. Whispers have suggested that the Japan Self-Defense Forces, for example, might deploy next to South Sudan.

---

[38] Yoichi Kato, *SDF's New Anti-Piracy Base Creates a Dilemma*, Asahi Shimbun, July 6, 2011.

[39] Defense of Japan 2009 at 130 (Ministry of Defense, Government of Japan, 2009).

[40] Defense of Japan 2010 at 252 (Ministry of Defense, Government of Japan, 2010).

B China

China's participation in counter-piracy operations is inseparable from the omnipresent story of the rise of Chinese economic and military power. In a December 2009 interview on the Ministry of Defense website, for example, retired Rear Admiral Yin Zhou suggested that the PLAN should consider establishing China's first overseas military base, most likely in the Middle East. Although Beijing clarified that China had "no plans for an overseas naval base," the proposal illustrated China's growing ability to project power.[41]

One of the most important edifices of PLAN power is China's counter-piracy deployments. The deployments to the western Indian Ocean mark the first out-of-area deployments for the Chinese Navy since the seven massive flotilla expeditions commanded by Admiral Zheng He from 1405 to 1433. Two PLAN destroyers and a supply ship have conducted anti-piracy operations in the waters off the Horn of Africa since December 2008. With the arrival of the advanced *Kunlun Shan* landing platform dock (LPD) in July 2010, the PLAN introduced a large, versatile expeditionary air-ground-sea capability to the western Indian Ocean.

In January 2012, China assumed control of a newly-formed coalition counter-piracy convoy consisting of warships from Russia, India, and other nations.[42] China commands the group for its first six months, until India takes over the duty. For China, assumption of command of the task force provides several benefits. First, the PLAN acquires valuable operational experience by working with many of the best navies in the world, witnessing everything from logistics and underway replenishment to maritime battle rhythm. Second, China can leverage the mission into its "peaceful rise" narrative, satisfying skeptical neighbors that China is a responsible player on the world stage. Lastly, China adds substantively to the effort to secure international sea lines of communication–particularly the lifeline extending from the Middle East oil fields to ports along China's east coast.

The out-of-area deployments are a major boon to China's power projection ability, since the combination of skill and equipment needed to successfully conduct replenishment at sea is one of the most difficult operations to orchestrate. The ability to deliver fuel, food, and supplies on the high seas and near distant shores is an important part of being able to maintain a continuing presence in the oceans. Underway replenishment or "UNREP"

---

[41] The Military Balance 2011 (Chapter Six: Asia) 195, 195 (2011).

[42] Keith Wallis, *PLA Navy Takes Initial Lead in Anti-Piracy Coordination*, South China Morning Post, October 21, 2011.

involves maneuvering a supply ship parallel to a warship, separated by a distance of about 50 meters, and off-loading supplies over a network of lines and hoses, while both vessels are transiting. In a 2007 UNREP study by the PLAN, a commander in charge of a logistics-support flotilla testified, "One minute on stage takes ten years of practice off stage."[43] From the first to the ninth escort mission of the first naval escort taskforce, China escorted 4,252 Chinese and foreign ships, and rescued 42 Chinese and foreign ships from pirate attacks in the western Indian Ocean. On October 2, 2011, PLAN Deputy Commander Ding Yiping stated that the tenth deployment to the Gulf of Aden "shows China's confidence and determination in fulfilling international obligations and safeguarding the security of maritime strategic channels."[44]

VI. CONCLUSION–VARYING APPROACHES, ONE GOAL

The incidence of successful piracy attacks in the western Indian Ocean is very high, but the multi-faceted counter-effort has yielded some positive results that provide room for cautious optimism. The International Maritime Bureau reports that during 2010, the number of attacks in the Gulf of Aden dropped "more than 50 per cent due to naval patrols and positive actions." Just as important, however, have been the adoption and implementation of shipboard anti-piracy measures by commercial industry, and the increasing trend toward embarked privately contracted armed security personnel (PCASP).

In the end, the only real solution to Somali piracy lies on land. Thus, the armed forces of Africa, which at first blush may be thought to bring the least to the fight against piracy, actually hold the key to ending it. The ground forces of AMISOM and the TFG, supported by outside training and logistics, are doing more to deter piracy and dismantle the business model than the warships over the horizon. The Kenyan incursion in the south of Somalia has similarly had a dramatic effect on denying shore-based safe havens to pirates. As the capability of the armed forces in nations surrounding Somalia increases, neighboring states will be able to provide a greater presence in the country. Eventually, however, the armed forces of neighboring African states may come to be seen by Somalis as outsiders. Thus, it is imperative that AMISOM receive maximum support from the NATO and the EU in order to build a viable TFG government and armed force.

---

[43] The Military Balance 2011 (Chapter Six: Asia) 195, 195 (2011).

[44] *10th Chinese Naval Escort Taskforce Sets Sail*, People's Liberation Army Daily, November 3, 2011.

In the meantime, nations continue to fight piracy at sea. The two nations of Asia covered in this chapter–the maritime power of Japan and the emerging naval power of China–view the Somali mission as an opportunity to showcase their naval capabilities. More importantly, the deployments signal a willingness and ability to project power outside Asia. China seeks to keep India off-balance and force the United States to contend with Chinese naval power in theaters such as the western Indian Ocean and Mediterranean Sea that historically have been devoid of PLAN warships. Japan is testing the boundaries of constitutional interpretation by establishing a semi-permanent military base in Djibouti–the first such effort to maintain a foreign footprint since World War II.

Much as the Asians are using piracy to signal intentions that go beyond mere maritime security in the Indian Ocean, so too are Europeans. Both NATO and the EU are optimizing the counter-piracy mission as part of their overall mission to maintain global stability and security. Thus, the counter-piracy mission is the maritime analogue of NATO's role in ensuring that the U.S. nation-building effort in Afghanistan does not fail. Similarly, the United States is using counter-piracy as a convenient way to test two concepts–the feasibility of the Cooperative Strategy to actually accomplish a "hard security" mission, and the role of U.S. Africa Command in being a powerful but benign presence in the continent that can deliver real security. Although nominally an "army" combatant command dominated by concerns of asymmetric land warfare, and staffed with Army Foreign Area Officers who have more experience on the continent than any of the U.S. armed forces, Africa Command is facing piracy as its first protracted test.

Ultimately, there is some irony that among the nations and armed forces involved in suppressing Somali piracy, the very weakest and least capable from an objective measure are likely to be the most successful. Thus, while the United States, NATO and the EU and Asian naval powers struggle to hold the line on Somali piracy, real success is being harvested by East African military forces working in conjunction with TFG irregulars. The combination of East African initiatives and the presence of private armed security personnel on board international shipping is proving to be the most effective response to the threat.

11. Operation Atalanta

Cédric LEBOEUF[1]

Piracy is a major concern for the Member States of the European Union (EU) and they have pushed the EU to take action. The counter-piracy measures taken by the EU have to be read in the light of the development of its current Common Security and Defense Policy.[2] During the 2000 Nice European Council Meeting, the EU adopted permanent political and military structures "to assume its responsibilities for crisis management as a whole."[3] Previously, the EU did not have a proper defence policy[4] or organizational structure. Defence policy was reserved to the competence of the member-states. The Political and Security Committee, the European Union Military Committee and the European Military Staff were created in 2001.[5] The establishment of these three entities constitutes the basis of the ability of the EU's action outside its borders, on its own behalf, implementing the resolutions of the Security Council of the United Nations (UNSC).

Until the entry into force of the 1999 Amsterdam Treaty, the EU declared for many decades the ambition of military autonomy in the theater of external operations. The EU had, however, no real capacity of intervention under its own banner. Pursuant to the Petersberg tasks, now included in the current Common Security and Defense Policy, the EU has the capacity to participate in United Nations (UN) peacekeeping operations. For all that, the EU is not master of its actions nor of the operational modalities. The voting rules as to the launch of a military operation demonstrate the lack of a central political power in Europe. When a military operation is concerned, Member

---

[1] Cédric Leboeuf, research fellow at the Center of Maritime and Oceanic Law (CDMO), University of Nantes, France.

[2] Formerly the European and Security and Defence Policy (ESDP).

[3] Council Meeting, Nice, Presidency Conclusions, 7, 8 and 9 December 2000, Annex VI

[4] *See* Morel J.-F., Cameron A., *Europe de la Défense: Le Cœur du Débat,* Paris, L'Harmattan, 2009, p 82; English version available under the title *European Defence. Breaking New Ground. Preface: Javier Solana.*

[5] Council Decisions of the 22 January 2001, respectively 2001/78/CFSP, 2001/79/CFSP and 2011/80/CFSP. Note that the last decision as to the EUMS has been amended by the Council Decision 2005/385/CFSP (May 10, 2005).

States are entitled to refuse to be bound by the decisions involving the use of civil or military forces. Indeed,

> when abstaining in a vote, any member of the Council may qualify its abstention by making a formal declaration . . . . In that case, it shall not be obliged to apply the decision, but shall accept that the decision commits the Union. In a spirit of mutual solidarity, the Member State concerned shall refrain from any action likely to conflict with or impede Union action based on that decision and the other Member States shall respect its position.[6]

This right not to be bound comes from the fact that the last members that entered the EU, formerly members of the Warsaw Pact, are more confident on these issues, vis-à-vis the United States allies.

The first two EU military missions date from 2003: Operation CONCORDIA, according to arrangements with the North Atlantic Treaty Organization (NATO), and operation ARTEMIS, from June to September, in the territory of the Democratic Republic of the Congo.[7] The EU gradually empowered its external actions modalities. Most of its members are also NATO members. Although the positioning of the states in one or the other Organization could be problematic at a political level, no such difficulty is raised from sea military operations. Absent as an actor at sea, the EU left to the Member States the conduct of all the operational aspects of the missions. The management of Operational Cooperation at the External Borders of the Member States of the EU (FRONTEX Agency) is a perfect example.[8]

The fight against piracy revises this premise and initiates a change in the ideological paradigm of the defense at sea. Until recently, the fight against high sea piracy and robbery was not a priority for the EU. The low number of attacks had only a marginal impact on the European economy and security. However, things changed in 2008. Particular attention was paid to the phenomenon following the "acts of piracy perpetrated in international waters off the Somali coast against a French yacht and a Spanish trawler which have again highlighted the seriousness of the situation in those waters."[9] In light of these events, discussions began about how the EU, in accordance with the Charter of the UN, could contribute to the establishment of "an effective

---

[6] Lisbon Treaty, art. 31 (ex-article 23 TUE).

[7] Map of the current EU operations: http://www.consilium.europa.eu/eeas/security-defence/eu-operations.aspx?lang=en.

[8] See Leboeuf C., *Contrôle et Gestion des Flux Migratoires aux Frontières Maritimes Sud de l'Union Européenne*, Annuaire de Droit Maritime et Océanique, Tome XXIX, 2011, pp 179-193.

[9] Council of the European Union, *Piracy off the Somali Coast,* 9436/08, Bruxelles, 15.05.2008.

system of collective security"[10] off the coast of Somalia and neighboring states.

EU INTEREST IN COUNTER-PIRACY ACTION

Over the years, European policies have taken a growing interest in the issue of piracy and armed robbery at sea. This interest is based on a set of economic, political, and military reasons. As an isolated phenomenon, piracy impacts a very large number of economic sectors and actors, which are directly and indirectly concerned. The fight against piracy also presents a major humanitarian issue. Since 2006, the UN World Food Program (WFP) has been feeding one third of the Somali population, about two million people a day. Sustainability and smooth running of this program is essential to avoid a further humanitarian disaster. However, since 2007, pirates have been attacking WFP ships, threatening the supply of food and the very survival of millions of people.

A quick review of the statistics of the transit of goods through the Suez Canal[11] reveals the potential impact of piracy on global trade. During the January-August 2011 period, 1.85 million tons of goods passed through this sea-lane. In 2010, 17,993 ships transited the canal. Being the shortest route between Europe and Asia, the Suez Canal is a strategic point. The crisis that resulted from the nationalization of the canal by G. A. Nasser in 1956[12] is an illustration of the canal's importance. Despite reopening for a few days in 1967, it remained closed until 1975. The closing of the channel during the Yom Kippur War led to an increase in distance of the sea routes of 20 to 30 percent. Between 1967 and 1975, the additional cost for maritime trade is estimated at $8 billion.[13] Nowadays, there is still a fear of closure due to a complex regional political situation. Compared to the extra costs that resulted from the closure in the 60's and 70's, such a situation would now entail much higher financial consequences. Although canal closure due to piracy is not a current fear, piracy threatens the very important Suez area and puts pressure on the safety and security of the crew, cargo, and ship itself, with additional costs for insurance. Some ship-owners are even choosing to go around the Cape of Good Hope, despite the additional ten days of transit time and the additional costs this entails. Thus, for some, the Suez Canal may as

---

[10] *Ibid.*

[11] See the Suez canal Traffic Statistics [online] : http://www.suezcanal.gov.eg/TRstat.aspx?reportId=3.

[12] Leading to the closing of the Suez Canal until 1975.

[13] Centre d'Etudes Supérieures de la Marine, *Suez, les Conséquences d'une Potentielle Fermeture,* Brèves Marine, n°123, February 2011.

well be closed. However, it is highly difficult to assess the impact of piracy on the Suez Canal's ship traffic in view of the global economic crisis.[14]

STATE INITIATIVES AND UN FRAMEWORK

Coping with the resurgence of the phenomenon of piracy in 2007, France was one of the first states that volunteered to provide military ships to ensure the safety of WFP in Somalia. To this end, Operation Alcyon was launched, to accompany these vulnerable humanitarian ships. This operation is orchestrated primarily by France, and then relayed by Denmark, the Netherlands and Canada. It consists in the boarding of military personnel on ships carrying food from Kenya (where the food is stocked) to Somalia. This targeted and personalized help aims at restoring the confidence and ensuring the sustainability of the cooperation of ship-owners of these chartered vessels. Meanwhile, the resurgence of acts of piracy are a growing threat to all the unprotected vessels transiting in the Gulf. The adoption of resolutions by the UNSC reflects the seriousness of the situation. Unfortunately, each resolution comes in response to particularly serious cases involving ships that have been under the French flag. The cases of the *Ponant* (2008), the *Carré d'As* (2009) and the *Tanit* operation (2009) have catalyzed the reaction of the International Society.

Considering the positive results of Operation Alcyon, the UN Security Council adopted Resolution 1814 (2008) that confirmed the pursuit of the protection measures for WFP convoys. Shortly after the *Ponant* attack, and under the influence of France and the USA, the UNSC adopted Resolution 1816 (2008) that increased the possibilities of intervention presented in Resolution 1814 (2008). Naval and air forces are allowed "to enter the territorial waters of Somalia and use 'all necessary means' to repress acts of piracy and armed robbery at sea . . . based upon that country's prior consent." Although Resolution 1816 (2008) states that third party states can intervene in the territorial seas of Somalia, Resolution 1838 (2008) "underscores in particular that this resolution shall not be considered as establishing customary international law." It allows the deployment of naval and air forces on the high seas, in the Somali territorial sea, and in the related air space. It also extends the protection measures for WFP convoys. This Resolution 1838 (2008) was made while piracy intensified. The Council underscored that "increasingly violent acts of piracy are carried out with heavier weaponry, in a larger area off the coast of Somalia, using long-range assets such as mother ships, and demonstrating more sophisticated organization and methods of attack."

This intensification also resulted in the reinforcement of the measures allowed by the Security Council in Resolution 1851 (2008) of December 16, 2008. Indeed, under the condition of reaching an agreement with the transitional Somali government, the states involved "may undertake all necessary measures that are appropriate in Somalia, . . . provided, however, that any measures undertaken . . . shall be undertaken consistent with applicable international humanitarian and human rights law." It also states that "the authorization provided . . . apply only with respect to the situation in Somalia and shall not affect the rights or obligations or responsibilities of Member States under international law, including any rights or obligations under UNCLOS, with respect to any other situation." However, this is executed without the Council having established the existence of a threat to international peace and security.[15]

Concerns and worries remain concerning the efficacy of court action and prosecution of the pirates. The *Report of the Secretary-General pursuant to Security Council resolution 1846 (2008)* of March 16, 2009 notes the policy of impunity the pirates benefit from in the region.[16] Resolution 1897 (2009) of November 30, 2009 reinforces these concerns by underlining the importance for

> flag, port, and coastal States, States of the nationality of victims and perpetrators of piracy and armed robbery, and other States with relevant jurisdiction under international law and national legislation, to cooperate in determining jurisdiction, and in the investigation and prosecution of persons responsible for acts of piracy and armed robbery off the coast of Somalia, consistent with applicable international law including international human rights law, to ensure that all pirates handed over to judicial authorities are subject to a judicial process.[17]

The Council Resolution 1918 (2010) of April 27, 2010 emphasises juridical gaps. It reminds the Member States of the necessity "to criminalize piracy under their respective domestic laws," while noting previous "cases

[15] Regardless of the condition laid down by Article 39 of the UN Charter: "The Security Council shall determine the existence of any threat to the peace, breach of the peace, or act of aggression and shall make recommendations, or decide what measures shall be taken in accordance with Articles 41 and 42, to maintain or restore international peace and security."

[16] Doc. S/2009/146, § 61.

[17] UNSC, Resolution 1897 (2009), § 12.

when persons suspected of piracy are released without facing justice." Finally, the improvement of the conditions for investigation, evidence search, and detention of pirates remains one of the priorities of resolution 1976 (2011) of April 11, 2011.

THE EU IMPLEMENTATION OF THE SECURITY COUNCIL RESOLUTIONS

The EU contributes to the implementation of the Security Council Resolutions in respect of Article 21 of the Lisbon Treaty.[18] On piracy issues, in its conclusions of September 15, 2008, the European Council establishes a coordination unit in charge of supporting the surveillance and protection activities carried out by some Member States off the Somali coast (EU NAVCO). It coordinates the activities of the military means sent over, and informs and increases the European shipowners' awareness of available operations that can secure the transit of their ships. This unit stayed in activity until the beginning of the Atalanta operation. On November 10, 2008, the EU Council adopted a joint action 2008/851/PESC on the military action of the European Union for contributing to the deterrence, prevention, and repression of acts of piracy and armed robbery off the Somali coast. Reaffirming its concerns about the increase of acts of piracy and armed robbery in this area, the EU Council, following Resolutions 1814 (2008), 1816 (2008) and 1838 (2008), introduced operation Atalanta. Initially planned for a 12 month period and then extended,[19] this operation aims for:

— the protection of vessels of the WFP delivering food aid to displaced persons in Somalia, in accordance with the mandate laid down in UNSC Resolution 1814 (2008), [and]
— the protection of vulnerable vessels cruising off the Somali coast, and the deterrence, prevention and repression of acts of piracy and armed robbery off the Somali coast, in accordance with the mandate laid down in UNSC Resolution 1816 (2008).

According to the joint action 2008/851/PESC, Atalanta also contributes to the surveillance of fishing activities. However, because fishing zones are hundreds of miles away from the transit zone in the Gulf of Aden, the solution of armed guards on board fishing boats has been preferred: whether they are soldiers (France) or working for private security companies (Spain).

[18] Treaty on European Union, art. 21 (General Provisions On The Union's External Action).

[19] On 7 December 2010, the Council of the EU extended the operation's mandate for another two years until 12 December 2012 (Decision 2010/766/CFSP). On 23 March 2012, the Council of the EU extended the operation's mandate until 12 December 2014 (2012/174/CFSP).

In order to execute its mission, Atalanta military forces can "take the necessary measures, including the use of force, to deter, prevent and intervene in order to bring to an end, acts of piracy and armed robbery which may be committed in the areas where it is present." Furthermore, naval forces shall

> in view of prosecutions potentially being brought by the relevant States under the conditions in Article 12, arrest, detain and transfer persons who have committed, or are suspected of having committed, acts of piracy or armed robbery in the areas where it is present and seize the vessels of the pirates or armed robbers or the vessels caught following an act of piracy or an armed robbery and which are in the hands of the pirates, as well as the goods on board.

At the start of the operation, naval forces covered "up to 500 nautical miles off the Somali coast and neighboring countries."[20] At the end of 2009, they covered "the exclusive economic zone, territorial sea, archipelagic waters and internal waters of the Republic of Seychelles." [21] Investigations concerning the juridical validity of this extension have been lifted by the adaptation of the Joint Action that does not refer anymore to the 500 miles zone. Indeed, the original Joint Action that funded the intervention of the EU according in particular to resolution 1851 (2008), had not been revised, leaving the operation mandate and missions unchanged.

Recently, negotiations have been engaged to increase the zone of action of EUNAVFOR. Competent European ministers are considering making an agreement with the Sultanate of Oman.[22] The aim would be to make a second extension that would allow EUNAVFOR to be present outside the Gulf of Aden in the Arabian Sea. Considering the piracy acts and robberies in these waters, it is evident that action must take place. However, experts agree that the zone defined in the actual Operation Plan necessitates a permanent presence of 83 vessels "in order to have always one vessel at one hour

[20] Council Joint Action 2008/851/CFSP, 10 November 2008, OJEU 12.11.2008, L 301/3, Article 1, "in accordance with the political objective of an EU maritime operation, as defined in the crisis management concept approved by the Council on 5 August 2008."

[21] Council Decision 2009/877/CFSP, 23 October 2009, on the signing and provisional application of the Exchange of Letters between the European Union and the Republic of Seychelles on the conditions and modalities for the transfer of suspected pirates and armed robbers from EUNAVFOR to the Republic of Seychelles and for their treatment after such transfer, JO L 315, 2.12.2009, p 35–43.

[22] Gros-Verheyde N., *Un Accord Entre l'UE et Oman en Préparation sur la Lutte Contre la Piraterie*", [online]: bruxelles2.eu, 14 October 2011. The agreement would let the EU forces to transit over its territory and would permit the use one airport to deploy the aerial means of surveillance.

reaction distance from potential attacks."[23] The Decision 2012/174/CFSP adopted by the Council establishes

> The area of operations of the forces deployed to that end shall consist of the Somali coastal territory and internal waters, and the maritime areas off the coasts of Somalia and neighbouring countries within the region of the Indian Ocean, in accordance with the political objective of an EU maritime operation, as defined in the crisis management concept approved by the Council on 5 August 2008. (article 1.2)

This extension targeting pirates on Somali soil needs to be clarified. The mission seems to be more offensive. Cohesion of the operation itself must be preserved. This cohesion must also be made with respect to other operations involved. Terms of the action on the coastal strip remain to be defined. Operational capabilities may also be questioned. European Rules of Engagement will have to be clarified, especially since the operation was based on a rather defensive mode that is supposed now to be radically transformed. Do the states agree to send troops under the European flag or will it remain under the responsibility of the state? The agreement of the EU Member States would probably not include a real intervention on land. Major General Buster Howes (UK), former EU Operation Commander of Operation EUNAVFOR-Atalanta, proposed in 2011 different actions including intervention on Somali soil.[24] Discussed by the Member States, this proposal had been abandoned. It had been preferred to use maritime means to target pirate logistical plots without sending troops into Somali territory. The recent change of mind of the EU States initiates the will to grant the EU an offensive vision. It still does not seem to deeply transform an EU operation lacking operational means. As a result, the territorial extensions of the operation raise two types of questions.

Juridical Dimension of Operation Atalanta: Mandates, Mission and Intervening States

On one side, from a strictly juridical point of view, the question of the juridical dimension of the EUNAVFOR Operation outside the zone defined by the Joint Action 2008/851/CFSP remains unclear. Even if EUNAVFOR is the naval representative of the external action of the EU, its juridical basis cannot stay incomplete. The divergence of the Member States concerning the use of lethal force during the Libyan crisis confirms the difficulty to accord

[23] Helly D., *Lessons From ATALANTA and EU Counter-Piracy Policies*, EU Institute for Security Studies, Seminar Reports, Paris, 23-24 March 2011 / Brussels, 17 June 2011, p 11. Although less than 40 are present in that area.

[24] Gros-Verheyde N.,*Atalanta vise les pirates à terre,"* [online]: bruxelles2.eu, 22 March 2012.

27 voices on external issues. Even if it seems that now all the Member States agree on the spatial extension of the Atalanta Mission, the establishment of Rules of Engagement might be restricted to the minimum. On the other side, the extension of the defined zone of action questions the efficacy of the fight against piracy and robbery acts. While numerous limits have been noted at the operational level, they will surely increase in the actual situation. The cooperation with other naval forces and regional operations in place is the only option. The combination of forces, especially for burden sharing between NATO and the EU, concerning the escort of WFP ships, should be reinforced. If the EU wants to proceed to a universal naval action, it can do it only within the context of an extended cooperation with local military forces. However, the observations made seriously call into questions the motivation of the different political forces.

Article 10 of the Joint Action plans the participation of organisations or states outside the EU, in accordance with article 37 (ex-art. 24) of the Lisbon Treaty. On April 21, 2009, a Committee of Contributors (CoC), composed by representatives of all the Member States and third states participating in the operation [25] was created. Without prejudice to the competencies of the Political and Security Committee, the CoC can unanimously adopt decisions concerning the day-to-day management of the operation. [26] As such, the participation of Norway in Atalanta was accepted by the EU in April 2009.[27] Croatia has participated in the operation since July 2009,[28] Montenegro since October 2009,[29] and, finally, Ukraine since March 2010.[30] The rules behind the participation of these third states, non-members of the EU, are defined by specific agreements between them and the EU. [31] Additionally, the EU develops different forms of cooperation and support with the coastal States concerned by the operation – the Seychelles, Djibouti and Yemen – through a bilateral or international framework. This work led with national, regional and international actors is one of the keys to success in the fight against piracy in this part of the world. Indeed, with the absence of a central political organisation, Somalia can neither carry out the surveillance of its territorial waters nor have pirates transferred for prosecution.

---

[25] PSC, Decision ATALANTA/3/2009, JOUE L 112 du 06.05.2009, pp 9-10.

[26] Abstention does not bar unanimity.

[27] PSC, Decision ATALANTA/2/2009, JOUE L 109 du 30.04.2009, p 52.

[28] Conseil de l'UE, Décision 2009/957/PESC, JOUE L 202 du 04.08.2009, p 83-89.

[29] PSC, Decision ATALANTA/7/2009, JOUE L 270 du 15.10.2009, pp 19-20.

[30] PSC, Decision ATALANTA/1/2010, JOUE L 083 du 30.03.2010, pp 20-21.

[31] See Agreement between EU and the Republic of Croatia, OJ L 202 du 04.08.2009, pp 83-89; Agreement between EU and Montenegro, OJ L 88 du 8.4.2010, pp 3-8.

The EU also plays a coordination role with other operations connected to Security Council Resolutions. There are between 30 and 40 ships present as part of the Combined Task Force 15, the NATO operation *Ocean Shield* or national actions (such as China, Russia, Japan, India), including about 20 for the European States. The size of the military forces engaged in EUNAVFOR varies according to the contribution of the Member States. The coordination and the cooperation between the different operations are essential to the efficacy of the fight against piracy and robbery at sea. Indeed,

> the danger is great that these processes will be conducted separately in a completely uncoordinated manner. EU and NATO countries only have one set of naval forces. Particularly in the current context of strained resources, neither organisation can afford to engage in a 'virility contest,' which would likely lead to the adoption of unrealistically ambitious goals and to unnecessary duplication.[32]

The Council has decided to create a Maritime and Security Centre for the Horn of Africa (MSC-HOA).[33] Placed under the authority of the Commandant of the Atalanta Operation, this centre has replaced the above-mentioned NAVCO. Further, on September 1, 2009, the Internationally Recommended Transit Corridor (IRTC) was implemented. The MSC-HOA aims for the dissemination of information to shipowners and ships "regarding the close support protection details for . . . transiting the Gulf of Aden. Ships are encouraged to conduct their passage through the IRTC in groups based on their transit speed."[34] As underlined by C. Ménard in a parliamentary report in 2009, it is an original contribution that offers for the first time and "in such a transparency, an information and intelligence service at the disposal of the principal economic actors concerned"[35] by piracy.

The Coordination of Naval Forces at the Interface Between National and Regional Interests: Universal Action and Military Autonomy

Following the recent events, a draft decision by the Council projected to name an EU special representative for the Horn of Africa at the end of October 2011. His mandates would include both a terrestrial and maritime approach in order to "promote a coordinated and coherent international approach with Somalia, also within the EU Training Mission in Somalia, the

---

[32] NATO, Comittee Report, Annual session 2010, *207 CDS 10 E bis - MARITIME SECURITY: NATO AND EU ROLES AND CO-ORDINATION*, § 95.

[33] See the dedicated website: www.mschoa.eu.

[34] ICC – IMB Piracy and Armed Robeery Against Ships Report, Annual Report 2010, p 21.

[35] Commission de la Défense Nationale et des Forces Armées, *Rapport d'Information sur la Piraterie Maritime,* 13 May 2009, p 53.

operation EUNAVFOR Atalanta, and the support given to the African Union Mission, in close cooperation with the Member States of the EU."[36]

Pursuant to Security Council resolution 1851 (2008), a Contact Group on Piracy off the Coast of Somalia (CGPCS) has been created. It is an *ad hoc* forum to discuss and coordinate actions conducted by the States and the international organisations working off the Somali coast. Five working groups (WG) have been established[37] to address the following focus issues:

WG 1: Military and Operational Coordination, Information Sharing, and Capacity Building

WG 2: Judicial Issues

WG 3: Strengthening Shipping Self-Awareness and Other Capabilities

WG 4: Public Information

WG 5: Financial Flows

About 70 countries and international organisations meet three times a year in plenary assembly in the United Nations and upon WGs' presented work. The important work done by the WG is transcribed during these plenary assemblies. The recent creation of a CGPCS Virtual Secretariat raises the question of the institutionalisation of the fight against piracy on the global scale.[38] We can underline the complementary action to MSCHOA led by WG 3 to facilitate the coordination between military forces and private organisations such as the World Food Program, fishing enterprises, insurances, shipowners, etc. In a recent communiqué, the CGPCS notes that "the operationalisation of three sub-regional Information Sharing Centres in Kenya, Tanzania and Yemen, facilitated by the IMO with the support of the European Union (EU) under the Djibouti Code of Conduct."[39]

---

[36] Original version: "promouvoir une approche internationale coordonnée et cohérente à l'égard de la Somalie, y compris dans le cadre de la mission de formation de l'UE en Somalie (EUTM), de l'opération EU NAVFOR Atalanta et du soutien apporté à la mission de l'Union africaine (AMISOM), en étroite coopération avec les Etats membres de l'UE," Conseil de l'UE, *Projet de Décision du Conseil Portant Nomination du Représentant Spécial de l'Union Européenne Pour la Corne de l'Afrique*, Bruxelles, 22 September 2011, SN 3546/1/11 REV 11 LIMITE.

[37] Originally, only four Working Groups were created. The establishment of the fifth working group has been considered necessary, in July 2011, "to focus on and coordinate efforts to disrupt the pirate enterprise ashore" (CGCPS, "Ninth Plenary Session of the Contact Group on Piracy off the Coast of Somalia – Communiqué," New York, 14 July 2011; available on the official CGCPS website : www.thecgpcs.org).

[38] See Guilfoyle D., "The Contact Group on Piracy off the Coast of Somalia: piracy, governance and international law." Paper presented at the workshop "Contemporary Maritime Piracy and the International Response, "Greenwich Maritime institute, London, September 2011; Bueger C., "The New Public Face of The Contact Group", 5 October 2011, [online] : http://piracy-studies.org/author/admin/.

[39] Contact Group on Piracy off the Coast of Somalia, Communiqué, 14 July 2011, New York.

From an operational point of view, the multilateral cooperation is a key for the success and efficiency of the mission. However, numerous undeclared tensions are persistent. As a NATO draft report underlines, "the monthly meetings of the Shared Awareness and Deconfliction group (SHADE), held in Bahrain, have provided a useful space for discussion and co-ordination of activities between the maritime industry and NATO, the EU, the US-led Coalition Maritime Force, and other involved countries."[40] The author of this draft report goes on and notes the preference certain states have for an action part of the EUNAVFOR rather than part of the NATO *Ocean Shield* because of the transfer agreement concluded with Kenya in March 2009.[41] This agreement was, however, denounced on September 30, 2010[42] because of the obstruction of the Kenyan judicial system.[43] Indeed, the terms of the agreement did not allow Kenya to deal with every case one by one: "Kenya will accept, upon the request of EUNAVFOR, the transfer of persons detained by EUNAVFOR in connection with piracy and associated seized property by EUNAVFOR."[44] The exchange of letters between the EU and the Republic of Seychelles, in December 2009, reckons that "the Government of the Republic of Seychelles may authorize the EUNAVFOR to transfer suspected pirates and armed robbers captured in the course of its operations in the exclusive economic zone, territorial sea, archipelagic waters and internal waters of the Republic of Seychelles."[45] The relocation agreement EU-Mauritian Republic of July 2011 gives a capacity to refuse the transfer: "Transfer shall not be carried out before the competent law

---

[40] Ameline N., *177 DSCTC 11 E – Nato Operations Under a new strategic concept and the EU as an operational Partner*, NATO, Committee Report, 2011 Annual Session, September 21, 2011, § 63.

[41] Annex of the Council Decision 2009/293/CFSP of 26 February 2009, Provisions on the Conditions of Transfer of suspected Pirates and Seized Property from the EU-Led Naval Force to the Republic of Kenya, OJ L 79, 25.3.2009, p 47-59.

[42] Ameline N., 1*77 DSCTC 11 E – Nato Operations Under a new strategic concept...*, § 66.

[43] J. Lang's UN report states (Report of the Special Adviser to the Secretary-General on Legal Issues Related to Piracy off the Coast of Somalia, S/2011/30, 25 January 2011, footnote 33): "By virtue of its decision of 9 November 2010, which was confirmed on appeal, the Mombasa High Court released nine defendants on the grounds that owing to the absence of universal jurisdiction over acts of piracy on the high seas. It was feared that that reversal in case law would permanently paralyse Kenya's legal action against piracy. In fact, the decision had been taken in accordance with the new Merchant Shipping Act adopted in late 2009 and was a result of a legislative deficiency that had been identified and will soon be corrected. The new legislation had only incompletely revoked the existing provisions of the Penal Code."

[44] Annex of the Council Decision 2009/293/CFSP of 26 February 2009, JO L 79, 25.3.2009, p. 47–59, §2 (a).

[45] Council Decision 2009/877/CFSP, 23 October 2009, on the signing and provisional application of the Exchange of Letters between the European Union and the Republic of Seychelles on the conditions and modalities for the transfer of suspected pirates and armed robbers from EUNAVFOR to the Republic of Seychelles and for their treatment after such transfer, JO L 315, 2.12.2009, p 35–43.

enforcement authorities of Mauritius decide within 5 working days as of the date of receipt of evidence as forwarded by EUNAVFOR that there are reasonable prospects of securing a conviction of persons detained by EUNAVFOR."[46] Still practiced, transfers to the Republic of Seychelles and the Mauritian Republic seem to show the necessity for cooperation based on reciprocal agreements and case-by-case analysis, even if many doubts remain about the efficacy of such a system.

The SHADE, quoted by the NATO Draft report is a forum through which NATO and EU naval unity forces cooperate and coordinate with each other. However, these practices show how daunting the challenge is. Indeed, only debates on the tactical issues can be discussed. The political sphere is not included as experts working for the forum underline:

> we make sure we don't raise discussions at the political level, otherwise it stops to talk. . . . there is the 'impression of a beauty contest between the EU, NATO and CMF.' It is the fourth time NATO and the EU simultaneously deploy forces in the same area and with the same mandate. . . . From an outsider's point of view, EU-NATO competition on piracy has grown and is a matter of concern for the industry. The EU and NATO also compete for media coverage and visibility and it was underlined that 'while success is not shared, failure is.[47]

Even though since the start of the two operations, the sharing of information has improved, cooperation seems to still be difficult.

Responsibility of the Member States During External Operations: Human Rights.

Rights and responsibilities have changed considerably with the creation of international organisations. The juridical nature of these new actors matters as it constitutes the condition for their responsibility at the international level. There are two views: either the international organisation is a simple instrument of its member states, or it is distinct from them. For the EU, the existence of its juridical nature cannot be questioned. It is based on its express and statutory recognition, of the recognition by third states and its

---

[46] Council Decision 2011/640/CFSP, on the signing and conclusion of the Agreement between the European Union and the Republic of Mauritius on the conditions of transfer of suspected pirates and associated seized property from the European Union-led naval force to the Republic of Mauritius and on the conditions of suspected pirates after transfer, 12 July 2011, JO L 254 du 30.9.2011, p. 1–6, Art. 3.1 of the Agreement.

[47] Experts quoted *in* Helly D., "*Lessons From ATALANTA and EU Counter-Piracy Policies*," EU Institute for Security Studies, Seminar Reports, Paris, 23-24 March 2011 / Brussels, 17 June 2011, p 11.

abilities to adopt conventional acts.[48] Especially through international conventionalism, the EU and its Member States are recipient and guarantor of the respect of international law. The development of the EU external operational ability and of its military involvement at sea, under the auspices of the resolutions of the Security Council, gives a chance to consider the rights and responsibilities from a new angle.

The collective use of force is a relatively new concept for the EU. The analysis of the factors surrounding the use of force enlightens the strong connection between the European forces of intervention and the local actors at the external level.[49] At the domestic level, there are interactions between politics and resources. The European naval forces feel these factors directly. They both put up with their effects and comfort them *in situ*. The driving force of European external politics in the Indian Ocean, EU-NAVFOR actions are conducted under the responsibility of the Member States. Beyond the connections established between the military forces and regional private and state entities, the framework for cooperation of the Atalanta operation do not relieve the Member States from their responsibility. Atalanta legitimates and reinforces the joint action of the Member States without engaging a direct responsibility for the EU. The intervening State is therefore likely to engage its own responsibility, even if rules of engagement were to be established in a cooperation framework at the European level. To evaluate the context of the operation and the actions of the forces matters to infer the repartition of responsibility according to the criteria imposed by international law. Although the question of attribution of responsibility rarely raises difficulties at the national level, it complicates when a state acts as a member of an international organisation that is allowed by the Security Council to use force.

It is crucial to consider the repartition of responsibilities between the international organisation and the Member States, according to the project of the International Law Commission (ILC) on the responsibility of international organisations.[50] Following the article proposed by the ILC, we

[48] Perez-Gonzalez M., *Les Organisations Internationales et le Droit de la Responsabilité*, RGDIP, 1988, pp 62-102; Charpentier J., *Quelques Réflexions sur la Personnalité Juridique des Organisations Internationales: Réalité ou Fiction?*, *in Le droit des organisations internationales. Recueil d'études à la mémoire de Jacques Schwob*, Bruxelles, Bruylant, 1997, pp. 3-17

[49] Engberg K., *The EU's Collective Use of Force. Exploring the Factors Behind its First Military Operations*, Dissertation presented for the Degree of Doctor of Philosophy, Insitutionen för freds- och konfliktforskning, University of Uppsala, Sweden, 2011, p 180.

[50] International Law Commission, *Report on the Work of its Sixty-Third Session*, Official Records, Sixty-sixth Session, Supplement No. 10 (A/66/10 and Add.1), 26 April to 3 June and 4 July to 12 August 2011, Chapter V, pp 52-172.

aim to analyse the repartition of responsibility between the EU and the Member States in the light of the act involving responsibility and the attribution of damaging conduct to the EU. We will first examine the conditions of attribution of conduct to an EU Member State, concentrating on the non-attribution.

THE NON-ATTRIBUTION OF CONDUCT TO AN EU MEMBER STATE IN THE CONTEXT OF THE ATALANTA OPERATION ACCORDING TO THE EUROPEAN COURT OF HUMAN RIGHTS

From the application of the ECHR to the European operation in the fight against piracy

Article 1 of the European Court of Human Rights (ECHR) calls upon parties to secure "to everyone in their jurisdiction" all rights and freedoms. The juridical competencies of the parties will be *a priori* the criterion that characterises the scope of application of the Convention. We will now present what the notion of jurisdiction covers for the ECHR. The European Court of Human Rights has differentiated the notions of territoriality and jurisdiction by establishing that "the notion of jurisdiction in this disposition is not limited to the national territory of the contracting parties. The responsibility of the contracting parties can be involved when action is led from their organs and happens on or outside their territory."[51] For our purposes, the core of the issue is not to know whether or not a ship is a territory,[52] but to know in which circumstances and with which criteria the ECHR applies to a ship that intervenes in international waters. In others words, does a state exert its jurisdiction on intervening ships in high seas?

The Court has not clearly answered this question. However, it has evaluated the respect of the norms of the Convention during the case of *Leray et autres c. France*. Concerning the shipwreck of a ship sailing under the French flag, which was coming from Mombasa (Kenya) off the Spanish coasts, "Judges did not notice a failure that could engage the responsibility of the State concerning the participation of the French maritime authorities to the rescue operations."[53] By deduction, the state can have its international responsibility engaged according to the Convention on a ship flying its flag

---

[51] ECtHR, *Loizidou v. Turkey (preliminary objections),* Judgment, 23 March 1995, § 62; See also ECtHR, *Drodz and Janouzek v. France and Spain,* June 26, 1992, § 91.

[52] Chaumette P., *Le Navire, ni Territoire, ni Personne*, DMF 2007, n° 2, pp 99-110; Van der Mensbrugghe, *Réflexions sur la Définition du Navire dans le Droit de la Mer. Actualités du Droit de la Mer.*, Ed. Pédone, 1973, p 64.

[53] CEDH, *Leray et Autres c. France,* 20.03.2002 (définitif), req. 44617/98, our translation.

on the high seas. We can conclude that the Convention applies to any ship that intervenes while sailing under one party state flag.

If the fact that a party State exercises its jurisdiction on a ship flying its flag does not call for explicit development by the Court, the question remains when it is about the application of the Convention during the intervention on a third ship flying a flag non part of the Convention. A characteristic example is the actions of capture and detention committed by the EUNAVFOR ships. On this point, C. Laly-Chevalier raises the question of place of action: "*quid* then when individuals suspected of piracy or robbery actions are arrested by soldiers on the pirate boat?"[54] A more detailed appreciation of the criteria is necessary to agree on how the state that apprehends pirates can exert its jurisdiction. A dearth of express jurisprudence on this matter requires the analysis of the rule and the letter of the Convention. C. Laly-Chevalier underscores that, according to J. A. Carillo-Salcedo, "it is not necessary for a stable juridical link such as the nationality or the place of residence to exist as it just requires the State to be able to exert a certain power on the person."[55]

This discussion brings us to the following point: the actions lead by ships of the States party in the ECHR, and the conduct of the piracy ships and persons to be placed under these States' jurisdiction. Article 1 of the Convention seems to generate a direct application of the ECHR to the vessels participating in Operation Atalanta. However, if a state is likely to engage its international liability according to this text, we have to reflect on the articulation of its responsibility with the one of the other Member States. As a regional actor allowed by resolutions 1814 (2008) and 1838 (2008) of the Security Council to take necessary measures to stop the phenomenon of piracy off the Somali coast, the EU has ruled on the conditions of the Member States intervention. In this context and considering the ECHR, we can legitimately wonder about a potential sole responsibility of the organisation concerning the actions conducted by one of its members.

The criteria for attribution of conduct to a Member State of the EU

---

[54] Original version: "quid alors quand les individus suspects d'actes de piraterie ou d'actes de brigandage sont appréhendés par les militaires sur le navire pirate?" Laly-Chevalier C., *Lutte contre la piraterie maritime et droits de l'Homme*, Revue Belge de Droit International, 2009/1, p 33.

[55] Our translation, original version: "il n'est pas nécessaire qu'existe un lien juridique stable comme la nationalité, la résidence ou le domicile, car il suffit que l'Etat puisse exercer un certain pouvoir sur l'intéressé."

Ibid. quoting Carillo-Salcedo, *Commentaire de l'Article 1er*, Pettiti Le. (dir.), *La Convention Européenne des Droits de l'Homme. Commentaire,* Economica, 1969, p 135.

The Convention does not state of any principle regarding the criteria of attribution of conduct of a State to the international organisation it belongs. This is logical as the Convention was originally open for signature only to Member States of the European Council and not to the EU.[56] It tended to appreciate the rightness of the actions of the State conforming to its own dispositions and independently from the status of member of a third international organisation. Also, the different protocols at the Convention did not intervene on this issue. We can therefore refer to the jurisprudence of the Court in order to understand what the implications of Member States who are part of the ECHR are for the EU in terms of responsibility.

In several cases, the Court raises the principle of *global control* as an interpretation of the notion of jurisdiction as presented earlier. First, it answers the question of attribution of conduct of a state actor to his state. In the *Loizidou* case, it says that "such control, according to the relevant test and in the circumstances of the case, entails her responsibility for the policies and actions of the 'TRNC.' Those affected by such policies or actions therefore come within the 'jurisdiction' of Turkey for the purposes of Article 1 of the Convention."[57] Later, in another judgment, it speaks on the role of responsibility within this global control:

> Having effective overall control over northern Cyprus, its responsibility cannot be confined to the acts of its own soldiers or officials in northern Cyprus but must also be engaged by virtue of the acts of the local administration which survives by virtue of Turkish military and other support. It follows that, in terms of Article 1 of the Convention, Turkey's "jurisdiction" must be considered to extend to securing the entire range of substantive rights set out in the Convention and those additional Protocols which she has ratified, and that violations of those rights are imputable to Turkey.[58]

The Court differently appreciates the notion of jurisdiction depending on the circumstances,[59] even if it came back sometimes to a territorial

---

[56] Protocol No. 14 to the Convention for the Protection of Human Rights and Fundamental Freedoms, amending the control system of the Convention, art. 17, May 13, 2004: "The European Union may accede to this Convention." For more details about a potential adhesion of the EU, see Sauvé J.-M., "*L'Adhésion de l'Union Européenne à la Convention Européenne de Sauvegarde des Droits de l'Homme et des Libertés Fondamentales*, intervention lors de la table ronde organisée par le Conseil des barreaux européens, 20 May 2011, Luxembourg, available at http://www.conseil-etat.fr/cde/media/document/DISCOURS%20ET%20INTERVENTIONS/intervention-ccbe.pdf.

[57] ECtHR, *Loizidou v. Turkey*, Judgment, 18 December 1996, § 56.

[58] ECHR, *Cyprus v. Turkey*, Application No. 25781/94, Judgment of 10 May 2001, § 77.

[59] ECtHR, *Loizidou v. Turkey (preliminary objections),* Judgment, 23 March 1995, § 71.

interpretation of the notion[60] as we discussed it earlier. The appreciation of the conditions of exercise of jurisdiction outside the national territory of a state allows the determination of the control and ultimate authority on actions or omissions.

On this subject, the joint cases *Behrami and Samarati* are particularly interesting. One case concerned the conformity of actions done by states party to the Convention regarding an operation allowed by the Security Council. The other one concerned actions conducted under commandment and unified control of NATO. In this case, the Court recognises a distinction between operations allowed and conducted "under the control of the UN" and operations only allowed by the Security Council. On that matter, it underlines that the quality of troop-contributing state does not necessarily exclude all authority and control from the international organisation in charge of the operational commandment.[61] Applied to the Atalanta operation, the logic of the Court would be that the EU could have its responsibility engaged as it offers only a framework of cooperation between the Member States. The chain of commandment shows that the military organs do not have real power to control contingents. The military staff of Northwood does not have direct military leadership *in situ*.[62]

EVENTS GIVING RISE TO INTERNATIONAL RESPONSIBILITY - CONTEXTUAL EXAMPLES FOR PIRACY

Pierre-Marie Dupuy defined the responsibility thusly: "through the illegal nature of the operative event. . . . One can describe as operative any fact attributable to the State and recognized as leading to the commitment of its responsibility."[63] Detailing his thinking, he cites the doctrinal traditional example of the boarding of a third state vessel, on the high seas, to deduce the existence of a liability without unlawful operative fact.[64] The fact giving rise to international responsibility must therefore be understood here as an

---

[60] ECRH, *Banković et Alii c. NATO countries*, Decision of 12 december 2001 (admissibility), § 63: "the Court finds clear confirmation of this essentially territorial notion of jurisdiction in the *travaux préparatoires* which demonstrate that the Expert Intergovernmental Committee replaced the words "all persons residing within their territories" with a reference to persons "within their jurisdiction" with a view to expanding the Convention's application to others who may not reside, in a legal sense, but who are, nevertheless, on the territory of the Contracting States."

[61] ECtHR (Grand Chamber – Admissibility), *Joint Applications Behrami and Samarati,* 2 May 2007, App. No. 71412/01 and No. 78166/01, § 133: "the key question is whether the UNSC retained ultimate authority and control so that operational command only was delegated."

[62] Council Joint Action 2008/851/CFSP, 10 November 2008, OJ 12.11.2008, L 301/3, Art. 17.

[63] Dupuy P.-M., *Le Fait Générateur de la Responsabilité Internationale des Etats*, RCADI, 1984-V, vol. 188, pp 25-26.

[64] *Ibid.* p 70.

act or inaction, that can be attributed to a vessel sailing under a European state flag, within the scope of the mandate and missions of the Atalanta Operation. Far from being exhaustive, the forthcoming examples will try to clarify certain legal aspects arising from the practice. They also will highlight the difficulty to coordinate regional and state acts with regard to different Rules of Engagement. We consider thus the case of abusing boarding on the international seas due to an incorrect identification of a suspected pirate ship. The second case describes the destruction of a vessel suspected of engaging in pirate activities.

The excessive or vexatious boarding in international waters

"The essential idea contained in the principle of freedom of the high seas is the prohibition of any interference with the navigation, in time of peace, of a flag towards any other flag."[65] As a customary exception to this principle, codified by the United Nations Convention on the Law of the Sea (UNCLOS), the boarding of a pirate ship, or one suspected of engaging in pirate activities, is allowed. Nevertheless, the practice reveals some operational difficulties as to the identification of a pirate ship. Dealing with the immensity of the sea, with the new and evolving pirate techniques, and with the use of fishing vessels or dhow as mother ships, ascertainment of whether a ship is a pirate ship is highly complicated and affects the decision-making of the authorities. The Rules of Engagement constitute the cornerstone of the framework of the intervention.

As recalled by Prof. Ph. Delebecque, since "if [UNCLOS] establishes distinct zones, it intends to enforce various rights and obligations."[66] However, he admits that due to the special character of piracy, it can be said that the Exclusive Economic Zone (EEZ) is on the high seas and, in this peculiar context, carries the same legal status. As such, piracy disrupts the traditional legal thinking. As being an exception to the customary international law of the sea, the phenomenon is not limited to a fixed area. The practice upsets the legal fictions of maritime zoning and involves an adaptation of the legal framework of the fight. The example of the right of reverse hot pursuit constitutes one of the best legal arrangements. Authorized by the Security Council, for the specific case of the territorial sea of Somalia, this right has been considered as a necessity to the effectiveness of the fight against piracy and armed robbery at sea. Warships are indeed authorized to

---

[65] Sentence attributed to Gidel, quoted by Treves T., *Intervention en Haute mer et Navires Etrangers*, AFDI, vol. 41, 1995, pp 651-75.

[66] Delebecque P., paper presented at the workshop "Europe facing maritime piracy," organized by the European Lawyer's Union, Marseille, November 2011.

board pirate ships in the territorial sea of Somalia for acts committed on the high seas.

The abusive or vexatious characteristic of boarding a ship on the high seas *is a product of* rocking the sovereignty principle. Freedom of navigation enjoyed by any vessel, under the Flag State Law, comes exclusively within the competence of the jurisdiction of the State whose Flag it flies. "The warship may proceed, over a ship that flies its flag, to the exercise of police powers on the high seas: the approach, the arrest, the investigation of flag, the visit, the rerouting, the seizure and the immobilization."[67] Under Articles 100 to 107 of UNCLOS, a military vessel may exercise these police powers with regard to any ship suspected of engaging in any pirate activity. Article 110 of UNCLOS provides that the boarding is authorized when the concerned ship is not a third state warship and is engaged in piracy. However, any excess is likely to engage the international responsibility of the intervening state. Note that the potential state responsibility remains even if the warship enjoys immunity from jurisdiction and execution. The state is indeed the last lever that is left to obtain compensation for the commission of an internationally wrongful act, such as boarding abuse.

The destruction of a ship suspected of carrying pirate activities and the ECHR

The unilateral practice of third states present in the area, like the Indian or the Russian fleets, provides examples of destruction of ships suspected of engaging in pirate activities. Sometimes, the destructed ship was not, in fact, a pirate one or had hostages on board. The military vessels of the two aforesaid navies meet rules of engagement which are radically different from those followed by the European states.[68] The behavior of the *INS Tabar* in November 2008 is a meaningful example underlining the importance of the interests at stake. An Indian navy frigate sunk a vessel suspected of engaging in pirate activities. The spokesman of the Indian navy explained that the concerned ship met the description of the typical pirate mother ship. However, the Thai trawler sunk had been attacked only shortly before. Sixteen sailors were on board, detained as hostages. Only one of them survived.

---

[67] Beurier Jean-Pierre (dir.), Droits maritimes, 2ème édition, Dalloz, Paris, 2009, p 114-17.

[68] Treves T., *Piracy, Law of the Sea, and Use of Force: Developments off the Coast of Somalia*, European Journal of International Law, 20 (2), 2009, p 399-414; Duda D., Szubrycht T., *The Somali Piracy New or Old Challenge for International Community*, International Journal on Marine Navigation and Safety of Sea Transportation, Nr. 3, September 2009, p 345-52.

The fact of sinking a pirate ship at sight, on the basis of relatively scant evidence, remains a quite common practice, which is sometimes desired.[69] It underlines the interest to having well-determined rules of engagement, sufficiently precise to avoid situations leading to the death of innocent people. Rules of engagement "are constituted from international law, domestic law, and policy considerations in order to refine and specify when force may be used, either in self-defense or in accomplishing a military mission."[70] Their disrespect, or even their respect, are therefore likely to engage the international responsibility of a state, especially in cases related to human rights. In the aforementioned *Tabar* case, the problem stemmed from the diplomatic sphere given the immunity enjoyed by the Indian military vessels and the absence of Human Rights Conventions in this region of the world. The rules of engagement correspond to a set of legal, or even moral, standards that the state undertakes to abide by. They are a practical and operational translation of the external legal policy of the State.[71]

"Everyone's right to life shall be protected by law." According to this article 2 of the ECHR, the state must refrain from causing intentionally and unlawfully the death of a man. This article implies that there is an obligation for the state to take all the necessary measures to preserve the lives of those within its jurisdiction. In this regard, the jurisprudence of the Court is constant. [72] The military status of a vessel that enjoys immunity from jurisdiction and execution in accordance with article 95 and 96 of UNCLOS does not mean an absolute irresponsibility of the flag state. The existence of state immunity for acts of authority is justified in international law by the role it plays. "Its benefits cannot be extended, by analogy to other subjects of international law"[73] without any express treaty provisions. The ECHR, in a decision by Marcovic, states that "the common term 'immunity' in [national legislations] means either a 'responsibility release' (in principle, it is a material limitation), sometimes a 'immunity from prosecution' (suggesting a procedural limitation) (*Judgment Roche*[74], §§ 119-121)."[75] In the Al-Adsani

[69] *See* Kirk M. US Senator for Illinois, *Report Ending Somali Piracy Against American and Allied Shipping,* [online]: kirk.senate.gov.

[70] Kraska J., *Contemporary Maritime Piracy,* Santa Barbara (US), Denver (US), Oxford (UK), Praeger, 2011, p 91.

[71] Lacharrière (de) G., *La Politique Juridique Extérieure,* Paris, Ed. Economica, 1983.

[72] *See among others* ECtHR, *L.C.B. v. UK,* 9 June 1998, 1998-III, p 1403; ECtHR, *Calvelli and Ciglio v. Italia,* no 32967/96; CEDH, *Leray et Autres c. France,* 20.03.2002 (définitif), req. 44617/98 (only in French); ECtHR, *Öneryildiz v. Turkey,* 30 November 2004, no 48939/99.

[73] Verhoeven J., *Droit International Public,* Précis de l'Université catholique de Louvain, Larcier, Bruxelles, 2000, p 742, our translation.

[74] ECtHR, *Roche v. UK,* [GC], 19 October 2005, no 32555/96.

[75] ECtHR, *Marcovic and others v. Italia,* 14 December 2006, no 1398/03, § 96.

case, the Court recognized that the state immunity is antithetical to the rule of the highest standards.[76] Even though the Convention requires the existence of an express provision excluding state immunity, other international courts recognize the superior value of human rights to the immunity of the state that are defined as "certain general and well recognized principles, namely: elementary considerations of humanity, even more exacting in peace than in war."[77]

Given these precedents, the presence of hostages aboard the pirate ship is not a condition that has to be taken into consideration under the international law of human rights. Right to life constitutes one of the most fundamental principles of the matter. Opening fire on a pirate ship and thus causing voluntarily the death of a man has to be considered as an internationally wrongful act. However, the right to life of the pirate and his *hostis humani generis* status form a complex balance of interests.[78] In fact, the number of pirates killed following the intervention of a European State is extremely low.[79]

The operational practice distinguishes the phases of the military action of the states involved in Operation Atalanta. Several legal frameworks are in force, as it pertains to the prevention or intervention. According to Gérard Valin, commander of the maritime area of the Indian Ocean from 2008 to 2009, the hostage is the key element that triggers the change of the legal regime of the military action. Indeed, "during the hostage-rescue missions, then we don't act as part of the ATALANTA Mission, the Operation comes under national command. It is the President of the Republic and the Chief of Defence Staff's responsibility to order the steps we must take."[80] The frame of interstate cooperation offered by the European Operation is limited to the

---

[76] Gaudreau J., *Immunité de l'Etat et Violations des Droits de la Personne: Une Approche Jurisprudentielle*, Graduate Institute of International Studies, Paper no 05/01, 2005, p 60.

[77] ICJ, *The Corfu Channel Case, Judgment,* 9 April 1949, I.C.J. Reports 1949, p. 22 ; ICJ, *Military and Paramilitary Activities in and Against Nicaragua (Nicaragua v. United States of America), Judgment,* I.C.J. Reports 1986, § 215.

[78] Note that some constitutions provide for the possibility of establishing the death penalty for anyone who would be found guilty of piracy. Example: Cypriot Constitution, art. 7 § 2: "No person shall be deprived of his life except in the execution of a sentence of a competent court following his conviction of an offence for which this penalty is provided by the law. A law may provide for such penalty only in cases of . . . piracy jure gentium."

[79] In comparison, on 6 April 2011, the Indian Navy counts 27 people killed, including 16 killed by mistake, six drowned after the delivery of the ransom *(Sirius Star)* and 10 after the liberation of the *Moscow University.*

(Source : Bruxelles2, "Bilan des opérations anti-piraterie (EUNAVFOR Atalanta, CTF, Otan, Inde Russie)," 6 April 2011, [online]: www.bruxelles2.eu.

[80] Proceedings Les Entretiens de Royan, *La Piraterie Maritime,* Brussels, Larcier, 2011, p 83, our translation.

prevention and deterrence of harmful damages. It thus brings states responsible to the fore, even if these acts can be qualified as an act of state precluding recourse to the national justice system.

CONCLUSION

Operation Atalanta is the legal reference frame for the coordination and cooperation of the European naval means acting against piracy off the Somali coast. Yet questions remain over the real intentions and political and economic interests that are pursued. As a universal action, the European operation carries out a mission of escorting the WFP ships. As an operation that aims at securing the energy supply and trade, particularly with Asia, it defends the economic interests of the EU and its Member States. Atalanta is thus at the intersection between the protection of the EU's own interests and the ones of the international community. The context of global economic crisis and strong interdependence between regional and national economies confirms the need for greater cooperation in the fight against a growing phenomenon, at least from a geographical point of view.

The legal ability of the EU to conclude conventional acts brings to the fight against piracy a criminal dimension. It provides a regional response to the prosecution of the captured pirates. However, the debate is still open on the location of the judicial treatment. Even if the aim is to give a judicial and cost-effective response, the regional judicial treatment of the pirates is opposed to the interests of victims and their families. However, the *Somalization* of the solution solves the issues rising from the minimal judicial guarantees afforded to any human being.[81]

Somalia, as a failed state, calls into question the modalities of the international response. Coping with a phenomenon that flows directly from the lack of organized central political power, the real curative solution is ashore and not at sea. If the realism of the solutions proposed by Jack Lang's report might be questioned, it nonetheless points out its origins and underscores the land-based character of the solutions.

Finally, it seems interesting to question the real effectiveness of a universal action of the international organisations and states that would aim at dealing with piracy on an area covering 70.8% of the planet. The disparity of the dangerous sea areas tempers these doubts. The spreading and extending radius of pirate action and their autonomy at sea tests the real capacity of the

[81] See ECtHR, *Medvedyev and Others v. France,* Judgment (referral to Grand Chamber), app. No. 3394/03, 10 July 2008 and ECtHR (Grand Chamber), *Medvedyev and Others v. France,* Judgment, app. No. 3394/03, 29 March 2010.

international community to respond. Can some international organisations, whose operations are based on the goodwill of the Troop Contributing Countries, really ensure safety and security, and prevent risks and threats in any place and at any moment? New technological solutions do exist and lay the foundations of a maritime permanent surveillance. The deployment of unmanned aerial vehicle enables a better orchestration of the naval means. New techniques for gathering evidence and information to authenticate a threat offer new ways. The elements necessary for the intervention, interception, capture and detention of vessels and / or suspected pirates become technologic. The difficulty of the investigations requires new options. Piracy, although brutal, is a source of renewal in legal and technical sphere.

12. Port State Control

Z. Oya Özçayir[1]

Introduction

Despite its relatively short history of application in the maritime world, port state control (PSC) has become the most effective control tool of foreign flagged vessels in national ports. The main discussion about the port state control system is whether it is a replacement for flag state control or not. Flag states have primary responsibility to safeguard against substandard ships. The national flag establishes the primary source of state responsibility for a ship.[2] As stated in Article 94 of the United Nations Law of the Sea Convention 1982 (UNCLOS 1982)[3] it is a flag state's obligation to ensure that their ships comply with the standards accepted by flag states under international law and conventions. Flag states' failure to eliminate substandard vessels from seas created a new control system called as port state control. Port state control did not come into practice to replace flag state responsibility, but to complement it. With time, port state control gained increasing support, and with frequent updates it is reflecting developments in the shipping world.

Since the *Erika*[4] oil pollution incident in France in December 1999, the port state control system went through major changes. This incident revealed the shortcomings of port state control practice; the vessel was inspected sixteen times by port state control officers (PSCOs) and twice by her flag state's controls inspectors and also went through vetting inspections undertaken by the major oil companies and classification society surveys. All

---

[1] Dr. Z. Oya Özcayir, Maritime Law Consultant & Member of Äzmir Law Bar, Turkey.

[2] *See generally* Z. Oya Özcayir, *Liability for Oil Pollution and Collisions*, 10-21 (LLP 1998).

[3] Article 94 establishes a flag state's fundamental duties and Article 94(5) requires flag states to take any steps necessary to secure observance with generally accepted international regulations, procedures and practices. United Nations Convention on the Law of the Sea Dec. 10, 1982, 1833 U.N.TS. 397 [hereinafter UNCLOS 1982].

[4] The International Tanker Owners Pollution Federation (ITOPF), Case Histories –ERIKA (France, 1999) http://www.itopf.com/information-services/data-and-statistics/case-histories/elist.html#ERIKA (last visited Dec. 1, 2011).

these controls were done before the vessel broke in two in the Bay of Biscay, France.[5]

The European Union (EU) maritime safety rules, named the *Erika I*[6] package, incorporated in the Paris Memorandum of Understanding (MOU) on port state control to step up the control of foreign ships in EU ports, and entered into force on 22 July 2003. Under the new rules port state control became compulsory for certain potentially hazardous vessels, member states were required to carry out inspections more frequently and systematically to run more extensive inspections for high-risk vessels such as gas, oil and chemical tankers. More importantly the concept of a blacklist was introduced to deny access to EU ports for certain ships. Apart from improvement of port state control activities, the *Erika I* package also dealt with the activities of classification societies and the phasing out of single hull tankers.[7] In December 2000, the European Commission adopted a second set of community measures on maritime safety, the *Erika II* package.[8] The new measures established a European Maritime Safety Agency (EMSA)[9] to facilitate implementation of the *Erika* I package, and established a vessel traffic monitoring and information system (SafeSeaNet).[10] It also dealt with rules for monitoring traffic in EU waters, identifying ports of refuge and creating a supplementary fund to provide compensation to the victims of oil pollution.[11]

While the preparation for prevention of incidents like *Erika* was going on, another oil tanker, *Prestige*,[12] broke in two and sank off the north-west coast of Spain in 2002. Following this incident the European Commission adopted a "communication on improving safety at sea" on 3 December 2001 to bring forward implementation of the *Erika I* and *II* packages and to introduce

---

[5] Malta Maritime Authority, *Report of the Investigation into the Loss of the Motor Tanker Erika on Sunday 12 December 1999*, at Executive Summary (2000).

[6] *See generally* The Commission of the European Communities, *Communication from the Commission to the European Parliament and to the Council on the Safety of Seaborn Oil Trade,* COM (2000) 142 final (Mar. 31, 2000).

[7] *Id.*

[8] *See generally* The Commission of the European Communities, *Communication from the Commission to the European Parliament and to the Council on a Second Set of Community Measures on Maritime Safety Following the Sinking of Oil Tanker the Erika,* COM (2000) 802 final (Dec. 6, 2000).

[9] http://www.emsa.europa.eu/ (last visited Nov. 27, 2011).

[10] *Id.*

[11] *Id.*

[12] The International Tanker Owners Pollution Federation (ITOPF), Case Histories –PRESTIGE (Spain, 2002) http://www.itopf.com/information-services/data-and-statistics/case-histories/plist.html (last visited Dec. 1, 2011).

specific measures for the carriage of heavy fuel oil and for liability, compensation and penal sanctions.[13] In the newly adopted *Erika III* package, Directive 2009/16/EC established a more ambitious regime by creating a new collective target for Europe as a whole to check all ships with more frequent inspections of high-risk ships.[14]

Although the *Erika* and *Prestige* incidents are not directly related to piracy they were major landmarks in the development of the PSC system and the lessons learned had a great influence on making PSC more robust and effective in combating substandard vessels with poorly trained crew that are generally more prone to piracy.

With a history going back more than 3000 years[15] piracy was a danger troubling the world's seas and then it faded away into the mists of the olden times. However, piracy made a strong return to the maritime scene and started to be reported in countries with civil wars, law enforcement problems and lack of resources. Somalia, on the Horn of Africa, has become the global piracy hotspot. Piracy has become a major problem in some parts of the world, but its devastating effects extend beyond the immediate threat to ships, crew, passengers on board and the cargo. The 1985 hijacking of the *Achille Lauro,*[16] the most high profile case of hijacking, drew worldwide attention to maritime terrorism. In response to this hijacking and to existing legal inadequacies, the 1988 IMO Convention on the Suppression of Unlawful Acts against the Safety of Maritime Navigation (SUA) was adopted.[17]

Terrorist attacks on September 11, 2001 had a marked impact on shipping legislation with regard to maritime security and started a new era in port state control. Following the attacks, the international maritime community realized the vulnerabilities present in the maritime transport system; the vessel, cargo,

---

[13] *See generally* Commission of the European Communities, *Communication from the Commission to the European Parliament and to the Council on Improving Safety at Sea in Response to the Prestige Incident,* COM (2002) 681 final (Dec. 3 2002).

[14] Directive 2009/16/EC of the European Parliament and of the Council of 23 April 2009 on port State control http://eur-lex.europa.eu/LexUriServ/LexUriServ.do?uri=OJ:L:2009:131:0057:0100:EN:PDF (last visited Dec. 1, 2011).

[15] Pirates! Fact and Legend http://www.piratesinfo.com/history/history.php (last visited Dec. 1, 2011).

[16] For detailed discussion of the *Achille Lauro* case *See generally* MALVINA HALBERSTAM, *Terrorism on the High Seas: The Achille Lauro, Piracy and the IMO Convention on Maritime Safety,* 82 AM. J. INT'L.L. 269 (1988) [hereinafter HALBERSTAM].

[17] Convention for the Suppression of Unlawful Acts Against the Safety of Maritime Navigation, Protocol for the Suppression of Unlawful Acts Against the Safety of Fixed Platforms Located on the Continental Shelf http://www.imo.org/About/Conventions/ListOfConventions/Pages/SUA-Treaties.aspx (last visited Dec. 1, 2011).

and ports. Within the international set-up, the world maritime community had to come to consensus to meet the challenges of ensuring maritime security and adopted the new SOLAS (International Convention for the Safety of Life at Sea) regulations on maritime security, and the International Ship and Port Facility Security (ISPS) code. The Paris MOU has been involved in the PSC aspects of the ISPS code from the early stages and considered security as a new area of work for port state control officers.[18] All of these developments represented a significant expansion of port state control activities from safety and environment, to include ship security inspections as well.

Ports are soft target areas not just for pirates, but also for terrorists. Today pirates do not limit themselves to the contents of the vessel, but instead ask for huge ransom payments. They have access to technology to gather information about the movements of vessels and they are often equipped with machine guns and rocket launchers. An attack on an oil tanker in a port may disrupt the world oil trade and cause large-scale environmental damage. The ISPS code makes it mandatory for ships and ports to have security plans, appoint security officers, keep security records and pass an audit to prove that the security plans can be put into practice. It is a comprehensive set of measures to enhance the security of ships and port facilities.

Starting with the ISPS code, maritime security has become a new area for port state control authorities to take care of. Port state control has been given responsibility not just for maritime safety and environmental protection but also for maritime security. Success of this application depends on effective and homogeneous application of port state control in all regions of the world especially where piracy activities are intensive and frequent.

Today piracy is not just a shipping problem, it represents a threat to vital trading routes, to national and international security. International law obligates states to co-operate to repress and combat piracy and gives them certain rights to seize pirate vessels and perpetrators. However, prosecution of piracy suspects does not occur as often as it should, either because governments are not party to relevant international conventions, do not have implementing legislation, or do not have the resources to handle such prosecutions. In order to prevent piracy, individual shipowners have been encouraged to take measures for their own protection. These precautionary measures include "Best Management Practices to Deter Piracy in the Gulf of

---

[18] http://www.classnk.or.jp/hp/SMD/isps/pdf/PSC/Press_Release20031215_e.pdf (last visited Dec. 1, 2011).

Aden and off the Coast of Somalia" (BMPs), [19] the Oil Companies International Marine Forum (OCIMF) guide on "Practical Measures to Avoid, Deter, or Delay Piracy Attacks." Deviation around the Cape of Good Hope to avoid the Gulf of Aden and the western part of the Indian Ocean, and hiring security guards are within the suggested measures. The International Maritime Organization (IMO) emphasizes that the employment of Privately Contracted Armed Security Personnel (PCASP) on board ships in the High Risk Area should not be regarded as an alternative to the BMP and other protective measures, and the use of PCASP should only be considered after a full risk assessment has been completed.[20]

BMPs were developed by shipping industry organisations in co-operation with naval operations. On the basis of these guidelines, shipowners are advised to install effective security equipment on board and register with international monitoring and advice centers in the region.[21] According to the UN Secretary General's report on piracy on October 2010, ships following BMPs had a significantly lower risk of being hijacked. [22] Expenditures associated with countering piracy attacks are quite costly. "Ocean's Beyond Piracy report on the Economic Cost of Somali Piracy" estimates that piracy cost nearly $7 billion in 2011. According to this study over 80% of the costs are borne by the shipping industry, while governments account for 20% of the expenditures associated with countering piracy attacks.[23] Considering the financial aspect of the counter piracy attack precautions and the efforts of all

---

[19] Industry Best Management Practices are designed to assist ships to avoid, deter or delay piracy attacks in the High Risk Area where pirate activity and/or attacks take place. For the purpose of BMP, the High Risk Area is defined as an area bounded by the Suez and the Strait of Hormuz to the North, 10 S and 78 E. In these guidelines the term "piracy" includes all acts of violence against ships, her crew and cargo, including armed robbery and attempts to board and take control of the ship, wherever this may take place. In August 2011, BMP4 booklet published to updates the guidance contained within the 3rd edition of the BMP document published in June 2010. For detailed information about BMP4 See http://www.mschoa.org/bmp3/Documents/BMP4%20Low%20Res_Sept_5_2011.pdf (last visited March 3, 2012).

[20] See IMO MSC.1/Circ.1405/Rev.1 "Revised Interim Guidance to Shipowners, Ship Operators and Shipmasters on the use of Privately Contracted Armed Security Personnel (PCASP) on Board Ships in the High Risk Area," p 1. MSC.1/Circ.1406/Rev.1 "Revised Interim Recommendations for Flag States regarding the use of Privately Contracted Armed Security Personnel on Board Ships in the High Risk Area," MSC.1/Circ.1408 "Interim Recommendations for Port and Coastal States regarding the use of Privately Contracted Armed Security Personnel on Board Ships in the High Risk Area."

[21] *Id.*

[22] UNSC, Report of the Secretary General Pursuant to Security Council Resolution 1897 (2009), S/2010/556, 27 October 2010, http://daccess-dds-ny.un.org/doc/UNDOC/GEN/N10/588/02/PDF/N1058802.pdf?OpenElement
(last visited March 4, 2012).

[23] Oceans Beyond Piracy, *The Economic Cost of Somali Piracy,* http://oceansbeyondpiracy.org/sites/default/files/economic_cost_of_piracy_2011_summary.pdf (last visited March 4, 2012)

shipowners to minimize costs, only well-operated vessels will follow the BMPs.[24] Substandard ships tend to be more vulnerable to pirate attacks than well-operated and maintained vessels.[25] According to the research done by the International Maritime Bureau (IMB), over one third of total hijacked vessels by Somali pirates in the year ending 30 June 2011 could be assessed as being substandard, either through their age or PSC record.[26]

Somali hijackings 1 July 2010-30 June 2011

	I July-31 December 2010	1 January-30 June 2011	TOTAL
Total Hijackings	24	21	45
Fishing Vessels	4	3	7
Dhows	2	1	3
Yachts	1	2	3
Commercial vessels of which:	17	15	32
Good ships	4	4	8
Fair ships	6	5	11
Old and/or substandard vessels	7	6	13

A well maintained vessel; installed with effective security equipment on board, and a crew well trained in counter piracy measures may be more successful in averting piracy attacks and hijackings. Such a vessel could only be run by a company which complies with all international ship safety and security regulations under the observance of flag or port state control. Where the flag state fails to ensure that its vessels meet national regulations and requirements of international agreements to which it is a party, PSC takes part in prevention of piracy by providing the last safety net.

---

[24] See, Sam Bateman, *Sea piracy: some inconvenient truths*, p. 16, http://www.unidir.org/pdf/articles/pdf-art2960.pdf (last visited March 4, 2012).

[25] *Id.*

[26] Sam Bateman, *Sub-Standard Shipping and the Human Costs of Piracy*, Australian Journal of Maritime and Ocean Affairs (2011) Vol 3(2), p 58.

BEGINNING OF PORT STATE CONTROL

The concept of port state control came to maritime law agenda when the Memorandum of Understanding between eight North Sea States was signed in Hague on 2 March 1978,to follow up the Convention Concerning Minimum Standards in Merchant Ships[27] which aimed to inspect vessels that entered the ports of member states.[28] The aim of the Hague Memorandum was the surveillance of seagoing ships in order to safeguard the requirements stated under this Convention, more commonly known as ILO Convention No. 147, and in other Conventions were met.[29] Just two weeks after the signature of the Hague Memorandum, the *Amoco Cadiz* incident happened.[30] The tanker *Amoco Cadiz* ran aground off the coast of Brittany following a steering gear failure and it released its entire cargo of 223,000 tonnes of light crude oil and 4,000 tonnes of bunker oil into heavy seas, over a period of two weeks. At the time of the incident the loss of marine life was the largest ever recorded after an oil spill. The result if this incident was "strong political and public outcry in Europe for far more stringent regulations with regard to the safety of shipping." [31] This incident showed the need that the Hague Memorandum be updated not just on working and living conditions, but also covering maritime safety and pollution prevention. [32] Following two ministerial conferences held in Paris by the ministers responsible for the maritime safety of 14 European countries the present Paris MOU on PSC was adopted and signed.[33]

The Paris MOU has been established as a model treaty upon which the other regions of the world have based their regional agreements on port state control. With the Paris MOU, a regular and systematic control of foreign ships started to be exercised by a regional group of port states. At present port state control is exercised by a group of Memorandum of Understandings in nearly every part of the world, as follows:

---

[27] Convention Concerning Minimum Standards in Merchant Ships, Oct. 29, 1976, 68 U.N.T.S. 17 [hereinafter ILO Convention NO.147].

[28] Dr. Z. Oya Özcayir, Port State Control, 121 (LLP 2nd ed. 2004) [hereinafter Özcayir]

[29] George Kasoulides, *Paris Memorandum of Understanding: A Regional Regime of Enforcement,* The North Sea: Perspectives on Regional Environmental Co-Operation 180, 180 (David Freestone & Tom Ijlstra eds., 1990).

[30] The International Tanker Owners Pollution Federation (ITOPF) Case Histories-A http://www.itopf.com/information-services/data-and-statistics/case-histories/alist.html (last visited Dec. 1, 2011).

[31] The Paris MOU on Port State Control, A Short History of Paris MOU on PSC, http://www.parismou.org/Organization/About_us/2010.12.28/History.htm (last visited Dec. 1, 2011) [hereinafter A Short History].

[32] Özcayir, *supra* note 19, at 121. A Short History, *supra* note 5.

[33] *Id.*

- Paris MOU 1982;[34]
- Acuerdo de Viña del Mar MOU 1992; (Latin American region);[35]
- Tokyo MOU 1993; (Asia-Pacific region);[36]
- Caribbean MOU 1996; (Caribbean region);[37]
- Mediterranean MOU 1997; (Mediterranean region);[38]
- Indian Ocean MOU 1998; (Indian Ocean region);[39]
- Abuja MOU 1999; (West and Central African region);[40]
- Black Sea MOU 2000; (Black Sea region);[41]
- Riyadh MOU 2004; (The Gulf region);[42]

The United States is not a party to any of the regional MOUs on port state control and undertakes port state control on a unilateral basis.

THE RULES THAT GOVERN PORT STATE CONTROL ACTIVITIES

The IMO Resolution A. 787(19)-Procedures for port state control- Last Amended in 1999 by Resolution A. 882 (21) and the Basic Guidance

The first resolution on procedures for the control of ships, IMO Resolution A. 466(XII) was adopted during the 12th IMO Assembly in 1981.[43] The first amendments to this resolution were made in 1995 by adopting Resolution A. 787(19), "Procedures for Port State Control,"[44] which was amended in 1999, by Resolution A. 882(21), which is the current version of IMO procedures for PSC.[45] Amendments to procedures for PSC continue in response to new developments in the shipping world. Following the amendments to the IMO instruments, which have entered into force or become effective since the adoption of resolutions A. 787(19) and A. 882(21), the IMO Sub-Committee on Flag State Implementation (FSI) 19th session agreed to the revised and updated procedures for port state control, 2011, for submission to IMO

---

34 http://www.parismou.org (last visited Dec. 1, 2011).
35 http://200.45.69.62/ (last visited Dec. 1, 2011).
36 http://www.tokyo-mou.org (last visited Dec. 1, 2011).
37 http://www.caribbeanmou.org (last visited Dec. 1, 2011).
38 http://www.medmou.org (last visited Dec. 1, 2011).
39 http://www.iomou.org (last visited Dec. 1, 2011).
40 http://www.abujamou.org (last visited Dec. 1, 2011).
41 http://www.bsmou.org (last visited Dec. 1, 2011).
42 http://www.riyadhmou.org (last visited Dec. 1, 2011).
43 Procedures For The Control of Ships, A. Res. XII/466 (Nov. 19, 1981).
44 http://www.classnk.or.jp/hp/SMD/ism/pdf/09_IMO/A.787(19).pdf (last visited Dec. 1, 2011).
45 International Maritime Organization, *Procedures for Port State Control*, (2001) [hereinafter PROCEDURES FOR PORT STATE CONTROL]. *See* http://www.classnk.or.jp/hp/SMD/ism/pdf/09_IMO/A.882(21).pdf (last visited Dec. 1, 2011).

Maritime Safety Committee (MSC) 89 and to IMO Maritime Environment Protection Committee (MEPC) 62 for approval, prior to submission to IMO 27th Assembly for adoption.[46] The draft Assembly Resolution on port state control was approved by the MEPC, 62nd session[47] and the MSC, 89th session[48] for adoption by the Assembly which took place on 21 November-31 November 2011 at the IMO headquarters in London.

IMO procedures are not mandatory and provide basic guidance to port states on how to conduct port state control inspections; they encourage consistency during these inspections and provide clarification for the procedure of assessment of deficiencies of a ship, its equipment or its crew.[49]

MOUs and Annexes:

The MOUs define the general frame of port state control in different regions. They refer to existing international agreements that are legally binding for states parties to MOUs, and provide a systematized process of enforcing these existing international rules. IMO and International Labour Organization (ILO) conventions provide the basis for port state control inspections.[50] A port state can only apply those conventions that have entered into force and which it has implemented for its own ships.[51] Because of the "no more favourable treatment" principle, ships which fly the flag of a state which is not a party to that convention, are not exempt from inspection.[52] If such ships become subject to a more detailed port state control inspection, the PSCO will follow the same guidelines as those provided for ships to which the relevant international agreements are applicable.[53] MOUs have been amended several times to accommodate new safety and marine environment requirements arising from the amendments made to the IMO Conventions.

The control of foreign flagged vessels by port states has been a feature of international maritime conventions long before the adoption of the Paris

---

[46] http://www.imo.org/MediaCentre/MeetingSummaries/FSI/Pages/FSI-19th-session.aspx (last visited Dec. 1, 2011).

[47] International Maritime Organization [hereinafter IMO], *Report of the Marine Environment Protection Committee on Its Sixty-Second Session*, IMO Doc. MEPC 62/24/Add.1 (July. 26, 2011).

[48] IMO, *Report of the Maritime Safety Committee on its Eighty Ninth Session*, IMO Doc. MSC 89/25 (May. 27, 2011)

[49] *See generally* PROCEDURES FOR PORT STATE CONTROL.

[50] Paris MOU on Port State Control, Principles, http://www.parismou.org/Organization/About_us/2010.12.28/Principles.htm (last visited Dec. 1, 2011).

[51] PROCEDURES FOR PORT STATE CONTROL, ¶ 1.2.3

[52] *Id.*¶ 1.2.2

[53] Paris MOU on Port State Control, Non-parties, http://www.parismou.org/Organization/About_us/2010.12.28/Nonparties.htm (last visited Dec. 1, 2011)

MOU, starting with SOLAS Convention in 1929.[54] The control of foreign flagged merchant vessels by port states has also been an important issue in many other international maritime conventions.[55] Therefore the powers used under the port state control system are not new, and it is the willingness to use these powers, and the organized and coordinated application of port state control, that constitutes a new concept for maritime law.

The EC Directives on Port State Control:

The 1995 Directive, 95/21/EC, is the core Commission policy in enforcing international rules on port state control which is designed to eliminate or deter substandard operators from trading in European waters.[56] It came into force on 1 July 1996 and made PSC mandatory in states which are members of the European Union. By 95/21/EC, the European Community incorporated the Paris MOU into its own legislation and thus provided a legal instrument for the port state control within the European Community. As stated under Article 20(1) of the Directive, each member state is required to implement the directive by introducing the relevant domestic legislation. Under Article 2 (1) of the Directive, reference is made to "the Protocols and amendments to these Conventions and related codes of mandatory status, in force at the date of adoption of this Directive under the definition of Conventions." The inclusion of this clause indicates that protocols, amendments and related mandatory codes, which should be applied by the member states, need to be continuously updated and specified.

On the basis of amendments made to certain conventions, 95/21/EC was amended by:

- Council Directive 98/25/EC of 27 April 1998 amending Directive 95/21/EC;[57]

---

[54] International Convention for the Safety of Life at Sea, May 31, 1929 136 L.N.T.S. 81 [hereinafter SOLAS].

[55] *See* International Convention on Load Lines, art.21, Apr. 5, 1966, 640 U.N.T.S 133 [hereinafter LL 66]; ART. 12; SOLAS 74/SOLAS Protocol 88, Ch. I, Reg. 19, Ch. IX, Reg. 6.2, Ch. XI-1, Reg. 4, Ch. XI-2, Reg. 9; International Convention for the Prevention of Pollution From Ships, as modified by the Protocol of 1978 relating thereto, art. 5 & 6, Feb. 16, 1978, 17 I.L.M 546 [hereinafter MARPOL 73/78], Annex I. Reg. 11, Annex II. Reg. 16.9, Annex III. Reg. 8, Annex IV. Reg. 13, Annex V. Reg. 8,Annex VI. Reg. 10; ILO 147, ART.4; International Convention on Standards of Training, Certification and Watchkeeping for Seafarers, art. X, July 7, 1978, 1361 U.N.T.S. 2 [hereinafter STCW 1978]; AFS 2001; Art. 11.

[56] Council Directive 95/21/EC of 19 June 1995 concerning the enforcement, in respect of shipping using Community ports and sailing in the waters under the jurisdiction of the Member States, of international standards for ship safety, pollution prevention and shipboard living and working conditions (port State control) [Official Journal L 157 of 07.07.1995] [hereinafter 95/21/EC].

[57] Council Directive 98/25/EC of 27 April 1998 amending 95/21/EC [Official Journal L 133 of 7.5 1998].

- Commission Directive 98/42/EC of 19 June 1998 amending Council Directive 95/21/EC;[58]
- Commission Directive 1999/97/EC of 13 December 1999 amending Council Directive 95/21/EC;[59]
- Directive 2001/106/EC of the European Parliament and of the Council of 19 December 2001;[60]
- Directive 2002/84/EC of the European Parliament and the Council of 5 November 2002;[61]
- Directive 2009/16/EC of the European Parliament and of the Council of 23 April 2009;[62]

INSPECTION COMMITMENTS AND RECENT CHANGES UNDER THE PARIS MOU

Under the port state control system, each of the MOU signatories agree that national surveyors of each state will undertake to make visits to a certain amount of foreign vessels visiting that state. Inspection rates are decided regionally and differ from one region to another.[63] As of 1 January 2011, the Paris MOU's initial inspection rate of 25 percent went through a dramatic change by a new commitment to inspect all High Risk Ships visiting its ports and anchorages in the Paris MOU region.[64] Under the New Inspection Regime (NIR) all ships visiting the region will be inspected with an inspection frequency depending on a risk profile assigned to each ship.[65] The targeting of ships is no longer based on a target factor, but on a Ship Risk

[58] Commission Directive 98/42/EC of 19 June 1998 amending 95/21/EC [Official Journal L 184 of 27/06/1998].

[59] Commission Directive 1999/97/EC of 13 December 1999 amending 95/21/EC [Official Journal L 331 of 23.12.199].

[60] Directive 2001/106/EC of the European Parliament and of the Council of 19 December 2001 amending 95/21/EC [Official Journal L 19 of 22 January 2002].

[61] Directive 2002/84/EC of the European Parliament and of the Council of 5 November 2002 amending the Directives on maritime safety and the prevention of pollution from ships [Official Journal L 324 of 29.11.2002].

[62] Directive 2009/16/EC of 23 April 2009 on port State control [Official Journal L 131 of 28.05.09].

[63] Paris MOU 1982: 100 per cent (visiting ports and anchorages in the Paris MOU as a whole), Acuerdo de Viña del Mar MOU 1992: 20 per cent, Tokyo MOU 1993: 80 per cent, Caribbean MOU 1996: 15 per cent, Mediterranean MOU 1997: 15 per cent, Indian Ocean MOU 1998: 10 per cent, Abuja MOU 1999: 15 per cent, Black Sea MOU 2000: 15 per cent, Riyadh MOU 2004: 10 per cent.

[64] Paris MOU, Paris adopts new inspection regime http://www.parismou.org/Publications/Press_releases/2010.12.22/Paris_MoU_adopts_new_inspection_regime.htm (last visited Dec. 1, 2011).

[65] Steamship Mutual Risk Alert, Paris MOU New Inspection Regime http://www.simsl.com/Risk-Alerts/RA18ParisMOUNewRegime.pdf (last visited Dec. 1, 2011).

Profile (SRP).[66] The SRP calculator calculates whether as ship is going to be considered as High Risk Ship (HRS), Standard Risk Ship (SRS) or Low Risk Ship (LRS).[67]

The risk profile is based on generic and historical factors.[68] Generic factors are ship type, flag, recognized organization and company; historical factors are inspection history of a vessel, deficiencies and detentions.[69] With this new regime, assessment of a vessel for inspection under the Paris MOU involves all components of the shipping world including performance of the company responsible for the International Safety Management Code (ISM) management as a new parameter. The Paris MOU web site provides a company performance calculator to evaluate the performance of the ISM Companies.[70]

Apart from regular inspections each year, major port state control regions carry out a concentrated inspection campaign (CIC) on an agreed topic as an effective tool for enforcement of relevant port state control requirements.[71] During these campaigns a PSCO checks certain specific items as well as the general routine PSC inspection. The website of relevant MOUs publishes a questionnaire detailing the additional areas to be inspected during the CICs together with the relevant information.[72] The areas which have paramount importance for effective implementation of port state control are repeated in the following concentrated inspection campaigns.[73] As co-operation between different regions, port state control is becoming more effective and CICs

---

[66] Paris MOU on Port State Control, Annex 7, Ship Risk Profile http://www.parismou.org/Content/PublishedMedia/8a663a6a-8980-45ee-a47d-e73d6c17cfb7/Paris%20MoU%20Annex%207%20Ship%20Risk%20Profile.pdf (last visited Dec. 1, 2011) [hereinafter ship risk profile].

[67] Paris MOU on Port State Control, http://www.paris mou.org/Inspection_efforts/Inspections/Ship_risk_profile/Ship_risk_profile_calculator (last visited Dec. 1, 2011)

[68] Ship Risk Profile, *supra* note 57.

[69] *Id.*

[70] Paris MOU, http://www.parismou.org/Inspection_efforts/Inspection/Ship_risk_profile/Company_preformance/Company_performance_calculator/ (last visited Dec. 1, 2011).

[71] Özcayir, at. 161.

[72] *See* Paris MOU, Concentrated Inspection Campaign, Structural Safety and Load Lines 1 September-30 November 2011 http://www.parismou.org/inspections_efforts/Inspections/Inspcetion_types/Concentrated_Inspection_Campaign/ (last visited Dec. 1, 2011).

[73] In 1998 and 2002 the maritime authorities of Paris MOU carried out the concentrated inspection campaigns on ISM Code implementation to verify that a safe management system had been established on board and in 2007 had another campaign to verify its effective implementation. http://www.tax-news.com/news/Paris_MOU_To_Conduct_Concentrated_Inspection_Campaign_28349.html (last visited Dec. 1, 2011).

could also be run as joint CICs.[74] By running joint and individual inspection campaigns the rules which are avoided by shipowners are recorded as continuous defects and are enforced in a more effective way.

Under the new NIR, any ship arriving or leaving ports and anchorages in the Paris MOU region has to comply with the following reporting obligations[75] for this information to be made available to the new PSC information database, Thetis, the new information system that supports NIR.[76]

- Pre-arrival notification: 72 hours before estimated arrival time for vessels due for expanded inspection. This includes all ships with a high risk profile and any passenger ship, oil tanker, gas or chemical tanker or bulk carrier which is more than 12 years old.
- Pre-arrival notification: 24 hours before estimated arrival time for every ship.
- Actual time of arrival.
- Actual time of departure.

If a vessel fails to comply with the relevant notification requirement, that vessel may be targeted for inspection, regardless of the period since her last periodic inspection, and penalties may be imposed by national authorities for non-reporting.[77] Like the present port state control regime, substandard vessels may be banned from the Paris MOU region, but with NIR, each refusal of access will be given for a predefined minimum duration and may also became permanent.[78]

PORT STATE CONTROL INSPECTIONS AND THE POWER OF A PSCO

A port state control inspection may be conducted by the initiative of the port state maritime authority, on a report or notification by another authority or a report or complaint by the master, crewmember or organization with a

[74] Launch of concentrated inspection campaign on structural safety and the International Convention on Load Lines beginning 1 September 2011 by Paris MOU and Tokyo MOU on Port Sate Control. Paris MOU, http://www.parismou.org/Publications/Press_releases/2011.07.21/Launch_of_concentrated_inspection_campaign_on_structural_safety_and_Load_Lines.htm (last visited Dec. 1, 2011).

[75] Paris MOU on Port State Control http://www.parismou.org/Inspection_efforts/Inspections/Frequently_Asked_Questions/Reporting_obligation/ (last visited Dec. 1, 2011).

[76] http://www.emsa.europa.eu/operations/maritime_survelliance/thetis.html (last visited Dec. 1, 2011).

[77] Paris MOU, Port State Control Reporting Obligations https://www.parismou.org/Content/PublishedMedia/613aa272-374d-4ead-9ba1-6acf5dc5a25c/Reporting%20obligation.pdf (last visited Dec. 1, 2011).

[78] Paris MOU on Port State Control, Section 4, Banning (last visited Dec. 1, 2011). https://www.parismou.org/Content/PublishedMedia/3e8bff04-7cca-4645-bd0a-f614eac8b2fb/Banning%20information.pdf.

legitimate interest in the safe operation of the ship. The inspections are required to be conducted in accordance with the provisions of the applicable conventions.[79]

The certificates carried by the vessels to provide proof of inspection and to demonstrate compliance with international standards are accepted as proof by the port authorities that the vessel is in compliance with the required standards.[80] However, if there are clear grounds that the condition of the ship, its equipment, or its crew do not substantially correspond with the particulars of these certificates,[81] or the crew members of the vessel, including the master, are not familiar with essential shipboard procedures relating to safety of the ship or the prevention of pollution,[82] then the PSCO may proceed on a more detailed inspection which may result in the delayed departure of the vessel or its detention.[83]

IMO port state control procedures, and regional MOUs, provide a list of examples of what might constitute clear grounds.[84] The absence of valid certificates or documents is considered a clear ground. However, the professional judgment of the PSCO is the decisive factor in examining the provided evidence to warrant a more detailed inspection. While the IMO guidelines and regional agreements serve as a consistent reference point, the professional judgment of a PSCO is ultimately used to determine the appropriate level of inspection in any given circumstance. The professional judgment of a PSCO gains more importance when a detention decision needs to be made. If deficiencies in a vessel are clearly hazardous to safety or the environment, the PSCO may detain the vessel, and has to make sure that those deficiencies are corrected before the vessel is allowed to sail.[85] The IMO guidelines and regional MOUs provide a list of deficiencies which are considered to be of such a serious nature that they may warrant the detention of the ship involved, but it is not an exhaustive list. Therefore the decision to detain a vessel is based on the professional judgment of a PSCO, and hence, despite all the provided guidelines to assist PSCOs in making such judgments, it is impossible to eliminate the subjectivity completely.

---

[79] PROCEDURES FOR PORT STATE CONTROL, ¶¶ 2.1.1-2.

[80] *See id.* ¶ 2.2.3.

[81] *Id.* ¶ 2.2.5.

[82] *Id.* ¶ 1.6.1.

[83] *Id.* ¶ 4.7.2.

[84] *See* Paris MOU on Port State Control, Memorandum of Understanding, Annex 9 Inspection Type and Clear Grounds http://www.parismou.org/Organization/2010.12.27/Memorandum_of_Understanding.htm (last visited Dec. 1, 2011).

[85] PROCEDURES FOR PORT STATE CONTROL, ¶ 4.7.2.

MARITIME SECURITY OVERVIEW AND PIRACY

The concept of security in the maritime sector came under discussion following the *Achille Lauro* hijacking.[86] On 7 October 1985, the Palestine Liberation Front took control of the *Achille Lauro* and its passengers, while the Italian cruise ship was en route from Alexandria to Port Said. They demanded the release of 50 Palestinians held in Israeli prisons and killed a disabled American tourist, and threw his body overboard with his wheelchair before the situation was resolved.[87] Following this incident the first question that needed to be answered was whether the seizure of the ship constituted an act of piracy or not. Following the *Achille Lauro* incident the question whether maritime terrorism falls within the meaning of piracy caused a considerable debate.

The answer to this question needed reference to existing international law on piracy. The notion of piracy first codified in the 1958 Geneva Convention on the High Seas (1958 Convention)[88] and later in the 1982 United Nations Convention on the Law of the Sea.[89] Article 15 of the 1958 Convention and Article 101 of UNCLOS Convention define piracy as:

(1) Any illegal act of violence, detention, or any act of depredation, committed for private ends by the crew, or the passengers of a private ship or a private aircraft, and directed:

(a) On the high sea, against another ship or aircraft, or against persons or property on board such ship or aircraft;

(b) Against a ship, aircraft, persons or property in a place outside the jurisdiction of any State.[90]

The definition under UNCLOS sets out the basic legal framework governing acts of piracy. *An illegal act of violence, detention or any act of depredation* will only fall within the definition of piracy under Article 101 of UNCLOS if it is committed by one ship against another, committed for private ends and committed on the high seas or in the exclusive economic zones (EEZ) of states.[91] The *Achille Lauro* incident could not be considered as an act of piracy, as the hijackers did not act for "private ends" because

---

[86] HALBERTSAM.

[87] Special Operations.Com, *Achille Lauro* Hijacking, Mediterranean Sea, October 1985 http://www.specialoperations.com/Images_Folder/library2/achille.html (last visited Dec. 1, 2011).

[88] Convention on the High Seas, Apr. 29, 1958, 13 U.S.T. 2312, 450 U.N.T.S. 82.

[89] United Nations Convention on the Law of the Sea, Dec. 10, 1982, S. Treaty Doc. No. 103-39, 1833 U.N.T.S. 397.

[90] Convention on the High Sea, at Art. 15; UNCLOS, at Art. 101.

[91] UNCLOS Art. 58(2), provides that the provisions on piracy also apply in the EEZ.

they were politically motivated, and the seizure of the vessel also did not meet the two vessel requirement.[92] This incident showed the weakness of the piracy international legal regime in dealing with acts of terrorism. It came to the attention of the maritime world that the development of international law relating to unlawful acts against ships was not as advanced as civil aviation.[93] Before the *Achille Lauro* incident, terrorism at sea had not been a serious international problem which led to lack of specific international rules on maritime terrorism.

Just over a month after this incident, on 20 November 1985, the IMO Assembly adopted a resolution,[94] A. 584(14), on "Measures to Prevent Unlawful Acts which Threaten the Safety of Ships and the Security of Their Passengers and Crews" directing the MSC to develop a circular on security measures "to ensure the security of passengers and crew on board ships." Under this resolution, governments, port authorities and administrations, shipowners, ship operators, shipmasters and crews are called on to review and strengthen port and onboard security, noting "the danger to passengers and crews resulting from the increasing number of incidents involving piracy, armed robbery and other unlawful acts against or on board ships." The MSC approved the circular (MSC/Circ. 443) titled "Measures to Prevent Unlawful Acts Which Threaten the Safety of Ships and the Security of their Passengers and Crew" on September 1986 for application on passenger ships engaged in international voyages of 24 hours or more, and the port facilities which service them. The circular recommended governments, port authorities, administrations, shipowners, shipmasters and crews to take appropriate measures to prevent unlawful acts that may threaten passengers and crews. It stressed the need for port facilities and individual ships to have a security plan and appoint a security officer. It gave a detailed description of

---

[92] H.E. Jose Luis Jesus, *Protection of Foreign Ships against Piracy and Terrorism at Sea: Legal Aspects*, 18 Int'l J. Marine and Coastal L. 363 (2003) at 388 [hereinafter JESUS]. *See* Documents Concerning the *Achille Lauro* Affair and Cooperation in Combating International Terrorism, 24 I.L.M. 1509, at 1554-57 for the opposite approach of U.S. Justice Department.

[93] In aviation the 1963 Tokyo Convention on Offences and Certain Other Acts Committed on Board Aircraft, Dec. 22, 1969, 20 U.S.T. 2941, 704 U.N.T.S. 219; the 1970 Hague Convention for the Suppression of Unlawful Seizure of Aircraft, Mar. 8, 1973, 22 U.S.T. 1641, 860 U.N.T.S. 105; the 1971 Montreal Convention for the Suppression of Unlawful Acts Against the Safety of Civil Aviation, Sep. 23, 1971, 24 U.S.T. 564, 974 U.N.T.S. 177. *See* Helmut Tuerk, *Combating Maritime Terrorism At Sea-The Suppression Of Unlawful Acts Against The Safety Of Maritime Navigation,* 18 U. Miami Int'l & Comp. L. Rev. 337 (200) at 343 [hereinafter TUERK].

[94] The Assembly Resolution A.584(14) titled "Measures to Prevent Unlawful Acts Which Threaten the Safety of Ships and the Security of their Passengers and Crew" was adopted on November 20th that year.

security measures and procedures to be adopted and details for security surveys to be conducted.[95]

The next action taken by the IMO regarding maritime security, came in the form of the "Convention for the Suppression of Unlawful Acts Against the Safety of Maritime Convention," known as the SUA Convention, and enacted in response to the *Achille Lauro* incident. It is only after the hijacking of the *Achille Lauro* that the term "safety" started to appear in IMO Conventions.

The SUA Convention addressed terrorism at sea for the first time.[96] It is directed at acts that endanger the safe navigation of ships[97] and it was amended in 2005 to include a framework for combating the proliferation of weapons of mass destruction and their delivery systems.[98] The main purpose of the SUA treaties is to ensure that appropriate action is taken against persons committing unlawful acts against ships and fixed platforms on the continental shelf.[99] In this context, unlawful acts include the seizure of ships by force; acts of violence against persons on board ships, and the placing of devices on board a ship which are likely to destroy or damage it.[100] The treaties include provisions for the absolute and unconditional application of the principle either to punish or to extradite persons who commit or have allegedly committed offences specified in the convention.[101]

THE CHANGING NATURE OF MARITIME SECURITY PROBLEMS

Everyone has an image of a pirate or pirate ship in their mind on the basis of movies they have seen or books they have read. Piracy had its peak days in the 17th and 18th century and seemed to be disappearing at the end of the

---

[95] IMO, Measures to Prevent Unlawful Acts Against Passengers and Crews on Board Ships, MSC. Circ./443 (Sep. 26, 1986) http://www.imo.org/blast/blastDataHelper.asp?data_id=3827&filename= msccirc443measurestoprevent.pdf (last visited Dec. 1, 2011).

[96] TUERK, at 337, 365.

[97] IMO, http://www.imo.org/OurWork/Facilitation/SUAConvention/Pages/Default.aspx (last visited Dec. 1, 2011).

[98] IMO, http://www.imo.org/OurWork/Security/Instruments/Pages/SUA.aspx (last visited Dec. 1, 2011).

[99] IMO, SUA Convention, (2006 Edition) at iii, Foreword.

[100] *See* Art. 3 & 3*bis* of the Convention for the Suppression of Unlawful Acts against The Safety of Maritime Navigation, 2005 (hereinafter 2005 SUA Convention) (Consolidated text of the Convention for the Suppression of Unlawful Acts against the Safety of Maritime Convention and of the Protocol of 2005 to the Convention).

[101] 2005 SUA Convention, Art. 10.1 "The State Party in the territory of which the offender or the alleged offender is found shall, in cases to which article 6 applies, if it does not extradite him, be obliged, without exception whatsoever and whether or not the offence was committed in its territory, to submit the case without delay to its competent authorities for the purpose of prosecution, through the proceedings in accordance with the laws of that State. Those authorities shall take their decision in the same manner as in the case of any offence of a grave nature under the law of that State."

19th century, and for the greater part of the 20th century, but unexpectedly in the 1970s and 1980s pirate attacks on ships started to increase.[102]

Today piracy may appear in many forms.[103] Piracy may take place in the form of theft to steal cash and valuables from the ship's safe and crew with a minimum use of force. These are considered as "armed robbery against ships" and not piracy under UNCLOS.[104] Despite the restricted definition of acts piracy "to the high seas" and "outside the jurisdiction of any State" under UNCLOS, many attacks take place when ships are in ports or at anchor and in territorial waters, inside the jurisdiction of a state.[105] Pirates who attack the vessels while they are underway seem to have better organizational background with better equipment, training and specific economic motives.[106] Modern 21st century piracy is benefiting from technological developments; pirates are using GPS[107] equipped speedboats armed with automatic weapons. Instead of having an interest in the cargo, they are keen on asking for huge amount of ransoms by attacking the ships and holding the crew hostage. They are supported by "mother ships," which enable them to

---

[102] JESUS, *supra* note 84, at 364. In response to increasing number of piracy attacks the International Maritime Bureau (IMB) Piracy Reporting Centre (PRC) was established in Kuala Lumpur in 1992 as a division of the International Chamber of Commerce (ICC). IMB Piracy Reporting Centre http://www.icc-ccs.org/piracy-reporting-centre (last visited Dec. 1, 2011).

[103] *See* Jayant Abhyankar, *Piracy and Armed Robbery at Sea, 97*-101 in Maximo Q Meijia Jr., Jinjing (Ed.). 97 ABYANKAR, Coastal Zone Piracy and Other Unlawful Acts at Sea (WMU, 2007).

[104] IMO, A 26/Res.1025, 18 January 2010, Resolution A.1025 (26) Adopted on 2 December 2009. (Agenda item 10) Code of Practice for the Investigation of Crimes of Piracy and Armed Robbery Against Ships "Armed robbery against ships" is defined in the Code of Practice for the Investigation of the Crimes of Piracy and Armed Robbery Against Ships (resolution A.1025(26), Annex, paragraph 2.2), as follows: ""Armed robbery against ships" means any of the following acts: (a) any illegal act of violence or detention or any act of depredation, or threat thereof, other than an act of piracy, committed for private ends and directed against a ship or against persons or property on board such a ship, within a State's internal waters, archipelagic waters and territorial sea; (b) any act of inciting or of intentionally facilitating an act described above."

[105] IMO, Reports on Acts of Piracy and Armed Robbery Against Ships, Annual report – 2010, MSC.4/Circ.169, 1 April 2011. http://www.imo.org/OurWork/Security/PiracyArmedRobbery/Monthly%20and%20annual%20piarcy%20and%20armed%20robbery%20report/169_Annual2010.pdf (last visited Dec. 1, 2011).

[106] Dana Dillon, *Maritime Piracy: Defining the Problem* SAIS Review vol. XXV no.1 (Winter-Spring) http://www.southchinasea.org/docs/Maritime%20Piracy.pdf (last visited Nov. 19 2011) [hereinafter DILLON].

[107] Joaquín Salido Marcos, *Modern Pirates Use GPS in Somalia*, May. 26, 2008. http://www.cafebabel.co.uk/article/24678/modern-pirates-use-gps-in-somalia.html (last visited Dec. 1, 2011). Chris Gayomali, *Pirates Now Using Blogs and GPS to Hunt Merchant Vessels,* June. 23, 2011 http://techland.time.com/2011/06/23/pirates-now-using-blogs-and-gps-to-hunt-merchant-vessels/ (last visited Nov. 27, 2011). Neal Ungerleider, *Somali Pirates Go High Tech,*June. 22, 2011 http://www.fastcompany.com/1762331/somali-pirates-go-high-tech (last visited Dec. 1, 2011).

launch attacks from a distance of up to 500 nautical miles.[108] Payment of significant ransoms is a major concern for the shipping world.[109] There has been an increase in the price of ransom during recent years.[110] In January 2010, a $ 7 million ransom was paid for the release of the Greek supertanker *MV Maran Centauros*[111] with a cargo of crude oil worth $162 million. In November 2010, the highest ransom on record, $ 9.5 million, was paid to Somali pirates for the release of a South Korean oil tanker, the *Samho Dream*.[112]

Following the terrorist attacks of September 11, 2011 the issue of security took priority in the international maritime agenda and the international community realized the potential of using maritime trading system for maritime terrorism. The international community recognized the need for including maritime security as part of the maritime transport policy. Today the international community as a whole feels the negative effects of piracy and maritime terrorism. Piracy poses a serious threat to the safety of navigation as well as to the marine environment, especially in the straits used for maritime navigation, and disrupts international trade. The inherent vulnerability of ports to terrorist attacks and criminal activities raised serious concern in the shipping community. With the adoption of the ISPS Code authorities could verify the identity of, and the potential risk posed by, a particular foreign vessel before it enters a port. Such exercise could help the authorities to identify and deter threats to international security.

APPLICATION OF ISPS CODE UNDER PORT STATE CONTROL

Following the 9/11 attacks the 22nd IMO Assembly acknowledged that terrorist attacks posed a threat for maritime trade and decided that the Organization should review measures and procedures to prevent acts of terrorism that threaten the security of passengers and crew and the safety of

---

[108] *See* Yvonne M. Dutton, *Bringing Pirate To Justice: A Case For Including Piracy Within The Jurisdiction Of The International Criminal Court,* One Earth Foundation Discussion Paper, February 2010, n. 1. http://www.oneearthfuture.org/siteadmin/images/files/file_52.pdf (last visited Dec. 1, 2011) [hereinafter DUTTON]

[109] *See* Dr. Z. Oya Ozcayir, *Piracy Part III, Ransom Payments and the US Executive Order on Somalian Piracy, (*2010)16 JIML 323.

[110] *See generally,* Anna Bowden, *The Economic Cost of Maritime Piracy,* One Earth Future Foundation Working Paper, December 2010 http://oneearthfuture.org/images/imagefiles/Cost%20of%20Piracy%20Final%20Report.pdf (last visited Nov. 19 2011) [hereinafter BOWDEN].

[111] Karl Wilson, *Terror on Waters,* China Daily Asia Pacific, Nov. 18, 2011 http://chinadailyapac.com/article/terror-waters (last visited Dec. 1, 2011)

[112] Rick Spilman, *Record Ransoms paid to Somali Pirates for MV Samho Dream & MV Golden Blessing,* Nov. 6, 2010. http://www.oldsaltblog.com/2010/11/06/record-ransoms-paid-to-somali-pirates-for-mv-samho-dream-mv-golden-blessing/ (last visited Dec. 1, 2011).

ships.[113] During the 22nd Assembly, held in November 2001, Resolution A. 924(22)[114] was adopted on review of measures and procedures to prevent acts of terrorism which threaten the security of passengers and crews and the safety of ships. A Diplomatic Conference was held in December 2002, which adopted a number of amendments to the SOLAS Convention, the most important of which is the new International Ship and Port Facility Security Code.[115]

Following 9/11, the European Community started the process of including maritime security related policies within maritime transport policy by adopting Regulation 725/2004[116] of the European Parliament, the Council of 31 March on enhancing ship and port facility. The general framework of the Regulation fully respects the ISPS Code and introduces security related policies within the framework of the European maritime transport policy as a primary legislation.[117] The US incorporated the ISPS Code into the national law under the Maritime Transportation Act of 2002 (MTSA).[118]

The ISPS code's aim is to ensure security of ships and port facilities through a risk management process; appropriate security measures need to be determined through an assessment of the risks to be made in each particular case. This risk management concept is represented in the ISPS Code through a number of minimum functional security requirements for ships and port facilities.[119] Shipping companies are required to designate a Company Security Officer (CSO) for the company and a Ship Security Officer (SSO) for each of their ships. The CSO is responsible for ensuring that a Ship Security Assessment is properly carried out, that Ship Security Plans (SSP) are prepared and submitted for approval by or on behalf of the flag

---

[113] IMO, ISPS Code, 2003 Ed. http://www.stlucia.gov.lc/nemp/agreements/ISPS_Code_en.pdf (last visited Dec. 1, 2011) [hereinafter ISPS Code].

[114] *Id.*

[115] *Id.*

[116] Regulation (EC) No 725/2004 of the European Parliament and of the Council of 31 March 2004 on enhancing ship and port facility security [Official Journal L 129/6 of 29.4.2004] http://eur-lex.europa.eu/LexUriServ/LexUriServ.do?uri=OJ:L:2004:129:0006:0091:EN:PDF (last visited Dec. 1, 2011).

[117] *See* David Kerr, *EU Maritime Security Policy Development and Its Current Status* at 121-128 in Maximo Q Meija Jr. (Ed.) Maritime Security and Crime (WMU, 2010).

[118] Maritime Transportation Security Act of 2002, 107th Congress Public Law 295, http://www.gpo.gov/fdsys/pkg/PLAW-107publ295/html/PLAW-107publ295.htm (last visited Dec. 1, 2011). As one of the major international marine insurance centers, the UK implemented the ISPS Code into English law by the Ship and Port Facility (Security) Regulations 2004 (SI 2004/1495). http://www.legislation.gov.uk/uksi/2004/1495/contents/made (last visited Dec. 1, 2011).

[119] ISPS Code.

administration and that once approved, the plan is placed on board each ship.[120]

Under the Code, there are 3 ISPS security levels which correspond to normal, medium and high threat situations. The SSP should indicate the operational and physical security measures that should be taken by those on board to ensure that it always operates at security level 1. The plan should also indicate how a ship's personnel could respond to security level 2 and security level 3 situations. Under level 1, minimum appropriate protective security measures shall be maintained at all times. Under level 2, appropriate additional protective security measures must be maintained for a period of time as a result of heightened risk of a security incident. Level 3 requires further specific protective security measures to be maintained for a limited period of time when a security incident is probable or imminent, although it may not be possible to identify the specific target.[121]

The ISPS Code consists of Part A, a mandatory section, with detailed security related requirements for Governments, port authorities and shipping companies; and Part B, a non-mandatory section, with a series of guidelines about how to meet these requirements. The aim of the measures is to provide a universal standard for preventing and combating terrorist acts in the international maritime transport sector. [122] The ISPS code applies to passenger ships and cargo ships of 500GRT and upwards, including high-speed craft and mobile offshore drilling units, as well as to port facilities serving such ships engaged on international voyages. SOLAS chapter XI-2, and Part A of the ISPS code, are mandatory since 1 July 2004, and starting from that date ships are required to carry a valid International Ship Security Certificate (ISSC) issued in accordance with the **ISPS Code.**[123]

The ISSC is subject to PSC and compliance inspections.[124] The legal reference enabling port states to exercise control on maritime security measures is regulated under the SOLAS Convention and the ISPS code. SOLAS Reg. XI-2/9 describes the control and compliance measures

---

[120] *Id.*

[121] *Id.* Port of Amsterdam, ISPS Code, http://www.portofamsterdam.com/Eng/Specials/(1150)-Port-Security/(1152)-ISPS-code.html#toc_2 (last visited Dec. 1, 2011)

[122] *Id.*

[123] *Id.*

[124] Sixteenth OSCE Economic and Environmental Forum - Part 1: "Maritime and inland waterways co-operation in the OSCE area: Increasing security and protecting the environment" Vienna, 28-29 January 2008, *IMO maritime security policy Background paper,* EEF.IO/3/08 23 January 2008 http://www.osce.org/eea/30455 (last visited Dec. 1, 2011) at. 5.

applicable to ships to which SOLAS chapter XI-2 applies.[125] These measures are described in three separate sections; control of ships already in a port, control of ships intending to enter a port of another contracting government, and additional provisions applicable to both cases.[126]

The ISPS Code Part B-4 states the security related responsibilities of contracting governments.[127] Regulation XI-2/9.1 deals with control of ships while in port of a foreign country. Under this section, duly authorized officers of contracting governments are given the right to go on board a ship to verify that the ship has a valid ISSC or interim ISSC issued under the provisions of Part A of the ISPS Code. A valid ISSC is accepted unless there are clear grounds for believing that the ship is not in compliance with the ISPS code.[128]

Regulation XI-2/9.2 applies to control measures to ensure compliance by ships intending to enter a port of another contracting state. If there are clear grounds that the ship is in non-compliance with the requirements of Regulation XI-2 or Part A of the ISPS Code the vessel may be denied of entry into port.[129]

"Examples of possible clear grounds under regulations XI-2/9.1 and XI-2/9.2 may include, when relevant:[130]

- evidence from a review of the certificate that it is not valid or it has expired;
- evidence or reliable information that serious deficiencies exist in the security equipment, documentation or arrangements required by chapter XI-2 and part A of this Code;
- receipt of a report or complaint which, in the professional judgment of the duly authorized officer, contains reliable information clearly indicating that the ship does not comply with the requirements of chapter XI-2 or part A of this Code;
- evidence or observation gained by a duly authorized officer using professional judgment that the master or ship's personnel is not familiar with essential shipboard security procedures or cannot carry out drills

---

[125] IMO, Annex, Guidance to the Masters, Companies and Duly Authorized Officers on the Requirements Relating to the Submission of Security Related Information Prior to the Entry of a Ship into Port, MSC/Cir. 1130.

[126] *Id.*

[127] *Id.*

[128] *Id.*

[129] *Id.*

[130] *See* ISPS-B/4.33 http://marsec.mardep.gov.hk/pdf/isps_code.pdf (last visited Dec. 1, 2011).

related to the security of the ship or that such procedures or drills have not been carried out;

- evidence or observation gained by a duly authorized officer using professional judgment that key members ship's personnel are not able to establish proper communication with any other key members of ship's personnel with security responsibilities on board the ship;
- evidence or reliable information that the ship has embarked persons, or loaded stores or goods at a port facility or from another ship where either the port facility or the other ship is in violation of chapter XI-2 or part A of this Code, and the ship in question has not completed a Declaration of Security, nor taken appropriate, special or additional security measures or has not maintained appropriate ship security procedures;
- evidence or reliable information that the ship has embarked persons, or loaded stores or goods at a port facility or from another source (e.g., another ship or helicopter transfer) where either the port facility or the other source is not required to comply with chapter XI-2 or part A of this Code, and the ship has not taken appropriate, special or additional security measures or has not maintained appropriate security procedures; and
- if the ship holds a subsequent, consecutively issued Interim International Ship Security Certificate as described in section A/19.4, and if, in the professional judgment of an officer duly authorized, one of the purposes of the ship or a Company in requesting such certificate is to avoid full compliance with chapter XI-2 and part A of this Code beyond the period of the initial interim certificate as described in section A/19.4.4. "

APPLICATION OF ISPS CODE TO PIRACY

In general the ISPS code could combat piracy against ships as it establishes a coastal zone security by preventing access of unauthorized persons to ships and port facilities. The ISPS code will have a particular impact especially on one type of piracy that exists in South-East Asia where some ships are hijacked and given false identity numbers. These vessels are then turned into phantom ships; the vessel is registered on the basis of false information provided to the authorities.[131] The hijacking of the product tanker *Petro Ranger* in the east of Singapore in 1998 was an example of this type of piracy. The vessel was owned by a Singapore national and had a Malaysian flag. It was attacked by Indonesians off the coast of Malaysia while she was

[131] For detailed information about phantom ships See Jayant Abhyankar, *The Phantom Vessel Phenomenon: An Update*, 149-156 in Maximo Q Mejia Jr., Jinjing Xu (Ed.) Coastal Zone Piracy and Other Unlawful Acts at Sea (WMU, 2007).

en route from Singapore to Vietnam, with diesel fuel as cargo. The cargo was transferred to another ship while at sea and the vessel was reflagged as a Honduran ship and renamed *MV Wilby* and proceeded to China, where the pirates were arrested and released after only a couple of months in jail.[132] Similarly, the *Alondra Rainbow* was hijacked by a gang of pirates armed with swords and guns in October 1999, soon after she sailed from Kuala Tanjung in Indonesia for Miike in Japan. On 14 November 1999, the vessel was located heading into the Arabian Sea named as *Mega Rama* and flying the Belize flag. On 16 November 1999, the vessel was captured approximately 300 miles south west of Mumbai. At that time India was a signatory to UNCLOS, but had not incorporated it into the national legislation. It was not a signatory to the 1988 SUA Convention. The Mumbai authorities managed to establish jurisdiction and charged the alleged pirates with 11 counts under Indian panel code provisions, and in March 2003 they were sentenced to seven years imprisonment.[133]

With the entry into force of the ISPS code, ships are required to have a ship identification number and, more importantly, a continuous synoptic record that provides a record of a ship's movement, changes of name, and owner. With such data, it will become more difficult to register ships with false documents and creating a phantom ship will be harder.[134]

One of the key features of efforts to combat piracy hijackings is crew training. Today many modern day crews have a polyglot nature and are assembled together at a short notice. In many cases the crew cannot even communicate with each other properly, let alone conduct anti-piracy drills as part of their safety training. With the ISPS code each company is obliged to develop a strong sense of security awareness, which means that basic security precautions need to be enforced and look out for suspicious persons and unusual occurrences. The application of the ISPS code, through PSC measures, will force shipowners to comply with the maritime security measures, and in return help them to counter piracy attacks.

CONCLUSION

Piracy is not a new issue for the shipping world and is not a problem for a number of states. It has been regarded as an international crime falling under

---

[132] Lloyd's MIU handbook of maritime security by Rupert Herbert-Burns, Walter Samuel Grono Bateman, Peter Lehr, p. 190, (Auerbach Publications, 2008).

[133] ABHYANKAR, See *supra* note 132, at. 99-101.

[134] Sam Bateman, *Sea Piracy: Issues in the Indo-Pacific Region*, at 23, http://www.navy.gov.au /w/images/PIAMA31.pdf (last visited March 4, 2012)

every state's jurisdiction under customary international law.[135] The *Achille Lauro* incident changed the perspective and drew worldwide attention to the prevention of maritime terrorism. The 9/11 events acted as a warning that ships might be used as a weapon, and ports could be soft targets with their open accessibility by water and land, and the tremendous amount of cargo they handle.

Today, maritime security at sea is an ever more important issue with the globalization of trade and the continuing freedom of movement on the high seas. The dependent nature of world economies means that any form of attack on the seas, either as piracy or maritime terrorism, would disturb world trade. Piracy and other maritime threats are heavy financial burdens on the international trade.

With a view of enforcing maritime security on the seas, the adoption of a new chapter in SOLAS on maritime security, the adoption of ISPS Code, and the SUA Conventions are important legal steps. However, like any other legal international convention, legal certainty can only be achieved on the basis of an adequate implementation of these instruments in national law. Effectiveness of legal measures depends on states' participation and implementation of these measures, which will in turn ensure that an effective legal framework is established to combat maritime terrorism and piracy.

Port state control supports the control process related to maritime security measures by acting as a mechanism for enforcement of maritime security measures in the port state control regions and by preventing sub-standard shipping practices. By preventing substandard vessels sailing on the oceans, the PSC system aims to make sure that well maintained and equipped vessels with better qualified crew will be the norm. These safety measures no doubt will help shipowners to fight piracy more effectively. However, the effectiveness of port state control inevitably varies from port to port, and will be better resourced in some parts of the world than in others. If port state control is used in an efficient way in regions where the most successful ship hijackings are taking place, it will become a more effective tool in combating maritime piracy and terrorism.[136] The Indian Ocean MOU on PSC covers many ships hijacked off the Horn of Africa. Despite this high piracy rate, PSC in that region is less effective than Paris MOU and Tokyo MOU regions. Vessel owners are aware of the fact that, with the growing amount

---

[135] I.A.Shearer, *Starke's International Law* (Butterworths 11th ed. 1994) 212. Ian Brownlie, *Principles of Public International Law* (Oxford University Press 7th ed. 2008) 229.

[136] *See* Sam Bateman, *Sub-Standard Shipping and the Human Cost of Piracy,* Australian Journal of Maritime and Ocean Affairs (2011) Vol 3(2) 57-61.

of legislation, it is becoming more expensive to run a substandard ship in Europe and USA. However, poorly maintained ships are still running in piracy prone areas where PSC is less effective. If shipowners know that running a substandard ship will cost more than the financial advantages they would gain, then there would be enough incentive to run a well maintained ship even in piracy prone areas.

13. THE GLOBAL INSURANCE INDUSTRY

Poomintr SOOKSRIPAISARNKIT[1]

Maritime piracy has come into sharp focus in recent years due to the situation in Somalia. A root cause of this has been explained and analysed by many contributors in this book and the author does not intend to repeat it here. To put it succinctly, as Mr. Justice David Steel put it, "Somalia is a failed state with no effective government or law enforcement. It is also one of the poorest countries in the world. This provides a fertile breeding ground for piracy conducted by fishermen living along the lengthy seaboard of Somalia."[2] But, piracy is not a new maritime peril. Its definition is given in rule 8 of the "Rules for Construction of Policy" (hereinafter "Rules for Construction") attached to the First Schedule of the Marine Insurance Act 1906 (MIA) of the United Kingdom. The same is adopted also in identical statutes in various parts of the world.[3] There, "pirates" are defined as "passengers who mutiny and rioters who attack the ship from the shore." This definition should be borne in mind in interpreting marine insurance contracts, unless the context otherwise provides.[4] This definition is also crucial when one comes to scrutinise the scope of cover provided in marine insurance policies since similar, yet different, risks may be excluded. Or otherwise, different types of risks may lead to different types of claims to be pursued.

---

[1] Assistant Professor, School of Law, City University of Hong Kong. The author would like to thank Mr. Lee Yu Heng, Daryl, LL.M. student, School of Law, City University of Hong Kong for his assistance in initial editing and reviewing of this work. Any errors or omissions are of the author alone.

[2] *Masefield AG v Amlin Corporate Member Ltd* [2010] EWHC 280 (Comm); [2010] 1 Lloyd's Rep. 509, [12].

[3] See for example the Marine Insurance Act 1909 (Cth) of Australia and the Marine Insurance Ordinance (Cap. 329) of Hong Kong. It is to be noted that the wording of the First Schedule of the Marine Insurance Act 1906 is derived from the old S & G Policy (Ship & Goods Policy) which was used prior to the introduction of the standard Institute Clauses. When the S & G Policy was first used is unknown but as early as 1791 the court was able to criticise its wordings. See Howard Bennett, *The Law of Marine Insurance* (2nd edn, Oxford University Press 2006) para 7.02.

[4] Section 30(2) of the Marine Insurance Act 1906 provides: "Subject to the provisions of this Act, and unless the context of the policy otherwise requires, the terms and expressions mentioned in the First Schedule to this Act shall be construed as having the scope and meaning in that schedule assigned to them."

This work seeks to explore the marine insurance industry's responses to piracy risks and examines the problems which marine assureds (primarily ship-owners and cargo-owners) face in securing insurances against piracy risks. To do so, it will start by distinguishing piracy risks from other types of marine risks which may be similar in nature, e.g. thieves[5] and barratry.[6] Then, it will outline types of insurance coverage available in the industry for piracy risk, including a rather new product available known as Kidnap & Ransom (K&R) insurance. Afterwards, this chapter will examine potential legal problems faced by ship-owners who may need to pay ransom payment and then make a claim upon marine insurers. Then, it will examine potential legal problems faced by cargo-owners whose goods may be delayed or even damaged due to the seizure of the vessel by pirates. Finally, it will look into the problems of loss of lives at sea due to pirates. This is a matter of rising concern following the increasingly common decision of ship-owners to employ armed guards on board. This work will then conclude by identifying existing problems faced by the shipping industry due to piracy and providing some suggested solutions. Whilst the title of this work is said to deal with the "global insurance industry," it must be mentioned here at the outset that the primary focus of this work will be on the English law. The reason is, as reported by a marine insurance broker firm, the London Market is still considered to be "the largest marine insurance market in the world."[7]

PIRACY RISK: IDENTIFIED

As mentioned earlier, piracy risk may be confused with the other two marine risks, namely thieves and barratry, despite these two terms also being defined in the Rules for Construction. "Thieves," as defined in rule 9, "do not cover clandestine theft or a theft committed by any one of the ship's company, whether crew or passengers." Barratry, as defined in rule 11, "includes every wrongful act wilfully committed by the master or crew to the prejudice of the owner, or, as the case may be, the charterer." For possible distinctions between theft and piracy, these were discussed extensively by

---

[5] In this work the terms "thieves" and "theft" are used interchangeably adopting the explanation of the learned editors of *Arnould's Law of Marine Insurance and Average* that the word "thieves" refers to the actors while the word "theft" refers to the act. See Jonathan Gilman and the others (eds), *Arnould's Law of Marine Insurance and Average* (17th edn, Sweet & Maxwell 2008) 1005, see in particular footnote number 176.

[6] For detailed analysis of these types of risks, see Baris Soyer, *Coverage Against Unlawful Acts in Contemporary Marine Policies*, in Rhidian D. Thomas (ed), The Modern Law of Marine Insurance Volume 3 (Informa 2009) 149.

[7] Codan Marine, *The Markets* <http://www.codanmarine.com/codanmarine/Page18337.html> accessed 15 August 2011.

the courts in both the United Kingdom[8] and in Singapore.[9] These cases are to be examined. For distinctions between barratry and piracy, there may be situations when crew members assist the pirates.[10] This again needs to be discussed, as a line has to be drawn.

Piracy and Theft

Traditionally, there was a need for a clear distinction between these two risks. "The distinction between the two perils in the past was necessary when piracy was excluded as a marine peril and was insured by a war risk underwriter under a war risk cover."[11] However, it is not entirely correct to explain a need for such a distinction solely in the context of the past. In fact, whether piracy risk falls either in marine cover or in war risk cover depends much on the market trend.[12] From the assureds' point of view, there appears to be certain advantages negotiating for piracy risk to be included in the war risk cover, rather than in the marine cover. First, the assureds can avoid deductibles for there may not be deductibles applicable to the war risk insurance claim [13] or such deductibles, if any, are almost negligible. Secondly, in practice, the basic annual premiums for the war risk insurance are relatively cheap in comparison with the basic annual premiums for the marine risk. The assureds can choose to declare to the war risk underwriter for each voyage to the piracy area and seek cover by paying additional

---

[8] *Athens Maritime Enterprises Corporation v Hellenic Mutual War Risks Association (Bermuda) Ltd* (*The "Andreas Lemos"*) [1982] 2 Lloyd's Rep. 483.

[9] *Bayswater Carriers Pte Ltd v QBE Insurance (International) Pte Ltd* [2005] SGHC 185; [2006] 1 SLR 69.

[10] Soyer (n 5) para 7.1.

[11] *Bayswater* (n 8) [40].

[12] Paul Todd, *Maritime Fraud and Piracy* (2nd edn, Lloyd's List 2010) para 1.055 citing Susan Hodges, *Law of Marine Insurance* (Cavendish Publishing 1996) 212 where the latter said that the risk of piracy "has, over the years, been shuttled back and forth…"

[13] Todd (n 11) para 1.054. In insurance practice, a "deductible" can be explained as "[t]he amount that is deducted from some or all claims arising under an insurance or a re-insurance contract. The practical effect is the same as an excess: the insured or reassured must bear a proportion of the relevant loss. If that loss is less than the amount of deductible / excess then the assured or reassured must bear all the loss (unless there is other insurance in place to cover the deductible). An increase in deductible should result in a reduction in premium." Lloyd's, "Glossary" <http://www.lloyds.com/Common/Help/Glossary?page=5> accessed 10 August 2011.

premiums.[14] For the present purpose, a distinguishing exercise here is useful for assureds, in light of which they would be able to determine under which insurance cover a claim should be pursued.

In *The Andreas Lemos* case, the vessel was insured for both marine risk (hull & machinery insurance) and war risk. The war risk was covered by the war risk association, the defendant in this case. The war risk insurance covered, among other things, risks excluded from marine risk cover by the existence of the "F.C. & S clause."[15] Both risks of piracy and theft were among exclusions listed in the clause. Therefore, the question for Staughton J. (as he then was) was whether the factual circumstances of the case fell under either of these risks.[16] The facts were thus: while the vessel was in Chittagong Roads, men with knives boarded it and took some of vessel's equipment. They were spotted by a crewman on watch while they were throwing equipment into the sea. The men got frightened and jumped into the sea when they saw ship staff coming with knives and pistols.[17] Mr. Mark Saville Q.C. (later Lord Justice Saville) submitted two reasons for the proposition that the loss was not caused by piracy. First, the loss "occurred within territorial waters . . ."[18] Secondly, "force or the threat of force is an essential element of piracy, and on the facts it could not be shown that any had occurred at such a time to cause the loss."[19]

Taking the first point, it is apparently anomalous to reconcile it with the definition of the piracy set out in the Rules for Construction, since from the definition the ship should be "attacked from the shore." But, again, the situation off the Gulf of Aden and in Somalia does not fit in well with the Rules for Construction as attacks there are mostly not "from the shore." A similar question was raised in the *Bayswater* case where the tug, which had

---

[14] As Bennett explains, "war risks cover is granted in return for an appropriately modest premium, but provision is made for the exclusion of such areas of high risk as may be designated at any time… An owner that wishes to trade in such an area is required to notify the insurer in advance and pay the appropriate, often substantial, additional premium assessed by reference to the prevailing level of risk. Compliance with the obligation to notify is often a condition precedent to the insurer's continued liability on the policy, so that breach automatically terminates the assured's cover." Bennett (n 2) para 6.41. In practice, the Joint War Committee at the Lloyd's Market Association (LMA) draws up and updates "Hull War, Strikes, Terrorism and Related Perils Listed Areas." The latest listed areas are contained in a circular JWLA/018 issued on 1 August 2011. This document is downloadable from Lloyd's Market Association, "Joint War Committee" <http://www.lmalloyds.com/Web/Market_Places/_nbsp_nbsp_Marine/Joint_War/Web/market_places/marine/JWC/Joint_War.aspx> accessed 10 August 2011.

[15] *The Andreas Lemos* (n 7) 486. 'F.C. & S' stands for 'Free of Capture and Seizure'.

[16] Ibid., 487.

[17] Ibid., 485-486.

[18] Ibid., 487.

[19] Ibid.

her hull insurance against both the risks of piracy and theft pursuant to the Institute Time Clauses (Hulls) 1/10/83,[20] was boarded by men carrying weapons. These men ordered ship staff to gather in the cabin with their hands tied for two nights. Afterwards, the ship staff were forced to jump overboard and these men took the tug away.[21] It was argued by the underwriter that, to constitute piracy, the tug must be "at sea."[22]

In a sense, such an argument is supported by a definition of "piracy" given in Article 101 of the United Nations Convention on the Law of the Sea (UNCLOS) 1982 as follows:

> Piracy consists of any of the following acts:
>
> (a) any illegal acts of violence or detention, or any act of depredation, committed for private ends by the crew or the passengers of a private ship or a private aircraft, and directed:
>
> (i) on the high seas, against another ship or aircraft, or against persons or property on board such ship or aircraft;
>
> (ii) against a ship, aircraft, persons or property in a place outside the jurisdiction of any State;
>
> (b) any act of voluntary participation in the operation of a ship or of an aircraft with knowledge of facts making it a pirate ship or aircraft;
>
> (c) any act of inciting or of intentionally facilitating an act described in subparagraph (a) or (b).

This Article was a re-production of Article 15 of the Convention on the High Seas 1958 (Geneva Convention), a predecessor of UNCLOS.[23] The Geneva Convention was heavily influenced by the work as early as 1932 of the research team from the Harvard University and also by the work of the International Law Commission.[24] The research team from Harvard University produced "Draft Convention on Piracy."[25] From the outset, there was no intention to touch upon the concept of piracy as set out in domestic laws. Instead, the intention was "to define . . . extraordinary basis of state jurisdiction over offences committed by foreigners against foreign interests outside the territorial and other ordinary jurisdiction . . ."[26] This attitude was

---

[20] Clauses 6.1.3 and 6.1.5.

[21] *Baywaster* (n 8) [9]-[13].

[22] Ibid., [7].

[23] Omer Elagab, *Somali Piracy and International Law: Some Aspects* (2010) 24 Australia and New Zealand Maritime Law Journal 59, 61.

[24] Barry H. Dubner, *The Law of International Sea Piracy* (Martinus Nijhoff Publishers 1980) 9.

[25] Harvard Research on International Law, *Draft Convention on Piracy with Comments* (1932) 26 Am. J. Int'l L. Sup. 739.

[26] Ibid, 760.

carried along into UNCLOS as evidenced in Article 105.[27] Criticisms have been made on the definition of piracy in UNCLOS itself which this work will not discuss further. Suffice it to say for the present purpose, considering an entirely different context in which the term "piracy" is defined, it was correct for Staughton J., upon referring to various authorities relating to international law, to hold that ". . . I see no reason to limit piracy to acts outside territorial waters."[28] The problem lies in what he said afterwards:[29]

> In the context of an insurance policy, if a ship is, in the ordinary meaning of the phrase, "at sea" . . . then for the business purposes of a policy of insurance she is, in my judgment, in a place where piracy can be committed. That view is supported to some extent by r.8 [referred to the Rules for Construction] . . . . It is not easy to envisage a ship being attacked by rioters from the shore when she is outside territorial waters . . . .

How far from the shore can a ship be attacked? What is the limit of "the sea" the judge referred to here? In the *Bayswater* case, the judge adopted the approach of Staughton J. and even went further and hinted that the limit can be ascertained as a matter of construction of a marine insurance contract and policy.[30] This approach does not exist in bringing further certainty. In the *Bayswater* case, there was a trading warranty limit within the policy and hence somewhat eased the judge's analysis. The same cannot be said for typical marine insurance policies with worldwide trading. Hazelwood raised a case of *The Salem*,[31] as an example of such difficulty in determining the sea[32] (even though the issue there discussed was not in the context of the piracy risk). The case involved massive fraud. A part of the cargo of oil was

---

[27] Article 105: "On the high seas, or in any other place outside the jurisdiction of any State, every State may seize a pirate ship or aircraft, or a ship or aircraft taken by piracy and under the control of pirates, and arrest the persons and seize the property on board. The courts of the State which carried out the seizure may decide upon the penalty to be imposed, and may also determine the action to be taken with regard to the ships, aircraft or property, subject to the rights of third parties acting in good faith."

[28] *The Andreas Lemos* (n 7) 490. A similar attitude was propounded as early as 1909 by Pickford J., which the Court of Appeal in the same case did not hold otherwise, that "[o]ne has to look at what is the natural and clear meaning of the word "pirate" in a document used by business men for business purposes; and I think that, looking at it in that way, one must attach to it a more popular meaning, the meaning that would be given to it by ordinary persons, rather than the meaning to which it may be extended by writers on international law." *Republic of Bolivia v Indemnity Mutual Marine Insurance Company, Limited* [1909] 1 K.B. 785, 790.

[29] Ibid.

[30] *Bayswater* (n 8) [83].

[31] *Shell International Petroleum Co Ltd v Caryl Antony Vaughan Gibbs* (*The "Salem"*) [1982] 1 Lloyd's Rep. 369.

[32] Steven J. Hazelwood, *The Peril of "Pirates" – All "At Sea"* [1983] LMCLQ 283, 286.

discharged at Durban at a "single buoy mooring" one and a half miles from shore.[33] The Court of Appeal, in construing the term "taking at sea" in the old S&G policy form, was of the opinion that the discharge did not happened at sea.[34] Hazelwood proceeded to argue that more of a concern should be a case happened in "large tidal estuaries."[35]

This somewhat reminded us of a case which divided the opinions of the judges in the High Court of Australia. The case involved an accident to an unfortunate lady who went parasailing with a free ticket received from her husband. She went along the estuarine waters of the Swan River in Australia.[36] The area was described in the case as "the interface between the ocean and a river, in which salinity changes are found . . . . The river has a permanent opening to the Ocean . . . . At some times of the year the estuary is salty and the other times it is fresh, the saltiness coming from the connection with the Indian Ocean."[37] The issue in the case was primarily whether the policy fell into the ambit of marine insurance. Therefore, the author is in agreement with what Hazelwood concluded at the end of his article:[38]

> Optimism in the ability of the courts to resolve such doubts is not encouraged . . . . Discovering when a vessel is far enough within port limits to cease to be "at sea" in the law of marine insurance may prove as great a mystery as knowing when, in the law of charter-parties, a vessel has "arrived" in port.

To avoid uncertainty and potential litigation, the question is whether it might be advisable for the underwriter to state clearly in the policy how "the sea" is understood by him. This may be done by analogue to how the Joint War Committee indicates the areas where war risk additional premiums are to be incurred. Or else, it might be advisable for the assured to

---

[33] *The Salem* (n 30) 371.

[34] Ibid., 374 (per Lord Denning M.R.), 378 (Kerr L.J.) and 383 (May L.J.).

[35] Hazelwood (n 31) 286.

[36] *Gibbs and Another v Mercantile Marine Insurance (Australia) Ltd* [2003] HCA 39; (2003) 199 ALR 497, [33].

[37] Ibid., [16].

[38] Hazelwood (n 31) 286-287. For complicated matter as to when the vessel is taken to be an 'arrived' ship in the context of the charter parties, see *E. L. Oldendorff & Co G.m.b.H v Tradax Export S.A (The "Johanna Oldendorff")* [1973] 2 Lloyd's Rep. 285 and *Federal Commerce and Navigation Co Ltd v Tradax Export S.A. (The "Maratha Envoy")* [1977] 1 Lloyd's Rep. 217. See in general John Schofield, *Laytime and Demurrage* (6th edn, Informa 2011).

simultaneously submit an alternative claim based on theft since "pirates are more than simple thieves."[39] This leads us to the second point.

In *The Andreas Lemos*, Staughton J. did not agree with the submission that the piracy has to occur on the high seas and he did not reject upon the facts that the incident happened at Chittagong Roads, "2.8 miles from the land, and within the port limits,"[40] was indeed the incident at sea. It was the second point, however, which caused the assured's case to collapse. For the judge held "that theft without force or a threat of force is not piracy under a policy of marine insurance."[41] From the facts, he categorised the situation as only a "clandestine theft."[42] Therefore, the case did not even fall within the ambit of 'thieves' as in rule 9 of the Rules for Construction.

Rose explained that the term "thieves" in this context has been construed as "assailing thieves."[43] Reference was made to a case of *La Frabrique de Produits Chimiques v Large.*[44] This case was about an insurance of cargoes on the warehouse to warehouse basis.[45] The thieves broke into the warehouse which was left unattended at night by breaking the padlocks and stealing some cargoes.[46] Whilst no violence was caused to any person, Bailache J. was of the view that there was the use of force or violence in this case. He said, "I do not think that the expression 'by violence' as used in this connection means that the assault must be committed upon some person."[47] The same can be said of piracy that there is always a form of violence in such case either to crewmen on board or to the vessel itself or to both. Taking this point, the learned editors of *Arnould's Law of Marine Insurance and Average* explain, "the use or threat of violence against persons appears to be an essential element of piracy; 'violent theft' extends to cases of breaking and entering, where violence is only directed against property."[48] But, accepting

[39] Lawrence J. Kahn, *Pirates, Rovers, and Thieves: New Problems With An Old Enemy* (1996) 20 *Tulane Maritime Law Journal* 293, 295.

[40] *The Andreas Lemos* (n 7) 486.

[41] Ibid., 491.

[42] Ibid. He described that in this case "force or a threat of force was used by the men to make good their escape." Soyer explained a possible rationale why the "clandestine theft" is excluded that "a theft of this nature has been considered to be entirely a result of negligence or carelessness on the part of the master; thus it lacks the element of fortuity." Soyer (n 5) para 7.6.

[43] F.D. Rose, *Marine Insurance Law and Practice* (LLP 2004) para 14.47.

[44] *La Frabrique de Produits Chimiques Societe Anonyme v Large* [1922] 1 K.B. 203.

[45] The warehouse to warehouse clause essentially extends the scope of marine insurance coverage starting from the time the goods leave the warehouse until the time the goods reach the consignee's warehouse. For a modern form of such clause, see for examples Clause 8 of the Institute Cargo Clauses (A) 1/01/82 and also Clause 8 of the Institute Cargo Clauses (A) 1/01/09.

[46] *La Frabrique de Produits Chimiques* (n 43) 205.

[47] Ibid., 208.

[48] Gilman and the others (n 4) para 23-33.

this as a point of distinction is not entirely without some doubts for violence may be used against both the persons and the property.

At least, as far as the theft is concerned, there appears to be no problem as to where the risk occurred – either at sea or not. But, this point does not present a line for distinction. The use of force or threat of force does not present a clear line either. It is submitted here that a thin line of distinction, if any, between the piracy and the theft is a "motive." This is also emphasised in the definition of "piracy" as in Article 101 of UNCLOS. As emphasised by Belinda Ang Saw Ean J., "the purpose of piracy is for personal gain,"[49] while the theft may be committed with the motive other than personal gain. A mere "hijacking for ransom" is unlikely to constitute a motive for thieves.[50] To some extent, this may be true in the context of most of the reported cases in the Gulf of Aden and off of Somalia. But, speaking of piracy more generally, this may not necessarily be the case. It may be that the pirates hijack a vessel in order to turn it into a "phantom ship."[51] So, again, the motive may not provide a definite line of distinction. The further question is at what point in time the motive is to be determined. At the time when the plan to hijack the vessel is carried out? When the action is done? The motive brings in further complexity because it again provides a distinction between piracy risk and the closely-connected, but yet different, risk, namely terrorism.[52] The case in point is *Republic of Bolivia v Indemnity Mutual Marine Assurance Company, Limited*[53] whereby a vessel was taken by a group of men who attempted to establish the "Free Republic of El Acre" in a once disputed area between Brazil and Bolivia.[54] Rejecting a claim based on

---

[49] *Bayswater* (n 8) [17].

[50] Todd (n 11) para 1.072.

[51] "The criminal groups use their network to find a suitable ship to be hijacked at sea. The cargo on board is downloaded, and disposed of through their smuggling network on the black market. The crew are either killed or abandoned. The ship becomes a 'phantom ship.'" XU Ke, *Myth and Reality: The Rise and Fall of Contemporary Maritime Piracy in the South China Sea* in Keyuan Zou and Shicun Wu (eds), Maritime Security in the South China Sea: Regional Implications and International Cooperation (Ashgate Publishing Group 2009) 81, 87. "a *phantom* ship or vessel is a term used within the International Maritime Bureau to describe a vessel which has no valid classification, is not registered with any recognised ship registry and is usually operated by criminals. It is employed as a vehicle for fraud on cargo-owners, the modus operandi being that, as part of a pre-arranged scheme to which the owners and/or master are party, shortly after leaving the port of shipment ostensibly bound for the port to which the vessel's cargo is contracted to be delivered, delays en route are reported during which the phantom vessel in fact proceeds to a new location to discharge her cargo and achieve her disappearance, usually by assuming a new identity." *NIMA S.A.R.L v The Deves Insurance Public Co Ltd* (*The "Prestrioka"*) [2002] EWCA Civ 1132; [2003] 2 Lloyd's Rep. 327, [10] (per Potter L.J.).

[52] *Bayswater* (n 8) [17].

[53] *Republic of Bolivia* (n 27).

[54] Ibid., 787.

the ground of piracy since the incident did not happen "at sea," all of the judges in the Court of Appeal endorsed the speech of Pickford J. at the first instance where he described the pirate as "a man who is plundering indiscriminately for his own ends, and not a man who is simply operating against the property of a particular State for a public end."[55] This work is not a place to discuss terrorism although there remains some doubt as to the piracy in the Gulf of Aden and off of Somalia, whether such may be seen as an act of terrorism. There appears to be a belief that: [56] "ties between various pirate groups and the Somali al-Shabaab Islamic group are on the increase, and that the latter group is linked to Al-Qaida. By way of illustration . . . the former provides military training for the latter, who in turn use pirate groups for smuggling weapons." Nevertheless, Elagab appears to be of the opinion that such belief is unfounded.[57]

So, as can be seen, there appears to be a very thin borderline to distinguish between piracy and theft. Apart from those points mentioned above, as observed by the learned editors of *Arnould's Law of Marine Insurance and Average*, whilst the actors in the event of theft are those outside the vessel, the players in the case of piracy can be those inside the vessel, i.e. passengers and ship staff.[58] In the case of the act done by the ship's staff, this is also relevant to the peril of barratry to be discussed below. At this stage, one would observe that the act of piracy caused by passengers and ship staffs are among not so many cases of the real risk of piracy, i.e. those with no question arise whether they can be classified as the incidents of theft as well.

Piracy and Barratry

Superficially, a distinction between barratry and piracy is clear and there appears to be no point for discussion. However, as noted by Soyer, "there are worrying reports indicating that members of the crew in some cases co-operate with pirates by giving the co-ordinates of the ship."[59] Although the matter is rarely heard of in the context of the pirates in the Gulf of Aden and off of Somalia, Leeson observed that pirates do have a practice of "conscription," i.e. persuading and at times forcing crewmen to become their members.[60] The worst of all, sometimes crewmen may even be pro-active

---

[55] Ibid., 791.

[56] Elagab (n 22) 64 citing Bruno Schiemsky, *Piracy's Rising Tide – Somali Piracy Develops and Diversifies* (February 2009) *Jane's Intelligence Review* 40-43.

[57] Ibid.

[58] Gilman and the others (n 4) para 23-33.

[59] Soyer (n 5) para 7.1.

[60] Peter T. Leeson, *The Invisible Hook: The Hidden Economics of Pirates* (Princeton University Press 2009) 134.

and join the pirates.[61] Certain issues deserve close scrutiny here. First, as pointed out by Soyer, coverage for barratry in the hull and machinery insurance contract is not without a condition. At least, the assureds must demonstrate due diligence.[62] The other point is in relation to a question of proof and unfortunately this is a rather complex one in the case of barratry.[63] These will be considered in turn. Secondly, when one imagines the situation where the pirates could board a ship due to certain faults or carelessness on the part of the crewmen, apart from a possible defence based on the lack of due diligence on the part of the ship-owner, the insurer may also allege incompetence on the part of the crewmen. Such allegation in turn bears directly upon a question of the seaworthiness of the ship. It should be reminded that in a voyage policy there is an implied warranty of seaworthiness of the ship.[64] Whilst there is no such implied warranty in a time policy, where it can be proved that the assured is privy to such unseaworthiness, the insurer is not liable for any loss "attributable to unseaworthiness." [65] So, here there is a question of how such crew incompetence is proved for there is a fine line between crew incompetence and a crew's mere negligence.[66] The other question is, of course, how the insurer can prove that the ship-owner is privy to such crew incompetence. This is not far from difficulty in the case where the ship-owner employs a third-party ship manager and such ship-manager in turn recruits crewmen. This part will deal first with the issue of barratry and then it will examine the seaworthiness aspect.

As far as barratry is concerned, a question has proved to be a complex one because in practice the underwriter often raises as a defence of "wilful misconduct" on the part of the ship-owner. Academic discourses pay much attention to the burden of proof in the event of alleged wilful misconduct.[67] In the context of this work, such discussions prove to be futile for it is hard to envisage that the ship-owner is co-operating with the pirates to take his ship and those crewmen he has employed and yet the ship-owner in turn is

[61] Ibid, 134-135.

[62] Soyer (n 5) para 7.59. See Clause 6.2.5 of the Institute Time Clauses (Hulls) 01/10/83, Clause 6.2.4 of the Institute Time Clauses (Hulls) 01/11/95 and Clause 2.2.5 of the International Hull Clauses 01/11/03.

[63] See a general discussion of the question of proof in Vasileios S.E. Tsichlis, *Causation Issues in Barratry Cases* (2004) 35 *Journal of Maritime Law and Commerce* 255.

[64] Section 39(1) of the MIA.

[65] Section 39(5) of the MIA.

[66] See in general Konstantinos Bachxevanis, *"Crew Negligence" and "Crew Incompetence": Their Distinction and Its Consequence* (2010) 16 (2) Journal of International Maritime Law 102. See also *Papera Traders Co Ltd and Others v Hyundai Merchant Marine Co Ltd and Another* (*The "Eurasian Dream"*) [2002] EWHC 118(Comm); [2002] 1 Lloyd's Rep. 719.

[67] See Bennett (n 2) para 11.60.

demanded a ransom payment. Still, the fact that a claim for barratry means alleged fraudulent or criminal conduct on the part of the master or crew attracts somewhat a more severe burden of proof on the part of the assured. Although it is well-known that a standard of proof in civil cases rests on the balance of probabilities, yet "the more serious the issue the higher will be the standard of proof required."[68] Indeed, in some cases involving alleged scuttling, being a form of barratry, the courts went so far to suggest that the same standard which is used to prove crime applies.[69] Unless the assured can trace a string of communications between one or more of the crewmen and the pirates, it is submitted that it is difficult for the assured to succeed on a claim based on the barratry. Bearing in mind the nature of the barratry risk, in general the assured has to adduce evidences as to the motive of the relevant master or crewmen.[70] The fact that some ship staff joined the pirates after the vessel got captured would not assist because such ship staff may be conscripted. Any communications between the ship staff and the pirates would hardly be done on the vessel as in these modern days vessels are equipped with modern equipment, for example, computers and satellite. Data can be retrieved by owners and relevant authorities. Such means of communication are therefore too risky. More to concern is perhaps some prior arrangement between ship staff and the pirates prior to their joining the vessel. This is connected with the next issue to be discussed.

As mentioned, the coverage for barratry is subject to a proviso, namely "due diligence." But, what does due diligence mean in this context? To put it slightly differently, due diligence as to what? Transposing these questions into the context presently discussed, does it mean due diligence to prevent barratry, i.e. complicity between the ship staff and the pirates? Or does it mean further to encompass due diligence starting from a process of selecting crewmen so as to ensure no inclination to act to the prejudice of the ship-owner? In practice, however, ship-owners may leave the matter of recruiting seamen with crewing agents. Mandaraka-Sheppard explained that underwriters tend to construe a lack of due diligence to mean a "personal

---

[68] Rose (n 42) para 15.34.

[69] "Scuttling is a crime, and the Court will not find that it has been committed unless it is proved with the same degree of certainty as is required for the proof of a crime." *Astrovlanis Compania Naviera S.A v Linard* (*The "Gold Sky"*) [1972] 2 Lloyd's Rep. 187, 192 quoting with approval the passage of Mr. Justice Branson in *Compania Naviera Vascongada v British & Foreign Marine Insurance Co Ltd* (*The "Gloria"*) (1936) 54 Ll.L.Rep. 35, 50.

[70] "That though the presence of a motive is not sufficient by itself to establish guilt…it is important to examine…whether the master or crew had any reason to destroy or damage the vessel for purposes of their own." *Continental Illinois National Bank & Trust Co. of Chicago and Xenofon Maritime S.A v Alliance Assurance Co. Ltd* (*The "Captain Panagos D.P."*) [1989] 1 Lloyd's Rep. 33, 43.

failure," akin to a "privity of the assured" adopted in s.39(5) of the MIA.[71] However, she argued that such a narrow interpretation does not accord with the recent trend. She referred to the Institute Time Clauses (Hulls) 01/11/95 whereby in Clause 6.2 the requirement of due diligence is extended to "Superintendents or any of their onshore management," in addition to a typical "Assured, Owners, Managers."[72] Still, under the Institute Time Clauses (Hulls) 01/11/95, the language does not seem to be wide enough to encompass the act of crewing agents. It is submitted here that, as far as barratry is concerned, the requirement of due diligence should start from the crew recruitment process. Cases involving scuttling repeatedly remind us of the significance of the crew selecting process. For example, in *The Michael*,[73] the second engineer who sank the ship was employed without the owner's awareness that he had been involved in the earlier scuttling of *The Gold Sky*.[74] Therefore, even with the use of the crewing agents, still ship-owners have to exercise due diligence in selecting reliable agents and have to supervise the crew selection process. Interpreting otherwise would forfeit the whole purpose of this due diligence proviso. Therefore, if in ignorance of the crews' past conducts, the ship-owner was not aware that the ship staff has been associated with the pirates, then the ship-owner should not be benefited from the claim based on barratry. The question is: if the pirates could capture the vessel with the assistance from the ship staffs, can the ship-owner make a claim on the ground of piracy?

One would be reminded that in marine insurance law there exists a rule of "causation." According to s.55(1) of the MIA, "the insurer is liable for any loss proximately caused by a peril insured against." A judicial interpretation of a proximate cause is an efficient or dominant cause.[75] If the pirates could capture the vessel due to the active assistance on the part of the ship staff, for example by informing the vessel's schedule, it is doubtful whether the causation should be attributed to the piratical act or the act of the ship staff. Of course, one has to distinguish such a circumstance from a situation where

---

[71] Aleka Mandaraka-Sheppard, *Hull Time and Voyage Clauses: Marine Perils in Perspective* in Rhidian D. Thomas (ed.), The Modern Law of Marine Insurance (Informa 1996) 47, 48. As for the "privity of the assured" in s.39(5), if the ship-owner is a company, the court has to be very careful in finding a directing mind of the company. See *Manifest Shipping & Co Ltd v Uni-Polaris Insurance Co Ltd and La Reunion Europeene* (*The "Star Sea"*) [1997] 1 Lloyd's Rep. 360, 366-367 (Court of Appeal) disagreed with *Manifest Shipping & Co Ltd v Uni-Polaris Insurance Co Ltd and La Reunion Europeene* (*The "Star Sea"*) [1995] 1 Lloyd's Rep. 651, 659-660 (Queen's Bench Division).

[72] Ibid.

[73] *Piermay Shipping Co S A and Brandt's Ltd v Chester* (*The "Michael"*) [1979] 2 Lloyd's Rep. 1.

[74] See *The Gold Sky* (n 68).

[75] See *Leyland Shipping Company, Limited v Norwich Union Fire Insurance Company, Limited* [1918] A.C. 350, 368-369.

the ship staff themselves turned to capture the vessel in which their act can be considered as the act of piracy as discussed above.

Even if the court will be ready to find that in the case of such the active assistance there exists concurrent causes, i.e. barratry and piracy, there is yet another hurdle to the assured's claim, for the assured has to pass the rule set out in *Wayne Tank & Pump v Employer's Liability*.[76] In this case, a fire occurred in a factory. The factory obtained a judgment in a separate action against the plaintiff in this case who installed new equipment into this factory.[77] The plaintiff therefore in this action claimed against the defendant under the public liability insurance cover. The Court of Appeal was inclined to the view that the dominant cause of the fire was improper installation of equipment.[78] Nevertheless, the Court of Appeal acknowledged the possibility of concurrent causes, i.e. the improper installation and the negligent conduct of the man who switched on the heating tape.[79] In such a case, the negligent conduct of the man was found to be within the scope of the cover while the improper installation was found to fall within the exception clause in the policy.[80] The Court of Appeal unanimously held that the insurer had no liability in such a case. In the speech of Lord Justice Cairns: [81]

> I do not consider that the Court should strain to find a dominant cause if, as here, there are two causes both of which can properly be described as effective causes of the loss . . . unless one cause is clearly more decisive than the other, it should be accepted that there are two causes of the loss and no attempt should be made to give one of them the quality of dominance. On this approach if one cause is within the words of the policy and the other comes within an exception in the policy, it must be taken that the loss cannot be recovered under the policy. The effect of an exception is to save the insurer from liability for a loss which but for the exception would be covered. The effect of the cover is not to impose on the insurer liability for something which is within the exception.

[76] *Wayne Tank & Pump Co Ltd v Employer's Liability Assurance Corporation Ltd* [1973] 2 Lloyd's Rep. 237.

[77] Ibid., 238.

[78] See ibid., 240 (Lord Denning M.R.), 245 (Roskill L.J.).

[79] Ibid., 239.

[80] The relevant exception clause reads: "The Company will not indemnify the Insured in respect of liability consequent upon…(5) death injury or damage caused by the nature or condition of any goods or the containers thereof sold or supplied by or on behalf of the Insured." Ibid.

[81] Ibid., 241.

It is true that in the scenario in our discussion, there is no clause to expressly exclude barratry from the scope of the cover. However, it is submitted here that by virtue of the clause which only states the extent of the coverage for barratry to the case of due diligence, by way of interpretation it necessarily means that barratry due to the lack of due diligence on the part of the ship-owner is excluded. Therefore, in the case there is a proof that the ship-owner did not exercise sufficient care in recruiting ship staff, the insurer should not be held liable for the loss. The question is: who has a duty to prove the existence or non-existence of such due diligence? Unfortunately, the legal position as to this is not entirely clear. As explained by Bennett:[82]

> If [due diligence proviso] constitutes an exclusion from the scope of cover, it will fall to insurers to prove a causally relevant failure of due diligence. If, however, the proviso is properly regarded as part of the definition of each of the perils insured...the onus will lie on the assured to demonstrate on a balance of probabilities that the loss did not result from a failure of due diligence on the part of any relevant person.

As construed above, the author is of the view that the due diligence proviso constitutes an exclusion from the scope of cover.

The situation can nevertheless be more complicated. Instead of proactively assisting the pirates, for example by giving the co-ordinates, the crew compromise security measures on board the vessel indirectly facilitating the boarding by the pirates. In such a case, there may arise certain scenarios depending upon factual evidence. In this case the clear motive of the crew can be proved, the ship-owner may have a good case based on barratry. Otherwise, the ship-owner may also have a good case based upon the "negligence of Master Officers Crew or Pilots," provided that there is no lack of due diligence on the part of the ship-owner.[83] Otherwise, the insurer may have a good case to deny liability based on the alleged unseaworthiness due to crew incompetence. Or else, the ship-owner may be found responsible if some security measures could not be maintained due to the failure on the part of the ship-owner to supply necessary equipment to implement such security measures.

In practice, various industry-based organisations have produced a document entitled *Best Management Practices for Protection Against*

[82] Bennett (n 2) para 11.71.
[83] See Clause 6.2.3 of the Institute Time Clauses (Hulls) 01/10/83.

Somalia Based Piracy (BMP)[84] containing some suggestions for ship-owners and masters. Whilst the legal status of such a document is unclear and it is questionable whether it has any bearing upon a seaworthiness obligation, for certain there exists another document which has significant implications. Compliance with requirements stated in this document must "lead to an improvement in the security situation and hence in the incidents of piracy."[85] The author is mentioning here the "International Ship and Port Security (ISPS) Code," which was added to the International Convention for Safety of Life at Sea (SOLAS) 1974.[86] It came into effect on July 1, 2004.[87] Despite piracy incidents having presented the threats to shipping community for a long time, it was the attack of the Twin Towers in New York on September 11, 2001 which triggered the ideas which led to the implementation of the ISPS Code.[88] The primary aim of the ISPS Code is "to provide a standardized, consistent framework for evaluating risk and for detecting security threats affecting ships or port facilities used in international trade."[89] Under the ISPS Code, ship-owners are required to make available on board their vessels a "ship security plan," which is "developed to ensure the application of measures on board the ship designed to protect persons on board, cargo, cargo transport units, ship's stores and the ship against the risk of a security incident."[90] Moreover, the ship-owner must designate a "ship security officer" for each vessel under its ownership. The responsibilities of the ship security officer include following and constantly reviewing the ship security plan, promoting security alert on the vessel, monitoring that sufficient trainings relating to the matters of security are provided to ship staff and also liaised with ship-owners and authorities on security issues.[91] Moreover, the ship-owner must designate a "company security officer" for each vessel within its ownership. The company security officer is responsible, among other things, for providing amendments to the security plan, liaising with the ship security officer, dealing with "deficiencies and non-conformities identified during internal audits, periodic reviews and

---

[84] Maritime Security Centre Horn of Africa (MSCHOA), "Best Management Practices for Protection Against Somalia Based Piracy" (BMP 4) <http://www.mschoa.org/bmp3/Documents/BMP4%20Low%20Res_Sept_5_2011.pdf> accessed 11 October 2011.

[85] Captain Pottengal Mukundan, *Piracy and Armed Attacks Against Vessels Today* (2004) 10 Journal of International Maritime Law 308, 311.

[86] Aleka Mandaraka-Sheppard, *Modern Maritime Law* (2nd edn, Routledge-Cavendish 2007) 281.

[87] Baris Soyer and Richard Williams, *Potential Legal Ramifications of the International Ship and Port Facility Security (ISPS) Code on Maritime Law* [2005] LMCLQ 515.

[88] Ibid.

[89] Ibid., 517.

[90] Ibid., 518-519.

[91] Ibid., 519.

security inspections" and arranging appropriate trainings to staff dealing with ship security.[92] As can be seen, the ISPS Code lays down a complex web of responsibilities among ship-owners, shore staff, and ship staff. No doubt, any non-fulfillment or any arrangement inconsistent with this and the security plan will bear negative impacts upon insurance.

Suppose that pirates could gain access to the vessel due to the failure to monitor the access to the vessel in breach of the ship's security plan and the ISPS Code, if such failure is due to the fact that the ship-owner has failed to provide appropriate training to ship staff or appropriate equipment such as CCTV has not been made available on board the ship, there is doubtlessly a good defense based on an implied warranty of seaworthiness on the part of the underwriter. Even in a time policy, it is likely that the ship-owner would be found "privy" or "turning a blind-eye" to such unseaworthiness.[93]

Suppose further that there is no question of lack of equipment and appropriate training has been provided by the ship-owner, it does not mean that the crew cannot be found incompetent as far as the matter of applying security measures is concerned for, as well-delineated by Cresswell J. in *The Eurasian Dream*, the crew incompetence encompasses "a disinclination to perform the job properly" as well as "physical or mental disability or incapacity."[94] So, if the ship security officer took a rather relaxing view and did not ensure proper drill on the ship for security check, this may amount to his incompetence. If the ship staff, knowing that the vessel has to pass through the piratical zone, feels so horrified that some security measures simply passed through their mind hence some security measures have not been carried out, such may fall upon crew incompetence. The problem, as well demonstrated in *The Eurasian Dream*, is that in practice ship-owners often focus on the commercial side of shipping, leaving the technical side, including crew recruitment, with third party ship managers or crewing agents. But, having regard to principal-agent relationship, "shipowners cannot hide behind their manning agents."[95] Therefore, to show due diligence both in preventing barratry and in escaping from alleged privity, it is imperative that ship-owners have to thoroughly involve in the crew recruiting process. It is perhaps not easy for anyone to realise whether a crew has such

---

[92] Ibid.

[93] "If a man, suspicious of the truth, turns a blind-eye to it, and refrains from inquiry – so that he should not know it for certain – then he is to be regarded as knowing the truth…." *Compania Maritima San Basilio S A v Oceanus Mutual Underwriting (Bermuda) Ltd* (*The "Eurysthenes"*) [1977] 1 Q.B. 49, 68 (per Lord Denning M.R.).

[94] *The Eurasian Dream* (n 65) [129].

[95] Bachxevanis (n 65) 122.

disinclination to perform the job properly or has mental disability. However, a proper interview may give some hints to the overall attitude. Likewise, a thorough investigation into work experiences of each crew member is equally vital. Ship-owners must also closely monitor all trainings to the crew arranged by their agents.

In light of a wide definition of incompetence as such, it becomes difficult for ship-owners to try to bring the matter into the scope of insurance coverage by arguing otherwise that one or more of the crew members were instead negligent. By this, the term "negligence" is used in the sense that "a crew member must fall below the expected standard of care required by the particular crew member."[96] For matters such as implementing defensive or security measures, these are joint responsibilities of all ship staff on board, from the master down the line of management to the bosun. Arguably, such a line of management starts from on-shore staff, especially the company security officer, and even ship-owners themselves. No doubt, the courts will take recommended industry standards such as the BMP into account and the failure to comply with the BMP will make it hard for ship-owners to insist that the ship staff were competent but negligent. There might be a rare situation where such negligence can be proved. For example, the ship-owner may be able to prove that the crew properly installed the razor wire around the vessel. But, at night before the incident, the crew failed to check that a part of razor wire around the vessel entrance went missing and hence the pirates gained access through such gap.

Overall, from the above analysis, one would observe that an attempt to make a distinction between the perils of "piracy" and "theft" faces certain difficulties. The analysis also transpires that the notion of what constitutes piracy risk as in the MIA may not sit easily with contemporary understanding. For example, limiting the piratical act to that which occurred "at sea" whereby an attack can be made from the shore appears unrealistic. At the same time, a claim for losses or damages due to the piracy incident can prove to be of particular complexity for the assured if one or more of the crew members were involved. The assured's claim on the ground of barratry may subject the assured to strict proof as to his due diligence. Even if such can be proved, still the assured's claim may be attacked via the other route, i.e. the alleged incompetence of the ship staff to prevent or deal with piratical situations. Suppose there was no involvement of ship staff and the piracy incident can be proved, the further question is of course what types of insurance coverage are available to relevant parties to such an incident.

---

[96] Ibid, 103.

COVERAGE FOR THE RISK OF PIRACY

As Thomas observes, in modern marine markets insurance coverage for piracy is extensive.[97] This part is intended to be a broad survey of such available coverage.

As briefly described in the earlier part, ship-owners have the benefit of insurance coverage for piracy risk in virtually all versions of standard form contracts which are available for hull insurance – both time[98] and voyage.[99] However, for cargo-owners who wish to insure their cargoes against piracy, the situation is quite different. Piracy risk is not specifically listed in standard form contracts dealing with cargo insurance. The Institute Cargo Clauses (A) are, however, recognised as providing the widest coverage, so-called "all risks,"[100] and the risk of piracy is thus taken to fall within their scope.[101] However, the same cannot be said of Institute Cargo Clauses (B) and (C) which are not "all risks." Instead, they list the range of risks they seek to cover, with Institute Cargo Clauses (C) providing the narrowest coverage.[102] This leads Thomas to conclude that, "there is no cover under [such] standard terms, but nothing to prevent additional cover for piracy being negotiated."[103]

Market practices and business reasons may dictate that the risk of piracy should be shifted away from the typical marine risk. Instead, it should perhaps be put in war risk even though piracy risk is particularly excluded in relevant standard form contracts dealing with war risks, especially as far as

---

[97] Rhidian Thomas, *Insuring the Risk of Maritime Piracy* (2004) 10 (4) Journal of International Maritime Law 355, 359.

[98] See Clause 6.1.5 of the Institute Time Clauses (Hulls) (01/10/83), Clause 6.1.5 of the Institute Time Clauses (Hulls) (01/11/95), Clause 2.1.5 of the International Hull Clauses (01/11/02), Clause 2.1.5 of the International Hull Clauses (01/11/03), Clause 9.1.4 of the Institute Yacht Clauses (01/11/85)., Clause 6.1.5 of the Institute Fishing Vessel Clauses (20/07/87).

[99] See Clause 4.1.5 of the Institute Voyage Clauses (Hulls) (01/10/83), Clause 4.1.5 of the Institute Voyage Clauses (Hulls) (01/11/95).

[100] Rhidian Thomas (n 96) 359.

[101] Clause 1 of the Institute Cargo Clauses (A) (01/01/82): "This insurance covers all risks of loss of or damage to the subject-matter insured except as provided in Clauses 4,5,6 and 7 below." This Clause is left unchanged in the Institute Cargo Clauses (A) (01/01/09). See also other similar standard form contracts include Clause 1 of the Institute Commodity Trades Clauses (A) (05/09/83), Clause 1 of the Institute FOSFA Trades Clauses (A) (01/07/85), Clause 1 of the Institute Frozen Meat Clauses (A) (01/01/86), Clause 1 of the Institute Frozen Food Clauses (A) (01/01/86), Clause 1 of the Institute Container Clauses (Time) (01/01/87).

[102] See Clause 1 of the Institute Cargo Clauses (B) and (C) (01/01/82). See similarly Clause 1 of the Institute Cargo Clauses (B) and (C) (01/01/09). See also Clause 1 of the Institute Frozen Food Clauses (C) (01/01/86), Clause 1 of the Institute Commodity Trades Clauses (B) and (C) (05/09/83), Clause 1 of the Institute FOSFA Trades Clauses (B) and (C) (01/07/85), Clause 1 of the Institute Frozen Meat Clauses (C) and 24 Hours Breakdown (01/01/86), Clause 1 of the Institute Coal Clauses (01/10/82), Clause 1 of the Institute Bulk Oil Clauses (01/02/83).

[103] Thomas (n 96) 360.

the hull insurance is concerned.[104] The Joint War Committee at the Lloyd's Market Association realised this practice, and as a result a clause extending piracy risk was recommended for use with the Institute War & Strikes Clauses Hulls – Times.[105]

Nevertheless, either on the basis of traditional marine risk or war risk, it is submitted here that the assured is likely to face difficulties during the claim process, especially for a claim for a paid ransom. There are some technical legal problems associated with such a process, in addition to the time and money that must be spent. Therefore, the insurance product known as 'kidnap and ransom' insurance (K&R) came to be in favour. Far from new, this type of insurance contract was introduced into the market by Lloyd's of London long before the recent rise in piracy.[106] However, there is no standard K&R policy wording available in the market and therefore the scope of coverage is a question of construction for each policy.[107] As described more generally by one of the marine insurance broker firms, the following losses are covered by K&R insurance:[108]

1. The ransom that has been paid
2. The loss in transit of the ransom.
3. The fees and expenses of security experts who specialize in advising clients on how to handle crises such as kidnap-for-ransom
4. Additional expenses including those for independent negotiator; a public relation consultant or interpreter; reasonable costs of travel and accommodation of the assured; plus all other reasonable expenses incurred subject to the insurer's approval.

---

[104] See in general Clause 4.1.7 of the Institute War and Strikes Clauses Hulls – Time (1/10/83), Clause 5.1.6 of the Institute War and Strikes Clauses Hulls – Time (01/11/95)., Clausse 4.1.7 of the Institute War and Strikes Clauses Hulls – Voyage (01/10/83), Clause 5.1.6 of the Institute War and Strikes Clauses Hulls – Voyage (01/11/95)

[105] Lloyd's Market Association, Joint War Committee, "Violent Theft, Piracy and Barratry Extension – for use with the Institute War & Strikes Clauses Hulls – Time 1/11/95" <http://www.lmalloyds.com/Web/market_places/marine/JWC/JWC_wordings/JW2005_003_Piracy_Extension_for_ITC_1995.aspx> accessed 19 October 2011. See in particular recommendation 1 that the piracy risk should be included as Clause 1.8 with the addition in Clause 1.7 for the coverage for "violent theft by persons from outside the vessel' and Clause 1.9 for 'barratry of Master Officers or Crew."

[106] "Lloyd's entered the K & R business following the highly publicized kidnapping of Charles Lindbergh's son in 1932. However, the specific line of insurance did not gain prominence until the early 1960s, following a rash of kidnappings of bank executives' wives." Meadow Clendenin, *"No Concessions" With No Teeth: How Kidnap and Ransom Insurers and Insureds Are Undermining U.S. Counterterrorism Policy* (2006-2007) 56 Emory Law Journal 741, 750.

[107] Ibid., 751.

[108] FP Marine Risks, *Marine Kidnap and Ransom Insurance* <http://www.fp-marine.com/news/articles/marine-kidnap-and-ransom-insurance> accessed 20 October 2011.

5. Legal liability to cover settlements or awards, fees and judgments imposed upon and paid by the assured as a result of an action for damages brought by or on behalf of any insured person, or his/their legal representative or shareholders, as a result of the kidnap. Defence costs incurred by the underwriters are payable in addition to the limit for legal liability.

In practice, brokers and underwriters are competing to sell K&R insurance by boasting that their services are provided in partnership with risk consultant firms.[109] K&R premiums are calculated based upon information supplied to the underwriter as well as on the basis of the limit of coverage which the assured desires to purchase. Information which the K&R underwriter typically requires, in addition to the standard vessel particulars, is the anticipated area of transit, estimated time of arrival and/or departure, the defensive measures available, type of cargo, and whether or not an armed guard will be employed to accompany the vessel.[110] The underwriter also inquires as to whether there is a plan for a convoy or group transit.

While K&R policies yield the benefit of reducing complication for ransom paid, they have also been criticised solely a "defensive device," and not a preventive measure. K&R underwriters "step in *afterward* and give [their] customers the best chance of coming out alive – with as little derring-do as possible."[111] Although K&R insurance surely helps resolve a symptom of piracy, it is certainly not the solution to the problem itself.

SHIPOWNERS AND THE ISSUES RAISED BY RANSOM PAYMENTS

Even if a ship-owner decides to not carry K&R insurance, he may have other means to recover a ransom paid. The Court of Appeal has confirmed that payment of ransom is not against public policy; the speech of Lord Justice Rix in this case deserves to be quoted in some length:[112]

---

[109] As noted by Willis, one of the London-based insurance brokers, ACE is partnering with Neil Young International Limited, Chartis is partnering with Clayton Consultants, Chubb uses The Ackerman Group, Great American Insurance Company and Hiscox use Control Risks, Liberty International Underwriter use Neil Young International Limited, PIA uses Corporate Risk International, Travelers uses ASI Global, QBE uses Terra Ferma. Willis Limited itself establishes a subsidiary company called Special Contingency Risks. See Willis Limited, "Special Contingency Risks (SCR)" <http://www.willis.com/Documents/Publications/Services/Special_Contingency_Risks/Marketplace_Realities_2010-SCR.pdf> accessed 20 October 2011.

[110] Skuld, *Kidnap & Ransom / Loss of Hire / Earnings Extension Request Form – Breaches* <http://www.skuld.com/upload/Products%20and%20Services/Ancillary%20covers/KnR%20Breach%20Application%20form.pdf> accessed 20 October 2011.

[111] Clendenin (n 105) 758.

[112] *Masefield AG v. Amlin Corporate Member,* Royal Court of Justice, U.K. (2011)

> There is thus something of an unexpressed complicity: between the pirates, who threaten the liberty but by and large not the lives of crews and maintain their ransom demands at levels which industry can tolerate; the world of commerce, which has introduced precautions but advocates the freedom to meet the realities of the situation by the use of ransom payments; and *the world of government*, which stops short of deploring the payment of ransom but stands aloof, *participates in protective naval operations but on the whole is unwilling positively to combat the pirates with force* . . . . In these morally muddied waters, there is no universally recognised principle of morality, no clearly identified public policy, no substantially incontestable public interest, which could lead the courts…to state that the payment of ransom should be regarded as a matter which stands beyond the pale, without any legitimate recognition. There are only elements of conflicting public interests, which push and pull in different directions, and have yet to be resolved in any legal enactments or international consensus as to a solution . . . .

There is much to be said on the Court of Appeal's condemnation on insufficient international governments' actions. More to be said as to the Court of Appeal's as well as Mr. Justice David Steel's optimistic belief in that the *modus operandi* of the pirates is merely for ransom.[113] There have been rising concerns that the pirates may change their strategy and start "killing."[114] Of note, is the incident of a French woman who was abducted by pirates and was killed.[115] This is not to mention some reported cases whereby the pirates used the hijacked vessels as 'mother ships' to further their operations.[116] These recent news may bear upon and indeed alter an analysis as far as the issues of constructive total loss or actual total loss are concerned. These are to be discussed in the next part where the question of

---

[113] *Masefield* (n 1) [19].

[114] CNN, *Fears Grow Over Somali Pirates' "New Tactics" After Kidnaps, Killing* <http://articles.cnn.com/2011-10-05/africa/world_africa_kenya-somali-pirate-tactics_1_somali-pirates-kenya-somalia-border-kenya-police?_s=PM:AFRICA> accessed 20 October 2011.

[115] The Guardian, *Kidnapped French Woman Taken to Somalia by Pirates After Sea Battle* <http://www.guardian.co.uk/world/2011/oct/02/kidnapped-french-woman-somalia-pirates> accessed 20 October 2011. The Guardian, *French Woman Kidnapped by Somali Militants Dies* <http://www.guardian.co.uk/world/2011/oct/19/french-woman-kidnapped-somalia-dies> accessed 20 October 2011.

[116] RiskIntelligence, *Implications of the Use of Hijacked Vessels by Somali Pirates* <http://www.riskintelligence.eu/dyn/files/newspage_links/6-file/Implications%20of%20the%20use%20of%20hijacked%20vessels%20by%20Somali%20pirates.pdf> accessed 20 October 2011.

cargo claims is discussed because these are points chiefly decided in the decision of the Court of Appeal.

Interestingly enough, the analysis of the Court of Appeal here stands in stark contrast to the position of President Barack Obama, who on April 12, 2010 released the Executive Order 13536 forbidding the payment of ransom to the pirates in Somalia.[117] So far as it is relevant, this Executive Order reads:

> (a) All property and interests in property that are in the United States, that hereafter come within the United States, or that are or hereafter come within the possession or control of any United States person, including any overseas branch, of the following persons are blocked and may not be transferred, paid, exported, withdrawn, or otherwise dealt in:
> (i) The persons listed in the Annex to this order; and
> (ii) Any person determined by the Secretary of the Treasury, in consultation with the Secretary of State;
> (A) to have engaged in acts that directly or indirectly threaten the peace, security, or stability of Somalia…

It remains to be seen whether the international community will adopt a similar attitude. This author respectfully submits that he is in entire agreement with Rix LJ's view that there has been no cohesive action among international governments as to the situation in Somalia. However, forbidding ransom payment is certainly not the way forward as it puts the lives of crewmen at risk. Apart from President Obama's Executive Order, the United States government has not yet come up with any ultimate solution to the existing problems in Somalia. In any event, this Executive Order is likely to have limited consequence to those who have connections with the United States; for marine insurance policies subject to English law, this Order should not present any impediment to ransom payment in light of the Court of Appeal's attitude.[118] Also, as observed by Soyer, "[t]he weight of authority is such that English courts would enforce agreements in cases where no issue of legality arises under the proper law of contract and

[117] National Archive, "Federal Register" <http://edocket.access.gpo.gov/2010/pdf/2010-8878.pdf> accessed 2 November 2011.

[118] "There appears to be little doubt that where a payment which is not itself illegal under any relevant law is made to secure the release of property, this can be recovered even though the persons demanding the payment are not acting lawfully in so doing. Thus, for example, payment to recover property from pirates or hijackers must, it is submitted, in general be recoverable." Jonathan Gilman and the others (n 4) para 25-21.

agreement was not made with the object of breaching the law of the place of performance."[119] Here, the place of performance being a failed state with no legal order does not seem to pose a concern. In reality, there have been many reported cases of ransom payments.

Apart from holding that the payment of ransom is not contrary to pubic policy, the Court of Appeal further affirmed the earlier decision in *Royal Boskalis Westminster N V and Others v Mountain and Others*[120] that the payment of ransom is claimable as "sue and labour expenses."[121] In the *Royal Boskalis* case a company which engaged in dredging work in Iraq entered into a "finalisation agreement" under duress in order to take its fleet and crewmen out of Iraq. The effect of this finalisation agreement was that large sums of money had to be paid for the ultimate benefit of the Iraqi government. Plus, further claims under the dredging contract had to be waived.[122] One of the issues before the court was whether the waiver of claim pursuant to the finalisation agreement amounted to a ransom which the company could claim as sue and labour expenses pursuant to s.78 of the MIA.[123]

Section 78 of the MIA is unfortunately a rather technical one, the language of which is hard to comprehend. So far as it is relevant to the point under discussion, the following sub-sections should be noted:

(1) Where the policy contains a suing and labouring clause, the engagement thereby entered into is deemed to be supplementary to the contract of insurance, and the assured may recover from the insurer any expenses properly incurred pursuant to the clause, notwithstanding that the insurer may have paid for a total loss, or that the subject-matter may have been warranted free from particular average, either wholly or under a certain percentage…

(2) ….

(3) Expenses incurred for the purpose of averting or diminishing any loss not covered by the policy are not recoverable under the suing and labouring clause.

---

[119] Soyer (n 5) para 7.51. Nevertheless, it has been noted that "the payment of pirate ransoms is technically illegal in Somalia," David Clarke and Mohamed Ahmed, *Exclusive: Somali Pirates Ransom Skirt U.S. Directives* <http://www.reuters.com/article/2011/08/08/us-somalia-piracy-ransoms-idUSTRE7772DW201108088> accessed 14 November 2011. The report showed that the funds in the amount of US$3.6 million prepared to be paid to the pirates in connection with the release of M/V *Yuan Xiang* were seized by Somali security officials.

[120] *Royal Boskalis Westminster N V and Others v Mountain and Others* [1999] QB 674.

[121] See *The Bunga Melati Dua* (n 111) [75].

[122] *Royal Boskalis* (n 119) 678-679.

[123] See ibid., 680.

(4) It is the duty of the assured and his agents, in all cases, to take such measures as may be reasonable for the purpose of averting or minimising a loss.

Thus, pursuant to s.78(1) it is necessary that the policy contains a sue and labour clause, but the effect of s.78(4) remains unclear for there is a view that this sub-section imposes a "statutory duty."[124] Nevertheless, such a clause is present in modern standard form contracts for hull insurance.[125] The rationale underpinning the concept of sue and labour, as explained by Rose, is that the underwriter usually has an obligation to indemnify (i.e. to pay) for any damage or loss caused by the perils covered by the insurance contract. So, if by the action of the owner or his agent, such loss or damage is reduced or even avoided altogether, such reasonable expenses incurred for such action are to be made recoverable from the underwriter, since such action is also in a sense for the interest of the underwriter.[126] Thus, in the context of ransom payment, it is readily imaginable that in the absence of such a payment the pirates would not release the ship, and the underwriter would then have to pay for the actual total loss of the ship due to the risk of piracy,[127] which as mentioned earlier is usually covered under hull & machinery insurance. Therefore, the payment of ransom, which is usually far less than the value of the vessel, is in the interest to the underwriter.

Although it has not received much attention and hence it remains unclear, the concept of sue and labour in fact came into existence before the MIA. Soyer suggests that on top of the ransom payment the "negotiation costs" should also be considered as sue and labour expenses.[128] Then, the question is whether the costs of employing armed guards on board can also be considered as sue and labour expenses. One concern is that any fight between armed guards and pirates may aggravate the loss or damage; such concern appears to underpin the International Group of P & I Clubs' initial reluctance

---

[124] See Rose (n 42) paras 20.33-20.38.

[125] Clause 13 Duty of Assured (Sue and Labour) of the Institute Time Clauses (Hulls) (01/10/83), Clause 11 Duty of Assured (Sue and Labour) of the Institute Time Clauses (Hulls) (01/11/95), Clause 11 Duty of Assured (Sue and Labour) of the Institute Voyage Clauses (Hulls) (01/10/83), Clause 9 Duty of Assured (Sue and Labour) of the Institute Voyage Clauses (Hulls) (01/11/95), Clause 9 Duty of the Assured (Sue and Labour) of the International Hull Clauses (01/11/02), Clause 9 Duty of the Assured (Sue and Labour) of the International Hull Clauses (01/11/03).

[126] Rose (n 42Z) para 20.25.

[127] Section 57(1) of the MIA: "Where the subject-matter insured is destroyed, or so damaged as to cease to be a thing of the kind insured, or where the assured is irretrievably deprived thereof, there is an actual total loss." Also, s.68(1) of the MIA: "Subject to the provisions of this Act and to any express provision in the policy, where there is a total loss of the subject-matter insured – (1) If the policy be a valued policy, the measure of indemnity is the sum fixed by the policy...."

[128] Soyer (n 5) para 7.44.

to recommend this measure to ship-owners. On the other hand, a former U.S. Navy Officer has observed that "[s]o far . . . not a single vessel thus equipped has been successfully boarded, or experienced any loss of life to crew or security-team members . . . ."[129] This observation must be taken with a grain of salt considering the observer's current association with a security company. In any event, one should be warned of what Rose explained: "the assured had a duty to take reasonable measures to avert or minimise a loss by a *peril which had begun to operate*."[130] Adopting also Soyer's logic on negotiation costs, it appears that sue and labour expenses are limited to any costs incurred for measures taken *after* the vessel was seized by the pirates in order to avoid or reduce subsequent loss or damage. In this sense, the costs of employing armed guards along with reasonable costs to carry out defensive measures appear to not be included among sue and labour expenses.

However, it is accepted that ransom payments are also claimable under another heading of claim, general average.131 If the decision is made to claim for ransom payments under general average, the assured will not be able to claim under the sue and labour expenses by virtue of s.78(2) of the MIA: "General average losses . . . are not recoverable under the suing and labouring clause." It is thus necessary to briefly examine the concept of general average. The concept is described in s.66(1) and (2) of the MIA:

> (1) A general average loss is a loss caused by and directly consequential on a general average act. It includes a general average expenditure as well as a general average sacrifice.
>
> (2) There is a general average act where any extraordinary sacrifice or expenditure is voluntarily and reasonably made or incurred in time of peril for the purpose of preserving the property imperilled in the common adventure.

The same is reflected in the York-Antwerp Rules, a set of standard rules governing general average that can be incorporated into a marine insurance contract.[132] To fall into the realm of general average, there must be a "common adventure," i.e. "more than one interest must be in peril."[133] Thus,

---

[129] Robert J. Bowman, *Time to Take a Harder Line Against Maritime Piracy* (SupplyChainBrain, 1 August 2011) <http://www.supplychainbrain.com/content/nc/logisticstransportation/transportation-distribution/single-article-page/article/time-to-take-a-harder-line-against-maritime-piracy/> accessed 4 November 2011.

[130] Rose (n 42) para 20.25 (emphasis added).

[131] "payment of ransom, in cash or kind, to obtain the release of ship and cargo is a general average matter." J.H.S Cooke and R.R. Cornah (eds), *Lowndes and Rudolf The Law of General Average and The York-Antwerp Rules* (13th edn, Sweet & Maxwell 2008), para A.68.

[132] See ibid, para 00.26. See also Rule A of the York-Antwerp Rules 1994 or 2004 version.

[133] Ibid., para A.53.

there is no general average in the event of the vessel sailing in ballast.[134] The interests recognised in general average are interests in ship, cargo, and freight.[135] Similar to the case of sue and labour expenses, such various interests must be in danger. In the piracy context, one would imagine of the situation of a cargo-carrying ship seized by pirates. In such a case, a ransom payment paid is considered an expenditure which is "extraordinary" in nature. There is also a suggestion that expenses incurred for ship searching are also claimable in general average.[136] Then, there appears to be no reason why negotiation costs should not be claimable in general average. Thus, the ship-owner who paid for a ransom, search expenses, and negotiation costs "is entitled ... to a rateable contribution from the other parties interested ... ."[137]

It is the process of seeking contribution which presents slight problems and inconvenience. In practice, unfortunately, the process of apportionment is a lengthy one. The author, from personal experience working in the maritime industry and from the experiences of his contacts in the industry, estimates that it might take up to half a year or longer to collect all the contributions, especially where many interests are involved, .e.g. where the ship is under a time-charter party with goods of various cargo-owners on board. In practice, the average adjuster is necessarily appointed. Various documents and communications must be examined. Moreover, as pointed out by Soyer, there might be room for other interests involved to argue that the pirates could seize the vessel due to the fault of the ship-owner in not maintaining the seaworthiness of the vessel.[138] This may prolong the process of apportionment. Further complications can arise if the ship-owner tries to collect security from cargo owners prior to release of their cargoes, unless a policy "absorption clause" is included,[139] and it "is now the exception to see a hull policy for an ocean going vessel without an absorption clause of some kind."[140] However, the absorption clause has been used traditionally in

---

[134] Ibid., citing *The Brigella* [1893] P. 189.

[135] See s.66(7) of the MIA.

[136] J.H.S. Cooke and R.R. Cornah (n 130) para A.66.

[137] See s.66(3).

[138] Soyer (n 5) para 7.47 citing Rule D of the York-Antwerp Rules 2004 which provides: "Rights to contribution in general average shall not be affected, though the event which gave rise to the sacrifice or expenditure may have been due to the fault of one of the parties to the adventure, but this shall not prejudice any remedies or defences which may be open against or to that party in respect of such fault."

[139] "the hull underwriter agrees to indemnify the assured (owner) for the general average expenditure, not merely the assured's proportion." Ibid., citing Clause 40 of the International Hull Clauses (01/11/03) as an example.

[140] J.H.S. Cooke and R.R. Cornah (n 130) para 50.33.

situations where "the general average expenses are relatively modest,"[141] and ransom payments have certainly not been so. Further, there is a limit to the amount the underwriter agrees to absorb.[142] Moreover, there is a question whether the ship-owner can collect general average contribution from the cargo-owner in the situation when, say, the negotiation with the pirates is protracted and the goods have perished by the time the ransom is paid. In that case, arguably, cargoes were not successfully preserved. This seems to go to the root of the general average concept in that the property "in the common adventure" was not successfully preserved. Thus, in the next section we consider how cargo-owners may claim for the loss of cargoes due to piracy incidents.

CARGO OWNERS AND CLAIMS FOR DELAY OR DAMAGE TO GOODS

In *The Bunga Melati Dua* case parcels of bio-diesel were carried on board the vessel. The vessel was captured on August 19, 2008 and was released some eleven days after payment of the ransom, which was over a month after it was captured. On September 18, 2008, the cargo-owner decided to submit a "notice of abandonment" to cargo-owners.[143] A notice of abandonment is a formal step taken by the assured to pursue a claim for a "constructive total loss" from the insurer.[144] The concept of constructive total loss is indeed unique to marine insurance and in *The Bunga Melati Dua* the cargo assureds treated it as an alternative route, while the primary contention was that the cargo automatically became an actual total loss upon the seizure of the vessel.[145] At this stage, it is necessary to consider both the concepts of constructive total loss and actual total loss.

Constructive total loss is defined in s.60 of the MIA, the relevant language of which is as follows:

> (1) Subject to any express provision in the policy, there is a constructive total loss where the subject-matter insured is reasonably abandoned on account of its total loss appearing to be unavoidable, or because it could not be preserved from actual

---

[141] Ibid.

[142] Clause 40.2 of the International Hull Clauses (01/11/03): "The Assured shall have the option of claiming the total general average…up to the amount expressly agreed by the Underwriters."

[143] *The Bunga Melati Dua* (n 111) [1].

[144] Section 62(1) of the MIA: "Subject to the provisions of this section, where the assured elects to abandon the subject-matter insured to the insurer, he must give notice of abandonment. If he fails to do so the loss can only be treated as a partial loss." Also, section 57(2) of the MIA: "In the case of an actual total loss no notice of abandonment need to be given."

[145] *The Bunga Melati Dua* (n 111) [15].

total loss without an expenditure which would exceed its value when the expenditure had been incurred.

(2) In particular, there is a constructive total loss –

(i) Where the assured is deprived of the possession of his ship or goods by the peril insured against, and

(a) it is unlikely that he can recover the ship or goods, as the case may be, or

(b) the cost of recovering the ship or goods, as the case may be, would exceed their value when recovered; or

(ii) …

(iii) In the case of damage to goods, where the cost of repairing the damage and forwarding the goods to their destination would exceed their value on arrival.

The subsequent section states: "Where there is a constructive total loss the assured may either treat the loss as a partial loss, or abandon the subject-matter insured to the insurer and treat the loss as if it were an actual total loss."

The language of s.60(1) of the MIA leads us to the complex area of the doctrine of abandonment. As observed by Tomlinson J., the term "abandonment" is confusingly used in two senses. In one sense, it refers to the tendering of a notice of abandonment as mentioned earlier. On the other hand, it also refers to "the cession to underwriters by the insured of their property and interest" in the subject-matter insured.[146] The use of the term in the latter sense is correct. Tomlinson J. explained further that "[b]y acceptance of notice of abandonment the insurer admits his liability to pay for a CTL [constructive total loss] and admits that the offer to cede given by the assured is validly made."[147] At this stage, only liability is admitted. The underwriter has a right subsequent to this to elect whether it will take over the interest in the subject-matter insured.[148] If the underwriter elects to take over the interest, "abandonment alters the property in the subject-matter insured and does so retrospectively as from the time of the casualty that generates the abandonment."[149] At least in hull insurance, it is rare for the underwriter to accept the notice of abandonment.[150] In *The Bunga Melati*

[146] *The "WD Fairway"* [2009] EWHC 889 (Admlty); [2009] 2 Lloyd's Rep. 191, [25].

[147] Ibid., [35].

[148] Ibid.

[149] Bennett (n 2) para 22.36.

[150] "However, at least in the hull market, a notice of abandonment is almost invariably refused for fear of liabilities that may attach to the insured property." Ibid., para 22.58.

Dua, the cargo-insurer rejected the notice.[151] However, as stated in s.62(4) of the MIA, "[w]here notice of abandonment is properly given, the rights of the assured are not prejudiced by the fact that the insurer refuses to accept the abandonment." Thus, rejection of notice of abandonment does not bar the assured from asserting his right and making a claim for total loss.[152] Nevertheless, considering the factual situation when *The Bunga Melati Dua* was seized, David Steel J. found that it did not give rise to constructive total loss and the claim on this basis was not pursued again when the case came to the Court of Appeal.[153]

As mentioned above, David Steel J. came to the conclusion that all the pirates of Somalia wanted was ransom payment. Therefore, there was no basis for constructive total loss because it could not be said that the prospect of the vessel and the cargo becoming an actual total loss would be unavoidable.[154] Additionally, there was no "abandonment" in the sense described above because, as the judge found, both the ship-owners and the cargo-owners at the time "had every intention of recovering their property and were fully hopeful of doing so."[155]

Bearing the pirates' motives in mind as well, the Court of Appeal agreed with the judgment of David Steel J. and proceeded to hold that there was no actual total loss in this case. Lord Justice Rix put it thusly:[156]

> [P]iratical seizure in the circumstances of this case, where there was not only a chance, but a strong likelihood, that payment of a ransom of a comparatively small sum, relative to the value of the vessel and her cargo, would secure recovery of both, was not an actual total loss. It was not an irretrievable deprivation of property. It was a typical "wait and see" situation…There is no rule of law that capture and seizure is an ATL . . . . The typical case of capture, by a nation's warship, subject to condemnation of a prize, is not an ATL, although it may mature into one. Piratical seizure, in the absence of a policy of ransom, may amount to an ATL, where the pirates escape with their prize for their own use and there is no prospect whatever of finding or recovering vessel or cargo: but where a chance of recapture remains

---

[151] *The Bunga Melati Dua* (n 111) [1].
[152] Rose (n 42) para 24.37.
[153] *The Bunga Melati Dua* (n 111) [2].
[154] *Masefield* (n 1) [57].
[155] Ibid., [56].
[156] *The Bunga Metali Dua* (n 111) [56].

even such a seizure will not give rise to an immediate ATL, and in any event that is very far from this case.

What, in truth, enabled David Steel J. and the Court of Appeal to find that there was neither a constructive total loss nor an actual total loss of cargo was the nature of the cargo in the case which was of a non-perishable type. After the vessel was released, the cargo could be discharged at its destination with only slight delay which affected the sale price.[157] Yet, the delay alone does not afford the insurance cover.[158] The outcome of this case would necessarily be changed if the cargo was perishable. One could imagine how apples or bananas on board the captured vessel would be after a month! In that case, no doubt there would be an incident of the actual total loss as the assured would be "irretrievably deprived" of cargoes.

In addition to the type of cargo, as discussed above, specific circumstances must also be taken into account in determining whether a claim for constructive total loss or actual total loss would be successful. For example, if it is believed that the captured vessel will be used by the pirates as a "mothership,"[159] the owners of cargoes on board such a vessel, and indeed the ship-owner itself, should be able to claim for constructive total loss or actual total loss of the cargoes and the vessel, from the cargo underwriters and the hull underwriters respectively.[160] The situation must be assessed on the date when the notice of abandonment is rejected. This is due to the practical reason that such a date is taken to be "equivalent to the commencement of proceedings; any facts discovered after that date which indicate that a constructive total loss had not occurred are . . . irrelevant in fixing the rights of the parties."[161]

The above analysis has demonstrated attendant difficulties for claims made for ransom payment and for damages or delays to cargoes. Even more of a rising concern is the loss of life of crewmen due to piracy. It is partly

---

[157] Ibid., [12].

[158] Section 55(2)(b) of the MIA: "Unless the policy otherwise provides, the insurer on ship or goods is not liable for any loss proximately caused by delay, although the delay be caused by a peril insured against." See similarly Clause 4.5 of the Institute Cargo Clauses (A) (01/01/82) or the Institute Cargo Clauses (A) (01/01/09).

[159] The term "mothership" is referred to "the very largest of merchant ships, fishing vessels and dhows…used to carry pirates, stores, fuel and attack skiffs to enable pirates to operate over a much larger area and are significantly less affected by the weather…" Maritime Security Centre Horn of Africa (MSCHOA) (n 83) 9.

[160] See Jonathan Gilman and the others (n 4) para 30.15.

[161] Robert Merkin and the others (eds), *Colinvaux's Law of Insurance in Hong Kong* (Sweet & Maxwell 2009) para 21.083.

pressure from crewmen demanding security that the employment of armed guard has received a relatively warm welcome from ship operators.

INJURY AND LOSS OF LIFE DUE TO PIRACY

In general, personal injuries and loss of life of crewmen are covered by a vessel's P&I Club.[162] Since practices among P&I Clubs do not vary to a great extent, for ease of reference, in this work the rules of the North of England P&I Club (NEPIA) 2011/12 will be referred to by way of example.[163] It is clearly stated in Rule 19(1) in relation to the "Liabilities in respect of Seamen" that the Club shall cover the assured for: "Liabilities to pay damages or compensation for death, personal injury, or illness of any Seaman of an Entered Ship and hospital, medical, funeral and other expenses necessarily incurred in relation to such death, personal injury or illness."

However, as pointed out by Mr. Nigel Carden of the UK P&I Club in his capacity as the Chairman of the Maritime Security Sub-Committee of the International Group of P&I Clubs[164] in his presentation to the European Commission,[165] tension is caused by the coverage for death or personal injury of seamen as mentioned above and the general exception to P&I coverage. The same is reflected in Rule 24 of the rules of NEPIA in relation to "war risks" that the P&I Club should not be liable for death or personal injury caused by:

(a) war, civil war, revolution, rebellion, insurrection or civil strife arising therefrom, any hostile act by or against a belligerent power, or any act of terrorism…
(b) capture, seizure, arrest, restraint or detainment (barratry and piracy excepted) and the consequences thereof or any attempt thereat;
(c) mines, torpedoes, bombs, rockets, shells, explosives or other similar weapons of war provided that this exclusion shall not apply to liabilities, costs or expenses which arise solely by reason of:

---

[162] The term "P & I Club" is a short-hand for "Protection & Indemnity Club." "P & I Clubs provide third party liability insurance for shipowners." Institute of Maritime Law, *Southampton on Shipping Law* (Informa 2008) 337.

[163] See The North of England P & I Club, "P & I Rules 2011/12" <http://www.nepia.com/cache/files/5451-1297174526/PIRules2011.pdf#zoom=70> accessed 14 November 2011.

[164] "The International Group of P & I Clubs is an association of the largest P & I Clubs, most of them originally based in the United Kingdom, with others in Scandinavia, Japan, and the USA....The main purpose of the International Group is the pooling of the cost of large claims…" Institute of Maritime Law (n 161) 340.

[165] Nigel Carden, *Piracy and Armed Robbery at Sea – How Best to Protect Seafarers Piracy and P & I Insurance* (presented to the European Commission at a seminar "Piracy and Armed Robbery at Sea – How Best to Protect Seafarers" held on 3 March 2010) <http://ec.europa.eu/transport/maritime/events/doc/2010_03_03_piracy/2010_03_03_igp-i.pdf> accessed 14 November 2011.

(i) the transport of any such weapons whether on board the Entered Ship or not or

(ii) the use of such weapons, either as a result of government order or with the written agreement of the Managers or the Directors, where the reason for such use is the avoidance or mitigation of liabilities, costs or expenses which would otherwise fall within the cover given by the Association.

The loss of life or personal injury to crewmen due to terrorism will not be covered and this is partly why the motives of the wrongdoers as to whether they acted as pirates or terrorists must be carefully parsed. Secondly, the P & I Clubs have concerns that the employment of armed guards may make the overall situation worse with "risk of escalated attacks with heavier weapons . . . ."[166] Additionally, there is a complication in demonstrating apparent danger to life and the appropriateness of any response.[167] Thus, the overall attitude of P&I Clubs is that they will examine each situation on a "case-by-case basis" in an attempt to identify "causation."[168] Of course, one can readily understand the mess in trying to ascertain whose bullets caused the death or personal injury to crewmen. This is further complicated as it is likely that the P&I surveyors and the local authorities will only reach the targeted vessel long after the fight. It is in part this that causes the hesitation of the P&I Clubs in providing the exact answer whether the armed guards should be employed to deter pirates.

The P&I Clubs have further concerns that the employment of armed guards may prove to be in conflict with the law of the Flag State of the vessel or of the Port State. In this respect, the International Group of P&I Clubs noted that the International Chamber of Shipping (ICS) has compiled information concerning laws of various countries in a document entitled "Flag State Rules and Requirements on arms and private armed guards on board vessels."[169] From the information so compiled, one can see that there is no consensus among states as to the employment of armed guards. Concern on the part of P&I Clubs is valid despite the P&I insurance cover being governed by the rules of each Club. Yet, the rules of the Club are still subject

[166] Nigel Carden (n 164).

[167] Ibid.

[168] Ibid.

[169] International Group of P & I Clubs, "Piracy – FAQs" <http://www.igpandi.org/downloadables/piracy/Piracy_FAQs.pdf> accessed 14 November 2011. See also The International Chamber of Shipping and The International Shipping Federation, 'Flag State Rules and Requirements on Arms and Private Armed Guards On Board Vessels: Combined ICS/ECSA Table' <http://www.marisec.org/Piracy%20Flag%20State%20Laws%20July %2011.pdf> accessed 14 November 2011.

to relevant law. For example, pursuant to Rule 6 of the rules of NEPIA, "[t]hese Rules and all contracts of insurance made by the Association shall be subject to and incorporate the provisions of the Marine Insurance Act 1906 . . . ." Further, s.41 of the MIA states that "[t]here is an implied warranty that the adventure insured is a lawful one, and that, so far as the assured can control the matter, the adventure shall be carried out in a lawful manner." As a matter of English law, this may not be of a concern in light of the recent United Kingdom government's more relaxed attitude for the employment of armed guards on British-flagged vessels.[170] It remains to be seen whether such an attitude will be extended to foreign-flagged vessels. Further, the question remains whether the warranty of legality in s.41 refers to English law alone. The learned editors of the latest edition of *Arnould's Law of Marine Insurance and Average* have drawn some support from the *obiter* of Phillips L.J. in the *Royal Boskalis* case where he stated that "[t]he warranty that the adventure shall be lawful and carried out in a lawful manner probably refers to English law, not foreign law."[171] Yet, this statement is inconclusive and there is no direct authority on the point. The unclear signals issued from various governments as to the use of armed guards, is, in a word, disturbing. Anemic language such as "encourage" or "discourage" does not provide much assistance.

In the event of a ship-owner's decision to employ armed guards, the International Group of P&I Clubs further advises that it is preferable for the armed guards to come in the form of "servicing members of a military force," which are also known as "Vessel Protection Detachments (VPDs)."[172] Also, the agreement with the security company should contain a requirement that the security company has its own public liability insurance and employer's liability insurance and, preferably, the contract should be "knock for knock."[173] This "knock for knock" provision is to the effect that "if . . . a crew member or armed guard is killed, in the absence of negligence the loss will fall where it lies . . . ."[174] In view of all of this uncertainty surrounding the use of armed guards, especially how P&I insurance cover will be affected, the only advice that can be given to ship-owners is that it is always prudent to maintain communication and seek advice from the ship's P&I

---

170 BBC, *Somali Piracy: Armed Guards to Protect UK Ships* (30 October 2011) <http://www.bbc.co.uk/news/uk-15510467> accessed 14 November 2011.

171 *Royal Boskalis* (n 119) 736 cited in Jonathan Gilman and the others (n 4) para 21-04, footnote 17.

172 International Group of P & I Clubs (n 168).

173 Ibid.

174 The Swedish Club, *PIRACY & USE OF ARMED GUARDS: Specific Contractual Provisions* <http://www.swedishclub.com/upload/Loss_Prev_Docs/Piracy/PIRACY_and_USE_OF_ARMED_GUARDS_-_Specific_contractual_provisions.pdf> accessed 15 November 2011.

Club in the event of any plan to employ the armed guards. This may include seeking advice on the recommended security companies or even involving the P&I Club in negotiating the contract with the security company.

As one can see, part of the reason why P&I Clubs cannot take a clearer stance on the issue of armed guards is because their use triggers many different relevant laws connected to the voyage. This is entirely outside the control of the P&I Clubs. Perhaps, the international community will determine whether there should be an international convention of some sorts providing certainty as to the employment of armed guards.

CONCLUSION

Piracy in the Gulf of Aden and off of the coast of Somalia not only poses challenges to the shipping industry worldwide, but also reveals the current limits of marine insurance law. It is abundantly clear that the characterisation of "pirates" provided for by Rule 8 of the Rules for Construction is insufficient for modern circumstances. This causes further issues of distinction between the risk of piracy and other risks such as theft and terrorism. As this author suggests, it might be advantageous for the global insurance industry to convene an industry-wide meeting and draft a clause delineating what piracy risk entails.

In recent years, there have been more international regulations dealing with the safety and security of ships. Ship-owners must ensure that they are well-acquainted with these regulations. Otherwise, their claims following an incident of piracy may be tainted by defences available to underwriters such as wilful misconduct or the breach of the implied warranty of seaworthiness. Whilst the modern standard form contracts widely used in the industry for hull & machinery insurance cover the risk of piracy, the process of recovery for ransom payment made by the ship-owner under either the sue and labour provision or the general average tends to be rather long and complicated. The global insurance industry has responded in the form of K&R insurance products. Of course, this is tied up with the question of whether the ransom payment is legal in the first place. At a minimum, the Court of Appeal in *The Bunga Melati Dua* has confirmed it is not against public policy.

Further, whether cargo owners can claim for either the actual total loss or the constructive total loss of their cargoes necessarily depends on the actual situation at the time, especially the type of cargo. It would be relatively easy for cargo owners to claim for total loss if their cargo is of a perishable type. However, the same cannot be said if the cargo is non-perishable. Under the current state of law, any consequences of delay must be absorbed by the cargo owners. Additionally, any loss of life or injuries to crewmen during a piracy incident are generally covered by the ship-owner's P&I insurance. However, the employment of armed guards on board the ship may give rise to complicated issues concerning the P&I cover. First, if the use of armed guards is prohibited by the laws of the flag state or the port state, this may go into the breach of the implied warranty of legality as in s.41 of the MIA 1906. Secondly, in event of a fight between armed guards and pirates causing deaths or injuries to crewmen, there is bound to be a complicated factual question of causation. This may be hard to determine considering that surveyors and the authorities will only arrive on the scene after the incident. Lastly, one should be reminded of the speech of Lord Justice Rix in the Court of Appeal in *The Bunga Melati Dua* whereby the Court clearly expressed dissatisfaction with the global community's response to the current piracy incidents off the Gulf of Aden and Somalia. Clearly, there will be no complications with insurance if there is no "risk."

14. The Role of Media and Communications

Edward GIRARDET

Introduction

This chapter explores the role of media and communications since the late 20th and early 21st centuries with regard to global maritime piracy. Essentially, it focuses on the way local and international media have reflected the causes and development of piracy in Somalia during the 1980s and early 1990s. It also highlights incidents elsewhere such as the hijacking of boatpeople in Southeast Asia during the late 1970s and early 80s,[1] assaults against sailing vessels and private yachts in the South China Sea, and rising attacks against ships and fishermen in West Africa.[2] Part of this assessment is based on the writer's own reporting experiences as a journalist covering humanitarian and conflict issues since early 1980 to the present in the Horn of Africa, West Africa and Southeast Asia.

Nevertheless, the bulk of local and international piracy coverage only came to the fore during the late 1990s and early 2000s as attacks against shipping became more prevalent. From 2007 onwards to the present, there has been regular coverage by news agencies, newspapers, radio, television and various Internet sites on the growing number of piracy incidents coupled with local, regional and international efforts to counter pirate activities, such as recent operations by Puntland marines against local pirates.[3]

The essay also specifically examines the impact of social media, such as Twitter, Facebook, Internet websites or mobile phone text messages, on the way pirates are able to operate today with regard to communicating ransom demands or managing their operations through contacts with the Somali diaspora, insurance companies and shipping firms. Furthermore, it looks at the manner in which the international community has galvanized its naval response to global piracy by publicizing messages of deterrent, notably blatant no-holds-barred YouTube segments, aimed at communities

---

[1] Edward Girardet, *Waves of Humanity Wash Across Southeast Asia*, The Christian Science Monitor, November 19, 1980. Plus other reports by Edward Girardet.

[2] Paige McClanahan, *Piracy on the rise off West Africa's Coast*, Christian Science Monitor, August 4, 2011.

[3] *Puntland Marines Conduct Anti-Piracy Operations Near Bossaso*, Allafrica.com, January 21, 2012.

supporting piracy in order to show what happens to those who indulge in the practise. More recently, with the spread of Somali attacks against tourists in eastern Kenya, it examines attempts by the Kenyan army, which intervened militarily in Somalia in late 2011, to use Twitter as a means of warning civilian populations of impending attack, but also as a means of threatening or intimidating pirates, kidnappers, and belligerents.[4]

And finally, this essay outlines public awareness initiatives in the print and broadcast media aimed at countries, such as the Philippines or Bangladesh, whose citizens constitute the bulk of seafarers who have been, and still are, affected by hijackings.

THE ORIGINS

During the early 1980s, Somalia was caught up in a ravaging humanitarian crisis resulting from a combination of regional drought and conflict over the Ogaden region between the mutually repressive regimes of Syad Barre in Mogadishu and Haile Mengistu in Ethiopia.[5] From the media point of view, this provoked considerable international attention but primarily as a result of humanitarian response rather than any particular interest in Somalia as a nation. To a lesser extent, there was a Cold War focus provoked by the fact that Somalia, a former ally of Moscow, had switched its allegiance to the United States as part of its confrontation against the Soviet and Cuban-backed regime in Addis Abeba. Washington carried out military manoeuvres in Berbera and other parts of Somalia as part of its engagement in the region, prompting additional media coverage.[6]

Already during the late 1960s, severe drought conditions had begun forcing tens of thousands of Ethiopians, many of them ethnic Somalis, to flee across the border into neighbouring Somalia. Following Somalia's defeat in the 1977-78 Ogaden War and the onset of further lack of seasonal rains in 1978 in eastern Ethiopia, even more people crossed the southeastern frontier into Somalia. By 1983, the Horn of Africa's refugee problem (over 2.5 million according to the United Nations High Commissioner for Refugees or UNHCR) was considered the worst in the world with Pakistan's hosting of Afghan refugees as second. Over 700,000 mainly women and children from the Ogaden region were living in 26 make-shift refugee camps in Somalia. Many suffered from chronic malnutrition and dehydration, but also malaria,

---

[4] *Kenyan/Somalia Twitter War*, MSNBC, November 3, 2011; The Guardian, December 13, 2011; Global Voices, January 13, 2012.

[5] Edward Girardet, *Desert War Refugees Inundate Somalia,* The Christian Science Monitor, July 2, 1980. Plus other articles and radio reports by Edward Girardet in 1980 from the Horn of Africa region.

[6] Robert I. Rotberg, *Somalia and US Strategic Interests*, The Christian Science Monitor, December 5, 1984.

tuberculosis and dysentery. Many families, too, had lost their primary means of survival, notably camels, cattle and goats.[7] This was aggravated further by the 1984-85 famine in the region.

The international press broadly covered Somalia's ongoing crisis, sometimes egged on by the relief agencies to portray it as a classic humanitarian disaster of biblical proportions. The *Christian Science Monitor, New York Times, Le Monde, Süddeutsche Zeitung* and other mainstream media regularly reported the situation, often at the instigation of UN and other relief agencies intent on promoting greater public awareness of the issue with organized field trips. While the bulk of this reporting was aimed at international audiences, some of it filtered back in the form of press reviews to the Somalis themselves via major broadcasters such as the *BBC, Voice of America* and *Deutschewelle.*

The BBC, particularly its widely heard Africa and Somali services, stood out as a principal provider of credible in-depth local or regional coverage for Horn of Africa populations given that both the official Ethiopian and Somali media were government-controlled. As elsewhere on the continent, most ordinary citizens listened avidly on their shortwave sets to outside international broadcasters. A small number of Somali newspapers and magazines operated out of Mogadishu, Hargeisa and Kisimayo, but none were independent. For the Mogadishu government, Radio Somalia served as its main vehicle of official information. The Barre regime had also set up a national television service funded by the West Germans, but in name only. No actual network ever managed to broadcast.

At the time, maritime piracy (as opposed to hijackings, cattle thefts or attacks by *shiftas* and other armed gangs in northern Kenya or parts of Somalia) was not a global problem. While there had always been periodic reports of pirates during the 1970s, 80s and 90s attacking fishing vessels, refugee boats or private yachts in Southeast Asia, plus attacks against anchored ships off Nigeria or Benin, organized piracy in Somalia had yet to emerge. Nevertheless, the roots were definitely there. But few journalists explored the broader connotations of the Horn of Africa crisis as an eventual source for piracy and other knock-on effects. This despite the fact that the humanitarian response was being heavily manipulated by the Ethiopian and Somali regimes prompting only limited efforts to remedy the region's more debilitating long-term problems, such as the lack of basic development.

---

[7] Edward Girardet, *Refugees Eke Out Marginal Existence in Dry Somalia*, The Christian Science Monitor, August 13, 1980.

Both governments sought to ensure the continued flow of outside aid funds, but also to hide what was going on behind the scenes. Select international relief agencies chose to turn a blind eye to government control of humanitarian response in order not to jeopardize their ability to work with crisis-affected populations. Millions of aid dollars disappeared through corruption or misappropriation by the military in Somalia and Ethiopia. In Ethiopia, for example, only Cultural Survival (a Boston-based NGO) and Medecins sans Frontieres dared speak out against forced population movements by the Addis regime during the early 1980s. MSF was expelled, while well over 60 aid organizations remained silent.

For the Syad Barre regime, it was a matter of encouraging more international support as a source of income for corrupt officials by maintaining Somalia in a constant emergency mode. The Somali dictatorship regularly inflated refugee numbers, sometimes 30%-50% more than those estimated by the UNHCR and other aid organizations. More refugees meant more money.

Barre also discouraged any aid initiatives that smacked of longer-term development as this might detract from the emergency atmosphere it was seeking to maintain. The regime's reluctance to have the foreign donors re-classify their support even went as far as to forbid reconstruction-style projects such as the re-planting of trees cut down by women foraging for firewood within 50 kilometers of the refugee camps. Hence, too, Barre's efforts to stifle any critics or media that sought to question the real reasons behind his country's predicament. Since coming to power in 1969 until his downfall in 1991, Barre conducted a reign of terror, such as the execution of opposition figures or threats against aid agencies, which further prevented any constructive approaches to helping the country emerge from its dire predicament.

More specifically, as highlighted by some media, Somalia and the rest of the Horn of Africa were suffering a problem that was also affecting much of the Sahel to the west, notably the worsening impact of drought on traditional pastoralism or nomadism. The nomad way of life during the 1970s had represented over 90% of Somalia's hard currency exports. By the mid-1980s, expanding desertification and declining precipitation combined with overuse of the land was thoroughly eroding this source of income. It was becoming clear that many nomads, who had lost their livestock, could no longer rely on their ancient way of life for survival. Nor could meat exports serve as a viable foreign currency earner. (The Saudi Arabian government had blocked Somali meat imports as a means of pressuring the Mogadishu government).

The land could simply no longer support growing populations of people and animals relying on diminishing supplies of grazing fodder and water.

Further drought was causing more livestock to die or to oblige their owners to sell off the few animals that remained at low prices. This meant that more and more people no longer had the means to replenish their herds once conditions improved. While humanitarian aid provided a temporary solution to their plight, it was clear that Somali nomads would have to find alternative means of survival. This meant that Somalia's problem was an inherent one exacerbated by political or conflict conditions that prevented any form of significant development.[8]

Nevertheless, despite the Syad Barre regime's emphasis on emergency response, a small number of development initiatives did manage to squeeze through during the 1970s and 80s as a means of providing Somali nomads with more diverse sources of income and food. This included relocating some 15,000 nomads during the 1973-75 drought to four coastal locations, such as Berbera and Hobyo, as part of an effort to turn them into fishermen. Other sporadic rehabilitation projects continued in the 1980s. Despite having one of the longer coastlines in Africa (1,000 km along the Gulf of Aden and 2,000 km on the Indian Ocean), Somalia had never really enjoyed a significant fishing industry. Most fishermen during the colonial period were Italians working with local Somalis as deck hands.

Media campaigns to promote this new form of life were limited and not particularly effective. Nevertheless, during the 1980s, Somali fishermen provided hotels, restaurants and the international community in Mogadishu, and other towns, with fresh lobster, shrimps, mackerel and tuna. Later efforts, such as a Japanese "from nomads to fishermen" project during the mid-1980s helped make boats available, but the industry never really took off. Reproduced data regarding project impact also remained highly questionable. Most fishermen focused on highly limited coastal pelagic fishing.

While reporting in Somalia during the 1980s and early 90s, this writer often visited the local markets to determine what produce was available. Compared to the Swahili coastline of Kenya and Tanzania with its vibrant fishing communities, the Somali industry remained a paltry one. Fishermen also had to compete with the imports of dried salted fish brought in from the Great Lakes region of Africa. Another problem was that fish did not

---

[8] Edward Girardet, *Somalia Starts Off on the Long Road to Economic Stability*, The Christian Science Monitor, October 7, 1985.

constitute a normal part of Somali food diets. And finally, few nomads knew how to swim and were thus wary of proceeding too far out with their boats.

Most Somalis at the time were not aware of the potential of their waters for fishing, and probably did not care. Nevertheless, reports by local and international media began to focus on two phenomena during the 1990s that appear to have contributed toward the development of piracy as a highly lucrative industry. They are also on-the-ground realities, which today cannot be resolved through the hammer of military force. Not unlike its failed approach with Afghanistan, much of the international community continues to regard Somalia's piracy as a security rather than an economic development or political issue.

As pointed out by select media, such as the *Toronto Globe and Mail*[9] or the US television programme *Democracy Now*,[10] Somali piracy did not arise suddenly or unexpectedly. For well over two decades, uncontrolled foreign fishing fleets from Europe and Asia regularly – and illegally - fished the nutrient-rich waters of Somalia. Certain commentators have pointed out that the lack of any effective government in Somalia, particularly following the outbreak of civil war in 1991, meant that no maritime limits were officially proclaimed. As a result, from the international law point of view, such outside fishing was not illegal.

Nevertheless, according to some estimates, foreign fishing reaped over 300 million US dollars a year in catches of tuna, shrimp, mackerel and lobster. This severely depleted local stocks, persuading affected coastal communities to demand compensation – without success - in the form of fishing levies from the foreign trawlers. Today, this competition from foreign boats is often cited by Somali pirates as a justification for resorting to attack ships off their coastline and demanding ransoms as a form of "tax."

While this may be correct, the international community today largely regards such "legal" or "justified" piracy as having crossed the line. As one London-based security analyst pointed out in a CNN report[11] on the US Seal rescue in late January, 2012 of two foreign aid hostages, including a US citizen, from pirates on Somali soil, the pirates are nothing more than "criminal bands" seeking profit for themselves, their communities and their investors. Commenting on the naval raid, US officials in Washington also referred to the pirate activities as "criminal" and that such activities against

[9] Andrew Lusztyk, Globe and Mail, July 21, 2011.

[10] Mohammed Abshir Waldo, Democracy Now, New York. 14 April, 2009.

[11] CNN News, January 15, 2012.

US citizens would not be tolerated.[12] Such "crossing of the lines" is also reflected by Canadian journalist, Jay Bahadur, who reported with Somali pirates in 2009 and published the book *The Pirates of Somalia* in 2011.

A second reason is that some western countries were using Somalia as a dumping ground for toxic wastes, particularly during the brutal civil war years where virtually every warlord could do what he wanted. According to various press reports, Somali warlords and select European companies had contracted with each other to dump several hundred thousand tons of toxic wastes in Somali waters and on land. With the 2004 Asian tsunami, tidal waves churned up these wastes, causing severe health problems among coastal communities in Somalia. This posed a serious environmental threat by causing higher than normal respiratory infections as well as mouth ulcers and bleeding. Media reports by the BBC and other international broadcasters highlighted these problems, which incited anger among local populations.

These two issues soon emerged as principal reasons of concern among Somalis directly affected. The first Somali pirates were reportedly men from these afflicted communities. Jobless and starving, they organized themselves into groups to demand payment from these outside interlopers. This eventually led to the involvement of mainland warlords and gangs, who, until then had blockaded roads, hijacked vehicles or attacked aid transports for revenue, and now saw piracy as a new and potentially lucrative means of income. They quickly assumed control of the business with their weapons, muscle and criminal approaches. Media reports have also cited the involvement of private investors – some of them part of the Somali diaspora, but others involved with the Mafia and other criminal groups - operating out of Europe, North America or the Gulf region. These provide the pirates with money, equipment, fuel and other means of support, but then expect to recoup their investment from the ransoms paid.

Various media reports have also suggested that the origin of armed Somali piracy was the result of different forms of international support to help local fishermen counter foreign exploitation of their waters. Some aid agencies have suggested that the European Union helped equip and arm the creation of a protective Somali coast guard, but that this programme was soon abandoned. Such involvement has produced names of piracy groups such as the "National Volunteer Coast Guard." A 2009 *Al Jazeera* report maintained that Hart Security, a private British company, provided military training to Somali fishermen in the 1990s to create a "Fishermen's Protection Agency."

---

[12] Anna Mulrine, *SEAL Team 6 Rescue in Somalia Frees Two From Pirates' Lair* (+video), Christian Science Monitor, January 25, 2012.

A major portion of this training was designed to teach them "how to handle weapons and board boats at high sea." These tactics are the same ones now used by pirates in their actions against international shipping. Apparently, this same company is now providing security for commercial maritime operators against the same pirates they once helped train.

Overall, there now appear to be two types of media narratives with regard to the pirates of Somalia. One is the victim of impoverishment whose predicament has justified his actions as a means of survival; the other is the nasty buccaneer out to exploit for profit whatever he can from passing ships. Clearly, ongoing war and lack of economic development since the 1970s have contributed to today's piracy, but so has basic greed by criminal gangs preying on international shipping.

Not surprisingly, the bulk of international reporting has focused on the impact of piracy on global shipping, rather than the illegal fishing or toxic waste dumping of the 1990s. Nor has there been much emphasis on Somalia's basic development or rule of law problems that afflict the majority of ordinary Somalis. Instead, media coverage has been stimulated by the hijacking of pleasure yachts, oil tankers and cargo vessels laden with goods worth millions of dollars.

One incident - the capture of a British yachting couple, Paul and Rachel Chandler off the Seychelles in October, 2009, and held for 388 days before being released after a ransom payment - received broad and often emotional media coverage, particularly by the British press. A video filmed by Agence France Press highlighted their predicament when a French journalist was allowed to accompany a doctor to visit the couple.[13]

MEDIA COVERAGE OF PIRACY TODAY

Ever since piracy off the Somali coast began to develop in the late 1990s and early 2000s, there has been broad local, regional and international media coverage of the issue in North America, Europe, Asia and Africa. But the bulk of this focus has been on security concerns, such as the need to contain piracy in the Indian Ocean region. According to Safer World, an international non-governmental organization working with grassroots groups in Somalia, an estimated 1,500-3,000 pirates operate off Somalia's coast. They typically range in age from 15 to 30 and are almost all unskilled and uneducated with the bulk of them originating from rural areas. In recent years, their ability to operate longer distances off the Somali coast has grown

---

[13] *Skeletal and Terrified: British Yacht Couple Reveal Cruelty of Their Somali Pirate Captors*, The Daily Mail, February 5, 2010.

considerably. Pirates have begun working from larger vessels, known as mother ships, which are stocked with food and fuel. This has enabled Somali pirates to operate as far away as the coast of India and the Persian Gulf.

"The solution to Somali piracy will be found on land, and will need to address the problem's root causes, not its symptoms," noted observer Andrew Lusztyk in the *Toronto Globe and Mail.*[14] This includes stimulating alternative livelihoods for the steady supply of young recruits who are unemployed, hungry and desperate.

According to Lusztyk, however, there has been a distinct inability of the international community to develop a serious strategy for dealing with piracy.

> There is a stubborn unwillingness to take a comprehensive action to Somali piracy, to investigate its root causes and work from there. Far simpler to populate the vast waters off the coast of Somalia with a smattering of international naval task forces and claim that progress is being made. But progress is not being made. If anything, the world is falling back on old-fashioned diplomacy - clumsy, ineffective, unsophisticated, ugly – and its costing time, money and lives.

In early 2012, major media such as CNN, BBC and other networks highlighted a 210-page report issued by the British House of Commons Foreign Affairs Committee, which severely criticized the international community for a lack of "clear leadership" and called for "decisive action" against the "growing problem of piracy off the coast of Somalia." Despite nine UN Security Council resolutions and three multinational naval operations, the counterpiracy policy has had limited impact, it maintained. "The number of attacks, the costs to the industry and price of ransoms have all increased significantly since 2007." Warning that there is no lack of targets, it stated that 90% of the world's traded materials are shipped by sea. Some 28,000 ships – 40% of this global trade – pass through the Indian Ocean, Gulf of Aden and Arabian Sea. Overall, the report added, the annual cost of piracy, including insurance, prosecutions, security and ransoms, is estimated at between $7-12 billion. Independent media reports, however, maintain that this figure could be far higher given the difficulties of assessing the real costs of naval counter-piracy operations in the Indian Ocean and elsewhere.

The report noted that average ransom over the past four years has risen from $600,000 to $4.7 million per vessel with 2011's total outlay reaching

---

[14] *Somali Piracy: The Solution is on Land, Not at Sea*. Globe and Mail, July 21, 2011.

$135 million. It warned that these payments should be a matter of deep concern for Britain and the entire international maritime community. Instead, the British government's response has been "disappointingly slow to track financial flows from piracy."

While some ships have begun taking more robust measures to defend themselves, the report noted, "pirates still face few repercussions for their actions." As stressed by some media in their coverage of the report, some 90% of captured pirates are released without charge. They also highlighted the report's demands that there is no reason why Britain could not assert jurisdiction over suspected pirates. Simply returning suspected pirates to their boats or to land "provides little long-term deterrence and has demonstrably failed to prevent annual increases in both the number of pirates going to see and in the number of attacks."

Furthermore, some media have linked piracy with the financing of international terrorism, notably al Qaeda. While refuted by the Central Intelligence Agency and other intelligence and security organizations as improbable, such associations with alleged terrorism serve to sensationalize the issue and detract from the real problems at hand. Most observers believe that piracy is organized more in line with local or international cartels seeking to profit from the situation rather than being deliberately cultivated as a terrorist tool. Certain terrestrial groups, too, are believed to extort "taxes" and other forms of income from the pirates.

Worldwide over the past four years, 3,500 seafarers have been taken hostage and 62 have been killed. Such realities have prompted considerable reporting among local or regional media in countries such as the Philippines - which relies on nearly 4 billion US dollars worth of remittances annually sent back by Filipino nationals working in the merchant marine industry. The Manila government is becoming increasingly concerned by the impact of piracy on the well-being of its seafarers, many of whom have been involved in piracy incidents and held on average for up to four months. According to some press reports, growing numbers of Filipinos have said that they will no longer return to sea as long as piracy remains a problem. Similar press reports highlighting the effects of piracy on seafarers have also appeared in Malaysia, Bangladesh and Sri Lanka.

Other countries, such as Yemen, which is just north of Somalia, have felt the impact of piracy against their fishermen. Yemeni fishermen are being increasingly attacked by Somali pirates, but also apprehended as suspected pirates by foreign naval vessels. The Indian Navy, for example, has intervened against a number of suspected pirate mother ships, but also

Yemeni fishing boats in 2011, incidents which have been broadly covered by the Indian press.

Tourism in the Indian Ocean region has also been affected by piracy. By Christmas, 2011, Kenya was suffering significant cancellations by tourists or tourist organizations fearful of attacks against the Swahili coasts by pirates, insurgents or criminal gangs. Because of security concerns, only two international cruise ships stopped off Mombasa in 2011. According to the *Nairobi Standard*,[15] an Abercrombie & Kent executive said that they have made considerable efforts to promote Mombasa as a cruise stopover. And yet, escalating piracy incidents along the western Indian Ocean rim have been forcing shipping companies to give the area a wide berth. Even Tanzania, further down the East Africa coast, has noted concerns for holidaying in Tanga, Dar-es-Salaam and Zanzibar. Warnings have appeared in the East African and other press, but also on numerous tourist-related websites and Facebook alerts.

Similarly, the Seychelles have been seeking to alleviate security concerns by developing a strategic partnership with China, which promises to use the islands as a base for operating against pirates. Local and international media have stressed that increased security by international naval operations could reduce the threat, particularly against wealthy tourists. But costs to the industry are rising. Cruise operators destined for Dubai have watched their costs rise for tourists seeking to transit the increasingly piracy-prone region. Sri Lanka, too, finds itself affected. While many seafarers are of Sri Lankan origin, tourists regard the island nation as a holiday area but are increasingly wary about coming because of press reports about piracy throughout the Indian Ocean rim.

At the same time, while Somalia and the Indian Ocean region are now regarded as the principal pirate zone, press reports continue to highlight attacks against boats in Southeast Asia, even though incidents have dropped dramatically. In 2000, piracy incidents in Southeast Asia accounted for 242 of the 469 recorded worldwide. At the time, Somalia represented only 22 – less than 5% - of the global total. By 2009, the situation had reversed with Southeat Asian pirates accounting for only 45 out of 406 incidents representing 11%, the lowest ever since 1994. According to local and regional media, counter-piracy efforts have been working, but incidents still persist, endangering both commercial shipping, fishermen and private yachts, suggesting that still not all is well.

---

[15] The Standard, December 27, 2011.

In many ways, the international response to piracy has brought different countries together or reduced political tensions. At least 20 nations are now involved in counter-piracy activities, including the US and Chinese navies. But regional players are also becoming involved, such as Iran. One such incident was the hijacking of an Iranian fishing vessel that had been commandeered by suspected Somali pirates in the Arabian Sea but was rescued by a US naval destroyer in early 2012. As pointed out by the *Times of India* (January 9, 2012), "the rescue came days just after Iranian leaders had warned the US to keep its warships out of the Persian Gulf" but that the Iranian foreign minister welcomed the "humanitarian gesture" of the United States. The US Navy detained the pirates, but indicated that the question now was where to send them for prosecution. By early 2012, it noted, over 1,000 pirates are under prosecution in about 20 different countries.[16]

At a recent maritime meeting at the International Labour Organization (ILO) in Geneva in December, 2011, several shipowners maintained that they thought the global media coverage of the piracy issue was relatively good. Where it could improve, some noted, might be in the area of "needs-based" information, notably better local and regional public outreach to alleviate concerns in countries providing seafarers to the industry. "There are a lot of families who are deeply worried about their menfolk departing on ships and yet know that they have no other choice," noted one corporate executive. "We have to show them that we are doing something about the problem and that we are deeply concerned about their safety."

At the same time, at least one naval observer, Retired Rear Adm. Terrence "Terry" McKnight, the former commander of the Combined Maritime Forces (CMF) and the Combined Task Force 151 (CTF-151) for counterpiracy operations, told the National Naval Museum in Washington that he thought the piracy problem in the Gulf of Aden was "overpublicized."[17] Commenting publicly, he noted that "we are fighting wars on two fronts in Iraq and Afghanistan with hundreds of thousands of troops involved. Yet world attention, particularly media attention, is drawn to Somali piracy in the Gulf of Aden which is a very minor problem in the large scheme of things." He maintained that only 29 pirate attacks had proven successful in 2009. "The ships that fall prey to the pirates are warned and counselled by the CMF in how to protect themselves. If they follow some simple procedures they can make themselves less attractive to piracy."

---

[16] Freep.com, January 12, 2012

[17] NNS, December 7, 2009.

With the spread of piracy across the Indian Ocean, but also West Africa, plus the deployment of naval ships and the trying of suspected pirates in German, American and other courts, there has been a distinct rise in media coverage of piracy. *The Financial Times* has tended to focus on the issue as an economic one, notably the impact of piracy on the shipping industry. Citing data from the International Maritime Bureau, it warned of record attacks against shipping in the months ahead leading into 2012.[18]

Other media coverage has focused on the rise of piracy in West Africa. In August, 2011, the *Christian Science Monitor* reported that there had been 15 reported pirate attacks off the coast of Benin in an area that witnessed just one attack between 2006 and 2010. In the most recent attack earlier that month, armed men boarded two Panamanian-registered ships. Italian- and Greek-owned diesel tankers were also targeted weeks earlier resulting in the killing of a Filipino seaman.[19]

As cited by the *Monitor*, Steven Jones, director of *Maritime Security Review*, maintained that this recent spate of attacks represented "a change of both scale and ferocity" of piracy in the Gulf of Guinea. "Gangs have boarded vessels in order to transfer oil from the tanker into their own small tanker vessels," he said, adding that in the past, attacks were largely motivated by "petty theft and pilferage." The pirates, he maintained, were believed to be Nigerian, perhaps from just one gang – and their push outwards toward Benin is believed to be a direct response to the successes of the Nigerian navy in their own territorial sea. He further noted that, unlike Somalia, where seafaring criminals demand ransoms for the people and goods they hold hostage, pirates in the Gulf of Guinea focus on stealing fuel, which they then sell for hefty sums on the black market.

The Nigerian fishing industry has been particularly devastated by piracy and other violence at sea. According to J. Peter Pham, director of the Michael S. Ansari Africa Centre, Nigerian fishermen, who represent a significant number of the employed for the country's poor, have suffered nearly 300 attacks between 2003 and 2008. While most West African countries are unable to police their waters, Nigeria has had some success in clamping down on piracy off its shores. This may be one reason why it is spreading to other areas where security is less effective. According to the *Monitor*, the International Maritime Organization is now working with countries in the region to create an integrated coast guard network to tackle piracy in West

[18] Financial Times, September 11, 2011.

[19] Paige McClanahan, *Piracy on the rise off West Africa's Coast*, Christian Science Monitor, August 4, 2011.

African waters. This concern regarding increased attacks against ships, particularly with regard to oil transports, is also increasingly reflected in Nigerian and other local press.

The trials of Somali pirates in the United States – the first since the American civil war – and in Germany – the first there in 400 years – have also shed light on the situation of piracy and counterpiracy efforts worldwide. Five Somali men were tried in 2010 in Norfolk, Virginia, charged with plundering, weapons possession and 12 other counts for their failed April 1 attack on a US Navy ship disguised to look like a cargo freighter. According to the *Associated Press*, they maintained that they were innocent fishermen who had been forced to help the pirates. In Hamburg, Germany, a court tried 10 Somali pirates accused of attacking the MS Taipan, 560 miles off the Somali coast. The Dutch Navy boarded the ship after a gunbattle and then handed the pirates over to Germany. According to *Agence France Presse*, the crew escaped harm by hiding in a "panic room." The newsgency further noted that decapitation used to be the punishment for pirates in the port city of Hamburg, but that now they faced a 15-year prison sentence instead.

While the trials have received ample press coverage, including by the BBC, VOA and other international broadcasters also transmitted on local Somali stations, some experts doubt that they will deter piracy. One comment cited by AFP, Ania Shortland, who studies piracy at the German Institute for Economic Research, suggested: "Spending three, five, even seven years in an European or American jail followed by political asylum – you can't do much better for a Somali man."

The successful release by Navy Seals of the two western aid hostages in late January 2012 unleashed a renewed flurry of debate about piracy in the media. But few sought to probe the real issues behind piracy as a growing world phenomenon. One CNN news commentator harped on them as being "thugs" while the term "pirate" appeared to be "too romantic."[20] Taking the issue out of context, there was little effort to explain why ordinary Somalis, many of them young illiterate men including former nomads, were resorting to piracy.

THE ROLE OF SOCIAL MEDIA AND TELECOMMUNICATIONS

But the role of the Internet, satellite and mobile phones coupled with more recent social media access in Somalia itself has meant that the pirates have been able to maintain close contact with the outside world. In many ways,

[20] CNN News, January 25, 2012.

Somalia remains one of the best connected countries in Africa. This has enabled the pirates to maintain close contacts with outside investors, but also maritime intelligence and insurance companies. Negotiations for ransoms and the release of hostages and ships are typically carried out by satellite phones or Skype and usually take three months to a year. (Skype data is more difficult for outside criminal investigators or intelligence organizations to penetrate). Contacts with the Somali diaspora are also close. Some diaspora constituents are closely involved with the organizing and coordination of hijackings, ransoms and payoffs in the United Kingdom, Canada, United States, Germany and elsewhere.

Pirate coordinators have become incredibly sophisticated even if the bulk of their cohorts are illiterate and uneducated local men from the mainland. Many pirate cartels are aware when and where ships will pass through or near their areas, whether they are travelling in convoy, what cargoes they are carrying and the size and nature of their crews.

The pirates also keep track of world events, notably which foreign nations are involved in the region with naval ships and the extent of their ability to prosecute or to crackdown on pirate activities. News or rumours of Russian and other naval forces killing suspected pirates or destroying mother ships with their crews left to fend for themselves have been reported on local airwaves. Whether such actions serve as a deterrent or threaten to make life more difficult for captured crews is not known. For the time being, it appears that keeping hostages alive makes good business sense, because they will not get paid if their wards are killed. Finally, pirates also monitor tribal and clan relations, because they themselves are sometimes hijacked by rival gangs. Recently, too, press reports have emerged of select authorities such as the government of Puntland or Somalia's Galmudug state conducting anti-piracy operations. Suspected pirates have been arrested and their weapons confiscated.[21]

The United Nations, which re-established an official presence in Mogadishu in late Janaury, 2012, also re-asserted to the media the need to clamp down on piracy but also to provide alternative sources of income and development among nomad or coastal communities with no other options. However, while security has allegedly improved in and around the Somali capital, no proper development can proceed until the country's horrendous security issues are resolved with rule of law and civil society effectively re-instated.

---

[21] Shabelle Media Network, Mogadishu. AllAfrica.com, December 28, 2011.

In early 2012, this writer tracked down no fewer than 20 Somali radio stations with Internet capabilities and website, some located in Somalia, Puntland and Somaliland, while others are being operated out of Switzerland, Canada and the United Kingdom. These include Radio Free Somalia, Radio Golis and Radio Lora, a Swiss-based webstation with music, news and re-broadcasts of the BBC and VOA. The radio stations provide regular coverage of pirate activities and international counter-measures. At the same time, there is a battle of the airwaves with stations struggling to cultivate audiences.

Most Somali-based stations are under operational restrictions by al-Shabaab, which forbids the broadcasting of music. Residents can now only hear music from the government-controlled station and a Kenyan-based radio station with an FM-transmitter in Mogadishu. Al-Shabaab also closed down BBC relay stations in five cities in southern Somalia, including the capital. The Islamists have sought to curb information content, including reports on the state of Somali piracy, which al-Shabaab has refused to condemn. The pirates are also known to be "taxed" by the insurgents who demand money in support of the "mujahideen" (holy warriors) of Somalia. Revenue from piracy has helped bolster local towns with shops full of goods and Internet cafes. Supplies provided to help captured seafarers also find their way into the local economy.

Twitter has also emerged as a key tool. The Kenyan military, which crossed into Somalia in October, 2011 in response to Somali kidnappings and killings of foreign tourists along the Swahili coast, began to use Twitter as a means of warning local populations of impending attacks and to intimidate Somali pirates, kidnappers, warlords and insurgents. Seeking to target those responsible for attacks on Kenyan soil, the Kenyan army made no distinction between who was a pirate and who an insurgent. This prompted a veritable Twitter war between the Kenyan army and al-Shabaab, an Islamist militant group reputed to have links with al-Qaeda.[22]

Despite posting more than 80 tweets in retaliation to the Kenyan military incursion since November, 2011, al Shabaab maintained that it would not respond to all. "Most comments are predictably ludicrous, irrational and uninspiring, and therefore do not warrant the time for a response," one of its tweets peevishly remarked. Most of its tweets are in English rather than Somali indicating that it is seeking to reach an international rather than a local audience. The al Shabaab tweets also prompted the US government to

[22] David Smith, The Guardian, December 13, 2011.

explore whether to shut down the organization's Twitter account given that Washington had outlawed it as a terrorist group in 2008.

Further sources of information regarding the situation within Somalia itself are provided by the few international humanitarian agencies able to operate on Somali soil, such as UNICEF and Médecins sans Frontières. The Office for the Coordination of Humanitarian Affairs (OCHA) regularly issues updates[23] (the Somali Situation Report) report based on on-the-ground observations by the aid groups. These help both the media and the international aid community to keep tabs on what is going on, including the impact of Somali pirate operations. These reports are regularly cited by Somali radio stations and other media.

An interesting new tool, particularly used by the international naval forces engaged in counter-piracy, has been YouTube. Even a cursory scan of the Internet reveals numerous videos of Russian, French, Dutch and other naval interventions against suspected pirates. One Russian video depicts the shelling and sinking of a pirate mother ship by naval guns. The ship receives a number of direct hits, bursts into flames and sinks. It is not clear whether members of the crew were still onboard. Nevertheless, the message is clear: this is what happens to pirates. And given that ordinary Somalis in the towns have access to the Internet, local media acknowledge that such YouTube videos are watched.

Over the past several years, there have been a number of international investigative television reportages into pirate activities. One Danish journalist contributed a dramatic, if not sensationalist, *ABC News 20/20*[24] report focused on Somalia's lawlessness but also how well-organized the pirates have become. Not only do the pirates have financiers, officers and soldiers, but they also have their own severe code of conduct. Furthermore, they are portrayed as contributors to the Somali economy.

International websites and travel advisories seek to keep merchant ships, cruise ships, independent yachtsmen and others updated on piracy in the Indian Ocean. These sites recommend when to travel and which shipping lanes to follow, and which organizations, including NATO, they need to remain in touch with. Even yacht race organizers are urged not to hold their regattas in high risk areas, such as the Persian Gulf. As part of the Volvo

---

[23] The Somalia Situation Report, OCHA http://ochaonline.un.org/somalia.

[24] ABC News, April 17, 2009.

Ocean Race, an armed ship had to transport five yachts through part of the Indian Ocean because of the piracy threat.[25]

Following the Chandlers' piracy incident, a BBC report[26] maintained that the British couple felt that they had not been adequately warned. In the Seychelles, where piracy has become a key concern, both the tourist board and local media ask visiting yachtsmen to be wary of proceeding toward the African coast in the western Indian Ocean or northwards toward Arabia, as piracy has now encroached into its own territorial waters. Over the past several years, local and international media have specifically highlighted the growth of piracy in the region. The Seychelles Maritime Safety Administration regularly stresses the need to be aware and specifically warned the Chandlers on at least two occasions to piracy risks associated with their planned journey. The Seychelles Radio Coast Station at Bon Espoir also provides ship-to-shore maritime communications alerts, so ships cannot claim not to have been informed.

Media coverage has specifically highlighted the roles of various naval forces in their actions against Somali and other pirates. But regional rivalries have also come into play between the Russian, Chinese and Indian navies. As pointed out by the South China Morning Post,[27] while there is a shared consensus to reduce conflict, there is also concern regarding mutual regional ambitions with different navies vying to accompany World Food Programme and other ships as part of their counter-piracy policies, but also vying for media coverage.

By late 2011, however, international media were reporting a rise in Somali piracy with 23 hijackings in the year so far, amid shipping industry warnings that the problem is worsening in the Indian Ocean. This was also because rains and rough seas during the Monsoon season between June and September make it harder for pirates to attack in small skiffs. Even if piracy worsens in 2012 and beyond, it is clear that informed reporting among local, regional and international media is crucial for keeping tabs on how the world community will counter piracy using a combination of security, and recovery and alternative income development initiatives.

---

[25] Financial Times, December 28, 2011.
[26] BBC World Service website, September 3, 2011.
[27] South China Morning Post, April 24, 2011.

IV. Law

15. CHALLENGES OF JURISDICTION AND PROSECUTION

Michael J. STEPEK[1]

Piracy is considered one of the first truly international crimes and has been governed by international law since the very inception of the concept. It is also one of only a few crimes considered a crime of universal jurisdiction such that any state is entitled to prosecute it. Universal jurisdiction allows a state to assert criminal jurisdiction over persons whose alleged criminal acts were committed outside the boundaries of the prosecuting state, regardless of nationality, country of residence, or any relation with the prosecuting country. A crime subject to universal jurisdiction is considered a crime against all, and accordingly any state is authorized to punish. The concept of universal jurisdiction is closely linked to the idea that certain international norms are *erga omnes*, or norms owed to the entire community. Under customary international law, two categories of crime are considered subject to universal jurisdiction: (1) piracy;[2] and (2) war crimes and crimes against humanity.

Given its long history and treatment under international law, one might reasonably expect that the legal infrastructure for addressing the crime of piracy would be well developed. Yet, if one looks at what is happening today, primarily in the Gulf of Aden and Indian Ocean, this is clearly not the case. Every day one reads stories about ships being hijacked and held for ransom together with their crews. In response, ship owners and operators have hired security personnel, trained crews to maneuver ships to avoid capture, and installed devices - of varying degrees of effectiveness - designed to repel pirates. In addition, national governments have contributed more and

---

[1] Michael Stepek is a partner in the London and Geneva offices of the international law firm of Akin, Gump, Strauss, Hauer & Feld LLC and Co-Chair of the Institute for Law & Development Policy in Geneva, Switzerland.

[2] Malcom N. Shaw, *International Law*, 593 (Fifth Edition Cambridge University Press) (2003) (citing *In re Piracy Jure Gentium* [1934] AC 586; 7 AD, p 213; D.H. Johnson, *Piracy in Modern International Law*, 43 Transactions of the Grotius Society, 1957, p 63; and G.E. White, *The Marshall Court and International Law: the Piracy Cases*, 83 AJIL, 1989, p 727. *See also* the Separate Opinion of Judge Guillaume in *Congo v. Belgium*, ICJ Reports, 2002, para 5) ("Universal jurisdiction over piracy has been accepted under international law for many centuries and constitutes a long-established principle of the world community.").

more naval resources to the area in an effort to prevent ships from being seized by pirates, and, when such efforts fail, to assist when one has been seized. The problem, however, persists and is actually becoming worse. Between January and June 2011 there were 177 reported attacks, of which 18 were successful. As of May 2011, 26 ships were held by pirates, with a total of 601 hostages.[3] The geographical area of the attacks extends to 2.8 million square miles in an area that is increasingly difficult for naval forces to patrol.[4] Even when naval forces are successful in detaining those suspected of piracy, it was estimated that by the end of 2010 ninety percent of pirates captured by national navies off the coast of Somalia had to be released because no one was prepared to prosecute them.[5]

This increasing problem is not caused by a lack of attention. Given the severity of the problem, attacks on shipping in the Gulf of Aden and the Indian Ocean are a recurring topic before the UN Security Council, and piracy is the subject of numerous Security Council resolutions. Beginning with Resolution 1816 (2008), the Security Council has considered the activities off the coast of Somalia as a threat to international peace and security and has repeatedly invoked Chapter VII in addressing the problem. In every resolution dealing with the issue, the Security Council expresses its continuing concern about the issue, emphasizes the importance of finding a comprehensive solution, commends those states that have amended their domestic law in order to criminalize piracy and facilitate prosecution, and notes its concern that other states have not yet done so.[6] Its second most recent iteration of these principles was in Resolution 2015 (2011), adopted by the Security Council on 24 October 2011 in which the Security Council also called upon the United Nations Office on Drugs and Crime (UNODC), United Nations Development Programme (UNDP), and other unnamed international partners to further their efforts to support the development of domestic legislation, agreements and mechanisms that would allow the

---

[3] S. C. Res. 306, S/2011/360 Annex I at ¶ 1, UN Doc. S/2011/360 (June 15, 2011).

[4] *Id.*

[5] UN Security Council Press Release 25 January 2011 SC/10164.

[6] For example, in Security Council Resolution 1976 (2011) 11 April 2011 S/RES/1976 (2011) ¶ 14, the Resolution recited: "Commending those States that have amended their domestic law in order to criminalize piracy and facilitate the prosecution of suspected pirates in their national courts, consistent with applicable international law, including human rights law, and stressing the need for States to continue their efforts in this regard," p 2; "Noting with concern at the same time that the domestic law of a number of States lacks provisions criminalizing piracy and/or procedural provisions for effective prosecution of suspected pirates;" p 2; "Urges all States, including States in the region, to criminalize piracy under their domestic law, emphasizing the importance of criminalizing incitement, facilitation, conspiracy and attempts to commit acts of piracy" ¶ 13.

effective prosecution, transfer and imprisonment of those apprehended and convicted.

Despite numerous general statements concerning the problem, and the clear need for a coordinated approach, few specific potential solutions have been identified, and only sporadic and overlapping efforts have been undertaken by various state, multi-state and non-state actors. One of the more specific efforts began in 2009, after the United Nations began, through the UNODC, a programme of assistance to states in the region to prosecute and imprison persons apprehended for attacks on shipping through the existing domestic court systems. In contrast to the use of existing courts, is the proposal to consider the establishment of specialized courts and prisons for Somali pirates both in Somalia and within other States in the region; this includes an extraterritorial specialized, anti-piracy court for Somalia, as referred to in the recommendations contained in the report of the Special Adviser to the Secretary-General on Legal Issues Related to Piracy off the Coast of Somalia.[7]

Whether or not these specific proposals and/or the general statements imploring individual states to amend their domestic law in order to criminalize piracy and facilitate prosecution of suspected pirates provide the correct solution, they must be reviewed in the context of how international law currently addresses the issue so that one can determine whether the international legal infrastructure needs to be improved upon. One hint of a potential problem derives from the nature of the law that defines it. Under customary international law, the crime of piracy is considered a breach of *jus cogens*,[8] the fundamental norms within the international community from which no derogation is permitted. Only piracy as defined by international law (piracy *jure gentium*), however, is subject to universal jurisdiction.[9] As will be discussed below, not every attack on shipping in the Gulf of Aden and Indian Ocean necessarily satisfies this definition. Further, even if one speaks only of acts defined in customary international law as piracy, not every state has invested its courts with universal jurisdiction with respect to this crime. States whose domestic laws grant their courts universal jurisdiction over acts of piracy include Australia, Belgium,[10] Canada, Denmark, Germany, Israel,

---

[7] S/2011/30 (2011).

[8] Yearbook of the ILC, 1966, vol. II, p. 248.

[9] Malcom N. Shaw, *International Law*, 593 (Fifth Edition Cambridge University Press) (2003).

[10] Belgium changed its universal jurisdiction law to an extraterritorial jurisdiction law that is similar to those of most other European countries in 2003 in response to international backlash against its exercise of universal jurisdiction and an unfavorable ruling by the International Court of Justice in the Case Concerning the Arrest Warrant of 11 April 2000 (*Democratic Republic of the Congo v. Belgium*). However, many cases continue under its previous laws.

Spain, and England.[11] Notably absent from this list, of course, are those countries from which modern day pirates tend to originate, and those nearer to where they ply their trade and which thus would have the greatest interest in eradicating the crime.

Accordingly, this chapter will briefly outline some of the challenges to jurisdiction over, and the successful prosecution of, attacks on shipping in the Gulf of Aden and Indian Ocean. It then discusses some of the efforts being taken to address the issue, and their potential for success given the underlying legal architecture. The chapter concludes with some thoughts on how these efforts might be improved.

I. CHALLENGES TO JURISDICTION AND SUCCESSFUL PROSECUTIONS AGAINST THOSE APPREHENDED FOR ATTACKS ON SHIPPING

Despite the size of the problem, and the ongoing efforts to eradicate it, there are several challenges to establishing jurisdiction over, and successfully prosecuting those apprehended for attacks on shipping. One of the principal challenges in this regard is that the international legal architecture relating to the problem is fractured in the sense that there is no single international instrument or source of international law that one can look to as a source of jurisdiction over, and proscription of, the various crimes associated with attacks on shipping, or the tools needed for the successful prosecution of them. Rather, there are several international instruments which address various issues, some of which were designed specifically for use in the context of attacks on shipping and some not. Moreover, these international legal instruments are intertwined with, and dependent upon, domestic legislation. Although this legal architecture identifies and sanctions multiple criminal acts associated with shipping, only the crime of piracy as defined in international law is subject to universal jurisdiction such that the other crimes need a jurisdictional nexus to the prosecuting state.

Additional challenges are presented by the practical challenges of investigating and collecting evidence for crimes with cross borders. Although some international legal architecture exists in this regard, it is not complete, or has not yet been implemented by ratifying states. Further, there is in some

[11] It should be noted that many of these countries have questioned their ability or the desirability of prosecuting suspected pirates under these laws, even while charging suspected perpetrators of crimes which are more controversially subject to universal jurisdiction, such as genocide. England, for example, has instructed its representatives not to capture suspected pirates of certain nationalities (Somalia being one), fearing that these individuals will be able to claim asylum under English law once on English soil for trial. To overcome this, the United Kingdom concluded an agreement with Kenya to the effect that any suspected pirates captured by a British ship that is authorized to do so will be transported to Kenya and tried there.

respects a lack of national will to take on the challenge of investigating, prosecuting and imprisoning those convicted of crimes which may have little to do with the countries being asked to undertake this burden. Each of these challenges are briefly discussed below.

A. The Current International Legal Architecture Concerning Piracy is Fractured

The current international legal architecture concerning acts of piracy has developed over time. Customary international law on the issue developed significantly at the beginning of the sixteenth and seventeenth centuries and continuing thereon, albeit with somewhat less urgency once the era of sailing vessels had come to an end, and naval warships at the time seemed to gain the upper hand. Given that the law of piracy developed at a time when the world was less complex, or at least one in which the states acting against piracy were protecting their own interests, it developed in response to those parameters as opposed to those parameters presented by the modern world and present day attacks on shipping off the coast of Somalia.

As will be seen below, the definition of the crime of piracy is not as broad as might generally be assumed from the colloquial use of the term. It is limited both by the specific nature of the act, its location, and the aim of the perpetrators. It also does not directly address conduct which is vital to the current flourish of attacks on shipping off the coast of Somalia, such as the financing of the perpetrators, nor does it address any of the modern practical legal issues that arise to challenge the prosecution of those apprehended. As a result, authorities looking for sources of international law to apply against conduct not directly addressed in the international law against piracy are generally referred to a series of international conventions that were designed to address other issues, and whose application to piracy is indirect, at best.

1. The Customary International Law Definition of Piracy as Reflected in HSC and UNCLOS

It is generally accepted by commentators today that the customary definition of piracy in international law is contained in Article 15 of the Geneva High Seas Convention of 1958 ("HSC") and reaffirmed in Article 101 of the United Nations Convention of the Law of the Sea of 1982

("UNCLOS").[12] Article 101 of UNCLOS (which is identical to Article 15 of the High Seas Convention) defines piracy as:

a) any illegal acts of violence or detention, or any act of depredation, committed for private ends by the crew or the passengers of a private ship or a private aircraft, and directed:

   i. on the high seas, against another ship or aircraft, or against persons or property on board such ship or aircraft;

   ii. against a ship, aircraft, persons or property in a place outside the jurisdiction of any State;

b) any act of voluntary participation in the operation of a ship of an aircraft with knowledge of facts making it a pirate ship or aircraft;

c) any act of inciting or of intentionally facilitating an act described in subparagraph (a) or (b).

Pursuant to this definition, piracy is comprised of: (i) an illegal act of violence or detention, (ii) undertaken for private ends, (iii) committed by the crew of one vessel against another vessel, and (iv) undertaken on the "high seas" or "in a place outside the jurisdiction of any state." Described as such, the definition has some potential limitations. Firstly, it is not clear what conduct is needed to determine the illegality of the act. Secondly, the definition requires "private ends," thereby potentially excluding acts committed for political motives. Thirdly, it requires two vessels, thereby excluding situations in which a crewmember or stowaway takes over a vessel from within. Finally, the definition requires that the act take place on the high seas, or in a place outside the jurisdiction of any state (*i.e. terra nullius*), thereby excluding acts that occur within a state's territorial waters, and also potentially excluding acts within a state's Exclusive Economic Zone ("EEZ")

---

[12] Although UNCLOS has been ratified by numerous countries, the High Seas Convention continues to be relevant for those states which have not. Eight states and the Holy See are not party to UNCLOS, but are party to the HSC: Afghanistan, Cambodia, the Holy See, the Islamic Republic of Iran, Israel, Malawi, Thailand, the United States, and Venezuela. Twenty-four states are parties to neither: Andorra, Azerbaijan, Bhutan, Burundi, Democratic People's Republic of Korea, Ecuador, El Salvador, Eritrea, Ethiopia, Kazakhstan, Kyrgystan, Libyan Arab Jamahiriya, Liechtenstein, Niger, Peru, Rwanda, San Marino, Syrian Arab Republic, Tajikistan, Timor-Leste, Turkey, Turkmenistan, United Arab Emirates, and Uzbekistan. *See generally*, Douglas Guilfoyle, *Treaty Jurisdiction over Pirates: A Compilation of Legal Texts with Introductory Notes*, p 4 para. 14 *available at* http://ucl.academia.edu/DouglasGuilfoyle/Papers/116803/Treaty_Jurisdiction_over_Pirates_A_Compilation_of_Legal_Texts_with_Introductory_Notes (hereinafter "Guilfoyle").

pursuant to Article 86 of UNCLOS, which *prima facie* excludes the EEZ from the high seas.[13]

None of these limitations are surprising given the historical context in which the customary international law of piracy evolved prior to its codification in the HSC and UNCLOS. In the *époque* of the sixteenth and seventeenth centuries, piracy was committed by ships of generally equal size to those of the naval vessels which would pursue them, in the search for gold, silver and other treasures as they were being transported from the new world to the old. Although there are historical incidents of such acts taking place in territorial waters, much of it occurred well outside them, or off the coast of land which was *terra nullius*, as legal concepts like EEZs did not yet exist, and large swaths of land existed that were not under the rule of any recognized sovereign.

In addition to codifying the customary international law on the crime of piracy, UNCLOS also codified the right of a military ship or aircraft to visit, inspect and seize any ship it has reasonable grounds to suspect of being engaged in piracy, as well as any suspected pirates. A pirate ship in this regard is defined as one intended "to be used for the purpose of committing one of the acts referred to in Article 101."[14] Accordingly, a military ship or aircraft has the right to arrest ships and persons intending future attacks. Whether this right to seize such ships and persons is coextensive with a violation of applicable law, however, is open to question as is discussed below. Finally, this right to visit, inspect and seize is also limited to the high seas, and does not extend into a state's territorial waters.[15]

Under international law, any state has jurisdiction to prosecute persons suspected of piracy found within their territory, regardless of any nexus between the state and the vessel, the victims or the pirates.[16] It is also possible that an act will violate the domestic law of a state based on that state's application of laws to its flagged vessels or citizens. For its part,

---

[13]Certain commentators disagree that this is the case. This line of thought points to Article 58(2) of UNCLOS which provides that: "Articles 88 to 115 and other pertinent rules of international law apply to the exclusive economic zone insofar as they are not incompatible with this Part." Under Article 56 of UNCLOS, coastal states enjoy sovereign rights for the purpose of exploring, exploiting, conserving and managing…natural resources" within the EEZ. Thus, it is not readily apparent that acts committed in an EEZ are *prima facie* excluded from the definition of piracy. *See generally*, Guilfoyle at p 2, paras. 6-7.

[14] UNCLOS Article 103.

[15] *See generally*, Guilfoyle at p 5.

[16] Ian Brownlie, *Principles of Public International Law*, 7th ed. (Oxford University Press 2008), at p 229. *See generally*, Guilfoyle at p 5.

UNCLOS provides for the seizing state to prosecute any suspected pirates.[17] It does not however, require that the seizing state do so.

2. Convention for the Suppression of Unlawful Acts Against the Safety of Maritime Navigation

Given the limitations posed by the definition of piracy in UNCLOS, other international conventions have been developed and agreed to address more contemporary iterations of the problem. Included in these are the Convention for the Suppression of Unlawful Acts Against the Safety of Maritime Navigation 1988 ("SUA Convention").[18] The SUA Convention arose from the *Achille Lauro* incident which exposed one of the limitations of the definition of piracy in the HSC and UNCLOS; namely, that the definition required that the act be committed by one ship against another. In 1985, the Italian cruise ship, the *Achille Lauro*, was captured by members of the Palestine Liberation Front off the coast of Egypt, and an American passenger was murdered. Given that the hijackers had boarded the ship before it left port, the attack did not fall within the definition of piracy and could not be prosecuted as such. Another relevant inspiration for the SUA Convention was General Assembly Resolution No. 40/61 which requested the International Maritime Organization ("IMO") to investigate the problem of terrorism aboard ships and to recommend measures to be taken to guard against this phenomenon, as at the time there was no such international convention that applied to the shipping industry. Its origins as such are not specifically directed against piracy. Rather, the SUA Convention was designed to be comprehensive in its prohibition of certain acts, avoiding arbitrary distinctions.[19]

For example, Article 3(1)(a) of the SUA Convention creates an offense which has particular relevance to the issue of piracy. It provides: "Any person commits an offence if that person unlawfully and intentionally: (a) seizes or exercises control over a ship by force or threat thereof or any other form of intimidation." This provision differs from the customary definition of piracy contained in UNCLOS and the HSC in that it does not require

---

[17] Article 105 states:

> On the high seas, or any other place outside the jurisdiction of any State, every State may seize a pirate ship or aircraft, or a ship or aircraft taken by piracy and under control of pirates, and arrest the persons and seize the property on board. The courts of said State which carried out the seizure may decide upon the penalties to be imposed, and may also determine the action to be taken with regard to the ships, aircraft or property, subject to the rights of third parties acting in good faith.

This is identical wording to Article 9 of the High Seas Convention.

[18] 1678 UNTS 221. 152 states are signatory to the SUA Convention as of 2 September 2011.

[19] *See generally*, Guilfoyle at pp 12 - 13.

"private ends," nor that it involve two ships - in other words, under the SUA Convention internal hijackings are covered.[20] The remaining provisions in Article 3 further delineate other, various acts of violence against shipping that qualify for prosecution. Moreover, under the SUA Convention, a person is considered as having committed an offence if the person attempts or abets any of the offenses in Article 3.[21] Further, there is no requirement that the offending act take place on the high seas. Rather, the SUA Convention applies to all ships that navigate or are scheduled to navigate outside the territorial sea of a single state.[22] Thus, the convention has wide application to acts taken against ships except in circumstances where a ship is not scheduled to navigate outside of the territorial seas of a single state.[23]

The SUA Convention also goes further than UNCLOS in that it obligates states to assert jurisdiction over the offenses in its Article 3. Under Article 6 of the SUA Convention, states have an obligation to take measures to establish jurisdiction over such offences by the flag state of the victimized ship, the state in the territory the event took place, including its territorial waters, or the state of citizenship of the person who committed the offence.[24] It also authorizes other states to assert jurisdiction if the act is committed by a stateless person whose residence is in that state, the nationality of any victim, or if the act is directed at a state itself.[25] Further, states must take jurisdiction of any alleged offender found in its territory if it does not extradite that person to any other state which would have jurisdiction under the convention. Article 8 of the convention further provides for the delivery of suspects to the nearest port.[26] In turn, a receiving state has an obligation to accept delivery of such suspects, unless it has grounds that the convention is

[20] *But see contra* Bahar, *Attaining Optimal Deterrence at Sea: A Legal and Strategic Theory for Naval Anti-Piracy Operations*, 40 Vanderbilt Journal of Transnational Law 1, at p 31-32 (2007).

[21] SUA Convention article 3(2): "Any person commits an offence if that person: (a) attempts to commit any of the offences set forth in paragraph 1; or (b) abets the commission of any of the offences set forth in paragraph 1 perpetrated by any person or is otherwise an accomplice of a person who commits such an offence."

[22] Article 4 provides:

1. This Convention applies if the ship is navigating or is scheduled to navigate into, through or from waters beyond the outer limit of the territorial sea of a single State, or the lateral limits of its territorial sea with adjacent States.
2. In cases where the Convention does not apply pursuant to paragraph 1, it nevertheless applies when the offender or the alleged offender is found in the territory of a State Party other than the State referred to in paragraph 1.

[23] *See Generally*, Guilfoyle at p 13.

[24] *Id.* at Article 6. *See also*, Treves, *Piracy, Law of the Sea, and Use of Force: Development off the Coast of Somalia*, 20 European Journal of International Law 399, at p 410 (2009).

[25] *Id.* at Article 6.2.

[26] Article 8.

not applicable to the acts giving rise to delivery.[27] Thus, once a state finds a suspect within its territory, whether by delivery to one of its ports as described above or otherwise, it must either extradite the suspect to a relevant jurisdiction for prosecution, or submit the case to its own local prosecutors.[28]

3. International Convention Against the Taking of Hostages

One of the unique aspects of piracy off the coast of Somalia is the apparent economic model for the criminal activity. Unlike piracy in other times and locations, piracy off the coast of Somalia involves the seizure of commercial vessels in order to hold it and its crew for ransom. Accordingly, another international convention that contains provisions potentially relevant to piracy off the coast of Somalia is the 1979 International Convention Against the Taking of Hostages ("ICTH") which has been ratified by 167 states. Article 1 of the ICTH requires states to criminalize the taking or attempted taking of hostages, without regard to the situation in which it occurs.[29] Article 1 defines the offense as follows:

> 1. Any person who seizes or detains and threatens to kill, to injure or to continue to detain another person in order to compel a third party, namely, a State, an international intergovernmental organization, a natural or juridical person, or a group of persons, to do or abstaining from doing any act as an explicit or implicit condition for the release of the hostage commits the offence of taking of hostages.
>
> 2. Any person who:
>
> a) Attempts to commit an act of hostage-taking, or
>
> b) Participates as an accomplice of anyone who commits or attempts to commit an act of hostage-taking likewise commits an offence for the purposes of this Convention.

ICTH further requires the signatory states to cooperate in the preventions of such offenses by, among other things, exchanging information to prevent the taking of hostages. It also obligates signatory states to take such measures as to establish jurisdiction over any offenses: (1) in its territory or on board a

---

[27] *Id*; *See generally*, Guilfoyle at p 18.

[28] The SUA Convention Article 10(1) provides: "The State Party in the territory of which the offender or the alleged offender is found shall, in cases to which article 6 applies, if it does not extradite him, be obliged, without exception whatsoever and whether or not the offence was committed in its territory, to submit the case without delay to its competent authorities for the purpose of prosecution, through proceedings in accordance with the law of that State."

[29] United Nations, Treaty Series vol. 1316 at p 205.

ship or aircraft registered in that state; (2) by any nationals of the state or those who have habitual residence there; (3) by any state which the act is to compel to do or abstain from doing any act; or (4) if the hostage is a national of that state. Further, it obligates states to establish jurisdiction over the offenses in cases where the alleged offender is present in its territory and the state does not extradite the suspect to another state that would have jurisdiction.

4. The UN Convention against Transnational Organized Crime

The UN Convention on Transnational Organized Crime ("TOC Convention") also contains offenses which could be potentially relevant to acts of piracy, despite the fact that it has its origins in the prevention of trafficking of women and children, the illicit manufacture and trafficking of firearms and transporting migrants by sea. Article 5 of the TOC Convention criminalizes participation in a criminal group, and as such mandates state parties to criminalize either or both of: (1) the agreement between one or more other persons to commit a serious crime for a purpose relating directly or indirectly to obtaining financial or other material benefit; or (2) conduct by which a person who takes an active part in criminal activities of the group or other activities knowing that it will contribute to the criminal aim. The TOC Convention further mandates the criminalization of aiding and abetting the commission of a serious crime involving an organized criminal group. An organized criminal group is defined in the TOC Convention as "a structured group of three or more persons, existing for a period of time and acting in concert with the aim of committing one or more serious crimes or offenses established in accordance with this Convention, in order to obtain, directly or indirectly a financial or other material benefit." The term "structured group" is itself defined as "a group that is not randomly formed for the immediate commission of an offense and that does not need to have formally defined roles for its members, continuity of its membership or a developed structure." As such, the TOC Convention has the potential to address the larger organization of persons who support and foster the criminal acts at sea.

Additionally, Article 6 of the TOC Convention mandates criminalization of the laundering of the proceeds of crime, and thus has the potential to address the financing of piracy. It includes in this mandate a fairly standard clause criminalizing the conversion or transfer of property with knowledge that it is the proceeds of crime for the purpose of concealing its origin or movement, as well as conspiracies, attempts, aiding or abetting or counseling the commission of such crimes to the extent allowed under national law.

Jurisdiction under the TOC Convention is to be established when the offense is committed within the state, or on board a vessel flying the flag of the state. Jurisdiction may also be established if the offense: (a) is committed against a national of that state; (b) is committed by a national of that state or by a stateless person having his or her habitual residence in its territory; or (c) the offense is either one established in accordance with Articles 5 or 6, with the exception of acts taken in conspiracy, aiding, abetting or counseling crimes in Article 6 which are excluded from this extended jurisdiction.

Finally, this convention contains numerous provisions that relate to cooperation in terms of obtaining evidence and prosecution. It contains an extensive regime calling on ratifying states to provide mutual legal assistance to other states at their request, which request cannot be declined without reason or for fiscal reason. It provides a general framework for joint investigations, special investigative techniques such as electronic surveillance, and cooperation between and among different law enforcement agencies. In an effort to assist prosecutions, it provides a framework for establishing an accused person's criminal record, the transfer of proceedings between jurisdictions, the transfer of sentenced person and the criminalization of the obstruction of justice.

5. International Convention for the Suppression of the Financing of Terrorism

To the extent that an act falls within the ambit of either the SUA Convention, or the ICTH, then the International Convention for the Suppression of the Financing of Terrorism also would have potential applicability to piracy, particularly in relation to its financing ("SFT Convention"). This convention is derivative of nine other international conventions including the two listed above, and mandates ratifying states to prohibit persons from directly or indirectly providing or collecting funds with the intention or knowledge: (a) that they be used to carry out an offense under one of the other conventions listed; or (b) any other act intended to cause death or serious bodily injury to a civilian or noncombatant with the purpose of intimidating a population or compelling a government to act. Attempts to do the same are likewise prohibited, as are those acting as accomplices, directors or participating in a group with a common purpose to commit an offense as described above.

Jurisdiction over such offenses is to be established when the offense is committed within the territory of the state, on board a vessel flying the flag of that state, or by a national of that state. Optional jurisdiction can also be established when the offense is directed against a national of that state, the state itself or government facility thereof, to compel the state to do or abstain from doing any act, or the offense is committed by a stateless person who has a habitual residence in the territory of the state or an aircraft operated by that state. The provisions of this convention do not apply where the offense is committed within a single state, the alleged offender is a national of the same state and is present in its territory, and no other state has a basis to exercise jurisdiction under the convention.

These then are the sources of international law which are most likely to provide support for the prosecution of those apprehended for attacking shipping off the coast of Somalia. In each case, regardless of whether the convention itself defines the proscribed act, successful prosecutions depend on domestic legislation as applied in national courts. As with the international legal instruments, this legal architecture is fractured.

B. The International Legal Architecture is Intertwined with and Dependent Upon Domestic Law

As we have seen from the above description of the various potentially applicable international conventions, there are numerous international legal concepts that must be incorporated into domestic law and reconciled with the existing constitutional and/or existing legal structure of the prosecuting country, notwithstanding the universal jurisdiction of any state over the crime of piracy. Unfortunately, to take as an illustration the situation off the coast of Somalia today, there is no country in the region that has incorporated all of the applicable provisions noted above into their domestic legislation. At best, countries have adopted provisions against the specific crime of piracy into their maritime legislation, but they rarely go beyond the accepted definition included in UNCLOS, and may not criminalize all the various acts and actors in an attack on shipping off the coast of Somalia. Even prosecutions for the crime of piracy itself, while recognized internationally, can face unforeseen challenges when pursued at the domestic level.

Kenya's prominent role in prosecuting suspected pirates detained off the coast of Somalia provides a good example of the complexity involved in incorporating the international legal architecture into its domestic law. Unlike many of the littoral states of the Indian Ocean, Kenya signed and ratified all of the multilateral conventions identified above as providing potentially useful provisions in the prosecution of piracy cases. It had also included the crime of piracy in its Penal Code. It had not, however, identified what acts had to have been committed in order to be charged with the crime beyond what is provided in UNCLOS. Although this did not stop a Kenyan court from convicting the first seven pirates who came before it,[30] it concerned the Parliament sufficiently such that it passed a new act addressing piracy in the form of the Merchant Shipping Act on 1 September 2009. This act repealed the previous definition of piracy in the Penal Code and replaced it, together with a definition of armed robbery, with a near reproduction of the crimes as contained in both UNCLOS and the SUA Convention.

Unfortunately, the enactment of a new law does not apply automatically to all those awaiting trial in Kenya, unless the charges are amended. This situation occurred in the case of nine suspected pirates apprehended in March 2009 after having attempted to board the German cargo ship *MV Courier*. The case was fixed for trial on October 22, 2009, but before it got to trial, the defendants made an application contesting the court's jurisdiction through a request for proceedings on an Order of Prohibition that would prevent prosecution. The defendants' theory was that the court did not have jurisdiction pursuant to Article 69 of the Penal Code given that no citizen or property of Kenya was involved, and because the arrest had been made on the high seas by the German Navy, taking part in operations in the Gulf of Aden. These facts, said the defendants, precluded liability under section 5 of the Penal Code which was limited to Kenya's territorial waters. In a ruling on the issue dated 9 November 2011, the court agreed and ordered release of the nine defendants.[31] The ruling is on appeal, and as of this writing had yet to be decided.

This situation is not to be taken as a criticism of the Kenyan court system. Other national court systems have grappled with these issues and struggled as well. In a pair of rulings in the United States, the courts reached opposite conclusions as to whether similar factual scenarios in which alleged pirates fired at US naval vessels, but who never boarded a third ship, constituted piracy or not. The crime of piracy under US law is not defined explicitly in a statute, but by reference to the law of nations.[32] In a decision dated August 17, 2010 a court held that an act of violence alone could not constitute piracy and dismissed the count.[33] Two months later, a second US court in the same district found that such conduct could constitute piracy, and the defendants

[30] The lack of a definition of the crime was the subject of an appeal against the initial conviction. The subsequent ruling on this appeal upheld the conviction on the basis that the crime, although not defined in the Kenyan Penal Code, was defined in UNCLOS. Hassan M. Ahmed v. Republic of Kenya, [2010] eKLR. *See generally,* Bahadur, *Pirate Law 101, A Short History of Kenya's Pirate Prosecutions*, December 10, 2011 Somalia Report, http://somaliareport.com/index.php/post/2263/Pirate_Law.

[31] *In re Mohamud Hashi and 8 others* [2010] eKLR.

[32] 18 U.S.C. § 1651.

[33] *United States v. Said*, 757 F. Supp. 2d 554, at 567 (E.D. Va 2010).

were convicted.[34] Both cases are currently on appeal to the United States Court of Appeals for the Fourth Circuit.

The above cases illustrate some of the problems in relation to the crime of piracy as defined in UNCLOS. The situation becomes even more problematic, however, for crimes related to piracy that would rely on one of the other international conventions which has been designed to address problems other than attacks on shipping. The organization and financing of piracy is a useful example of these additional challenges. Piracy is not undertaken spontaneously, nor is it cost free. Although the basic tools for a near shore attempt may not be beyond the means of ordinary fishermen, the logistical requirements required for the longer-range attacks beg the question as to who provides the financing for them.

There certainly is sufficient money to be gained from the attacks to warrant interest from unscrupulous persons. In a special report in 2011, the Financial Action Task Force ("FATF"), an independent, inter-governmental body that develops and promotes policies to protect the global financial system against money laundering and terrorist financing, found what appeared to be three basic means of financing piracy for ransom: (1) a single funder for the whole operation; (2) a shareholder or cooperative structure in which individual pirates invest in the operation and share the proceeds; and (3) a syndicate or committee structure formed by several investors similar to those employed in conventional organized crime.[35] The same report estimated the practice to be highly lucrative, estimating that the total ransom money paid to Somali pirates in the years from 2006 to 2010 totaled US$ 180 million, with individual ransom payments in excess of US$ 9.2 million in 2010.[36] With this amount of money at stake, and with the organizational similarities to conventional organized crime, the flow of financing should be a prime target for anti-piracy efforts.

This is perhaps particularly so given the relatively large supply of young men who may face limited economic opportunity in their home country. If one accepts this as true, then they can be easily replaced should they be captured or killed in an assault. Thus, a far more productive approach to the problem would be to focus on the senior persons in the organizations. These persons are not likely to set to sea in a small boat where they could be apprehended by the navies patrolling the Gulf of Aden or Indian Ocean.

[34] *United States v. Hasan*, 747 F. Supp. 2d 599, at 640-642 (E.D. Va 2010).

[35] Financial Action Task Force, *Organized Maritime Piracy and Related Kidnapping for Ransom*, p 17 (2011).

[36] *Id.* at p 18 (2011).

These are the persons who stay on shore, and thus are outside the range of arrest unless they are in a state that has legislation which would outlaw the specific acts they undertake, and a government which could undertake to arrest them.

This aspect of piracy is potentially covered by the SFT Convention, but as with UNCLOS, the SUA Convention, and the other multilateral conventions, there is no consensus on this, and not all countries which have ratified this convention have clear domestic legislation applying the provisions. For example, although Kenya is a signatory to the SFT Convention it has no specific legislation enacting it into domestic law; rather its provisions are covered, to varying degrees, by a plethora of existing provisions in Kenya's Penal Code which a prosecutor would have to argue are applicable to any given instance of pirate financing. Other countries in the region fare no better. For example, the Maldives is also a signatory to the SFT Convention. In a report on its observance of standards and codes for anti-money laundering and combating of the financing of terrorism released just recently, the International Monetary Fund found that it suffered from several deficiencies.[37] Although the Maldives has criminalized money laundering, it only does so with respect to proceeds of offenses listed in its Drugs Act. The provision of finance and property for the commission of a terrorist act only constitutes aiding and abetting the commission of the underlying act. There are no laws or procedures in place to freeze terrorist funds or assets of persons in line with UN Security Council resolutions.

Once again, this is not to criticize the Maldives unnecessarily. It is simply used as an example to illustrate that although the international legal architecture may include provisions against the various offenses involved in the crime of piracy or other illegal acts of violence against merchant shipping, these provisions must still flow through national legislation which may or may not effectively carry out their purpose. To the extent that the various provisions in the international legal architecture themselves come from several different conventions dealing primarily with other issues than piracy, it becomes exponentially more difficult.

Moreover, relying on domestic law alone for criminalizing the act faces a substantial cross border problem in that an organization leader who takes acts which might be prosecutable in one state, but who is located in another state where the acts are not prosecutable will likely be outside the reach of the first

---

[37] International Monetary Fund, *Maldives: Report on Observance of Standards and Codes – FATF Recommendations for Anti-Money Laundering and Combating the Financing of Terrorism*, IMF Country Report 12/2.

state, barring any extradition treaty between them. The harmonization of domestic legal provisions, and laws providing a method by which these persons are within reach of the prosecuting authorities, is a function of a well designed multilateral convention. Yet, if the multilateral convention does not itself clearly address the issues, there is little hope that the confusion can be cleared up through each state's expression of its criminal laws.

C. Universal Jurisdiction is Limited to Piracy As Defined by Customary International Law and UNCLOS

In addition to the definition of the crime of piracy, issues of jurisdiction also present challenges to successful prosecutions as well. Although much is written about the universal jurisdiction over the crime of piracy, universal jurisdiction only extends to acts falling within the customary international law definition of this crime. Thus, attacks on shipping in Somali territorial waters are not subject to such jurisdiction. Moreover, other crimes which are committed in relation to an attack on shipping require jurisdiction pursuant to the other international conventions identified above. Almost invariably, these require some nexus to the prosecuting state. This issue is being addressed at both the international and domestic levels.

At the international level, the UN Security Council has, in effect, extended the crime of piracy to cover the territorial waters of Somalia. As discussed above, the international legal architecture provides for interdiction of pirates on the high seas under UNCLOS, but it does not allow the military of one state the right to interdict pirates in the territorial waters of another sovereign state. This situation may work fine when the sovereign, in whose territorial waters piracy occurs or to which pirates return, has the capacity to arrest and prosecute them, but a problem arises when it does not. Somalia of course faces this very problem as it has very little such capacity on land, and almost none at sea.

In order to fill the enforcement vacuum in Somali territorial waters, the Security Council has passed resolutions under Chapter VII of the UN Charter permitting third states to enter Somali territorial waters to repress piracy and armed robbery at sea, including but not limited to boarding, searching, and seizing vessels engaged in or suspected of engaging in acts of piracy, and to apprehending persons engaged in such acts with a view to such persons being prosecuted. For example, in Security Council Resolution 1916, the Security Council:

> Decides that for a period of six months from the date of this resolution, States cooperating with the TFG in the fight against piracy and armed

robbery at sea off the coast of Somalia, for which advance notification has been provided by the TFG to the Secretary-General, may:

(a) Enter the territorial waters of Somalia for the purpose of repressing acts of piracy and armed robbery at sea, in a manner consistent with such action permitted on the high seas with respect to piracy under relevant international law; and

(b) Use, within the territorial waters of Somalia, in a manner consistent with action permitted on the high seas with respect to piracy under relevant international law, all necessary means to repress acts of piracy and armed robbery.[38]

The Security Council resolutions authorizing entrance into Somali territorial waters were passed upon the request of the Somali Transitional Federal Government ("TFG"), and they are careful to recognize the sovereignty and territorial integrity of Somalia over its territorial waters.[39] Resolution 1816, and each resolution since, states that its contents are not intended to create customary international law and instead are limited to the circumstances in Somalia.[40]

The Security Council thereafter further extended its authorization to states to enter the Somali mainland with the same goal in mind. Whereas previous resolutions specifically defined the *ratione loci* to Somali territorial waters, Resolution 1851 specifically refers to taking appropriate measures in

---

[38] *E.g.* S/Res/1816 (2008). *See also*, S/Res/1846 (2008); , S/Res/1851 (2008); S/Res/1897 (2009);, S/Res/1950 (2010); S/Res/2020 (2011).

[39] S/Res/1976 (2011) p 1: "Reaffirming its respect for the sovereignty, territorial integrity, political independence and unity of Somalia."

[40] *See, e.g.*, Resolution 1897 (2009) 30 November 2009 ¶ 8:
Affirms that the authorizations renewed in this resolution apply only with the respect to the situation in Somalia and shall not affect the rights and obligations or responsibilities of Member States under international law, including any rights or obligations under the Convention [the United Nations Convention on the Law of the Sea of 10 December 1982], with respect to any other situation, and underscores in particular that this resolution shall not be considered as establishing customary international law; and *affirms further* that such authorizations have been renewed only following the receipt of the 2 and 6 of November 2009 letters convening the consent of the TFG.
Resolution 1950 (2010) 23 November 2010 ¶ 8: *Affirms* that the authorizations renewed in this resolution apply only with respect to the situation in Somalia and shall not affect the rights or obligations or responsibilities of Member States under international law, including any rights or obligations, under the Convention, with respect to any other situation, and underscores in particular that this resolution shall not be considered as establishing customary international law; and *affirms further* that such authorizations have been renewed only following the receipt of the 20 October 2010 letter convening the consent of the TFG.

Somalia.[41] This provision followed the incursion of French Special Forces onto the mainland in order to capture six of the pirates that had attached the French-flagged commercial sailing yacht *Le Ponant*.

This grant of access by the Security Council and TFG may cover, for the time being, an ambiguity that could impact third states' ability to exercise jurisdiction over crimes committed in attacks on shipping once the grant of access expires or is withdrawn, given that there is an existing ambiguity over the demarcation of the Somali territorial sea. In 1972, Somalia passed a law established a territorial sea of 200 miles.[42] It subsequently ratified UNCLOS on 24 July 1989, which assumes twelve miles as the maximum width for the territorial sea. Notwithstanding its ratification of UNCLOS, it is not clear whether it ever repealed its 1972 domestic legislation. As a result, the extent of Somalia's territorial sea is not entirely clear. The Security Council's resolutions authorizing access to Somalia's territorial seas to repress piracy and armed robbery as if they were on the high seas avoids the issue for the time being. Should the Security Council, however, choose not to renew its resolutions in such regard, or the TPG withdraw its support for them, there arguably will be confusion as to just where the Somalia territorial sea ends, and where universal jurisdiction begins. Fortunately, for the time being at least, the Security Council and the TFG have sidelined this particular issue by extending the grant of access to Somalia's territorial seas for an additional 12 months until November 2012.[43]

At the domestic level, individual states are also addressing the challenges posed to prosecution by jurisdictional issues. For example, Kenya's new Merchant Shipping Act has addressed this by including in its terms a specific jurisdictional provision that provides for jurisdiction over acts of violence against ships in a manner similar to the SUA Convention.[44] It provides that any person who: (1) seizes a ship or exercises control over it; (2)

[41] S/Res/1851 (2008) at p 3 para. 6: In response to the letter from the TFG of 9 December 2008, encourages Member States to continue to cooperate with the TFG in the fight against piracy and armed robbery at sea, notes the primary role of the TFG in rooting out piracy and armed robbery at sea, and decides that for a period of twelve months from the date of adoption of resolution 1846, States and regional organizations cooperating in the fight against piracy and armed robbery at sea off the coast of Somalia for which advance notification has been provided by the TFG to the Secretary-General may undertake all necessary measures that are appropriate in Somalia, for the purpose of suppressing acts of piracy and armed robbery at sea, pursuant to the request of the TFG, provided, however, that any measures undertaken pursuant to the authority of this paragraph shall be undertaken consistent with applicable international humanitarian and human rights law.

[42] *Law on the Somalia Territorial Sea and Ports 1972*, available at http://faolex.fao.org/docs/pdf/som4925.pdf

[43] S/Res./2020 (2011).

[44] It also specifically defines the act of piracy in accordance with UNCLOS. The Merchant Shipping Act, 2009 at Article 369.

intentionally destroys or damages a ship or its cargo; (3) commits acts of violence likely to endanger its navigation; or (4) places any device on it which is likely to destroy it or damage its cargo, falls within the new law regardless whether the ship is in Kenya or elsewhere, whether the act takes place in Kenya, and whatever the nationality of the person committing the act.[45] This jurisdictional provision goes further than the SUA Convention in that the SUA Convention generally provides for jurisdiction of such acts in instances where they take place in the prosecuting jurisdiction either by being on one of its flagged vessels or in its territorial waters, or by a national of that state.[46] Given the scope of jurisdiction in the new law, its consistency with Kenyan and international law has been questioned by at least one Kenyan commentator.[47]

Indeed, the extension of extra-territorial jurisdiction by any state to criminal acts with no nexus to it raises issues of international law particularly when there is no customary international law providing for universal jurisdiction of the acts proscribed. Bear in mind that the new Kenyan Merchant Maritime Act, and others which might follow its lead, extends its extraterritorial jurisdiction beyond piracy as defined by customary international law. It extends this jurisdiction to those acts which fit the definition of armed robbery at sea as well. Whether Kenya or any other state can exercise such authority consistent with international law, or whether it should do so, is open to question and thorough analysis. One potential check on this broad assertion of extraterritorial jurisdiction to be considered, of course, is that of international comity. To the extent that countries impose their criminal law over defendants with no nexus to them, those countries expose their citizens to being treated in the same manner by other countries. Principles of international comity may partly explain why other states have not yet extended the principle of extraterritorial criminal jurisdiction in terms of maritime security as far as Kenya at present.

---

[45] *Id.*, at Article 370(1), (2) and (4).

[46] The SUA Convention Article 6 provides:

1. Each State Party shall take such measures as may be necessary to establish its jurisdiction over the offences set forth in article 3 when the offence is committed:
a. against or on board a ship flying the flag of the State at the time the offence is committed; or
b. in the territory of that State, including its territorial sea; or
c. by a national of that state.
2. A State Party may also establish its jurisdiction over any such offence when:
a. It is committed by a stateless person whose habitual residence is in that State; or
b. During its commission a national of that State is seized, threatened, injured, or killed; or
c. It is committed in an attempt to compel that State to do or abstain from doing any act.

[47] *See* Gathii, *Jurisdiction to Prosecute Non-National Pirates Captured by Third States Under Kenyan and International Law*, Loyola L.A. Int'l & Comparative Law Rev. Vol. 31:363 (2009)

D. Although The International Legal Architecture Addresses Some of the Challenges in Investigating and Collecting Evidence for Prosecutions, These Provision are Neither Complete nor Have They Been Implemented by All Ratifying States.

Given that the arrest of suspected pirates is being carried out by the navies of various countries and the prosecution of those apprehended typically is being undertaken elsewhere, there are substantial challenges posed by the collection of evidence and the transmission of it to the prosecuting authorities. Naval officers are not trained as criminal investigators, nor are they necessarily aware of what steps need to be taken in order to ensure that the evidence collected is legally admissible in the prosecuting state's courts. Without admissible evidence, of course, there can be no successful prosecution even if one were to get beyond the other challenges outlined above. These practical problems are evident in the statistics concerning the rate of transfer from apprehending navies to prosecuting authorities. Of a total of 286 reported attacks in 2011, only four resulted in the transfer of persons in their custody to a regional state for prosecution.[48]

Given its importance, this issue has received some attention at the international level. The first UN Security Council Resolution authorizing third party states access to Somali territorial waters to repress piracy called upon all states, in particular flag, port and coastal states, states of the nationality of victims and perpetrators of piracy or armed robbery at sea, and other states with jurisdiction under either international law or national law to cooperate in the investigation and prosecution of those apprehended in a manner consistent with international human rights law.[49] This resolution was supplemented a year later, given the Security Council's concern with the dramatic increase in the incidents of piracy and armed robbery at sea, by the threat to ships bringing humanitarian aid to Somalia, and the greater sophistication, daring and geographic expansion of attacks.[50] The Security Council specifically noted the lack of capacity, domestic legislation and clarity about how to dispose of pirates after capture had hindered more robust action and sometimes led to the release of those apprehended without prosecution. It addressed this concern by inviting all states and regional organizations fighting piracy off the coast of Somalia to facilitate the investigation and prosecution of those detained by concluding special agreements, or arrangements with countries willing to take custody of pirates

---

[48] S/2012/50 at p 3.
[49] S/Res./1816 (2008) at p 3 paragraph 11.
[50] S/Res./1850 at second preambular paragraph.

in order to put the latter's law enforcement officials on the seizing ship.[51] These "shipriders" were to come particularly from countries in the region, and hopefully would help ease the transition of the investigation and collection of evidence on the scene to the prosecuting authorities.[52]

Other efforts in this regard have also been made. In particular, at a sub-regional meeting organized by the IMO and held in Djibouti in January 2009 to discuss the protection of vital shipping lanes, the IMO adopted a resolution urging participant governments to implement a code of conduct concerning the repression of piracy and armed robbery against ships in the western Indian Ocean and the Gulf of Aden (the Djibouti Code of Conduct), and to designate a national focal point to coordinate timely and effective information flow among participants. In several substantive provisions, the Djibouti Code of Conduct largely follows the provisions of UNCLOS. It defines piracy in the same terms as UNCLOS, and it further addresses the concept of "armed robbery" in Article 2.[53] Relying on these international legal provisions, the code of conduct puts a focus on regional efforts to address the problem. Its Article 7 also addresses the issue of shipriders which are referred to as "embarked officers."

Despite the Security Council's encouragement, and the Djibouti Code having specifically included the posting of domestic law enforcement officers on naval ships in its provisions, the use of shipriders or "embarked officers" does not appear to have gained widespread use such that the challenge can be said to have been met. For example, in response to a letter dated 27 April 2011 from the United Kingdom's Foreign Secretary to the Foreign Affairs Committee of Parliament, MP Henry Bellingam, responded with written testimony to questions the letter posed in relation to piracy off the coast of Somalia. In it he reported that:

> The UK continues to encourage regional states to deploy shipriders on warships in the Indian Ocean, not least in order to simplify questions of jurisdiction (the shipriders can

---

[51] Id. at p 2 paragraph 3.

[52] It further encouraged all states and regional organizations to consider creating a centre in the region to coordinate information relevant to piracy and armed robbery at sea, and to increase regional capacity with assistance from the UNODC to implement both the SUA Convention and the TOC Convention in order to effectively investigate and prosecute piracy. S/Res/1851 16 December 2008, at paragraph 5.

[53] It defines armed robbery as: "(a) unlawful act of violence or detention or any act of depredation, or threat thereof, other than an act of piracy, committed for private ends and directed against a ship or against persons or property on board such a ship, within a State's internal waters, archipelagic waters and territorial sea" or "(b) any act of inciting or of intentionally facilitating an act described in subparagraph (a)."

> assume jurisdiction on behalf of the regional state from the outset), but regional states so far remain non-committal, including due to continuing gaps in prison capacity until such a time as post-trial transfer to Somali prisons becomes a reality.[54]

Notwithstanding the success *vel non* of shipriders, none of the international conventions fully address the practical issues of the collection and transmission of evidence. To be sure, these issues perhaps are not the most interesting when it comes to discussions of international law, but they have very real consequences on the successful prosecution of those accused. Despite the practical nature of this challenge, international law can serve a useful function in helping to harmonize or provide order to the issues. These types of issues are often addressed in bilateral mutual legal assistance treaties, although there also are some multilateral treaties that deal primarily with specific offenses and others which deal with a range of offenses. Examples of multilateral conventions which apply to a range of offenses which would be most relevant to the topic at hand, include the Council of Europe's Convention on Mutual Assistance in Criminal Matters which entered into force in 1962 (which has subsequently been supplemented by the Convention on Mutual Assistance in Criminal Matters of 29 May 2000 in order to incorporate the best practices developed over time), and the Commonwealth Scheme for Mutual Assistance in Criminal Matters, which is an instrument applied in the context of the British Commonwealth. The UN has also developed a Model Treaty on Mutual Assistance in Criminal Matters, the purpose of which is to provide a suitable basis for negotiations between states that do not have a bilateral treaty and which have different legal systems.

The TOC Convention also provides a framework for cooperation between prosecuting authorities. This is clearly a useful feature of the convention. Unfortunately, not all the littoral states to the Indian Ocean and Gulf of Aden are party to it. Moreover, for several which are, not all have yet implemented key features of it. For example, one of the most fundamental manners in which to facilitate the process of cross-border investigation and collection of evidence, is to identify a central authority that shall receive or send all such requests. In international practice generally, requests for assistance have typically been done through *letters rogatory* which emanate from the judicial authority of one state to another, requesting that it perform one or more

[54] *Piracy off the Coast of Somalia*, PIR 08, 21 July 2011 Session 2010-12 located at http://www.publications.parliament.uk/pa/cm201012/cmselect/cmfaff/writev/1318/m08.htm.

specified actions. These requests were typically transmitted through diplomatic channels such that the request is typically certified by the competent national court in the requesting state, and then passed on to the state's Foreign Ministry who then passes the request on to the competent judicial authorities in that state. Naturally, the numerous steps required for communication through diplomatic processes, and the time spent in doing so, hinder the effectiveness in getting the required information in a timely manner.

In order to streamline this procedure, the TOC Convention provides that each state is to designate a central authority which shall receive requests for assistance directly, which can execute such request, and which can transmit them to the competent authorities for execution.[55] The convention also provides for direct requests through the International Criminal Police Organization in urgent cases where the state parties agree. Other multilateral legal assistance treaties go further than this approach and actually allow direct contact between judicial authorities with the territorial competence for initiating and executing them, thereby avoiding central authorities and other middlemen. Examples of such conventions are the Schengen Agreement in Europe, or the European Union Convention on Mutual Legal Assistance in Criminal Matters. Despite the obvious advantages these types of streamlined exchanges provide, few of the littoral states to the Indian Ocean and Gulf of Aden, which are party to the TOC Convention, have notified the United Nations of their central authorities. As such, any requests for legal assistance must be made through diplomatic channels, with all the delay and uncertainty associated therewith.

Notwithstanding requests for legal assistance with investigations or the collection of evidence, none of the conventions address issues of suspect transfer from the apprehending authority to the prosecuting authority. Issues involved in such transfer also can greatly affect the success of piracy prosecutions. It has been widely reported that there are several bilateral memoranda of understanding which have been signed among western governments and governments of littoral states of the Indian Ocean. The Kenyan government has purportedly signed agreements with both the United Kingdom and the United States. The Government of the Seychelles purportedly signed a bilateral agreement for the handover of pirate suspects with the Government of the United Kingdom. The actual terms of these agreements, however, are less widely reported. As a result, it is difficult to know on what basis these agreements are made, whether they are effective, and how they might fit into a coordinated effort to tackle piracy in the region.

[55] TOC Convention at Article 18, para. 13.

It stands to reason that some of these agreements may be more effective than others. Yet, without knowing the specific terms by which they operate, it is difficult for others to learn which terms work best and to emulate them. Further, to the extent that persons can build on the successes of others, it is more likely than not that subsequent agreements can be improved should they be able to build upon the experience of previous efforts. Collective experience, for example, could provide a baseline for terms of such agreements that would be consistent with international law, such that individual states would only need to ensure that the agreement's terms satisfied their national laws.

E. Successful Prosecution is Intertwined and Dependent on National Will

The various international conventions that have potential application to the problem are only as good as the domestic will and the domestic legislation that is undertaken to enact and enforce them. Herein lies another challenge. In the past, successful efforts to eliminate acts of piracy were conducted by the states whose interests were directly affected. In the sixteenth and seventeenth century, Barbary pirates raided British vessels in the Mediterranean, to the Atlantic, and into the English Channel and the Irish Sea, impeding Britain's trade with the rest of the world and taking the crews as slaves. Before the age of flight, and for an island nation, it comes as no surprise that the British navy was intent on patrolling its sea lanes and rooting out the problem. In more modern times, when acts of piracy threatened shipping in the Malacca Straights Singapore, Malaysia and the Philippines composed a joint response. Again, given that these countries' interests were directly affected and that they had the resources to patrol their own sea lanes and coasts, it was not surprising that they undertook to alleviate the problem.

Piracy now taking place off of the coast of Somalia, however, arises from within a country which does not yet have the capacity to patrol either its land coast or territorial sea, nor does the piracy which emanates from its shores implicate directly the interests of any particular nation or those of a few which have the capacity to take control of the problem. Rather, the problem affects several countries in relatively small numbers. Geographically, the whole of the Indian Ocean is affected with attacks having taken place from 3.74 degrees east off the coast of Tanzania, to the 76.4 degrees east off the coast of India, to as far north as 17.8 degrees north near the Straits of Hormuz in the Arabian Sea, to as far south as 46.6 degrees south off the coast of Mayotte.[56] As such, the attacks on shipping are not geographically confined to the coast of one particular country whose national interests would be severely impacted by the problem. Similarly, attacks are not focused, intentionally or by accident, on the shipping or trade emanating from or directed at any one country. To the contrary, the problem is one that affects international trade more generally, with multiple states and multiple actors within those states being impacted to differing degrees.

Not surprisingly, each state has taken relatively more interest in matters when its vessels or citizens have been attacked, or its national interests are otherwise concerned. This type of conduct takes many forms. For example, when *Le Ponant*, a commercially operated luxury cruising yacht, was seized by Somali pirates on April 4, 2008, French Special Forces tracked the pirates to the town of Jariban and captured them after payment of a ransom by the yacht's owner and the release of the hostages. Thereafter, the six pirates were transferred to Paris for trial. Similarly, Somaliland limits its jurisdiction over piracy cases to those which have a connection with Somaliland. Even further, Somaliland refuses to take custody of those persons convicted of piracy unless the pirates originated from Somaliland, despite the fact that Hargeysa prison was constructed by the UNDP to hold those convicted of piracy.[57] Although Somaliland's position on prisoners may be changing, as potentially indicated by a statement made by the Somaliland Minister of Foreign Affairs and International Cooperation on 11 December 2011, declaring Somaliland ready to accept prisoners who come to Somalia under the terms of a prison transfer agreement between the governments of Somaliland and the Seychelles,[58] these examples illustrate how states limit their involvement to cases which concern them.

Apart from the instances when a developed state's vessel or citizens are attacked, there is not one particular nation that has taken the lead in countering the problem. Rather, it is being pursued as a collective effort. Although richer nations have devoted resources in the form of their navies patrolling the Gulf of Aden and the Indian Ocean, none have stepped forward in the important role as willing prosecutor of the crimes, or jailor of the convicted, unless it was their vessel or citizens attacked. This role is being accepted, to differing degrees by countries which happen to be in the neighborhood, such as Kenya, the Seychelles and Mauritius. The fact that these nations are undertaking this role almost certainly has had an effect on

[56] International Maritime Bureau, IMB Piracy and Armed Robbery Map 2011, http://www.icc-ccs.org/piracy-reporting-centre/imb-live-piracy-map/imb-live-piracy-map

[57] http://somaliareport.com/index.php/post/415/Somaliland_Opens_Pirate_Prison_with_UN_Funding.

[58] S/2012/50 at p 12, fn. 16.

the rate of successful prosecutions, if for no other reason than that it increases the legal issues involved given that the suspected pirates originate from elsewhere and are arrested by the navies of multiple other countries. For example, when the seizing country and the prosecuting country are not the same, there needs to be hand-over agreements negotiated between the two countries involved, which agreements must be consistent with both countries' laws. Physical evidence must be obtained and handled by the apprehending naval personnel in a manner that is acceptable to the prosecuting country, and the multinational crews of foreign flagged vessels likely need to be made available at a future date to provide testimony for prosecution. The very multinational approach taken to address the problem is itself the source of several practical challenges.

Moreover, states must also contend with international human rights implications on exercising jurisdiction. There are fears that once arrested and on board a western warship, or transferred to a western nation trial, the suspects will demand asylum, or that laws in the prosecuting state will prevent the return of the suspects or convicted persons to their country of origin. As a result of the human rights considerations, there are multiple reports of suspected pirates avoiding prosecution, and who are instead set ashore uncharged. This happened when the Danish warship *Absalon* captured ten suspected pirates off the coast of Somalia. Unwilling to transfer the captives back to Denmark for trial and concerned that the suspects risked torture and the death penalty from other available courts if surrendered to them, it released them, as Danish law prohibits the extradition of suspects when they may face the death penalty.[59]

Indeed, the captain of the *Absalon* was faced with a poor choice of alternatives. He could not release the suspects to countries who he feared would not provide them treatment consistent with international human rights obligations, and he could not have transferred them back to Denmark for trial as this likely could not be done in a manner that was consistent with the suspect's rights under the European Convention on Human Rights ("ECHR"). The captured suspects came under the protection of the ECHR as soon as they came under the effective control of Denmark's naval vessel. Moreover, ECHR jurisprudence has clarified that the capture and detention at sea of suspects for later transfer to another state's court violates the suspect's human rights under certain circumstances. In *Medvedyev and Others v France*, the European Court of Human Rights found that a two week

[59] *See generally*, Treves, *Piracy, Law of the Sea, and Use of Force: Developments off the Coast of Somalia*, 20 European J. of Int'l Law 399, at pp 408-409

detention of suspected drug traffickers violated Article 5(3) of the ECHR which, among other things, provides that arrested persons "shall be brought promptly before a judge or other officer authorized by law to exercise judicial power."[60] It would not have been surprising then for a similar ruling to have been issued against Denmark should it have decided to transfer the suspects back to Denmark for trial.

Naturally, no one wants a system which would ignore the human rights of others even if they are suspected of criminal activity. The varied rights provided by western countries to those apprehended by their navies, the practicalities involved in transferring those persons from warships to prosecuting courts, and the fact that most suspects originate from lands where they might face treatment inconsistent with those rights, however, have implications for the potential success of subsequent prosecutions.

II: A REVIEW OF SPECIFIC ACTIONS AND RECOMMENDATIONS MADE TO ADDRESS THE CHALLENGES OF JURISDICTION AND PROSECUTION OF PIRACY OFF THE COAST OF SOMALIA

In order to address the various challenges outlined above, several actions and/or recommendations have been made. The question though is whether they are likely to resolve the various challenges. This section of the chapter will briefly address this.

One of the most specific recommendations, and the most comprehensive, calls for the establishment of specialized anti-piracy courts either in Somalia or in a neighboring country. In 2010, the UN Security Council undertook a process to support the aim of prosecuting and imprisoning persons responsible for piracy and armed robbery at sea off the coast of Somalia, and requested the Secretary-General to report on possible options. After deliberations on this report, the Security Council commissioned a report to "identify any additional steps that can be taken to assist States in the region, as well as other States, to prosecute and imprison persons who engage in piracy, and explore the willingness of States in the region to serve as potential host for any of the options for potential new judicial mechanisms," and it appointed a Special Advisor to compile it.[61] This report was compiled and delivered to the Security Council in January 2011 (the "Special Advisor's Report").

---

[60] ECHR Application no. 3394/03, 22 April 2010. *See also*, *Rigopoulos v. Spain*, ECHR Application No. 37388/97 12 January 1999. *See generally*, Treves, *Piracy, Law of the Sea, and Use of Force: Developments off the Coast of Somalia*, 20 European J. of Int'l Law 399, at pp 408-409; Osiro, *Somali Pirates Have Rights Too*, ISS Paper 224 July 2011.

[61] SG/A/1260.

The Special Advisor's Report made a series of 25 proposals designed to address the problem from several perspectives, including operations, counter-piracy measures, judicial and correctional measures, and development measures. In particular, the report proposed to make Somalia the focus of the judicial solution through the establishment of both specialized antipiracy courts in Somaliland and Puntland, and an extraterritorial Somali specialized court.[62] Other variations on this proposal for specialized courts have since been made, including a "piracy chamber" comprised of judges from littoral Indian Ocean countries applying their own national laws with the power to interact with foreign navies and to incarcerate those convicted,[63] as well as placing specialized courts to be created by the Security Council on a ship sailing off the coast.[64]

Certainly the proposal to place specialized courts in Somalia, if it were carried to a successful conclusion, could resolve some of the jurisdictional challenges to a successful prosecution given the nexus between Somalia and those committing attacks against shipping off its coast. Other jurisdictional problems would nevertheless remain, even if such court were located in Somalia such as those created by the uncertain delimitation of the Somali territorial sea. Naturally, to the extent that the court is not located in Somalia, the jurisdictional challenges remain in full, and would likely need to be resolved by the Security Council.

Beyond jurisdictional issues, however, it is difficult to see these proposals as a realistic alternative given the current legal architecture. The weak link in the chain of contingencies to the success of the idea is also one of the first; namely, that there does not exist a clear source of law, international or domestic, for the all the criminal offenses arising in and contributing to attacks on shipping off the coast of Somalia to be prosecuted. Although the crime of piracy is defined and accepted as a matter of international law, as can be seen from the preceding discussion, this does not mean that there is clarity on the issue at the domestic level as attested to by the two competing U.S. district court decisions and the Ahmed case in Kenya. The situation in Somalia is less developed, and domestic laws against the crime of piracy are

[62] S/2010/394 (2010).

[63] Chivers, *Captured Pirates in Legal Limbo*, International Herald Tribune, January 30, 2012.

[64] Dubner and Henn, *On Selecting A Judicial System(s) to Try Sea Pirates – An Interesting/Necessary Exercise But is it Enough to Deter The Attacks/Hijackings?*, 42 J. of Maritime Law & Commece 569 (2011).

not yet fully defined. This situation is complicated further by the relative lack of capacity in the judicial sector.[65]

Moreover, beyond the crime of piracy, matters become even more opaque. Although one can find support in international law mandating the criminalization of the types of criminal activity included in the attacks on shipping off the coast of Somalia today, these international conventions are not signed or ratified by all the littoral Indian Ocean states. At present, Somalia has not signed the SUA Convention, the ICHT or the TOC Convention, nor has it ratified the SFT Convention. Moreover, those international conventions which would apply more to the persons who organize and finance attacks on shipping, as well as laundering the proceeds thereof, do not themselves define the criminal acts proscribed. Rather they rely either on domestic legislation to define the criminal acts, or on other international conventions. This is not to say that Somalia does not have any existing legal architecture to prosecute those apprehended. It does, and prosecutions take place and convictions are made. By not being party to the international conventions on the various challenges to repressing and prosecuting all the acts associated with attacks on shipping, however, it is not coordinated with other nations in combating a problem that extends beyond its borders. This inevitably leads to breakdowns in investigations and prosecutions.

Other than the proposals for specialized anti-piracy courts, there are several programmes of various organizations, each of which deals with discrete issues. The UNODC, for example, has a counter-piracy program ("CPP") which, among other things, focuses on assisting countries in providing fair and efficient trials and imprisonment in both the Somali region and in Somalia itself through the existing criminal justice systems in these countries.[66] Its mandate includes of course the goal of developing all parts of the criminal justice systems of East Africa, and its efforts encompass a broad range of activities from providing specialist training courses to detectives in Kenya, organizing regional prosecution programs in Kenya, the Seychelles and most recently in Mauritius which are designed to provide support for the police, prosecutors, court and prison staff with the processing of piracy cases, to the hiring and providing interpreters to the courts for use at trial. It also sponsors legal training workshops such as its most recent workshop on rules of engagement, organized together with the IMO, which covered the

---

[65] *Id.* It was estimated in the report that less than five percent of the 76 existing judges in Puntland and the existing six prosecutors have had legal training. Out of Somaliland's existing 120 judges and 40 prosecutors, only five percent have legal training.

[66] Counter-Piracy Programme, *Support to the Trial and Related Treatment of Piracy Suspects*, Issue 7, September/October 2011.

fundamentals of international maritime law such as maritime zones and the right of safe passage, as well as the use of force in specific situations.[67]

The IMO also has been active in developing measures to assist in the effort. In addition to the Djibouti Code of Conduct, in May 2011 the IMO's Legal Committee circulated to all IMO members four short papers concerning: (1) the elements which could be included in national legislation on piracy pursuant to UNCLOS; (2) an overview of the international conventions within the UNODC's competence and which may contribute to the establishment of a legislative framework for conducting piracy prosecutions; (3) the elements of the SUA Convention which complement UNCLOS regarding piracy; and (4) comments on the analysis of the UNODC with regard to those instruments which serve as a basis for prosecuting pirates.[68] Although these materials are useful and a good start in educating states about the various sources of international law that can be used to develop domestic legislation, they were circulated more as an adjunct to the IMO's counter-piracy programme rather than because the issues covered therein were a focal point of it. The circular letter itself refers to the materials as ones which "might be useful" to states that are either developing national legislation on piracy or reviewing existing legislation.[69]

Notwithstanding the excellent work and intentions of all these organizations, they all try to address the challenges through the existing international legal architecture. Given the existing architecture, however, it is not readily apparent that these efforts have a realistic chance of success at improving the ability of states to prosecute those persons apprehended in connection with attacks on shipping off the coast of Somalia, which is needed as any effective program at reducing and preventing the activity. The various international legal instruments available for guidance are not focused on the issues that arise out of attacks on shipping off the coast of Somalia, nor are they applicable in all littoral states of the Indian Ocean and Gulf of Aden. Instead, they, and particularly those that would assist in the

[67] The CPP also includes one of the few efforts focused on ameliorating the causes of piracy rather than dealing with the effects of it. In this regard, the CPP has initiated an advertising effort in Puntland which is trying to persuade the local population that piracy is bad for their society and against Islam. This effort is based on the experience of the people of the village of Eyl which recently rid themselves of criminal gangs using the village as a base for their pirate enterprise. The effort uses radio and television as well as visits from elders and clerics to locations to deliver its message. Included in this message of course is the news on arrests and convictions of pirates.

[68] IMO, Circular letter No. 3180, 17 May 2011.

[69] The Contact Group on Piracy off the Coast of Somalia serves as another international forum to develop and implement national counter-piracy policies and programs. These working groups are focused on topics related to military and operations coordination, judicial issues, strengthening shipping self-awareness, public information and the financial flows which support and finance pirate attacks.

investigation and prosecution of the organizations involved in the attacks, are addressed to terrorism and organized crime generally. As such, they do not serve as a clear starting point by themselves for the harmonization of domestic laws needed to prosecute the criminal acts associated with, and including, the crime of piracy. Consequently, it seems more likely than not that they will result in a patchwork response to the challenges rather than an organized coherent approach to a complex and cross-border problem. Indeed, this seems to have been the result so far.

III A POTENTIAL WAY FORWARD

A more effective starting point then would appear to include a study of the methods by which states could unify or harmonize their domestic laws. Although harmonization will not resolve all the challenges to successfully prosecuting those involved in attacks on shipping, they would potentially ease some of the current problems being faced. The methods by which to harmonize the law in this area of course can take several forms, and warrants its own specific chapter or articles devoted to the topic. As such, a full discussion of these methods is well beyond the scope of this chapter. Nevertheless, there are certain observations one can discern readily from the preceding discussion

The various existing international conventions are of course already an attempt to harmonize the domestic law. Each of the international conventions discussed above devises normative regulations by which each ratifying state then has the responsibility to incorporate into its domestic law and practice. They each elaborate provisions as to conduct that a state should prevent and sanction, and they elaborate provisions on when states should exercise jurisdiction over this conduct. As we have seen from the above, however, the challenge in this approach is that the normative regulations must be translated into domestic law and procedure in a clear and cohesive way. Unlike other international conventions which set forth such normative regulations, however, because there is no single international convention relating to the various issues arising out of attacks on shipping, not all of which are specifically addressed to attacks on shipping, the norms appears do not appear to be as effective in guiding states in the development of their domestic law then such norms normally would be. Thus, these particular international conventions by themselves do not appear to be an effective response to the challenges posed by attacks on shipping.

This begs the question as to whether there should be drafted and negotiated a new international convention that would address specifically the full range of criminal conduct associated with attacks on shipping, or what is colloquially referred to as piracy. This would undoubtedly help to clarify the issues, and potentially would provide clearer guidance to individual states in the formulation of their domestic laws. A new international convention is not a quick or simple solution, however. It likely would be several years before this could be accomplished, and the instrument would then be subject to further potential delays while states decide whether to sign and ratify it. Moreover, much of the work has already been done in that there already exist several international conventions that address the various issues arising from attacks on shipping. These conventions are all in force, although not all have been signed and ratified by all the countries in the region most affected by the attacks on shipping in the Indian Ocean and Gulf of Aden. International diplomatic effort is probably better spent on persuading the states which have not yet ratified the appropriate treaties, or for those who have ratified but not yet fully implemented them to do so, rather than embarking on a new international convention entirely.

An alternative to a new international convention may be to add a protocol to an existing international convention which states can then agree to. This option, however, suffers from similar obstacles presented by the status quo, or the drafting and negotiation of a new instrument. There is not any one international convention addressing all the criminal acts arising out of attacks on shipping. As such, there is no obvious convention to which one could add a protocol.[70] Trying to develop a protocol that would address all of the criminal acts associated with attacks on shipping might thus create more confusion rather than less. Further, drafting and negotiating a protocol, while perhaps not as complicated as a new convention, is neither simple nor quick, and would require substantial diplomatic effort.

Another alternative approach which might build upon the provisions of the international conventions already in place and in a manner that could more effectively guide states in the formulation and codification of their own legislation, might be to devise model laws to serve as guides for local adaptation, and/or uniform laws to be incorporated by states into their domestic legislation. The model law of course would be based upon the normative regulations provided in the various international conventions applicable to it,

[70] Further, one of the international conventions discussed above already has a protocol attached to them which focuses it further away from criminal acts associated with piracy. For example, the SUA Convention has already has a Protocol of 2005 to the Convention for the Suppression of Unlawful Acts against the Safety of Maritime Navigation which criminalizes the intentional transport of any material, equipment, or software that is intended to be used to produce a biological, chemical, or nuclear weapon.

providing, it is hoped, a streamlined method by which domestic legislatures would be able to secure passage of similar legislation in their national legislative bodies. This approach appears to have been specifically rejected by the UNODC, however, in favor of its providing assistance to countries individually.[71] In its view, this approach allows it to provide more detailed advice so as to more effectively tailor it to the specific demands of the legal system it was asked to support. Although one can certainly understand the rationale behind this approach, there is nothing that would prevent the UNODC from providing such specialized advice even if such a model law existed. The reference to such a model law by the relevant authorities in the state being advised in advance of any meeting with outside legal experts would seemingly assist those authorities in understanding what is required of them more than if they have not seen such model legislation in advance.

Somalia itself suggests that this approach might pose one of the better methods by which to deal with the problem. Even though attacks off the coast of Somalia became increasingly more common in the last decade, Somalia's Penal Code and Code of Criminal Procedure does not expressly prohibit piracy, let alone the related criminal acts arising from attacks on shipping. Instead, those accused of piracy have been tried under the Penal Code provisions that refer to the detention of persons for the purpose of robbery or extortion. A bill criminalizing piracy and intended for application throughout the country was developed in association with the UNODC, and the relevant persons from the TFG, and the governments of Puntland and Somalia have met over the draft since spring 2010. The Parliament of Puntland subsequently adopted the bill on 18 December 2010. The Parliament of Somaliland has also debated the measure, and it is in the process of being amended with a goal of it being enacted by June 2012. Although the author understands that the specialized anti-piracy legislation does not expressly address acts undertaken to finance attacks on shipping, and that it is foreseen that further revision of the Penal Code and code of Criminal Procedure will also be needed in any event, the provision of draft anti-piracy legislation to the relevant authorities in Somalia has already achieved some success. The creation of a model uniform law to address all the criminal acts associated with attacks on shipping which could be used throughout the region, may yield similar positive results.

These regions of Somalia of course share a legal tradition already, and thus might understate the challenges that would be faced when trying to incorporate a model law into an entirely different system. There is little

[71] LEG 98/8/2 18 February 2011 at para. 1.

question that such challenges exist. Yet, it is difficult to see how reference to a model law would not help the local authorities in the relevant states review and revise their domestic legislation so that it incorporates what is needed for effective prosecutions. They will know better than consultants from outside their jurisdiction what modifications to a model law will be needed to be made in order to make them consistent with their national laws and procedures, whereas the outside legal consultants can help with ensuring that modifications to the model law remain grounded in the international legal architecture to advise them with best practices which the consultants have learned to be effective in their experience.

The development of a model law to provide for a more uniform approach to the investigation and prosecution of criminal acts associated with piracy also may also obviate the need and additional cost associated with the establishment of specialized anti-piracy courts. Although this is certainly one way to approach the problem, it seems duplicative of existing courts. The reasons typically given for the lack of effective prosecutions is not so much that there is no court available to try the suspects, such that new courts are needed. Rather, the typical explanations offered for ineffective prosecutions are the uncertain state of the law by which to investigate, collect evidence or prosecute the suspects, as well as challenges in the transfer of suspects to prosecuting states. If that is true, then it makes sense to focus more effort on ensuring that the substantive and procedural laws of the prosecuting countries are sufficient to ensure a just result. It is of course also true that investment needs to be made in general court capacity in the region as well, but this capacity is arguably better built into the current domestic legal systems where it might also be used to address other crimes when crimes associated with piracy might recede from prominence.

IV CONCLUSION

Too often, piracy is treated as being comprised of a single issue with an obvious solution that any state can enforce. As with many things, the reality is not that clear. Attacks on shipping off the coast of Somalia present a much more nuanced legal problem with various levels of actors in various locations, undertaking various criminal acts. It thus presents challenges that are belied by the association of the term "piracy" with the concept of universal jurisdiction to which it is always linked. Effective prosecution of those involved in attacks on shipping requires a coordinated multinational response. This coordinated response will be difficult if not impossible given that international law, as it exists currently, does not aide the harmonization among the various countries taking part in the effort to restrain and prosecute those persons and organizations involved in the attacks. Given the state of international law, law at the domestic level is not always clear, thereby impeding a state's ability to prosecute those apprehended.

Indeed, without a clear definition of the criminal activity one seeks to prevent, it is difficult to expect any court, whether pre-existing as part of a functioning judicial system or created to address the problem of "piracy" specifically, will have much success. As such, any attempt to ameliorate the difficulties in prosecuting the persons and organizations conducting and coordinating attacks on shipping should include efforts to harmonize domestic laws and procedures. The need for such efforts, however, does not appear to have received as much attention as it should, notwithstanding the excellent work being undertaken by state governments and various international organizations combating the issues arising from attacks on shipping.

16. THE NEW FRENCH LAW ON PIRACY

Valérie BORÉ EVENO[1]

Some gestation periods can be long. Sixteen months of parliamentary work were necessary before giving birth to the recent French law on the fight against maritime piracy, officially proclaimed January 5, 2011.[2] It must be said that this new legislation was highly anticipated as it became urgent to strengthen the capacity of the French state at sea, in a context of increasing acts of piracy in the Gulf of Aden and off the Somali coast.

Is it necessary to be reminded of the ever-increasing figures in the reports of the International Maritime Bureau? In the year 2010 alone, 445 attacks were reported worldwide (an increase of 10% in one year). Pirates captured 53 ships and 1181 sailors, the vast majority of them in the northern Indian Ocean. The number of incidents reported since the beginning of 2011 unfortunately seems to confirm this inflationary trend.[3] Since 90% of the global transport of goods is by sea, piracy poses a serious threat not only to the safety of persons and goods but also to the freedom of maritime commerce. Despite the various naval forces in place in the region as part of the international fight against this scourge, whether under the command of the European Union,[4] NATO, other coalitions, or independent naval forces,[5] the efforts undertaken at the international level have unfortunately not

[1] Valérie Boré Eveno is a lecturer at the Faculty of Law and Political Sciences at the University of Nantes (France) and member of the Centre Maritime Law and Oceanic (CDMO).

[2] Loi n° 2011-13 of January 5, 2011, "relative à la lutte contre la piraterie et à l'exercice des pouvoirs de police de l'Etat en mer," *JORF*, 6 January 2011, p 374. Presented in Conseil des ministres September 2, 2009 and filed the next day before the Sénat, the bill was adopted by it on first reading May 6, 2010. Subsequently amended by the Assemblée nationale on first reading November 25, 2010, it was finally adopted on December 22 by the Sénat on second reading without further modification. For more details on the dossier législatif and the content of parliamentary debates, see the website Légifrance: http://www.legifrance.gouv.fr.

[3] *See* IMB Live Piracy Report on the website of the IMB Piracy Reporting Centre (http://www.icc-ccs.org/piracy-reporting-centre).

[4] The European Union launched in December 2008, the military operation ATALANTA, also called EU-NAVFOR or Task Force 465 (Joint Action 2008/851 CFSP of November 10, 2008). Originally scheduled for a term of one year, it was extended for one year in 2009 and for two years in summer 2010.

[5] In addition to the Combined Task Force 151 (US), a number of independent naval forces (Russian, Chinese, Japanese, Indian or South Korea) have also been deployed in the region.

managed to curb this phenomenon.[6] The lack of domestic legislation against piracy is certainly an obstacle to the success of this battle. Indeed, despite the recognition by international law of universal jurisdiction over acts of piracy, the authorities of a state who capture suspects without having specific criminal laws for prosecution of piracy are usually obligated to release them without the pirates ever being brought to justice.[7] According to the recent report of the Special Adviser to the Secretary-General of the United Nations on Legal Issues Related to Piracy off the Coast of Somalia,[8] "more than 90 percent of the pirates apprehended by States patrolling the seas will be released without being prosecuted." This inevitably fosters a sense of impunity and emboldens the perpetrators.

However, international pressure has steadily increased since politicians realized that the punishment (and its deterrent effect) was an essential component in this fight. The United Nations Convention on the Law of the Sea (UNCLOS, or Montego Bay Convention), [9] which provides an international legal regime for the suppression of piracy,[10] states in Article 100 that all states shall cooperate in all possible ways in the suppression of piracy. The International Law Commission also noted, at the time of the codification of maritime law, that "any State having an opportunity of taking measures against piracy, and neglecting to do so, would be failing in a duty laid upon it by international law."[11] If some discretion is left to the state regarding the measures to be taken for this purpose, the lack of national legislation on maritime piracy is increasingly stigmatized by international bodies. Thus the United Nations Security Council gave, as early as 2008, a much more restrictive interpretation by holding that article 100 meant "a

---

[6] We'll not linger, here, on this important issue, which has already been the subject of many studies. *See* A. Bellayer-Roille, *Montée en Puissance de la Lutte Contre la "Piraterie" Maritime. Sus à l'Hostis Humani Generis!*, Annuaire de Droit maritime et Océanique, T. XXVII, 2009, pp 309-331; J. Ashley Roach, *Countering Piracy Off Somalia: International Law and International Institutions*, *AJIL*, 2010, vol. 104, afl. 3, pp 397-416; MD Fink and RJ Galvin, *Combating Pirates Off the Coast of Somalia: Current Legal Challenges*, *NILR*, 2009, pp 367-395.

[7] *See, e.g.*, a case judged by Cour d'appel d'Anvers (Belgium), 19th July 1985. Pirates who attacked Belgian nationals on the High Sea weren't criminally judged since the Belgian Law didn't provide for repression (example quoted by L. Luchini, *Droit de la Mer*, Tome 2, vol. 2, Pedone, Paris, 1996, p 176, quote 384).

[8] Submitted by Mr. Jack Lang to the Secretary General, the report was presented to the Security Council January 25, 2011. It is available on the website of the United Nations, Official documents of the United Nations (ODS): http://documents.un.org/ (Symbol : S/2011/30).

[9] Opened for signature by states on 10 December 1982, the United Nations Convention on the Law of the Sea is in force since November 16, 1994. It gathers 162 states parties now (20 September 2011), including France for which it came into force on May 11, 1996.

[10] *See* Articles 100 to 107 of the Convention, and Article 110, which we will discuss later.

[11] *See* International Law Commission, *Articles Concerning the Law of the Sea and Commentary*, *YILC*, 1956, vol. II, p 282 (art. 38).

cooperation to the fullest possible extent in the repression of piracy."[12] It also urged states party to the 1988 Convention for the Suppression of Unlawful Acts Against the Safety of Maritime Navigation (SUA) to fully fulfill their obligations under said Convention[13] and to cooperate with the Secretary-General and the International Maritime Organization to build judicial capacity for the successful prosecution of persons suspected of piracy and armed robbery.[14] The Council has since repeatedly insisted on the need for states involved in the struggle to acquire the necessary legislation to ensure the prosecution of persons suspected of piracy.[15] The United Nations General Assembly has also, in turn, called upon all states to take appropriate measures to facilitate the arrest and trial of persons accused of acts of piracy and to adopt national legislation to this end.[16] In the absence of an international court with jurisdiction to try the pirates, their punishment is in the hands of the domestic legal systems.

While some states legislated against piracy long ago,[17] others have done so only recently.[18] These laws are far from homogeneous, both in respect to the penalties handed down and in the very definition of piracy, which may itself be distinguished from the definitions given by international law or by professional maritime practice. While France has had legislation on piracy for a long time, with its Law of April 10, 1825 for the safety of navigation and maritime commerce,[19] the provisions of this law became obsolete and did not meet the criteria set by UNCLOS. After its repeal in 2007,[20] the crime of piracy as such no longer existed in French criminal law. The fact that several cases directly led the French authorities to address this lack, such as the *Ponant*,[21] *Carré d'As*,[22] and the *Tanit*,[23] is certainly one of the reasons that the French legislature readdressed the issue.

---

[12] Resolution 1816, 2 June 2008.

[13] According to this Convention, adopted by the International Maritime Organization at Rome on 10 March 1988 and came into force in 1992, states parties (157, including France) are required to criminalize the act of seizing or exercising control over a ship by force or threat thereof or any other form of intimidation. The Convention also devotes the principle of "extradite or prosecute." However, some states have considered that the SUA Convention applies only to acts of terrorism.

[14] Resolution 1846, 2 December 2008. *See also* Resolution 1851, 16 December 2008, preamble and § 15.

[15] *See* Resolution 1918, 27 April 2010 and Resolution 1950, 23 November 2010.

[16] *See* Resolution 64/71, 12 March 2010, §§ 72-73.

[17] This is especially true for the United States with a law dating back over 100 years.

[18] The Seychelles have adopted such a law in May 2010. Legislative reforms were also undertaken in Belgium, Spain, Japan, Maldives and Tanzania.

[19] Law No. 1825-04-10 of April 10, 1825 for the safety of navigation and maritime commerce defined the status of "pirate" by the position of captain of a ship or belonging to a crew engaged in a series of acts that the law stated, and is sanctioned by life imprisonment.

[20] The law of 1825 was repealed by Law No. 2007-1787 of 20 December 2007 on simplifying the law.

[21] French cruise ship *Le Ponant* was boarded in the Gulf of Aden 4th April 2008. After the crew held hostage was freed by force, some pirates have been handed over to French justice.

The context has changed dramatically from one where, during the medieval period, France suppressed piracy through maritime laws which were very dissuasive.[24] During that period any and all means were deemed acceptable to capture the *hosti humani generis* and punish him in an exemplary manner after an oft-expedited trial. It was as if, in engaging in criminal activity, the pirate had ceased to be human. Thus, those who were "lucky" enough to escape hanging or the breaking wheel usually found themselves condemned to the galleys for life. Maritime piracy has indeed long been considered a scourge, deserving of universal reprobation.[25] As Blackstone pointed out in 1769, "piracy or sea robbery is a crime against society: a pirate is the common enemy of mankind, and as he gave up all benefits of government and society . . . by declaring war on mankind, mankind must in turn declare war on him."[26]

If the main issue of this fight against piracy is no longer defined in the same terms today, it is partly because the evolution of human rights sheds new light on the subject.[27] Despite his crimes, the pirate retains his status as a human being, holder of fundamental rights and freedoms. It is then entirely legitimate and even necessary that the state authorities take a strong stand against piracy in order to effectively combat its spread; however, the end cannot justify the use of any and all means. States parties to the European Convention on Human Rights, in particular, are thus obliged to ensure to everyone within their jurisdiction the free and full exercise of those rights and freedoms, regardless of the circumstances and with the only limitations being those within the Convention. This is especially true when a deprivation of liberty is at stake. France knows this all too well, as it was recently

---

[22] A French sailing yacht, the *Carré d'As*, was attacked Sept. 2, 2008 in the Gulf of Aden by Somali pirates. After freeing two French nationals taken hostage, the French forces were able to brought six pirates to French justice.

[23] The sailboat the *Tanit* was also boarded off Somalia April 4, 2009. Following an attack launched by French soldiers, one of the French hostages and two pirates were killed. Three other attackers were delivered to the French courts.

[24] The order of the Admiralty in 1584 condemned the pirates to the breaking wheel (also known as the Catherine Wheel). The order of the king of the September 5, 1718 established the death penalty with confiscation of their property. As to the sentence of the instigators and accomplices, the text provided for the galleys for life. *See* T. Ortolan, *Règles Internationales et Diplomatie de la Mer*, T. 1, Henri Plon, 4ème éd, 1864, p 211.

[25] *See* D. Gaurier, *Le Crime Contre l'Humanité est-il une Notion Nouvelle? Le Pirate, Ennemi du Genre Humain*, *ADMO*, tome XVIII, 2000, pp 173-192.

[26] W. Blackstone, *Commentaries on the Laws of England*, Book Four, Clarendon Press, Oxford, 1769, p 71

[27] *See* C. Laly-Chevalier, *Lutte Contre la Piraterie Maritime et Droits de l'Homme*, *RBDI*, 2009-1, pp 5-51. *See also* D. Guilfoyle, *Counter-Piracy Law Enforcement and Human Rights*, *ICLQ*, 2010, vol. 59, pp 141-169.

convicted on this point by the European Court of Human Rights. In the *Medvedyev*[28] case the Court ruled that detention on board French ships had no legal basis. While this case involved drug traffickers intercepted on the high seas, the ruling was transposable to the case of pirates being held for transfer to a competent judicial authority. Thus, the European Court asked the states concerned to improve the framework for police intervention on the high seas.

This situation has forced the French legislature to combine the implementation of international rules in the fight against maritime piracy with the rights and freedoms that the French state committed itself to when it signed the European Convention on Human Rights. These two requirements, while not necessarily contradictory although coming from quite distinct considerations, are reflected fairly clearly throughout the eight articles comprising a new French law. The first objective of the text is indeed to adapt French legislation to the rules designated in UNCLOS, which, as noted by the European Court of Justice, are not directly applicable.[29] Several texts in effect will be modified by the new legislation: Act No. 94-589 of 15 July 1994 on procedures for the exercise by the state of its police powers at sea (as amended by Chapter I of the new law), the Criminal Code and the Code of Criminal Procedure (Chapter II), and the Defense Code (Chapter III of the Act).[30] The integration of the suppression of acts of piracy in that Act and the addition of a section in the Defense Code allow this mission to be integrated into the State's action at sea. Also, to comply with the objections raised by the European Court of Human Rights, the new legislation now provides expressly for the hypothesis of a deprivation of liberty for the crew during the rerouting of an intercepted vessel and tries to frame it within a system designed to prevent arbitrary interference with individual liberty.

It is from the perspective of these two objectives: adapting to international rules on piracy while complying with the requirements of European law on human rights, that this paper will examine the contents of the new French

---

[28] The first case (July 10, 2008) has been confirmed by the Grand Chamber (Mar. 29, 2010, *Medvedyev et Autres v. France*, req. n° 3394/03).

[29] *Cf.* ECJ, June 3, 2008, *Intertanko Ea v. Secretary of State for Transport*, aff. C-308/06, *Rec.* I-4057. In this case (about the assessment of the legality of a European directive on the harmonization of criminal sanctions against that "Intertanko" opposed to the provisions of the United Nations Convention on the Law of the Sea), the Court held that "UNCLOS does not establish rules intended to apply directly and immediately to individuals and to confer upon them rights or freedoms capable of being relied upon against States, irrespective of the attitude of the ship's flag State." *Id.* at 64.

[30] The text of the Act is composed of five chapters including the provisions for child victims of acts of piracy, who are recognized as a Ward of the State (Chapter IV), and the provisions Final (Chapter V).

legislation on the fight against maritime piracy, in order to evaluate the adjustments made, to appreciate the merits and to assess its relevance to the purpose. It is indeed "in light of" international maritime law that the legislature has decided to reintroduce the concept of piracy into French law (I), while ensuring that the legal framework of police operations in this domain meets the requirements of the European Court of Human Rights (II).

I-THE REINTRODUCTION OF THE CONCEPT OF PIRACY INTO FRENCH LAW IN LIGHT OF INTERNATIONAL MARITIME LAW

Having disappeared in 2007, piracy once again figures in French law. The law of January 5, 2011, however, does not specifically define it. In its Article 1[31] it refers expressly to the definition in the United Nations Convention on the Law of the Sea (A). It also does not criminalize piracy as such but merely states the criminal offenses that are constitutive (B). It is precisely these offenses, if recorded by officers of the Navy, which may be subject to "quasi-universal jurisdiction" that the law now accords the French courts in the matter, as is allowed by maritime law (C).

A. The definition of piracy "inspired" by UNCLOS

The revised version of law No. 94-589 of July 15, 1994, on procedures for states exercising their police powers at sea, dictates that the mechanisms relating to the fight against piracy (new Title 1) apply to "acts of piracy under the United Nations Convention on the Law of the Sea" (UNCLOS). Thus it relies explicitly on the definition of piracy stated in UNCLOS, which was signed in Montego Bay on December 10, 1982, even if, as can be seen, the essential elements slightly differ.[32]

Even though the customary definition of piracy remained somewhat ambiguous,[33] Article 101 of UNCLOS has indeed given clearly defined characteristics to these acts, with different elements that help differentiate similar offenses which tended to be assimilated in the past. This definition is not new since the text of 1982 essentially reproduces that of the 1958 Geneva Convention on the High Seas.[34] Piracy is understood primarily as:

---

[31] This article is the one which introduces a Title I of the Law No. 94-589 of 15 July 1994 on procedures for the exercise by the state of its police powers at sea.

[32] This is also the definition that was adopted by other recent legislations, such as the Belgian Law of 30 December 2009 on the fight against maritime piracy, (*Moniteur Belge*, January 14, 2010, p 1483 and p 1485) or the Seychelles' Penal Code (Penal Code Amendment No. 5, Supplement to Official Gazette, 11th March 2010).

[33] *See* L. Lucchini, M. Voelckel, *op. cit*, pp 159-160.

[34] *See* Article 14 of the Geneva Convention on the High Seas of April 29, 1958, *Treaty Series*, vol. 450, p 11.

> any illegal acts of violence, detention or any act of depredation, committed for private ends by the crew or the passengers of a private ship or a private aircraft, and directed [either] on the high seas, against another ship or aircraft, or against persons or property on board such ship or aircraft, [or] against a ship, aircraft, persons or property in a place outside the jurisdiction of any States.

Two other types of acts, which constitute accessory, can be assimilated according to the text as either complicity ("any act of voluntary participation in the operation of a ship or of an aircraft with knowledge of facts making it a pirate ship or aircraft") or incitement to commit such acts or their facilitation.

If the scope is limited to the principal act (violence), it should be noted that the place where it is committed is an essential element of the very restrictive definition of piracy as stated in UNCLOS. It must indeed have been committed "on the high seas," and secondly "in a place outside the jurisdiction of any State."[35] Without reiterating the entire text of Article 101 of the Convention, Article 1 of the new law places emphasis on the condition *ratione loci* by specifying that the acts covered by the new law are those committed, firstly, "on the high seas" and secondly "in the maritime areas not under the jurisdiction of any State." The wording adopted by the legislature seems at first glance to be consistent with the text of the Convention. However, a closer look reveals a certain misunderstanding or awkwardness in the handling of the concept of piracy as considered in international law, that could lead to confusion when qualifying the act. While it is clear that the offending violence, committed on the high seas, are acts of piracy, the reference in law to "maritime areas not under the jurisdiction of any State" leaves some doubt. The question is not the terminology used by UNCLOS, which again, refers to the high seas as "a place outside the jurisdiction of any State." If UNCLOS is not referring here specifically to a "maritime space," this reflects the original intention of the codifiers to include among the places likely to be the playground of pirates what is called in international law, *terra nullius*, or land that belongs to no one.[36] Due to the

---

[35] Article I of the new first Title I of the Act of July 15, 1994: "in the maritime areas not under the jurisdiction of any state" (our translation). Note: The third hypothesis, mentioned in the law relating to acts committed in the territorial waters of a state, will be discussed later.

[36] In any case, this is the sense that seemed to give the International Law Commission while explaining that in 1956 it had considered "primarily for the actions of a ship or aircraft on an island forming a terra nullius, or on the coast of an unoccupied territory," *Yearbook ILC*, 1956, Vol. II, p 282.

lack of titles that would give power over the territories, suppressing acts of piracy committed in this territory would indeed fall under universal jurisdiction. Moreover, the fact that UNCLOS refers in this case to acts directed "against . . . persons or property" without specifying that they must necessarily be "on board" ships or aircraft (unlike the same acts committed on the high seas), reinforces the idea that they can possibly be committed "on land."

It is true that alternative interpretations of this provision of article 101 sometimes stray from this original meaning, and infer that the wording is making a willing reference to maritime areas which do not fall under full state sovereignty (unlike the internal waters, archipelagic waters and territorial sea) nor belong to the high seas which are in the international zone. Allusion is made here to the Exclusive Economic Zones (EEZ), to which the question has sometimes arisen as to whether the acts committed that otherwise meet the criteria of piracy could be characterized as such under UNCLOS. The answer falls under common sense and can find its legal basis in the text of the Convention. Article 58, § 2 of the Convention states that "Articles 88 to 115 and other relevant rules of international law apply to the Exclusive Economic Zone in so far as they are not inconsistent with this Part. [Part V on EEZ]." The rights that the coastal state may exercise in the EEZ are only recognized for essentially economic ends,[37] and third-party states continue to enjoy extensive freedoms in this zone, including the freedom of navigation. There is, therefore, no reason for the rules relating to the suppression of piracy in the chapter devoted to the high seas to not apply in a state's Exclusive Economic Zone as well.[38]

---

[37] Article 56 UNCLOS (Rights, jurisdiction and duties of the coastal state in the exclusive economic zone):

1. In the exclusive economic zone, the coastal State has: (a) sovereign rights for the purpose of exploring and exploiting, conserving and managing the natural resources, whether living or non-living, of the waters superjacent to the seabed and of the seabed and its subsoil, and with regard to other activities for the economic exploitation and exploration of the zone, such as the production of energy from the water, currents and winds; (b) jurisdiction as provided for in the relevant provisions of this Convention with regard to: (i) the establishment and use of artificial islands, installations and structures; (ii) marine scientific research; (iii) the protection and preservation of the marine environment; (c) other rights and duties provided for in this Convention.

However, the fact that the coastal state is now authorized to exercise, in its EEZ, the "sovereign rights" or "jurisdiction" in economic matters, only fuels the confusion in this regard and highlights the outdated character of the expression.

[38] *See* J.-P. Pancracio, *Droit de la Mer*, Paris, Dalloz, 2010, p 455. *See also* L. Lucchini et M. Voelckel, *op. cit*, pp 164-165, recalling in this regard in the Geneva Convention on the High Seas, the reference to "any other place outside the jurisdiction of any State" was intended at the time, to exclude only internal waters and territorial sea (EEZ concept did not exist yet).

While Article 1 of the law analysed does not rule out this hypothesis, since its objective is most certainly intended to integrate it by citing the famous "maritime areas not under the jurisdiction of any state." The fact remains that the reference to these seems redundant and quite indicative of the confusion mentioned, as is also clear from the legislative record.[39] What is more delicate is that at the same time it ignores the *terra nullius* that had justified, originally, the conventional precision concerning the place where the act was committed, which restricts even more the definition given by the Convention, even if the hypothesis of being in such a situation today remains rather theoretical.

Furthermore, another awkwardness appears in the third hypothesis of localizing acts that, according to the new law, may be subject to the new initiative in the fight against piracy. In the same article, it refers also to "piracy" (as according to UNCLOS still) committed, "when international law allows, in the territorial waters of a State." However, the international law in question - at least if it is considered within the framework of UNCLOS, as the law does - does not qualify these actions as of acts of "piracy" but equates them to robbery or armed robbery. By referring only to acts committed "on high seas" or "in a place outside the jurisdiction of any State." Without reiterating the entire text of Article 101 of the Convention, Article 1 of the new law, the Convention of 1982, implicitly but undoubtedly presupposes that the same type of offense that would take place in the territorial sea or internal waters of a state would escape classification as international piracy (and the resulting universal jurisdiction). It would come under only the exclusive jurisdiction of the state concerned, under its territorial jurisdiction. Thus, only that state would be entitled to determine an act of piracy and to carry out the prosecution, if of course it willed to do so. Thus, even though the offense may be physically identical, and even if the procedures and the consequences strictly equivalent, it would however be a different legal regime that would result, in principle, from this difference in qualification. Moreover, a similar act committed on the high seas, and which meets the *ratione loci* definition of piracy, but where the perpetrators manage to escape into a zone under sovereignty, if it does not lose it's legal qualification, would in principle escape third-party state jurisdiction, which has no jurisdiction over the area. The "right of hot pursuit," as designated in Article 111 of UNCLOS does not apply to this situation because if it can continue out into high seas, it must have originated in waters under the

[39] *See* in particular the explanatory statement of the law, which states that "the provisions of this title shall apply to acts of piracy on the high seas and maritime areas not under the jurisdiction of any State is to say in the exclusive economic zone."

sovereignty of the pursuant coastal state, and cease once the pursued vessel manages to take refuge in the territorial sea of another state, which may be the flag state.

All of these rules would obviously pose no problem if the coastal state with the jurisdiction over where the pirates are found always assumed its responsibility for maritime safety and criminal prosecution of the acts mentioned. But it is quite different when it is unwilling or is unable to perform this task, as is the case with Somalia.[40] Therefore, in such a case, either the "failed" state consents to let foreign troops enter its territory to intercept the pirates, or the pirates find refuge in total impunity. In April 2008, the *Ponant* case highlighted this loophole in international law,[41] which, shortly afterwards, the United Nations Security Council attempted to address by adopting Resolution 1816.[42] Adopted on the basis of Chapter VII of the UN Charter, the resolution extends the scope of the legal regime on piracy on the high seas to the territorial waters of Somalia. It exceptionally allows, in agreement with the Somali government, foreign maritime forces to enter the territorial waters of Somalia to suppress piracy in the same manner as if they were on the high seas.[43] Valid for an initial period of six months but regularly renewed thereafter[44] and even extended to the land territory of Somalia,[45] the authorization to exercise a reverse "right of pursuit," as it has sometimes been described, integrates fully with the new international instruments in the fight against maritime piracy put into place in recent years. However, according to the Council, "this resolution shall not be considered as establishing customary international law" and is therefore limited to the case of Somalia.

---

[40] About the "failed" or "failing" states issue, *see* C. D. Classen, *Failed States and the Prohibition of the Use of Force*, *in* J-M. Thouvenin, C. Tomuschat, *Les Nouvelles Menaces Contre la Paix et la Sécurité Internationales*, SFDI, Journée Franco-Allemande, A. Pedone, Paris, 2004, pp 128-139. More specifically on Somalia A. Lelarge, *La Somalie Entre Anarchie et Piraterie*, *JDI*, 2010, n° 2, pp 450-474.

[41] After negotiating the release of hostages and paying the a ransom, the French authorities justified their entry into Somali territory by advancing the argument that the intervention was authorized by the Transitional Federal Government.

[42] Resolution 1816 (2008) June 2, 2008.

[43] The requirement that states be "permitted to intervene" (that are those who cooperate with the Somali government and whose names have been formerly disclosed to the Secretary General of the United Nations) might seem superfluous within the framework of the implementation of coercive measures adopted under Chapter VII of the Charter (the agreement of the state concerned might not in principle be necessary), but can be explained by taking into account the particularly complex political context of Somalia.

[44] *See* Resolutions 1838 (2008), 1846 (2008), 1851 (2008), 1897 (2009). Resolution 1950 (2010) renewed the previous authorizations for a further twelve months period.

[45] Resolution 1851 (2008), point 6.

As is reflected in the preparatory work of the law of January 5, 2011, it is of course this type of authorization that it refers to when it evokes the possibility of intervention in state territorial waters. The criticism that was raised did not disappear though, because, through the exemptions granted, it is not the qualification of acts of piracy that is exceptionally extended to acts committed in the zones under sovereignty, but only the exceptional regime which is applicable to them. The United Nations Security Council did not err in reserving, in the previously evoked resolutions, the term "piracy" for acts classically defined as such by UNCLOS, and by employing the expression "armed robbery" to refer to crimes committed in the territorial waters of Somalia, where it exceptionally allows pursuit. In contrast, in order for the new legislative plan to combat piracy to be applied to acts committed in territorial waters where international law permits action by third-party countries, it must be understand that these would be described as acts of piracy, not "armed robbery."

It is clear that the geographical condition posed by UNCLOS no longer fits with the need to fight against acts that otherwise meet all other criteria of piracy. Whether committed on the high seas or in zones under state sovereignty, the facts may be identical, but the legal regime that results will be quite different. Other approaches that are broader in terms of piracy have been used.[46] The fact remains that the terms used in French law only imperfectly correspond to those resulting from UNCLOS, in contrast to the willingness of the legislator, which makes the definition of piracy even more ambiguous.

Furthermore, without contradicting international law, the reference to only "territorial waters" may, in turn, seem somewhat restrictive. For example this provision could make an arrest impossible in the archipelagic waters of an archipelagic state which would have been allowed by the Security Council. A new concept designated in Part IV of UNCLOS, the archipelagic waters are a special category of maritime space located between the domestic waters and the territorial sea of an archipelagic state and which have the particularity of falling completely under the sovereignty of the latter (even though they could have previously been covered by the zone of the high seas). This hypothesis could present itself in the case of archipelagic states which, like the Seychelles, are affected by criminal acts committed by pirates but that could

[46] Thus, the International Maritime Bureau does not draw any consequences of the distinction between acts of piracy and acts of armed robbery at sea. On the "multiple approaches" of piracy, I J.-P. Pancracio, *op. cit.*, pp 446-450.

not, according to the restrictive definition chosen, be described as piracy.[47] Only a teleological interpretation of the text of the law, viewed in the light of the objectives thereof, the intention of the legislature and applicable international law, could possibly overcome this difficulty.

In reference to the definition in UNCLOS, the legislature may have wished to avoid the emergence of certain discrepancies between domestic and international law with regard to the meaning given to the notion of piracy. This was achieved in only half measure. This approach avoids all the difficulties of interpretation associated with other components of piracy, which are regularly highlighted by the doctrine,[48] which will inevitably spring forth during the legal qualifying of the facts by the domestic courts. So arises, among others, the issue of the qualification of the acts of violence against oil platforms (while Article 101 of UNCLOS evokes only acts committed against a ship or aircraft), or also that of assessing the condition based on the existence of "private purposes," which involves the search for a psychological element (intent or motive) that may prove difficult in practice (and sometimes difficult to distinguish from terrorism, a political crime by goal but which can prove identical to piracy in its mode of execution[49]).

Furthermore, even though it reintroduces the notion of piracy into French law, the new law does not establish an autonomous violation as such as it links it to diverse offenses already defined in the penal code, specifying the legal framework of their prosecution in the specific context of maritime piracy. But can it then be considered that the provisions of UNCLOS have actually been implemented?

B. The determination of criminal offenses constituting acts of piracy

Rather than proceeding with a revision of the penal code to accommodate the criminalization of piracy and thereby fully harmonizing French criminal law with that of UNCLOS, which would have been more consistent in terms of legal logic, the French legislature chose another option. To clarify the material scope of misconduct which the new system is intended to apply to, the Act of January 5, 2011, in Article 1,[50] lists the criminal offenses which are already illegal under French law, but which will apply to the new

---

[47] One of the amendments introduced by the representative Christian Ménard before the National Assembly in the first reading, also planned to complete the wording used in the bill by this reference, in addition to territorial waters, the "archipelagic waters," where also "if international law allows it." This amendment, which would at least be clear, however, was not retained.

[48] *See* L. Lucchini et M. Voelckel, *op. cit*, pp 159-174.

[49] *See, e.g.,* F. Odier, "Piraterie et Terrorisme Maritime," *Droits Maritimes et Défense,* Actes du Colloque du Ministère de la Défense, 1996, p 82.

[50] This list of offenses is now embedded in Article 1-II of Title I of the Act of July 15, 1994.

legislation, if they can legally be defined as acts of piracy in the sense defined above.

It should be noted that even before the concept of piracy was reintroduced into French criminal law, certain acts of piracy could well be punished on the basis of it. Thus, the offenses of injury to life or property, such as kidnapping, forcible confinement, extortion, robbery, hostage taking or murder, remained convictable. However, these are offenses which could constitute acts of piracy. Moreover, the mere possession of or taking control by force of or threat of violence to a ship was already an offense punishable by twenty years of imprisonment under Article 224-6 of the Criminal Code. The ability to prosecute those who were guilty of such offenses, even when they could be assimilated into piracy under international law, however, was dependent on the usual limits for the exercise of state powers, especially with regard to their personal or territorial affiliation with the French state, and could only take place in accordance with the contingency of common law. Their inclusion in the new framework of the fight against maritime piracy will give to them legal significance of a different magnitude, thereby letting them benefit from the broader opportunities open for law enforcement by the relevant provisions of UNCLOS.

It is, therefore, these criminal acts likely to constitute acts of piracy that the legislature has attempted to identify by inserting them into the new Title I of the Act of 15 July 1994 on procedures for the exercise by the State of its police powers at sea. Three categories of offenses are thus listed. They concern: 1) hijacking of aircraft or vessels, 2) kidnapping and unlawful confinement, and 3) participation in a criminal conspiracy.

With specific reference to hijacking[51] the new law states that the cases referred to are those involving "at least one vessel or aircraft directed against a vessel or aircraft."[52] It should be noted here then that the attack of an aircraft on another aircraft could be characterized as an act of maritime piracy! This qualification, following an amendment by Representative Christian Ménard, rapporteur of the bill to the National Assembly, does not contradict the definition of article 101 of UNCLOS. It is nevertheless surprising,[53] especially since this possibility is not mentioned in the rest of

---

[51] Offenses under articles 224-6 to 224-7 and 224-8-1 of the Penal Code.

[52] "at least one ship or aircraft against a ship or aircraft" (our translation).

[53] This is a hypothesis "rather unlikely," as it was stressed during the parliamentary debates (could be taken into account an attack on a seaplane with another aircraft). *See* Report of Mr. Dulait, on behalf of the Committee on Foreign Affairs, Defence and Armed Forces Bill, as amended by the National Assembly on the fight against piracy and exercise police powers of the State at Sea, No. 151, December 7, 2010, p 14.

the text as the police powers authorized later are mentioned only with respect to offenses committed "on board or against the ships mentioned in Article L.1521-1 of the Defense Code." However, while Article 224-6 of the Criminal Code envisages as a possible seizure the theft of a stationary platform situated on the continental shelf, the new law does not place this offense among those that could constitute an act of piracy. Since this type of attack has been on the rise in recent years, particularly in the Gulf of Guinea, one could have expected that the new legislative framework would be applied to it, but ultimately French law here merely aligns itself with the definition embodied in UNCLOS, which does not cover this offense under acts of piracy.

The second category of offences adopted by the new law, abduction and illegal restraint, as well as communication of false information,[54] are also applicable in this legislative framework when the offenses precede, accompany or follow a hijacking of ship or aircraft. The hostage taking that often accompanies acts of piracy and which is in marked increase in recent years can thus be regulated within the new framework. As for participation in a criminal conspiracy,[55] the third offense category selected by the law, it also falls within the scope of the new legislation when it is intended to prepare the aforesaid acts, whether the hijacking of vessels, abduction or illegal restraint. This criminalization will thus allow for prosecution of persons who, without necessarily having participated in the violence, have contributed to the preparation of the act, particularly as regards its sponsors.

All of these offenses can now be "searched, recorded and prosecuted" under the conditions of Title I of the Act of July 15, 1994 as amended by that of the January 5, 2011, that is to say by applying the new framework for the fight against maritime piracy. Note however that some offenses that could be considered as participating in piracy, such as extortion, are not included in the list. For the sake of simplicity, the legislature has in fact selected only the most serious offenses. This pitfall could have been avoided if the legislature had chosen to make piracy a crime in itself, directly transposed from the provisions of UNCLOS. For, as some have already pointed out, "many offenses are likely to consist in an act of piracy, but none of them can be specifically and completely assimilated to it."[56] Choosing not to make piracy a specific offense, but rather to draw on an existing set of offenses was

---

[54] Offenses under articles 224-1 to 224-5-2 and 224-8 of the Penal Code.

[55] Offenses under articles 450-1 and 450-5 of the Penal Code.

[56] AC Dumouchel, *Contenu et Dernières Avancées du Projet de Loi Français de Lutte Contre la Piraterie*, *DMF* 2010, n° 720, p 962: "many offenses are likely to consist in an act of piracy, but none of them can be specifically and completely assimilated to it" (our translation).

justified, especially during the impact assessment of the bill, in the wish not to upset the balance of the penal code offenses and the fact that this would in any case not have been enough, since the law of July 15, 1994 would have needed to be modified in order to identify the authorities authorized to establish and seek out crimes of piracy. It is also true that the conventional definition of piracy does not provide specific guidance regarding the types of violent offenses. Nor does it specify the means that can be employed to exercise them, nor their intensity. The law therefore is based on existing general criminal offenses by trying to encompass all the most plausible scenarios, which presents the advantage of acting on a consistent penal law, even if the law loses coherence. This technique is also the same as that which was previously used for terrorism, with the "common law offenses in connection with a terrorist organization."

The new legislation also strengthens the penalties against the crimes mentioned, the maximum penalty for these offenses ranging from twenty years imprisonment to life imprisonment, depending on the aggravating circumstances (hostage taking, kidnapping ending in death, the victim being a minor, etc.). Thus, the new Article 224-6-1 of the Criminal Code (added in Article 4 of the Act of January 5, 2011) provides that where the hijacking of an aircraft or vessel is committed by an organized gang, the penalty is increased to thirty years imprisonment (instead of twenty), together with a period of firm imprisonment. Until now, only the provisions of the Criminal Code relating to abduction or illegal confinement of people envisaged the commission of such acts by an organized gang as aggravating circumstances (thirty years or even life imprisonment particularly in cases of abuse of the victims or their use as hostages). Henceforth, the crime of hijacking an aircraft or ship committed by an organized group (which is in practice, the most likely case) is thus an aggravating circumstance and falls under the yoke of the specific procedures applicable to the crime and organized crime, as do crimes of conspiracy or non-justification of resources equal to lifestyle, when in connection with such an offense.[57] Life imprisonment is also always a threat to the perpetrators of these crimes if loss of life is involved or if they are accompanied by acts of torture or barbarism,[58] which has apparently become a common practice of Somali pirates for some time now.[59]

Though the new law works towards a general increase in penalties for this type of offense, it is not clear whether this will deter potential pirates who are

---

[57] Title XXV of the Criminal Procedure Code, amended by section 5 of the Act of January 5, 2011.
[58] Articles 224-2 and 224-7 of the Penal Code.
[59] *See Les Armateurs Très Inquiets Face au Développement de la Piraterie*, *Mer et marine*, 8 February 2011.

more attracted by the lure of money than concerned by the potential consequences of their actions, especially given the conditions of poverty in which they mostly live. It was also necessary, moreover, that French courts be authorized to judge them, which, until recently, was subject to restrictive conditions relating to the classic pattern of allocation of national jurisdiction guided by the principle of the law of the flag. The new law breaks new ground in this respect since, taking advantage of the exceptional authorization given by international law if the acts genuinely meet the definition of piracy, it gives the French courts "quasi universal" jurisdiction to judge such acts.

C. The recognition of the "quasi-universal" jurisdiction of the French courts to try perpetrators of piracy

Before the law of January 5, 2011, “pirates” were not completely unknown to French courts which already had the power to handle their legal treatment, provided that there was a nexus with France that yielded jurisdiction. Individuals who committed acts amounting to piracy could be condemned by the French courts on the basis of existing offenses (kidnapping, robbery, hostage taking, for example), but only if they acted in the territory of the Republic; in territorial waters for example (although in this respect we can no longer speak of piracy under international law . . .), or even against ships or persons of French nationality, unless they themselves were French citizens.[60] In other words, the jurisdiction exercised here was either territorial or personal (passive or active), but by no means universal. This is illustrated mainly by cases such as the *Ponant*,[61] the *Carré d'As*,[62] and the *Tanit*,[63] which were able to be brought before French courts after the pirates were arrested by French armed forces.[64] However, when such acts occurred outside the territory of the Republic and did not involve nationals or French

---

[60] *See* articles 113-3 and 113-7 of the Penal Code.

[61] *See*, in that case, the judgments of the Chamber of Criminal Court of Appeal of Paris (April 6, 2009) and the Criminal Chamber of the Court of Cassation (September 16, 2009 (No. 09-82777)) and the remarks of S. Touzé, in the chronicle of French jurisprudence, *RGDIP*, 2010, No. 4, pp 904-937.

[62] Six Somali pirates captured in the case of the *Carré d'As* were indicted in Paris September 25, 2008 and charged with hijacking the ship, kidnapping, theft and receiving stolen goods. See the judgments of the Criminal Chamber of the Supreme Court February 17, 2010 (comments of P. Bonassies, *DMF* 2011, No. 726, pp. 569-572) and May 11, 2011 (Légifrance site: http: / / www.legifrance.gouv.fr).

[63] Three pirates arrested in this case are currently subject to proceedings before the French courts, for “misuse of the ship” and “arbitrary detention and kidnapping by organized gangs.” They should be tried in Rennes.

[64] Paradoxically, they may not have been convicted in these cases of acts of piracy as such, the concept has meanwhile disappeared from our legal framework.

ships, jurisdiction of the French courts could not be established due to the lack of recognition under French domestic law.

Article 105 of UNCLOS, however, offered France a new opportunity to bring pirates to trial in a court of law. This article provides that "every State may seize a pirate ship or aircraft, or a ship or aircraft taken by piracy and under the control of pirates, and arrest the persons and seize the property on board." However, if international law permits the use of restraint with respect to this, this can only be at the service of law. All pirates need to be duly tried. This is precisely the aim of what follows in the same article, which is our sole concern here,[65] when it states that "the courts of the State which carried out the seizure may decide upon the penalties to be imposed, and may also determine the action to be taken with regard to the ships, aircraft or property, subject to the rights of third parties acting in good faith." A perfect example of exclusive jurisdiction of the state's flag on the high seas, piracy is thus subject, according to UNCLOS, to a system of universal suppression, completely outside of common law. Independent of the relationships usually developed on a domestic level and their jurisdiction, the courts and any apprehending state can then, according to international law, suppress piracy regardless of the nationality of its perpetrators, the ship or of the victim, even if the acts were committed on the high seas. Universal jurisdiction is clearly recognized on an international level, aiming to try acts of piracy in courts of law.[66]

In the absence of an international court with jurisdiction over pirates, the criminal prosecution of the pirates can only occur in domestic courts. Hence the need for the states concerned to adopt legislation on piracy. However, Article 105 of UNCLOS makes it clear that "the courts of the State which carried out the seizure may decide upon the penalties to be imposed."[67] Thus, there is no requirement for state authorities that have done so to call on its domestic courts. This is simply an option left open to the discretion of the states concerned and not a binding obligation for them. For example, nothing prevents the state responsible for the seizure of the pirate ship to agree with a

---

[65] We will come back later on the police powers so granted on the high seas to all States as far as piracy is concerned.

[66] The "universal jurisdiction" can indeed be defined as "demonstrated ability to the courts of any state to try offenses committed abroad, regardless of the location of the offense and the nationality of the perpetrator or the victim" ("aptitude reconnue aux tribunaux de tout Etat à juger des faits commis à l'étranger, quels que soient le lieu de l'infraction et la nationalité de l'auteur ou de la victime" *in* J. Salmon [Dir.], *Dictionnaire de Droit International Public*, Bruxelles, Bruylant, 2001, p 212).

[67] In contrast, the Convention for the Suppression of Unlawful Acts against the Safety of Maritime Navigation (SUA), which can also be used in the fight against piracy, provides for the obligation to "prosecute or extradite."

third-party country to hand over an accused for trial, provided of course that said action meets relevant constitutional and international obligations.[68]

In any event, by reinstating the offense of piracy into French law, the legislature could have given the French courts broad jurisdiction in this area. However, a more moderate position was preferred, due to the risks the recognition of such a universal jurisdiction would pose. Other than the fact that it could quickly lead to congestion in the courts, even while they are far removed from the where the actions take place, the Belgian and Spanish precedents have shown that by recognizing an absolute universal jurisdiction for their courts, in this case genocide, it could cause major diplomatic incidents, while having only limited judicial efficiency. The extent is such that these countries have had to renounce the universal jurisdiction.[69] The French legislature therefore considered that universal jurisdiction was "an instrument to be used with caution"[70] and it had to avoid the same disappointing examples that their neighbor states became.[71]

It is true the new law expands the jurisdiction of the French courts by giving them the authority to try acts committed outside French territory, even if the nationalities involved (ships, pirates, the victims) have no connection with France.[72] It takes advantage of the possibility offered by Article 105 of UNCLOS. However, it adds two conditions which limit its scope. The jurisdiction of French courts will only be retained if the perpetrators (or associates) of acts of piracy were arrested by competent French agents and failing agreement with the authorities of another state to exercise court

[68] For a study on the application of universal jurisdiction for piracy, see especially E. Kontorovich and S. Art, *An Empirical Examination of Universal Jurisdiction For Piracy*, *AJIL*, 2010, vol. 104, afl. 3, pp 436-453.

[69] *See* J. Rios Rodriguez, *La Restriction de la Compétence Universelle des Juridictions Nationales: les Exemples Belges et Espagnols*, *RGDIP*, 2010, No. 3, pp 563-595.

[70] In the words of French Senator André Dulait in his Report No. 369 (2009-2010) made on behalf of the Foreign Affairs Committee and filed March 30, 2010: "un instrument à utiliser avec précaution."

[71] Note that Belgium had also wished, in its new legislation on piracy, to finally establish a limited extraterritorial jurisdiction, may be somewhat cooled by its previous experience. *See* the two above-mentioned Belgian laws of 30 December 2009 on the fight against maritime piracy. *See also* the commentary of L. the Hardÿ de Beaulieu, "Les lois du 30 décembre 2009 relatives à la lutte contre le piraterie maritime", *Revue de droit pénal et de criminologie*, 2010, vol. 90, n° 7-8, pp 854-877. For a comparison between French law and Belgian law (considered more "progressive"), *see* P.-A. Janssens, *La Loi Française de Lutte Contre la Piraterie Maritime à l'Epreuve des Mesures Pionnières Adoptées par la Belgique*, *DMF*, 2011, n° 726, pp 544-551.

[72] It should be noted that so far, the jurisdiction over offenses committed outside the territory was admitted into French law (articles 689 and following of the Code of Criminal Procedure) in respect of certain acts (such as torture or terrorism) only under two conditions: based on an international convention and the alleged offender "is in France."

jurisdiction.[73] If for example, another state accepts jurisdiction, particularly the state to which the perpetrators or victims belong, or if the pirate ship sails under its flag, those apprehended could then be turned over in order to be tried. France has been able to opt for this solution with respect to Somalia, as it regularly delivers alleged pirates to local authorities in the region of Puntland. But this second condition primarily aims to take into consideration the case of agreements concluded by the European Union, as part of Operation Atalanta, with certain third-party countries such as Kenya,[74] the Seychelles, or more recently the Republic of Mauritius (agreement signed July 14, 2011). These states have in fact accepted, as a result, that suspects be transferred onto their territory in order to be tried by their courts. If the will to favor a regional judicial treatment of persons suspected of piracy clearly is reflected in this context,[75] the "almost universal" jurisdiction resulting from the legislation is not more present than the opportunities offered by the provisions of UNCLOS as the scope is more limited.

The legislature must, however, in the event that jurisdiction of French courts be established, specify the courts with the jurisdiction to try these and related offenses.[76] Depending on the situation, it would be in the case of mainland France, the High Court of the Maritime Prefect or that the court which corresponds to the port where the vessel was diverted to. In the case of French overseas territories, the trial court of the Government delegate for the state action at sea or that which corresponds to the port where the vessel was diverted. The new law also refers to the concurrent jurisdiction of the courts under the Criminal Procedure Code or special legislation. It refers specifically in this context to Article 706-75 of said Code, relating to inter-regional specialized courts. These have a recognized expertise in organized crime and have resources and skills that are undoubtedly better suited to the gravity of the crimes in question here, particularly with regard to the offense of ship hijacking committed by gangs, which is now included in the list in Article 706-73 of the Code of Criminal Procedure.[77] The trend towards the specialization of courts as designated in the new law should in any case allow more effective treatment of piracy cases by the judges sensitive to this problem.

---

[73] Article 5 of the new Title I built into the law of July 15, 1994: "à défaut d'entente avec les autorités d'un autre Etat pour l'exercice par celui-ci de sa compétence juridictionnelle."

[74] Agreement of March 6, 2009 since denounced by Kenya in March 2010.

[75] In this regard, see also the proposals made by Jack Lang, in its report cited above, for a "Somaliazation" of the solutions.

[76] Article 6 of the new Title I built into the law of July 15, 1994.

[77] *See id.*

By broadening in this way the jurisdiction of its courts, the new French legislation therefore adapts, certainly with some nuances and hesitations, to the international legal framework established in this domain. And it is in order to overcome the legal obstacles to the prosecution of suspected pirates that the legislature has decided, as encouraged by international law, to integrate into France's domestic law the concept of maritime piracy, while taking into account the particularities of its law enforcement system. However, the objective of the international definition of piracy is not only to allow national courts to try the perpetrators. It is also, and perhaps above all, to assert the need for action against a barbarian act that ignores the elementary principle of humanity.[78] Is there not, in this context, a paradox in trying to protect the human rights of detained pirates? Yet this is what the legislature has sought while defining in the Act of January 5, 2011, the legal framework that will now dictate operations against maritime piracy, under the watchful eye of the European Court of Human Rights.

II- The Legal Framework for Anti-Piracy Operations Under the Control of the European Court of Human Rights

While French law had no specific legal framework to allow State authorities to exercise the full police powers that international law accords them when dealing with the fight against piracy, the new legislation is now enriched with a new legal framework to guide the actions of officials in this area (A). While it is based on the International Law of the Sea, the operational framework has nevertheless been accompanied by a specific legal basis for the detention of suspects on board vessels in order to meet the expectations of the European Court of Human Rights (B). If, in this context, a number of procedural guarantees have been made to the individuals thus detained, it is nonetheless fair to question their ability to meet all the requirements in this area (C).

A. The extension of the legal framework for State action at sea

The inclusion, in the Act of July 15, 1994 on procedures for the exercise by the State of its supervisory powers at sea, of a new pillar dedicated to the fight against maritime piracy, extends to the regime of maritime intervention operations that was so far only applicable to operations involving drug

[78] *See* L. Lucchini et M. Voelckel, *op. cit*, p 173: "l'acte barbare qui méconnaît les principes élémentaires d'humanité."

trafficking and illegal immigration on the high seas.[79] However, unlike these other two pillars, the control measures and enforcement envisaged here in the fight against piracy can be employed for vessels without a flag or vessels flying a foreign flag, without the necessity of obtaining the prior consent of the flag state. French naval forces are then explicitly authorized to act in accordance with international law.

The latter, it must be recalled, establishes the principle of freedom of navigation on the high seas, only the flag state may exercise powers of control and enforcement over its ships. However, Article 110 of UNCLOS recognizes a few exceptions to this principle, since it permits the vessels of third states to exercise their "right of visit," without the prior consent of the flag state and also where specific treaties provide for it. This can be exercised only when there are reasonable grounds for suspecting that the vessel is engaged in the slave trade or piracy, that it is used for unauthorized radio broadcasts, is without nationality or actually has the same nationality as the vessel that shall inspect it though flying a foreign flag, or is refusing to show its flag. With respect only to piracy, Article 105 of UNCLOS specifies, as pointed out above, that "every State may seize a pirate ship or aircraft, or a ship or aircraft taken by piracy and under the control of pirates, and arrest the persons and seize the property on board." The impact of these provisions should be qualified, however, because the usage of the word "may" certainly helps found the basis for the jurisdiction of the state of the ship involved, but does not impose any obligation.

Therefore, by linking these operational powers into domestic law, the legislature does not really respond to a legal constraint; it is only making use of the opportunity which it was given, to use some of its powers in areas where the principle of the law of the flag generally forbids it to do so. In the absence of legislation introducing into French law the provisions of UNCLOS, serious doubt existed as to whether France had a comprehensive legal framework appropriate to all the powers it was nevertheless authorized to exercise. For this reason, it is likely that the French legislature has taken the case law of *Medvedyev* as a forerunner developing all of its legal regime concerning police operations at sea (and not only that relating to deprivation of liberty, which we will examine next). Continuing on from this, the new legislation will indeed provide clarification regarding both the preconditions for the operation and the authorized police powers and the agents authorized

[79] The law of 15 July 1994 had already been amended in 1996 (Act No. 96-359 of 29 April 1996) to allow the suppression of drug trafficking on the high seas under Article 17 of the Vienna Convention of 20 December 1988 and by Law No. 2005-371 of 22 April 2005 organizing the fight against illegal immigration by sea in accordance with the Palermo Protocol.

to act, giving them a solid legal basis so that they can carry out their work according to well established rules of law.

As regards the criteria for justifying an intervention, several factors warrant attention. The first condition, relating to the reality of the offense, provides that authorized measures may be employed when the offenses constituting piracy "were committed," "are being committed" but also "are preparing to be committed." In doing so, the law seeks to address a legal problem sometimes encountered by naval vessels when they want check ships that, without being caught in *flagrante delicto*, are nevertheless suspected of planning acts of piracy (this is particularly the case for support ships, commonly known as "mother ships," which serve as a rear base for boarding skiffs). Up to the present, in the absence of initiation of its execution, French law did not allow them to punish such acts. Now, authorized officers may proceed legally with measures of control and enforcement, even when the offense is not yet established.

Moreover, the criterion adopted to allow government intervention at sea relies on the existence of "reasonable grounds" for suspecting such acts of piracy, while the original text of the bill, more restrictive, required the presence of "serious reasons" for having such suspicions.[80] The initial formulation was nevertheless more consistent with the wording of Article 110 of UNCLOS mentioned above, which allows for the boarding of a foreign ship on the high seas only if it has "serious reasons" for suspecting that the vessel is engaged in piracy. While "grounds" and "reasons" for suspicion may be considered as synonymous terms, the adjective "reasonable" allows for a certain freedom in the interpretation of the term while the word "serious" calls for a more rigid interpretation. The condition ultimately adopted by French law for the implementation of control measures and enforcement against suspect vessels therefore appears more flexible, less demanding, than that enshrined in the French version of UNCLOS,[81] the objective put forward being here again to better address the operational requirements.[82] It should also be noted that, while it is intended to strengthen

[80] The amendment passed by the Chamber of Deputies at first reading is the result of an amendment proposed by the deputy Christian Ménard, rapporteur.

[81] It is true that the English version of the Convention using the term "reasonable ground" in section 110 could argue for a less restrictive reading of this condition.

[82] If grounds for suspicion of piracy are not difficult to demonstrate when the perpetrators of acts of piracy are effective, evidence of preparation for the offense may actually be more difficult to make when it has not yet been committed, especially when the material for the attack could have been thrown overboard by pirates feeling identified.

the capacity for repression of piracy, this wording is consistent with that used in the fight against drug trafficking and illegal immigration by sea.[83]

The legislature also relaxes the condition linked to the nationality of the ship victim, which should be included in the list in Article L. 1521-1 of the Defence Code,[84] covered by the provisions relating to the exercise by the State of its police powers at sea. Indeed, this article is subject to a substantial change in Article 6 of the new law. It always designates firstly the French ships, for which the personal jurisdiction of the State will of course be exercised (law of the flag), in compliance with international law. But alongside foreign vessels for which the Defense Code recognises the powers of the State in the maritime areas under French sovereignty or jurisdiction, and on the high seas as permitted by international law (as is the case for piracy), the legislature added the hypothesis of "ships hoisting no flag or stateless."[85] Moreover, in addition to the actions authorized, in agreement with a foreign state, when it concerned a vessel within the maritime areas under the sovereignty of the latter (and where the territorial jurisdiction is expected to take precedence over personal jurisdiction), the new law adds the more general hypothesis of vessels flying the flag of a state which has requested the intervention of France or approved its request for intervention,[86] which broadens the scope of the exercise by the state of its police powers at sea. In contrast, foreign warships and foreign government ships used for non-commercial purposes are not affected by these measures, which comply with Articles 95 and 96 of UNCLOS which grants them complete immunity from jurisdiction as regards any state other than the flag state.

Once these conditions are met, what are the police powers exercisable by authorized officials? The new law refers specifically to the execution of control measures and enforcement provided in three sources of law: international law, Title II of Book V of the first part of the Defense Code and the Act of July 15, 1994 concerning the terms of the exercise by the State of its police powers at sea. Once again we find the relevant rules of international law mainly in UNCLOS, but possibly also in the resolutions of the United Nations Security Council. The "right of visit" enshrined in Article 110 of UNCLOS not only gives to warships and military aircraft the right to board a pirate ship met on the high seas, but also the right to conduct a

[83] Articles 13 and 20 of the Act of July 15, 1994.

[84] New Article 2 of Title 1 of the Act of July 15, 1994.

[85] Note that according to Article 104 UNCLOS, "become a pirate ship or aircraft. The retention or loss of nationality is determined by the law of the State from which such nationality was derived."

[86] New "4" added to Article L. 1521-1 of the French National Defence Code.

verification of the titles authorizing the ship's flag and, if suspicion remains, that of further examination on board the ship. Such control measures were already included in the Defense Code, allowing particularly conducting a verification of the ship's identification (art. L. 1521-3), ordering a visit (art. L. 1521-4) and, if necessary, its rerouting (Article L. 1521-5). In case of refusal to comply, it is also authorized, in accordance with international law, the pursuit of foreign ships (art. L. 1521-6) and even the use of force (Article L. 1521-7). The new law also authorizes "the rerouting of the vessel to a position or a suitable port to proceed with more detailed observations if necessary and to hand over the arrested persons and the objects and documents which were the subject of provisional measures."[87]

Article 105 of UNCLOS also authorizes the seizure of the pirate ship (or aircraft), as well as the arrest of persons and seizure of property on board. Note that while the ultimate objective of the Convention is to "maintain order, security and tranquility on high seas,"[88] the measures authorized here fall clearly within the context of the exercise of a judicial police power, since they are directly concerned with a specific criminal offense. It should nevertheless be emphasized that the seizure considered here has a precautionary aim: it is not to grant title, but simply to substitute the authority of the captain of the vessel seized, with the authority of the captain of the government ship. This objective is transcribed in the new version of the Act of July 15, 1994 via the opportunity for authorized officers to exercise the right of access to "take any precautionary measures" with regard to objects or documents that appear related to the commission of the offenses referred to "to prevent them from recurring, or being renewed."[89] In practice, the objects in question are primarily assault weapons and other equipment used by pirates, such as grappling hooks. Note also that coercive measures may be taken against persons on board (including restrictive measures or deprivation of liberty), which we will of course come back to and which are now framed by the new provisions of the Defense Code relating to the procedure for detention on board.[90]

---

[87] Article 3-A of Title I of the Act of July 15, 1994 as amended, "le déroutement du navire vers une position ou un port appropriés pour procéder le cas échéant à des constatations approfondies ou pour remettre les personnes appréhendées ainsi que les objets et documents ayant fait l'objet de mesures conservatoires."

[88] *See* L. Lucchini et M. Voelckel, *op. cit*, p 175, "assurer l'ordre, la sécurité et la tranquillité sur la haute mer."

[89] Article 3 of Title I of the Act of July 15, 1994, "pour éviter qu'elles ne se reproduisent ou se renouvellent."

[90] Section 3 completing the single chapter of Title II, Book V, the first part of the Defence Code. *See below* (B).

It should be emphasized that the only persons authorized by law to carry out (or to have carried out) the authorized control and enforcement measures are commanders of warships and aircraft responsible for maritime surveillance.[91] This clarification is consistent with the UNCLOS which states in Article 107 that "only by warships or military aircraft, or other ships or aircraft clearly marked and identifiable as being on government service and authorized to that effect." As the State is liable for these measures, they must be undertaken with the authority of government officials. This is why the law states that operations will be conducted under the authority of the maritime Prefect, as regards operations carried out off of the mainland,[92] or, overseas, under that of the Government Delegate for state action at sea.[93] It is also envisaged that these operations be conducted under the designated authority of a civilian or military command in an international context. This specific reference aims explicitly to include in the scope of the law the actions of the crews of French ships engaged in international operations, as is the case with Operation Atalanta in the European Union, and therefore subject to another operational chain of command.

These same commanders of warships and military aircraft responsible for maritime surveillance, as well as the Navy officers on board these vessels, can carry out acts which are normally performed by judicial police officers. They will have received for these duties, however, a special authorization in accordance with conditions laid down by decree in the Council of State.[94] The acts in question, now proposed in section 4 of the new Title I of the Act of July 15, 1994, concern in particular ascertaining the offenses and the search for and apprehension of perpetrators and their accomplices. Note that, unlike the procedure laid down in the fight against drug trafficking and illegal immigration, the law makes no provision here, with regard to piracy, for the obligation to inform the public prosecutor of these operations in advance. Only in the event that these agents wish to seize objects and documents related to the commission of the offense need they obtain prior authorization and here again, except in cases of "extreme urgency."[95]

---

[91] Article 2 of the new Title I built into the law of July 15, 1994.

[92] Decree No. 2004-112 of February 6, 2004.

[93] Decree No. 2055-1514 of 6 December 2005 for New Caledonia, French Polynesia, Reunion, Guyana, French West Indies and Saint-Pierre and Miquelon.

[94] *See* Article 4 of Title I of the Act of July 15, 1994. The wording of this provision is strictly the same as the one used in articles 16 and 23 of the Act which are respectively subject to the decrees No. 97-545 of 28 May 1997, the suppression of drug trafficking and No. 2007-536 of April 10, 2007 for offenses committed on immigration.

[95] This exemption is the result of an amendment to the draft adopted by the Government senators, once again to take into account operational constraints.

The new law also envisages the possibility that these agents carry out the destruction of certain vessels.[96] These vessels must have been used to commit the offenses in question, be "lacking a flag," and there should be no "conceivable technical measures for permanently preventing the renewal of such offenses."[97] The law of July 15, 1994 already provided for such a possibility in the fight against drug trafficking and illegal immigration overseas. This is now extended to the fight against piracy on the high seas, with the stipulation that it can only be done "in accordance with the international agreements and treaties in force."[98] This implies, in particular, ensuring that such an operation does not produce debris that could interfere with navigation. The goal here is once again to take operational constraints into account, the "mother ships" and skiffs used by pirates being sometimes difficult for the warships to transport. Members of Parliament have, however, seen fit to regulate this option even more, by providing for the need to obtain prior authorization from the Public Prosecutor and to proceed only after the objects or documents relating to the commission of the offences have been seized.[99] The stated objective here is to avoid potential claims against the commanders of the vessel or naval officers, while ensuring the preservation of evidence.

The conclusion is clear: the legislature has extensively exploited the opportunities provided under international law concerning the exercise of police powers on the high seas, within the context of maritime piracy. However, if international law allows for the use of force in regard to piracy, this can only be at the service of the law. If the law calls for all suspected pirates to be brought before a judge, it also mandates that this time of transition not occur in an arbitrary manner, at least in legal systems that have made a commitment to the protection of human rights and fundamental freedoms. That is why these police actions, from the moment they affect the person that is the pirate, must be conducted in compliance with these commitments.[100] It is also to take into account the considerations and

[96] This possibility was introduced by senators in the first reading on a proposal of Mr. André Trillard.

[97] *See* Article 4 of the new Title I built into the law of July 15, 1994, "de mesures techniques envisageables pour empêcher définitivement le renouvellement de ces infractions."

[98] Taking account of Article L. 218-44 of the Code of the environment, notwithstanding Article L. 218-43 authorizes the dumping of ships, by the representative of the State at sea, in respect of treaties and international agreements.

[99] Amendment proposed by the member Christian Le Bris and members of the Socialist Group, and completed by the Government.

[100] Note here that the "Convention for the Protection of Human Rights and Fundamental Freedoms" of 1950 (hereinafter "European Convention on Human Rights") is not the only international instrument protection of human rights which France must comply with when its authorities exercise their police powers at sea.

criticisms raised by the European Court of Human Rights with regard to shortcomings in the French system pertaining to detention on board ships,[101] that the legislature decided to endow it with the legal framework that it was lacking.

B. The establishment of a legal basis for detention on board ships

Even before its scope was extended to the fight against maritime piracy, the procedural framework governing the operations of the French state at sea was already subject to criticism from the European Court of Human Rights. Indeed, it has twice condemned France in the *Medvedyev* case[102] for failing to comply with Article 5, § 1 of the European Convention on Human Rights. This article, on the right to liberty and security, explicitly states that "no one shall be deprived of his liberty," except in the limited cases listed in the article and "in accordance with a procedure prescribed by law." Among the situations where a deprivation of liberty may occur is notably "the lawful arrest or detention of a person effected for the purpose of bringing him before the competent legal authority on reasonable suspicion of having committed an offence or when it is reasonably considered necessary to prevent his committing an offence or fleeing after having done so." (Article 5, § 1(c)). It is useful to recall that the case concerned the interception off of Cape Verde by the French authorities of a ship flying the flag of Cambodia (The Winner) which was suspected of narcotics trafficking. The crew members were detained on board in the custody of soldiers for thirteen days, the time it took the ship to reach the rerouted port of Brest and to hand the suspects over to the authorities. What France was mainly criticized for in this case was not having at the time a "legal basis" organizing the conditions of detention on board a ship, contrary to the requirements of the general principles of rule of law and legal certainty.[103]

However, while such measures of restriction or deprivation of individual liberties may be implemented by the commanders of government ships against persons apprehended in contexts other than drug trafficking, in reality

[101] Note however that at all stages of the fight against piracy involving a link with people, not just to situations where retention measures are implemented against alleged pirates, international standards in this area must be taken into consideration. On all these issues, *see* the aforementioned Articles of C. Laly-Chevalier and D. Guilfoyle.

[102] After the first stop, dated July 10, 2008, the case was referred to the Grand Chamber, which adjudicated on March 29, 2010 (*Medvedyev and other c / France*, Appl. No. 3394/03). For a critical approach of the first case, see note to S. Touzé, in the Chronicle of international jurisprudence, *RGDIP*, 2009, No. 2, pp 205-215. On the second case, see Ph. Weckel same chronicle, *RGDIP*, 2010, No. 3, pp 651-660.

[103] *See* § 62 of the Judgment of July 10th 2008, and § 102 of the Judgment of March 29th 2010 mentioned above. We'll discuss later the other ground of illegality based on the fact that the control exercised by the prosecutor could not be considered as a proper "judicial authority."

they are implemented whenever the state intends to conduct a police operation at sea, especially in cases of arresting pirates. Deprivation of liberty is indeed inevitable in this type of situation from the moment the ship's course on which the suspects are found is prescribed by the French military, regardless of the level of restriction on freedom of movement they are subject to inside of the ship itself. In order to prevent future similar convictions at the Court of Strasbourg automatically punishing these measures, and in order that they be adopted as part of the fight against piracy as they are in other areas, it was first necessary that France acquire a legal basis for arrests at sea.

By placing, in Article 1 amending the Act of July 15, 1994, as a condition to the execution of control or enforcement measures, "on reasonable suspicion," the committing of or preparing of the offenses mentioned above, the new law responds in itself to one of the requirements laid down in Article 5, § 1(c). Under this article, the arrest and detention of an individual in order to bring the person before the competent judicial authority is allowed only if there is "reasonable suspicion" of the commission of an offense or "reasonable grounds to believe" in the need to prevent it.[104] This rationale is not, however, sufficient, since it already existed in the fight against drug trafficking and that has not prevented the European Court ruling that there was in this case a lack of legal basis. It has instead placed particular emphasis on the fact that to satisfy the general principle of legal certainty, "it is therefore essential that the conditions for deprivation of liberty under domestic and/or international law be clearly defined and that the law itself be foreseeable in its application, so that it meets the standard of 'lawfulness' set by the Convention."[105] However, the Act of July 15, 1994 on procedures concerning the state supervisory powers at sea, as well as the Defense Code, only provide for the implementation of control and enforcement measures "in accordance with international law," without expressly authorizing the deprivation of liberty.[106] As for the International Law of the Sea, it also

[104] *See* ECHR, August 30th, 1990, *Fox, Campbell and Hartley c / UK* case, § 32.

[105] *See*, *Medvedyev* case, 2010, § 80 and among others, the decision of 25 June 1996, *Amuur c / France*, Rec. 1996-III.

[106] If the CMB is considering a possible compensation for the ship visited if the suspicions are proved unfounded (Article 110 § 3), as well as the implementation of international responsibility of the State in case of arbitrary seizure (Article 106), the Convention remains fairly quiet with regard to safeguards governing the exercise of police powers. Article 110 of the CMB is indeed limited to admit that the discussion must be carried out with all "possible consideration" without giving further details as to the methods to be used. *See* decision of 1 July 1999 by the International Tribunal for the Law of the Sea in the *Saiga* case, § 155: In the absence of precision in the Montego Bay Convention, ITLOS had invoked the customary principle of the "considerations of humanity" to define the conditions of the boarding.

remains silent on the framework for deprivation of liberty, even if the UN Security Council has repeatedly stressed, in the above-mentioned resolutions on the situation in Somalia, the fact that enforcement should be "consistent with applicable international human rights law."[107]

To address these concerns it was essential to secure the transfer process, by ship, of persons suspected of crimes within the context of state actions at sea. As this concerns measures which could include the deprivation of liberty, legislation became necessary. This is why Article 6 of the Act of January 5, 2011 complements the single chapter of Title II of Book V of the first part of the Defense Code with section 3 specifically devoted to the "measures taken against persons on board ships." It defines a *sui generis* system adapted for confinement to ship of persons apprehended within the context of state actions at sea that reaches well beyond acts of piracy since, by extension, the framework will also apply to other pillars of the state exercising its police powers at sea, including the fight against drug trafficking. As shown in the preamble of the Act, this is expressly to provide for the possibility of a deprivation of liberty for the crew during the rerouting of an intercepted ship, and to precisely define it and to frame it within a system providing adequate protection against arbitrary interferences as regards the right to freedom, all in order to comply with the objections raised by the European Court of Human Rights in the case of *Medvedyev*.

As stated now in Article L. 1521-11 of the Defense Code, "necessary and appropriate" enforcement measures against persons on board can be decided on by the commanders of ships. The reasons for their implementation are specifically listed as they must be employed only "to ensure their holding, the preservation of the ship and its cargo and personal security."[108] When ordered enforcement measures include a restriction or deprivation of liberty, the law provides for a staggered procedure in several phases, involving various external authorities. Article 1521-12, states that the authorities empowered to decide on such measures must refer the matter to the maritime Prefect, or if they operate overseas, to the government representative for state actions at sea.[109] These authorities then have the responsibility of notifying as soon as possible the public prosecutor with territorial jurisdiction. To extend

[107] *See* in particular resolutions 1851 (2008) and 1918 (2010) previously mentioned.

[108] Original version: "d'assurer leur maintien à disposition, la préservation du navire et de sa cargaison ainsi que la sécurité des personnes."

[109] Note that a decree of May 9, 2011 (No. 2011-505) precises that in the maritime areas that do not fall under the jurisdiction of a maritime Prefect or a governmental Delegate for the action of State overseas, the commander of sea area exercise the functions delegated by the Government to implement these provisions.

these enforcement measures on ships beyond the first forty-eight hours, the prosecutor must, at the request of the commanders, refer the matter to the relevant national liberty and custody judge. It is this judge who now, before the expiration of this period (assuming it is referred as soon as possible given the constraints related to the remoteness of the vessel), rules on the possible continuation of measures to a maximum period of five days (exactly one-hundred-twenty hours after the expiration of the above). It may however be renewed under the same conditions throughout the entire time necessary to ensure that the persons in custody be delivered to the competent authority.[110]

Moreover, in order to take into account situations where these persons are transferred by air rather than by sea, the Senate saw fit, in its review of the text on first reading, to add that this system may also be applied on land or on board an aircraft.[111] It was also made clear that, upon arrival on French soil, the persons subject to the enforcement measures would be put at the disposal of the judicial authority.[112] Note also that this procedure should, in principle, be applied regardless of the operational framework (national or international) in which the suspected pirates were arrested and regardless of whether the court processing be carried out by France or not. This means that if the commanders of French ships intercept suspected pirates as part of Operation Atalanta, they will follow this procedure, even if the European Staff decides in the end to use the transfer agreements concluded by the European Union with third countries.

In this way the new legislation has attempted to fill the legal vacuum that existed in French law regarding detention on board ship, in order to meet the criteria set by the European Court of Human Rights. However, Article 5, § 1 of the European Convention on Human Rights does not only require the existence of a legal basis as the basis for arrest or detention. It also requires that this legal basis be of "quality," that is to say "sufficiently accessible and precise, in order to avoid all risk of arbitrariness."[113] Does the new legislation provide adequate safeguards on this issue for individuals, suspected pirates in particular, who are the subject of enforcement measures during operations by the State at sea?

---

[110] Article L. 1521-14 of the French National Defence Code.
[111] Article L. 1521-17 of the French National Defence Code.
[112] Article L. 1521-18 of the French National Defence Code.
[113] ECtHR, *Amuur c / France*, *supra*, § 50 and 53, pointed out in Case *Medvedyev* of 2008, § 53.

C. *The uncertainties relating to procedural safeguards for persons detained on board ships*

To further secure the procedure, the law provides new safeguards to govern the deprivation of liberty on the sea, taking into account the operating environment characterised by the physical distance from judicial authorities. In addition to preserving the rights of suspected pirates (which was not, it must be noted, the main concern of the legislature), the objective regularly raised during the parliamentary debates was to avoid allowing the perpetrators of the offenses to invoke nullity of procedure, in France or before the European Court of Human Rights, in order to escape punishment. Do the precautions set out in the new law ensure the adequate protection and legal certainty necessary to prevent arbitrary infringements of the rights and freedoms of the persons concerned by public authorities? If the efforts undertaken in this regard are undeniable, certain weaknesses concerning the guarantees to individual liberties provided by law can still be found, particularly in terms of European law on human rights and the requirements of the Strasbourg Court.

Regarding first of all the introduction of the liberty and custody judge into the proceedings, it must be noted that it was clearly presented as a measure intended to draw from the consequences of the first ruling by the European Court on *Medvedyev*. It had considered in this case that if the detention measures on board had been placed under the control of the prosecutor of the Republic, the latter could not be considered a "judicial authority" in the sense that the legal precedent of the Court gives to this notion.[114] Even if, by adopting a more subtle argument concerning the status of the public prosecutor, the High Court did not see fit to return this argument in the final decision (the lack of legal basis in itself constitutes a violation of Article 5, § 1), it has clearly reiterated that the magistrate before whom the person deprived of liberty must be brought promptly, "must offer the requisite guarantees of independence from the executive and the parties, which precludes his subsequent intervention in criminal proceedings on behalf of the prosecuting authority."[115] The Court refuses to admit judicial authority to public prosecutors in the sense of Article 5, § 1(c) of the Convention, particularly because of the lack of independence of the latter with regard to the executive.[116] Under these conditions, it is likely that the sole control of

---

[114] ECtHR, 5th Sect., July 10, 2008, *Medvedyev c / France*, Appl. No. 3394/03, § 61. See also *Amuur* case cited above, § 53.

[115] ECtHR, GC, March 29, 2010, *Medvedyev and other c / France*, Appl. No. 3394/03, § 124.

[116] ECtHR, Judgement of December 4, 1979, *Schiesser c / Switzerland*, Series A No. 34, §§ 29-30.

the public prosecutor on the procedure for detention on board appeared insufficient in the eyes of the Court.[117]

The liberty and custody judge henceforth intervenes in the control of custodial measures on board ships. But will this be enough to satisfy the requirements of European law on human rights? In particular, the issue of the transit time of the detainee on board to the judicial authority could become the focus of discussion. The brevity of time taken for the suspect to be brought before the judicial authority is indeed one of the essential requirements laid down by Article 5, § 3 of the European Convention on Human Rights, which requires that anyone arrested or detained "shall be before a judge promptly or other officer authorized by law to exercise judicial power and shall be entitled to trial within a reasonable time or to release pending trial." While it is foreseen in the law that "upon their arrival on French soil," the persons concerned will be brought to the judicial authority.[118] But at no time does this expressly state that the capturing ship head directly to a French port, with no stops other than which is necessary for the transfer. Among the objectives to the enforcement measures taken against persons on board (including the restrictions and deprivations of liberty), Article L-1521-11 evokes only "to ensure their holding, preservation of the ship and its cargo and personal security," but not that of delivering them as quickly as possible to the judicial authorities. It is true that the distance and the uncertainties of the journey may be such as to explain the difficulty of meeting the requirement of promptness.

Moreover, the Strasbourg Court adopted an adjustable interpretation of this condition to time, depending on the circumstances of the case. Thus, in the case *Medvedyev,* it did not accept the applicants' complaint that they were not "promptly" brought before a judge. The trip lasted thirteen days, followed by two to three days in custody. The Court took the view that the deprivation of liberty undergone by the applicants was justified by "wholly exceptional circumstances," including "the time it took inevitably the [vessel] to reach France."[119] It therefore held that this case was very similar to the case

---

[117] The ECHR has confirmed its position in the *Moulin* case, in which it held that, because of their status, the public prosecutors in France do not present enough independence vis-à-vis the executive (ECtHR, 23 November 2010, *Moulin France v. France*, Appl. No. 37104/06). We must also remember that the French Cour de cassation itself has recently followed the position of the Strasbourg Court, acknowledging, in the case of Philippe Creissen, that the prosecution does not have the guarantees of independence and impartiality required by Article 5 § 3 ECHR to be considered a "judicial authority" according to the meaning of this provision (Cass. Crim., December 15, 2010, No. 10-83674).

[118] Article L. 1521-18 of the French National Defence Code.

[119] *Medvedyev* case, 2008 aforementioned, § 68.

Rigopoulos Against Spain, discussed a few years earlier, in which it had recognized a material impossibility to "physically" bring the applicants before such an authority in a shorter time period (sixteen days in this case).[120] The Court nevertheless made it clear in the same case that swift and automatic judicial review allows the assurance of significant protection against arbitrary behavior, specifically secret detention and ill-treatment,[121] mainly during the first hours of detention, where the risk is at its maximum.[122] The fact that according to the new law, control of arrests in the early hours remains under the public prosecutor, and that this figure is not a "judicial authority" in the conventional sense of the expression could still pose some problems. In their dissenting opinion issued under the second ruling on *Medvedyev,* the minority judges stressed in this regard the distinctions between the circumstances of the case and the *Rigopoulos* case, including the fact that in the latter it was a Central Court of Instruction, not the public prosecutor, which oversaw the proceedings on the day of the arrest and that it presented guarantees more protective of the rights of the detainees.[123] Given the narrow majority (nine votes against eight) with which the Court ruled on this issue, it is not sure that it will not one day change its position, nor that the guarantees foreseen in the law completely meet conventional requirements.[124]

Furthermore, the fact that measures for restricting or depriving liberty may be renewed by the liberty and custody judge, admittedly in increments of a

---

[120] ECtHR, *Rigopoulos v. Espagne* (déc.), no 37388/97, CEDH 1999-II. This case concerned the interception on the high seas by the Spanish customs police of a ship under the Panamanian flag and carrying the cocaine and the detention of its crew for sixteen days, the time of his convoy to a Spanish port. The Court concluded manifestly ill-founded the complaint under Article 5 § 3, arguing that "the circumstances are quite exceptional . . . of the case, one can not conclude that the time elapsed between the time of the detention of the applicant and its presentation to the judge exceeded the speed as designed in paragraph 3 [of the] article [5]."

[121] ECtHR, 29 November 1988, *Brogan and others v / UK*, Series A, No. 145-B, § 58. The Court found in this case a violation of Article 5 § 3 by considering a four days and six hours custody beyond the time limits allowed by this article.

[122] *Medvedyev* case, 2010, cited above, §§ 118-120.

[123] *See*, in *Medvedyev* case of March 29, 2010, the joint partly dissenting opinion of Judges Tulkens, Bonello, Zupancic, Fura, Spielmann, Tsotsoria, Power and Poalelungi.

The very next day its crew members were informed of their situation and advised of their rights. Within two days the court had ordered the crew to be remanded in custody. On the following day they were apprised of that decision and invited to name the persons they wanted to have informed of their detention. This information was communicated to the respective embassies of the States of which the crew-members were nationals. Three days after the boarding, the independent investigating court issued an order regularising the crew's situation in accordance with the Spanish Code of Criminal Procedure. One week after the interception, the applicant had access to the services of a lawyer.

[124] For a dissenting opinion, *see* Luc Briand, *Lutte Contre la Piraterie Maritime: la France Renforce son Arsenal Législatif*, *Gazette du Palais*, 20 janvier 2011, n° 20, p 8.

maximum of one-hundred and twenty hours but "during the time necessary for the people concerned to be submitted to the competent authority,"[125] without a maximum time limit being set, can also leave the fear of more criticism from the European Court of Human Rights. At the first reading, the Senate had not wished to add an amendment to introduce a maximum period of thirty-two days for the custody on board of persons apprehended through an act of repression,[126] considering that the incorporation of such a time limit into the law could pose practical difficulties, and that the authorization by the liberty and custody judge to extend this measure every five days was such as to provide all necessary guarantees for the duration of the measure. Such a maximum period of detention, based on that provided for the detention of illegal aliens, would constitute an additional guarantee. This is the solution that neighboring Belgium chose to follow in their new legislation on the fight against piracy, setting a maximum period of one month for detention on board.[127]

The new law does try however to set out other safeguards to protect the rights of individuals detained. In particular, it is expected that, within twenty-four hours from the beginning of the restriction or deprivation of liberty, a health examination be made "by a qualified person."[128] Relatively succinct, this exam can be performed by anyone who has received medical training, such as a nurse. If it concerns assessing the overall health of the individual at the time of their apprehension by the crew, the goal is also to undoubtedly prevent any possible challenge based on ill-treatment during the judicial phase. Furthermore, the medical examination itself is only mandatory within ten days from the first health examination.

But what happens if there is no doctor on board and that detention lasts longer than 10 days? It is true that in practice, at least on large vessels that have a doctor on board at all times, it is likely that the first examination will be carried out by a medical officer. It remains though that this provision, which takes into account, certainly, the material conditions in which the Navy operates, is probably less protective towards the person apprehended than the measures that are provided for during the custody phase, the medical examination in this instance taking place right from the beginning of the

---

[125] Article L-1521-14 of the French National Defence Code, "durant le temps nécessaire pour que les personnes en faisant l'objet soient remises à l'autorité compétente."

[126] This amendment was introduced in the Senate by Didier Boulaud, Jean-Louis Carrère, Michel Boutant.

[127] Aforementioned Act of 30 December 2009 on the fight against maritime piracy and to amend the Judicial Code. *See also* the comments above, note 70.

[128] Article L. 1521-13 of the French National Defence Code.

measures. Also it is provided that the liberty and custody judge be able to ask the public prosecutor to provide an account of these health and medical examinations, which had to have been transmitted to the latter in advance in order to assess the situation of the person concerned. The liberty and custody judge can even order a new health examination.[129] Certainly there is an extra judicial guarantee here, but it is not automatic, as the judicial authority must make the request and that, in the eyes of the European Court of Human Rights, the public prosecutor is not such a figure.[130]

In addition, since it is expected that the liberty and custody judge communicate with this person if, of course, the technical means permit, would it not also have been possible to provide access for people interested in a lawyer, in line with the requirements of Articles 6, § 1 and Article 6, § 3 of the European Convention on Human Rights (right to a fair trial)? It should be remembered that the Strasbourg Court no longer hesitates to sanction those states, including France,[131] when their legislation does not provide for a lawyer to be present at the first stage of police custody.[132] While people detained aboard a ship in transition to the territory are not yet quite at the stage of custody, the risk of being condemned by the European Court indeed exists. Did it not also criticize the standards outlined by the French Government, in the first *Medvedyev* ruling, for not regulating the conditions of deprivation of liberty on board, "in particular the possibility for the persons concerned to contact a lawyer or a family member?"[133] While it may indeed be difficult to bring a lawyer on the ship, it would be equally difficult for the public prosecutor and the liberty and custody judge to get aboard. Such guarantees would however, be quite able to draw upon the possibilities offered by new communication technologies.[134] Protection of the right to counsel in the new law appears even weaker as the information for the detainees on the reason for their deprivation of liberty is not fully guaranteed. It is, however, expected that the order by the liberty and custody judge be communicated to the person concerned "in a language they understand"[135] and the law in this meets the requirements of Article 5, § 2 of the European Convention on Human Rights. But it ignores the right for the detainee to be

[129] Article L. 1521-15 of the French National Defence Code.

[130] *Supra.*

[131] ECtHR, Judgement of 14 October 2010, *Brusco v. France*, Appl. No. 1466-1407.

[132] ECtHR, GC, Judgement of November 27, 2008, *Salduz v. Turkey*, Appl. No. 36391/02, § § 50-62 and Judgement of 2 March 2010, *Adamkiewicz v. Poland*, No. 54729/00, § § 82-92.

[133] *Medvedyev* case, 2008, § 61.

[134] *See* G. Poissonnier, note under ECtHR, 10 July 2008, No. 3394/03, *Medvedyev*, *Gazette du Palais*, October 26, 2008, No. 302, p 13.

[135] Article L-1521-16 of the French National Defence Code.

informed "in the shortest period of time possible" of the reasons for their arrest and the charges against them, since if the order must be communicated to the maritime prefect "in the most brief amount of time," there is no time limit however, imposed on the latter to ensure its transmission to the applicant. More broadly, does not the fact that the court order of the liberty and custody judge is "not subject to appeal"[136] enter clearly into conflict with Article 5, § 4 of the European Convention on Human Rights which provides that "everyone who is deprived of his liberty by arrest or detention shall be entitled to take proceedings by which the lawfulness of his detention shall be decided speedily by a court and his release ordered if the detention is not lawful?"

It is also surprising that the legislature did not wish to consider the hypothesis of the liberty and custody judge deciding on the release of those subjected to the restrictions of liberty. The argument made during the parliamentary debates that such a decision would be unlikely had problems being convincing, except to admit the facade of the role of the judge assigned to the seat in the course of this procedure. "Such a question is not at all theoretical," as rightly pointed out Luc Briand, Judge and Administrator of Maritime Affairs.[137] If for example, the evidence would prove insufficient or impossible to transmit in due time, the liberty and custody judge has little choice but to rule for release.

Among the other "weaknesses" of the text, the rejection of the amendment proposed before the Senate by Robert Badinter (and again in the Assembly by Gilbert Le Bris) concerning the conditions of transfer of suspects to other states is regrettable. It was intended to supplement Article 5 of the Act of July 15, 1994 by requiring that suspected pirates not be handed over to the authorities of a state "where the penalty incurred be more severe than in France or where the legislation or the internal situation of the State concerned does not guarantee them a fair trial." This meant to prevent the possibility of pirates being sentenced to death, knowing that there exists in the areas concerned, states that have not abolished the death penalty. However, it was felt that the inclusion of these guarantees was not useful, since they already figure in French and international norms, and in the agreements between the European Union and the countries concerned. Such a provision would still have brought an additional guarantee to the rights of suspected pirates detained and a certain coherence with the provisions of

---

[136] Article L-1521-16 of the French National Defence Code.

[137] Luc Briand, *Lutte Contre la Piraterie Maritime: la France Renforce son Arsenal Législatif*, Gazette du Palais, 20 January 2011, n° 20, p 8.

Article 696-4 of the Code of Criminal Procedure, which provides such a condition for extradition. Is this an exacerbated conception of Human Rights? Is this protection which comes at the expense of real victims, whether they are sailors who are taken hostage or more generally of all those who suffer from this threat that hinders the exercise of freedom on the high seas, whether ocean carrier crews or fishermen? The truth is that it is not certain that the array of measures adopted make France entirely safe from other litigation, initiated by organisations or individuals, which would result in being condemned anew by the European Court of Human Rights.

More generally, some suggest that it would be better to merely reform the Code of Criminal Procedure rather than adding new offenses to the scope of procedures with a military dimension. More adequate protection against risks of the arbitrary could have been given to individuals who, under French jurisdiction, would be subject to enforcement action outside the territory.[138]

The military dimension of the new legislation concerning piracy comes up elsewhere, as in the provisions for the children of victims of piracy, who can themselves be recognized as "ward of the Nation" in the same conditions as for children of war victims.[139] This is a retroactive provision as it benefits the victims of acts of piracy committed since November 10, 2008, date of the beginning of Operation Atalanta. Between this date and the date when the new law came into force, only one French citizen died as a result of an act of piracy, which occurred during the liberation of the French yacht *Tanit,* in April 2009, leaving an orphan.[140] This generous provision should enable the latter to be granted the rights assigned to wards of the Nation. If they cannot certainly be held liable for any indiscretions committed by their parents, the question can nevertheless be asked concerning the possible relief of liability that such a measure could lead to in respect to intrepid adventurers.[141] There is concern also of a sort of injustice due to the very definition of piracy. It is only once territorial waters have been exceeded that the offenses

---

[138] *See also* Pascal Beauvais, *L'affaire du Ponant: les Pirates à l'Abordage de la Procédure Pénale Française*, *JCP G*, n° 7, 15 February 2010, p 184.

[139] The amendment, introduced at the initiative of the Government, was set out in Article 7 of the Act, which refers to Title IV of Book III of the Code of military disability pensions and war victims. Initially reserved for children of fallen soldiers, the category has gradually been expanded to include, for example, children of people who died in exile, or the children of victims of terrorism.

[140] The *Tanit* was boarded by Somali pirates on April 4, 2009, in the Gulf of Aden. Negotiations for the hostages' release (taken from the frigate *Floreal*) were unsuccessful, an attack was launched by French naval commandos on April 10, 2009. One of the French hostages and two pirates were killed during the operation.

[141] As recalled by MP Gilbert Le Bris during the debates in Committee, the occupants of the *Tanit* had been warned that they entered in an area infested with pirates and they have been advised to turn away, but they ignored these warnings.

corresponding to ship hijacking and kidnapping fall under the domain of piracy. This means that while the children of victims of acts similar to piracy but committed in territorial waters are *a priori* deprived of the same support that benefit those for whom the same acts took place on the high seas. The provision of the law can in this respect seem incomplete.

The new French law on the fight against piracy is therefore not perfect, but what text could be in these circumstances? The preoccupying concern of the development of piracy off the Somali coast has highlighted the need and urgency to improve the mechanisms to fight against this scourge, with order and certainty. Within the twenty-five proposals put forward by Jack Lang in his recent report to the Security Council of the United Nations,[142] figures prominently encouragement for all states to criminalize piracy as defined by UNCLOS and to develop universal jurisdiction of such acts, while adopting a legal framework for detention offshore that complies with international rules regarding human rights and is compatible with operational constraints. This is unquestionably what the French parliament attempted by clarifying the legal framework for operations against maritime piracy. But, pulled on one side by the international obligations of France under UNCLOS and on the other by its European commitments with respect to human rights and fundamental freedoms, it had to compose a text which is, at times, only precariously balanced. In this perilous balancing act, the legislature made great efforts to meet these two requirements, at the risk of leaving some gaps and imperfections. The legal framework applicable to operations against maritime piracy that results is, however, reinforced by this new law. It yet remains to be seen what practical consequences will result from its application.

---

[142] http://documents.un.org/ (Symbol : S/2011/30).

17. United States Law on Piracy

Timothy STEIGELMAN[1]

Piracy, which is an offense subject to universal jurisdiction, is also a crime under the domestic law of the United States. With the recent anti-piracy efforts in the Gulf of Aden and surrounding waters, more alleged pirates are ending up as defendants in American courts. Pirate prosecutions have already caused an inevitable increase in decisional law, updating an area of U.S. municipal law that had festered for a century without major developments. Strikingly, two federal judges on the same court came to opposite conclusions on the meaning and application of America's piracy statute.

This piece will explore the American law of piracy, focusing on recent developments. The statutory definition of piracy will be examined, involving a discussion of the elements of the crime. Certain elements of the crime are a point of contention within the federal courts today, so a detailed examination will explore the two decisions mentioned above and the reason for the judges' contradictory conclusions.

Elements of Piracy Under U.S. Law

Piracy is a federal crime under U.S. municipal law. United States Code lays out a deceptively simple definition of piracy: "Whoever, on the high seas, commits the crime of piracy as defined by the law of nations, and is afterwards brought into or found in the United States, shall be imprisoned for life."[2] However, the second element of the crime is a mere tautology: piracy is committed (under U.S. law) if someone commits piracy (under international law). Little wonder that it is this enigmatic question-begging statute that now confounds the federal courts.

I. High Seas

Turning to the first element, even "high seas" is not as clear as it seems. Location on the high seas is ambiguous, as "high seas" might mean only beyond the low water mark of the United States, or it may mean beyond the

[1] J.D., University of Maine School of Law, *summa cum laude*; M.A., University of Maryland; Diploma, United States Naval War College; B.S., United States Naval Academy.

[2] 18 U.S.C. § 1651 (2011).

low water mark of *all* nations. In other words, if an otherwise piratical act were committed in the territorial seas of a third party nation, is it within the "high seas" under the statute, and therefore prosecutable as piracy under U.S. law?

The answer is probably yes—piracy may still occur under U.S. law in the territorial seas of other nations. At least one pirate was executed under U.S. law (in an American court superimposing Spanish punishment on American law) for a piratical act committed in Dutch waters.[3] The court explained that

> [p]iracy is a crime not against any particular state but against all mankind. It may be punished in the competent tribunal of any country where the offender may be found or into which he may be carried. The jurisdiction of piracy unlike all other crimes has no territorial limits. As it is against all so may it be punished by all. Nor does it matter that the crime was committed within the jurisdictional 3-mile limit of a foreign state, "for, those limits, though neutral to war, are not neutral to crimes."[4]

One might call this the "domestic" definition of high seas, defining the high seas completely in reference to one nation's own territorial seas.

The contrary view might be called the "internationalist" view. Under international law, the "high seas" are beyond the territorial seas of all nations.[5] For example, an otherwise piratical act committed in Canadian territorial waters would not have occurred in the high seas as that term is traditionally understood under international law. Under the internationalist view, then, the high seas element of the crime of piracy would not be met, and the defendants could not be prosecuted in an American court.

One commentator reviewed these competing schools of thought and argued that because of this conundrum, the term "high seas" should be removed from the American statutory definition of piracy. "As used in [18 U.S.C.] section 1651, [the term 'high seas'] does not appear to have the jurisdictional meaning it has acquired in international law, but rather . . . attach[es] to *any*

---

[3] *See People of the Philippine Islands v. Lol-lo and Saraw*, 43 Phil.Rep. 19, 22-23 (1922).

[4] *Id.*, *quoting U.S v. Furlong*, 18 U.S. [5 Wheat.] 184, 200-201 (1820). *See also* 46 U.S.C. § 761, the Death on the High Seas Act (DOHSA); *Dalrymple ex rel. Dalrymple v. Fairchild Aircraft Inc.*, 575 F.Supp.2d 790, (S.D.Tex. 2008); *Sanchez v. Loffland Bros. Co.*, 626 F.2d 1228, 1230 & n. 4 (5th Cir. 1980) (per curiam) (because DOHSA extends a wrongful death action for death occurring in territorial seas of foreign nations, U.S. law may equate the term "high seas" to mean "international high seas or foreign territorial seas").

[5] United Nations Convention on the Law of the Sea (UNCLOS), art. 86, Dec. 10, 1982, 1833 U.N.T.S. 397.

waters beyond the low water mark" of American shores.[6] The author goes on to support the internationalist view, desiring "the term ['high seas'] to be used in its correct treaty sense," or else deleted from the statute altogether.[7]

Perhaps the best understanding is that the term "high seas" may mean something different under international law than it does under American municipal law. That seems to be the case in the use of "high seas" elsewhere in U.S. Code,[8] so it stands to reason that "high seas" as used in section 1651 is shorthand for "waters beyond U.S. territorial seas," even while the term is somewhat narrower under international law.[9]

II. Piracy Under "The Law of Nations"

Under American law, the second element of the crime of piracy is that the defendant "commits the crime of piracy as defined by the law of nations."[10] The meaning of this phrase, incorporating by reference the "law of nations" to define a statutory crime, is the crux of the disagreement now swirling through the U.S. courts.

A. Background on Criminal and Appellate Procedure

For international readers unfamiliar with the American legal system, a brief introduction to the American system is in order. A prosecutor—here, a lawyer for the United States government—brings an indictment against a criminal defendant. In these piracy cases, the defendant is already in government custody, often transferred to civilian imprisonment after being captured at sea by U.S. or allied naval forces.

After whatever pretrial motions may be exchanged, the case moves forward to trial. A piracy defendant is likely unable to afford his own counsel, so the government provides defense counsel at government expense. If there is no conviction, the defendant is released. If there is a conviction, the case proceeds to sentencing, and the convicted defendant is sentenced to a prison term or fine according to sentencing guidelines.

Appeals are usually brought after trial, but interlocutory appeals before final judgment may be attempted as well. The discussion of the two cases below will discuss the procedural posture of each case going into the appeals.

---

[6] Samuel Pyeatt Menefee, *"Yo Heave Ho!": Updating America's Piracy Laws*, 21 Case W.Int'l.L.J. 151, 163 (1990).
[7] *Id.*
[8] *See* discussion of DOHSA, *supra*, n.3.
[9] *See* Menefee, *supra*, n.5, at 163 n58.
[10] 18 U.S.C. § 1651.

B. U.S. v. Said

In the early hours of April 10, 2010, the amphibious landing ship U.S.S. Ashland came under attack while transiting the Gulf of Aden. The offending vessel was a small skiff, commonly used by pirates in the area. With rounds incoming, the Ashland's crew returned fire, killing at least one person on the skiff, and setting it on fire. Ashland crewmembers spotted at least one AK-47 type rifle in the skiff; crewmembers rescued individuals from the burning skiff, and those rescued became the defendants in *U.S. v. Said.* Among other crimes, the defendants were charged with committing piracy under U.S. federal law.[11]

Before trial even commenced, defense counsel moved to dismiss the piracy charge. Their rather clever (if unoriginal) argument was that the federal statute criminalizing piracy "as defined by the law of nations" requires that defendants must stand accused of boarding a vessel, or taking control of it, or stealing something from the vessel. Because the indictment makes it clear that the defendants never got aboard the Ashland, no robbery or other piratical act under the law of nations occurred, so even if the pleadings were proven, the government would not be able to prove piracy.[12] In other words, the motion to dismiss argued that this was not piracy, but merely attempted piracy, so charging the complete crime is inappropriate in a case of attempt. The municipal statute incorporates the law of nations for its definition; if international law requires a theft to complete a piracy, there could be no piracy proven under the charges which do not, themselves, allege a theft.

The court agreed with the defendants, dismissing the piracy charge in a twenty-one page order.[13] The court relied on U.S. Supreme Court precedent from 1820 to interpret the federal criminal statute on piracy; the earlier decision in turn construed the forerunner to the current section on piracy. The key turn of phrase that the *Said* court focused on is that "all writers concur, in holding, that robbery or forcible depredations, *animo furandi*, upon the sea . . . is piracy."[14]

The *Said* court held fast to the simple arithmetic of piracy equals robbery at sea, concluding that "the Government simply fails to cite to one case in United States jurisprudence in which the Defendant was criminally prosecuted for 'piracy in violation of the law of nations,' for conduct that fell

---

[11] *U.S. v. Said*, 757 F.Supp.2d 554, 556-57 (E.D.Va. 2010).
[12] *Id.* at 557.
[13] *See id.* at 2:10-cr-00057-RAJ-FBS, Doc. 94 (E.D.Va. Aug. 17, 2010)(original docketed Order).
[14] *Said*, 757 F.Supp.2d at 559, *quoting U.S. v. Smith*, 18 U.S. (5 Wheat.) 153, 161-62 (1820)(Story, J.).

short of robbery or seizure of a ship."[15] The court goes on to review drafting committee notes, legislative history, and other statutory sections to buttress its conclusion.[16] Furthermore, the court shows that scholars have recently come to different conclusions as to whether attempted plunder at sea is consummated piracy. With the state of international law apparently so unsettled, the court concludes, it would be unfair to hold a defendant criminally liable for a crime—piracy—where "defendants in United States courts would be required to constantly guess whether their conduct is proscribed by § 1651."[17] The court dismissed the piracy charge, and the case continued on as to the other charges.

C. U.S. v. Hasan

In the early hours of April 1, 2010, the frigate U.S.S. Nicholas came under attack in the Indian Ocean, somewhere between Somalia and the Seychelles. The crew of the Nicholas returned fire on the small attacking vessels, and the attackers fled. The Nicholas pursued and stopped its former attackers, and found and detained the larger seagoing vessel that had housed and transported the small attack craft to the point of attack (the "mothership"). The individuals detained from the attack craft and the mothership became the defendants in *U.S. v. Hasan*.[18] Like in *Said,* the *Hasan* defendants were charged with a panoply of offenses, including piracy.

Also like in *Said*, the *Hasan* defendants filed motions to dismiss the piracy count arguing that, even if true, the allegations charge merely an attempt, not a consummated act, which does not constitute piracy under the law of nations, so piracy cannot be proven on the allegations of the indictment. Recall that this was precisely the same argument on which the *Said* defendants won dismissal of their piracy charge. *Said* was decided on August 17, 2010, and the *Hasan* opinion was not released until October 29, 2010; the *Hasan* court was certainly aware of the outcome of *Said,* and even refers to that then-recent decision.[19] Nevertheless, despite following the *Said* decision by less than two months, and even though both judges sit on the same federal court,[20] the *Hasan* court came to the opposite conclusion, holding that unlawful violence at sea, even without a consummated robbery, is piracy.

---

[15] *Said*, 757 F.Supp.2d at 562.
[16] *Id.* at 562-63.
[17] *Id.* at 566.
[18] *U.S. v. Hasan*, 747 F.Supp.2d 599, 601 (E.D.Va. 2010).
[19] *Id.* at n.2.
[20] Judge Raymond A. Jackson decided *Said*, and Judge Mark Davis decided *Hasan*. Both jurists preside at the U.S. District Court for the Eastern District of Virginia, and have chambers in the Norfolk division. Despite their colocation, the two judges came to opposite results on the same question.

In retaining the piracy charge, the *Hasan* court takes a long view of the municipal statute, starting with the provision in the U.S. Constitution that allows for the piracy statute in the first place.[21] The court then "examine[s] the [U.S. Constitution] Framers' understanding of piracy at the time of the nation's founding, and review[s] the unique characteristics that have for centuries distinguished piracy from all other crimes."[22]

The court painstakingly analyzes the history of piracy under domestic and international law, directly addressing the confusion inherent in piracy as both a municipal and an international crime. The court starts from the position that although "general piracy" [23] is a crime of universal jurisdiction, Congressional enactment does not increase the scope of general piracy; in other words, the United States cannot exercise universal jurisdiction over crimes that are not piracy under international law.[24]

The *Hasan* court proceeds to analyze the previous iterations of the piracy statutes under municipal law, starting in 1790 and proceeding through several revisions through 1820 and beyond. The court stops to detail the factual and procedural history of the British case *In Re Piracy Jure Gentium*, where the Privy Council ruled that robbery is not a necessary element of the crime of piracy under international law.[25] The court completes its survey of the law by reviewing treaty law on point, culminating with the UN Convention on the Law of the Sea (UNCLOS) and its definition of piracy.[26]

Revisiting the parties' arguments, the court next examines old American case law to put context on the *Smith* decision. With no binding precedent on point and even a fair amount of case law pointing against a narrow reading of *Smith*, the court declines to leap just yet; instead, the court explores the possibility that as the law of nations evolves, general piracy evolves with it, and so too does the American municipal statute criminalizing piracy.[27]

To emphasize the necessity of an evolving law of piracy, the court sets up an interesting possibility: a reading of piracy under municipal law that is forever wedded to its nineteenth century enactment would, in some circumstances, make enforcement impossible. When the piracy statute was initially passed, the law of nations recognized territorial seas out to three

---

[21] *Hasan*, 747 F.Supp.2d at 604-05; *citing* U.S. Const. art. I, § 8, cl. 10 (the "define and punish" clause, specifically mentioning piracy).

[22] *Hasan*, 747 F.Supp.2d at 604.

[23] The court distinguishes between "general piracy," meaning piracy under international law, and "municipal piracy," meaning piracy as defined in domestic law. *See id.* at 606.

[24] *Id.* at 606-12.

[25] *Id.* at 617, *citing In re Piracy Jure Gentium*, [1934] A.C. 586, 586-88, 600 (1934).

[26] *Hasan*, 747 F.Supp.2d at 619-21, *citing* UNCLOS art. 101.

[27] *Hasan*, 747 F.Supp.2d at 622-25.

nautical miles from the low water mark. In the early twentieth century the limit was expanded to twelve nautical miles. Consider that the major reason for universal jurisdiction over pirates is that the high seas are beyond the reach of all nations, so all may prosecute the crime. That justification no longer makes sense if the historical "law of nations" expects the high seas (and universal jurisdiction) to begin at three nautical miles, but modern international consensus is now twelve nautical miles. It is therefore possible that under a static view of the "law of nations," a person could be convicted of piracy for acts committed at seven nautical miles out to sea—unquestionably within U.S. territorial seas—even though no modern conception of international law considers seven nautical miles to be the high seas.[28]

Further underlining the need for a developing law of nations, the *Hasan* court points to the ban on the slave trade as a poignant historical example for why a developing law of piracy is not only necessary, but already understood in American law. The U.S. Congress outlawed the slave trade in the language of piracy, equating slave traders to pirates, but requiring a nexus to the United States. The *Hasan* court points out Congress's tacit understanding that the United States could not exercise universal jurisdiction and prosecute slave traders under general piracy where the movement to stop the slave trade was not yet an international norm.[29] When Spanish and Portuguese slave ships were impounded and the owners demanded compensation for the freed slaves, Chief Justice Marshall ruled for the claimants. The ruling resulted because the slave trade was not yet internationally condemned, so there could be no universal jurisdiction over slave traders; without a nexus to the United States there was no jurisdiction over them so municipal law could not be exercised over the slave traders. The *Hasan* court points out that Chief Justice Marshall further indicated that international law may continue to change, and with it, the power to prosecute general piracy may change as well.[30]

If the law of nations can change for municipal law purposes, and if UNCLOS embodies the current law of nations, the UNCLOS definition of piracy is essentially incorporated into municipal law and its elements are effective against the defendants.[31] Because the UNCLOS definition of piracy includes within its sweep any act of violence committed on the high seas

---

[28] *See Hasan*, 747 F.Supp.2d at 625.
[29] *See Hasan*, 747 F.Supp.2d at 628.
[30] *See Hasan*, 747 F.Supp.2d at 629, *citing The Antelope*, 23 U.S. (10 Wheat.) 66 (1825).
[31] *See Hasan*, 747 F.Supp at 633-41.

without governmental sanction,[32] and the complaint charges the defendants with committing violence on the high seas, proving allegations in the indictment will prove the charge of piracy.

Perhaps the most striking part of the *Hasan* decision—other than its complete rejection of *Said*—is that the court explicitly allows that its detailed analysis of universal jurisdiction is unnecessary to the result reached. Because the alleged target vessel was the U.S.S. Nicholas, America could exercise its sovereignty by prosecuting the alleged attackers without resort to universal jurisdiction.[33] The discussion of universal jurisdiction, therefore, is dicta, and the court admits as much. So much useful, well-considered dicta may be one jurist's attempt to correct a perceived error in this area of law, and the only candidate that comes to mind is the close precursor decision of *Said.*

It is also worth noting that the *Hasan* court goes out of its way to explain why international law is properly part of the decision. As most legal readers in America are aware, there is an argument currently in vogue in certain ideological circles that looks askance at American courts relying on international law. Addressing this concern, the *Hasan* court states foreign case law is pertinent here because piracy is one area "where Congress has specifically chosen to define a crime by reference to the 'law of nations.'"[34]

D. On Appeal: U.S. v. Dire

Both *Said* and *Hasan* were appealed to the U.S. Court of Appeals for the Fourth Circuit, an intermediate federal appellate court. The appeal for *Hasan* was heard under the name *U.S. v. Dire.*[35] The *Said* appeal was held in abeyance pending decision in *Dire.*[36] One commentator who neatly summarizes the oral argument predicts the court will affirm *Hasan* (now *Dire*).[37] Affirmance would allow for developments in the international law of piracy to apply to the municipal law of piracy. More immediately, that holding would conclusively answer the question that robbery need not be committed to complete the crime of piracy.

---

[32] UNCLOS, art. 101(A)(1), *but see Hasan*, 747 F.Supp.2d at n.33.

[33] *Hasan*, 747 F.Supp.2d at n.8.

[34] *Id.* at n.16.

[35] Oral argument can be heard through the links on the Fourth Circuit's website (http://www.ca4.uscourts.gov/) (last accessed November 30, 2011).

[36] *U.S. v. Said*, 10-4970, Doc. 50 (4th Cir. April 20, 2011)(Order).

[37] Kevin Walsh, Oral Argument in U.S.S. Nicholas Piracy Case, Opinio Juris (Sept. 22, 2011) (http://opiniojuris.org/2011/09/22/oral-argument-in-u-s-s-nicholas-piracy-case/).

III. WHAT IS THE RIGHT RESULT?

The decision coming out of *Dire*, controlling both that case and *Said*, cannot support both lower court decisions. Therefore if there is to be a ruling on piracy, either the *Said* court's static view of international law will prevail, or the more malleable, evolving view from *Hasan* will carry the day.

Reasonable people can—and already have—disagreed about the right result in these two piracy cases. An interesting comment about the development of piracy law in the United States is from an academic article that predated the *Said* decision by only a few months. Almost presaging the court in *Hasan*, the article concludes that: "Legal doctrines on universal jurisdiction and state action developed both directly and indirectly from cases involving piracy. Moreover, through *Smith*, the Supreme Court recognized that international sources, such as the teachings of foreign scholars, could be used in American courts to determine the meaning of American laws."[38]

It would be a bizarre result if municipal piracy, having been a font of change and evolution in U.S. law, were now trapped in the eighteenth century understandings of its original enacting assumptions. I am left with the conclusion that on balance, the *Hasan* court is probably correct. Contemporary international law should be considered, especially considering that the "law of nations" is explicitly incorporated into the municipal statute.[39] The forthcoming decision by the Fourth Circuit will hopefully squarely answer this issue. Regardless which side prevails, it will help clarify United States law in this area, so enforcement and prosecution of piracy can proceed with more certainty in the future.

---

[38] Joel H. Samuels, *Troubled Waters: Combating Maritime Piracy with the Rule of Law: Article: How Piracy Has Shaped the Relationship between American Law and International Law*, 59 Am.U.L.Rev. 1231, 1264 (2010).

[39] For another commentator coming to this same conclusion, *see* U.S. v. Abdi Dire Oral Argument, Piracy and the Law (http://piracyandthelaw.blogspot.com/2011/09/abdi-v-dire-oral-argument-and-some.html) (Sept. 25, 2011).

18. A Holistic Approach to Piracy: Toward a Public Order of Human Dignity through Corporate Social Responsibility

Gwenaële PROUTIÈRE-MAULION

The global economy has led to "a disconnect between the global economic and financial systems, and the legal standards of dominant States. It has brought about the end of the myth of the State and the ability of the State to define the legal framework and the forms of creation of law. [1]" The resurgence of piracy, in the context of the social and political crisis which is presently occurring in Somalia, is indeed a particularly striking example of the end of the ability of the State to define the legal framework for its intervention. Indeed, despite the implementation of important capabilities to fight against piracy at the international level, this phenomenon was mistakenly assumed to be disappearing. It has resurfaced unexpectedly and is now growing dramatically. An International Maritime Bureau (IMB) report indicates that between January and September 2011, 352 attacks have been recorded worldwide, of which 56% were by Somali pirates, who are now expanding their operational area into the Red Sea, the Indian Ocean, and the Arabian Sea, although these latter operations were less successful: attempts to capture ships succeeded in only 12% of cases (24 ships) against 28% in 2010 (35 ships). However, the fact remains that Somali pirates have significantly increased the number of operations (199 from January to September compared with 126 for the first 9 months of 2010), while at the same time, acts of piracy are increasing in West Africa [2]. From Togo to Nigeria to Cameroon, attacks on commercial vessels, oil tankers, or offshore platforms are more and more frequent (19 attacks in 2011 against only one recorded in 2010).[3]

---

[1] A. Baylos Grau, *New Areas of Regulation in Globalization: Transnational Corporations and International Framework Agreements*, in Corporate Social Responsibility and Transnational Economic Globalization, coord. I. Daugareilh, Bruylant, 2010.

[2] IMB Report, July 2011.

[3] This has also led Benin and Nigeria to launch during late September 2011 a program of joint maritime patrols.

Intrinsically linked to the history of navigation, piracy is a phenomenon with a long ancestry. Once connected to the control of the oceans and struggles for naval power, it now reveals a new face, one that illustrates a particular aspect of globalization. Indeed, piracy has reappeared in a context of economic globalization and internationalization of shipping that constantly tempts impoverished people, who are struggling to meet basic needs, with the possibility obtaining previously unreachable Western and Asian wealth. In a battered Somalia confronting clan struggles, the capture of vessels transiting off the coast is a source of income and power, redefining not only the structure of Somali society, but also the global governance of maritime traffic off the Horn of Africa.

At a time when letters of marque were closely related to piracy and the construction of States' naval power, enabling them to assert their supremacy over maritime areas, today the resurgence of the threat of piracy demonstrates how the globalization of shipping routes can no longer allow a unilateral state response. As the ship is now at the core of the internationalization of legal relationships (registration of ships in countries with which they have no real economic link, multi-national crews, distance from headquarters, legal water crossings of territorial waters, exclusive economic zones, or high seas), the fight against piracy requires a comprehensive approach that transcends individual States.

A Comprehensive and International Approach

The legal framework regulating the fight against piracy is also an international framework encouraging cooperation between States as it was set by the United Nations Convention on the Law of the Sea (UNCLOS), art. 100-108 and art. 110 - cf. Annex IX. The Convention gives every State the power to apprehend people or ships "in the high seas or in any other place outside the jurisdiction of any State" for acts of piracy, and to bring them before its courts (Art. 105).

Therefore, the Convention confirms the availability of universal jurisdiction for the repression of piracy, even if the State of nationality of the pirates or the flag State still retains the ability to exercise its own criminal jurisdiction. However, it does not automatically confer criminal jurisdiction over the vessel and seized property to acts of piracy, nor does it require the capturing State to exercise jurisdiction in any case. The State may still determine to what extent it will exercise any jurisdiction over piracy. It can choose to claim jurisdiction over captured pirates, the ship and the goods seized, or else to restrict its jurisdiction to more limited cases, for example when the hijacked ship or victims are its nationals, or when the piratical acts injure physical or legal persons of its nationality.

In accordance with Article 100 of the Convention, which gives States a duty to cooperate, other legal measures (such as a resolution of the Security Council of the UN) that are specifically directed against piracy, could help to resolve the issue of the jurisdiction. In addition, a judicial cooperation or extradition agreement could give a "non-capturing" State, which had established its criminal jurisdiction in the matter, the ability to judge a pirate caught in the territory or territorial waters of another State.[4] Since the fight against piracy occurs on the high seas, a space of regulation with no territorial roots, the construction of legal standards must take place at the international level, and therefore result in a transfer of the State's ability to define the legal framework of the fight against piracy to an international authority. This legal framework has also led, in recent years, to a plurality of national, European,, and international actions, resulting in the adoption of resolutions by the UN Security Council or the multilateral mobilization of armed forces, both of which are extensively discussed in this book. All these initiatives have so far shown a constant concern not to sacrifice respect for human rights to security for international commerce.

While this coordinated response is undoubtedly yielding results, as the number of successful attacks is declining, it fails to address the issue of piracy. In addition, the proliferation of initiatives and stakeholders could begin to undermine the coherence and effectiveness of these measures. Due to a lack of coordination and in the short term, these initiatives might not result in an overall synergy, but rather in a multiplicity of uncoordinated legal standards. Moreover, the multiplication of stakeholders creates the risk of a lack of a coherent process, and could lead to a loss of energy in the absence of a unified action program and clearly identified voices. A middle way between military cooperation and overall governance of the high seas thus remains to be clarified. For example, policy coordination between the CFT-151 and EU-NAVFOR is yet to be implemented, although both forces already work together organizationally.[5]

---

[4] Ch. Ménard, *Information Report on Piracy, National Assembly of France*, n° 1670, May 2009.

[5] Helly D., "Lessons from *ATALANTA* and EU counter-piracy policies," EU Institute for Security Studies, Seminar Reports, Paris, 23-24 March 2011 / Brussels, 17 June 2011, p. 1

SHIPOWNERS IN THE FIGHT AGAINST PIRACY: DEVISING NEW FORMS OF ACTION

While the world community is witnessing a newly emerging form of governance of maritime areas, the question of social responsibility of shipowners should also be considered. This is so despite the industry's often prioritizing profitability even if it means taking dangerous routes and exposing their crews to the risk of an attack, rather than extending routes or increasing the cost of maritime shipping. The development of maritime [flows ???] and containerization has already resulted in a reduction of crews, which increases the workload on board, and also the vulnerability of ships and their cargo. The transit through the Gulf of Benin and the Gulf of Aden now exposes seafarers to important psycho-social risks that impact their working conditions by creating situations of extreme stress when passing through the risk area.

An increasing number of European companies are promoting their corporate social responsibility strategies as a response to a variety of social, environmental, and economic pressures. They aim to send a signal to the various stakeholders with whom they interact: employees, shareholders, investors, consumers, public authorities, and NGOs. In doing so, companies are investing in their future and expect that the voluntary commitment they adopt will help to increase their profitability. By stating their social responsibility and voluntarily taking on commitments which go beyond common regulatory and conventional requirements, which they would have to respect in any case, companies endeavor to raise the standards of social development, environmental protection, and respect of fundamental rights, and embrace an open governance, reconciling interests of various stakeholders in an overall approach of quality and sustainability.

Most definitions of corporate social responsibility describe it as a concept whereby companies integrate social and environmental concerns in their business operations and in their interaction with their stakeholders on a voluntary basis. However, being socially responsible means not only fulfilling legal expectations, but also going beyond compliance and investing "more" into human capital, the environment, and the relations with stakeholders. The experience with investment in environmentally responsible technologies and business practice suggests that going beyond legal compliance can contribute to a company's competitiveness. Going beyond basic legal obligations in the labor sphere, e.g. training, working conditions, management-employee relations, can also have a direct impact on productivity. It opens a way to managing change and to reconciling social development with improved competitiveness.[6]

As actors in the global economy, shipowners should be participants in the fight against piracy, not only in ensuring the security of transit, but more to ensure the protection of fundamental social rights at work. From this point of view, the possibility of shipowners' liability, in case of a successful pirate attack, appears as an instrument of law enforcement but also as a source for redefining the concepts of economic efficiency and speed that influence the choice of maritime routes.

Further, health and safety at work have traditionally been approached mainly by means of legislation and enforcement measures. However, the trend of outsourcing work to contractors and suppliers makes companies more dependent on the safety and health performance of their contractors. Companies, governments, and sector organizations are increasingly looking at additional ways of promoting health and safety, by using them as criteria in procuring products and services from other companies and as a marketing element for promoting their products or services. These voluntary schemes can be seen as complementary to legislation and control activities by public authorities, as they likewise aim at promoting a preventive culture, i.e. higher levels of occupational safety and health.[7] Corporate social responsibility allows transnational companies to display the values that underpin practices and normativity deployed globally on objects and spaces legally unregulated.[8]

The globalization of the economy currently relies upon international economic law principles and procedures that are in the exclusive interest of companies. However, it is not unreasonable to suggest that corporate social responsibility can also provide better involvement of stakeholders in developing regulation more respectful of human rights. If the owners are now experiencing the effects of globalization in terms of economic gains, recall that the basics of corporate social responsibility can also remind them that they have obligations to their employees. It is therefore essential to mobilize this concept in order to make them more involved in the fight against piracy, especially to reduce the social and psycho-social risks faced by seafarers. Choosing less dangerous routes, or participating financially in support of the

---

[6] H. R. Bowes, Social Responsibility of the Businessman, New York: Harper and Brothers 1953; Commission of the European Community, Green Paper, Promoting a European Framework for Corporate Social Responsibility, COM (2001) 366 final.

[7] Ibid.

[8] I. Daugareilh (dir.), *Corporate Social Responsibility and Transnational Economic Globalization*, Bruylant 2010, p. XI.

cost of the fight against piracy are illustrations of new aspects of corporate social responsibility.

The impact of globalized trade increasingly leads to a consideration of the ethics of globalization. One hopes that taking account of the cost of human risk caused by acts of piracy will encourage actors to consider the need to rethink the production of law as no longer in a national context, but at an international level promoting universal respect for fundamental rights. In this way, the concept of corporate social responsibility, the only means able to mobilize the social, governance, and human rights aspects of dealing with the problem of piracy,[9] appears to be a new prism for understanding the involvement of shipowners in the fight against piracy, as a basis for a possible international harmonization.

REESTABLISH THE LAW OF THE FLAG

This evolution in the production of legal standards should, in particular, lead to a necessary overhaul or reconstruction of the concept of the law of the flag. The system of incentives for cooperation established by the CMB are, indeed, an exception to the concept of law of the jurisdiction of the flag State that had been the only rule applying on the high seas. However, it is clear that the flag State can no longer play the central role in the production of legal standards, as the massive use of flags of convenience has led to flagging most commercial vessels in States which are lax in supervision and investigation of the labor and working condition of seamen on board and which do not respect international conventions, particularly with regard to health and safety.[10] What guarantee can a flag of convenience State then offer to victims in a prosecution, trial, and then remedy?

In France, maritime labor law has long been a precursor in the labor relations field. But on the international scene, recent decades have seen the deterioration of working conditions on board ship. The quest for the lowest social cost has led shipowners to disregard safety rules and the qualification of the crew and to offer increasingly weak compensation to seafarers. This phenomenon is exacerbated by the development of shipping and the trivialization of flags of convenience.

Until now, the link between the ship and the State whose flag it flies was founded upon the principle of criminal jurisdiction of the flag State. This

---

[9] Ibid.

[10] J.P Beurier (coord), *Maritime(s) Law(s)*, Dalloz Action. Paris, 2008, 2è éd., n° 321-41 et s. See the following for the economic aspect of the flag of convenience's development - P. Guillotreau (coord), *Mare Economicum*, PUR, Rennes, 2008, p. 267 et s.

solution was required, as the flag reflected the existence of a link between the ship and the State; it allowed the State to "effectively exercise its jurisdiction and control administrative, technical, and social issues."[11] However, the practice of open-registry has been emptying the law of the flag of all its substance.[12] Flags of convenience allow shipowners to choose an attachment that is almost fictitious to escape rules deemed too restrictive, in particular in terms of labor costs, welfare, safety, or tax. In case of conflict, the ship remains subject to the law of the flag State although it has no real economic link with that State. The situation thus has an appearance of regularity, even though this practice has led to the legalization, on a large scale, of something which is a fraud on the law. Yet, this reflects the irresponsibility of States when they fail to fulfill their international obligations as flag States.

It is the same regarding criminal jurisdiction assigned to the flag State when the State does not observe its international obligations. Blindly retaining this principle threatens the rule of law. Current practices in open registry countries not only call into question the legitimacy of the law of the flag as a connecting factor in international disputes,[13] but also the ability of these States to fight against maritime crime. International society can no longer tolerate that the law of the flag becomes the pledge of a virtual immunity for pirates. This also explains why the European Union has an agreement with Kenya, the Seychelles, and Mauritius, to transfer captured pirates so they can be tried in accord with accepted criminal procedures and human rights. Globalization of trade, threats, and legal standards clearly shows that the law of the flag is no longer appropriate today to manage all the situations related to the operation of a ship.

Economic issues related to maritime transport security have for the first time, caused States to effectively cooperate to stem the phenomenon of maritime piracy. This is an innovative form of action in both the political will, clearly and consistently displayed, and the means used. But beyond that, the fight against piracy, like any fight against maritime crime (pollution, illegal unregulated fishing, abandonment of seafarers, illegal immigration, human trafficking, etc.) renders ensuring human rights and rights at work more necessary than ever. In its own way, the fight against piracy could eventually help to rebuild a new approach to the law of the flag. It would be futile to think that this phenomenon will not persist in the coming years. Thus such a reconstruction is not only desirable, it seems inevitable in an

---

[11] Article 5 of the Geneva Convention on the High Seas of 28 April 1958, Article 94 of UNCLOS.

[12] J.P. Beurier (dir), *Maritime (s) law(s)*, Dalloz Action, Paris, 2008, 2è éd., n° 115-12 et s.

[13] G. Proutière-Maulion, *Criminal Competences in the Field of Maritime Incident, About the Collision of Trawlers by Cargo Ships*, L'observatoire des Nations-Unies, Aix-en-Provence, n° 16, 2004.

international context marked by the globalization of threats, to relinquish a rule that previously depended on the supremacy of the State as a conquering sea power.

IMPLEMENT THE LEGAL INSTRUMENTS OF THE INTERNATIONAL LABOR REGIME

In the fight against piracy, legal instruments that are traditionally brought to bear derive from the international law of the sea and from regulations of the International Maritime Organization. But, too often, we forget that it is also possible to use other legal principles. Reconstructing the law of the flag is a necessary path. It is also possible to draw on concepts from international labor law. In fact, the International Labor Organization's Maritime Labor Convention (MLC) of 2006 provides comprehensive rights and protections at work for the world's more than 1.2 million seafarers.[14] The Convention aims to achieve both decent working conditions for seafarers and to secure the economic interest in fair competition for quality shipowners. An estimated 90% of world trade is carried on ships, and seafarers are essential to that trade. The 2006 Convention consolidates and updates more than 68 international labor standards related to the maritime sector adopted over the last 80 years. The Convention sets out seafarers' rights to decent conditions of work on a wide range of subjects, and aims to be globally applicable, easily understandable, readily updatable, and uniformly enforced. It was designed to become a global instrument known as the "fourth pillar" of the international regulatory regime for quality shipping, complementing the key conventions of the International Maritime Organization (IMO).The fight against the degrading working conditions in this sector required the adoption of a new international instrument adapted to changes related to the globalization of trade in order to promote the emergence of a public international social order based on respect for a certain minimum of standard-setting rules. This agreement has a major ambition: promoting social justice in the maritime sector by using labor law as a spearhead for the protection of seafarers. It aspires to become a legal standard of reference for building a new framework for social relations accepted by the various maritime stakeholders. But, even if the Convention becomes a new legal framework there are currently no provisions dealing with piracy.

---

[14] Marin M. et Charbonneau A., *The Maritime Labour Convention 2006: Towards a Codification of International Maritime Labor Law?*; DMF, p 110 et s; PROUTIERE-MAULION G., A. Charbonneau et P. Chaumette, *De Maritieme Arbeidsconventie van de IAO van 2006 en de conventie nr 188 over de arbeid in de visserij*, Arbeidsrechtelikje annotaties, 2009/2, pp. 95-122.

A resolution adopted in 2006 by the International Labor Conference, at its 94th (Maritime) Session, [15] after the adoption of the Maritime Labor Convention (MLC) of 2006, urges the Governing Body of the International Labor Office (ILO) to request the Director-General to work closely with the International Maritime Organization and the United Nations in encouraging all member States to ensure that adequate measures are introduced to prevent the continued incidence of cases of piracy and armed robbery in many parts of the world, and to prevent the increasing violence directed against seafarers that is associated with such attacks, as well as the trend to hold seafarers hostage for ransom.

In 2012, the "Guidelines on operational procedures for the promulgation of maritime safety information concerning acts of piracy and piracy counter-measure operations" were adopted. These operational procedures provide specific additional guidance for naval and military authorities involved in the gathering and interpretation of information on acts of piracy and piracy counter-measure operations. A piracy attack warning should be broadcast as an "URGENT" NAVAREA or Coastal Warning immediately on receipt of the source information, and at a minimum at the next scheduled broadcast and for as long as the information remains valid. But an amendment of the MLC to this effect is still awaited.

CONCLUSION

The globalization of risk calls for international normative regulation. The resurgence of the phenomenon of piracy is a perfect example of this evolution. Nevertheless, while the production of international legal standards in the maritime sector has been traditionally approached from the angle of ship and transport safety, it is now time to rethink the production of international legal standards in terms of the safety of seafarers. Along this path, using the concept of corporate social responsibility to redefine the rights and obligations of shipowners and to rethink the law of the flag is a way of restoring the rights of seaworkers, and more broadly the human rights at the heart of the debate. From this perspective, the modification of the MLC 2006, should be a way to assign a new role to the ILO in the fight against piracy. Promoting compliance with ILO conventions and promoting the concept of corporate social responsibility is thus a way to involve all the maritime stakeholders in the fight against piracy without placing the burden only on the States. This is also a way to highlight the issue of the respect of the seafarer's dignity and the need to guarantee them decent working

[15] Wcms_ O88131

conditions in a sector dominated by issues of economic competitiveness.

If the current resurgence of piracy can be perceived as a consequence of the globalization of trade, this is also true of the degradation of working conditions on board vessels. On both sides, pirates and seafarers are primarily victims of a globalization not mindful of social justice. That is why the fight against piracy requires not only a militarized response, but also the construction of a world public order of human dignity.

CONCLUSION

PIRACY AND THE PUBLIC ORDER OF THE OCEANS

Charles H. NORCHI

The preceding chapters are a collective appraisal of the maritime piracy problem, including the goals, and actual and potential outcomes bearing on the public order of the oceans.[1] The particular goals specified by the contributors can be aggregated to three. First, a goal of minimum order of the oceans would eradicate incidents of unauthorized coercion and violence perpetrated by non-state actors on the seas. States have a variety of coercive mechanisms and naval assets in place to contain and manage piracy incidents such that world public order is minimally threatened. This is a continuation of long-standing world community piracy policy, with adjustments reflecting contemporary global security threats that became especially salient from September 11, 2001. A second, mid- level goal, would move beyond piracy containment to eradicate all such incidents with the explicit aim of defending and maintaining world public order. This goal would require a combination of, (1) coordinated political will of State elites, (2) the enhancement of the multinational maritime security apparatus, and (3) robust sanction strategies accompanied by the exercise of State jurisdiction and prosecution. A third, higher order goal, would be an optimum public order of the oceans. Achieving that goal would require a more holistic approach addressing the root causes of piracy on land and sea while integrating development and human rights into the existing counter-piracy maritime security program. An optimum world order would strive to maximize the shaping and sharing of values in the service of human dignity. The trends, as described by the authors of this book, indicate the present level of goal achievement.

[1] Public order is that feature of the world social process in which decisions are made from perspectives of authority - by individuals expected to make them in accordance with the fundamental policies of the community. They are achieved through established procedures and through accepted structures. The individuals who make these decisions have sufficient bases in power to put them into operation. These are the authoritative decisions of the community and therefore law. See, Myres S. McDougal, and Associates, Studies in World Public Order (1960).

TRENDS IN MARITIME PIRACY

The most salient contemporary trend is the recrudescence of piracy off the coast of Somalia. However, as described in these pages the piracy phenomenon dates back to the origins of human political organization with periods of abatement. It was known to the European and Persian worlds as underscored in this book by Dominique Gaurier, and to the Eastern World as explained by Fozia Lone. Gaurier notes that the Roman lawyer and orator Cicero, condemned pirates as *hostis humani generis* as the enemy of all mankind. In 1817 Lord Stowell declared in the case of the *Le Louis*, pirates are "the enemies of every country, and at all times; and therefore are universally subject to the extreme rights of war."[2] In the 1927 *Lotus Case* before the Permanent Court of International Justice, Judge Moore captured the prevailing world view of the time writing that a person charged with piracy "may be tried and punished by any nation into whose jurisdiction he may come."[3] Thus the world community from ancient times has asserted a policy of minimum order of the oceans, fundamental to which have been claims to suppress unauthorized coercion, termed "piracy," as applied to high seas vessels. The trends in piracy policy are reflected in custom, case decisions and eventually codified international law.

Despite those long-standing policies, in the early part of the 21st Century, governments, international organizations, the shipping industry and myriad actors are engaged in a war against pirate organizations that have emerged as increasingly sophisticated private armies operating in littoral and international waters. Pirates usually launch in skiffs from a mother vessel and employ AK 47s and Rocket Propelled Grenades (RPG) directed at the bridge to force vessel's master to stop. When a vessel stops the pirates board and hijack it.[4] A High Risk Area as designated by Military Forces and the Shipping Industry now covers vast Indian Ocean space bounded by the Suez Canal and the Strait of Hormuz to the north extends to the Mozambique Channel in the South.

The trends include escalation of the numbers of pirates emerging from the hinterlands and participating in attacks, the intensification in the violence and sophistication of weapons and the increasing sophistication of operations using advanced technologies and communications systems. Edward Giradet writes in these pages that use of "…the Internet, satellite and mobile phones coupled with more recent social media access in Somalia itself, has meant

---

[2] *Le Louis*, [1817] 2 Dods. 210, 244.
[3] The Case of the SS *"Lotus"*, PCIJ 1927, Series A, No. 10, 3, at 37 *et seq*.
[4] See Tom Tulloch, this volume.

that the pirates have been able to maintain close contact with the outside world." As Puntland President Mohamud Farole writes in the Forward to this book, "The pirates are becoming more violent and cunning, and they are increasingly using sophisticated technology, such as GPS satellite phones, and international connections, including foreign-based brokers, facilitators and ransom money transporters," and he points to "...the worrisome trend of growing ties between pirates and al-Shabaab."

The effects of maritime piracy bearing on wealth are appraised by Chassot, Chassot, Guillotreau, Kaplan and Vallée who write in this volume that, " maritime piracy is costing the international economy between $7 and $12 billion annually." And they write that the impact upon fishing has been intense, noting that, "since April 2008, when the first piracy attacks against tuna purse seiners operating in the Indian Ocean occurred, vessels have been deterred to harvest in some fishing zones... the productivity of vessels has decreased by 50% since the extension of piracy acts up to 500 nautical miles off the Somalia coast, an area encompassing the most productive fishing grounds of the Indian Ocean." However, beyond maritime security and global commerce contemporary piracy affects seafarers overwhelmingly who may be taken hostage and traded between groups until a ransom is paid. The picture is captured by Tom Tulloch who writes that "in February 2011 Somali pirates held 30 merchant vessels in anchorages off the east coast of Somalia and 664 innocent merchant seamen hostage."

IMO Secretary-General Efthimios E. Mitropoulos has stated,"piracy and kidnapping have blighted the maritime community for too long and it is seafarers who bear the brunt."[5] Piracy greatly affects the well-being of seafarers and their families. Hostages may be held for a year in unsanitary conditions of malnutrition and subjected to torture and may die. And many seafarers suffer inadequate labour conditions as noted by Gwenaële Proutière-Maulion. Patrick Chaumette observes that all the suffering from piracy incidents falls disproportionately on seafarers. Indeed, weak and adequate protection for seafarers is itself a threat to shipping, global commerce and world order. Protecting and saving the seafarers is a critical public order of the oceans goal.

To protect seafarers, and to insure they will continue to work in high risk zones, ransoms are paid and the amounts have been increasing. Simon Delfau writes in this volume that the average payment in 2012 was $5.4 million and that "total ransom payments for 2009 and 2010 are estimated

[5] IMO Secretary-General Efthimios E.Mitropoulos, *Situation Unacceptable IMO Launches Anti-Piracy Agenda for 2011*, IMO News, Issue 1, 2011, p 11.

around US$415 million and that by November 2011, ransom payments paid by shipping companies to Somali pirates in 2011 had already reached nearly US$110 million." He explains that ransoms paid directly by shipowners (usually dropped by plane) and subsequently the owner seeks reimbursement from a Kidnap and Ransom (K&R) insurer and with each ransomed paid, the K&R insurance premium increases. Because in 2008, the Gulf of Aden was designated as a War Risk Area by the Joint War Committee the Indian Ocean became a War Risk Area in January 2011 meaning additional insurance premiums for the industry.

K&R is an important tool that enables ransom payments for seafarers while restoring certain costs to the ship owner. Poomintr Sooksripaisarnkit writes in this volume that this kind of insurance contract was introduced into the market by Lloyd's of London long before the recent rise in piracy, and he underscores that there is no standard K&R policy available and thus the scope of coverage is a determined in the construction of each policy. Protection & Indemnity Clubs (P & I Clubs) provide third party liability insurance for shipowners adding to operating costs. As Tulloch notes, "the ransom payments are but a small part of the overall economic impact of piracy. Increased insurance rates for merchant vessels; the added costs to shipping companies to avoid high risk areas, to hire security teams and to "harden" vessels against attack; the costs to deploy and sustain naval forces, and the prosecution costs, as well as the secondary economic impact to local tourism and fishing industries and regional investment. "

Yet although States deploy substantial naval assets to protect shipping, including the thirty-five percent of the world's oil and gas and half of world's container traffic steaming through the Strait of Bab el-Mandeb to the Gulf of Aden and the Indian Ocean while policing ever vaster ocean spaces, the trends indicate that few of the postulated goals are met. As to maritime piracy, the strategies in pace have produced a minimum order of the oceans

MARITIME PIRACY CONDITIONS: LAND, POWER AND LAW

General and specific conditions have shaped the trends described. Certain derive from socioeconomic and geopolitical realities, others derive from decisions made by global elites. They correspond to outcomes on land, to power-based strategies, to the constitutive process and its decision outcomes. Consider the conditions shaping piracy outcomes pertaining to land, power and law.

Our existing minimum order of the oceans is connected to conditions on land. For all the necessary focus on the oceans, piracy is also a land-based problem. James Kraska writes in this book, "while the threat of piracy poses a relatively minor inconvenience to most states, the effect on East Africa has been devastating—tantamount to a blockade." Poor economic development and socio-political instability are the conditions that spawn piracy.[6] Somalia is an extremely poor and a failed state where, in the south especially, people live with an expectation of violence. There has been no effective central government since 1991 when President Siad Barre was deposed. The Transitional Federal Government (TFG) established in 2004 exercises minimal control and is in a struggle against Al Shabaab insurgents. The State is weak, the culture is strong, and disparate groups wield power to gain control over territory and institutions.

The autonomous Government of Puntland is relatively calm, but also facing Al Shabaab incursions from the south. Geography presents a formidable challenge. Like the rest of Somalia, there is minimal road infrastructure and pirate groups are among isolated valleys, mountains and along a coast line that is very difficult to monitor. In the Forward to this book, The President of Puntland outlines genuine steps his government has undertaken to confront piracy, but he underscores the constraints owing to a lack of capacity. He writes of the "need to develop alternative livelihoods for coastal communities affected by piracy and illegal fishing." The prevailing conditions encourage vulnerable youth to join pirate organizations or al-Shabaab.

Although development is desperately needed and people are poor, pirates fully engage the modern media environment employing social media such as Twitter and maintaining contact with the diaspora. Edward Giradet writes that , "in many ways, Somalia remains one of the best connected countries in Africa. This has enabled the pirates to maintain close contacts with outside investors… Negotiations for ransoms and the release of hostages and ships are typically carried out by satellite phones or Skype and usually take three months to a year. …Pirate coordinators have become incredibly sophisticated even if the bulk of their cohorts are illiterate and uneducated local men from the mainland."

There are few effective sanctions to modify unauthorized behavior whether of pirate organizations or al-Shabaab. With poverty and limited means to sustain a dignified life, the opportunity cost of choosing to become a pirate is low. It is a decision to pursue a specific value- wealth- even if that pursuit is fraught with personal risk. And as Tulloch writes in this volume, "what

[6] See Chassot, *et al*, this volume.

constitutes an acceptable level of risk to a Somali pirate bears no resemblance to a western understanding of risk." From the pirates' standpoint a successful operation generates positive wealth outcomes in marked contrast to otherwise impoverished conditions. Hence the analysis presented by Chassot *et. al.* is very pertinent as they underscore that pirate behaviour can be considered rational, citing Peter Leeson's neologism "*pirational* choice."

Pirate behavior follows the maximization postulate which "holds that living forms are predisposed to complete acts in ways that are perceived to leave the actor better off than if he had completed them differently."[7] Choices, and the strategies employed to implement those choices, are deliberate decisions intended to improve one's stakehold from the standpoint of the decision-maker. The decision to engage in piracy is a rational choice calculated to maximize a stakehold as measured against other choices. That trend continues. And it is both an individual and collective choice, hence Chassot *et. al.* consider the nature of the pirate enterprise as a firm characterized by investment, wealth-maximization and the spread of risk. It should be added that pirate organizations are of a culture charaterized by close kinship and custom with robust operational codes. And pirates pose, at least instinctively, the same question as the beneficiaries of globalization: "Who gets what, how, where and why?"[8]

POWER

While international law depends on global expectations of authority, the efficacy of the system depends upon a power process that is a component of all law -the sanctioning process that protects the integrity of the system of public order. [9] Expectations of effective control are fundamental to the establishment of law in any community. Authority joined with control establishes and maintain processes of authoritative decision which amount to public order.[10]

---

[7] "The postulate draws attention to the actor's own perception of the alternative act completions open to him in a given situation." *See,* HAROLD D. LASSWELL, A PRE-VIEW OF POLICY SCIENCES (1971).

[8] Harold D. Lasswell, *The Structure and Function of Communication in Society*, in Lyman Bryson, ed., The Communication of Ideas, (1964).

[9] "Sanctions are patterns of conduct employed in a social context with the expectation of influencing conformity to a norm of the context." Richard Arens & Harold D. Lasswell, In Defense of Public Order: The Emerging Field of Sanction Law, Columbia University Press (1961).

[10] Myres S. McDougal and W. Michael Reisman and Andrew Willard, *The World Process of Effective Power: The Global War System* in M.S McDougal and W.M. Reisman, eds., Power and Policy in Quest of Law 353 (1985).

Mahnoush H. Arsanjani and W. Michael Reisman appraise maritime piracy as "..a problem of the restoration and maintenance of public order rather than as a *stricto sensu* legal problem"[11] and consider seven specific sanctioning strategies:

(1) *Preventing* imminent discrete public order violations;

(2) *Suspending* current public order violations;

(3) *Deterring*, in general, potential future public order violations;

(4) *Restoring* public order after it has been violated;

(5) *Correcting* the behavior that generates public order violations;

(6) *Rehabilitating* victims who have suffered the brunt of public order violations; and

(7) *Reconstructing,* in a larger social sense, in order to remove conditions that appear likely to generate public order violations.[12]

Arsanjani and Reisman write that, "the common denominator of each of these strategies …is to protect, reestablish, or create a public order characterized by low expectations of violence and a heightened respect for human rights.[13] Features of the existing counter-piracy strategies discussed in this volume merit review and adjustment as urged by the authors.

The instruments of power authorized for the application of maritime piracy law are described and appraised by many contributors to this volume. As James Kraska writes in these pages, "manned and unmanned aircraft are operating from South Africa to India, patrolling against roving gangs of Somali pirates. Thirty nations have deployed naval and maritime law enforcement forces to the region … The nations that have sent forces to the region are interested in suppressing maritime piracy, but they do so within a distinct political and strategic context." This includes NATO which maintains a Combined Task Force (CTF 508).There is also Combined Task Force 151 (CTF 151) a multinational task force to counter maritime piracy in the Horn of Africa established in January 2009 by the commander of naval forces for U.S. Central Command and based in Bahrain. The counter-piracy effort is coordinated via regular Shared Awareness and Deconfliction (SHADE) meetings in which all parties participate. At-sea coordination between the different groups, the independent deployers (Russia, China,

---

[11] Mahnoush H. Arsanjani & W. Michael Reisman, East African Piracy and the Defense of World Public Order, in Hestermeyer ,*et al*, Law of the Sea in Dialogue 137 (2011).

[12] See also, Richard Arens and Harold D. Lasswell, In Defense of Public Order: The Emerging Field of Sanction Law,199-201 (1961)

[13] Mahnoush H. Arsanjani & W. Michael Reisman, East African Piracy and the Defense of World Public Order, in Hestermeyer ,*et al*, Law of the Sea in Dialogue 139 (2011).

India, Japan and Malaysia) and the merchant vessels is achieved via a secure Internet based system called Mercury.[14]

The European Union (EU) is present with EU-NAVFOR an Operation Atalanta that protects shipment of humanitarian aid to Somalia with the World Food Programme (WFP) and the African Military Mission in Somalia, cooperates to deter acts of piracy and armed robbery at sea in the Red Sea, Gulf of Aden and part of the Indian Ocean, and protects vulnerable shipping. The taskforce also monitors fishing activities off the Somali coast. Cédric Leboeuf , writes in these pages that "collective use of force is a relatively new concept for the EU."

China has dispatched a naval unit consisting of two destroyers and a supply ship to the Gulf of Aden on an anti-piracy mission to primarily protect Chinese ships and crew on board, as well as ships carrying humanitarian relief material for international organizations, including the World Food Programme. The Chinese Navy has escorted about three thousand merchant vessels since deploying the first unit to the region in 2009.[15]

A key component of the power arrangements are mechanisms that facilitate intelligence and coordination. These include IMO initiatives whose Assembly first adopted a resolution concerning piracy in 1983. The IMO has played an integral role in the development of regional cooperation agreements including ReCAAP, MOWCA and the Djibouti Code of Conduct and the world of its Maritime Safety Committee (MSC) write Arthur Bowring, Alexander McKinnon and Patrick Chaummette . The Contact Group on Piracy off the Coast of Somalia (CGPCS) was created pursuant to Security Council resolution 1851 (2008). This *ad hoc* forum with five working groups discusses and coordinates actions conducted by the States and international organizations working off the Somali coast. "The Maritime Security Centre – Horn of Africa (MSCHOA) was established on 8 December 2008 by the European Union Naval Force (EU NAVFOR) Somalia with support from the shipping industry pursuant to UN Security Council Resolutions 1814 (15 May 2008), 1816 (2 June 2008) and 1838 (7 October 2008).

Port State Control (PSC) is another preventive strategy writes Dr. Z. Oya Özçayır, especially in relation to the International Ship and Port Facility Security (ISPS) code. Port state control is integrated in the control process as

[14] See Tom Tulloch, this volume.
[15] Li Yancheng, "Chinese Navy escorted over 3,000 merchant vessels in Gulf of Aden", *People's Daily Online*, 10 March 2011 <http://english.peopledaily.com.cn/98666/101812/101886 /7314838.html>.

a mechanism for enforcement of maritime security measures in capable and networked ports and by preventing sub-standard shipping practices. The PSC system aims to ensure sure that well maintained and equipped vessels with better qualified crew are the norm. Thus PSC is a strategic mechanism to control piracy, particularly under an expanded view that includes armed robbery. A key PSC problem is the lack of capacity in less developed countries in regions where pirates operate. Port authorities and port state control offices share information. The International Maritime Bureau (IMB), a specialized division of the International Chamber Of Commerce (ICC) maintains a 24 hour manned Piracy Reporting Center that makes real time data available to the maritime community. In sum, there are ample mechanisms for the sharing of intelligence, both in civilian and military sectors.

An effective preventive measure includes the Best Management Practices for protection against Somalia based Piracy (BMP-4), revised in 2011 and implemented by the shipping industry. These practices, as detailed in the this volume, have been a helpful preventive strategy, though not perfect. The IMO International Ship and Port Facility Security Code (ISPS Code) stipulates another preventive strategy whereby vessels are to be equipped with Ship Security Alert Systems (SSAS) to be activated in event of attack. As Simon Delfau explains, vessels are equipped with Automatic Identification Systems (AIS). AIS allows all vessels in the vicinity equipped with the system to receive reciprocating information.

There is increasing resort to the private sanctioning capacities of private maritime security companies (PMSC).[16] The International Chamber of Shipping (ICS) acknowledged the use of armed guards to combat piracy in February 2011, and in October 2011 the Government of the United Kingdom announced plans to license armed guards for merchant ships in pirate-infested waters. Delfau writes, "shipowners use PMSCs because they do not have any other choice, as military forces are unable to ensure security in the whole High Risk Area." And as Martin Murphy observes, " given that naval capacity is being cut, there is a real concern that armed guards will become a permanent feature for all ships transiting "at risk" areas worldwide." The P&I Clubs are concerned that the employment of armed guards may prove to be in conflict with the law of the Flag State of the vessel or of the Port State. Poomintr Sooksripaisarnkit writes, "... if the use of armed guards is prohibited by the laws of the flag state or the port state, this may go to the

[16] Defined by IMO Circular MSC.1/Circ.1405/Rev.1 as "Private contractors employed to provide security personnel, both armed and unarmed, on board for protection against piracy."

breach of the implied warranty of legality and the in event of a fight between armed guards and pirates causing deaths or injuries to crewmen, there will be complicated factual question of causation. This may be hard to determine considering that surveyors and the authorities will only arrive on the scene after the incident."

The Security Association for the Maritime Industry (SAMI) is working on standards and accreditation processes for PMSCs in line with the IMO guidance.[17] The Swiss Government and the International Committee of the Red Cross (ICRC), have produced the *Montreux Document* which addresses legal concerns arising from the use of private military and security companies, including respect for international humanitarian law including by " private military and security companies to protect merchant shipping against acts of piracy." [18] The International Ship and Port Facilities Security (ISPS) Code stipulates that "[a]t all times the Master of a ship has the ultimate responsibility for the safety and security of the ship."[19] As Bowring and McKinnon write, "[F]rom a practical point of view, if a ship is carrying experienced security personnel or navy personnel, it may be difficult for a master to enforce control during a pirate attack." Still, no vessel utilizing private armed guards security team has been taken by Somali pirates.

In August 20122, The Round Table of International Shipping Associations wrote to United Nations Secretary General Ban Ki-Moon urging the "....establishment of a UN Force of Armed Military Guards that can be deployed in small numbers onboard merchant ships." A United Nations peacekeeping operation on board private vessels require UN Security Council action and could produce a tectonic shift in counter-piracy sanctioning. One aim of The Round Table proposal is to, "... restrict the growth of unregulated privately contracted armed security personnel," according to the writers. In contrast with private security firms, a UN force would be bound by the laws of war, humanitarian law and human rights law and would be trained in the observance and implementation of associated norms and rules and would possess the privileges and immunities of UN civil servants while performing their duties.

There is precedent for UN maritime peace enforcement. Since 2006 the United Nations Interim Force in Lebanon (UNIFIL) has included a UN Maritime Task Force. A UN Maritime Force deployed onboard merchant

[17] For more information refer to <http://seasecurity.org/standards-accreditation>.
[18] The document was finalized by consensus on 17 September 2008 by 17 States.
[19] *See* Guidance Regarding the Provisions of Chapter XI-2 of the Annex to the *SOLAS Convention* as amended, pt 4.10.

ships could be ad hoc, on-call or standing force. From the creation of the United Nations, States have been allergic to the creation of a UN standing force as control of the military instrument is am attribute of State sovereignty upon which the functioning of the United Nations depends. The most politically palatable mechanism is likely a maritime peace enforcement mission of limited scope (ad hoc) and limited duration designed for counter-piracy contingencies.[20]

With the maritime security architecture in place, the instruments of power in support of law, why is not a fully effective sanction? There have been challenges of coordinating the proliferating mechanisms and instruments. And as Martin Murphy underscores, "The problem has been that no more than 30 warships – supported by even fewer aircraft - have been at sea at any one time, too few to adequately patrol the vast spaces involved. The number has usually been nearer 20, when 50 was estimated to be the minimum needed to patrol the Gulf of Aden alone." Murphy emphasizes, "navies have rarely been able to exert sufficient dissuasive pressure at sea alone; to be effective they have had to deny pirates access to their bases on land." …Governments "have refused to sanction operations to neutralize pirate bases, forcing navies to confront the problem solely at sea." Yet, acting under Chapter VII of the Charter of the United Nations, the Security Council decided in Resolution 1816 that states cooperating with the Transitional Federal Government of Somalia could enter and use the territorial waters of Somalia for the purpose of repressing acts of piracy and armed robbery at sea, in a manner consistent with such authorized action on the high seas.[21] Resolution 1846, which renewed the initial authorization, extended its application from states cooperating with the Transitional Government to include regional organizations and this has been renewed.[22]

Recently, the EUNAVFOR mission has expanded, and thus Leboeuf observes the "area of operations of the forces deployed … shall consist of the Somali coastal territory and internal waters." He argues "this extension targeting pirates on Somali soil needs to be clarified," observing "that the mission seems to be more offensive." EU and member State counter-piracy operations are complicated by a problem of State versus international organization responsibility. Cédric Leboeuf writes of the question of State responsibility" " EU-NAVFOR actions are conducted under the responsibility of the Member States. Beyond the connections established

[20] See Charles H. Norchi, *Could Blue Berets Beat Piracy?* Lloyd's List, November 29, 2011.

[21] SC Res 1816, UNSC, 5902nd mtg, UN Doc S/RES/1816 (2 June 2008) para 7.

[22] SC Res 1846, UNSC, 6026th mtg, UN Doc S/RES/1846 (2 December 2008) para 10; SC Res 1950, UNSC, 6429th mtg, UN Doc S/RES/1950 (23 November 2010).

between the military forces and regional private and state entities, the framework for cooperation of the Atalanta operation do not relieve the Member States from their responsibility. Atalanta legitimates and reinforces the joint action of the Member States without engaging a direct responsibility for the EU." Leboeuf observes that "any excess is likely to engage the international responsibility of the intervening state." Hence there are sanctioning constraints.

Martin Murphy makes the point that, " states have, one by one, begun to back away from their claim to monopolize the use of force at sea, because they are no longer willing to provide their navies with the resources necessary to do so. Western navies, in particular, have been forced to make a choice: either prepare to fight high intensity war, or secure the seas. The relentless decline in escort ship numbers makes clear the choice they have made." James Kraska writes, "The naval coalition, being relatively cost-ineffective, is the wrong tool for the job of suppressing piracy, even at sea.... The answer is not to concentrate high-end warships, but rather to create a diffuse network consisting of private security and small boat coastal security and naval forces."

LAW

Consider the authoritative decisions that power-based sanctions are intended to support. The counter-piracy legal framework is fraught with pathologies in that the sanctioning strategies of prevention, deterring, restoring, correcting and rehabilitating discussed above, are imperfectly performed. The legal architecture of our unorganized global arena is designed to generate stable patterns of authority and control and to limit the options of actors in the global social process. This includes pirates. All States are authorized to take measures against piracy irrespective of the national character of the offending ship. UNCLOS calls upon all States to cooperate in the repression of piracy [23] and provides for universal jurisdiction over acts for acts of piracy "in the high seas or in any other place outside the jurisdiction of any State."[24] The decision to exercise jurisdiction resides with the discretion of the capturing State.

Somali piracy has been the subject of UN Security Council resolutions beginning with Resolution 1816 of 2008. The Security Council has considered the activities off the coast of Somalia as a threat to international peace and security and thus has invoked Chapter VII of the United Nations

[23] UNLCLOS, Art. 100
[24] UNCLOS, Art. 105.

Charter. Security Council Resolution 1918 (2010) urged Member States of the necessity "to criminalize piracy under their respective domestic laws," while noting previous "cases when persons suspected of piracy are released without facing justice." Matters of investigation and detention of pirates was a priority of Security Council Resolution 1976 (2011). Resolution 2015 (2011), calls upon the United Nations Office on Drugs and Crime (UNODC), United Nations Development Programme (UNDP), and international partners to further efforts to support the development of domestic legislation, agreements and mechanisms that would allow the effective prosecution, transfer and imprisonment of those apprehended and convicted. There are myriad counter-piracy prescriptions that authorize action. Yet as Michael Stepek writes in this volume, "there is a clear need for a coordinated approach, [yet] few specific potential solutions have been identified, and only sporadic and overlapping efforts have been undertaken by various state, multi-state and non-state actors." Stepek summarizes the constitutive and sanctioning process limitations as follows:

(1) The current international legal architecture concerning piracy is fractured,

(2) The international legal architecture is intertwined with and dependent upon domestic law,

(3) Universal jurisdiction is limited to piracy under customary international law and UNCLOS,

(4) The international legal architecture addresses some of the challenges in investigating and collecting evidence for prosecutions, but they are neither complete nor have they been implemented by all ratifying states,

(5) Successful prosecution is intertwined and dependent on national will.

Although the crime of piracy is well-founded in international law, as Stepek notes, "not every state has invested its courts with universal jurisdiction with respect to this crime." He continues, "the international legal architecture relating to the problem is fractured in the sense that there is no single international instrument or source of international law that one can look to as a source of jurisdiction over, and proscription of, the various crimes associated with attacks on shipping, or the tools needed for the successful prosecution of them." He urges the strategic use of international instruments specialized to related problems that could implicate piracy including the 1979 International Convention Against the Taking of Hostages, The UN Convention on Transnational Organized Crime, and the

International Convention for the Suppression of the Financing of Terrorism.

Obviously it is the State that must seize and prosecute a pirate. Stepek emphasizes that this is where the system breaks down, "there is no country in the region that has incorporated all of the applicable provisions noted above into their domestic legislation. At best, countries have adopted provisions against the specific crime of piracy into their maritime legislation, but they rarely go beyond the accepted definition included in UNCLOS, and may not criminalize all the various acts and actors in an attack on shipping off the coast of Somalia. Even prosecutions for the crime of piracy itself, while recognized internationally, can face unforeseen challenges when pursued at the domestic level."

States have revised and modernize older anti-piracy laws. "In the absence of an international court with jurisdiction over pirates, the criminal prosecution of the pirates can only occur in domestic courts, hence the need for the states concerned to adopt legislation on piracy, writes Valérie Boré Eveno. Thus in France, "politicians realized that the punishment (and its deterrent effect) was an essential component in this fight." Hence a new law was promulgated combining the implementation of international rules in the fight against maritime piracy with the rights and freedoms that the French state has undertaken under the European Convention on Human Rights.

Boré Eveno writes that "The new law breaks new ground ... taking advantage of the exceptional authorization given by international law if the acts genuinely meet the definition of piracy, it gives the French courts "quasi universal" jurisdiction to judge such acts." But the jurisdiction of French courts will only be retained if the perpetrators (or associates) of acts of piracy were arrested by competent French agents and failing agreement with the authorities of another state to exercise court jurisdiction. If for example, another state accepts jurisdiction, particularly the state to which the perpetrators or victims belong, or if the pirate ship sails under its flag, those apprehended could then be turned over in order to be tried. France has been able to opt for this solution with respect to Somalia, as it regularly delivers alleged pirates to local authorities in the region of Puntland. Boré Eveno underscores that the new French legal maritime piracy framework "unfolds under the watchful eye of the European Court of Human Rights."

In the United States Justice Story wrote in the 1820 case *United States versus Smith,*"The common law...recognizes and punishes piracy as an offence, not against its own municipal code, but as an offence against the law of nations (which is part of the common law) , as an offence against the universal law of human society, a pirate being deemed an enemy of the human race."[25] In this book Timothy Steigleman discusses the recent American experience, and explains that "Piracy is a federal crime under U.S. municipal law... 'Whoever, on the high seas, commits the crime of piracy as defined by the law of nations, and is afterwards brought into or found in the United States, shall be imprisoned for life.'[26] However, the second element of the crime is a mere tautology: piracy is committed (under U.S. law) if someone commits piracy (under international law)." The cases Steigleman analyzes do not present a picture of clarity with respect to United States law in this area. He notes that future cases should serve as a better guide so that enforcement and prosecution of piracy can proceed with more certainty. This also underscores the lack of experience, even in the developed West, in prosecuting piracy cases.

Tom Tulloch writing in these pages expresses a widely shared observation. "For centuries piracy was treated very harshly indeed, with pirates being executed when caught, their vessels sunk, and their hideouts destroyed. Nowadays however, in our more enlightened times, such ruthlessness is frowned upon. Pirates today are treated as civilian criminals, with all the expansive interpretations of individual human rights inherent in that status. If pirates are captured they must be tried in court, however there is no international court in place with the authority to do so." Today, a State choosing to exercise jurisdiction must be concerned about the wider international human rights implications. A suspect may demand asylum in the capturing State and may have a well-founded fear of persecution in his country of origin. A State that does exercise jurisdiction and decides to prosecute faces the challenge of collecting evidence, witnesses including naval experts, translating proceedings, ensuring the rights of the accused, a lengthy trial and possible incarceration. Instead, following capture some pirates have been set ashore uncharged. Until a coherent system is in place enabling the application of counter-piracy prescriptions that exist, the "catch and release" trend is likely to continue.

There are clear limitations to existing piracy sanctions at the international and national levels. Current strategies support only a minimum public order of the oceans. Arsanjani and Reisman write that "strategies dealing with modern piracy should develop around the one strategy which recommends itself for its feasibility: prevention, stopping piracy during its occurrence.

[25] 18 U.S. (5 Wheat.) 153, 161 (1820).
[26] 18 U.S.C. § 1651 (2011).

The direct suppression of piracy that is, directly preventing pirates from boarding ships is crucial. That necessarily means a reversion to the types of self-help that were used by merchantmen plying the seas in earlier centuries."[27] As naval assets are redirected from pirate infested waters, so long as the political will of States to exercise jurisdiction remains tepid, if the UN Maritime Force proposal is shelved, there may well be an increased use of private security mechanisms as public sanction substitutes. However the burden on States to insure respect for humanitarian law and human rights will remain.

THE FUTURE AND THE ALTERNATIVES

Dr. Gaurier asks in these pages, "this increasingly complex problem presents increasingly complex questions. Is piracy merely a crime? Could it be, for some destitute peoples, just a means of subsistence? Or is it becoming, through funding, arms, and commissioning, a means to further a vague ideo-religious cause in the region?" Piracy incidents are claims. They are claims to wealth and perhaps more. They are also events that demand the attention of decision-makers which activate a response that can implements and perhaps creates international policy.[28] As discussed throughout this book, authoritative international policy has long evolved in response to piracy incidents. However international law is dynamic and prescriptions do not remain constant. Conflicting demands, expectations and a stream of outcomes spawned by international incidents can lead to termination over time. The critical factor is elite response to piracy incidents. If present trends continue with inadequate sanctioning and ineffective application of power in support of law, existing piracy prescription will corrode into *lex imperfecta.*

Puntland President Farole writes that, "Somalia has begun to export its problems – particularly piracy and terrorism." And the prospect of common interests and alliances among militant and insurgent groups is a troubling projection. Murphy, writes, "it is the destabilizing potential of militant Islamist groups al-Shabaab, in Somalia, and al-Qaeda in the Arabian Peninsula (AQAP), in Yemen, and the possibility that they might find some common cause, that worries many outside the region most." Al-Shabaab has reportedly sworn to support AQAP and to exploit the opportunity for the conflicts on either side of the Gulf of Aden to become "increasingly

[27] Mahnoush H. Arsanjani & W. Michael Reisman, East African Piracy and the Defense of World Public Order, p 156 in …

[28] See, W. Michael Reisman, *Private Armies in a Global War System: Prologue to Decision*, in Myres S. McDougal, W. Michael Reisman, eds., International Law Essays (1981)

intertwined." This is concern is underscored by Simon Delfau who writes, "the development of the political and security situation in Yemen is very worrying. If Yemen becomes a *Somalia bis*, security in the Gulf of Aden will become particularly difficult to ensure, threatening even further one of the world's most important sea passages."

So long as human dignity in desperate coastal communities remains unfulfilled, value demands and legitimate claims remain unmet, these communities are excluded from the benefits of the 21st Century globalization and that is a recipe for the further expansion of piracy. If conditions and critical factors remaining unchanged present trends will generate a situation of drastic interruption of global shipping, spiraling costs for the industry and consumers, and even heavier burdens falling upon seafarers and their families. And as Murphy emphasizes, "pirates' actions have raised serious concerns about international security regimes, the changing balance of power in the Indian Ocean and a reordering of the balance between state and private security in the maritime domain that has not been seen for nearly two centuries."

The sociologist Daniel Bell wrote, "the future is not an overarching leap into the distance, it begins in the present."[29] So what must be done in the present to achieve an alternative future? James Kraska writes that, "any long-term solution will have to involve the African states." This means capacity building as urged by Claude Ichalanga in this volume. This requires stabilizing the TFG, supporting new coastal maritime forces to combat piracy in more tranquil autonomous Somali States such as Puntland, and it means implementing intensive international development and institution-building and educational programs.

The Special Adviser to the Secretary-General on Legal Issues Related to Piracy off the Coast of Somalia, has proposed a court system that would comprise specialized piracy courts in Puntland, Somaliland and an extraterritorial Somali court that would eventually be transferred to Mogadishu. The piracy courts would possess concurrent jurisdiction.[30] The Puntland specialized court and the extraterritorial court would have universal jurisdiction under the counter-piracy law. International support for a legislative framework for the proposed system, to train judges in the application of the new legislation, and to monitor trial proceeding, pretrial detention, and imprisonment would be critical. A counter-piracy law was

[29] Daniel Bell, *The Year 2000- the Trajectory of an Idea*, Daedalus, 639 (summer 1967).

[30] See, Report of the Specail Advisor to the Secretary-General on Legal Issues Related to Piracy off the Coast of Somalia, S/2011/30.

adopted by the Parliament of Puntland on 18 December 2010, a similar measure is pending in Somaliland, but it has not been adopted by the Parliament of Mogadishu. The present burden on prison systems discourage States from becoming involved in the prosecution of pirates. Enhanced correctional capacities would help end the practice of "catch and release." Transfer agreements, effective bilateral treaties that would facilitate the transfer of apprehended pirate suspects, are an essential strategy.

Contributors to this book offer a number of recommendations under the rubrics of development, security and law. Among the recommendations under the rubric of development:

- Build a viable TFG government and institutions,
- Build on the Somali tradition of "bottom-up" governance,
- Engage autonomous Somali political entities,
- Introduce and scale up community driven development programs,
- Engage Somali women's groups and Imams,
- Introduce small-scale infrastructure projects such as clinics, schools, roads, air-strips and electrical capacity,
- Create job opportunities in sectors that are locally identifiable,
- Support immediate and long term education programs,

Among the recommendations under the security rubric:

- Attack known pirate land bases in partnership with the TFG and regional governments,
- Target pirate leaders,
- Employ coastal and littoral vessels rather than high end warships,
- Disrupt pirate support networks, primarily those that supply weapons, fuel, outboard motors, skiffs and other equipment, imported from Yemen and the Gulf,
- Intelligence should focus on piracy finance networks within Somalia and abroad,
- Enhance support to the African Union Mission in Somalia (AMISOM),
- Assist responsible regional administrations, such as Puntland, to build counter-piracy capacity.

Among the recommendations under the rubric of law:

- Pressure States to ratify and implement all appropriate treaties,
- Devise model laws to serve as guides for local adaptation, and/or uniform laws to be incorporated by states into their domestic legislation,

- Provide technical assistance for piracy transfer agreements
- Enhance technical assistance to build penal and prison capacity,
- Convene a joint shipping insurance industry-wide to delineate what piracy risk entails,
- Overhaul the law of the flag,
- Fully implement Maritime Labor Convention standards.

President Farole, writes, "the future of Somalia depends on the continued development of the regional administrations like Puntland, and our ability to combat the two greatest threats to stability: piracy and terrorism, the latter generally perpetrated by al-Shabaab.... It remains vitally important that the international community develop genuine partnerships with Somali institutions to advance the process of stabilization, state building and reconstruction. Dealing with piracy alone – for example, through international military action – will not suffice, as piracy constitutes simply a part of the whole problem in Somalia."

Clearly, in addition to maritime security efforts, eradicating piracy requires capacity building. This means penal system capacity, legal capacity, maritime protection capacity, and economic capacity including alternative livelihoods. Piracy roots must be attacked on land while the symptoms are attacked at sea. As with the poppy farmers of Afghanistan, a challenge is to identify and implement alternative livelihoods for the pirates of Puntland, and to target the delivery of development resources to local entities and autonomous regions that are reasonably tranquil and demonstrate a commitment to join the world community to defeat piracy.

TOWARD AN OPTIMUM ORDER OF THE OCEANS

In the 2011 *Masefield* case concerning the vessel *Bunga Melati Dua*, Lord Justice Rix wrote, "There is thus something of an unexpressed complicity: between the pirates, who threaten the liberty but by and large not the lives of crews and maintain their ransom demands at levels which industry can tolerate; the world of commerce, which has introduced precautions but advocates the freedom to meet the realities of the situation by the use of ransom payments; and the world of government, which stops short of deploring the payment of ransom but stands aloof, participates in protective naval operations but on the whole is unwilling positively to combat the pirates with force."[31] This is an accurate picture of piracy and

---

[31] *Masefield AG v. Amlin Corporate Member,* Royal Court of Justice, U.K. (2011)

our mininum public order of the oceans. But the future is not a prisoner of the present; an optimum public order of the oceans is achievable.

There are choices to be made and decision-makers should be guided by the principle of human dignity meaning that every human being possesses and a right to optimal self-realization through the sharing of all social values. Thus Gwenaële Proutière-Maulion in this volume urges that piracy also be conceived as a consequence of the globalization of trade, that it implicates the degradation of working conditions on board vessels and that a holistic approach would incorporate social justice goals. This is essential to achieving the optimum order goal, a world public order of human dignity.

Yet achieving those higher order goal requires attacking the roots of piracy on land and the symptoms at sea. Thus a double barrel strategy is necessary, or a what Proutière-Maulion terms a holistic approach. Fozia Lone writes that "poverty plays a significant role in piracy and thus a pure procedural approach to this problem can never exterminate it." She cites Carlos Andres Perez, the President of Venezuela who opening the Third United Nations Conference on the Law of the Seas, stated" the seas could not be permitted to be used in such a way that a few countries benefited from it while the rest live in poverty, as had been done with the rich of the land."[32] Peaceful enjoyment of the seas requires scaled-up development for poverty alleviation, training and educational programs and foreign investment. Power alone will not defeat maritime piracy.

In their seminal work, The Public Order of the Oceans, [33] Myres S. McDougal and William T. Burke wrote, "The historic function of the law of the sea has long been recognized as that of protecting and balancing the common interest, inclusive and exclusive, of all peoples in the use and enjoyment of the oceans, while rejecting all egocentric assertions of special interests in contravention of general community interest." [34] The authors' key idea was the inclusive use and enjoyment of the oceans for all people. A common interest goal is framed in the preamble of the 1982 United Nations Convention on the Law of the Sea as "the desirability of establishing… a legal order for the seas and oceans which will facilitate international communication, and will promote the peaceful uses of the seas and oceans, the equitable and efficient utilization of their resources,

---

[32] *See*, Warioba (United Republic of Tainzania) Third UN Conference on Law of the Sea, Official Records, Vol I, UN Publications Sales no E 75, v. 3 (New York, 1975) 36.

[33] *Myres S. McDougal & William T. Burke*, The Public Order of the Oceans: A Contemporary International Law of the Sea, 1962 (1987, with new introductory essay).

[34] Id at 1.

and the study, protection and preservation of the marine environment."[35] Maritime piracy, the causes and symptoms, contravenes our common interest of the oceans. It is hoped that this volume will stimulate creative thinking for the reader and for all who care about the oceans. It is hoped that this volume will provide fresh perspectives from diverse standpoints for decision-making that will achieve of an optimum order of the oceans.

[35] Preamble, United Nations Convention on the Law of the Sea, signed at Montego Bay, Jamaica 1982.

APPENDIX

INDIAN OCEAN
Arabian Sea
Bay of Bengal
Gulf of Aden
South China Sea
Celebes Sea
Timor Sea
Strait of Malacca
Equator
Tropic of Capricorn (23°27')
EGYPT
SUDAN
ETHIOPIA
KENYA
SOMALIA
UGANDA
TANZANIA
RWANDA
BURUNDI
ZAMBIA
MALAWI
MOZAMBIQUE
ZIMBABWE
BOTSWANA
MADAGASCAR
COMOROS
SEYCHELLES
SAUDI ARABIA
YEMEN
OMAN
IRAQ
IRAN
SYRIA
AFGHANISTAN
PAKISTAN
INDIA
NEPAL
MALDIVES
CHINA
MYANMAR (BURMA)
THAILAND
LAOS
VIETNAM
CAMBODIA
INDONESIA
PHILIPPINES
2009

Impression & brochage sepec - France
Numéro d'impression : 03163120710 - Dépôt légal : juillet 2012
IMPRIM'VERT®